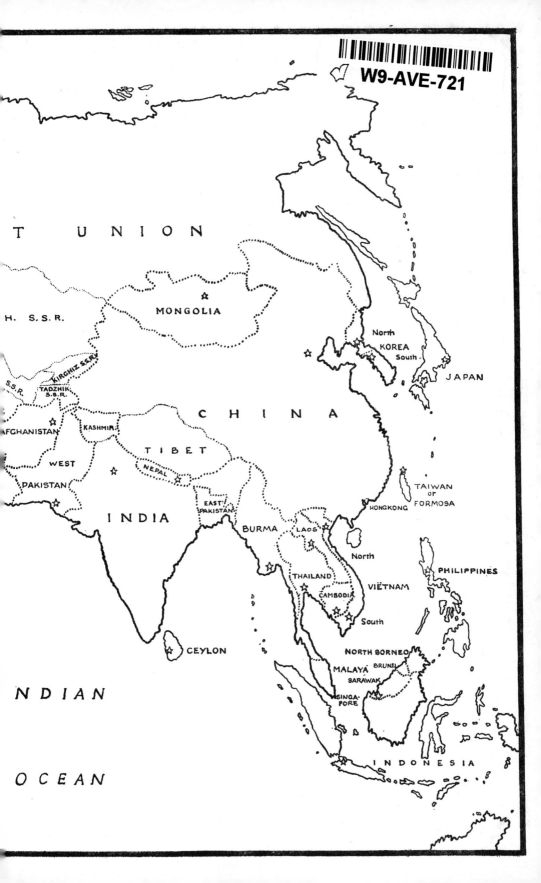

THE ASIAN CENTURY

THE ASIAN CENTURY

A History of
Modern Nationalism in Asia

BY

JAN ROMEIN

Professor of History in the University of Amsterdam

IN COLLABORATION WITH
JAN ERIK ROMEIN

TRANSLATED BY R. T. CLARK

WITH A FOREWORD BY
K. M. PANIKKAR

UNIVERSITY OF CALIFORNIA PRESS
Berkeley and Los Angeles 1962

University of California Press
Berkeley and Los Angeles
California

First published in Dutch under the title
DE EEUW VAN AZIË
in 1956

German translation DAS JAHRHUNDERT ASIENS, *1958*
This edition translated from the German and
with an additional section ('Last Period')
first published 1962

—

PRINTED IN GREAT BRITAIN

FOREWORD

by K. M. PANIKKAR

TILL the period of European dominance over Asia, there was no Asian history as such. Asia consisted of three cultural areas, the Islamic, the Hindu-Buddhist and the Sinic, each continental in its proportions. Separated by deserts and impassable mountains, the relations between these areas were limited and intermittent. The dominance which the Western nations exercised over them in the nineteenth century and in the first half of the twentieth gave to Asian political developments a unity which entitles it to be considered a definitive period of history.

Outside these broad regions of culture lay the vast steppes of Siberia which for long did not enter into the history of Asian peoples. Though from the time of Yarmak Timofevitch's ride across the Ural into the khanate of Siber, this northern half of the Asian continent gradually began to emerge into history as Siberia, it is only in the nineteenth century that the great demographic movement which was destined to transform northern Asia into a new cultural area began to assume considerable proportions: and it was only after the Russian Revolution that the Asian republics of the Soviet Union became the fourth constituent unit of the Asian continental system.

Thus Asia achieved what may be called a pattern of Asian history only in the nineteenth century when from the Ural to the Pacific and from the Arctic to the Indian Ocean, the entire continent came under European dominance.

This of course is not to say that the great cultures of Asia before the nineteenth century had no independent history or that they did not contribute to the general current of world development. Among the Islamic peoples, as also among the Chinese, there was a well-developed historical tradition which was not less important than the tradition developed in Europe. Like the Europeans, the Chinese and Islamic historians treated the rest of the world only so far as it touched their own development. It is only in the nineteenth century that a change became visible. The dominance of the West (including Russia and America) gave to the whole world a sense of unity and Western scholars began to interest themselves in the histories of Asian countries. To begin with, they were only looked upon as appendages of Europe. As a leading Western historian observes: 'Even countries with an important and well-documented history like Persia or China' were of interest only in terms of 'what happened when the Europeans attempted to take them over'.[1] The situation began to undergo a change when the countries of Asia, through a dual process of assimilation of ideas and resistance to power, emerged in the middle of the twentieth century as independent nations. In the first part of the twentieth century only Japan counted in world politics as an independent Asian nation. By the middle of the century there was no country in Asia which continued to be under foreign domination. Asian history had thus

[1] *What is History?* by E. H. Carr (Macmillan & Co. Ltd.)

achieved the status of an independent section in world history which even the most Europe-centred historians could not neglect.

*   *   *   *

It is not the independence of the Asian states but the transformation of Asian societies through the assimilation of modern science and technology that gives significance to this period of Asian history. This undoubtedly was the outcome of the massive contact of Europe with Asia in the nineteenth century. Though Europe and Asia had known each other from very early days, this kind of large-scale impact is of recent origin. Europe's knowledge of Asia before the eighteenth century was indeed marginal. No doubt the Greeks and the Romans had, of course, intimate knowledge of Western Asia and Alexander even reached as far as the present frontiers of India. Roman merchant ships seem to have sailed up to South China. But such knowledge of peoples and civilizations as these activities indicate was marginal and vague. It may also be true that some idea of the religious beliefs and philosophies of India had penetrated to the West by the second century A.D. as is witnessed by a recognizable summary of Hindu philosophical systems in a Latin work of the period entitled 'The Refutation of all Heresies' published in Rome. The *Romaka Siddhanta* or the Roman school of Indian astronomical science equally bears witness to the influence of the West on India at this early period.

The interest of Rome in trade with the East declined after the barbarian invasions and in the early middle ages there was very little curiosity in Europe about Asia. A great challenge to Christianity and Europe had emerged in the seventh century in West Asia and the Islamic world which spread out from Persia to Spain interposed during this period a barrier between Europe and the rest of Asia which the West was able to circumvent only when Vasco da Gama reached Calicut in 1498. Islamic Asia was looked upon by the European states as enemy territory and though during the later middle ages Islam exercised considerable influence on the cultural development of Europe, it also proved an effective barrier for closer contacts between Asia and the West.

Such was the prevalent ignorance about Asia that Archbishop Montecorvino after a stay of a few months in South India in the thirteenth century reported to Rome that the people of India knew how to count only up to five and had no developed language. It is true that the court of the great Khans was visited by many European adventurers and a few Christian priests and that Marco Polo wrote about the marvels of China after many years of stay in Kublai Khan's empire. But it would be an error to argue from this that the European states had any but vague notions about Asia. Marco Polo's descriptions of China were not only not accepted at their face value but were treated as the result of too luxuriant an imagination. It is only after Europe came to have greater knowledge of China through direct contacts some centuries later that Marco Polo came into his own.

How vague Europe's conception was about Asian lands may best be seen in the ideas of medieval writers about the Christian kingdom of Prester John. It was alleged to lie beyond the Persian mountains and sometimes was even identified with the Tatar empire. The original missions to the court of the great Khans were sent in the belief that the monarch was a Christian with whom the West could forge an alliance to break the might of Islam and thus recover the holy land and at the same time eliminate the threat to Christendom. In fact it would be true to say that in spite of the numerous travellers from Europe who visited the different countries of the East, very little was known in Europe about non-Islamic Asia, except that spices came from India and silk came from China.

With the discovery of the sea route to the East by Vasco da Gama and the entry of Portuguese ships into the Pacific through the Malacca Straits begin the first real encounter between Europe and Asia. The ships of the Portuguese roamed from the sea of Japan to the ports of the Red Sea and established trading centres at Macao, Malacca, Colombo, Goa and other coastal areas. While they controlled the navigation of Asian seas and enjoyed a practical monopoly of foreign trade, it would be wrong to think that the Portuguese brought Asia and Europe face to face with each other. The Portuguese were established only with small coastal tracts. Even their missionary effort, except to some extent in Japan, was limited to the fisher folk on the coastal areas. They made no attempt to understand the Asians. In the succeeding century the Dutch, the British and the French followed in the footsteps of the Portuguese but in their case also for another century and a half there was no proper encounter between Asia and Europe. The Moghul empire in India and the Manchu empire in China were at the height of their power while Turkey which ruled over the vast territories of the Middle East counted as a Great Power, till Prince Eugene in the opening decades of the eighteenth century struck the first serious blow to Ottoman power in the Danube valley. Of the European nations, only Russia was spreading over the vacant steppes of Siberia and reaching out to the Pacific.

*　　　*　　　*　　　*

The eighteenth century witnessed the first awakening of interest in Europe, about the societies and civilizations of Asia. During this period the work of the Jesuit scholars in China revealed to the European public the imposing structure of Chinese civilization. At the end of the century, Sir William Jones, Charles Wilkins, Colebrook and others opened up the mysteries of Sanskrit language and literature and embarked on a programme of translation which familiarized the West with the philosophical speculation of the Hindus. It is, however, necessary to emphasize that at this period, the process was altogether one-sided. Apart from a group of intellectuals in Calcutta, who mainly through the influence of the missionaries, developed an interest in Christianity, there was neither in India nor in China any curiosity about Europe and its peoples. In fact the extent of this ignorance may be judged from the famous letter that one of the best-instructed and liberal mandarins of his day, Imperial Commissioner Lin, wrote to Queen Victoria at the time of the

Opium War. The British Queen whose warships were threatening the Celestial Empire was to him only the chieftainess of a tribe in the outer regions. People in India through the experience of over a century had a better idea of the strength of European nations: but it could not be said that even they had a better idea of the sources of European power. The developments in science and technology which revolutionized life in Europe in the eighteenth century and provided the Western nations with economic power and military strength sufficient to dominate the most powerful nations of Asia and exploit their natural resources aroused neither interest nor curiosity among either the Chinese or the Indians. In fact it is recorded that the Chinese plenipotentiaries negotiating the treaty of Nanking after the first Chinese war, when taken to inspect British battleships were under the impression that the wheels of the ships were turned by the action of bullocks concealed in the hulls of the vessels! The only exception to this total lack of curiosity about the sources of European strength was provided by Japan, where a remarkable band of scholars known as the Rangkusha group continued to work with heroic persistence to master through the Dutch language the latest scientific knowledge of Europe. They continued this quest for a century and a half, so that even the reactionary Shogunate, awakened to the changed situation following the total defeat of the Chinese in the Opium War, was able to undertake a serious inquiry into the causes of British victory. The national movement in Japan which led to the Meiji Restoration was the result of the Japanese people's realization of the real nature of the danger that faced them.

As Professor Romein rightly points out, by 1850 the Western domination of Asia was complete. For over half a century after this, the great nations of Asia excepting Japan were prostrated by a sense of impotence. In India, the Indian National Congress which had come into being in 1885, was asking for no more than minor administrative reforms and for some limited association with the British in the government of the country. In fact the leaders of the national movement in India in the second half of the nineteenth century had no desire for independence and were inclined to look upon British rule in India as 'a gift of a benevolent providence'. In China the sense of political impotence against the dominance of 'the barbarians' of the West was equally widespread. The great viceroy Li Hung-ch'ang, writing to the Empress at the time of the Boxer rebellion, expressed this point of view. In a remarkable letter, Li pointed out how resistance to Western power was worse than useless at the time, and till the conditions changed co-operation with imperialist nations was the most fruitful line to follow.

*   *   *   *

The significant fact about the last two decades of the nineteenth century is the discovery of Europe by Asia. More and more young men from India and China began to visit Britain for studies. Students from the Middle East flocked to Paris and the universities of Germany provided special attraction to those whose nationalism made them unwelcome in London and Paris. The beginnings of large-scale industry in Shanghai, Calcutta and Bombay introduced Asians to the methods of modern business organization. This discovery of Europe by Asia, though begun at the end of the nineteenth century, became important only in the twentieth. The new movement which was to end with the withdrawal of European nations from Asia and to start the great states of the continent on a revolutionary career, destined to transform their ancient societies and take them into the era of science and technology, may be said to have started in 1902. As E. H. Carr, the historian of the Russian Revolution, puts it in his Trevelyan Memorial lectures: 'The story begins with the Anglo-Japanese alliance of 1902, the first admission of an Asiatic country to the charmed circle of great European powers. It may perhaps be regarded as a coincidence that Japan signalized her promotion by challenging and defeating Russia and, in so doing, kindled the first spark which ignited the great twentieth century revolution.'

This twentieth century revolution in Asia was not only a political upsurge, as many people are inclined to consider. From the very beginning, it had three aspects: political independence, mastery of science and technology, and social transformation. It is worthwhile to recall and emphasize that the political agitation following the partition of Bengal (1905) had as one of its major activities the popularization of science and technology. The Jadavpur College of Engineering, which today is a full-fledged university, was established at that time by the National Educational Council of Bengal and this may well be claimed to be the first awakening of national conscience to the values of modern science. The establishment of the Indian Institute of Science in 1909 as a centre of higher scientific studies and research through the munificence of Jamshedji Tata was the outcome of his realization of the integral relation between science and industry.

The second aspect of this triple revolution, the transformation of the ancient, stratified and seemingly unchanging societies of the East, also started at this time. This is a process which is by no means yet complete; but Chinese students (May the 5th movement) marching under the banners of 'Down with Confucius', Gandhi making the abolition of untouchability a major plank in his political programme and the Indonesian Princess Kartini demanding freedom for women, were unmistakable signs of this major revolution. The reforms of Rama VII in Thailand which modernized the social life of that kingdom, the more radical measures of Atatürk who replaced the *shariat* with a new code of laws borrowed from Europe, the abortive reforms in Afghanistan under Amanulla, are sufficient evidence that this movement for the transformation of society as a necessary foundation for political emancipation was one of the major characteristics of this period of Asian history.

Like the cultivation of science and technology, this programme of social change is a continuing movement. In most of the Asian countries political independence has provided an impetus for major social changes. In China the revolutionary urge of Communism has violently uprooted the ancient and inherited social structure of that country, and the present effort to replace it by something new based on Communism, Marxist-Leninism and the 'Thoughts of Mao' may be considered part of a continuing revolution. In India the endeavour has been to transform society by the process of legislation, assisted both by changes in the distribution of wealth and by the sharing of political power by all classes. Adult franchise has been in India as much an agency of social upheaval as an instrument of politics.

No less significant is the peaceful social transformation of Japan in the short period of fifteen years after her defeat in the great war. The Meiji restoration, for all its spectacular results, was in essence a conservative revolution – more interested in the dynamics of political, industrial and military power and in the utilization of science and technology for that purpose than in social progress. The post-war period saw the second revolution which in some ways is more significant than the first, for it represented an upsurge of the people and a transformation of the social basis of Japan which the Meiji restoration did not attempt to do. The logical evolution of the Meiji restoration into an alliance between big business and militarism, led Japan away from the general trend of Asian history in the period before her defeat in the great war. It was a heavy price she had to pay but no one who has watched the emerging pattern of Asia will deny that post-war Japan represents a phenomenon of the highest importance in new Asia.

Two factors have contributed to this continuing revolution in social and economic affairs. The first is the reaction to foreign domination – the desire not so much to imitate the imperial races but to demonstrate that given the opportunity to modernize and to assimilate the new sciences and technology, the subject peoples of yesterday can be as good as their former rulers. The second is the impact of the Russian revolution and the scientific and industrial achievements of Soviet Russia. The social and economic revolution of more than two-thirds of Asia in area and half of it in population, including Siberia, the Central Asian Republics of the U.S.S.R., Mongolia, China, North Korea and North Vietnam represents Marxist ideology and Communist industrial and social pattern. That is a fact which no student of Asian history can overlook. Over 750 million people (650 million in China alone), half of Asia's total population, follow the Communist way. That in China, North Korea and North Vietnam this has within the course of the last decade and a half created a new and unprecedented situation in social life and economic development due to the dynamic influence of Communism and Soviet power is too obvious to be denied. But in recognizing the far-reaching importance of the Communist revolution in China, North Korea and North Vietnam, the outside world has been inclined to overlook the development in the Soviet Asian republics. Today Siberia, it is said, has a population of twenty-five million, mainly of Russian stock. The new plans for the cultivation of virgin soil, and the development of power resources in this vast territory would almost certainly result in a rapid increase in population. In the same manner the Central Asian republics of Russia which, not many centuries ago, were great centres of culture, have of late shown evidence of a vigorous revival. It may be true, as many European observers point out, that these Central Asian republics are not really independent but in many respects represent only a new variation of colonial authority. What Professor Romein has to say in this connection is both pertinent and wise. 'The coming of the socialist revolution', he says, 'of new and foreign ideas and techniques naturally are not incompatible with an eventual Russian Imperialism. The penetration of the Russians, even if they are revolutionary Russians, the entire assimilation of regions like Turkistan to the economy and culture of the U.S.S.R., have in a sense to be considered colonial. But the emancipation of women, tractor factories, hygienic houses for the peasant and other things may not in the least be romantic but they are the coveted signs of modern civilization: even by 1940 Soviet Asia was different from the other countries of Asia, free and unfree alike.'

In fact the Soviet transformation of Siberia during the last forty years is paralleled only by the conquest of the wild west by the U.S.A. in the nineteenth century. It has undoubtedly added dimension to Asian history in a way which sea-oriented Western writers have not yet begun to realize. When this fact is viewed in the light of re-emergence of the old Central Asian states in their modernized Soviet version, no one who studies the history of new Asia can fail to realize that a slow if steady shift is taking place in the balance of the Asian continent.

It will thus be seen that the history of Asia in the twentieth century can no longer be treated only in so far as it affected the activities and interests of Western states. It has achieved universal significance and has now to be recognised as being right in the main stream of human development. But, unfortunately, no major European historian before Professor Romein ever attempted to put the whole problem into perspective. There have been many perceptive studies of Europe's relations with different regions of Asia, the Middle East, South and South-East China, China, Japan and the Far East. There have also been some attempts by Western scholars to evaluate developments in Soviet Asia. But so far as I know, Professor Romein's is the first work which takes the whole of Asia within its range and relates the three ancient cultural patterns of the continent with the new and emerging pattern of Soviet Asia.

Professor Romein is one of the leading historians of Holland. Among his major works are a standard history of the Netherlands in twelve volumes, and a comprehensive study of European expansion entitled *The Era of Europe*. He is also one of the co-authors of the VIth volume of UNESCO's *Cultural and Scientific History of Mankind*. That so distinguished an author would be objective in his judgement and meticulous in the presentation of his facts need not be emphasized. What I would venture to emphasize is the masterly way in which Professor Romein has woven strands of different colours into a single piece of tapestry both impressive in its design and beautiful in its texture.

AUTHOR'S PREFACE

In my book *Aera van Europa* the story is told of the departure in Europe from the 'common human pattern'[1] which elsewhere was still dominant; that departure began with the Greeks, was continued in the Renaissance and was completed in the 'Enlightenment', the Industrial Revolution and the French Revolution. In this departure the author believes he has found the final cause of the temporary domination of Asia by the Europeans.

The history of the national movement in the countries of Asia in the twentieth century, which is the subject of this book, is in a sense a continuation of what was set forth in that earlier work. The awakening of Asia – the name usually given to this complicated play of phenomena, tendencies and developments – is, as it were, the appearance in Asia of this process of departure which was originally confined to Europe. As it became 'European', Asia rediscovered itself and at the same time the departure ceased to be a departure. Thereby Asia took the most significant step forward on the road to the unity of mankind, the prospect of whose realization now lies before us. In the place of the centuries-old Asia a new Asian century opens before us.

This development provokes a variety of reflections. When the West invaded the East, it acted from purely selfish motives. The East could not do other than seek to defend itself. Neither Europe nor Asia could foresee that the final result of the conflict would be the unifying of the world. One is tempted to ask what suffering mankind would have been spared if that had been foreseen, and an effort been made to bring about that development by peaceful means.

There have been those who condemned this aggression. Some seventy-five years ago at the beginning of the great drama whose end we are now seeing – in December 1885 – a member of the French Chamber, Jules Delafosse, attacked the new imperialist regime in Indochina; he was speaking in a debate on an eventual evacuation of Tonkin by the French. His speech was of such significance that I quote from it here. 'He who seeks to colonize Asia', he said, 'is dreaming of a utopia. He creates a dangerous situation. He has not considered fully that the peoples of Asia are like ourselves, that they have known a culture which is older than ours, that they have retained the memory of it and take pride in it. They have been in turn conquerors and conquered, and now demand to resume their fight for freedom. It is not hard to prophesy that once they come under the influence of our culture, they will, thanks to the urge towards liberty which is everywhere affecting the world, quickly find awakening in themselves that desire for independence which is

[1] The attention of the reader is directed to my essay on 'The Common Human Pattern' in the *Journal of World History*, iv. 2 (1958).

at once the predominant aim and the honour of a people. They will be roused to anger and their anger cannot but carry the day, for it is the eternal prerogative of freedom to be everywhere victorious. I am convinced that before fifty years have passed there will not be a single European colony left in Asia.'

These memorable words extend and deepen our argument. He who merely rejects force does not reckon with the fact that in history what seems to be a curse is often a hidden blessing, and what seems a blessing is later revealed as a curse. That occurs so often that we must ask whether there is a possibility of other ways than these contradictory ones. The answer to the question whether the French politician was right or wrong is not at all simple. No doubt he was right when he warned us of the dangers of colonialism, when he saw the cause of that danger in the fundamental equality of peoples. He was right in his prophecy of what the ultimate end would be. But was he also right when he confined himself to a simple rejection of colonialism and recognized equality as a fact without drawing any conclusions therefrom, when he wished to leave Europe to be Europe and Asia Asia? Here he was wrong. He only seemed to see into the future because, living in the past, he rejected the present.

Had he actually seen into the future he would surely have proposed some form of co-operation between Europe and Asia which would have been at once the cause and the consequence of the unity concealed beneath the antagonisms, a co-operation which would have been powerful enough to prevent war and at the same time to secure freedom, a co-operation – to quote the famous Dutch historian Huizinga – in a 'pandaemium' to take the place of that 'pandaemonium' which existed then and which exists today. But no one can demand from anyone that sort of insight into the future. Even today, co-operation between East and West is more a wish than a reality. Men make their own history; even if they know their aims, the final result is hidden from them. With curse and blessing alike, only the outward appearance is known and not the reality behind either. The historian, therefore, can do no more than establish that the mutual hostility was necessary so that the possibility of co-operation could be recognized. Only in anticipation of a better future can one put up with a tragic past. Only when it is demonstrated that the unity of the world is the final achievement of the actual world conflict which this book describes, only then will one be able on both sides to forget and, what is infinitely more important, to forgive. It is therefore the author's desire that his book will speedily lose the topicality which it has.

That topicality no one will deny. But the problems with which we are concerned go deeper. It is a question of more than simply expelling the foreign masters. That 'more' was expressed not so long ago by Walter Lippmann, the well-known American journalist and one of those who best know our contemporary world. On the occasion of the visit to the United States of the Indonesian President Sukarno in May 1956 he wrote in the *New York Herald-Tribune*: 'What gives this revolution' – and he meant the revolution described in this book – 'its strength and its flexibility is its purpose of wiping out the results of the three-centuries-old rule of the "whites" and at the same time of ending the economic and technical back-wardness of the former colonies. Sukarno declared that he would carry through this revolution by democratic methods but added that the most important thing was that it be carried through – even by totalitarian methods.' Lippmann went on to say: 'The revolution is being carried through from Morocco – or so it seems – to Formosa and Japan. And in this whole great area the West is on the defensive while all the key positions which it still holds are under attack. The impression one has is that the Western nations are now fighting rearguard actions, the French in North Africa, the British in the Near East, the Americans in Formosa and so on.'

This book will give a concise account – the first, so far as the author is aware – of a historic development which can be regarded as unique in three aspects – in its extent, in its shortness as compared with its significance and in its results. Only such an account can do justice to this fact of uniqueness. Naturally the book has the defects of a first attempt. The author can only hope that none the less what he does give will compensate for his omissions.

Of the numerous difficulties in the way there are only two of which the reader should know how they were resolved.

The first is the definition of the area to be dealt with. The development in North Africa west of Egypt is left undiscussed; the treatment of this sub-ject would need a special study. Even with that omission the task was hard enough. Besides, had it been included, the rest of Africa where the same process is now visible could not have been left unconsidered. The author, therefore, confined himself to Asia including Egypt; that country is included for reasons which will be indicated in the book itself. None the less, in order to emphasize the continuity of the whole front 'from Morocco to Japan', the most important events on this left sector of the front will be given in the chronological survey.

The second difficulty was theoretical in character and so the harder to resolve. The author wished to write a history of modern Asian nationalism and not a history of modern imperialism. Yet these are inseparable inas-much as the latter is the chief cause of the former. That, however, means that imperialism must be described as the colonizing peoples saw it, and still see it today; otherwise the nationalist reaction would not be comprehensible. That does not imply that the author thinks their view of the matter is untrue. He agrees with what Sir Stafford Cripps said: 'You have only to look in the pages of British imperial history to hide your head in shame', and would add that the colonial history of other nations provokes a similar verdict; the words of the Founder of Christianity (Matt. xix, 24): 'It is easier for a camel to go through the eye of a needle, than for a rich man to enter into the kingdom of God' hold good not only for the individual but also for the nation. None the less, the picture given in these pages is not a complete one. Although imperialism in the form of domination by force and exploitation cannot in any way be defended, the author does not deny that milder aspects of it are visible in the motives, practice and attitude of individual governors and in the general development of self-government in many colonies. Nor should the direct and indirect advantages which some of the victims of colonialism drew from the conditions which colonization created be over-looked. Materially, many improvements were made: disease was combated, education furthered, ports, roads, bridges and irrigation works constructed. And, just as the author does not doubt that the Asians of today who are still struggling for complete independence must regard imperialism and colonialism as being as brutal as ever, so he does not doubt that in the future Asian historians will point out those milder and progressive aspects once co-operation – in the equality of which we have spoken – has become a reality.

But to progress to that point *one* condition must be fulfilled which is not fulfilled today. The West must understand that true objectivity in the judging of human phenomena depends – to quote my friend Pos, the young Dutch philosopher who died too soon – on integrating into a higher unity the conflicting interests and values, and that, naturally, is possible only if these interests and values – including one's own – are regarded relatively. It is only this objectivity which will free us from the particularism of the past and lead to that order of world citizenship the creation of which is the task of our times, or, to put it more simply, when the West frees itself from its delusion of superiority. But that remains a pious wish so long as we fail to recognize that man has morally to conquer himself in order to break through the barriers of the group to which he belongs 'by nature' and to achieve his integration in humanity itself.

This condition, as we have said, is not yet fulfilled. If there do exist signs that in principle the concept of the completely equal worth of all races and classes gains ground steadily, it is clear that it has not yet fully penetrated to the ruling classes, especially those of the West. Sometimes one has the impression that up to now the Vatican is the only power in the West which has fully realized the fundamental significance of the revolution in Asia – and acts accordingly.

This is a scientific book in the sense that every statement has been repeatedly controlled with the aid of the best material available, that the author has devoted more than thirty years to his task and that, in 1951–2 as a result of his stay in Indonesia, short as it was, as guest professor he had the opportunity to subject his views to the test of direct experience. But like any other historical work it is a construction of the human mind and will and feeling enter into it, thus giving it the character of a valuation. For the final basis of such an enquiry are, as no less an authority than Georg Jellinek [1] once said, not certain knowledge but a confession of faith. So the author confesses – without fear of being misunderstood by unprejudiced readers – that, when he wrote, his thought was of a better future for mankind and that he intended to make his contribution towards the coming of a better world.

Finally, for this English edition the author has to acknowledge his thanks to Dr J. M. Pluvier who was so kind as to help him in collecting the material for, and in the editing of, the last chapter containing a survey of the developments in the field since the Bandung conference.

[1] In his address as Pro-rector *Der Kampf des alten mit dem neuen Recht*, (Heidelberg 1907).

CONTENTS

INTRODUCTION

I

THE ASIA OF THE CENTURIES

WHAT were the essential characteristics of Asia, that section of the world into which the Europeans broke about A.D. 1500 and where from 1800 onwards they established colonial domains, domains which they believed would be permanent, but which, a century later, began to crumble and by the middle of this century had with a very few exceptions disappeared?

About sixty centuries ago river cultures arose in South and East Asia in the valleys of the Tigris and the Euphrates, of the Indus and the Ganges, of the Hoang-ho and the Yang-tse. Over the centuries these cultures spread from the valleys where they originated. The migrants brought with them the art of the cultivation of the soil, an art which demands of its users a relatively high degree of development, for cultivation depends on irrigation while the existence of proper irrigation works implies the establishment of central organs of administration. These migrant peoples were several times in their history the victims of invasion from the northern nomad areas. These nomads considered themselves the natural lords of the territories they overran. But conquest did not mean the disappearance of the cultures the invaders found. Rather these cultures were taken over and the new social structure which conquest created enabled them to reach even higher levels. There arose a caste which lived on the farmers and could devote itself primarily to the task of defence. But it also devoted itself to cultural tasks. Warriors and priests indeed ruled over the peasants, but they were there to protect them when necessary and to satisfy their loftier needs. Which task was the more important it is hard to say.

It is clear that in Southern Asia there did exist in many places and in very ancient times an intense spiritual life; in the case of the Middle East, India and China we have evidence of it in the sacred writings. Even if we did not have these, we could conclude that it did exist by the simple fact that it was in Asia that all the great religions originated. The process took many centuries but, relative to the length of man's history, a remarkably short time.

In India the religion of the Hindus – Hinduism or Brahmanism – was originally a local phenomenon, but as it spread to Farther India and Indonesia it acquired full right to be called a world religion. It has innumerable aspects, but common to all of them is the teaching which demands a higher morality by the doctrine of the transmigration of the soul and its rebirth in a higher form, if a life of moral goodness has been led. Still more important, because it is not just confined to India but has found the majority of its followers in China, is Buddhism, the religious ethic preached by the Buddha in the fifth century B.C. in reaction against the stagnation of Brahmanism. Today the adherents of the various Buddhist sects are estimated at

about 200,000,000, although in India there are now only some 30,000
Buddhists. Japan, in addition to Buddhism, has Shintoism, which combines
religious practices with a doctrine of moral obligation in which stress is laid
on social conduct and especially on the conduct of the subject towards the
emperor and the fatherland.

This fifth century is a very productive period in the religious history of
Asia. About 500 B.C. the Chinese philosopher Confucius began to expound
a doctrine which today has no fewer than 300,000,000 adherents. His is perhaps more an ideal ethic than a religion in the strict sense of the word, but
it is also a religion if the word 'religion' is used in its original sense of 'bond'.
From its origin until the present day the Confucian doctrine is the bond
which holds together its adherents because they all have the same conception
of what are the greatest human values. About the same time Zarathustra
appeared in Persia, teaching that history is a war between good and evil in
which good will eventually triumph. His teaching has not become a world
religion. Its adherents today number no more than 100,000 – the Parsees in
India who are the descendants of those who for their faith were driven from
Persia after the Moslem conquest. But the influence of his thought on
Christianity is undeniable; the Christian conception of God and Satan is
very akin to the Persian's.

Also about this time the prophets were teaching in what is today Israel.
Out of the religion of the Hebrews with its strict monotheism and its expectation of a Messiah they created the very special religion which we know as
Judaism. Because it arose in a very small country, and because of the many
persecutions of which the Jews were the victims, its adherents today number
barely 12,000,000, but the two latest great religions both arose from Judaism.

Last but one in time is Christianity. Although because of its history it can
be called European, it is none the less of Asian origin. Of all the great
religions it has the greatest number of followers – some 750,000,000; it must
be added, however, that the differences between Roman Catholicism, Ortho-
doxy and Protestantism are so great as to appear unbridgeable and that Protestantism itself is split into a number of mutually hostile sects.

The last world religion is Islam, which was founded in Arabia by Mohammed in the seventh century A.D. and brought back monotheism in its most
rigorous form. Today there are in the world some 350,000,000 Moslems, so
that in numbers Islam takes second place after Roman Catholicism. Partly
by conquest, partly by trade, Islam has spread from Arabia as far as
Morocco in the west, Central Africa in the south, South China and the
Indonesian archipelago in the east and in the north to Northern India,
Pakistan and Central Asia.

If we call these world religions it is, in part at least, to emphasize the importance of this southern part of Asia for the history of mankind, especially
because they still play a part in the awakening of Asia. The rise of so many
religions in so short a time is witness to the fact that the age was one of
turmoil, so much so that some scholars consider those few centuries immediately before and after 500 B.C. to mark a definite turning-point in history.
We are still very much in the dark about the origins of these religions. But

they testify to the fact that Asian history is not one of stagnation. It is a popular fallacy that Asian history shows little or no movement, a fallacy that obstinately persists mainly because European scholars, perhaps without being aware of it, use the rapidity of change in their own small area as a standard for areas very much larger. It is definitely a misconception to regard Asia as stiffly immobile. It is, however, a comprehensible one, for Asian methods of production are so fundamentally different from those of Europe. For centuries Asia presented the same economic picture – the patient cultivation of rice, corn or maize, producing roughly the same annual harvest, a sequence broken only by periodic drought and its consequence, starvation. Throughout Asia society was ordered on this unchanging agrarian basis despite variations of detail according to geographical situation. Asia indeed is like the sea. When the waves are whipped up to great size by the tempest, it is only the surface of the sea that is disturbed; the lower depths remain unaffected. So in Asia violent movements – rebellions, conquests, the rise and fall of kingdoms, the endless succession of ruling races – affected only the upper classes, while the lower remained for centuries unmoved. But it is here that the comparison ceases to apply. The surface movement of the sea has nothing to do with the calm of the depths. In Asian history the movement in the upper classes resulted from the immobility of the society in which they ruled. Because of the incapacity of Asian methods of production to develop, the ruler could do nothing, even if he wished, to raise his subjects' standard of living and so inevitably had to plunder them as he strove for power. If his plundering overstepped the limits of the peasants' endurance, revolt followed. If the revolt was successful, the reigning dynasty was either got rid of – in which case the leader of the revolt succeeded to its power – or it was so weakened that power later fell either to a native pretender or to a foreign enemy. In the latter case the victor added the shattered realm to his own empire, and there it remained until at the given moment his time too came and his empire fell to pieces.

This static agrarian basis, which is so different from the dynamic development of Europe since the end of the Middle Ages, with its yearly growth in industry and the consequent rise in the lower classes' standard of living, was the fundamental cause of the sharp division in Asia – existing even today – between rich and poor. As a result of what is by European standards a total failure of industry because of the unimportance of trade as compared to agriculture, there arose in Asia for the most part no free middle class such as in Western Europe filled the gaps between the two extremes. There was, of course, in Western Europe a clear distinction between prince and peasant, between noble and artisan, but the movement between the classes was, and is, progressive. Compare this with the monstrous difference still existing in Asia between the magnificence of courts and palaces, with their pomp and brilliance, and the huts of the peasants and the mean houses of the artisans and small merchants. Europe has never understood the art of domination as Asia has. That is why when Eastern and Western diplomatists negotiate, the latter come off the worse; it is not by chance that the Westerner talks of 'Asiatic cunning', cunning that is not simply the product of weakness.

Just as little is it accident that in the West we speak of 'Oriental splendour' and think of the East in terms of the fairy tale. It is not a fairy-tale world that is revealed, but the hard reality of sheer unlimited plundering of the subject masses, though it may not be altogether wrong to identify oriental wealth with a sort of unfulfilled dream. That wealth compared with the poverty of the rest of the population was infinitely greater than anything Europe or America has known. That is true not only of the great rulers – a sultan of Turkey, a shah or the Great Mogul; it is just as true of the Persian satrap, the viceroy, or warlord, of China and the shogun of Japan. They did live in palaces so large as to be almost small towns built at relatively small cost because labour was so cheap; the labourer earned no more than was necessary to keep him alive, settle down and have children, and in Asia what was necessary was very little. If the palace did cost more, forced labour made the peasant work for nothing. The exploitation of the masses is incontestable. It resulted in the heaping-up in the palaces of treasure of gold and silver, ivory and precious stones, each piece more costly than the other because of the refined sense of beauty of the Asian craftsman. And by the very law of exploitation whatever was squandered on favourites male and female, the treasure came back to the ruler or, if not to him, to his sons and successors.

Chinese literature abounds with tales of the absolute power and the spendthrift way of life of the great magnates who are not yet wholly of the past. That power was so unlimited that it continued on the death of the possessor. In India, the widows of the great were condemned to die with their husbands in the purifying funeral flames, and these women were so imbued with the sense of duty to their omnipotent lords that if they did not go joyfully to the pyre, they did go to it with devotion. There was no widow-burning in China, but the lot of woman there was no less ruled by law and custom; the binding of the feet is dumb witness to the fact that the Chinese woman's highest destiny was to be a domestic pet. So, if to a less degree, the veil of the Moslem woman was equivalent to denial of her right to live a free life of her own.

But all this power and wealth was not simply squandered, re-accumulated and squandered again. True, power and wealth did not, as in the later Europe, serve to increase production. But it was often spent in the service of higher culture and education, the possession of only a few no doubt, but none the less remarkable. Part of what the people produced by, as the Old Testament has it, the sweat of their brow, went to the priests and was dedicated to their maintenance and to that of the magnificent temples which in proud extravagance had been raised to the glory of the gods. Another part the priests, or a section of the educated laity, devoted to education and the increase of knowledge. The first observatory was constructed by the Chinese emperor in Pekin three hundred years before there were any in Europe, and four hundred years before Jesuit missionaries brought with them what were then the modern instruments of the West. What the Chinese mandarins, the Persian court poets, the Buddhist monks did over the centuries for art and literature cannot be told in a few words, but it can be summed up in one word – everything.

In all this power, wealth and culture the mass of the people had no share –

except, of course, that it was their toil which created the power of the ruler, the wealth of the upper class and the leisure which the scholar and the artist needed. Asian poverty is as proverbial as Oriental luxury. The peasant and the labourer were rewarded for painful toil at the treadmill of their lives with lack of the barest necessities, with a child mortality of as much as 88 per cent, often with the necessity of selling their daughters. In China these daughters became the slaves of the landlord; in Japan they became geishas. Often the man of the people had to sell himself – in Singapore he became a rickshaw man – to be for all his life the slave of another and end it an opium den. Everywhere in Asia the masses suffered disease, starvation, death. If any of them had the luck to have a bit of land of his own, enjoy a good harvest, have a tiny house with a vegetable plot, a goat, or even a cow, it was almost inevitable that every two years catastrophe took it all from him. There would be a bad harvest, a usurer who demanded payment on a debt incurred on a future harvest, a troop of soldiers who destroyed everything as they went plundering through the countryside; it is no accident that in China the most hated of all professions is the soldier's. With nothing of his own left, he paid with his poverty for the pride and good living of the rich. Sometimes, as in India, his misery was made harsher still by his being excluded from society altogether, by being a pariah.

No social revolution, no technical improvements brought change in his circumstances. For centuries agricultural methods remained just as they had been when the first cultures arose. In mountainous or desert areas water was the costliest article; only the rich could afford it because they owned the wells and so had power. In the valleys water made the land fruitful, but there was the perpetual danger of flood. Tools, pumps, ploughs, hunting and fishing tackle, proas and junks remained just as they were when the first pioneers with their astonishing inventiveness made them. Skill in their use made up for the lack of machinery. Housing remained in a pitiful state – tents in the agricultural areas, caves as in the Afghan hills. Men did not strive to better themselves as did the peasants and workers in later Europe, who made their own betterment their main objective. Had not their forefathers lived as they did as far back as memory could go and were they not worthy of reverence? So the Asian thought.

Thus lived the Asian masses, generation after generation, century after century, living in A.D. 1500 just as they had lived in 1500 B.C., uncoveting, undesiring and so renouncing the effort to gain an existence worthy of a human being.

II

INVASION FROM THE WEST

THE date A.D. 1500 in the preceding paragraph was deliberately chosen. The mass of the people in Europe then lived under conditions scarcely better than those under which Asians lived, but at that date there began to be completed a fundamental change which was to alter radically many of them. The change began in Athens at that historical turning-point about 500 B.C. already mentioned and, two millennia later, Europe overleaped its boundaries and began that expansion which took European sailors to America in the west and to Asia in the east – first simply to trade, then to protect trade and then, so far as was possible, to rule.

European scholars in their pride at the achievements of their ancestors have greatly exaggerated the Western predominance in Asia as far as the years between 1500 and 1800 are concerned. For centuries after that first date Asian trade was able to fight the threatened Western monopoly. Domination over Asia was not by any means complete; it was the Western invader who adapted himself to the East rather than *vice versa*. None the less the fact remains that Portuguese, Spaniards, Englishmen, Frenchmen and Dutchmen went eastward and that neither Chinese nor Indians landed in Europe nor – in historic times at least – did Japanese or Malays land in America.

For long, and particularly in the West, men were inclined to attribute the conquest of virtually all the 'coloured' peoples by the 'whites' to a definite sort of inferiority in the coloured races or, what is the same thing, to a superiority in the white – that is, the European – races. That view is right to a certain degree, for it is hard to see why conquest was possible if the European had not, to some extent and in a definite way – that is, technically and militarily – been superior to the vanquished peoples. But there is a flaw in the reasoning. It accepts as proven fact what is not proven; first, that this superiority came from the character of the European and was not the result of other causes, and, second, that this character always existed and would continue to exist. If the matter is regarded objectively, nothing is left of the innate superiority of the European peoples, the 'whites'. Historically the European domination lasted only a very short time, roughly only for the past three centuries. The constant tendency, when dealing with history, to project the past into the present, has obscured the relative shortness of European expansion, and given Europeans themselves the idea that their domination was a necessary result of European superiority and so would be permanent; it was quite arbitrarily assumed that the racial characteristics and the nature of the European peoples were unalterable.

History itself justifies the Asians and those Europeans who regard the racial question as of lesser importance and give greater weight to social and economic circumstances. During the European Middle Ages, i.e. between 400 and 1400, Europeans were so far from dominating other races and peoples that it is more correct to consider this period as one in which Europe was on the defensive, notably against the Arabs and the Mongols. Only when the first stage of capitalism was reached, with the consequent creation of national states at the end of the Middle Ages, was Europe possessed of a weapon with which she could not only repel attack but herself pass to the offensive, a weapon powerful enough to let her dominate the earth. The special characteristic of Europe, and particularly of Western Europe, is not just the rise of capitalist methods of production but their complete victory. Elsewhere that development was scarcely even begun; fully developed capitalism outside Europe came always from abroad. Here is an historical problem of the first magnitude which, despite all the acumen with which it has been examined, is still in no way solved.

History does not wait for the solution of problems of theory. This century has shown that capitalism and Western rule are not eternal. If it is true that the kernel of the whole Asian question from Cairo to Kamschatka lies less in the difference between races than in the difference in methods of production and the resultant difference in the standard of living, then we must enquire more closely into the nature and consequences of the ensuing conflict.

When the European development reached its climax about 1800 in the Industrial Revolution and the French Revolution, with the resultant liberation of unknown energies, the influence of the West was decisive for the future of Asia. In the nineteenth century Asia had no choice save between rejection and conformity, and latterly only the second choice was possible. Then came the stream of cotton goods from Lancashire which disrupted the Asian village community. Then came the opium war with China and the forcible entry into Japan. Then came the construction of the Suez Canal which so shortened the passage to Asia. Then came the steamship and the railway constructed with Western capital and by Western technology.

Still more effective was Western influence after the rise of imperialism, i.e. after the productive capabilities of Europe had through industrialization reached such a height that the need for raw materials and for markets for their products became a problem for the Western nations. Because of this ever-growing industry and extending trade there came such an accumulation of capital that in its turn capital investment became a problem. European capital flowed to whatever region offered the greatest possibilities of gain – that is, not to the Western nations suffering from a surfeit of capital, but to all the undeveloped land wherever it might be. It was laid out in railways, canals, ports and finally in industry as well. This capitalism invaded the colonial regions, and so everywhere began the supersession of pre-capitalist methods of production.

For the sake of simplification we use the phrase 'undeveloped lands'; in the literal sense there was of course no such thing. Virtually every land to which Western colonizers came already contained people who got their living by their own methods. Capitalist expansion did not develop on a universal plan in lands still lying fallow in order to exploit them for the benefit of humanity, but simply first to find a market for excess production, then to procure raw materials and thirdly to obtain cheap labour. The primaeval forests of Brazil, the deserts of Africa and the steppes of Asia were of little use in the attainment of these three aims. Imperialism came only where there was gain to be made, above all to South and East Asia. In all the exploited colonial and semi-colonial areas there arose what has been called a 'dual economy'. After the railways came the airlines, which opened all these lands to modern traffic. And with the traffic arose modern towns with sewage systems and fresh-water supplies and in the countryside modern factories, dams, port facilities, mines, oilwells, indeed everything which only Western technology could construct.

It would be to take a short view to say that there was here only a matter of profit-making, and that the question whether Asian culture could at the same tempo absorb European civilization was never taken into consideration. Such absorption was naturally the more difficult in proportion to the genuineness and solidity of the existing culture. To accommodate its own native culture to industrialization had taken Europe three hundred years, and that not without loss. Asia was given just a tenth of that time. It is not surprising then that the westernization of Asia shook the Asian social order and the centuries-old cultures to their foundations, and that the inevitable process of readjustment meant deep dislocation and violent outbreaks.

The new economy whereby the aggressive capitalism of the West attacked and shattered the traditional pre-capitalist Asia of peasants and workers was the basis for a revolution of an extent not so far known in her history. That revolution found its most notable expression in resistance against the bringers of the revolution, against Europe, and with the more reason in that capitalism treated the Asian peoples shamefully, and beyond and above economic exploitation there was the suppression of nationalism and the humiliation of the individual.

Was imperialism, however, no more than an evil? Human relations are never so simple as that. Imperialism was an evil so far as capitalism is an evil. But it was also a good in so far as capitalism too has its good side. On earth man must live on what the earth can produce, and the more men multiply the more intensively must the earth's resources be exploited. This intensification of exploitation of what the earth produces and of those riches which have been accumulated in it in the course of millions of years is called the development of production. Now it is clear that no single kind of production in history has been so effective in exploitation as capitalism and its imperialist phase has meant nothing less than the increase of production throughout the world. Even if unwittingly, imperialism has drawn the countless millions of non-Europeans into the modern production process which with all its temporary material sufferings none the less opens out every possibility.

If history is not to be falsified it must be admitted that European and American colonialism and imperialism had virtually no other aim than profit, but it must also be admitted that the very effort to make profit led to the extinction, or at least the combating, of the worst evils from which Asia suffered; nor should it be contested that in place of these evils others arose often as unintended as unexpected. The capitalist invasion has often been described as the gold trimmings on the beggar's cloak of Asia, and rightly, for the trimming often was of gold. People from the land must be educated in modern fashion if a modern social system is to become possible. That meant high schools and universities. Workers in modern factories must be able to read and write and understand something about the machines which they work. That demands technical as well as general schools. If the tobacco and sugar fields, the coffee and tea plantations, are to produce more, the workers must understand something about their products. That means some agricultural training. If it is undesirable that the worker be an absentee half the time because of sickness, then hygienic conditions have at least to be improved – that is, there must be an adequate water supply; the population must be taught hygiene; information centres and hospitals must be set up. And that does happen – too slowly, indeed, on too small a scale, too haltingly – but happen it does. And where it happens, disadvantages come with it. The population increases more quickly than does the provision of food. The excess of population leaves the land. Where there is industry it is proletarianized; where there is none it is pauperized.

There is, however, one circumstance outwith the range of this balancing of good and evil. The process of modernization in Asia created a group of Europeans who, because of the work they undertook, took a different attitude to their Asian fellow-being and helped to awaken him. He would indeed have awakened without their aid, but awakening would probably have come later and more slowly. That awakening is expressed in the European word nationalism. Asian nationalism awakened by Western imperialism has roused millions from their centuries-long sleep and so warned the world of a new stage of development. The imperialism of the Western industrial states has swept over the tropical countries like a flood destroying great cultures in its foaming course, reducing the peoples to a great mass of the exploited, but from the mud which high water leaves behind there arises nationalism from which comes a new culture, a new society, as soon as the flood subsides. May it be seen that a liberated Asia will be able to do what the West could not do, reap the benefits of modern production technology without getting entangled in the works of its own machines.

III

RELIGION AND NATIONALISM

In the preceding section we have met more than once with the term nationalism; we have not yet said what it means. We can give no definition nor are history and the other social sciences fitted to supply one. Simple definitions can be easily grasped, but they are not of much use here, for human, and so historical, phenomena are always much too complicated to admit of explanation in our limited vocabulary. If one attempts an adequate definition it will be itself so complicated that only a reader who knows the phenomena thoroughly will understand what we are trying to say. If, in the following sections, we learn to know the phenomena which collectively we call nationalism, then we will know what nationalism means. In other words, historical concepts can be understood only if we are sufficiently acquainted with the phenomena on which these concepts rest; in the same way we know and learn to understand our fellow man.

Here we must say a word about the relation between religion and nationalism, for, in the awakening of Asia, both concepts play an important role. Nationalism is more than the simple stirring of the population of a country, or of a group in that population, towards the attainment of political independence. It is also more than a striving towards economic independence of the foreigner. It is more than loyalty towards the national state itself though it includes that. Further, nationalism is not an eternal permanent concept. We know a Western nationalism and an Eastern one, a nationalism of the sixteenth century, one of the nineteenth and yet another of the twentieth. They are all in a sense different, yet so akin that we apply the same term to all of them.

Nationalism is, then, a historical phenomenon. There was a time when it did not exist. In Europe it first showed itself in Germany in the time of the ill-famed Thirty Years' War (1618–1648). That was in part a war of religion: that is, in the state and in society religion was the most important factor. Roughly after 1650 and especially after the French Revolution (1789) nationalism to some extent took the place of religion. That should not be interpreted in the sense that religion disappeared; it simply no longer remained the spiritual basis of the social order. There arise new national states whose inhabitants belong to different religions, e.g. Germany, Britain, Holland, Switzerland and the United States of America. That nationalism could replace religion to a certain extent as a ruling principle results from the fact that the many human needs which in other societies were satisfied by religion, could now be satisfied in part at least by nationalism; that is, there is in nationalism a religious element or, better, nationalism is in a sense itself a religion. That nationalism has to some extent taken the place of religion has up to now been considered as a European phenomenon, and when it is seen in Asia about 1900 is regarded as an import from Europe. That is not at all certain. It is possible that at a certain stage in its growth each nation develops nationalist tendencies. If that is true then, as in Europe from 1600, so in Asia from 1900 nationalism may have arisen of itself at a period when not only the ruling classes but broad strata of the population had gone so far in their development as to begin to interest themselves in the concerns of their state and their society.

After this theorizing let us return to historical facts, and cite some cases of the connection between religion and nationalism – a European case, a Moslem, an Indian, a Burmese and a Japanese case. The original Christian Church has had two schisms. The first was in 1054, and had as consequence the establishment of the Eastern Church in Southeastern Europe and in Russia. The second, the Reformation, came in the middle of the sixteenth century and resulted in a division between Northern Europe which became Protestant, and Southern Europe which stayed Roman Catholic, and we may note the remarkable fact that this second schism occurred roughly at the same time at which we begin to detect a growth of nationalism in Europe. The chief direct cause of the Reformation was the abuses and superstitions in the old church. But nationalism, particularly in Germany, Britain, Holland and Switzerland, was possibly as important a factor. Before the Reformation much money flowed from believers in these countries to the Papal court. That annoyed the nationalists. They wanted to keep it in their own lands; they wished also to control church and religious affairs themselves. Remember this was the beginning of the period of mercantile capitalism when national capital could already claim a direct influence on production.

The great reform movement in Islam – our second case – began in central Arabia, the cradle of Islam, in the eighteenth century. Mohammed Abd el-Wahhab (c. 1702–1791) founded a sect there which sought to purify Islam from the abuses which had crept into it, by introducing a simple puritan – by derivation, virtually equivalent to pure – way of life. At the same time the Wahabites sought to combat European influences, to which they ascribed the abuses which they were trying to remove. There was exaggeration here. The Europeans have been the cause of many abuses, but not of all the evils in the world. All human and divine institutions, since they are managed by men, are exposed to corruption and all religions show from time to time efforts at reform. The sultan in Constantinople, who was the temporal and spiritual head of Islam, tried to suppress the Wahabite movement but without success. At the beginning of the nineteenth century the Turkish governor of Egypt undertook a regular campaign against the Wahabites, occupied Mecca and Medina (1803–6) and threatened Damascus and Syria. And the great nationalist Ibn Saud, from whom Saudi Arabia takes its name, belonged to the Wahabite sect.

A sect akin to it arose (1887) in North Africa; it called itself Senussi after its original leader Mohammed Ali el-Senussi. Its adherents spread all over North Africa and were opposed both to the suzerainty of the sultan and to the encroaching Europeans. In 1901–2 they fought against the French; in 1914 there was a mass revolt against the Italians who had taken Libya from Turkey (1911–12), and it was no accident that, when Mussolini sought to found an African empire, the Senussi were his opponents. They had their centre at Kufra, a little west of the Egyptian frontier. Mussolini overran their territory, with the usual colonial atrocities. But the defeat of the sect in 1931 did not mean the defeat of its ideas; ideas are not destroyed by bayonets. If Islam today is once again an inspiring and driving factor from Morocco to New Guinea – no matter how one judges the policy of the various Moslem groups – that is due largely to the Wahabites and the Senussi.

Besides this negative defence against the West and against all that can be called modern, there was, and still is, in Islam a tendency to try to make head against the West by partial acceptance of modern ways; this is the positive defence. This is the movement which found much support in Egypt and in India through the teachings of Jamal ed-din al Afghani (1838–1879). In Egypt it was Mohammed Abduh (1849–1905 and from 1899 Grand Mufti) who, in the belief that there was no conflict between Western science and Islam, sought to give a 'modern' interpretation of the teaching of the Koran. In India it was Sir Said Ahmed Khan (1817–1898), the founder of the Moslem University in Aligarh, who thought that Islam, which was so 'natural', could not conflict with the laws of science and so opened the way to Western ideas. The Indian Moslem Said Ameer Ali, in his book *The Spirit of Islam* (1891), appealed to a new interpretation of the Koran to support his modern ideas on slavery, polygamy and divorce. He recalled the historical fact that the beginning of a modern science in Europe was the work of Arab scholars. Mohammed Iqbal (1873–1938), who inspired the later idea of Pakistan, appealed to Bergson and Nietsche in his new conception of Islam, just as in Turkey Zia Gok Alp, in his investigation of the religious institutions of Islam, appealed to Comte and Durckheim; he is still today the honoured spiritual father of Turkish nationalism.

It is remarkable that this modern tendency in Islam is strengthened in practice by the belief that the reforms which each reformer strives for are to be found in the Koran if it is only read rightly. If on the one hand that means a tendency towards secularization, on the other it means continued attachment to the old beliefs, and this double inspiration – the puritan and the modern – constitutes the greatest driving force of the politico-religious nationalist movement in the Moslem world.

Our third case is the renaissance of Hinduism, and this too is intimately connected with the modern nationalist effort. The first figure one thinks of is Swami Vivekananda (*ob.* 1902), in whose teaching Eastern and Western influences are inseparably united. Educated on Western lines he fell like many younger men under the spell of Sri Ramakrishna, a mystic *yogi* and saint in the old Hindu tradition. In the 'nineties he spent three years in America and Europe, and so reached a synthesis which amounted to a belief that the East must take over the material achievements of the West, while the West must receive Hinduism from the East. In his view Hinduism was the religion which recognized the relative truths in all other religions. His speeches at the Congress of Religions in Chicago are the first conciliatory yet challenging answer to Western missionary activity. Tilak, the pioneer of Indian nationalism, took the same view. But he added something important. In his *Gita Rahasha* ('The Mystery of the Bhagavad Gita'), which he wrote in prison, he re-interpreted the teaching of this holy book of Hinduism. It did not, as had hitherto been asserted, teach the rejection of the world; rather it was in its own way a book which taught a dynamic social ethos, a social activism – that is, it taught just those lessons which would save India. And so closely in this new and modern interpretation is it bound to the nationalist movement that it can be said that all the great leaders in India's struggle for independence – Nehru is the one exception – have felt compelled to add their commentaries to Tilak's. Among them Annie Besant, by her translation of the *Bhagavad Gita* and through the educational work of her Theosophical Society, as well as by her personal share in the independence movements of nationalism and Hinduism, helped to bind each the closer to the other.

The fourth case is the revival of Buddhism in Burma. In the days of British domination it had been deprived of its official status and had become torpid. But when the national movement began to penetrate to the mass of the people, revival began. It was the *pongyi*, the Buddhist priest, who in days of old had brought the elements of knowledge to the villages and who now resumed religious teaching and spread nationalism. This union of religion and national revival is seen best in the calling of the great Buddhist Oecumenical Council in Rangoon in 1956 by U Nu the premier, on the occasion of the celebration of the Buddha's birth two and a half millennia earlier. It marked a notable revival of the old Buddhist council tradition. The first council had been held immediately after the Buddha's death, the second by Asoka in the third century B.C. and the third by Kanishka in the second century A.D.

The last case is Japan. The original religion, Shintoism, the way of the gods, was originally a sun-cult. Between the eighth and the nineteenth centuries Shintoism was of less importance than the Buddhism imported from China. But between 1868 and 1912 reformers appeared who preferred national Shintoism to international Buddhism, and sought to return to the original purity of their own tradition. As Japan modernized herself politically and economically, Shintoism became the State religion and developed a complete politically-tinged philosophy whose basic concept is that the Japanese as an individual is nothing; Japan and the emperor are everything. It was symbolic that the American occupation (1945) abolished Shintoism as the State religion. Thus, in a very different form to that shown by Christianity and Islam, here too there was a remarkable revival of both religion and nationalism.

A.C.—2

IV

THE POLITICAL AND SOCIAL REVOLUTION

IN addition to this connection between religion and nationalism there is another factor which, though of a very different kind, is so general that in order to avoid repetition we must deal with it in this introduction. This is the general complex of political and social strivings which we call the Asian revolution. There is nothing special about it; all the revolutions of earlier times of which we know, from the Dutch revolution in the sixteenth century to the general European one of the nineteenth, have a social as well as a political aspect. In them all the form of government was more or less radically altered, and as a result a new class temporarily or permanently became dominant. The decisive difference between them and the revolutions of our own century – the Russian, the Chinese and the Asian – is this: in the earlier revolutions the leadership was in the hands of a single class, the bourgeoisie, and the political and social demands were on a single plane; in the later that is not so. In them the social demands were not put forward by the bourgeoisie alone, but also by the peasants and workers, and they were not always the same demands. Something in the nature of a breach in the revolutionary front is indeed seen in the earlier revolutions; the iconoclasts in Holland, the levellers in the English revolution, were from the social point of view more radical than the Dutch burghers or Cromwell. In the French revolution the secret society of the 'Equals' (1796–7) is proof of a definite discrepancy between the main current of the revolution and its undercurrents; the conflict ended with Babeuf's execution. Still plainer is the lower middle class current in the February revolution of 1848, and in the suppressed June rising, while the Commune of 1871 is entirely the work of the radical lower and lowest classes; the Commune lasted for ten weeks before it was crushed by the mass of the bourgeoisie.

The Russian revolution is the classical example of the second type. Even in the abortive attempt of the bourgeoisie to seize power in 1905, peasants and workers played not only a great, but a creative, part. When, twelve years later, in March 1917, the bourgeoisie made the attempt again, it was plainly shown in November that its proletarian 'comrades' in the struggle against Czarism had become so powerful as to seize power themselves and put an end not only to Czarism but to the bourgeoisie as well. The tempo of the Chinese revolution was slower, but its nature is precisely the same. The war between the Chinese bourgeoisie and feudalism lasted fifteen years (1911–1926) if we regard as its end the reuniting of the empire under Chiang Kai-shek. But the victory was of relatively short duration. Twenty-five years later Chiang had to flee from his proletarian opponents to Formosa.

Comparison of the earlier revolutions and those of our own time show that it is the time factor that is decisive. The former, the bourgeois, revolutions had time to develop; in today's revolutions the proletarian follows hard on the heels of the bourgeois revolution or at least can do so, and particularly in Asia where the bourgeoisie is no stronger than it was in Russia or in China. Above all, even where it is strongest, i.e. in India, it is weak in numbers as compared to the mass of the population. Also, everywhere in Asia it is young. While the European bourgeoisie took four centuries (1350–1750) to prepare itself for the exercise of power and then had two centuries in which to exercise it without being seriously threatened either from 'above' or from 'below', the Asian bourgeoisie had only four decades.

This difference in time raises a series of problems which still further emphasize the weakness of the Asian bourgeoisie. Even as a ruling class it cannot in so short a time gain the prestige which the European bourgeoisie possessed long before it became a ruling class. In Asia, money as such generally confers no direct social prestige, and so the Asian bourgeois, just as his European counterpart long did, imitates the feudal class either by putting his money into landed property or wasting it in extravagant living; he never put it, or enough of it, into commerce or industry as capital, i.e. as productive investment for the building up of a modern industry and the transport facilities such industry needs.

This creation of a modern industry and a communications system itself constitutes a serious problem, for it seems to be the only way in which the standard of living of the masses can be raised. That is the more insistent as today the masses multiply rapidly; the death rate falls – for South, Central and East Asia on an average by 28 per 1000 – but the birth rate shows no material fall, being still 41 and 45 in these regions. Here, too, comparison between the industrial revolution in contemporary Asia with the earlier one in Europe is instructive. If we accept 1750 as the date of the beginning of the industrial revolution in Britain, British industry has had two centuries in which to develop. For other countries it is a shorter period – a century and a half for France and the United States, a century for Germany and half a century for Russia and Japan. We may ask whether revolution can go quicker, but we must also ask whether Asia will be allowed half a century, if the rapidity of the increase in its population will not mean that its standard of living will not rise but fall. One thing seems clear, that the peasants and workers will urge their social claims the more vigorously if their standard of living rises slowly.

Here too we are faced with the problems which industrialization always brings, but which are far more serious in the Asia of today, for there the social revolution is already in progress and the national revolution is scarcely yet ended. We have already mentioned one, its own bourgeoisie's lack of accumulated capital. Really decisive aid neither the Western nor the Eastern 'bloc' can, or is willing to, supply, despite all the fair words and promises of each. The Soviet Union also is faced with the task of building up an industry while lacking a class which can finance it out of savings. Indeed, there the State has to 'save' by lowering the standard of living of its people while holding before their eyes a social ideal. A non-Communist regime cannot do that, and besides, the great majority of the Asian masses live in a condition of such abject poverty that that measure, even if one wished, could not be applied to them.

But even granted that this capital in the required amounts was available in a foreseeable time, men are not so quickly accustomed to the regulated work which is unavoidable in modern production methods. Here again we may see from the history of Europe that this adjustment process takes time. Even there it is not so long since the worker refused to adjust himself. The normal labourer or the worker at home who, if he has got so far as to be able to do so, can himself fix his hours of labour, the peasant who goes to the field only when there is a definite task to be done, does not overnight become a factory worker who has to be punctually at his place, and work without pause since otherwise he will be dismissed.

In my view it is in this complex of problems that we must seek the explanation of what I call the 'double face' of the modern Asian bourgeois and particularly of the modern Asian intellectual who most clearly displays it though he may not be aware of its causes. His position is 'split' and has a double aspect. First, the bourgeois stands between the present and the past, a position creating a revolutionary situation which in Asia assumes a special form, for there the very modern present and the virtually still feudal past are much farther apart than the few years of transition would lead us to expect. Secondly, and more important, there is the fact that, as a result of the speed at which the national revolution has been completed and at which the social revolution threatens to be completed, the position of his class is 'split'. While it was more or less revolutionary so long as it was a question of obtaining national independence, it tends to pass over to the opposition when it comes to making a social revolution.

Thus the leaders of the political revolution in Asia find themselves in an extremely difficult situation, and one would be inclined to say that the problems facing them are insoluble were it not for the fact that history does not know of an insoluble problem. There will be a solution but no one can predict its nature. We can, however, make one assertion of a general kind. Nothing in history is either completely advantageous or completely disadvantageous. The disadvantage of the tempo, at which the Asian revolution is being completed is now clear to us; it is the speeding up of its political and social sides which is so prolific of contradictions. But the advantage is just as clear. The same tempo will also shorten the difficult transition period towards a new and more stable situation.

V

GEOGRAPHICAL AND HISTORICAL DIVISIONS

BEFORE we pass to the history of Asia in the last half-century and, in particular, of the national movements in this period, it would be well to study this continent a little more closely on the map. In this greatest of the five continents – the figures are for 1950 – there lives a population of 1,300,000,000. In Europe there is one of 500,000,000; in America of 325,000,000; in Africa of 185,000,000, and in Australia and Oceania of 12,500,000. Asia has a third of the earth's land surface and more than half the world's population.

Of the Asians as many as 90 per cent live in South and East Asia, i.e. the area from West Pakistan up to and including Japan. This is the area which produces nine-tenths of the world's rice, where the yearly rainfall is at least 50 cm. From the point of view of climate, Asia is sharply divided between the dry north and west and the moist south and east. If we call this moist area, which is densely populated, the 'inner zone', and the generally thinly populated north and west the 'outer zone', then, on a conventional map which shows mountain and desert, the frontier between them can be easily traced. A no man's land of desert and steppe stretches along the northern and western frontiers of the inner zone, which is marked by the steppe-like highlands of Afghanistan, the snowclad Himalayas, the barren tableland of Tibet, the desert of Gobi, and the hills and coniferous forests of Eastern Siberia north of Manchuria. If he flies over it, the traveller will see from the Arabian Sea to the Sea of Japan nothing but sand, stone, snow and rough grass and trees. This division into zones is as arbitrary as any other attempt to expound a complicated reality in a simple formula. Actually in the outer zone there is a series of centuries-old, fertile oases like the valleys of the Tigris and Euphrates, the coasts of the Mediterranean and the Russian area southeast of the Sea of Aral. Nor when we come to the inner zone could anyone call the Indian desert or the wastes of Borneo thickly populated agricultural areas. But such deviations apart, the frontier we have outlined is of great value to the comprehension of Asia past and present, possibly of greater value than the state frontiers which have been drawn arbitrarily enough.

The meaning of inner and outer here is naturally subjective. An inhabitant of Cairo, Teheran or Samarkand would be inclined to name the zone in which he lives the inner zone, and call Southeast Asia the outer zone, but considering that, in the latter, 90 per cent of Asians live, our nomenclature seems preferable.

When we come to geographical frontiers, the frontiers of Asia are in the east washed by the waters of the Pacific; near the coast that ocean has other names – the Bering Sea, the Sea of Okhotsk, the Sea of Japan, the Yellow Sea, the South China Sea. For our purpose these local names are without significance, for the waters all belong to the Pacific in which lie Japan and the Philippines; on the boundary between the Pacific and the Indian Oceans lies Indonesia. Here Asia is separated from the other continents by the Indian Ocean, and here too it is of no significance that the ocean east of India is called the Gulf of Bengal, that to the west of India the Sea of Arabia, the Persian Gulf and the Red Sea. Nor does the northern boundary present any difficulty. Although the traveller by air along the coast of the northern frozen sea would find it difficult to tell what was land and what was water in these icy regions, on the map the frontier can be easily traced along the coast line from the Bering Straits to Novaya Zemlya. The western boundary is less easy to define. Although in earlier times the frontier between European and Asiatic Russia was drawn along the Ural Mountains and the river Ural which flows into the Caspian, the scientist nowadays tends to draw it from Novaya Zemlya southward along the Urals to the sources of the Pechora; from there, southeast to the frontier of the Soviet Republic of Kazakstan in the neighbourhood of Petropavlovsk (long. 70°); farther west along the Kasakstan frontier and so to the Caspian at the mouth of the Volga. From the Caspian, which can be regarded as a Russian inland sea, the line turns westward south of the Caucasus to the Black Sea, along the northern coast of Turkey and the east coast of the Mediterranean to the Suez Canal and the Red Sea, which between Aden and Jibuti runs into the Indian Ocean.

The frontier between Europe and Asia so far as the Russian part of it is concerned is no natural frontier; it has been fixed by history and is first and foremost a politico-economic frontier. On the average the Urals are so low that they do not, as, for instance, do the Himalayas, form a barrier to traffic, and the Ural river is of no importance. Europe is separated from Asia by history, not by nature. Were it not for history, Europe would still be what it was for centuries – a series of Asian peninsulas.

We can from the general picture proceed to describe the countries in the two zones, the history of whose awakening is the subject of this book. It must be said that a comprehensive history of Asia is not possible to write in the framework which we have laid down; the narrative deals only with the most important countries and the emphasis is on the development of nationalism. It is with the following countries that I propose to deal – in the inner zone Burma, China, the Philippines, India, Indonesia, Japan, Korea, Malaya, Siam; and in the outer, Afghanistan, Egypt,[1] Irak, Persia, Israel, Jordan, Lebanon, Saudi Arabia, Russian Asia, Syria and Turkey.[1]

Having made a division in space we now have to make a division in time, i.e. in history. The half-century (1900–1950) can be divided into five periods. The first is from 1900 to 1914, the period of the 'awakening' of Asia in the narrower sense of the term. The terminus here is the outbreak of the First World War. Later we shall explain more fully why that war had so tremen-

[1] For the reasons for the inclusion of Egypt v. p. 93.

dous an influence on Asia; here we merely note that up to its outbreak many Asians hated the European, but were still so much under the influence of his assured bearing, his air of domination, that respect was greater than hate. Without exaggeration it may be said of these fourteen years that, as a result of the improvement of the administration which was coincident with the beginning of industrialization and the increase in the number of native officials, dependence on, as well as attachment to, the Western rulers increased rather than diminished. When, however, Asia saw that on the battlefields of France and Russia the Europeans were destroying themselves – the terrible figure of eleven million dead was as well known in Asia as in Europe – respect suffered a heavy blow. The Asian peoples began to despise the Europeans for their lust of power and especially for their lack of self-control. Then, too, the war brought about an economic upheaval. As its demands on the peoples of Europe were drastic in the extreme, few industrial products reached Asia and fewer agricultural and mining products went to Europe, and of what was shipped much was sent to the bottom of the sea by German cruisers and submarines. Here was the reason for a sudden progress in industrialization, notably in Japan and India, thus opening up new possibilities for Asia's nationalist bourgeoisie and the creation of a new Asian self-consciousness.

The second period – 1914 to 1919, the war years – we can call the era of the 'deglorification' of the West. From 1919 onward Asian self-consciousness found fresh expression and the Asian peoples demanded the fulfilment of the pledges which the colonial powers had given during the war in order to secure their co-operation. There was a similar situation in Europe, where the workers did not get what had been promised them in the times of danger. This connection between the Labour movement in Europe and the anti-colonial movement in the colonies – the reaction to government breaches of faith – should not be forgotten when we study the liberation of Asia.

During the war the Russian revolution had begun (1917), which had a greater power of attraction to all the Asian peoples because of its renunciation of all Russia's imperialist positions, e.g. in Persia and China, which were outside the Russian frontiers proper. As a direct consequence, revolts on a large or small scale broke out in Asia and particularly in Egypt.

The third period is that between 1919 and 1941. In the former year there was a sort of reaction, an attempt to restore Western rule in Asia and capitalist power over the Asian working class; the latter attempt had its parallel in Europe. In the first years of this period – really up to 1928 – the Russian revolution and the USSR which had emerged from it were still weak. During the period of civil war (1918–1922) the new state was hard put to it to maintain itself against counter-revolutionary armies led by Czarist generals and the armed intervention of Britain, France, Japan, the United States and Poland. In Europe the war was over. The revolutionary workers' movement was everywhere crushed and the colonial governments of Britain, France and Holland had their hands free to repress any national movement which during the war had arisen in Asia. None the less the new ideas survived in spite of Western suppression and we may call this period in the awakening of Asia one of action and reaction.

The fourth period is once again a war period. The Second World War broke out in Europe on September 3, 1939; in Asia on December 7, 1941, with the Japanese attack on Pearl Harbour; it ended on August 14, 1945, with the surrender of Japan. That period, one of only 2194 days and nights, changed Asia politically more than all the previous hundred years had done. As a result of the Japanese conquest of broad stretches of the China coast, of all Farther India – i.e. Indochina, Siam and Burma – of Malaya with Singapore, of Indonesia, the Philippines and all the islands of the Pacific west of Midway – i.e. from Attu in the Aleutians to Funafuti in the Ellice group – all Southeast Asia was involved in a common misery in which to some extent India, Pakistan and the Middle East shared. What had happened in the First World War happened again on a larger scale in the Second. Because of the German aggression in Europe, which was almost entirely overrun by Hitler's armies, the colonial governments were so weakened that they had once again to think in terms of the independence of their Asian colonies. But the difference between that situation and the one in 1919 lay in the fact that the West was totally, or very largely, unable to maintain its rule over great areas of Asia. This fourth period we call 'storm over Asia'.

The fifth period, i.e. from 1945 onward, is certainly no less important than its predecessor, but it must be rather differently treated. It is so short that it belongs to the present and not yet to history; we have on it a great mass of facts, but cannot yet make historical judgements. To judge of the events of the post-war period we must wait some years until we know what political freedom meant to the liberated peoples.

We can, of course, make some sort of judgement now, but it cannot be a permanent one. That is why the history of this fifth period is left to a concluding chapter which is called 'fulfilment and disillusion', fulfilment because nearly all the Asian countries attained either full or partial independence, disillusion because they found that independence did not solve all their problems. In any scientific project, the solution of a problem creates one or more new problems; that is true here and need cause no surprise. In the struggle for independence all the groups in the colonial lands worked together more or less harmoniously; today the groups are in conflict with one another – here violently, there less so; there is conflict between the feudal upper class, with whose help the Europeans and Americans still endeavour to maintain their rule, and the middle class, conflict between the middle class and the workers and peasants. If we can perhaps foresee the result of that conflict, the course it will take is for the time being not known to us.

Some readers perhaps will ask why this historical study begins with the year 1900 when, as we saw, Western domination had already lasted so long. The answer is that actually it was in 1900 that the nationalizing or modernizing process began. To explain it we shall use the two concepts made familiar by the British philosopher and historian A. J. Toynbee, who made the concepts of challenge and response the basis of his investigation of the causes of the rise and fall of civilizations.

The aggression of the West was the challenge to Asia, and the various reactions to it the response Asia made. In the first three and a half centuries of colonial history the challenge was weak and only here and there was there response. The Dutch attack on Jakarta in 1619 was a weak challenge. Blood was indeed shed, but two foreign ships and the establishment of a foreign fort hardly constituted a dangerous threat. As a result of the industrial revolution the challenge throughout the nineteenth century became much stronger, and then so strong that Asia was stunned and there was no response. The Anglo-Chinese opium war of 1839 was typical. Opium was a British product made in India. China sought to prevent its import and was humiliatingly forced to raise the bar. This challenge shocked Asia, but not permanently; half a century later she slowly recovered and sought a response to the challenge. That was about 1900, the last year preceding the coming of the twentieth century, which was to be the century of liberation.

In principle, two responses were possible to the Western challenge. If we compare the ships, soldiers and merchants who discovered Asia to burglars, the peoples thus assailed could either lock their houses and so try to avoid loss, or they could endeavour to ward off the burglar until they could take over Western techniques and fight him with his own weapons. Japan is an outstanding case of both responses. In 1543 the Portuguese landed in Japan; in 1600 the Dutch came, in 1602 the Spaniards and in 1613 the English. Resistance grew. In these merchants and priests the Japanese saw the pioneers of Western aggression. Between 1600 and 1612 various anti-Christian measures were taken, and in 1639 the shogun Yemitsu completed the process by expelling all foreigners from Japan. Only Chinese and Dutchmen were allowed to remain as merchants, and the latter were confined to Deshima, a small artificial island in Nagasaki Bay. The policy of national isolation lasted until, roughly, 1850.

After the opening up of Japan by the Americans (1853-4) Japan began to prepare the second response. It was virtually completed by 1900; Japanese technology no longer lagged behind – or not very much behind – the West. In 1895 a Great Power, China, was defeated; the Japanese army, be it noted, was built on German lines. In 1902 came the Anglo-Japanese Alliance and so Japan became a Great Power, and in 1904-5 she astonished the world by defeating Russia. That defeat made a deep impression all over the 'coloured' world; even in far-away African villages where no one could either read or write, tomtoms and fire signals told the villagers that one of the most dreaded Western powers had come off the loser in a war with a relatively small Asian country. In the first period Japan used its strength to repel the foreigner; in the second to make her own what the foreigner possessed, and in both cases remained true to herself.

So the responses, however different, even contrary, they may be, had the same result for the West and it is not surprising to see all the Asian peoples to a greater or less degree using both methods though not everywhere on the Japanese model; often the defence was tentative and uncertain as was the 'dewesternization' involved. It was difficult to create these responses because naturally European imperialism put every obstacle in the way of their creation. In the first case defence was answered by stronger attack; in the second obstacles were put in the way of the industrialization of the colonial lands and the creation of a middle class. The best example of initial irresolution and weakness is Turkey, which lies so close to Europe; the best example of a clear response to challenge is Japan, which is equidistant from Europe and America.

First Period 1900–1914

THE AWAKENING OF ASIA

I

THE TURKISH EMPIRE

In a history of nationalism the Turkish Empire is a special case and a particularly interesting one. Here the Western powers, for reasons which we shall discuss later, placed no obstacles in the way of nationalism; indeed they fostered it, an attitude which had its bad as well as its good side. In the Middle Ages (c. 400–1400) waves of invaders from Asia had attacked Europe, from the Huns in the fourth century to the Ottoman Turks in the fifteenth. From Europe's point of view the most famous are the Huns, Mongolian nomads from north of the Caspian Sea who broke into Europe about 370; the Avars, Turkish nomads who in the sixth century used Hungary as a base for their predatory raids; the Tatars who between 1300 and 1500 held all Russia under their sway, and finally the Ottomans whom nowadays we simply call Turks.

The Ottomans reached Asia Minor about 1200, and subdued the Anatolian peasants who then inhabited it. They took their name from Osman I (1290–1326), the founder of an empire and a dynasty that lasted until 1922. On May 29, 1453, under Mohammed II, they captured Constantinople, the capital of the East Roman or Byzantine Empire, pressed forward into Europe and in the following centuries succeeded in occupying a not inconsiderable part of it. In the sixteenth century, when the Turkish Empire attained its greatest expansion, the Turks ruled from the Persian Gulf to the gates of Vienna and from the Caspian to Algeria. The European inhabitants of this empire, the peoples of the Balkans and Hungary, were mainly Christian and as a result Western influence on the Turkish minority was already considerable when, in the eighteenth century, the collapse of the empire had slowly but surely begun. The mixed feelings, admiration as well as fear, which Europe had for the Turks gradually changed; the Turk was despised and underestimated. The collapse is marked by a series of military disasters of which the repulse from Vienna in 1683 was the first and the total defeat in the First World War the last. Each war with Austria or Russia ended with loss of territory. In the nineteenth century the sultan was called 'the sick man' – the expression was first used in 1684 – and before that century was out European Turkey would have been lost had not the rival powers, France, Britain and Russia, contrived to prop up the falling empire. First to cast off the yoke were the Serbs and the Greeks, who attained independence in 1830. Then it was the turn of the Montenegrins, the Bulgars and the Roumanians (1878). Egypt was occupied by the British in 1882 on the ground that occupation was necessary for the defence of the sea route to India *via* the Suez Canal (opened in 1869). The problem of the Canal is a thorny historical one which is still acute and is an excellent example of how the study of history can help towards the comprehension of our own times. A similar problem was presented by the Straits. In the nineteenth century Russia coveted Constantinople, first, because to the Orthodox Church it was a holy city and, second, because of the desire for free passage between the Black Sea and the Mediterranean; it was Britain which stood in the way of the realization of the Russian dream, again because of her preoccupation with the sea route to India. None the less Britain sought to weaken the Turkish Empire. The Armenian atrocities were a pretext and we find Russia and Britain rivalling each other in fostering Armenian nationalism just as they had fostered Greek and Serbian, Bulgar and Roumanian nationalism.

Egypt was rather a special case. Here as early as 1769 the viceroy Ali Bey had proclaimed Egypt independent, and Mohammed Ali and his son Ibrahim had awakened, or rather shocked, the Egyptian nation out of its centuries-long sleep, not indeed out of love for it, but to be able to wage a modern, Western sort of war. Their efforts had results. In a single generation between 1821 and 1847 the population rose by 75 per cent. If we are not to some extent aware of this early history, the work of later Egyptian politicians like Zaglul Pasha, Nahas Pasha who risked defying the United Nations on the question of oil supplies for Israel *via* the Suez Canal, and Nasser who nationalized the Canal, cannot be understood.

By 1900 the Turkish Empire was politically and economically in the hands of the European powers. Banks, factories, shipping, ports, roads, posts and customs were all constructed with Western capital and managed by the West. The sultan got all the loans he wanted but at heavy rates of interest, which in the last resort was paid by the Turkish peasant and the subject races. The whole customs system, the salt and tobacco monopolies and many other taxes were under Western control. Nor was it only Britain, France and Russia who battened on the Turks; Germany, too, took the imperialist road, and naturally, for, just like the Japanese militarists, the Turkish militarists had unbounded confidence in Germany's military capacities, especially after the German victory over France in 1870. The Franco-Prussian war was an offensive war whose very modern character – e.g. the Prussians made great use in their operations of the telegraph – caused amazement and anxiety. In 1903 the Germans got the concession for the building of the Bagdad railway from Scutari (mod. Uskudar on the east side of the Bosphorus opposite Istanbul) *via* Konia, Aleppo and Mosul to Bagdad and Basra. There was consternation in Britain where the German concession was seen as an attempt to extend German power to the oilfields of Mosul and the Persian Gulf. Britain, therefore, sought to hinder the building of so dangerous a railway and to counter German influence while cleverly making use of the 'capitulations'; these were treaties which placed the subjects of certain Western powers outside the power of the Turkish laws. These capitulations, known also in China and in other colonial lands, were abolished in Turkey in 1914 when the Germans were striving to get Turkey to come in on their side in the First World War and Germany's foes feared any such development.

A caricature of the time shows the sultan sitting on a bomb and smoking his hookah in apathetic content. But in 1906 things began to move. This time revolt came not from the subject peoples but within Turkey itself. Mustapha Kemal (1880–1938), then a junior officer who later was to become the first president of the Turkish Republic, joined other revolutionaries in a secret society called 'Fatherland'. Its foundation was at the outset merely a symbol; other societies were in being, notably the Committee for Union and Progress which had been in existence since 1891; this was the organization of the so-called 'Young Turks' and its programme was modernization of the state, a liberal democracy with a parliament and the abolition of the capitulations.

The Young Turk agitation was notable in two respects. Its leaders grasped what other reformers in the East either did not grasp at all or grasped too late, that it was not enough just to become westernized but that further steps had to be taken. They believed that the first thing to be done was to make the state genuinely Turkish; that is to say, they were nationalists. There was nothing remarkable in such an aim in itself, but the consequences were certainly remarkable and that is why the Young Turk revolution is so special a case. In the actual conditions the principle of nationalities, if applied, meant the end of the unity of the Turkish Empire and the reduction of a great empire to a tiny Turkish state in Asia Minor, the only part of that empire inhabited only by Turks. But the dissolution of the empire was not what these Turks wanted. So when they had succeeded in carrying through their revolution they oppressed the national minorities with no less zeal than the sultan had showed. To the European challenge the Young Turks gave the wrong answer.

On July 6, 1908, rebellion broke out at Rezna in Macedonia organized by Niazi Bey, one of the most important organizers of revolt in Turkey. Macedonia was then a frontier district inhabited by Bulgars, Serbs and Greeks, and the rising was the result of the Anglo-Russian plan to separate it from the Turkish state. As a result of this *coup d'état* Abdul Hamid II (1876–1909) was compelled to bring into force the constitution of 1876 which he had let remain a dead letter. The sultan did not resist; he declared that he had been deceived by his ministers, and was not made to abdicate. All over the empire there were stormy demonstrations by the oppressed nationalities, who thought that the hour of freedom had struck for them as well. Austria lost no time, but immediately took advantage of the troubles in Turkey to annex Bosnia and the Herzegovina; had it been foreseen that the annexation would become one of the causes of the First World War, perhaps the Austrians would not have carried it through. In April 1909 the conservative elements attempted a counter-revolution in Istanbul, but within five hours it was suppressed by the Army of Liberation. In these five hours the sultan conducted himself so foolishly that he was deposed and sent into exile; his weak brother Mohammed V (1909–1918) was put on his throne. Parliament now passed a series of measures reforming the administration and dealing with economic questions, but the reforms did not go very far. Disillusioned, Mustapha Kemal withdrew from politics and devoted himself to modernizing the army, but never for a moment did he abandon his aim of a smaller, but a national, Turkish state.

There was unrest throughout the empire. Risings in Albania, in Armenia and in Arabia were put down with a good deal of bloodshed. In 1911 Italy took advantage of the situation to seize Tripolitana, the Libya of today, and then part of the Turkish Empire. Here in 1912 Mustapha Kemal won his first victory at Tobruk. It was a fruitless victory, for now Montenegro, Greece, Bulgaria and Serbia attacked Turkey (First Balkan War, October 1912 – May 1913), which suffered defeat and loss of territory. Tripolitana became an Italian colony and remained so until 1943. The Turks would have been driven completely out of Europe had not the victors quarrelled over the spoils. Bulgaria, which had contributed most to the Turkish defeat, wanted all Macedonia, a demand which did not please her allies. Now they attacked Bulgaria and found willing helpers in the Turks. The sultan and the government indeed hestitated and were prepared to abandon Adrianople and Albania; the result was a fresh *coup d'état* on January 23, 1913, under the leadership of the extreme nationalist Enver Pasha. In the Second Balkan War (June–July 1913), fought by Bulgaria against Greece, Serbia, Roumania and Turkey, the Turks recovered Adrianople. In this operation the German General Liman von Sanders was the real commander; he had been appointed to organize the Turkish army, an appointment which was one of the minor causes of the First World War since the French, and particularly the Russians, disliked the presence of a German general in foreign territory. In the same year the first Pan-Arab Congress was called by Arab students in Paris; it demanded full political rights for the Arabs and an effective share in the administration of the Turkish Empire.

In 1914, on the eve of the First World War, the national movement in Turkey entered on a new phase. The British feared that, if war came, the Turks would take Germany's side and they sought – another instance of the way in which the Western powers encouraged nationalism – to gain the favour of Hussein, sherif of Mecca, by a comprehensive offer of 'Arab emancipation' and a 'free Arab nation'. Hussein was the Turkish ruler of the Holy Places, but as an Arab an opponent of the Turks. They offered, if the need arose, to come to his help against the Turks. In the end Turkey did come in on the German side. The need thus arose, and the result was the independence of the Arab countries. Of Hussein's sons, Abdulla became king of Transjordan and Faisal king of Irak; the British have now to endure the consequences throughout the Middle East of their pro-nationalist Arab policy.

We conclude this section with two general observations. At this stage there was no real popular movement in Turkey. The national movement was the work of officers and intellectuals. This is, in fact, a general phenomenon. The resistance of Asia to Europe can, as a rule, be divided into three phases – a feudal phase in which the aristocracy and the upper class form the core of that resistance; then comes a second phase which has a character of its own because of the increasing resistance of the intellectuals often supported by the soldiers, and only then comes the third phase when we see a genuine popular movement in which the workers and peasants as well rise against the colonial powers.

On the other hand, we should not underestimate the awakening of the areas ruled by the Turks; we may note the growing number of newspapers which made their appearance between 1904 and 1914. In Lebanon the number rose from 29 to 168; in Syria from 3 to 87; in Palestine from 1 to 31; in Irak from 2 to 70, and in the Hejaz where there was none in 1904 there were 6 in 1914. In the whole Arab area there were ten times as many newspapers in 1914 as there were in 1904. In addition there were the newspapers run by exiles which were distributed throughout Turkey by certain foreign governments, those who by the capitulations had their own posts with which the Turkish police could not interfere. Thus the Europeans helped to spread revolutionary literature, rightly believing that thereby they weakened the Turkish Empire. They did not see that they were also undermining their own position; confident in their superiority, they did not think that the nationalism they aroused would be later turned against them. The average politician has no such insight into the future; no one in London, Paris, Berlin or St Petersburg ever imagined the rise of a Mustapha Kemal, a Nahas Pasha, an Ibn Saud.

II

THE JAPANESE EMPIRE

It was Japan which gave to the challenge of the West an answer which was at once negative and radical. In the sixteenth century all foreigners except the Chinese and the Dutch were expelled by the shogun; the latter were confined to the tiny island of Deshima (some 2100 sq. yds.). For two centuries their trading post was the only point of direct contact between Japan and the West. When in 1853 and again in 1854 an American naval squadron under Commodore Perry anchored in Edo Bay near Uraga and demanded free entry for American shipping to a number of Japanese ports, the policy of isolation clearly could no longer be carried out, especially as for some time more and more Japanese had been saying that isolation, perhaps useful in its day, now brought loss rather than gain since in the end the Japanese could learn much from the West. The government of the shogun yielded to the American demands (Treaty of Kanagawa, March 1854). The protection of Japan from the foreigner, which was in the main the work of a reactionary nobility, was abandoned; mediaeval Japan had to go with it. The system of the shogunate, whereby the shogun, a representative of the military aristocracy, ruled instead of the emperor, was played out. On January 3, 1868, the emperor Mutsuhito (1867–1912) himself took over the government. On November 14th he delivered to his court a speech on the modernization of the country – the summoning of a parliament, the rallying of public opinion by social and economic measures, the abolition of the excessive privileges of the nobles. In his speech were two significant points. First of all, he urged the Japanese to collect all the knowledge the world offered for the upbringing of the new empire and, second, he declared that every Japanese must be given the opportunity to place all his capabilities at the service of the community.

The astonishment at such a notable and decisive step took time to pass, and at a suitable moment the adherents of the deposed shogun sought to turn back the wheel of history (January 27, 1869), but within five months the imperial troops were masters of the situation. At first a little doubtfully, and then with greater conviction, Japan took the path of westernization.

A wrong impression of this change has often been given by those who see in it nothing but sheer imitation, even mimicry. Actually everything which was taken from the West was taken in consonance with Japanese conceptions and convictions. The army was modelled first on the French and then on the German, for the lightning victory of the Germans over the French in 1870 had created a profound impression in all countries. The navy, for which Dutch advisers had originally been provided, was modernized on British lines. Japan was not like Turkey. The latter was a country inhabited by different peoples with different status and different languages. In Japan there was no super-national state to be destroyed by modernization; Japan was a national island kingdom which began to seek possibilities of expansion overseas and to create an empire. In the 'seventies Japan annexed the Kuriles, the Bonin islands and the Ryukyu archipelago; in 1895, as a result of her war with China, she added the Pescadores and Formosa to the empire.

On January 30, 1902, the treaty of alliance with Britain was signed in London; in it the special interests of Japan in Korea were recognized. For Japan the treaty meant her recognition as an independent power and as a valuable ally. In Britain many thought it humiliating that proud Albion should become the ally of a non-white power, yet it was seen to be necessary, for Russia was so pressing eastward that British trade interests in China and soon possibly in Japan itself would be endangered if there was no such treaty.

Then the inevitable happened. The Russians, the only Europeans threatened by the expansion of Japan, invaded North Korea, and when the Japanese retort came – the attack on February 8, 1904, on Russia's naval base at Port Arthur – no one could grasp the fact that it was a storm signal for the whole of modern Asian history. On May 1st the Japanese army attacked the Russians on the Yalu. A passage from one of the many articles which fifty years after correctly estimated this historic episode may be quoted:

'A river valley only a mile or two wide. The western banks are steep and stony; the eastern gently sloping hill-country. The Yalu flows in several beds to the Yellow Sea; the main branch of the river is some 1400 yards wide. Tiger Hill in the north on the west bank dominates the ground. Here on the Yalu on May 1, 1904, on the frontier between Manchuria and Korea, the "land of morning quiet", a non-white nation defeated a European power in the first battle of the Russo-Japanese war. That war Russia lost; Japan won it. What is the significance of that? Russia was still a Great Power and Japan not yet one. But for the nations of Asia the battle of the Yalu and the war are unforgettable. Admittedly the whites in their wars with coloured peoples had taken some bad knocks. Did not the naked Zulus wipe out a British detachment at Isandlhwana and had not an Italian expeditionary force been cut to pieces at Adowa by the Abyssinians?

'But the Yalu was a very different event. During the night the little yellow men had thrown bridges across the main stream; in the Russian trenches they could hear the rattle of the traffic crossing them. The Japanese had little material, so pressed Chinese junks into service and used the ploughs of Korean peasants as anchors. Soon a small body of them had occupied Tiger Hill, to which the Russians, it seems, attached little importance. When day came, the Russians saw long lines of Japanese shoulder to shoulder crossing the nearest river bed, the water up to their chests. There was a dreadful silence, for the Russians did not open fire. A Japanese officer said: "It is terrible to have to wait for the enemy to open fire."

'The Japanese won the battle, which ended in the late afternoon. They had cut off part of the Russian army, but one of the tough Siberian rifle battalions had counter-attacked and let it escape through a mountain pass. . . . On this spring day 4000 dead and wounded lay in the fields round Tjurenteben, among them barely a thousand Japanese . . . a victory for the yellow race. True the men who shouted "banzai" as they fought were 35,000 against 15,000 Russians, but it is the whole art of war to be the stronger on the battlefield. And Japan had done everything to ensure that. Her people were made enthusiastic for the war; everything was carefully prepared, and her troops marched hundreds of miles through Korea in the cool spring months. An Asian country was not only the victor but the victor deservedly.'

The war went on. The great battle at Liao-yang in Manchuria lasted from August 25th to September 4th, but it brought decision on land. The Russian colossus with the feet of clay was driven back towards Mukden. On January 2, 1905, Port Arthur surrendered. A Russian fleet of thirty-two ships which had come round Asia from the Baltic to the Sea of Japan was destroyed by Togo in the Straits of Tsushima. The Russians could do no more, and in the treaty of Portsmouth, due to the mediation of the American president, Theodore Roosevelt, it was agreed that Korea should be a Japanese sphere of influence – annexation followed in 1910 – that southern Sakhalin which lies over against the Siberian coast should go to Japan; Japan also got the Chinese peninsula of Liautung with Port Arthur – it was not returned to China until 1945 – and finally Manchuria was recognized by both sides to be Chinese territory.

None the less the treaty was not popular in Japan because there was no provision for reparations. On this critical issue the Western powers were solid against Asia, and this attitude was maintained, for the West always held it advisable that Japan should not become powerful enough to take over the leadership in Asia. But the war had shown with deadly clarity that Japan had indeed awakened.

That there was another Japan than that of the army and the imperialists was shown in the same period. At the International Socialist Congress in Amsterdam in 1904 – that is, during the war – the Japanese delegates shook hands with the Russian in order to show that, even if their countries were at war, the workers of both countries were allies not in the war of states but in the war of classes. The leader of the Japanese delegation was Sen Kata-yama. On his return he and his colleagues were arrested for 'treason to the nation' and in 1907 a demonstration for their liberation was brutally dispersed by the police.

Meantime Japan, from being a nation of peasants in 1868, had become an industrial state. In 1871 the first newspaper appeared. In 1872 the first railway was opened from Tokio to Yokohama. In 1890 there was already 200 factories working with steam-driven machinery and the steamship tonnage rose from some 150,000 tons in 1893 to a million and a half tons in 1913. In 1906–7 seventeen private railway lines were nationalized, thus permitting the development of a profitable railway system. In the same year, 1907, a high tension electric line was constructed between Yamanashi and Tokio right through the tiny farms of the peasants, who now could use electric light and power in the later-developed home industry. But at the outset it was the great textile concerns which benefited most from the cheap electricity supplied quickly by the swift-flowing mountain streams with their great waterfalls. And as the worker did not cost the employer much – the trade unions were then of no great significance – Japan could prepare an economic offensive, particularly against the British cotton industry, an offensive that embraced all East and South Asia and extended farther westward to Ethiopia and even to Europe.

Most important in this context was the fact that Japanese industry was concentrated as a direct result of its sudden development. In 1900 the Nippon Kogio Ginko, the industrial bank of Japan, was founded. It invested the hitherto unproductive capital of the rich townsfolk in industry, which was almost entirely controlled by the four great family trusts with State support, the so-called Zaibatsu. The notable feature of the development of Japan is that the feudal organization of society was so little disturbed by the arrival of capitalism, perhaps simply because everything happened with such suddenness.

When we turn to the peasant we must make it clear that his condition remained bad, indeed even worse than before, as a result of the increase in population and the distribution of land. It had been customary when a peasant died for his land to be divided among his sons. Up to the Meiji period, the period of so-called enlightenment which began in 1868, the government had compulsorily kept down the number of children. The practice of infanticide was normal in Japan and as comprehensible as in the case of many Polynesian islands before the Europeans colonized them, for an isolated island could support only a limited number of people. The generally accepted morality in Japan in these centuries held that it was immoral to have more than two or three children – a useful example of the truth that human morals can alter even in so important a matter, for in modern Japan the ideal was to have as many children as possible since that now seemed to be profitable to the country.

As a result of birth limitation and infanticide the population of Japan between 1650 and 1850 remained stationary at about 25,000,000. 1868 altered all that. Birth limitation stopped; soaps, inoculations, maternity care – according to the rules of modern hygiene and medical science – became ordinary things in the life of the Japanese. The factories were now attracting the workers who could not get work on the land. The result was that the population rose and rose rapidly. By 1910 it had doubled; in 1930 it was 65,000,000, in 1945 75,000,000 and in 1952 85,000,000.

This gigantic increase in population certainly was not the only, perhaps not even the most important, factor in the adoption of an aggressive policy. The chief cause was the need of Japanese industry for raw materials and fuel – iron, coal and petrol. None the less it can be said that expansion became necessary as a result of the increase of population. The workers' wages remained low, since for every worker lost there were ten to replace him. That applied both to men and women. The daughters of the poor peasant were sold in thousands to the factories, which employed a veritable army of women. The girls who could not stand factory conditions – and

these were the reverse of pleasant – became prostitutes or, riddled with consumption, went home to die.

As in other countries, so in Japan, members of the ruling classes felt
drawn to the workers. In 1903 Tojohiko Kagawa (b. 1808 and later head of
the Ministry of Social Affairs), who could no longer bear the miserable
condition of the common people, became a Christian. He believed then that
in the West everything was better, the living conditions of the worker and
religion. Aided by Sotohiko Mazuzaki, he did much for the proletariat in
the towns where conditions were worst, and especially in Shinhawa, the
most horrible quarter of the port of Kobe; they also brought help to the poor
peasants. It may be true that social problems of this kind cannot be solved
by the goodwill of the upper strata; these classes as a whole seem ready to
make substantial concessions only when they are compelled to do so. None
the less it is due in great part to these two reformers that the trade union
movement became so important to the Japanese working class.

How far Japan was influenced by foreign countries is seen in the fact that
in the period 1900–1914 it was the United States which, without intending
it, did most to further the modernization of Japan. That becomes comprehensible if we look at the map, and especially if we remember the history
of the United States in these years. In the area of the Pacific which today
can be called without much exaggeration an 'American inland sea', the
Europeans had been less intrusive than elsewhere. Later the Americans
turned to China and so created a tension between British and American
imperialism which has not yet disappeared. And if China was the first great
area of contact between the two Western Great Powers, South America was
the next, while, at the present time it is in the Near East, the Middle East
and Africa that the focal point of conflict lies.

The term 'American imperialism' is justifiably used. About 1900 America
too began to move overseas. If we cannot call the opening up of Japan
imperialism – after all it was a question only of a couple of coaling stations
for the new shipping line from Shanghai to California – it was quite clearly
imperialism when, in 1898, the 'liberation' of Cuba from the yoke of Spain
brought the island under the economic domination of the United States.
But a protectorate over Cuba was not the end. Opportunity, they say, makes
the thief; equally opportunity turns a nation's eye to expansion. As a further
result of the Spanish-American war the United States got Hawaii and Guam
in the Pacific and also the Philippines, whose inhabitants were taught in a
bloody guerrilla war that they too now lived in a colony. In 1900 the United
States was not only the most modern industrial state in the world but had
also become the strongest power in the Pacific. What that meant to Japan
expanding and modernizing itself with great speed can easily be understood;
it was at once a threat and a portent.

But not only in high politics was there change, but in small things as well,
and some of these are of historical import. In 1905, for instance, the baseball
team from the Waseda University founded by Count Okuma went on a tour
through the United States. In those days sport was becoming ever more
important and a sporting victory or defeat became a matter of national

honour and prestige. In America the Japanese team went from defeat to defeat. From that moment sport became a national concern in Japan. Did not Shintoism require that every Japanese must strive his utmost to serve the Fatherland? Swimming became obligatory in the schools; skiing and skating became part of military training and was practised in Japan in Asia with the same doggedness as in European Germany.

Again, a relatively trifling matter arose in 1905 which seriously wounded Japanese feeling and so influenced history. In San Francisco the children of Japanese immigrants were forbidden to sit in the same school classes as the children of white Americans. That was the first step in a process of discriminating racial legislation in the western United States. They led in 1908 to the 'gentleman's agreement' in Tokio, whereby Japan of her own free will limited the number of immigrants to America. But that did not suffice. In 1913 the State of California passed a law which forbade the Japanese to acquire landed property. This and similar regulations were as distressing as wounding to the some ten thousand Japanese who then lived in California and had as farmers or gardeners cultivated considerable areas of unoccupied land. It does not require much imagination to understand the indignation in Japan. To that challenge we know the response—the war of 1940. Here was a foreshadowing of the Second World War before the First had begun.

III

THE CHINESE EMPIRE

IN China the response to challenge was different. Here we find two national characteristics which in Turkey and Japan had either very minor significance or none at all. The first is the Chinese feeling of superiority. China is the land of the oldest continuous culture and had been for fifty centuries the most important state in East Asia. Typical of that feeling is the tale of the first steamship on the Yang-tse in 1870. When the Chinese saw on its waters this odd product of the Western barbarians they were not at all impressed, re- marking that two millennia earlier they had experimented with something similar; it was nothing more than the result of a passion for innovation. Secondly, China reacted differently because of her almost complete defence- lessness; here there was no aggressive tradition, probably just on account of the feeling of superiority.

In history everything hangs together, which is the reason why the study of it is so difficult and at the same time so fascinating that, once begun, it can never be abandoned. The course of events in Japan naturally could not fail to have great influence on China. To the challenge of the West the Chinese originally adopted the same type of resistance as did the Japanese. But it was inwardly more intense though outwardly less thorough because, as a result of the excessive self-confidence in its eternal and unique culture, its size, and its hundred millions of inhabitants, it could risk more than could tiny Japan. Big China certainly was, before the Europeans began to break up the decaying empire. Did it not as late as the middle of the nineteenth century stretch from Saigon to north of the Amur and from the east coast of Formosa to the snow- peaks of the Pamirs? And who had so many subjects as the ruler of the Heavenly Kingdom? In 1900 the eighteen provinces of China proper alone had 400,000,000 inhabitants and the rest of the empire another 50,000,000. More exact figures are not available for, although there were many censuses held in China, they were always held in connection with military service or taxation and so are not reliable.

Again, China's isolation was not nearly so complete as Japan's. In the eighteenth century we hear of a considerable trade with Russia, although the enormous extent of the Siberian steppe seemed a greater obstacle than the Great Wall. It brought to China quantities of furs and salt at the same time as British and Dutch were exporting tea and porcelain and much else from Canton. As early as 1557 the Portuguese had a settlement in Macao which has maintained itself to this day. In 1784 the first American ship appeared but the foreigner, the 'barbarian', was still of little account; he could not have Chinese servants in his house, and after his trading business was finished he had either to go home or to the Portuguese free port in Macao. That was a very different situation from that which existed later, when in the parks in the Western concessions one could read 'Dogs and Chinese forbidden'. Semi-legally, Western influence was spread by the Roman Catholic, and especially by the Protestant, missionaries. In the mission schools the Chinese children heard of foreign countries, learned geography and history and a good deal about the economic prosperity which the industrial revolution had brought to Europe and America, about the position of the peasant and of woman in other lands, about the achievements of the West in medicine and hygiene; above all, in that century, the nineteenth, the most important of all, scientific-ally, the West had achieved much in technology, in biology, in chemistry and in medicine which was completely unknown in China. Just as important, perhaps more important, was the connection with the West created by the import of cheap cotton goods: without realizing it, and certainly without wishing it, the Chinese peasant was made a slave of the West.

But no matter how profitable the trade was, even if carried on under many restrictions, the West was not content. In 1842 the British had breached the Chinese wall, which was steadily ever more broken through. In Japan the West had appeared in 1854 almost as a suppliant; in China it came as an invader. The reasons for the Opium War (1839–1842) – the British ultimatum demanded the right to import Indian opium – were in the highest degree unjust and immoral; the seizure of Hongkong (1842) was sheer robbery and the conditions under which by the Treaty of Nanking (1842) a number of ports were forcibly opened to European trade were not much better.

The response to challenge now took other forms. In 1850 there broke out the notorious Taiping rebellion, a peasant rising which was aimed as much against the native landed proprietors and the Manchu dynasty as against Western encroachments. The spiritual leader of the rebellion was Hung Hsiu-chuan who had incorporated certain Christian elements into his teaching – an interesting case of the connection between religion and nationalism with which we dealt in the introduction. The attempt of the emperor to crush the reform movement only caused it to be directed against himself, an easy transition since his dynasty (1644–1912) came from North Manchuria and was always regarded in China proper as being more or less a foreign one. But, even if the dynasty had been a native one, things would not have been any different. Chinese history shows that always, when the pressure on the people becomes too great, there are anti-dynastic risings. The leaders of the risings become the new rulers, who rule until the pressure exercised by them in turn becomes intolerable; the new dynasty, now become old, is then declared deprived of 'the mandate of Heaven' and the same process begins all over again. Under the able leadership of Yang Hsiu-ching the whole country between Nanking and Canton rose. The rebels made Nanking their capital, but their armies failed to organize defence properly or to introduce an orderly administration. The population was not sufficiently inspired to action and the revolt was much too local although it occupied half the country. Yet it did not surrender until 1864. That surrender British and Americans had done much to secure, and, what was worse, the white nations had seen that in 1850 the Chinese Empire was a ruin and so new ultimatums could be issued to it. The Treaty of Tientsin (June 1858) inflicted fresh humiliation. Two years later French and British troops entered Pekin, and in 1861 China was forced to create the 'Tsung li Yamen', a central organization for the conduct of foreign relations. Thereafter the number of treaty ports and of foreign commercial houses rose steadily; in 1900 there were nearly a thousand of the latter with some 20,000 employees. More and more Roman Catholic and Protestant missionaries came in and foreign loans increased.

Technical modernization, which had almost exploded in Japan, was accomplished only slowly in China. The first railway came up against the opposition of the people. When in 1876 the ten-mile-long line from Shanghai to Wusing on the coast was taken in hand, the peasants threw the rails into the sea because they thought that the graves of their ancestors would be disturbed. It was not until 1888 that the first Chinese train ran from Tientsin to Tangshan (75 miles). Underwater cables had been laid in 1871 from Vladivostok *via* Shanghai and Hongkong to Singapore, and along the coast lighthouses and modern harbours were built, mostly by the British. Thus, and at first, very slowly, China began to awake from her torpor, and so began a new period which, if it destroyed much that was worth preserving, yet did, at least in principle, create new possibilities of a better existence for the millions of miserably poor Chinese.

The great shock which shattered the old China and allowed a new China to arise was the Sino-Japanese War (1894–1895). The struggle was fought out in the main in Korea and South Manchuria; its consequences, partly embodied in the Treaty of Shimonoseki, were fateful. Korea, then a part of China, was declared independent; that meant the very near possibility of a foreign occupation either by Russia or Japan and either possibility was dangerous. The Chinese island of Taiwan, which is generally known by its Portuguese name of Formosa, became Japanese territory. That was very nearly as dangerous as the loss of Korea. The stategic importance of the island was seen not only at the time of the Japanese occupation, which lasted until 1945, but above all after that, when under Chiang Kai-shek it became an American naval base. After Japan had got her share of the booty at Shimonoseki, the Great Powers proceeded to further extortions. They took all they could. In 1898 Germany 'leased' the port of Kiauchow on the Yellow Sea with its hinterland. Russia, which had in 1860 occupied the Maritime Provinces between the present Vladivostok and the Amur, now received Port Arthur with the right to connect this naval base with the Trans-Siberian railway by a new line running through Manchuria. France leased Kwangchow (on the South China Sea in Kwangtung province), thus rounding off her occupation of Indochina taken from the Chinese in 1885. The British were content to take Kowloon opposite Hongkong, and Weihaiwei on the Shantung peninsula, from which they could keep an eye on Port Arthur, Kiauchow and Korea; all this was in return for the aid which the Great Powers had given to prevent complete spoliation by Japan. China received a French loan of 400,000,000 francs at 4 per cent with the customs as security, and there now began a competition for mines and railways, each more profitable than the other to the foreigner.

The reaction to all these humiliations was the attempt at reform by the radical Kang Yu-wei (1858–1927) and a group of students from Canton who had studied abroad (1898). Their plan was expounded in a classic pamphlet published (1898) by Chang Tse-tung, of which over a million copies were sold. Besides railways and ever more railways, Western weapons for the imperial army and a modern fleet, the reformers asked for the establishment of a university in Pekin. The Chinese mandarin was well educated and possessed great knowledge, but that knowledge was confined to literature and ethics, while science and, above all, natural science received very little attention. Possibly China could have been modernized without more bloodshed had not the dowager empress, the Regent Tsu-hsi, feared that the weak emperor would permit the reforms to which he had agreed, to be carried out; if they were, her own position in the empire would be lost. Here once again we see how personal considerations of little importance influence world history, not indeed in the sense that an individual can really alter the course of history, but in so far as an individual can either help or hinder the historical development. Tsu-hsi arrested the emperor, declared him by decree to be illegitimate and feeble-minded, and all the reform measures were annulled; only Pekin University remained. As a result everything stayed as it was, or rather was worsened, for the Chinese people sank into extreme misery. Once again the reactionary court misused the Chinese zenophobia for its own interests. That is seen in the Boxer rising of 1900, an attempt at a revolution made by the secret society of the Boxers which had been formed a short time before to combat Western influence and the privileges of the foreigner. When the German ambassador was murdered and the rebels besieged the foreign legations in Pekin, Europe thankfully accepted the chance of military intervention. The German General von Waldersee was placed as 'General World-marshal' at the head of an international army and the rebellion was bloodily suppressed. After the Boxer protocol of 1901 there were more humiliating demands, more concessions. The imperial court and the reformed Tsung li Yamen accepted everything, for they knew that now they could not rely on the Chinese people but only on foreign bayonets to maintain themselves in power. The disruption of China went on. In 1904 came the British expedition to Tibet, which was declared autonomous though Chinese suzerainty was recognized at least in name. Note in passing that the Chinese had reached Tibet in 42 B.C. and from the beginning of the eighteenth century had politically been its masters. When in 1950 it again incorporated Tibet into the empire as an autonomous province, Mao Tse-tung's government was only following a centuries-old tradition.

China had in 1905, in part at least, to bear the bitter consequences of the Russo-Japanese War. Japan acquired the privileges of the Russians in South Manchuria and Port Arthur. Nor were the Americans behindhand, though for them it was a question not of Chinese territory but of the Chinese market. Their sympathies with the Chinese were certainly not greater. In 1904 they so tightened up the immigration laws that in fact Chinese could no longer emigrate to the United States.

Even if the day of liberation must inevitably have come, it is not unthinkable that the humiliation of China would have lasted much longer had there not been born in 1866 a man who more clearly than others recognized the desperateness of the situation in which his people were, who grasped the fact that more was needed than just political resistance to the West, and who understood that only a social revolution could arouse in the Chinese people the energies needed to enable them to turn Western methods in their own way to the advantage of their country.

This was Sun Yat-sen (1866–1925), a man whose name is as closely tied with the Chinese revolution as Lenin's is with the Russian, Kemal Ataturk's with the Turkish, Gandhi's with the Indian and Sukarno's with the Indonesian, a man with the impatience, but also with the patience, of the revolutionary. Born during the horrors of the Taiping rebellion, he was the son of a peasant. As a medical student – he studied in Honolulu and Hongkong – he got his first political impressions when the French occupied the rest of Indochina, attacked the Chinese port of Foochow and burned the whole merchant fleet of junks. As a Southern Chinese he was against Pekin and the Manchus; he became convinced that the corrupt dynasty in the north was the first obstacle on the way of modernization and so formed in 1894, after the model of many similar societies, the secret society of Hsin Tsung-hui, a society for the renewal of China. A first rising in Canton (1895) failed. Sun had to flee abroad, and now organized the Chinese in Honolulu and San Francisco, thus coming into contact with many of his rich fellow countrymen. That even abroad he was not safe from imperial vengeance was shown in 1896, when he was abducted by the Chinese legation in London and was kept imprisoned there for twelve days. It was evident that the intention was to get him back to China and hang him there. But the legation was no more energetic than the Government, and, with the help of British friends, he escaped, returned to China and risked another rising at the time of the Boxer rebellion. Once again he failed and had to flee again, but the prospects seemed much rosier than before. At the first rising he had been an unknown rebel; now he was looked upon by many as a revered, popular leader who was getting money from every quarter for a final trial of strength with the hated government. In 1905 we find him in Japan, where thousands of Chinese students were finding refuge, and here he created a new revolutionary organization, the Tung Meng-hui, which had cells everywhere including Brussels, Paris and Berlin, and was the direct ancestor of the famous – and infamous – Kuo Min-tang.

A new rising (1906–1907) – we have already said that a revolutionary needs patience – was suppressed by the Government police, but things were now different. In Kwangtung an army of 60,000 men was ready to rise. Possibly under the influence of the 1905 revolution in Russia, Sun broadened his anti-Manchu programme; it became directed towards nationalism, democracy and socialism. The crisis came in 1911 because of an arrangement come to by the Government whereby Chinese owners of Chinese railways were expropriated so that their property could be used as security for foreign loans. In the years just before this the Kuo Min-tang had found many supporters among the rich Chinese bourgeois both at home and abroad, and for them this was the last straw. The revolution broke out in Hankow on October 10th and by the end of the year China was a republic.

But human affairs are a complicated business. The old China had received a dangerous shock, but it was not totally shattered. Sun was elected president but, six weeks later, in order not to imperil the national unity, he withdrew in favour of Yuan Shi-kai, a soldier trusted by the court who had already played a dubious role in the events of 1898. Had it not been established later that the right wing of his own party forced him to withdraw, Sun might well have been blamed for committing a gross blunder when he agreed to the doubtful solution of a republic by the grace of the emperor. Again he had to be patient. It is the really great politician who combines great courage and deep insight – the two qualities are seldom found together – but even he can do no more than the circumstances permit. In this sense it is true that politics is the art of the possible, even if, in order to gain the possible, the impossible must be attempted. In this uncertain situation – the old China destroyed, the new in process of formation – China, the old Heavenly Kingdom, entered the First World War, which can be said to be the real beginning of the twentieth century.

IV

INDIA-PAKISTAN

UNDER British rule India and Pakistan were a single political unity, called in Britain 'India' and in other countries 'British India' or 'Nearer India'; to avoid confusion we shall use the last name to describe the subcontinent until the end of British rule. It was originally a geographical rather than a political name. In 1600 the British East India Company was founded in London, and the similar company in Amsterdam (founded in 1602) was called the United East India Company. Both had 'East Indian' in their titles because the Europeans called Southeast Asia the 'East Indies' in contrast to the Central American islands discovered by Columbus in 1492 and annexed by Spain which were called the 'West Indies'.

The companies' activities in Asia meant in fact political intervention and conquest with the aim of ruining the existing and flourishing internal trade. The efforts at expansion were not just adventurous. If Europe had then at her disposal gold as well as the products which Asia needed, then trade would have remained 'innocent'. That was not the case and finally, in Nearer India, as in Indonesia, the political power of the companies became so great and so oppressive that the State supported them and eventually took over from them. In Indonesia Java was the point of departure for political conquest; in India it was Bengal and, just as in Java Batavia became the capital of European political domination, so in Bengal Calcutta became the capital. Not until the beginning of the twentieth century did New Delhi take Calcutta's place.

The British were not the only white invaders of Nearer India. The Portuguese were there and also the French. The former appeared as early as 1498 when Vasco da Gama, having rounded the Cape of Good Hope, landed on the coast of Malabar. They had been trading and intriguing there for a century before the British arrived. The French were much more dangerous competitors then than they are today; our present generation has virtually no experience of a really strong France. France bled to death in the First World War, a war which was too strong a challenge to let her make an adequate response. But from about 1640 until the years from 1900 to 1914 France was the most important European power, and not merely for political and military reasons. All new ideas came from France; French literature was the richest of all; French art among the richest; the Royal court in Paris was the model for all other courts, just as the French bourgeoisie of the nineteenth century was a model for all other countries; Paris was the capital of the world. But that France is now no more than a legend.

In the Seven Years' War (1756–1763) the British, not without difficulty, drove the French from Nearer India; from that time the latter held only Pondi-cherry, Chandernagore and a few other scattered tiny colonies, where, curiously enough, their rule lasted longer than did that of the British in British India. The conquest of the independent native states took place for the most part between 1782 and 1817. First to go was the realm of the Great Mogul ruled by a Moslem dynasty which, in the sixteenth and following centuries, had conquered the greater part of Nearer India. This British con-quest was called the establishment of the *Pax Britannica*. The taking over of the East India Company by the British Government in 1868 came rather later than the similar taking over in Indonesia; there the Dutch East India Com-pany had disappeared before the end of the eighteenth century. British rule, in the proper sense of the term, lasted less than a century.

The British Government had two reasons for dissolving the company. The first was of a foreign political nature. All through the eighteenth century Britain feared that the French might return and when, as a result of the col-lapse of the Napoleonic Empire in 1815, that fear vanished, fear of Russian influence took its place. This fear of Russia was at the bottom of the wars against Afghanistan (First Afghan War 1839–1842; Second Afghan War 1878–1879). The second reason was an internal one and the direct cause of the disappearance of the company – the great mutiny of 1857–1858. The company's army was composed in the main of Moslem soldiers and these, like the Hindus, feared that they would be compelled to become Christians; here is another example of the connection between religion and nationalism. The immediate cause of the mutiny was the introduction of the Enfield rifle whose cartridges, as the sepoys believed, were greased with cow's and pig's fat. Moslems do not eat pig's flesh; Hindus do not eat cow's flesh. On May 10, 1857, the mutiny began in Meerut and in a very short time spread over all the north and centre of the land; Delhi was occupied by the rebels. In Cawnpore the British garrison was massacred, an easy feat, for the majority of the British troops had been sent to the Crimea. As usual, the revenge of the British when reinforcements came was still more terrible. The most famous episode is the siege of Lucknow; the decisive military event was the recapture of Delhi. The Hindu troops from Bombay held out longest. They were only 4500 strong and were led by a twenty-year-old girl, Kakshmi Bai, the Ranee of Jhansi, whose name is still revered in India. Another guerrilla leader, Tantia Topi, perhaps the ablest of the rebel chiefs, was hanged in April 1859. From that year the British rule remained firmly established for over fifty years, with the co-operation of the highest social classes. The great mutiny belongs to the first phase of the awakening of Asia; it was a rebellion, a war of independence under aristocratic leadership.

In 1877 Queen Victoria took the title of Empress of India. All this Euro-pean presumption furthered the growth of unity among the colonial peoples. In 1885 there was founded the society which in the long run was to set Nearer India free – the Indian National Congress, usually referred to simply as 'Congress', an organization which at the outset found its members from the rising middle class and had the support and the sympathy of the Government. In its own land, the British ruling class is very clever in dealing with and controlling movements towards reform; that is why social development in Britain has been so remarkably slow. In Britain much can be altered without really being altered and much can be maintained while really being changed. This was the lesson the British ruling class learned from its centuries-long domination in its island kingdom; Sir Winston Churchill is, perhaps, the last of the type. The first leaders of Congress were Dadabhai Naoroji (1825–1917), the author of *Poverty and un-British Rule in India* and for many years a member of the British Parliament, Sir Surendranath Bannerjea (1848–1925) and Gokkale, the friend and predecessor of Gandhi.

An early reformer was Ram Mohan Roy (1772–1833). Swami Dayananda Saraswati (1824–1883) was a reformer of a different kind, who in 1875 founded the Arya Samaj, one of the most significant Hindu modernization movements of the period. The first great radical leader who opposed the moderate wing of Congress led by Gokkale was Bal Gangadhar Tilak (1856–1920), by far the greatest predecessor of Gandhi. Tilak was a student at the British University of Bombay and was imbued there with modern Western ideas. None the less he did not hesitate to form a society to prevent the killing of cows – the special reverence of the Hindu for the holy cow is well known – and against the prohibition of child marriage, not because he approved of child marriage but because prohibition was a British measure and he wished on any terms to bring into the anti-British movement the broad masses of his people. Thus deliberately he sought to bring the national movement into its third phase. It is characteristic of his international vision, so far as the Indian resistance went, that at the demonstrations which he led he displayed pictures of the champions of Italian nationalism Mazzini and Garibaldi; it was in the years from 1860 to 1870 that Italy obtained her freedom from long foreign domination, notably the Austrian. In general Tilak's policy, in contrast to Gokkale's, was one of 'self-reliance, not mendicancy'. In 1907 Tilak was arrested and imprisoned, a step which, as is usual, inflamed rather than damped down the movement for freedom.

About 1900 a number of factors further helped on that movement. Starvation has never been, and still is not, an unusual condition in Nearer India. Thirty-five per cent of the population then did not possess any land of their own; peasants and small farmers possessed on an average not quite two and a half acres. The great landed properties and high rents were, and are, obstacles to the development of modern farming methods. Periodic bad harvests when the rains came too late made agrarian economy still more uncertain; the eighteen great famines between 1875 and 1900 cost 26,000,000 lives. Three failures of the harvest (1896, 1900 and 1902), much greater than was usual, were veritable catastrophes and these, with the plague that ravaged the land in 1896, showed up the real character of British domination; it was directed to taking profit from India, not to profiting India and its inhabitants. The defeat of the Italians in Abyssinia (1896), though to a lesser extent, had the same effect as the defeat of Russia by Japan (1905). The obvious conclusion was drawn; the white men are not invincible. Shortly after the Russo-Japanese War, the Curzon plan for the partition of Bengal provoked the first great clash between the national movement and the British administration. In itself the plan had its justification; a province of 80,000,000 inhabitants was much too big. But the dividing line followed the linguistic line and so divided the intellectuals and the nationalist leadership. Apparently one of the aims of the plan was to convince the Moslems that the British found them more trustworthy allies than the Hindus.

The fires rose higher. For the first time there was a boycott of imports from Britain, particularly cotton goods. In 1907 the first bomb was thrown. Shortly before that the extremists had called a congress in Surat. It was not surprising that Tilak was arrested, since at it he demanded full independence. The moderates disavowed the extremists, but the British had to make some concessions. These were contained in the Indian Councils Act of 1909, known as the Morley-Minto reforms from its sponsors John Morley, the well-known Liberal leader and at that time Secretary of State for India, and Lord Minto, who was viceroy from 1905 to 1910. The reforms did not go far; they implied only a very gradual beginning of the indianization of representative bodies and of the administration. Finally, however, the national movement won the victory in Bengal. The Bengali-speaking area remained a unity; the non-Bengali districts in West and South Bengal (Bihar and Orissa) were made a separate province. In their own peculiar way the British had made their contribution to the liberation of Nearer India; the East Bengal of the Curzon plan had virtually the same boundaries as the East Pakistan of today, from which we may deduce that Moslem-Hindu religious rivalry had its effect on the national movement.

That is seen in other events including the founding of the All-India Moslem League by the nabob of Dacca, Viquar al Mulk, and the mission of the Aga Khan to the Viceroy. That was in 1909, and in the same year the British Government carried through the division of the electorate between Hindus and Moslems, the so-called 'communalism'. The Moslem League and the Hindu Congress fought each other like cat and dog, but, so far as the national movement was concerned, their efforts ran on parallel lines. It was, for instance, the Moslems whose anti-European feelings were stimulated by Turkey's loss of territory in the Italo-Turkish War and the First Balkan War. Thus on the eve of the First World War Britain was not the sole ruler of Nearer India; the national movement had become a powerful factor with which the British Government had to reckon.

Just as in Japan's case, a relatively unimportant incident occurred whose effect was greater than was then realized. In May 1914 the Japanese ship *Kamagata Maru* sailed into the port of Vancouver. She had on board Gurdit Singh and four hundred other British Indian subjects, mainly Sikhs and Moslems, who proposed to make trial of the position of would-be immigrants from India under the American immigration regulations. They were not allowed to enter the United States – another insult to Asia. When the ship returned to Calcutta there were riots; eighteen people were killed. Hatred

A.C.—3

of the whites grew, for it was not only the United States which refused entry to Indians. What Gandhi experienced in South Africa about race discrimination should not be forgotten. For years he had fought for the position of Indians there; that was well known in his own country. Outside South Africa he was just a relatively obscure lawyer.

V

KOREA, FORMOSA, THE PHILIPPINES AND INDONESIA

It may displease some readers that Indonesia does not get a separate section to itself, since Indonesia, the greatest island power in the world, is the fourth in population among the Asian countries; only China and India have a much larger number of inhabitants. Economically, and especially where agricultural production is concerned, Indonesia cannot be passed over; in 1950 it was the largest producer in the world of pepper, quinine and kapok; the second or third largest of natural rubber and tin-ore; the fourth of coffee, tea, cocoa and palm-oil; the fifth of rice and the seventh largest of cane-sugar and bauxite. Economically and politically Indonesia has the role of middleman between South and East Asia and because of her position, between two oceans, will no doubt become an important sea power. The reason why in this part of my book it gets a lowlier place than, for instance, Japan, is that as a Dutch colony it played as insignificant a role as Holland itself.

Nothing need be said here about the strategic importance of Korea; history, and particularly recent history, has demonstrated it. In the early hours of June 25, 1950, the war we call the Korean War broke out on the famous 38th parallel; the subsequent intervention of the West, notably of the United States, and the counter-intervention of China showed Korea still to be what it had been for half a century, one of the most important strategic points of the Pacific area.

Traditionally, Korea's history as a political unity goes back to the third millennium B.C. and, if for a time China's influence was strong, the kingdom of Korea remained, until the nineteenth century, to a certain extent independent. For Japan the existence of a flourishing half-Chinese peninsula so close to her west coast was an invitation to aggression. In 1592 the Japanese undertook a great invasion but were driven back, for one reason, by the possession by the Korean navy of what was, to all appearances, an armoured battleship – a most interesting development for that time when bows and arrows were still the fashionable weapons, and one characteristic of the high state of culture of the Koreans at that date; in the same century the Koreans were using movable metal type and had evolved an alphabet unique it seems in its completeness. But Japan remained dangerously near and after their successful attack on China in 1895, the Japanese compelled the vanquished to recognize Korea's independence for their own, rather than for the Koreans', advantage. Chosen – the Japanese name for the peninsula – became a typical case of a province to a greater extent than did the colonies of the European type. Any impartial investigator will admit that here Japan far outstripped her European teachers. In the Anglo-Japanese treaty of alliance of 1902 Britain recognized Japan's special interest in Korea very much against Russian wishes; for Russia had much less to fear from an independent Korea than from a Japanese one. Russia objected to the presence of Japanese troops, but had to abandon protests when the bill of reckoning came in for her underestimation of Japan as a military power.

Although in the war of 1904–1905 Korea remained formally neutral, a Japanese army arrived and it became a Japanese protectorate. The Koreans, who knew very well the bitter significance of the word protectorate did not yield to the conquerors. They turned to foreign countries who gave them no help. Embittered, they did all that remained for them to do, for no one can deny an oppressed nation the right to rebel. In the general rising in 1907–1908 10,000 were killed. The Korean army was dissolved; the emperor compelled to go. But the fire of freedom glowed brighter and after a Japanese governor-general, Count Hirubimi Ito, was assassinated in Harbin in Manchuria by a Korean, Japan annexed the country outright. Japanese became the official language, a burdensome and, in its arrogance, humiliating measure, but not unbearable for the illiterate majority. More burdensome was the attempt to suppress Korean culture and religion. In the fourth century, Korea had accepted Buddhism and, if this religion in the course of the centuries had been gradually ousted by Confucianism, the Koreans had no more desire to be the victims of Shintoism than of the piratical policies of Japan. Their forests were hewn down, their iron-ore and coal were exported on foreign ships and the peasants, overwhelmed with debt, had to produce by the sweat of their brows the rice and cotton which the Japanese needed. Only the big landlords, particularly in the north of the country, and part of the bourgeois merchant class were prosperous, especially after Japan in her own interests had to some extent industrialized the north in about 1915. But until 1945 the hate of the Korean for the Japanese remained unaltered.

Formosa, in Chinese Taiwan, i.e. the land of terraces, which is now the last stronghold of the Chinese 'nationalists' against the Communist domination on the continent, is an island off the southeast coast of China about the same size as Holland and separated from the mainland by the ninety-mile-wide Formosa Strait. The original inhabitants, whose language belonged to the Malay group, offered a good deal of resistance to the Chinese invasions in former days and remained independent until the seventeenth century. Then came the intermezzo of the Dutch colonization settlement at Fort Zeelandia near the modern Tainan; its establishment served as the reason for the Chinese annexation (c. 1680). The Formosans in the following centuries were driven into the hills by Chinese immigrants, so that by 1895, when the Treaty of Shimonoseki gave it to Japan, it was in fact a Chinese island. The Chinese population, ignoring high politics, declared Taiwan independent and was crushed after heavy fighting by the soldiers of Japan. The new masters exploited it just as they did Korea after 1910. Rice, tea, sugar and jute went to Japan. When the Japanese Mitsui company proceeded to cut down the forests, the Lichi rising made its frantic protest. It is only towards the end of the First World War that we can speak of a genuine national movement, but by that time there was nothing left to oppress.

Let us now, since we are so near China, make a detour to Hongkong. This trading port, a British crown colony, was only a deserted rocky island, a resort of fishermen and a refuge for pirates, when in 1841, during the Opium War it fell into British hands and, marvellous to relate, the British are still there. In the period 1900–1914 there was not the slightest chance for the Chinese there to shake off the British yoke.

The Philippines were discovered in 1521 by the Portuguese Fernão de Magelhães on his circumnavigation of the globe (1519–21). In the sixteenth century they were occupied by the Spaniards, who founded Manila in May 1571 and named the archipelago after Philip II. Culturally the colony had to a very large extent become Spanish by the time Spain and the United States went to war (1898) over Cuba. The Spaniards lost the war on all fronts, and on December 10th of that year the Philippines, by the Treaty of Paris, were surrendered to the United States.

In the last days of Spanish rule a national reform movement had been started among the Filipinos under the Liga Filipina (founded 1892), which was directed particularly against the economic and spiritual influence of the Catholic monasteries. One of the foremost of its leaders was Dr Jose Rizal, an ophthalmic surgeon of world-wide repute, an able ethnologist and a painter and sculptor of considerable merit. During the rising of 1896–1897 under Emilio Aguinaldo, Rizal, the greatest of Filipino nationalists, was executed by the Spaniards. The rising was crushed, but when in 1898 the Spanish fleet in Manila harbour was destroyed by the Americans, Aguinaldo organized a national army of liberation which helped the Americans to defeat the Spaniards.

Aguinaldo acted as he did in the belief that he was fighting for Filipino independence, but the new masters had other ideas; the Philippines were annexed by the United States. Aguinaldo rejected American sovereignty, declared (1899) the Philippines an independent state and began a guerrilla war in which for three years he held at bay a strong American expeditionary force.

Meantime it was seen that American rule differed from European colonialism to this extent that the United States Government quickly granted a degree of self-government. When General MacArthur, the father of the MacArthur of the Second World War, suppressed the rebellion and took Aguinaldo prisoner, his captive bowed to the situation and ordered the war to stop. By 1902 the Philippines had their own administration. The first chamber was elected by the United States, the second by the Filipinos themselves. Only the Congress in Washington had the right of veto. Then followed economic reforms, including the expropriation of part of the estates of the rich monasteries, and further political reforms like the separation of church and state. When elections were held to the law-making body, the united nationalist parties, the Partido Union Nacionalista, won some 50 per cent of the seats.

In 1909 there was a development which was abnormal in a colonial area. By law – the so-called Payne-Aldrich Tariff – the Philippines were granted free entry for their products, especially sugar and tobacco, into the United States, at first on a smallish scale, latterly, from 1913, without restriction. This typically modern American policy meant, on the one hand, the possibility of a relatively high standard of living for the Philippines, and, on the other, it bound the land economically, and therefore politically, to the United States, and as political freedom increased, these bonds were strengthened in the same measure; this was a development very different from that in Indonesia where political freedom was much more restricted and where the native citizens were as far as possible prevented by the Dutch from entering the field of production. In the Philippines it was not the genuine Filipinos who benefited most from the flourishing trade with America, but the old Spanish families and the Chinese middle class. The peasants remained poor, for the feudal structure of the country was substantially maintained, It was – and remains – the 'cacique', the estate agent of the great landowners, to whose pipes the peasant had to dance because the 'cacique' was the only person who could advance the cash the latter needed.

To conclude this section we must just note the most important aspects of the rise of the national movement in Indonesia between 1900 and 1914. In 1900 the immense majority of the Indonesians were 'tanis' – i.e. small peasants and fishermen – or worked as coolies on the European sugar and tobacco plantations, the tea and coffee fields, and at the growing of pepper and quinine. In Java particularly, where two-thirds of the Indonesian people live on what is only 7 per cent of the area of the archipelago, the discrepancy between the amount of the rice harvests and the size of the population became ever greater. During this period the fertility of the land seemed to have reached its limits, unless there were gigantic schemes of irrigation and, while the European plantations swallowed up more and more land, the population of the islanders rose terribly disproportionately. It grew, indeed, like the rice. From 4,000,000 people in 1800, it had risen by 1875 to 18,000,000 and to 29,000,000 in 1900. The position of the noble official class was still as uncontested as that of the Dutch, while the Chinese, just as in Malaya and the Philippines, formed a definite, but not universally beloved, group of middlemen.

About 1900 one may note both a weakening and a strengthening of Dutch rule. Between 1895 and 1905 the so-called pacification of the outer provinces took place, made notorious by the war against Lombok (1894) and the last phase of that against Atjeh (1896–1904). As long ago as 1871 the sultan of Atjeh had asked Turkey for help against the Dutch. Turkey had other matters to think about and no help came. But resistance to the Dutch went on until finally it was cruelly and terribly suppressed by General van Heutsz.

The only redeeming feature of the subjection of the whole archipelago is that Van Heutsz and his men, without either knowing it or wishing it, laid the foundations of the unity of the republic of today.

Atjeh was a typical case of the first, the feudal, phase of the national movement. On a casual look it may seem absurd to link the primitive bands of Atjeh armed with their old muskets with the later organized movement for independence. For history, however, there is connection, for here we see the evolution from simple defence to the creation of a free modern nation. Here we have the two phases of the Asian-European conflict, just as in the case of Gandhi and contemporary India, and in the case of China from the Taiping and Boxer risings, through the Red Army revolution in South Kwangsi, to the China of today.

Those who regard the awakening of Indonesia as a consequence, though undesired, of the so-called 'ethical policy' which the Dutch inaugurated in 1901, put the cart before the horse. The real basis of the ethical policy was not ethics but simply economics. The situation began to change definitely in the 'seventies. In a country where there was nothing but illiterates there was no possibility of creating a modern administration, modern rubber plantations, roads, shipyards, railways and sugar refineries. So a number of irrigation schemes were launched; primary schools were established and a ministry of hygiene created. The true nature of the ethical policy is revealed by the fact that these developments were not paid for by the coconuts which in the nineteenth century Holland exported from Indonesia, but in the main from taxes levied on a population which had been educated enough to understand their significance.

The ethical policy was a policy of regimentation and it remained so. In colonial affairs phrases like 'a declaration of coming of age' were used to conceal from the users and from other people that the development of the colonies and their inhabitants was desirable only to the definite extent of serving the needs of modern industrial concerns, and the consequent modern system of administration. The conflict between desire for this development to go on and the desire to prevent it or at least to slow it down is the source both of national movements and of the tactics of suppression used by the colonial governments.

The first signs of a national movement in Indonesia were among the Chinese who, wherever they are born, remain Chinese. It was a reaction to Japan's attainment of equality with the European powers. By the Anglo-Japanese treaty Japan had become a Great Power, and so, in the statistics of the Dutch East Indies had to figure among the European and not among the Asian states. The Chinese began to build their own schools and took a prominent part in the revolution in China in 1911.

Among the native Indonesians the movement began between 1908 and 1911. We may pass over the emancipation efforts of Raden Adjeng Kartini (1879–1904), the daughter of the ruler of Djapara, for she was concerned in the main with the education of women, and regard as the first sign of 'the beautiful stream' among the Javanese aristocracy the foundation of the Budi Utomo in 1908. Although there were radical elements in it, it was moderate in its aims, making propaganda mainly for better education; it hardly ever touched on politics before 1918.

The general picture first fundamentally changed in 1912 when the Sarekat Islam was founded. This was originally a co-operative trade association which was principally concerned to combat the economic monopoly of the Chinese, for the Chinese yoke bore even more heavily than the Dutch. None the less the genuine nationalist movement was born; like a tempest it swept through Java; in Djakarta its membership rose to 12,000 in a few months, a remarkable feat. Even if its demands were not very definite, it was the first Indonesian organization of which the Europeans took notice and which caused them anxiety, especially because of the double character it had, the national and the religious. The cry of an official to the Queen of the Netherlands: 'Sarekat Islam is stirring up the people; we are losing our colonies', was a gross exaggeration. Yet, though fear causes blindness, this official to some extent saw clearly enough; it was at least an impressive opinion when it is compared with what the Dutch newspapers in Indonesia were saying.

Of scarcely less importance was the Muhammadija, a modern Moslem organization which was founded in 1912. The Muhammadija was non-political, loyal to the Dutch government and by means of a revival and requickening of the tradition of Islam hoped to modernize Indonesia socially and economically. It is parallel to the efforts made in many Moslem circles in other countries.

The young national will found expression in the same year in a third section of the people, the Eurasians. It is worth noting that this group, which appeared to be the first ready for emancipation, was because of its position between the races, an insignificant factor in the struggle for independence.

These events, the first signs of the tempest which was to carry away the old colonial domination, were in great measure a reaction to the system of administration and its consequences. Although improvement was its aim, the methods of that system were regarded as further encroachment; for instance, the war in Atjeh, the conquest of the other provinces and the reforms of the time in the regions still sovereign as a result of which the sultans were directly subjected to Dutch rule. Half-consciously the future was being prepared, and in proof that Indonesia in its awakening looked beyond the frontiers, there was the reaction in 1911–13 to the Italo-Turkish War and the Balkan Wars. The Indonesians were on the Turkish side in the first instance from religious motives, but it was as much an instinctive political choice felt rather than understood – for Asia against Europe.

VI

INDOCHINA, MALAYA, THAILAND AND BURMA

THE name Indochina is used here to denote the four independent states of North Vietnam, South Vietnam, Cambodia and Laos. Vietnam, the land of the Annamites and the biggest, most productive and most densely populated part of the country, was formerly divided into three provinces, North, Central and South Vietnam, which, up to 1950, were called Tonkin, Annam and Cochinchina. We cannot call Indochina a real political unity, especially after Vietnam has been split in two by the guerrilla war between the semi-French regime of Bao Dai and the Communist regime of Viet Minh.

At the beginning of the nineteenth century, Indochina was ruled for the most part by the emperor of Annam. Culturally it was a province of China and recognized the suzerainty of the Chinese emperor. An 'unoccupied' territory in Asia attracted the Europeans. In 1858 Spaniards and Frenchmen arrived and, with less delicacy than they showed in other regions, desired to make the acquaintance of the inhabitants. On a sunny morning ships' guns were thundering on the coast of Tourane and the first French shells fell on the future colony; Indochina was now experiencing what had already befallen half of Asia. One after another the Chinese provinces yielded to French superiority, Cochinchina at once, Cambodia five years later, Annam and Tonkin in 1884 and 1885. The last to go was Laos – earlier called Lane Xang, the land of the million elephants – which, after a long conflict with Thailand (Siam), became a French protectorate. By 1887 the various regions were already united for administrative purposes in the 'Union indochinoise'.

From 1897 to 1902 the governor-general was the well-known French politician Paul Doumer. It cannot be denied that in his day there was progress in modernization. Railways, canals and dams appeared; the new capital Hanoi on the Red River had a big modern quarter. The native rulers, save in Cochinchina which became a colony, were maintained. The majority of the population was Annamite, who felt themselves bound by many ties to China whence, about 100 B.C., their culture had come. They lived in the three coastal provinces: Tonkin, Annam and Cochinchina; then, as now, three-quarters of the total population lived there. It was their fruitful delta regions – on the Red River in the north, on the Mekong in the south – that the French had most exploited, a fact which made the loss of them in our own day a grievous blow. It is unpleasant to have to wage a colonial war as the French and their German mercenaries had to do in Vietnam, but it is much worse to be driven out of a colony which produces $3\frac{1}{2}$ per cent of all the natural rubber in the world and 3 per cent of the rice. In religion the Annamites are partly adherents of Confucianism, while the poorer and less densely populated states of Laos and Cambodia are overwhelmingly Buddhist and Taoist.

However stout resistance may have been before it was broken, Indochina was firmly in French hands by 1900, but from the days of the Russo-Japanese War (1904–1905), the colonial fruit began to rot on the tree. Indochina entered the first phase of the nationalist movement, the opposition offered by the princes and the nobility and the humbler class of the mandarins who derived very little advantage from all their book-learning. A secondary cause of discontent was the treatment by the French of the emperor of Annam, Thanh Thai; they said he had become insane and compelled him to abdicate and in 1907 exiled him. But of all the burdens, and especially for the peasants, the greatest was the indirect taxation and the French monopolies including salt, opium and alcohol. It need cause no surprise that in 1906–8 many conspiracies were discovered – and many others were not discovered. They were inspired often from Japan – at this period was not Sun Yat-sen preparing the Chinese revolution in Japan? – and were financed by the princes and the nobility. It is no more surprising that the resistance was forcibly suppressed. The protests of the Young Annamite movement remained unanswered.

Meantime the second phase of the awakening was being prepared through the French policy of assimilation, which sent many Annamite students to Paris, who returned to strengthen the modern spirit in the resistance. What did this assimilation policy amount to? Each European nation has its own methods of colonization. The Dutch feared to make Dutch the language of the primary schools, not in order to keep the natives down but because it was held that the native culture must remain intact. The British, on the other hand, introduced their language very early as the language of instruction in the Indian schools, while leaving the Indians in cultural matters a free hand, whereas the French believed that no one can be thought educated who does not speak, think and feel French. In the French view even European peoples were on a lower scale if they did not know French, which at that time was an international language and the only language of diplomacy. How strongly the French are ruled by this prejudice may be seen from the fact that it still exists.

In Indochina, the influence of China and the Chinese kept pace with the rate of conquest, especially in the south where Cochinchina was a real stronghold of Chinese merchants and intellectuals. In the economic sphere, the Annamites in Tonkin were less dominated by the Chinese, and in the valley of the Red River and in the highlands it was the Europeans who exploited the sugar and coffee plantations and the coal, tin and zinc mines.

Thus by 1914 the subjective and objective pre-conditions for the winning of liberty already existed; objective because of foreign rule, subjective because of the growing self-consciousness of the Annamites. None the less a shock was needed to set the ball rolling. That shock was administered by the First World War.

The name Malaya is used in these pages for the region which is now the Malay Federation with Singapore, i.e. the British part of the Malay Peninsula. It was colonized in the fourteenth century by Malays from Sumatra. At the beginning of the sixteenth century the Portuguese occupied Malacca on the famous straits of that name and made it one of the earliest European settlements in East Asia. They had got the trade in tin and spices well organized, when, in the first half of the seventeenth century, they were driven out by the Dutch who kept trade with the whole peninsula firmly in their hands for a hundred years. About 1800 the British arrived, obtained the island of Penang from the sultan of Kedah as a trading place, and in 1824 took over Malacca from the Dutch in exchange for Bankahulu (Benkulen) on the west coast of Sumatra. Meantime Stamford Raffles had built the first houses and fortifications of Singapore (1819). Malaya was recognized as British territory when Penang, Malacca and Singapore became officially crown colonies under the name of the Straits Settlements; in this area are all the big towns. From then Britain pushed farther on. Between 1874 and 1895 the whole area between Penang and Singapore came under British rule, that is, the native states of Perak, Selangor, Negri Sembilan, Pahang and Johore. The first four were incorporated in a federation but Johore was not included, nor were the states separated from Siam in 1909 – Perlis, Kedah, Kelantan and Trengganu, which all lie on the northern frontier of modern Malaya. This was the last British acquisition in the peninsula.

It is now time to see how the inhabitants reacted to the British occupation, for it was an occupation. The four federated states, as well as the five non-federated states, had only a semblance of self-government. If we are to summarize the complicated history of nationalism in Malaya it can only be done in answer to the question: how did the British manage to stay in Malaya until 1957? Had not the European regimes been driven out of all other Asian areas of any importance? The answer may be found in Malayan history.

Before the First World War, Malaya as it is today was inhabited by three very different races. According to present figures, 42 per cent of the people are Chinese, 40 per cent Malays and rather less than 10 per cent Indians, both Hindu and Moslem; in Singapore four-fifths of the population are Chinese. The percentages were pretty much the same before 1914. Of the three races the Malays are either nobles or small farmers and fishermen. The workers in the tin mines, the ports and the rubber plantations are Chinese and Indians. The Chinese, as elsewhere in Southeast Asia, are also merchants and planters. This mixture of races was a great obstacle to the growth of the national movement and the British often used the fact that the Chinese were in the majority as justification for the continuance of their rule; the Malays had to be protected against the threat of Chinese domination.

Just as confused as the ethnic-social was the political situation. The division of the country into nine small states and a crown colony was all to Britain's advantage, and that she could rule this rich country almost until today is due to the fact that the Roman rule of *divide et impera* was easier to apply here than anywhere else.

A third cause was the intensive economic exploitation in which Britain had so great an interest. No less than two-thirds of the cultivated area is taken up by the rubber plantations, which – and this is true of the pre-1914 period in some considerable measure – now produce almost 45 per cent of the world's rubber, about 10 per cent of its palm-oil and copra, and roughly a quarter of its tin. And all its produce is for the most part shipped through one of the greatest of world ports, Singapore.

The fourth and last cause of the weakness of nationalism in Malaya is that the national movement had to be the work of the economically weak Malay minority. Like the Indonesians they had been converted to Islam in the thirteenth century, and during the British domination the movement was predominantly Moslem and, until the end of the Caliphate in 1924, pan-Islamic. None the less there did exist modern elements comparable to the Muhammadija in Indonesia; the British who understand the art of ruling better than any other people, posed as the champions of Islam. Again, the many Indians and Arabs who had become rich by trade, and from the economic point of view were the masters of the Malay peasants and fishermen, also were Moslems. In a word, the Malays of Malaya, the only natural representatives of its nationalism, often were confronted by hidden enemies and that is of great significance to any political movement. The people desirous of freedom will not be content to feel unfree; it will learn to know who its opponents are.

Thailand, the former Siam – 200,000 square miles of mountain and plain, two-thirds of it covered with tropical forest but elsewhere a land of ricefields and rubber plantations – was inhabited at a very early date. In the sixth century the Khmer peoples who lived in the northeast of the country came under the influence of Hindu culture. In the eighth century the northern river valleys in the neighbourhood of Chiang Mai were the centre of the kingdom of Haripundjaja. Its civilization went under in the thirteenth century when it was overthrown by an invasion of the Thai peoples from present-day Yunnan in southern China. These invaders still rule Siam and it is after them that the country is officially called Thailand. The new state was from its beginnings founded on Hinayana Buddhism and on Chinese political institutions. Ajuthia, north of Bangkok, was its capital. The period from the fourteenth to the eighteenth century was chequered with wars with China and Burma, but Thailand none the less expanded and in the latter century it stretched from the banks of the Mekong in the east to the coasts of the Indian Ocean in the west. The first encounter with Europe was an idyll compared to what followed. The Portuguese and Dutch sailors who reached its coasts were concerned only with trade and were thus not very dangerous. It was the French who about 1680 provoked a series of civil wars as a result of which all Europeans were expelled. Siam shut out the foreigner just as Japan had done.

In 1782 a new dynasty, the one ruling today, succeeded in uniting the country. Meantime the Europeans had not disappeared from the scene and in 1826 the British were able to conclude a limited trade treaty. This was the beginning of fresh contacts between a mediaeval country and the coal and steel civilization on the North Sea. In the reign of Rama IV, Phra Chom Klao Mongkut (1851–1868), the first European consulates were established on the wooded banks of the Chao Phraja river south of the capital Bangkok. At first they could only be approached by water and it is symbolical that the first modern road in Thailand was built at this period to connect the consulates with the royal palace. Mongkut was the first king of Siam to realize that the West meant more than warships; he felt – as Japan felt at the same time – that his country could maintain itself against Europe only if it became partly Europeanized. He made intensive studies of Western culture, a fact brought to the notice of the British because it was, preferably, the British consul who was dragged from his bed in the middle of the night to discuss a matter of geography or the exact translation of a word into English. He had an English governess in his palace who taught his children and wives English and told them of foreign lands and people. Thus Thailand began to awaken as a result of royal studies, of the curiosity of the harem, of a glance at a map of the world, an English book or a lump of coal.

Meantime the French were concerned lest the British alone should skim the cream from the milk. In 1893 they made Laos, which had earlier belonged to Siam, a French protectorate. 1896 was a bad year for Thailand. The British and French agreed to a settlement of what was then called the Siamese question; both guaranteed the independence of Thailand. That had an excellent sound, but it meant in practice that Siam became a buffer state between British India, of which Burma was then part, and French Indochina. It is an old story. We may recall the guarantee of the independence of Korea, China, Afghanistan and Persia, which simply signified: If I can't have, you won't either. It did not mean that the jealous powers – even if they did not admit jealousy, they thought in its terms – left the contested area in peace. On the contrary, both sought to increase their influence in Siam and in 1907 it was divided into two 'spheres of interest', a French sphere to the east of the Menam and a British to the west. The state of Siam can be compared to that of Afghanistan, which played the part of a buffer state between India and Russia, and to that of Persia which suffered the same fate.

None the less there was progress, for in Rama V, Phra Maha Chulalongkorn, the land found a radical modern ruler (1868–1910). Roads were built and canals and railways (1893); a post and telegraph service was set up in 1883. Slavery was made more tolerable and in 1905 abolished altogether. The army, the administration of justice and the taxation system were all modernized. That was at once the condition and the consequence of a centralized administration implying limitation of the power of the nobility which in many parts of the country made its own laws and rebelled against Bangkok. What Chulalongkorn could not prevent was the British landgrab of 1909, when the provinces of Kedah, Kelantan, Trengganu and Perlis were detached from Siam.

Rama VI Vadjiravudh (1910–1925), who had studied in Britain, continued the work of modernization. Chulalongkorn had a harem with nine hundred wives and female slaves in it, wives who were so sacred that one of them was drowned because no one dared to go to her help. Rama VI established monogamy for himself and everyone else. The irrigation of the ricefields was improved and modernized, the Buddhist calendar was replaced by the European, unpaid labour was diminished and, in 1917, the first students arrived at the new university in Bangkok which was named after the great Chulalongkorn.

But there were two serious obstacles in the way of genuine modernization and genuine independence. The first consisted of the 120,000 Hinayana-Buddhist monks, the great majority of whom had few modern ideas and who were constantly influenced by the nobility in a reactionary sense. They had the whole educational system in their hands and encouraged the people to resist modernization. In 1921 education was made compulsory and State schools were opened. The second was the economic ties with Britain from which all capital came. More than half the exploited forests, especially those with teak and ebony, belonged to British subjects. The great rubber plantations were owned by British companies, though the actual managers might be Chinese. But the inhabitants of Thailand remained peasants and fishermen. The country lived on rice, and more was exported from it than from any other country except Burma. For these peasants who were the genuine Thailand, the new age was not a sunny one. The supersession of the old natural economy by the modern money economy caused many of them to fall into debt and many peasants had to sell their land, often to Chinese.

Burma, which lies between China and Thailand in the east and India and Pakistan in the west, has much in common with Thailand. In the north there are the forested mountain chains, in the south a fruitful plain with ricefields; the whole country is watered by the Irrawaddy, as Thailand is by the Menam. Historically the two countries are akin. In the third century Hindu peoples, in their efforts at expansion, had founded trading posts on the coasts of Tenasserim and on the great rivers. From these modest beginnings arose small kingdoms which spread Buddhist culture among the Tibetan-Burman peoples in the Irrawaddy valley. Like Thailand, Burma was overrun by invaders from Yunnan fleeing before the horsemen of the Mongol prince Gengis Khan, who at this period was in possession of almost all Asia and a part of Europe; his empire stretched from Pekin to Poland and from Bagdad to the Siberian forests. From then on the political status wavered between that of an independent country and that of a subject province of China; the scales were swayed by wars with China.

At the beginning of the fifteenth century a notable Italian, Niccolo de Conti, made a voyage to Asia as far as Sumatra. About 1435 he visited Burma. He returned to Europe a Moslem, and it was his reports which led the Portuguese to the Irrawaddy in 1519. They came as usual for spices, but were quite ready to hire soldiers to Tabin Schwehti the lord of Taunghu, some 150 miles north of present-day Rangoon. This prince was thus enabled to conquer a great part of the country and in 1546 was crowned king of Burma. The time was not yet ripe for a dangerous European invasion, for the Dutch and British, who set up trading posts in 1619, took their departure in the same century.

The real conflict of Europe and Asia, so far as Burma is concerned, starts in the nineteenth century. During the eighteenth century Burma had been steadily freeing herself from China and had roughly reached her present frontiers when, in 1823, King Badjidaw (1819–1837) annexed Manipur and Assam on the frontier of the East India Company's possessions in Bengal. In three wars the Burmese troops with their out-of-date equipment were beaten by the modern army of the British. In the First Burmese War (1824–1826) they lost Assam, Arakan and the Tenasserim coast; in the Second (1852–1853) Rangoon and in the Third (1885) Burma had to give up altogether and a year later became part of British India, remaining such until 1937 when it became a crown colony with some degree of self-government.

So Burma was a British colony – really a British-Indian one, for at this period what the Chinese were to Thailand the Indians were to Burma. The valuable forests were in British hands; the teak was hewn and sawed up by Indian labourers and shipped abroad on British ships. The lead and zinc mines were already of international importance, but the miners were Indians, the technicians Indians or British and the directors were British. The owners of the ports, railways and shipyards lived in London and Calcutta. There were more Indians in Rangoon than Burmans. The few factories, some rice-flour mills and the sawmills were worked with British capital. The Burman remained a peasant and a small one. Two-thirds of the cultivateable land was ricefields, on which from 4 to 5 per cent of the world crop was harvested; Burma is the world's biggest exporter of rice. And again – the listing becomes wearisome – it was the British, the Indians and the Chinese who as landed property owners, bankers and merchants made the greatest profits. Equally the administrative officials were not natives. The nobility were now of hardly any importance and there were only a very few native-born intellectuals. So the movement for independence grew very slowly, the more so because nationalism was disrupted by anti-Indian and anti-Chinese tendencies. The Russo-Japanese War and an outbreak of plague (1905) helped to rouse the country from its apathy. In 1907 a medical institute was established; in 1906 a 'Young Men's Buddhist Association' was formed on the model of the Y.M.C.A. Very much as was the case with the Sarekat Islam in Indonesia, the national movement showed definitely religious traits with all the strength but all the weaknesses that that implies. Here too, as in Indochina, a shock was needed before nationalism could really become an independent factor; here too it was the same shock that was administered – the First World War.

VII

AFGHANISTAN AND IRAN

So far we have dealt with the inner zone of Asia – that is, the area which has the densely populated agricultural states, the area where rice grows. Now we turn to the outer zone in the period 1900–1914, and first to Afghanistan and Iran (Persia); the latter then appears mainly in the role of a buffer state between the British Empire in Nearer India and the Russian Empire in Central Asia. It is also one of the oldest cultural areas in history.

There is not much to say about Afghanistan – a national movement had not yet begun in the period 1900–1914 – were it not for the fact that that country is so good an example of the way in which the Great Powers used Asian countries for their own purposes, countries which either by their geographical situation or by their mineral resources invited intervention, such as Korea, Thailand, Irak with its wealth of oil, and smaller lands still, Cyprus, for instance, and Formosa. Afghanistan was in a situation which invited its neighbours to intrigue. In the west and south it is bounded by what is today Pakistan and was then British India, in the west by Persia and in the north by Russian Central Asia. There was not much to be got out of the country either by Britain or Russia. Although it is a relatively large country – it is some 250,000 square miles in area – most of it is barren mountain, steppe and desert, and only north of the Hindu-Kush, towards the Amu Daria and in other river valleys, is there cultivateable land – roughly 5 per cent of the total area. The population, then about 11,000,000 to 12,000,000, was sparse and extremely primitive; the nomad shepherds who formed a considerable part of it lived in tents, others lived in caves and others in huts without any comforts. Certainly it was neither the maize, the dates, the wool, nor the cotton which made Afghanistan politically interesting in the nineteenth century; it was so because of the ambitions of Russia and Britain.

For many centuries until the eighteenth, Afghanistan was ruled partly by princes from the Indus region, partly by Persians and partly by the kingdom of Bokhara which is now the Soviet Republics of Turkmenistan, Usbekistan and Tadjikstan. About A.D. 800 the Afghans became Moslems and the population today is 90 per cent Sunnite and 10 per cent Shiite; the latter are doctors, merchants and intellectuals in the towns. About the beginning of the eighteenth century there was a movement towards independence originating from Kandahar which, thanks to the decline of the empires which then ruled Afghanistan, ended in victory. In 1750 the Afghans took Lahore and Delhi, over 600 miles from Kabul, and about 1775 Afghanistan reached its greatest extent, stretching from East Persia in the west to Delhi on the Ganges in the east. At the beginning of the nineteenth century the frontiers had begun to recede and in 1835, when the head of the Barakzai tribe Dost Mohammed took the title of amir of Afghanistan, the kingdom's frontiers were roughly those of the present day. The Barakzai dynasty ruled until 1929 and was able to steer successfully between the two rocks, the military power of Russia and that of Britain.

In Dost Mohammed's reign the Persians, urged on by Russia in order to check the growing influence of the East India Company, invaded Afghanistan in 1837. The result was not that expected in St Petersburg, for Britain embarked on the First Afghan War (1839–1842). Dost Mohammed was deposed and brought to India. Under Shah Sujah, British influence was secured by a virtual occupation. In 1841 there was a rising. Two British envoys were murdered; the British had to evacuate Kabul and the retreating army was massacred in the Khyber Pass. Shah Sujah was murdered and Dost Mohammed was able to return. He realized that the British must not be given too much offence, and so in 1855 he signed a treaty with them in Peshawar and just at the right time, for next winter the Persians took Herat, the only town of any importance in western Afghanistan. Britain now declared war on Persia, and in the peace of Paris of 1857 Persia recognized the 'independence' of Afghanistan; the boundary between the two countries was finally settled in 1872. France also had intervened but to no purpose. Making use of the alleged 'independence' of the sultan of Muscat, she armed ships flying his flag and sent weapons and munitions to Persian Baluchistan to help the Persians. In itself the incident had no significance; we recall it to indicate the methods the Great Powers used towards each other while they lived together in peace and friendship.

We now reach the time when the historic situation arises of two powers each grudging the other a country, the situation, say, of Korea in 1895 and Thailand in 1893. In 1878 a number of Russian officers arrived in Kabul and got the amir to sign a mutual assistance treaty. Scarcely had this Russian mission departed when the British embarked on the Second Afghan War (1878–1879), in which they occupied three-quarters of the country. By the treaty of Gandamak Britain obtained the Khyber Pass, which is the only road of military value connecting Afghanistan with British India. The amir received an annual subsidy of £60,000 but had to agree to let his foreign relations be controlled by the Government of India. Afghanistan then was a mediaeval wilderness and in no sense a modern state; the amir in Kabul had no authority over the wandering hill peoples. Led by the mullahs, resistance to the British flared up again and British Indian troops had to be used to quell it. Meantime Russia was increasing the number of Cossack regiments on the frontier and the amir Abdurrahman (1880–1901) adopted a policy of equilibrium between the bear on the Amu Daria and the lion on the Indus. He also laid the foundations for the modernization of the country by forcibly unifying it and, as far as he could, as he tells us in his autobiography, furthering the growth of a middle class.

If we look for an example of how a mountain country which is of little value to anyone can raise the temperature of world politics to boiling point we can find it in Afghanistan at the time of the Pendjeh incident. In 1885 Russian and Afghan troops were involved in fighting on the still rather indeterminate northern frontier. The result was a serious Anglo-Russian crisis during which Britain occupied a port in Korea to serve as base for an attack on Vladivostok. It did not come to war, but the conception of making Afghanistan a buffer-state was again very much to the fore and in 1895 an agreement was made on the frontier between Afghanistan and the Pamir highlands in Russia. The result is still visible on the map; in the northeast Afghanistan possesses a sort of 'blind appendix' barely thirty-one miles wide and some 185 miles long which divides the Pamir district from Kashmir (then part of British India).

Under the weak government of Habibulla (1901–1919), who preferred to take the advice of his harem and the reactionary mullahs than trust to his own certainly limited understanding, European ideas kept penetrating the country. The material results were trifling – two factories and some schools. But the connection with Britain, who had to protect the frontiers, and her control of Afghanistan's international relations became stronger. The amir's subsidy was doubled. In 1907 the picture changed. Britain, who formerly had fear of France and later of Russia, now felt herself threatened by Germany's economic expansion in Asia, e.g. in the plans for the Bagdad railway. The entente between Paris and London, a reaction to German policy, dates from 1904 and was followed by the Anglo-Russian entente. This, reached in 1907, concerned especially Persia and Tibet, but it also concerned Afghanistan. Russia declared that she would not interfere with that country. Thus when the First World War broke out, Afghanistan was to all intents and purposes a British colony and had not yet awakened.

Iran, called Persia until 1935, is a much more important country than Afghanistan. There is first of all her political expansion in classical times and not less her great significance in the cultural history of mankind – one need think only of Zoroaster and Omar Khayyam – which has given her world fame. The Iran of today, the heartland of this historic culture, has an area of 628,000 square miles – that is, more than Spain, France and Germany together. According to official estimates the population is about 18,000,000. Of its area nearly 70 per cent consists of desert and steppe, often salt steppe, on which only sheep can graze. Genuine forest, partly pine forest, is found in the cooler hill country south of the Caspian. Land suitable for agriculture takes up only $6\frac{1}{2}$ per cent and is for the most part not dependent on irrigation; it is found in the few river valleys and the lower slopes of the hills. But, much more important than dates, figs and almonds and politically much more dangerous than wheat, cotton and oranges is what lies beneath the soil – oil. Iran is indeed synonymous with oil. It produces 6 per cent of the world's oil and is inferior only to the United States, Venezuela and Soviet Russia.

In 1901 a New Zealander, William Knox d'Arcy, for £20,000 sterling and 16 per cent of the profits, got a concession for the exploitation of the oilfields in four-fifths of Persia; the concession was for sixty years. D'Arcy made many fruitless borings before, in 1908, the field of Mashid-i-Sulaiman between

Isfahan and the Tigris was discovered. The Anglo-Persian Oil Company was formed in 1909 as a result of this discovery. This was the company which later was called the Anglo-Iranian Company and was nationalized by Iran in 1951. By the Anglo-Russian agreement of 1907 Persia was divided into two spheres of influence; the northern half of the land a Russian one, the southern a British one. Persia reacted to the European invasion more vigorously than did Afghanistan. Why this was so will be more easily understood if we take a glance at her history. Long, long ago, in the morning twilight of history (4000–3000 B.C.), a notable and highly developed culture arose in Susa and Persepolis in the southwest of what is today Iran; in many respects it is comparable to that existing in Mesopotamia. The peoples who made it – the level they attained has been demonstrated by excavation – must have been about 1800 B.C. overrun by a people belonging to the Indo-Germanic speech-group who form the kernel of the population today. The new nation quickly expanded; about 550 B.C. the Persian Empire was one of the greatest in the world, stretching from Cyrenaica, Egypt and the Bosphorus to the Indus and the Sea of Aral. No more than any other was the Persian Empire immortal, and two centuries later it had become so weak that it fell victim completely to Alexander the Great. In 331 B.C. he conquered Iran, the core of the empire; he was the first European, whose name we know, to reach the Indus. If Persia recovered from the European invasion – it formed a barrier which the armies of Rome could not break through – it was never again politically and militarily what it once had been. Yet once again it was an oasis of culture in the long period after the Arab conquest in A.D. 648, until 1258, the period in which it was converted to Islam. The next foreign rulers were the Mongols, who overthrew the caliphate of Bagdad in 1258 and ruled Persia and three-quarters of Asia until the fourteenth century. When Persia recovered its freedom again, it was consolidated under the native dynasty of the Seffyids (1501–1756), which deepened the Shiite colouring which Islam took on in Persia. Hemmed in between the Turkish Empire and Afghanistan, Persia was unable to prevent itself being forced back to what are virtually its present-day frontiers in east and west. Only in the north, in Caucasia and the plains of Turkestan, was there prospect of movement, and of that prospect Persia was deprived by the arrival in the nineteenth century of Russian Cossacks. In 1812 Russia annexed the present republic of Azerbaijan and Baku. The Kadjar dynasty (1794–1925) could not make head against this Russian forward movement. In 1850 Russian horsemen appeared in the plain of the Syr Daria west of the Sea of Aral, and it was only British threats that prevented further losses after, in 1885, Russia had brought South Turkestan, which was officially Persian, under its sway.

Even if now the frontiers were officially respected, the number of British and Russian concessions within them grew steadily. In 1896, in the reign of the shah Muzaffer ed-din, the process was plainly seen; because of Persia's need of money, tariffs, railway and oil concessions were handed over with the production of salt and tobacco to the foreigner, and as at this time the British were relatively weak after the Boer War, Russian influence grew stronger.

In 1905 revolution broke out against the weak rule of the shah. The leaders were the mullahs and the merchants who were inspired by the pan-Islamic ideas of Jamal al-Din al'Afghani, a great Persian intellectual and propagandist who had edited an Arabic review in Paris and had very great influence on the intellectual life in the Moslem lands. The revolution was directed chiefly against the corrupt minister Ain al-Dawla, whom the people held responsible for the steadily increasing foreign pressure. The left wing of the revolutionaries had what we call liberal leanings. Imitating the Young Turks, these liberals called themselves the Young Persians. They were persecuted by the Government and, as in Turkey, we see the West inclined apparently to support these liberal tendencies partly out of democratic sympathies and partly because it was thought, and rightly, that a modern liberal regime would be easier to do business with than a regime that was both corrupt and reactionary. That was the case in Persia, where the British could hope with the aid of the liberals to stem the growth of Russian influence. Little objection could be made to such ideas, so long as Asian nationalism failed to see that a genuine modernization was possible only when the colonial, or as in the case of Persia, the semi-colonial status was ended – that is, when the nation became fully independent. Thousands of the Young Persians fleeing from the police took refuge in the gardens of the European embassies, especially the British one, where they were safe for the time at least, since Persian sovereignty did not reach so far.

None the less the movement, encouraged by the Europeans, attained such strength that the shah had to concede the chief demands of the revolutionaries just as the sultan of Turkey had to do when his time came. The hated minister was dismissed and in August 1906 the shah made the still greater concession of recognizing the right of the nation to have a parliament. This was Asia's second parliament. Tokio had the first; the Turkish parliament sat in Constantinople, i.e. in Europe. In October the first parliament of Persia, the Madjlis, met; it passed a constitution of the customary type just as the Japanese and the Turkish parliaments had done. All this upset the shah so grievously that at the end of December, a few days after he had signed the constitution, he died.

His successor, Mohammed Ali (1907–1909), was just as little pleased with this burdensome modernization. The feudal organization of society had many advantages for the nobles, and there need be no surprise that, though they favoured anti-Westernism, they would have nothing to do with the idea that the West could be warded off only by the adoption of Western ideas, even if there were cases to prove that it could be, as in Japan, in China during the Hundred Days and in Thailand. It is not easy to think ourselves into these mediaeval conceptions. But the situation of Asian feudal nobles in earlier times was that they had an uncontested right over everything possessed by their subjects beyond what satisfied the bare needs of the latter. Thus the harvest of the peasant was his own, but if there was a particularly fruitful one, the excess belonged to the ruler. A particularly productive cow, an exceptionally beautiful wife had the same fate. It is not mere accident that in Javanese one single word has the threefold meaning: demand, take and steal.

The ruler who acted so was still a just ruler, neither tyrant nor despot. He only became the latter when he took from his subjects the bare necessities even to the extent of condemning to death an innocent man in order to acquire his property. There was only one answer to such excesses—conspiracy or assassination. Such rights strike us as odd. Yet if the taxation system of a modern state is examined we might find that the difference between then and now is relatively slight. There is, of course, this difference. For a feudal ruler there is no distinction between his private and public purse, while a finance minister and a member of a truly democratic parliament will not enrich himself by high taxation. Taxes are levied on the whole to the benefit of the community or at least to what the minister, the government and the parliament consider to be the benefit of the community.

The Persian minister, Atabeg-i-Azam, ruled entirely in the spirit of the reactionary shah. The Young Persians were only the more active; Atabeg-i-Azam was assassinated and the shah forced to yield to the citizens. The formation of a liberal ministry under Nasir-al-Mulk (1907) meant a new attack on the old regime. In the August of that year the contents became known of the Anglo-Russian agreement by which Persia was economically divided. This was sad news for the Persians, or at least for the enlightened among them, who were not deceived by the provision in the treaty for 'the principle of the independence and integrity of Persia'. In mid-December the opposition to the shah became too much for him. He attempted a *coup d'état* and arrested the liberal prime minister. But revolts occurred everywhere in the angry country and again he had to give way. At the end of June 1908 he tried it again, this time with the support of Russian bayonets. The czar, who in 1905 had had to suffer a revolution in Russia, was no champion of constitutions and democracy. Everywhere the Cossacks broke the resistance. Many liberals were murdered; parliament was dissolved and a state of siege declared in Teheran. Only in Tabriz were the Cossacks and the shah's troops baffled.

In this fortress city in Northern Persia the whole population rose on news of the outbreak of the revolution in Turkey (July 1908). Here we may see the difference between a revolution which is the work of certain groups and one which, as in the case here, is supported by the whole population; against a stone wall the greatest of tyrants can make no progress. It was not until February 1909 that a Russian army after a grim slaughter won back the city for the shah. In another part of the country the revolution, though hard pressed, was not destroyed. In June 1909 a certain Ali Kuli Khan of the Baktiari tribe marched on Teheran, restored the constitution and finally expelled the shah who had given so painful an example of how reactionary rulers threatened by a revolution can betray their own country by bringing in foreigners to do their dirty work.

The son of the expelled shah, Sultan Achmed (1909–1925), succeeded his father; he was still a child. He was at the beginning of his reign under the influence of the radicals. Later he was at least an original monarch who got the name of the 'merchant shah' because in time of famine he hoarded grain and other foodstuffs and sold them at a high price to the people. True, modernization proceeded under foreign advisers but none the less it made great strides. W. Morgan Shuster, an American, received from Parliament virtually dictatorial powers to put the national finances in order and organize a taxation enquiry. The natural result followed. He met with opposition from the Russians, who encouraged the ex-shah, who had fled to Russia after his deposition, to make an attempt to return to power. He landed at Astrabad on the southern shore of the Caspian but was besieged by Government troops. When two Russian ultimatums demanding the dismissal of Shuster had been rejected by the Madjlis, czarist troops again invaded the country. That happened in 1911, the year of unrest. The Persia that was vanquished was still too little modernized to offer energetic resistance, and both from a military and intellectual point of view was virtually helpless against the foreigner. It was the First World War which so kindled the national movement as to determine the fate of Persia.

VIII

THE ARAB COUNTRIES

AFTER the Turkish Empire had been shattered in the First World War new states appeared, with which we must now deal; these are the so-called Arab countries – Arabia proper, Syria, and the area which now contains Irak, Jordan and Israel.

There must be few readers who do not know why these are called Arab lands. Their inhabitants are overwhelmingly Moslem Arabs who were left in them after the dissolution of the Arab empire under which they had lived for centuries. Europeans are sometimes inclined to confine the word 'Arab' to the peoples of the oases in the sandy deserts of the Arabian peninsula but, a year after Mohammed's death in A.D. 632, the Arabs broke out of Arabia and invaded Syria. Like the wind of their own deserts, they swept into Egypt and Mesopotamia, and by 700 had created an empire stretching from the Sea of Aral and the Indus in the east, to the Atlantic coast of Morocco and the Straits of Gibraltar in the west. In 711 they landed on Gibraltar and built a castle on the famous Rock, which takes its name from the Berber leader Tarik ibn Zijad (Gibraltar = Jebel-al-Tarik : the hill of Tarik). Spain and Portugal were conquered and it was not until 732 that the Moslem offensive in the west was checked at Poitiers by the chivalry of Charles Martel. A little earlier, in 717, that offensive was checked in the east by the victorious defence of Constantinople. In the fifteenth century, Spain was recovered for Europe and what was left of the empire in North Africa was annexed by the Turks along with the other Arab lands, but the Arab-Islamic culture had had time to spread to and penetrate all the conquered countries.

Between 1900 and 1914 the whole Arab world was under foreign rule, first under the sultan in Constantinople, Abdul Hamid, and later (from 1908) under the Young Turks, whose rule was no gentler. At the beginning of the century the Hejaz railway was laid between Damascus and Medina. The construction took from 1900 to 1908 and was the work of German engineers; this was one of the signs of the growing German intervention in Turkey and a move in the game against British policy. The concession had been obtained during the State visit of Wilhelm II to Constantinople and the Arab lands in 1898. It was on this visit that that unbalanced political romantic had proclaimed himself the protector of Islam. The Turkish Government paid no attention to this bombast; it regarded the railway simply as a means of controlling its empire militarily and as a link in case of war between the Suez Canal and the Red Sea. Though no one in Constantinople intended that it should, the new railway actually aided the emancipation of the Arabs just as did the new army training grounds where German officers trained the

future leaders of the Arab revolt. The intentions of men have often other
consequences that they intend or even suspect. Bad intentions can have good
results; unfortunately the converse is equally true.

In the Turkish province on the Mediterranean coast known today as the
Lebanon, an illegal Arab movement was in existence as early as 1880. Called
the Beirut movement, after the town in which it started, it sought to rouse the
inhabitants against the hated Turks. The answer of the Constantinople
government was censorship, espionage and terror in severer form than of
old, because at that time parts of the empire were being seized by the
insatiable Europeans, Tunis by the French in 1881, Egypt by the British in
1882. Things were made too hot for the rebels, and the leadership of the
movement was transferred to Paris; here in 1904 the 'Ligue de la Patrie
arabe' was founded. The head of it was Nadshib Azuri, a Moslem freemason
who in the review which he edited spread the ideas which Turkish policy
was trying to root out in Syria. In 1905 he wrote the first book produced by
the Arab national movement. As might have been expected, the Arabs had
great hopes of the Young Turks, and the general excitement over the revolution of 1908 was the beginning of romantic illusions on Ottoman-Arab
brotherhood. At this time Hussein ibn Ali (1853–1931), one of the Arab
leaders, was appointed Grand Sherif of Mecca. But, after Abdul Hamid had
tried to make a counter-revolution in 1909 and the resistance of Albanians
and Armenians to the tyranny of Constantinople had assumed forms dangerous to the state, the new rulers of Turkey showed themselves, as far as
the nationalities were concerned, as reactionary as the sultan. The 'brotherhood' was speedily dissolved. The oppression of the Arabs continued, no
greater indeed than before but with greater consequences. It ought never to
be forgotten that modernization means better organization, and better
organization means greater capacity for action whether for good or ill.

As a result of all these happenings a great number of new societies
appeared, some recognized officially, others secret ones. One of the best
known was Al-Muntada al Adabi (founded in Constantinople in 1909), a
literary club whose members were mostly students; its aim was to promote
cultural contacts between Arabs. Students play an important role in all
nationalist movements in Europe as well as in Asia, and the Arab students,
the 'flower of the nation', had been relatively well-educated. They could
deal with things critically, but they were also full of idealism and that enthusiasm characteristic of the immature which prevents one from seeing
the other side of the medal. Also recognized by Constantinople was the so-
called Decentralization Party (founded in Cairo in 1912), the first genuine
political Arab organization; its aim was local self-government. An important
illegal society was Al-Kahtanija (founded in 1909), whose aim was the creation of a dual monarchy, an idea derived from the then existing Austro-
Hungarian Dual Monarchy; it advocated a Turco-Arab monarchy in which
Arabia would be a separate kingdom, but with the same monarch as Turkey
had. Its most prominent member was Aziz al-Misri, one of Arabia's greatest
leaders. As a Turkish officer he had taken part in the revolution of 1908;
now as head of Al-Kahtanija he brought many officers over to the Arab

resistance movement. His activities came to the notice of the government. He was arrested in February 1914 and condemned to death. A formidable agitation was the result; mass demonstrations, especially in the towns of Egypt, demanded his release. It was due to British intervention that a judicial murder was prevented, for the British were then seeking, by every possible means, to gain Arab friendship now that German influence in Turkey was beginning to appear really threatening. The sentence was reduced to one of fifteen years' imprisonment. Aziz, however, was soon released; he went to Egypt where he was made Inspector-General of the Army. When the Arab revolt broke out he was again its military leader.

Thus, in the years from 1900 to 1914, there was an actual Arab national movement. Among the Arab upper class and especially among Arab officers there did exist a desire for the independence of their country; it was irrepressible. Odd, is it not, that we may abhor war and militarism, yet when we study history we have to admit that war is often a step towards progress in the sense that war's acute danger and permanent threat teach men to organize. A leader in war has to make a quick assessment of the chances; he has to train soldiers; he has to be always on guard and act at the right time. Every sort of discovery and idea has been the direct or indirect consequence of a war. But modern war has no longer this character. Because of the increase in productive power, in transport facilities, in scientific work, in population, the capitalist society – and also the socialist society – has become so complicated that the dormant qualities and the new ideas which formerly could be awakened only in or through war are now daily and urgently needed in peace-time.

In the Arab lands, then, there did exist the beginnings of a movement in favour of a national Arab state, but its leaders were either abroad or working underground. An observer could only see that Turkish rule was still unbroken and that European influence, especially British influence, was increasing rather than diminishing. At the outset it was the south and east coasts of the Arabian peninsula which most interested the British. Here behind its barrier of sand and desert there was a region which was very far distant from Constantinople, but very near indeed to the sea-lane to British India. In 1839 the British had seized Aden, a safe coaling station and the point of entry for southern trade to the Red Sea. Its seizure was also a reaction to the expansionist ambitions of the then ruler of Egypt, Mohammed Ali, who was anti-British as well as anti-Turkish. Later, partly in the nineteenth century, partly in the period with which this section of the book deals, various coastal districts ruled by an independent sultan or sheikh became British protectorates – Hadramaut, the 'land of the burning sun' thought of as a protection for Aden; Oman and Muscat on the Persian Gulf; the Bahrein Islands, now an oilfield with many refineries but then merely an archipelago made militarily important by its situation, inhabited only by pearl-fishers and lemon-growers, and finally, in November 1914, Kuwait, due south of the fertile valleys of the Tigris and the Euphrates. That was no bad choice, for today from its 1200 square miles Kuwait produces 2 per cent of the world's oil.

Meantime in Central Arabia the rival dynasties of Rashid and of Saud fought out their inter-tribal quarrel. Abd al-Aziz ibn Al Saud, who later united Arabia under his rule, expelled the Turkish garrison from the coastal district of al-Hasa south of Kuwait, but in the Shammar where the Rashids reigned, Turkish influence increased. In the First World War a fine opportunity was offered Ibn Saud and he took wise advantage of it.

But the part of the Turkish Empire which at this period demands closer study is Palestine. Palestine is very much like the other provinces, just as stony and barren, but it was here that the Jewish state was to be re-established. When our period begins, in 1900, Jewish immigrants were already beginning to stream in, mainly from Eastern Europe, from the Ukraine, Poland and Roumania, where there was violent anti-Semitism; but also from Spain and Morocco, from Aleppo and Bagdad, from Georgia, the Yemen and Persia, even from Turkestan and India. They settled first of all in the towns – Jerusalem, Haifa and Jaffa; later, they went on the land. The Jewish population, which in 1800 amounted only to some 8000 rose to 85,000 by 1914, i.e. to be 13 to 14 per cent of the total population of the country as against slightly over 8 per cent in 1800.

The reader is well aware that here the Jewish people once had their own state; about 1000 B.C. Jerusalem became its capital. Here between the Mediterranean, the Dead Sea and the Lake of Tiberias were laid the foundations of the Jewish and the Christian religions. With the deportation to Mesopotamia of the whole population of Judah by Nebuchadnezzar of Babylonia (586–538 B.C.) begins the long period of foreign domination – by Persians, Egyptians and Syrians, and finally the rule of Rome. Irritated by the resistance of the people, the Roman army devastated the country, and during the first century A.D. the surviving Jews fled to every quarter of the known world, to Egypt, to Mesopotamia, to Europe. Their fate was something worse than oppression, war or colonization, which every nation experiences at one time or another, for from then on the Jews had no homeland. Exiled wanderers on the face of the earth, they were for centuries hated and despised by the peoples among whom they lived. They suffered least in Britain and Holland, partly because of the reverence of the Calvinism dominant there for the Old Testament, partly because of a tolerance induced by commercial reasons. Meantime Palestine became an Arab land, first as a part of Arab kingdoms, later as a Turkish province.

Plans for the return of the Jews to the land which in a sense still was theirs, date back to the sixteenth century. But it was in the nineteenth century that an event occurred in France which indirectly led to the birth of a new Jewish state. This was the notorious Dreyfus case. On October 15, 1894, Dreyfus, a Jew and a captain in the French army, was arrested and accused of treason; it was alleged that he had betrayed military secrets to the Germans. In December he was convicted by a court martial and sentenced to banishment to Devil's Island on the coast of French Guiana. But the truth could not be hidden, and France was divided into two camps, wild anti-Semitic agitation on the right, violent indignation on the left. It was the article 'J'accuse' by the novelist Emile Zola, in Clemenceau's paper *l'Aurore* which revealed the machinations of the French General Staff and made the Dreyfus case *the* case of the century. In 1906, it may be added, the verdict was reversed and Dreyfus restored to the French army with the rank of major.

What connection has this with the future of Palestine? During the case there lived in Paris the correspondent of a great Viennese newspaper, Theodore Herzl (1860–1904), a Jew. Deeply affected by the anti-Semitic excesses which he had not believed could possibly happen in France, Herzl organized in 1897 a Jewish international congress which met in Basel in summer. It was the first time in the eighteen centuries of the Diaspora that representatives of the Jewish people assembled together to make plans for the return to their old home. It was the birth of the Zionist Movement. The name was taken from Zion, one of the names of the Holy City and used by Christians and Moslems as well as by Jews; Jerusalem in Hebrew is Yerushalim, in Arabic el-Kuds.

The most important section of its programme was the demand that European Jews be allowed to settle in Palestine. The Turkish Government was, however, fully occupied by other problems, and was in any case not particularly inclined to let in new minorities. The negotiations dragged on. The Jews of Eastern Europe urgently needed a place of refuge, and for a moment Herzl had the idea of finding another land of settlement, Cyprus, for instance, or Sinai. When in April 1903 news came of new and terrible pogroms in various Russian towns, Herzl went to the highlands of Kenya near Nairobi where the British Government had offered land. Kenya was far away from Palestine, but an independent territory under a Jewish government could exist there. During the controversy whether or not Kenya should be chosen, Herzl died and the Zionist movement at once split into two groups. The core of the movement held fast by Palestine; the opposition, led by the English Jew Zangwill, sought a Jewish home elsewhere. Between 1905 and 1915 this section of the movement made a series of suggestions involving Libya, Irak and South America, but objection was raised to all of them. In the ghettos of Europe the burning desire of the Jews for a land of their own where they could live in safety became steadily more demanding, but no other land would they have but Canaan, which they had entered three and a half millennia ago.

As early as 1880 Russian immigrants had established themselves on the land near Jaffa, but it was only with the help of the proverbially rich Rothschilds that they could maintain their farms and vineyards. About 1905 the picture altered considerably and an important new element in Jewish colonization made its appearance. The period of reaction and terror in Russia which followed the revolution of 1905 drove a horde of immigrants to Palestine; they also affected the policy of the Zionist organization. The earlier colonists in the towns and on the land had become employers, with Arabs as their workers. In the countries from which they had fled they had been barred from all occupations except that of trade and the intellectual professions. Among the newcomers, it was the socialists who grasped the fact that without peasants, carpenters and masons no national state could exist. In 1908, at Kinnereth on the Lake of Tiberias, the first modern farming colony was founded under the guidance of experts and without Arab labour. A year later, in nearby Degania, a Russian intellectual, Aaron David Gordon, founded a second similar colony. With his passion for nature and for work on the land in the open air, Gordon was the chief inspirer of the creation of many collective farms with a socialist or communist look; in their economic structure they are comparable to the kolkhozes of Soviet Russia. These *kibbutsim* (sing. *kibbuts*), as they are called today, were remarkable. In one a former Russian professor grew oranges; in another a merchant from Berlin ran a chicken farm; in others, exiles from Poland, Roumania, Portugal and Persia grew wheat. The land of the *kibbutsim* was held in common and the grain and other harvests, corn, oranges or wine, sold on a common account. The individual owned only a vegetable garden, some hens and sheep and perhaps a cottage. In 1914 about 90,000 acres were colonized and put under cultivation.

All this semi-legal colonization took place under the formal rule of the sultan in Constantinople and under the actual control of the local sheikhs who regarded the immigrants with no favourable eye. When we come to the period 1914–1918 we shall see how the Jews, at least on paper, recovered the home of which they had been deprived for nearly two thousand years.

IX

EGYPT AND THE SOUDAN

ALTHOUGH the Suez Canal and the Red Sea seem to form the frontier of Asia there are several reasons for considering Egypt as a part of that continent. The first is that the Nile valley in 1900–1914, as compared with all other Moslem countries, had progressed furthest in nationalism and by its nationalism had inspired great stretches of Asia and notably the neighbouring Arab lands. Secondly, throughout its history Egypt has looked to Asia. The link between the Nile oasis of the Pharaohs and foreign lands was – apart from the sea routes – the forty-two-mile-long landbridge between the Mediterranean and the Red Sea, rather than the waste land of Libya and the Sahara to the west and the wide barren steppes of brushwood or grass of the Sudan in the south. Things might indeed have been otherwise; though hot seas of sand, stony plateaus and grass plains do not *alone* determine the history of a country. None the less it is nature herself which makes us for the purposes of this book consider Egypt as part of Asia. The natural barriers on her western and southern frontiers were a decisive factor in isolating Egypt from the rest of Africa and in the development of Egyptian contacts with the east, that is, with Asia.

Without the muddy waters of the Nile Egypt herself would be simply desert. Today 20,000,000 people live there close-packed together, for only a thirtieth part of the country is made fruitful by the Nile mud, a thick stratum some 22 feet deep which has been deposited by the river over the centuries. The Egyptian state of today has an area of 386,198 square miles. Of that area – and then only because of irrigation, for no rain falls – about 14,000 square miles is cultivated, an extent roughly equal in size to Holland. On the banks of the river the Egyptians live on an average 1300 to the square mile, that is, denser than Java with its 800 to the square mile; it is, in fact, the most densely populated area in the world. Though it is but a tiny part of Egypt, the fellaheen and land owners in this little strip produce 1 per cent of the world's wheat, rice and maize, and 5 to 6 per cent of the world's cotton; cotton comprises four-fifths of Egypt's export trade.

Egypt – its European name comes from the Greek — has an unusually long history, unusual particularly if we define history, as opposed to prehistory, as the age for which we have written sources. The old Egyptians wrote on paper manufactured from the pith of the papyrus plant. It is exceedingly durable, for masses of it with writing on it have been dug up from under the sand. Historical sources go back as far as 4000 B.C. The response of the Egyptian culture to the challenge of the capricious Nile was made over many centuries. During the rule of the Fourth Dynasty (2650–2500 B.C.) it reached a level not hitherto known. It is its 'modern' works of art which have made Egypt immortal. The three famous sandstone pyramids southeast of Cairo, built under this dynasty, are the eternal witnesses to the artistic and technical ability of the old Egyptians.

The first great invasion of which we know something more than just legend was that of the Hyksos, a horse-using people from the east coast of the Mediterranean. Between 1700 and 1600 B.C. they occupied the Nile Delta and they did Egypt the service of introducing the horse. To the Egyptians their rule appeared as a short period of servitude. But when the Persians under Cambyses invaded the land the die was finally cast. The Egyptians were now condemned to twenty centuries of foreign domination. In 330 B.C. the Macedonians under Alexander the Great supplanted the Persians. They ruled for three centuries and, though the romantic love affair between the beautiful Cleopatra VII and Julius Caesar saved their rule for a time, in 30 B.C. Egypt became a Roman province. When the Roman sun set, the Arab sun arose. In A.D. 640 Egypt was conquered by the Arabs, and Islam took root and bore fruit. From this period, one of permanent significance, date el-Kahira or Cairo (founded 968), which soon after became the capital, and the famous university of al-Azhar (founded about 970). Arab rule proper came to an end in the middle of the thirteenth century, when Egypt was ruled in reality by the Mamelukes who were Turkish and Circassian slaves in the Arab army who had reached high rank. They were, in fact, the sole masters of the country until, in 1517, Egypt became a Turkish province; it remained so for four hundred years.

To realize why it was in Egypt that Asian nationalism made greater progress than elsewhere we have to go a little deeper into a complicated history. In 1799 when Napoleon undertook the Egyptian expedition with the intention of using Egypt as a base for attack on the British in Nearer India, there arrived in Egypt as commander of an Albanian force a certain Mohammed Ali. He was a tobacco merchant from Kavalla and in 1805 was made governor of Egypt by the sultan. In the Turkish sense he was a bad governor for, having at a banquet in the citadel of Cairo massacred all the Mamelukes, he ignored the sultan and Egypt became in fact an independent country. He created an army of his own and built a fleet which he used several times to attack Turkey. It was in his reign (1811–1848), on the other hand, that cotton-growing began in the Nile valley. He was the first ruler of a dynasty which ended as ignobly with Farouk as it had begun so splendidly with him.

Under the khedive Mohammed Said (1854–1863) and still more under Ismail (1863–1879), Egypt began to be modernized and acquired much of the Western technical skills. That was dangerous to freedom, for it was accomplished with the aid of European loans. The first railway from Alexandria to Cairo was opened, and on April 29, 1859, work began on the Suez Canal. It is possible that Egypt might have retained her relative independence had not, about 1880, the coils of modern imperialism fastened round her; it was from Africa particularly – other available territory had for the most part been partitioned among the powers – that imperialism envisaged a rich return. For those who do not know Africa's bloodstained history it may be recalled that in 1880 4 per cent of that continent was in European hands –

the coastal regions of the south and west. Some thirty years later, in 1912, when Italy acquired Tripoli, 96 per cent of it was colonial or semi-colonial territory. The 4 per cent that now remained free was composed of Ethiopia and Liberia, the small negro republic on the Ivory Coast, created by American goodwill. When we speak of modern imperialism we mean in particular British and French imperialism, for these powers obtained the lion's share. When the former German colonies were partitioned in Versailles in 1919 between Britain and France – Togo, Cameroon, Southwest Africa and what is now Tanganyika – the British and French possessed almost three-quarters of Africa.

About 1880 the two powers were suspiciously interested in Egypt. If it was the French who built the Suez Canal, it was the British who obtained the country. In the agreement which created the Anglo-French entente of 1904, London got a free hand in the Nile Valley, while in return Paris got the same in Morocco. The Suez Canal, finished in 1869, was a vital part of the new sea route between Britain and India. By the old route round the Cape of Good Hope Bombay was some 12,500 miles from London; by the Canal it was only 7200 miles. Was not the ninety-three-mile-long canal through the sands of Egypt necessary to Britain? British bases had already been established on that route – Gibraltar (1704), Malta (1800), Cyprus (1878) and Aden (1839). Then again the British had invested much loan money in Egypt and, when the khedive in 1875 got into financial difficulties, they acquired all the shares – nearly 50 per cent of the total issue – which he held in the Suez Canal Company. Here was a second reason for intervention, and the third was just as simple – cotton; oil – today Egypt produces only $\frac{1}{2}$ per cent of the world's supply – was then of no significance. By 1881 the British invader had gone too far – at least in the opinion of a great number of Egyptian officers. When one of them was dismissed from the army they rose in rebellion in February, and compelled the Government to dismiss the Minister of War who was under European influence and replace him by a nationalist. The movement was led by Ahmad Arabi (1839–1911). It was the first clear evidence of the existence of a national consciousness, inspired by the Persian Jamal al-Din [1] who had come to Cairo in 1871 and preached resistance to the West; he advocated the learning of European methods and their application in order to be able to defend Egypt against the West.

In January 1882 London and Paris delivered an official warning to the Cairo government with the aim of strengthening the position of the khedive against the nationalists; as so often was the case, the reactionaries were the only supporters of the European imperialism. The warning only further discredited the khedive, for the powers did not proceed to action. The Liberal Prime Minister Gladstone was opposed to imperialism which he, unlike Disraeli, held to be 'ungentlemanly', while the French feared international complications. On June 12, 1882, there were risings in Alexandria and fifty Europeans were killed. Various observers accused the khedive of having inspired them in the hope of forcing Britain to intervene; such methods are not unknown to politics. At any rate the British fleet bombarded Alexandria,

[1] v. supra, p. 84.

allegedly to destroy the fortifications which the nationalists had constructed. British troops were landed and took possession of the Canal. On September 13th the nationalist forces under Arabi were defeated at Tel el-Kebir, and Cairo was occupied two days later. Arabi was deported to Ceylon – he did not return until 1901 – and the British remained. From 1883 to 1907 Egypt was a semi-colonial territory under the rule of the Resident and Consul-general Sir Evelyn Baring (later Lord Cromer). Cromer was of those genuine empire builders such as history, and especially colonial history, knows so well. They do not in one sense rule badly; they put the finances in order; they modernize the economy; they utilize the natural resources; and out of a mediaeval feudal kingdom they make a relatively modernized unified state. But, consciously or unconsciously, they do all this in the service of foreign bondholders and capitalists and pay little attention to things just as necessary, education for instance, and local self-government.

Under Cromer the British pressed on to the Upper Nile to the then independent Soudan. Kitchener, who later defeated the Dutch Boers in South Africa (1900), destroyed in 1898 at Omdurman the army of the successor of the Mahdi Mohammed Ahmed from Dongola who sought to make the Soudan independent of Egypt. The result of the campaign against the Mahdi, begun in 1883, was that a mixed Anglo-Egyptian rule over the Soudan was created, the so-called condominium. Actually that meant British rule and it was a Briton, Sir Reginald Wingate, who was the Soudan's first governor – over a land of some 970,000 square miles ranking in size between India and Indonesia, a land of grassy plain, woods and papyrus marshes; thanks to the Nile, 1 per cent of the world's cotton production is harvested here and much gum arabic. The British had two motives in taking it over, the need to control the Nile waters and – recognizing an historical necessity – to keep out their rivals.

The Nile is some 4000 miles long. Its source is the Kagera river, which rises about 150 miles south of the Equator in the mountains between Lake Tanganyika and the Victoria Nyanza and was discovered in 1876 by Stanley. The Kagera flows straight through the great Lake Victoria Nyanza into the Soudan where it is called the White Nile (Bahr al-Jebel). The Nile proper begins at Khartoum, where the White Nile is joined by the Blue Nile (Bahr el-Asrak) and with the Atbara farther north brings the floods on which the cotton fields depend. Both the Blue Nile and the Atbara rise in Ethiopia in the neighbourhood of Lake Tana, where between June and August there is heavy monsoon rain.

The Nile – that is, the water of the Nile – was in 1880 the private possession of Egypt. All the water, except what is evaporated by the heat, flows north-ward to the cotton fields; in its whole course there was nowhere any people who tried to hold it back and use it to enrich their own land. The British in Egypt would have had very little reason to annex the Soudan had not the armed forces of other powers appeared on the horizon. It was very clear to them that here lay a threat to the uninterrupted flow of water to the north. Could not the French, the Germans, the Italians and the Belgians build dams just as well as the British who had built the Aswan dam in 1902? The cotton, indeed all Egypt, was in danger. The whole valley of the Nile had to be in British hands. Only Ethiopia remained untouched, but was compelled, like the Italians who had occupied Eritrea in 1882, to recognize the area of the Blue Nile and the Atbara as a British sphere of influence. Uganda too, where the Germans were the first to arrive, became British. The King of the Belgians, who had acquired the Congo in 1885, was informed that the Nile must remain British just as the Congo was Belgian. The frontier was drawn on the watershed between the Congo and the Blue Nile. All the powers accepted the British position. The only possibility of trouble arose when the French pressed on from the west. After the capture of Khartoum, Kitchener advanced by forced marches southward along the Blue Nile. At Fashoda (today Kodok) on the 10th parallel he found a French force under Captain Marchand. This was the most dangerous crisis in Anglo-French relations in the years before 1914 and, had the French Government, then in the throes of the Dreyfus case,[1] not given way, war possibly would not have been avoided.

That in summary is the history of the Anglo-Egyptian Soudan. After the Second World War world attention was twice called to it. The first time was when Egypt claimed the Soudan which lately had become independent; the second when the Soudan proclaimed its independence of Egypt. Nationalism conquered the African peoples no less than it had earlier done the Asian.

In Egypt, to which we must now return, two important events happened in 1906. The first was that, after a British ultimatum to Turkey, the Sinai peninsula became Egyptian territory. The second was the Denshawi incident, which inflamed the native nationalism. Some British officers hunting near the village seem to have aroused the anger of the fellaheen, who attacked them and killed one of them. The British commander-in-chief demanded exemplary punishment; four of the peasants were hanged and others publicly flogged. Even Cromer himself described their punishment as 'unduly severe'. Hatred of the foreigner which was thus aroused gave the incident its special significance. All the respect which the British had earned for relatively democratic measures vanished like snow before the sun. A violent press campaign followed and the vague feeling of resistance became a genuine liberation movement. In October 1907 the Hizb al Uma, the 'Party of the Nation', was founded by Saad Zaglul (1860–1927) and in December, at the time of the first Nationalist congress, the Nationalist party Hizb al-Watan was revived on the initiative of Mustapha Kamil, who had a short time before returned from France where he had been studying; it was this party which more than any other was anti-British. Kamil's death in 1908 was a very sensible loss for awakening Egypt; he had close ties with the Young Turk Committee of Union and Progress. His funeral, which became a demonstration, considerably impressed even anti-Egyptian British eyewitnesses.

Some months later the khedive appointed as minister-president a certain Butros Ghali, a Copt – that is a member of the Christian Church of Egypt; he it was who was judge at the Denshawi trial. This provocation – it could not be anything else in an Islamic country under foreign occupation – was a new signal to the resisters throughout the land. Neither censorship nor terror could

[1] v. p. 90.

save Butros Ghali from assassination by a nationalist; they may even have helped to inspire the assassin.

The growth of nationalist feeling under the relatively mild government of Eldon Gorst (1907–1911) made London feel that a more energetic rule was needed and Kitchener (1911–1914) of Boer war and Soudan fame was sent out. He dealt firmly with unrest, but also made some liberal concessions. Thus in the summer of 1913 a democratic electoral system and a modern constitution were introduced. In 1914 the first real Egyptian parliament met, and nationalism would perhaps have come to maturity had not the outbreak of the First World War compelled Britain to keep Egypt firmly in her hands. The danger of a German attack on the Suez Canal from Turkey was soon seen to be a real one. The situation of Egypt then was not unlike that in the Second World War when Rommel's tanks threatened the land from the west. Parliament was again dissolved; the khedive was compelled to declare war on Turkey and on December 18, 1914, Egypt became officially a British protectorate. That was a kindly name for a sad reality. It meant that a kingdom which, besides the name, had its own government and its own financial administration could have no international relations of its own. Everything concerning the foreigner – war, for instance, or trade – was decided by the occupying power. This was the situation in which Egypt found herself at the end of the first period of Asian awakening.

Second Period 1914 – 1919

THE 'DEGLORIFICATION' OF THE WEST

I

THE FIRST WORLD WAR

ON a hot summer's day, June 28, 1914, a Serbian exile in Bosnia shot dead an Austrian archduke at Saraievo, then an Austrian town near the frontier of Serbia, the kernel of what is now Yugoslavia. At first, it all seemed to be a very local affair without any other consequence than the condemnation of the assassin, Gavrilo Princip. His name indeed is significant. Behind the assassination lay ideals, ideals of nationalism. Thousands had imagined themselves doing what Princip actually had done. Tens of thousands had the like sentiments, but it was only on that day that dreams became intention and intention became act. In a given situation the desires of the many can release forces which have effect on history, even on world history. The assassination had the same effect as tropical rains have on treeless hills, destructive rather than productive; the streaming rains turn to torrents, the torrents to muddy floods which rage through the valleys. Princip was condemned; Austria presented demands to Serbia, demands which could not be accepted, for they struck at the very independence of the country. After the ultimatum came the declaration of war, and after that a punitive expedition against the Serbs. Germany supported the Austrians; Russia began to mobilize (July 30th); France and Germany ordered mobilization in the afternoon of August 1st. On that fateful Sunday at 7 p.m. Germany declared war on Russia because Russia had not answered Germany's demand that the troops be demobilized. The flood from the Balkan hills was flowing over all Europe. On August 3rd Germany declared war on France; on the 4th Britain declared war on Germany. Thus came what is known as the 'First World War', because in an age when imperialism encompassed the entire earth its effects were not confined to Europe.

Officially the great conflict lasted for 1,553 nights and days. The 'cease-fire' was sounded on November 11, 1918, at 11 a.m., in the muddy trenches of Northern France.

Originally a conflict between the Great Powers of Europe, it became a general war. By the summer of 1918 only a few small nations of Europe were still neutral – Holland, Switzerland, Denmark, Sweden, Norway and Spain. Africa, as Europe's nearest colony, was involved from the outset; only independent Ethiopia escaped it. Canada and the United States were fighting, and of all the Latin American states only Mexico and the Argentine were really neutral. In Asia the colonial lands were automatically involved, while of the independent states only Persia and Afghanistan were nominally neutral. Indonesia was the only important Asian colony which remained outside the war, thanks to the neutrality of Holland.

What was the special significance of the war for Asian history? We have seen when dealing with the period 1900–1914 that, in the lands of the outer zone between Egypt and the Bering Sea, and in the inner zone between Japan and India, the educated class had met the European challenge with the response given by Turkey and Japan, with the call: Learn from the West in order to fight the West. History, even for those who believe in a divine dispensation, is the work of men. To understand history means to understand men – that is, to be able to put oneself in another's place, to enter the lists oneself. How would we have reacted? How would I have thought, if I had been in these days an Egyptian or a Chinese? A partial acceptance of Western ideas implied for many Asians a situation which psychologically was difficult to work out. It is the nature of man to admire and hate at one and the same time. This leads often to a feeling of insecurity, and such insecurity hinders the development of that self-consciousness which is the primary precondition of freedom. How this development would have been accomplished had there been no world war is difficult to tell. At no time in history can we say: If *this* had not happened, then *that* would have been different. We call this the 'if' point of view; *if* this or that had not happened. In the most favourable circumstances we can only say: This is what *did* happen, and what happened later we must try to understand as one of the consequences of that earlier event. Thus we can assert that in 1918 Asian self-consciousness had greatly developed as compared with prewar days and we can explain this phenomenon as a consequence of the fact that in the war and because of the war the Asians had more or less found a way out of the dilemma of the necessity at once of hating the West and of adopting its methods. The main impetus towards this escape may be found in the fact that, during the war, the Europeans began to be despised. Despite and hate are very much akin. Neither word is to be taken to mean that in 1918 every Asian hated and despised every European. All that is meant is that the general feeling, often unconscious, can best be expressed by these two words.

It may be asked if wars inevitably lead to this despite. Possibly not. So far as Asia is concerned, the kernel of the matter lies in the fact that the white peoples had claimed to possess a very special culture which, for the benefit of mankind, must be spread to Asia and other colonial areas. The 'white men's wars' served to do so. But the war of 1914 fell even on Europe as a thunderbolt. It had been believed in these years that a really dangerous conflict between the European powers was unlikely. When none the less war did come, the Asian said, or rather thought: You whites claim to be better than us, but you aren't. Your God is supposed to be a God of love, but there is nothing of this love in your actions. You pretend to bring culture to Asia, but all you bring is technology. Possibly you are the more skilful masters of the natural world; you know more and produce more than we do, but only in the material sense. Perhaps your culture is useful, although that is debateable; but what advantage is it to master nature if you cannot master yourselves?

Less laudable manifestations of European culture such as were revealed, say, by the films, caused the Asian second thoughts, and he began to think: I am now ready to take over your methods because of their obvious advantages in certain domains, but I have a higher aim; I stand for the liberation of Asia, for the improvement of my own people. We must remember that to the Asian the gulf between Christianity in the ideal sense and the average European must have seemed greater than it was in reality. Generally speaking the active Christians in Asia were above the average – the Roman Catholic and Protestant missionaries. The other Europeans were generally below the average – soldiers, officials, planters and merchants, and of these the two last classes had only one aim, to become unlimitedly rich in a limited time.

On the other hand the war took from the Europeans the self-confidence which had so filled them since 1900. Many began to feel doubts of the value of Western culture. Not a few asked their consciences whether Europe was not on the wrong path. Had a culture which threatened to degenerate into mutual destruction the right to impose itself on other peoples? What was the final result of all the manufacture, the expansion, the intellectual and artistic accomplishment of the West? Europe felt exhausted and the innumerable readers of a book like Spengler's *The Decline of the West* (published in 1918 but conceived and written sometime before the war) were attracted to it by the pessimism of its title, the title which revealed the way of thinking of its gifted author.

Besides these psychological changes – the growing self-confidence of the Asians and the declining confidence of the Europeans – there appeared during the war quite as important a change in the material sphere. Asia began to have its own industry. The reasons are not hard to find. The First World War was different from, and worse than, all earlier wars. It caused greater loss, demanded more lives; it was absolute or, as we say today, total. That is why contemporaries called it a world war. It was not a world war in the sense that the second one was. Actually it was a war between the German cultural bloc (Germany and Austria-Hungary) and Britain, France, Russia and, later, the United States. Outside Europe the war raged only in the Middle East because Turkey was involved as a result of her alliance with the Central Powers. For four years there was no decision, while Northern France, Northern Italy and Russia experienced its full horror. For four years the million-strong armies lay dug in, ever vainly trying to break the enemy lines in costly offensives. Two examples will give an idea of its terrible character. On February 21, 1916, the Germans opened a great offensive against Verdun. By the time they were thrown back on the defensive in July, the French had lost some 270,000 men, the Germans some 250,000. Meantime, on another part of the front, the battle of the Somme had begun in July: it ended in November bogged down in rain and mud, with the dismal result that the Allies had gained some 300 square miles of ground to a depth of some six miles, of little strategic value, but the British had lost 400,000 men, the French 200,000 and the Germans nearly half a million. The war cost in all 10,000,000 soldiers' lives.

The war made the most extreme demands on the Great Powers. Every factory, the whole transport system, the miners and the farmers worked only for the insatiable, tottering fronts. The revolution in armaments shows its total character. The Germans used gas – chlorine – on April 22, 1915, at Ypres; the British first used the tank on September 15th on the Somme. The German submarine blockade of Britain began in February 1915; unrestricted submarine warfare, which brought in the Americans, began two years later. With the entire economy of Europe being directed towards war purposes, there were now fewer products to export to the East, and when they were available there was little possibility, as a result of the German blockade and lack of shipping, of carrying them to lands so far away. The result was that in these dark times for the West, a native industry began to arise in Asia, such as Japan, but so far no other Asian nation, had been able to create. This crisis in the trade relations between Europe and Asia went farther and deeper than earlier ones. Here was the beginning of a structural change in Asian-European relations which had seemed so stable; here was the economic basis for a middle class in the Asian countries.

The third factor in the awakening of Asia in the war years was a political one. The Great Powers were in these years in no position to suppress resistance movements in the colonies. They had to do something, and what else remained for them to do but to make promises, perhaps not of liberation but of self-government. Naturally these promises were not meant to be kept; they were made on the assumption that, when better times came for Europe, they could be withdrawn – that must now be admitted – and so the pre-war state of colonial rule be restored. But what happened was that the alluring promises worked strongly on the consciousness of Asians, and there was a similar effect when the reactionary sequel in 1919 showed how they had been deceived. The hate of masters, now revealed as treacherous, which had been once concealed by respect was now made painfully visible.

There was a similar development in Europe itself. The European governments had to make promises not only to the colonies but to their own people as well, especially to workers and soldiers who had, and especially in 1917 and 1918, been moved to stay at their posts in the factory and the battlefield by higher wages and by the prospect of gaining greater political power. In 1917 it appeared that the French soldier had had enough of fighting. Only a ruthless maintenance of war discipline prevented the breaking down of the front. As with the people of Asia the European worker became more self-confident as a result of far-reaching promises and temporary concessions, and as a result of disillusionment later the bourgeois was the more hated and despised. There is a certain kinship between the national movement in the colonies and other Asian lands and the workers' movement in Europe. Both had the same enemy, the bourgeoisie which wished to regain its prewar position. The kinship is the closer, for in Asia too, as a result of the beginning of industrialization, a workers' movement in the modern sense appeared. The worker of the West was a model for the worker of Asia. That made the psychological situation easier, for the worker in Shanghai, Jakarta and Bombay did not need to hate the European worker; all belonged to the oppressed classes and so felt themselves united against the oppressor. Resistance to the bourgeoisie meant for the European worker social resistance against capitalism, and, especially in the defeated countries Germany, Austro-Hungary and Russia, the socialist awakening was a veritable *levée en masse*. In many cases the official socialist parties were extremely moderate. and so it was the Communists who by risings and revolts sought to prevent a return to the *ancien régime*. Examples of that are the mutiny in the German High Seas Fleet in Kiel on October 28, 1918, which spread throughout Germany in early November resulting in the establishment of Workers' and Soldiers' Councils on the Russian model; the Spartacist rising in Berlin in January 1919 which was bloodily suppressed; the Communist Republics in Bavaria (April 1919) and in Hungary (summer 1919). We have still to mention the most outstanding example, that afforded by Russia, the only country in Europe in which, despite all the efforts of its enemies, the revolution was never crushed. On November 7, 1918, the Bolshevik revolution broke out in what is now Leningrad; we shall devote a separate section to it, not only because of its importance to Russia, but because of the enormous influence it had, and still has, on Asia, particularly in the modernization of the largest part of Northern Asia, i.e. Siberia which was then virgin land, in the revolutionizing both of the culture and the economy of Central Asia, the Moslem area between the Caspian and China, and finally, because of its influence, if indirectly, on the rest of Asia.

We can deal with this at relatively short length, for a whole library of books has already been written about it. For instance, one aspect of the fruitful influence of the Russian revolution on Asia was the fact that besides the national problem, i.e. the question of independence under a native government, the social problem became a compelling reality. What was to be the state of the worker and the peasant in the independent state? Further, what was quite as decisive in the modern history of Asia, the Bolshevik revolution had shown that the bourgeois phase of national liberation in many lands and many circumstances can be dispensed with.

A second country where the changes during the war and as a result of it were of decisive importance for Asia was the United States. There was first of all the arrival of that country in the front row of Great Powers. We have seen a foretaste of this in the American occupation of Cuba and the Philippines. But the war of 1914–1918 altered the relations between Europe and America more fundamentally than it did those between Europe and Asia. America entered the war on April 6, 1917, in reaction to the German threat to wage unrestricted submarine warfare even against neutral countries. The Anglo–French armies were then demoralized and weary, and the million fresh soldiers from America, who arrived at the front in the summer of 1918, played a decisive part in breaking German resistance. The United States sent enormous shiploads of war material to the Allies and in the winter of 1918, Europe found that America had become a rich land; from a debtor it had become a creditor nation. In earlier days Europe had loaned money to the United States; indeed, the American railways and American industrialization had largely been financed by British and Dutch capital. Things were now different and American dollars flowed into Europe. Now for the first time the United States had the power as well as the desire to carry out a grand scale policy of imperialism in Asia, particularly in the Pacific, not perhaps quite on the same scale as Europe had done, for the United States had no colonial tradition and its economic and social structure was different; its policy however, did not in any material way differ from that of Europe. 'Dollar

A.C.—4*

imperialism', as it is called, appeared at the outset benevolent enough – to a certain extent and up to a certain point that policy was less dangerous and less crudely reactionary – but none the less another wild beast bent on plunder was ravaging the Asian garden.

If all that has been said affords good reason for devoting a series of chapters to Asia during the First World War, the fact that the war itself, though fought mainly in Europe, was fought partly in Asia, reinforces that view. There were campaigns in Asiatic Turkey – in Arabia, in what is now Syria, Israel, Jordan and Irak – and in Persia and Egypt. Turkey fought on the German side; on the Allied side China and Japan each played a part in the war. In the long development of over half a century which we call the awakening of Asia, the First World War can no more be neglected as a factor than can the Second.

II

THE TURKISH EMPIRE

WHEN the First World War broke out in August 1914 between the Central Powers and Britain, France and Russia, other states had to decide whether to remain neutral or join in the war, and, if the latter, on which side. Turkey quickly found an answer. The War Minister, Enver Pasha (1881–1922), one of the extremists who led the *coups d'état* of 1908 and 1913, and to a less degree Talaat (1874–1921), and Djemal, over-estimated Germany's military power and economic resources, great as these showed themselves to be. Did not the German armies within a few weeks reach the heart of France? Earlier, in summer 1914 – the initiative came from Turkey – a secret military treaty had been signed with Germany. On the critical day of August 1st, when Germany declared war on Russia, the treaty had been signed. After mobilization had been nearly completed, a Turkish squadron without warning bombarded the Russian Black Sea ports of Odessa and Sebastopol (October 29th). The czar declared war on Turkey on November 2nd and Britain and France followed suit on November 5th. Enver's pro-Germanism was not illogical, for it was Britain which was at the time most dangerous to Turkey, much more than Germany was; it is, of course, a matter for surmise what the results of a German victory would have been. It was Britain, too, who at once took action in the annexation of Cyprus (occupied in 1878 and since virtually a British colony) and the proclamation of a protectorate over Egypt (December 18th) in order to secure the Suez Canal. Before that, Australian and New Zealand troops had landed in Egypt. Britain had then a relatively small population (about 35,000,000, roughly the same as Java), but in the centuries of her colonial domination had learned the art of making her subjects overseas fight for her.

The three Turkish ministers won over the sultan in his capacity as caliph for the idea of the Holy War (jehad). Enver perhaps dreamed of a pan-Turkish empire. Outside Turkey the Moslems cared very little for the caliph, a fact that made it the easier for Kemal Ataturk later to abolish the caliphate. Liman von Sanders wanted the Turks to attack the Ukraine which, once taken from Russia, would be a grain reserve for Germany; Hitler planned to make it such in the Second World War. The notorious desire of Germany to possess the fertile Ukraine is one of the classic instances of the influence on history of geographic and economic factors, just as classic as that of the influence of the limitless areas of Russia with their mud and snow and their appalling winter temperatures; the bitter effect of these on military operations was learned by Napoleon in 1812 and by Germany in both world wars.

Sanders' view was contested by Enver, who decided to attack Russia through the Caucasus. In December he launched an offensive in the district of Kars, in the northeast of present-day Turkey, between Batum and Mount Ararat. That area had been occupied in 1829 by Russian Cossacks, but became Turkish again after the Crimean War; in 1878 it became finally Russian. The only result of the Turkish offensive was another massacre of the Armenians who lived there; Russians no less than Turks had savagely mistreated them in earlier days. When it was realized that no invasion of Russia was possible through Caucasia, the Turks sought, as had been foreseen in London, to strike at Britain by an attack on the Suez Canal. The railway from Asia Minor to the Hejaz, built with the money of Turkish believers, performed now a service which these had not at all expected; for the railway was hardly more than a stone's throw from Suez through the desert of Sinai. But the defence was obstinate (February 3–4, 1915) and Turkish troops failed to capture the Canal.

At this time, things seemed to have reached deadlock on the Western Front. The British, therefore, took the offensive in the Mediterranean. It was Winston Churchill who got the plan accepted for a landing on Gallipoli, the peninsula on the northwest side of the Dardanelles which links the Black Sea with the Mediterranean. The plan was to advance from Gallipoli and take Constantinople, put Turkey out of the war and open the Straits to traffic to and from Russia. Churchill (b. 1874) had served under Kitchener at Khartoum, had been a war correspondent in the Boer War, and was now First Lord of the Admiralty, but he underestimated the Turks. The British attack was not only a threat to the Turkish Empire but deeply wounded the awakening nationalist feeling. The Turkish troops fought like lions when British, Australasian and French troops sought to advance inland. The British Commander-in-Chief Ian Hamilton, who had as a guest of the Japanese witnessed the Russian defeat on the Yalu, telegraphed home that at any moment the victory would be won. But a moment later the landing had failed; it was an officer named Mustapha Kemal who brought the news to Liman von Sanders. It was a black day for the Allies, a brilliant one for the Turks. None the less, victory on Gallipoli could not prevent the downfall of the Turkish Empire. During the battle a bullet hit Kemal's pocket watch; the watch saved Kemal's life and preserved him to be, as Kemal Ataturk, the founder of modern Turkey. Britain sent more troops to no avail; demoralized by the fierce resistance which they had not expected, exhausted by the heat and lack of water, the British were finally defeated at Sari Bair in August. Later events were only an epilogue, prolonged because those responsible for them would not give up their illusions. The invaders evacuated the peninsula in December. The plan had led to a bloody defeat; the result, which is important to world history, was that Russia had now no hope of being supplied by its Allies. It must be remembered that the two traffic lanes used in the Second World War were not available in the first. Theoretically the route by way of Persia and the Caspian was open, but Persia had no railways and the route via Murmansk in North Russia was made exceedingly dangerous as a result of U-boat activity. Gallipoli was one of the causes of the Russian collapse, and it is notorious that the Bolshevik revolution was the result of the military defeat of the czar's troops.

Meantime the war had spread also to Mesopotamia, the Irak of today. In order to protect the Persian oilfields, British troops had landed at, and occupied, Basra (November 1914). What had started as a local operation developed in the following summer to a full-scale expedition to take Bagdad. In June 1915 the Turks were defeated at Kut el-Amara, some ninety miles south of that city. Although, in April 1916, the British garrison of 10,000 men in Kut had to capitulate to the Turks, Bagdad none the less was still in danger. The mistake made by the Young Turks when they joined the Germans was now plain. Germany had penetrated deeply into France and Russia, but it took all their force and energy to remain there. Bulgaria, in October 1915, had entered the war on the side of the Central Powers, but Roumania was ready to join the Allies; in December she declared war on Germany. In London, Paris and St Petersburg it was thought that the time had come to divide up the Turkish Empire. In April 1916 a secret treaty was signed whereby Russia was to get Constantinople and Armenia; Arabia was to become an independent state; Britain was to have Mesopotamia as a sphere of influence and the Mediterranean ports of Haifa and Acre; the French, spheres of influence in Syria and Southern Anatolia; Palestine was to be under international control.

The rest of the war can be quickly dealt with. Neither the Turkish counter-offensive against the Suez Canal in the summer of 1916 nor the later operations in Mesopotamia, where Bagdad capitulated in March 1917, could save the sultan's empire. When, in October 1917, Allenby suddenly attacked Palestine from the south, it was the end for Turkey. On December 8th Allenby entered Jerusalem. The only route of escape left the Turks was the road by which they had come centuries before. In September 1918, when the defeat of Germany was as clear as that of Turkey, the great British offensive began at Megiddo (Tell el-Mutesellim), some thirteen miles southwest of Nazareth. The Turkish line was broken and the Turkish army dissolved. Damascus fell on October 1st; French marines took Beirut (October 7th) and Homs and Aleppo were occupied.

The consequences were soon seen. In mid-October the new – and last – sultan Mohammed VI (1918–1922) dismissed Enver and Talaat and appointed a new grand vizier who telegraphed asking the all-powerful American President to intervene. He got no answer; Wilson possibly thought it not worth the trouble of sending one. Townshend, who had been captured at Kut, was now set free and he set things in train for the signing (October 30th) of an armistice at Mudros on the island of Lemnos. The island lies close to Gallipoli and the coveted Straits, and the British had stayed there after the evacuation of the peninsula. The defeat was complete. The Turks had to open the way to Allied ships, for the British and French governments wanted to crush the Russian revolution by way of the Black Sea. All prisoners had to be returned; the army and navy were to be demobilized; relations with the Central Powers were to be broken off and all Turkish territory was to be made available to the Allies for possible further operations against the Central Powers.

For Enver and Talaat the collapse was the signal for flight. Enver went east, became an emir in West Turkestan and fell in battle against the Bolsheviks. Talaat was murdered by an Armenian in 1921, and if ever a murder, even a political murder, was justified, this one was; if there was any single man who stood out as a persecutor of the Armenians it was Talaat.

Meantime, on November 13th, an Allied fleet anchored off Constantinople and on August 20, 1920, a peace treaty was signed at Sèvres, near Paris, between Turkey and the Allies. But before that much had happened in Turkey, with which we will deal when we come to the period 1919–1941. The great Turkish Empire, for four and a half centuries a Moslem fortress threatening Europe at her very doors, was now in fragments; a new Turkish national home arose. The old empire was large, but because of the divisions in it had become weak; the new was small but compact, a national state without large minorities; it was destined for a great future. In 1918 everything seemed lost and it seemed that nationalist Turkey would fight a hopeless battle. The great Islamic empire had collapsed; the only really independent Islamic area was occupied by the Europeans. The Hejaz, Arabia, Palestine, Transjordan, the fruitful land of Irak, Syria, Egypt with her riches, Mecca, Medina, cotton plantations and oilfields, all were lost. At this crisis Turkey seemed entirely abandoned to Western imperialism. Even if it was admitted that Egypt had not been part of Turkey since 1914, the fact remained that between 1914 and 1918 Turkey had been deprived of two-thirds of her territory and half her population. And that was not all. All the imperial provinces had disappeared and even the heartland of Anatolia was not left intact; great parts of it in 1919 were occupied by the Italians and the Greeks.

Yet in the darkness of that night the grey light of dawn became visible. The signature of the sultan on the dictated treaty of Sèvres was a further inspiration to the freedom fighters under Kemal Ataturk. It was their movement which created the national state of Turkey, a state inhabited only by Turks. It was small, confined in a small land which was mostly mountain and barren steppe, but spiritually it was made strong by the national ideal which was its basis. World history knows other surprising reversals of fortune, but only a few are so amazing as the Turkish. The Bible tells us that man must lose his soul to keep it; in these years Turkey gave proof that the saying is true.

III

THE ARAB COUNTRIES

AFTER the Turkish Empire disappeared from the map, the so-called Arab lands were virtually blank sheets of paper. What would be written on them? Would all these sandy deserts, oases and oilfields, the birthplace of Islam, fall completely victim to the West or would national states arise? The answer to these questions is of world-historical significance. Forty years after the First World War had ended, the voice of the Arab League in the international chorus was not to be mistaken.

We had no occasion to mention the names of the Arab leaders in our account of Turkey in the world war. These emirs and kings, however, deserve mention, for it was they who managed to prevent their domains becoming French or British colonies. We have already heard of Hussein ibn Ali (1853-1931), the Grand Sherif of Mecca, and of Abd al-Aziz ibn al Saud (1880-1953), the King of Nejd in the centre of the Arabian peninsula. We have still to mention Hussein's three sons – Faisal (1883-1933), Abdullah (1882-1951) and Ali; all three took part in the Arab war of independence.

When the Constantinople government on October 29, 1914, began hostilities by the naval attack on Russia's Black Sea ports, Hussein at once (October 31) sought to get into touch with Kitchener, now Secretary of State for War. It may indeed have been Kitchener who made the first approach. The truth on this point may be of interest in a full study of Anglo-Arab relations, but it is enough for our purposes to say here that each side needed the other. Towards the end of the nineteenth century, Britain had abandoned her traditional policy of looking after 'the sick man on the Bosphorus', and had substituted for it a policy of seeking to gain influence in the Arab lands at Turkey's expense. Her intervention in the Aziz al-Misri incident in February 1914 is a good example of her efforts to win the affections of the Arabs rather than of the Germanophil government in Constantinople.[1] In London the possibility was seen of creating a defensive zone against Turkey between Egypt and the Persian Gulf in which the Arabs would hold the central section. On his side Hussein thought that he might be able with British aid to free Arabia from the Turkish yoke. Faisal, who distrusted the British, was against the plan of an Anglo-Arab alliance; Abdulla was for it; their father hesitated.

In the negotiations the Arabs held strong cards, for the British position was in a way critical enough. If the Arabs responded to the sultan's call to a holy war, then the British troops throughout the Middle East would be in a difficult situation. The Suez Canal, Aden, Persian oil would no longer be safe. London tried to drag out the negotiations, but did assure the Arabs

[1] v. p. 88.

that they would guarantee their independence if they rose in rebellion. Britain was hardly in earnest and the Arabs, particularly Hussein and Faisal, saw through this double-dealing, but they both thought that so favourable a chance should not be missed. Meantime the Constantinople government drew its own conclusions and when Hussein learned of its plans for his assassination, his hesitation vanished.

In March 1915 he sent Faisal allegedly to Constantinople, but actually to Damascus, the headquarters of the illegal organization of the Young Arabs, al-Fatat, founded in 1911 in Paris. There Faisal at first took a pro-Turkish attitude through fear of too great a British influence, but soon agreement was reached on the basis that the Arabs should trust neither British nor Turks but should try to use this unique opportunity by becoming temporary allies of Britain. This was all laid down in what is known as the Damascus protocol (summer 1915), the chief points in which were co-operation with Britain and revolt against Turkey on condition that the whole Arab area became an independent state, naturally with the abolition of the capitulations; Turkey had at the beginning of the war (September 7, 1914) declared them to be no longer valid. In January 1916, a few weeks before the Allies had to evacuate Gallipoli, the British accepted Hussein's terms or, rather, pretended that they would. Only the position of Bagdad and Basra and the French sphere of influence in Syria was left undefined.

But Hussein, Faisal and the al-Fatat were not the only Arabs. In the interior of the peninsula there was the powerful Ibn Saud in Nejd. As the British Government always liked to have more than one iron in the fire, it had as many agents in Nejd as with Hussein in the Hejaz; the only difference was that the latter came from London, the former from Delhi. Whether there was any difference depended on what suited the British book. This time there was a difference. The Indian Government and Ibn Saud signed in December 1915 an agreement – ratified in July 1916 – whereby all Arab areas on the Persian Gulf were recognized as the independent domain of the latter. This was a concession obviously irreconcilable with the promise made to Hussein that he would have rule over all the Arab lands, but the British Government took no notice of that; as if neither posts nor telegraphs had ever been invented, it declared that it had no knowledge at all of what the government in Delhi was doing.

Hussein, who was not aware of this particular double-dealing, started the Arab rebellion in the Hejaz on June 5, 1916. The Turkish garrison in Medina was cut off; the Hejaz was declared independent; the garrison in Mecca surrendered within a month. In mid-December Britain recognized Hussein as king of the Hejaz. Meantime the British army had laid down a railway line and a pipeline across the Sinai desert, and Allenby had begun the offensive which was to end in the winter of 1918 with the destruction of the Turkish army. In this campaign the Arabs played an important part. The Jehad had indeed become a reality, but it was not the sort of Jehad that the sultan had expected.

The direct cause of the rebellion was the events in Syria, where the Turkish commander-in-chief, the notorious Djemal, sought to liquidate the Arab nationalist movement by methods of sheer barbarism. Executions and mass deportations of the Arab populations were regular occurrences; at least 300,000 Syrians died between 1915 and 1918 from the terror or from starvation. When it is remembered that the communications between Turkey and the south pass through Syria the savagery is in a way comprehensible, for a general revolt in Syria would have cut the most important line of supply of the Turkish army. It was the same in Palestine. Here there were Jewish immigrants as well as Arabs and these could limit Djemal's freedom of movement. He therefore issued an order forbidding the Jewish settlements to be guarded, in other words, he ordered pillage by Beduin and bandits, deportations, compulsory service in the Turkish army and all sorts of petty annoyances which such a regime decrees – for instance, the banning of Hebrew street names. The German occupation in Europe during the Second World War and the Dutch in Indonesia between 1945 and 1949 behaved precisely similarly.

One result of Turkish tyranny was that thousands of Jews fled to Egypt where they were formed into Jewish regiments; many of them took part in the Gallipoli campaign and in Allenby's offensive. When Palestine was liberated it was found that the number of Jewish inhabitants had fallen from 90,000 in 1914 to about 55,000 in the winter of 1918, one of the countless tragedies which have in its long history overtaken the Jewish people, and none the less tragic because it is less known than many of the others.

In the Anglo-Arab operations between the rising in the Hejaz and the fall of Damascus, the mysterious Colonel Lawrence – known later as Lawrence of Arabia – played a considerable part. He was an Englishman, but genuinely pro-Arab; he spoke Arabic and appreciated Arab culture. He devoted himself entirely to the Arab cause. Scholar, explorer, political agent, author and soldier, Lawrence (1888–1935) was originally an archaeologist and had done interesting work in Egypt. In the summer of 1917 he was the unofficial chief of staff of Faisal's and Hussein's guerrilla army. In July he attacked Akaba on the Red Sea in the south of the Negeb desert, and even more than Allenby he was the military genius of the final offensive. In 1918 he was only thirty.

But the Arab-English idyll was rudely shattered when the publication by the Bolsheviks of the secret treaties showed how Hussein and Ibn Saud had been betrayed. Deeply disillusioned in his pan-Arab hopes and by the attitude of the British Government, Lawrence withdrew and even changed his name. In 1922 and 1923 he served as a private soldier under the name of Ross and later called himself Shaw. When his bitter experiences, his ambition and all his disappointments were but past history, he wrote of it all in the famous *Seven Pillars of Wisdom* (1926); a year later a shorter version appeared under the title *Revolt in the Desert*. In 1935 he was killed in a motor accident. His romantic figure made a deep impression in Britain. As a rule British policy is not very sympathetic to hero-worship, but it would seem that its pro-Arab leanings in the Arab-Jewish conflict later was due in the last instance to Lawrence's influence. The young Lawrence seems to have been a little naïve and even blind. Much earlier than he did, Hussein realized that the British were playing a double game, and rightly distrusted them all through the war. On July 14, 1915, Hussein sent an official letter to Macmahon, then high commissioner in Egypt and the Soudan, in which he presented the Damascus protocol as the basis for further negotiations. Unofficially he received a somewhat obscure reply in which the keypoint of his letter, freedom for all Arabs south of the 37th parallel, was not mentioned. He made himself plainer, and on October 24, 1915, received a less ambiguous answer in which the British gave way all along the line – at least in words – and only to some extent reserved western Syria for France. It was this second letter which brought the Arabs in on the Allied side, and we can rightly call it the most important document of Arab nationalism.

The later history during the war and after is one of the ugliest episodes in the diplomatic history of the West. One would like from sheer shame to ignore it were it not so valuable an example of the methods of Western imperialism. That does not imply that all Arabs were angels. Hussein himself was so obsessed with his own ambitions that in October 1916 he had himself crowned 'king of all the Arabs' as if Ibn Saud did not exist. He was only king of the Hejaz, and even that title he had to give up in 1924. Faisal was for a short time king of Syria (1920), as we shall see later;[1] he had to flee, for the French and British had other plans, but next year he became king of Irak (1921–1923). Abdulla we shall meet later as emir and then king of Transjordan, the state now called Jordan; his rule lasted from 1921 to his murder in 1951. Ali's ambitions were never realized. In the winter of 1924 he succeeded his father Hussein, who had been driven out of the Hejaz because of the tyranny of his rule, but the Hejaz was invaded by Ibn Saud. Hussein's dream had finally dissolved and Ibn Saud united under his rule the whole of the Arabian peninsula except for the British coastal zones on the Sea of Arabia. The peninsula got the name of Saudi-Arabia in 1932.

But now let us return to the European intrigues. The secret treaty of April 1916, between Britain, France and Russia was worked out in detail in the Sykes-Picot agreement of May 9, 1916. Sykes a British diplomatist, Picot a French one, settled the details of this 'thieves' bargain'. We need not describe the plan as it affected Russia, for after the 1917 revolution the new rulers renounced all claims in these areas. France was to get the greater part of Syria and also South Anatolia, i.e. what is today southern Turkey and the Mosul area. Oil! Britain was to get southern Syria, i.e. Palestine, and also Irak. The rest of the Arab lands were to be free in name, actually they were to form a federation under concealed colonial rule.

At the outset these designs succeeded fairly well. Kemal indeed drove the French from Turkey and the oil from Mosul was carried in British and not French ships, but Irak, Syria and Palestine were anything but free states. But between the wars there were such changes that European intervention became generally less. None the less, whatever may be thought of European diplomacy, the plans for the Arab lands were no more than an unscrupulous bargain which was in direct contradiction to the promises given to Hussein and Ibn Saud. Understandably, the Sykes-Picot agreement was to be kept

[1] *v. p.* 173.

secret, and it remained secret until in December 1917 the Bolsheviks found a copy of it in the archives of the Russian Foreign Office and promptly published it. When Hussein learned about it he hesitated again. He asked Britain for an explanation and received the usual evasive answer. It was an exaggeratedly friendly answer such as the British Foreign Office thought necessary, since, almost simultaneously, the Balfour declaration of November 2, 1917, was published, in which the prospect of obtaining a 'Jewish home' in Palestine was dangled before the eyes of the Zionists. This was a further shock for the Arabs everywhere, and its effects are still felt. But the Jews were not less indignant, and with some right, for they had been promised a house of their own and it was now plain that the owners would live in London with their factor in Jerusalem and that the house itself had already been let to the Arabs.

That was bad, but worse was to come. In the spring of 1918 seven influential Arab leaders in Cairo demanded that Britain should declare in principle its policy in the Near East. Again the British cheated them. Naturally, it was answered, Britain would keep its word, naturally its policy was based on the principle of the 'self-determination of peoples' – that magic formula of Woodrow Wilson under cover of which French and British carried on so many of their intrigues. As a result, the Arab guerrillas fought on as fiercely as before. In November 1918 the same tactics were applied after a series of incidents in Syria and Irak. Yes, London repeated, all would turn out as had been promised, and the French agreed. That is now only history. The breaking of their pledges by the Europeans could not prevent the spread of independence; deceit is the weapon of the weak. World history seems always to take revenge on those who lie in hope of altering it, and that in a sense perhaps is what is called 'the justice of history'.

When in 1918 the rotting empire of Turkey collapsed, the Arab countries were already set on the path of independence, and after the weakening of Europe in the Second World War there could be no going back.

IV

THE RUSSIAN EMPIRE

WE have already discussed some of the factors which influenced the growth of the independence movement in Asia. But the one event which was possibly of greater importance than any of them was the Russian revolution – that of November 1917 – and to a rather less extent the revolutions of March 1917 and of 1905. If the effect of these on an Asia already in turmoil is at the outset difficult to distinguish, yet when today Mao has made China the second great communist state in the world, a history of modern Asia is meaningless if it lacks a history of the Russian revolution. Is it not the case that three-quarters of Asia and 45 per cent of Asians are ruled by ideas first conceived in Leningrad and Moscow?

Four events brought down the Russian Empire of the czars and the great landowners who oppressed dozens of peoples in Europe and Asia. There was the defeat in the Russo-Japanese War, its immediate sequel the 1905 revolution, and the two revolutions of 1917. No great empire, no human construction, simply falls of itself. A government can be terribly weakened by the corruption and incompetence of the governing classes through the misery and discontent of its subjects, but to bring it down requires either attack from abroad or the evolution within of a revolutionary class which consciously sets as its aim the undermining and the fall of the existing regime. Both – the shock from without, the shock from within – we have noticed in Turkey, the Young Turk revolution of 1908 and the attack by the British and Arabs in the First World War. The course in Russia was not dissimilar; there the shocks were simultaneous both in 1904–5 and in 1917.

What is today the Union of Socialist Soviet Republics (USSR) – usually called the Soviet Union and, with less accuracy, Russia – has an area of just over 8,708,000 square miles, i.e. it is about half the size of Asia and thrice the size of the United States. Within its frontiers lies a seventh of all the cultivated land in the world, or, if one excludes Greenland and Antarctica, a sixth. Its inhabitants number about 200,000,000. It borders on Norway, Finland, Poland, Czechoslovakia, Hungary, Roumania, Turkey, Iran, Afghanistan, China, Mongolia and Korea. It is separated from Japan and America by narrow straits – the Bering Strait is about sixty miles wide – and from India and Pakistan, south of the Pamir highlands, by the 'blind appendix' [1] of Afghanistan which is at many points only sixteen to seventeen miles wide. Stretching from the Baltic to the Eastern Pacific – that is, from 20° E. Long. to 170° W. Long. – it is a realm on which the summer sun never sets;

[1] v. p. 82.

at the period when day and night are equal, dawn is beginning on the Bering Strait and it is night in Kaliningrad in the west. It is a realm in which the steel works and cornfields of the Ukraine and the fishing ports and oilwells of Sakhalin are some 5600 miles apart, and its natural resources and the number of its inhabitants are roughly equal to those of the whole of the North American continent as far as the Panama Canal.

At the beginning of this century the Empire had pretty well the same frontiers as the Soviet Union of today. The one difference of importance is that in czarist days Finland and Poland were part of Russia. The population, naturally, was smaller. The census taken in the winter of 1897 gave a population of 125,640,000; in 1914, on the eve of the First World War, it was 142,400,000, of whom 12 per cent were Asians.

How did this powerful European-Asian – or, as it is often called, Eurasian – Empire arise? What were the sources of the political unity of all these peoples and countries from the deserts of Turkmenistan to the snow-clad forests of Northern Siberia, from the fruitful cornfields of the West to the volcanoes of Kamschatka. How and when did a wilderness become an empire? Far back in history in what we now call the European part of the Soviet Union, i.e. in Russia proper, there lived a number of Slav peoples which originally, like all Europeans, came from Asia. It was in their lands that we must locate the starting points of the Russian state. One of these points was the Grand Duchy of Kiev which, as tradition says, was founded by Scandinavians in the ninth century A.D. The Kievan kingdom was converted to Christianity in the tenth century by Byzantium, and in the succeeding centuries possessed a relatively highly developed culture. From various causes, such as the changes in the trade routes and the invasions of Asian nomads, it fell into decay in the twelfth century and politically and economically was pressed back to the regions in the north to the Russian Mesopotamia in the thick forests of the Upper Volga.

In the thirteenth century the Mongol Tatars invaded Russia and in 1240 burned Kiev to the ground. For two centuries Russia was part of the astonishingly wide Mongol Empire between the China Sea and the Mediterranean. Despite the oppression of the invaders, the Grand Duchy of Moscow grew in the shadow of the Tatar domination. The city of Moscow is first mentioned in the chronicles of 1147. In 1300 the Duchy was barely 200 square miles in extent, but it gradually annexed the surrounding districts and in 1480 Ivan III was able to refuse to pay tribute to the Mongols who were now weakened and on the retreat. Then Russia came to birth and in the following centuries its territory rapidly increased. In the thinly populated Russia of that time, west of the Urals and north of the Caucasus there lived in the fifteenth century some 2,000,000 people. The kingdom expanded in three directions: east, south and west. All three expansions began in the sixteenth century. In the south the frontiers of Persia were reached in 1870. The expansion eastward, until halted on the Yalu in 1904 by Japan, will be dealt with in detail later. The western frontier was very fluid, and here expansion took rather the character of defence against the rest of Europe. Here the Russians were threatened chiefly by the German knightly orders which had in the twelfth century occupied the so-called 'Baltic lands' on the southern coasts of the Baltic; further by the great kingdom of Poland which in the fourteenth and fifteenth centuries reached from the Baltic to the Black Sea with frontiers perilously close to Moscow, and finally by the Swedes who in the second half of the seventeenth century possessed virtually all the Baltic coasts. Peter the Great was the first to reach the Baltic and 'open a window' to the West; in 1703 in the marshes of the Neva the new capital and port of Petersburg was founded, and shortly after that the Swedes were finally defeated. At the end of the eighteenth century the frontier was roughly what is today the frontier between Poland and Russia. In the early summer of 1812 the *Grande Armée* of Napoleon, 450,000 strong, invaded Russia. At Borodino on the Moskwa the emperor broke through the Russians under Kutusov. In the middle of October the exhausted French army, now reduced to 100,000 men, decided for fear of the winter to evacuate Moscow, which had been abandoned and set on fire by the Russians. When Napoleon suddenly appeared in Paris in the night of December 18–19th it was already known there that only 15,000 half-frozen men had got back to Europe by the tottering bridges of the Beresina. Poland was now Russian territory; Finland had been acquired shortly before.

Within a few centuries Russia had risen from being an insignificant duchy to be the biggest kingdom in the world. That was unprecedented growth, but inside the country the development in more than one sense had failed to keep pace. When Peter the Great (1682–1725) came to the throne Russia was a mediaeval state. If, on the one hand, he tried to europeanize his country – a task in which Holland made an important contribution in spheres like shipping and printing – it was, on the other hand, in his reign that the originally free peasants were finally bound to the land as serfs of the nobility without land of their own. The form of government remained an absolute monarchy 'mitigated by assassination' as a famous French writer of the eighteenth century noted. If Catherine II (1762–1796) had plans for a constitution, the advent of the French revolution made her conceal them. The modernization plans of Alexander I (1801–1825) also remained on paper. A revolt made by liberal officers – the so-called Decembrist rising – was suppressed in a few hours. Admittedly, for reasons of which the defeat in the Crimea was one, the peasants were liberated in 1861; some 312,000,000 acres of land belonging to the great magnates was divided among some 50,000,000 people. But, unlike what happened in Western Europe and North America, Russian agriculture between 1800 and 1930 was by and large mediaeval, i.e. it was not mechanized and it was quite unscientific. Stolypin's agrarian reform in 1906 – he sought to introduce modern capitalist methods – could not bring material change. Because of the resistance of the great landowners, the desire of the peasants for more land could not be met. At the time of the First World War, the 18,000,000 peasant families were living on some 500,000,000 acres, while over 380,000,000 acres was still in the hands of the nobility, the monasteries and the imperial family. In 1905, the period of the first revolution, 10,500,000 peasants had the same amount of land – 200,000,000 acres – as

30,000 big landowners. In November 1917 the great majority of the peasants were ready for a revolution.

It was not only in the domain of agriculture that Russia lagged behind the Western powers. When war broke out in 1914, Russia was from the economic point of view a colony of Western Europe, just as Siberia and Turkmenistan were colonies of Russia. Nine-tenths of the Russian mines, railways and metal factories were financed and managed by foreigners. In 1914 there were only 3,000,000 workers employed in the mines and factories, that is, just as few as in the United States in 1820.

About a quarter of the Russian Empire belonged, and geographically belongs, to Europe. Although 90 per cent of the population lived then in European Russia, Russia had most of the characteristics of an Asian power, of a semi-colonial feudal state. It did have a bourgeoisie which looked to the West, to France, Britain and Germany, and tried to implant Western ideas and institutions, a parliament, for instance; Russia did not obtain one until 1905. It is characteristic that these liberals called themselves *Zapadniki*, i.e. westerners, to distinguish themselves from the so-called slavophils who thought that the Slav peoples should be preserved from Western influence.

If there had been no Japanese it is possible that the reactionary czarist rule would have maintained itself without much loss until its final disappearance in 1917. But Japan could not put up with Russian ambitions in the Far East; it declared war in February 1904, the war that is famous as the Russo-Japanese War, in which Russia suffered defeat after defeat. For Russia, at least for official Russia, that was a great humiliation which evoked from the liberals violent protests against the incompetence of the regime, protests in which the workers in the big cities joined. It is true that one cause of the defeats at Port Arthur, Mukden and Tsushima was the great distance which separated the theatre of war from the heart of the empire. But another cause was as clearly corruption; for instance, great packages of tins filled with sawdust instead of meat were sent to the front. Besides, the arrogance and incapability of the governing class made their own contribution to the disaster.

As a result all Russia was in a ferment when on January 22, 1905, an event occurred which raised the revolutionary excitement to fever heat, the event of 'Bloody Sunday'. Led by the priest Gapon, who was later murdered when found to be a police spy, a great crowd of Petersburg workers marched that morning to the czar's palace to present a petition. The Cossack guard received orders to fire; seventy dead and 240 wounded were left on the deserted street. The czar yielded and again published plans for modernization but that did not avail him much. Between June and August there were revolts everywhere. Peasants murdered landlords, burned down their mansions and divided up the land. There were mutinies in the army and in the fleet, of which the most notable was the mutiny at Odessa on board the cruiser *Potemkin*; in 1926 Eisenstein made a famous film of it. In August the czar made a further concession; an Imperial Duma, a parliament, would be granted. That was not enough. It merely added fuel to the fire and at the end of October came the general strike and the creation of the first soviet – workers' council – to lead the strike in Petersburg. Things were now really dangerous for the regime and once again concessions were announced. By the October manifesto of October 30th Russia got a constitution, i.e. the façade at least of representative government. The liberal Witte became prime minister. Part of the liberals, the so-called Oktobrists, professed themselves satisfied; the progressives, who formed the Constitutional Democratic party (K.D. or Kadet party), were still critical. The workers stayed revolutionary. They were led by the Social Democratic Labour party in which the Bolsheviks formed the left wing. As is known, the word Bolshevism means majority; the term dates from the second congress of the Social Democrats in London in 1903 when Lenin's fraction (Vladimir Iliitch Ulianov, 1870–January 21, 1924), got a majority over the Mensheviks, the minority men.

As soon as the Government had got back sufficient soldiers from the Far East, it proceeded in December to the arrest of the Petersburg soviet. Two hundred members were arrested, including their chairman Trotsky (Lev Davidovitch Bronstein, 1879–1940). In reply Lenin organized a workers' rising in Moscow (December 22, 1905–January 1, 1906); the army remained loyal and the rising was bloodily suppressed after fierce street fighting. Throughout the winter punitive expeditions were sent all over the country and crushed whatever semblance of resistance remained. Meantime the czar had got big loans from Britain and France by the aid of which he could continue to rule without a parliament. The reaction triumphed. Four Dumas met, but that meant nothing at all; the real government was the court, the landowners and the church, and in a great decision like the declaration of war on Germany in August 1914, the workers and the great majority of the peasants had as little to say as had the minorities in Poland, Finland and Asia.

In 1917 the attack from abroad and the attack from within coincided. The German offensives had placed the enemy in occupation of large tracts of Russia, in particular Poland and a considerable part of the Baltic provinces. Internally, on March 8, 1917, trouble broke out in Petrograd, the city which until 1914 had been called Petersburg. Now, in vivid contrast to 1905, the universal agitation was protected by the soldiers, four-fifths of them peasants who wanted nothing save to return to their holdings and their cattle; this is the problem that eternally confronts a peasant army. The Duma refused to accept its dissolution, and set up (March 12th) a provisional government which was predominantly liberal, with Prince Lvov as premier and in which A. F. Kerenski (b. 1881), the sole representative of the socialists, was minister of justice. Nicolas II (1894–1917) abdicated (March 15th). The provisional government, which seemed fairly radical at the outset, could not yield to the popular desire to end the war. On the contrary, Kerenski, who in May had become minister for war, tried to restore the shattered front. His famous offensive in summer was just another great defeat; the Russian losses were nearly a million. The German General Staff, which knew the tremendous importance of completing the ruin of Russia – if they could end the war in Russia the whole of the German forces could be directed against France – had meantime sent back to Russia in a sealed train *via* Germany the revolutionaries who lived in exile in Switzerland – Lenin and other Bolsheviks like Zinoviev, Lunacharski and Radek; they arrived in Petrograd on April 16th.

Trotsky returned to Russia in May from the United States and Canada, and Stalin (Josif Vissarionovitch Djugashvili, b. in Georgia 1879, d. in Moscow March 5, 1953) came back from Siberia. The Bolshevik agitation was now much stronger and more conscious of its aims, particularly after Lenin published his programme of 'all power to the soviets' – these were already in existence as a second government – the ejection of the bourgeois government of Kerenski, the ending of the war and the division of land among the peasants.

In July, when the Germans again attacked, the Bolsheviks attempted a coup in Petrograd but the time was not yet ripe for that. Many of them, including Trotsky, were arrested. Lenin fled to Finland where, in a house in the middle of a firwood beside one of Finland's many lakes, the recognized leader and prophet of the revolution bided his time.

Kerenski meantime had taken over the premiership from Lvov, and in September Kornilov, the first of many 'white' – i.e. counter-revolutionary – generals, tried to seize power. The Kornilov *putsch* was speedily crushed, mainly by the intervention of the workers' battalions of Petrograd. This was grist to the mill of the Bolsheviks, who were seen now to be the only vigorous defenders of the revolution. Lenin believed the hour had come. Early on November 7th the third revolution broke out; it was *the* Russian revolution. Commanded by the Bolshevik, i.e. the Communist, party, the garrison of Petrograd and the sailors of Kronstadt rose and the workers' Red Guard occupied the Government buildings, stormed the Winter Palace and arrested the members of the Kerenski government. Later in the day the second congress of soviets recognized the revolution and handed over executive power to the Communist party. The revolution is known as the October revolution, since by the old Russian calendar it took place on October 25th; the old Julian calendar was replaced by the Gregorian on February 14, 1918. In the same way one will often find the March revolution called the February revolution.

In the government which Lenin formed, Stalin was commissar for the nationalities and Trotsky minister of foreign affairs. The events in Petrograd, which were simultaneous with risings in Moscow and some other cities, the division of the land by the peasants – in all, nearly 6,000,000 square miles of landed property was broken up – the general desertion at the front and the return of the soldiers mark the beginning of a new era not merely for Russia but, in a sense, for the world.

It should cause no surprise to find that the first period of the Russian revolution was an exceptionally difficult one, both for the Communist party and for the Russian people as a whole. The plan of the revolution was simple, to free Russia from feudal, and especially czarist, oppression. Let us repeat, Russia was a great power in Asia but at the same time it was a semi-colony of the West. As socialists in principle, the Bolsheviks at once nationalized the banks and the big factories, and took control of the land and of foreign trade. The foreign debts incurred by the old regime and by Kerenski's government were repudiated. That meant, of course, that no more aid from abroad could be expected. And not only that, it meant, also, the fierce hostility of the bankers and industrialists of Western Europe, who saw that they were losing not only money but also a huge market and possibilities of capital investment. Did not this revolution also threaten the alleged security of the capitalist system, all the illusions of the capitalist class, undermine its whole conception, and wreck its world more than any other revolution had done? At the outset Britain, France and America could not intervene, for they were still at war with Germany and Turkey. The Germans had followed in the wake of the retreating Russians and now occupied more great stretches of Russia; Narva, a little over ninety miles from Petrograd, fell on March 4th, 1918. The Bolsheviks were now faced with the question whether or not to go on fighting. Lenin said: No, for only in the absence of war can we secure the fruits of the revolution. The soviet government removed to Moscow, which before Peter the Great had been the capital, and at Brest Litovsk, close to the present Russo-Polish frontier, a treaty was signed between the Bolsheviks and the Germans by which what was formerly Russian Poland and Finland, the granary of the Ukraine and all the border provinces where non-Russian minorities lived, e.g. the Baltic provinces and Transcaucasia, were given up. The Germans were now in the heart of Russia, a case of frank, imperialist expansion. All the big towns in the Ukraine were occupied and in May Sebastopol, the great naval base on the Black Sea, fell into their hands.

Worse was to come. The counter-revolution of the Don Cossacks under Kornilov in December 1917 and the landing of the Japanese at Vladivostok in the same month mark the beginning of the terrible period of civil war and intervention in which the Bolshevik government more than once nearly went under. There was heavy fighting all over the country. The Red Army, organized mainly by Trotsky, faced in the Ukraine and the Caucasus the White Russian armies of Kornilov, Denikin and Wrangel, and in Siberia the notorious counter-revolutionary Admiral Kolchak, who was called 'the Regent'. In February Kolchak was shot by the Bolsheviks at Irkutsk, and the counter-revolution was finally broken in Russia when Wrangel was compelled to evacuate his army to Istanbul.

But before that, as if civil war was not bad enough, interventionist armies came from all quarters – French, British, Poles, Czechs, Americans, Japanese and Germans. Not until 1922 did the Japanese leave Vladivostok; they left North Sakhalin only in 1925. On December 30, 1922, the Union of Socialist Republics was officially proclaimed; it embraced Russia proper and the Asian districts, the Ukraine, White Russia and Transcaucasia.

These two periods, the revolutionary period and the period of civil war and intervention, are of incalculable significance for the awakening of Asia – one need only mention China – if only because of the liquidation of the great estates and the intervention of the West as if Russia really were only a colony. But it was also significant because it marked the end of Russian imperialism in Asia and Europe. In Europe Poland, Finland and the Baltic States were recognized as independent, and, by the agreement on a degree of independence for Transcaucasia, the region south of the Caucasus. For Asia it meant that all the old claims on Turkey were abandoned, that Russian troops were withdrawn from Northern Persia and the frontier districts of Afghanistan, and that all rights and privileges were surrendered in Manchuria and other parts of China. The policy may have been followed simply because of the necessities of the times, but in principle and in its consequences it was anti-imperialist, and led in many Asian lands to a re-estimation of Russia such as was never completely effaced.

In the Asian districts of Russia also the czarist heritage was abandoned. The peoples of Turkmenistan, the Moslem area, and Siberia did not indeed get freedom in the sense of independence, but the era of stupid efforts at russification was over. The policy of Stalin on the nationalities meant that the language and culture of the various peoples was recognized and protected. On the other hand, however, the strong links between religion, culture and society that are so characteristic of Islam were destroyed. In spite of that we may state that, by the nationalities policy as well as by the planned industrialization of the Asian districts, the welfare of the peoples as well as their education was permanently furthered, especially if one looks at the surrounding countries. We say 'permanently' advisedly, for what held true of Russia proper held true also for them. The Soviet Union neither could not nor wanted to borrow abroad, so capital had to be found by extreme economy for factories, blast furnaces, universities and tractors. That at the outset meant less bread, fewer houses, less wood on the fire. The soviet republics were no gardens of Eden and, as compared with the countries of Western Europe, they were very much less than free. But the word 'free' has many meanings. If to the intellectual it means that he can freely express his opinion, to the Asian peasant it means a little more grain, milk and hygiene, instead of constant lack of all three. Thus with all its restrictions and hardships the socialist state seemed like a shining and guiding light to the great majority of the Asian peasants and workers.

V

JAPAN, CHINA, MONGOLIA AND KOREA

WE have already seen how Japan took advantage of the gap in time between the Russia of the czars and the Russia of the soviets, and how on December 30, 1917, they landed at Vladivostok. The name means 'ruler of the east', and that Japan as its possessor had now become. It was the third great attempt on the continent, the great dream of the Island Empire since 1894, or at any rate since 1904. One can, of course, consider the War of 1904–1905 as a war of defence. Had not the czar at that time sought to conquer Korea once and for all, Korea which is so near Japan? Had not Russia intervened in the Sino-Japanese War in 1895? Had not the Russians acquired Port Arthur in 1897, Manchuria in 1900 and, at the same time, had not the first train run over the Trans-Siberian railway to Vladivostok?

At any rate, Japan did look enviously towards Eastern Asia. If the wish to conquer was not made actual until 1931 in the invasion of Manchuria, long before that things were happening which pleased neither Russia nor China nor the Western powers. When on August 23, 1914, Japan declared war on Germany, no regard was paid to Chinese neutrality. It was not only the German islands in the Pacific that were seized, but also the German possessions in Shantung, particularly in the leased territory and the port of Kiauchow on the Yellow Sea which had become German in 1898; its garrison surrendered after a siege of a month. Secondly, Japanese trade took the place of the German. That was possible because between 1900 and 1914, as we have shown,[1] Japan had built up its own large-scale industry which in certain branches, cotton goods for instance, could compete with its German and British rivals. The creation of the trust embracing the two great family businesses of the Mitsui and Mitsubishi dates from 1893. The war period naturally was a very profitable one for Japanese industry. No chances were neglected. German prisoners-of-war interned in Japan were put to the production of beer by European methods; the result was the well-known Asahi beer which is as good as any German beer. Also, very great fortunes were made by supplying munitions of war to Russia. Before 1914 Japanese warships were built mostly in British yards and all Japanese locomotives came from America, but in 1919 Japan was building cruisers and locomotives in Japanese yards. Great industrial concerns arose and the whole country was like a great bowl from which the capitalists took the rich cream, leaving the skimmed milk to the workers; the latter are not supposed to have needs.

If one has anything, one wants more; the desire of Japan's industrial barons to extend their sway on the continent grew; they coveted the coal of Manchuria and Shantung, the cotton and rice of the Yangtse valley. In the

[1] v. pp. 52 sq.

years after the 1911 revolution China was completely helpless and in Japan it was thought that a war was unnecessary, for what was desired was to be had for the asking. The result of that was the 'Twenty-one Requests' which Japan made to China in January 1915. They were suspiciously like demands and are, indeed, the start of Japanese aggression against China and the rest of the Far East. They can be divided into five groups – the taking over of German rights in Shantung; extension of the Japanese lease in South Manchuria to ninety-nine years plus freedom of trade in that area; the half of the shares in a series of iron and steel works and mines; the assurance that no part of the Chinese coast would either be leased or surrendered to another power, and the acceptance of Japanese advisers in the political, military and financial spheres. It was at once intervention and robbery. The Japanese aims were frankly avowed and were now clear as daylight. Japan wanted to replace Western with Japanese imperialism.

This Japanese ambition in the end showed itself to be illusion, though in the Second World War it came very near to realization if only for a moment. Its enormous importance for world history is undeniable. Entirely contrary to design, Japanese imperialism was a great factor in the achievement of freedom by China and other Asian countries. In some twenty years of continuous skirmishing and war with Japan, China finally grasped the necessity of defending itself against Western imperialism. That was seen later. In 1915 this was not China's reaction. Yuan Shi-kai, who became president of the Chinese Republic in 1912 in place of Sun Yat-sen, sought to make use of the national defeat to further a treacherous plan of his own. He said that things would continue to go wrong without an emperor, and tried in a palace revolution (December 1915) to make himself emperor. A counter-revolt in Yunnan foiled this cunning, but foolish, plan; modernization had made too much progress to let it succeed. None the less it seemed to show that the 1911 revolution has been premature, and part of the responsibility for this must fall on the West, whose intervention had shown up the incompetence of the imperial regime. And all the conflicts which had further plunged China into division and chaos were in the last resort the consequences of a single set of circumstances which 1911 had brought into existence, the existence of a republican regime which wanted to make China a modern capitalist country without being able to do so or being prepared to break completely with the feudal basis of society.

It was a difficult time for China, an apparently endless period in which the war lords (the tuchuns) fought each other, the governor of one province against the governor of another, one army against the others, all at the expense of the peasantry and all inflamed by the foreigner – by Britain and Japan before 1914 against America and then by Britain and America against Japan, while the Pekin government became simply a reactionary camerilla, the so-called Anfu party (1917) which could maintain itself only with the help of Japanese money and Japanese bayonets.

The declaration of war on Germany (August 14, 1914) had only a few real gains to show. German exterritoriality and German concessions naturally disappeared and naturally that pleased Britain and France. But China's entry into the war had no military results at all, even if China did send some labour battalions to France, Mesopotamia and Africa. But when the Russian revolution broke out, and Japanese, British and American troops landed at Vladivostok, the Japanese sought to draw the Chinese into the anti-communist front. Officers from Tokio trained Chinese troops for the war in Siberia. The success was not quite what was expected, but in its way not unimportant. The Russian revolution, to be sure, was not to be halted, but for the first time China had some modern troops. When the great civil war in China broke out in 1927 Chiang Kai-shek, and later Mao Tse-tung, were able to make good use of the knowledge and experience gained from the Japanese instructors. Here again is something which was a factor in China's awakening, a development quite contrary to the designs of foreign powers. We do not know whether history has a meaning of its own or just follows a destined path, but we can again state that it always leads somewhere – in this case to the awakening of China. An impartial study of the facts teaches us that everything aids the general process, even the measures taken by those who want to halt it or turn it in another direction. For instance, neither the Dutch nor the Japanese wanted an independent Indonesia. Yet what was the end-result of all their efforts and reforms, all the compulsion and terror? The independent republic of Indonesia!

In 1916 Sun Yat-sen returned from exile and drew up his great programme of construction and modernization. He went on the assumption that he could get foreign capital for his plan without letting his country become a semi-colony. In rather naïver form, his effort much resembled the plans which the Soviet Union tried to work out, but had to abandon as illusory. In Versailles Sun asked the powers to give him just so much money as *one single day* of war had cost them. He, too, had to abandon his plan and, unlike the Bolsheviks, he was not in a position to awaken without foreign intervention the energies of his own country for modernization. Perhaps he was naïve, but he was still a very great man, i.e. a man who grasped the fact that he must learn from reality before he could influence it. His bitter experience in Versailles in 1919, where both he and his plan were virtually ignored and where the European masters instead of giving back to China the former German concessions in Shantung handed them over to the Japanese, caused Sun to think that he should not go to the foreigner for help, but turn to his own country and there not to the bourgeoisie but to the workers and peasants. As head of the rival government in Canton in 1920 he was the first to try to draw these classes into active participation in the revolution.

When we deal with Chinese history we must never forget that we are dealing with a giant country. If we reckon in the outer provinces like Tibet it is as big as Europe; it is twice as big as India with Pakistan and holds a quarter of the total world population. It is a country in which the sugar fields of the island of Hainan off the coast of South China is, as the crow flies, some 1560 miles from Pekin, while Pekin is some 940 miles from the snow peaks of the mountains on the Amur in North Manchuria. If we leave the thickly populated districts, the distance between Eastern Manchuria and Western Tibet, where the Indus and the Brahmaputra have their sources, is more than 3000 miles. For the period with which we are dealing we can declare with a probability that is virtually certainty, that the chaotic and sanguinary disruption of China was the result primarily of the social struggle intensified by foreign intervention, but at the same time we must recognize that the huge extent of the country and its wretched communications were also factors of great importance. Even in 1920 it was not possible to go from Canton to Shanghai by train.

Both factors had much to do with the events in Outer Mongolia. It was the first soviet republic outside the frontiers of the Soviet Union and in an area which for centuries had been a Chinese province. The People's Republic of Mongolia, as the land is now officially called, has today a population of about 2,000,000; the majority are Mongols, but there are 100,000 Russians and 50,000 Chinese. There are at present great plans for agricultural development, but the country is still typical of the Asian outer zone. It is a land of sheep, camels and horses; there are 700,000 camels in it, a number against which the few factories and mines can hardly be put in the scales. It is separated from China by sandy and stony deserts and barren steppe in which, as evidence of the mortality of all that belongs to earth, one can still see the sand-covered ruins of what were once flourishing towns. The beauty that existed here was over and already buried in the sands before the first Chinese chroniclers had put pencil to paper. It was the powerful Gengis Khan (c. 1155–1227) who gave the country its name and made it world-famous through the conquests of the Mongol cavalry armies in all Asia and a great part of Europe. Under Kublai Khan, in the second half of the thirteenth century, the Mongol realm was the greatest empire known to history which was without access to the sea. At the period of the Yuan dynasty (1260–1368), Kublai Khan and his sons ruled over China; the expulsion of the Mongols was the work of the first emperor of the Ming dynasty. The Mongol forays into China across the Great Wall during the fifteenth and sixteenth centuries were only minor incidents. In its later history other powers drew Mongolia into their field of power – Pekin, Petersburg, Tokio and Moscow. The semi-nomads of Mongolia came more and more under Chinese sway. In the seventeenth century they recognized the suzerainty of the Manchu emperor in Pekin and in the following centuries were nominally Chinese subjects in approximately the same position as Sinkiang and Tibet, then both parts of the Chinese empire. Things changed only in the period with which this book deals. In 1907, the year in which Britain and Russia were dividing Persia and Tibet, Russia and Japan were acting similarly in Northern China; Tokio's annexation of Korea was recognized, while Russia got a free hand in Mongolia. Russia recognized the Chinese Republic on condition that Mongolia became an independent province, officially part of China but actually a buffer state between Russia and China. It was the domain of a Russian resident who exercised his functions from Urga, spreading the influence of Russia to Tannu-Tava in the northwest, to Sinkiang, or Chinese Turkestan, in the west, and to Tibet in the southwest, where it met the British. Ruled by Buddhist monks and nobles, Mongolia awaited its hour.

The tempest of the First World War set everything in motion. In 1919 Outer Mongolia was temporarily occupied by General Hsu Chu-seng, one of the barbaric warlords of North China, allegedly to prevent the spread of Bolshevism. The plan was a Japanese one. In Siberia the Red armies were fighting with the 'White' and foreign armies. When Kolchak was shot by a Red firing squad, one of his subordinates, Baron Ungern-Sternberg, tried to make a counter-revolution. Driven out of Siberia he arrived in Outer Mongolia, where in 1921 he took Urga, the Ulan Bator Choto of today. Ungern-Sternberg, half Russian, half Hungarian, claimed that he was a descendant of Batu, Gengis Khan's grandson, who had besieged Budapest in 1240. His dream was to revive the Mongolian Empire. 'As earth cannot exist without heaven, so nations cannot exist without kings' was one of his poetic, but not very clear, ideas. His deeds were more prosaic. Having in May 1921 slaughtered all the Chinese in Outer Mongolia, he resumed his war with the Bolsheviks and marched to Lake Baikal to cut the Trans-Siberian railway and hand over Eastern Siberia to the Japanese. It was not to be. Close to the frontier of his brand-new empire he came up against a cavalry detachment commanded by Budjenny, who is today a marshal of the Soviet Union. The baron was beaten. During his flight he was attacked by Mongol herdsmen and left in the desert, where Russian troops found him. After brief proceedings before a people's court, he was shot.

The Bolsheviks realized how easily their republic could be attacked from Outer Mongolia, and momentarily 'forgot' their policy of anti-imperialism. On June 6, 1921, 6000 Red troops crossed the frontier. It was soon realized that there was no need to occupy the country. Led by native Mongol revolutionaries like Sukebator, Choibalsan and others, the small peasants rose against their noble masters, and that same summer the Soviet Republic of Mongolia was set up, formally independent, actually an autonomous province of the Soviet Union, even if in 1924 Chinese sovereignty over it was again admitted – in theory.

But to come back to Japan. A feature of the awakening of Asia, and not the least important feature, was the rise to self-consciousness of the mass of the workers who now demanded consideration of their rights as human beings and a definite minimum in wages, sustenance and housing. During the war the numbers of workers in industry had doubled; the agitation among them had also doubled. The result, or one of the results, was the first Labour Law of 1916, which forbade children under twelve to work in the factories and limited young workers between twelve and fifteen years of age to a twelve-hour day; two days off per month were granted. Social legislation met the same obstacles as it did in Europe about 1900. The manufacturers, who were apprehensive of lower production and higher expenditure without realizing that in the long run better working conditions lead to higher and relatively cheaper production, were against it; Parliament, through franchise restrictions representative really only of the ruling class, feared strikes and rebellions – they accepted social legislation but were very slow in passing it. There were nowhere any labour inspectors and so no control over what did happen in the factories, and the exceptions laid down in the law of 1916 were so numerous that the law was no more than mere appearance; it could even be called deception.

All that was not hid from the workers and they sought to compel the manufacturers and the port authorities to undertake genuine modernization, and, with the only weapon left to those who are economically weak, sought improvements through combination and strike action. The so-called 'Peace Law' of 1900, by which all striking was made illegal, could not prevent the growth of the unions, especially during the war. The great Workers' Confederation, established on the initiative of the labour leader Bundchi Suzuki in 1912, was in 1916 reorganized as a real trade union. It fought all along the front against an industry which had got rich overnight and its secret police; the secret police is not an invention of the later war years but goes back to 1916. During the struggle the workers got an insight into their own situation; through newspapers, pamphlets and public meetings socialist ideas seeped in. Nor did it escape their notice that, while the profits of the manufacturers had risen formidably, for the dock workers and those in the cotton plantations the only result of the boom had been a rise in the price of rice. By 1918 it was too much. Some fisherwomen in the south plundered a rice store and this was the signal for a series of rice revolts. Fearing a general rising, the Government, whom the riots embarrassed while the war lasted, ordered the police not to intervene in the many illegal strikes. Strike action even spread to munition depots and a mutiny among the troops was the consequence.

The political results were soon made visible. Baron Terauchi, the prime minister and a former governor-general of Korea, was not equal to handling the ever-growing labour movement and he was replaced by Hara, the first non-noble premier of Japan. Here was a new breach in the feudal tradition. Again, in March 1919, after a great mass demonstration in Tokio, the electoral laws were revised. The number of voters was doubled, rising from one and a half to three million; for a population of 55,000,000 or, if you include Sakhalin Formosa and Korea, of 77,000,000 it was not a very great number. But as compared to earlier conditions this was a great reform; the reactionary principle that peasants and workers should have no say in the governing of the country had gone by the board.

When the war was over and the peace conference met in mid-January 1919, Japan, as an ally of Britain since 1902 and a Great Power, was invited, and at it things on the whole went very well for the Japanese. Japan got the former German concessions in China which it had tried to force China to surrender in the 'Twenty-one Requests', and all the German islands in the Pacific, and gladly accepted a seat in the League of Nations. But when Japan asked the Assembly of the League to declare that no race was inferior to any other, the 'Big Three' of that day – President Wilson of the United States,

Lloyd George, the British prime minister, and Clemenceau the French premier – could do nothing else but reject it. Probably they thought that they could in this way postpone the emancipation of Asia and Africa; perhaps they merely yielded to a national instinct, but they certainly had no idea how much by their rejection they increased the pace at which all the Asian peoples, no matter how much they differed from each other, became united in their dislike of the 'whites' whether they were European or American.

Meantime Japan did more for the awakening of Asian nationalism on a large scale by the fact that she had asserted herself as a 'non-white' Great Power, and on a smaller by her colonial policy in Korea and Formosa. Korea, annexed in 1910, was dealt with in a barbaric manner as a province in the worst sense of that word. Anyone who has studied Japanese policy in the peninsula will certainly not maintain that it is only the 'whites' who are inclined to oppress other peoples. The savage national rising of March 1919 in which Korea declared herself to be independent was only the most violent phase of a long resistance. The preparations for revolution may have escaped the notice of the Japanese intelligence but, once it started, its suppression was an easy matter for the occupying power. According to Korean sources 7000 patriots lost their lives for their country's independence during the Japanese counter-action. Martyrs do not die in vain. Japan seemed to realize that Korea had been all too drastically governed. A civil administration took the place of military government and the country would have had self-government in a sense if the Koreans had only moderated their desire for independence. Naturally they did not; no people can. The *fata morgana* of self-government drove the nationalists further on the road to freedom.

Lest we go over the limits which we have set for this book we shall only briefly deal with the Pacific islands which were declared at Versailles in May 1919 to be Japanese mandated territory, and with the other islands which have played so dramatic a role in the modern history of the Far East and of the whole world. The names of Guadalcanal, Tarawa, Bikini, Okinawa, Iwojima are now known to more than their inhabitants and a few ships' captains.

The modern history of the Pacific islands is the history of European invasion. On September 25, 1513, the Spanish Admiral Vasco Nuñez de Balboa, crossed the isthmus of Panama and south of it found a sea unknown to Europeans; he called it the Pacific. In the autumn of 1520, Magellan's three Portuguese ships sailed round the toe of South America through the straits that still bear his name and through the Pacific to the Philippines. Then, like bees attracted by honey, the Europeans swarmed in from every quarter. Micronesia and Melanesia were discovered and explored by the Spaniards in the sixteenth century from the Philippines in 1521 to the distant New Hebrides in 1606. Polynesia – that is, roughly, the islands east of 180° Long. W. – became known in the seventeenth and especially in the eighteenth century by the voyages of British, French and Dutch. Samoa and the unique

Easter Island (real name Rapa Nui) were discovered by the Dutchman Roogeveen in 1721 and 1722; rich Tahiti by a French expedition about 1770; Hawaii by that great and humane Englishman Captain James Cook. In the eighteenth century the Europeans thought they had found here the earthly Paradise. Sailors deserted in crowds to the desirous nymphs of the palm-shaded islands and, as the ships' captains wanted little more of their friendly inhabitants than water and fresh coconuts, the islands until well into the nineteenth century remained unoccupied by Europeans.

But about 1880 a new era began, the era of modern imperialism, the era of the division of the world between the Great Powers. As Africa was by and large divided into a French and a British part, so the Pacific was divided between Germany and Britain. If we divide the Pacific into four quarters along the Equator and the international date line, the eastern and southern quarters are on the whole British. The only notable exceptions are Hawaii (USA) and Tahiti (French). The northwestern quarter was German – Northeast New Guinea and the Bismarck Islands (1884), the Marshalls and the Solomons (1885), the Marianas, the Palm Islands and the Carolinas (1889). In this quarter only Guam, Marcus and Wake were American.

So we return again to Japan. In 1919 Japan got all the German possessions north of the Equator and awakened 1400 Pacific islands from their slumber. It turned them into fortresses for a Japan which, as a result of the self-slaughter of the Europeans in the First World War, had become the third sea power in the world and the first power in Asia.

VI

THAILAND, INDIA-PAKISTAN, INDONESIA, INDOCHINA, MALAYA, PERSIA AND AFGHANISTAN

THE ferment in Asia was not confined to the countries with which we have been dealing, though these were revolutionary and of greater direct political importance both from the Asian and from the international point of view. We shall try first to sketch briefly the picture of the rest of Asia; first Siam, the Thailand of today; then India-Pakistan, the core of British India; then the French colony of Indochina and the British colony of Malaya – all in the inner zone of the thickly populated rice countries. In the outer zone there is only the theoretically independent state of Persia (the Iran of today) and Afghanistan. The sequence of these states looks arbitrary, but it corresponds to the degree in which the First World War furthered their awakening most in Thailand, the eastern neighbour of British India, least in Afghanistan, its neighbour in the west. The Philippines, at this period an American colony; Burma, then a part of British India, and Egypt, still occupied by Britain, will come into the sequence in the third period.

For many centuries Thailand was relatively free from European encroachment, but about 1880 things turned out just as in Africa and the Pacific at that time. In 1886 Burma became British and French troops were pressing into Laos. After London and Paris had reached a general political and military agreement in the *entente* of 1904, Thailand maintained its already restricted independence only by being a semi-colonial buffer state between British bayonets on the Salween and in Malaya and French in Laos and Cambodia. Only the upper classes had been to some degree modernized, and in the First World War Thailand had importance merely as a rubber and timber reservoir for the British. The government of Rama VI tried at first to stay neutral, but on July 22, 1917, it declared war on Germany and Austria. It was in a manner only a gesture against two countries of whom the majority of the Siamese people had never even heard. But it was a protection against the threat of a Franco-British occupation, and it was also a practical way of getting rid at least of German and Austrian extraterritorial rights. The tiny expeditionary force which went to France in the summer of 1918 was a mere nothing beside all the American divisions then in action on the tottering German front in Northern France.

It is worth while delaying at this point for a moment. The fact that these Asians came to distant and mysterious Europe was of itself of importance.

They passed through the villages and towns of France on modern roads. Everywhere they saw factories, motor cars, farm machinery. They now for the first time saw the European at home, got to know the French peasant and the French worker. But they also saw Europe at its lowest, bleeding to death in mud behind barbed wire amid all its real or alleged civilization. When in 1919 they returned to Thailand and its ricefields, they were full of the new modern ideas, longed for all that Europe had and what their villages, their wives and daughters never had had.

They had the same ideas, the same desires as all the other 'coloured' troops on the fronts in Europe – Berbers from Algeria and Morocco, negroes from the valleys of the Niger and the Senegal, and the some 120,000 men from British India who in fighting units or labour battalions had been in Europe, Mesopotamia, Palestine, Egypt and the German colonies in East Africa.

What are today the states of India and Pakistan became definitely British in 1850 – or appeared to be so. Burma was added in 1886 and British India became the biggest colony in Asia apart from the colonial parts of the Russian Empire. In 1914 it had about 325,000,000 inhabitants, a third of the population of Asia. It was a land with 600,000 villages of small peasants – three-quarters of the total population – illiterate, constantly harassed by grain shortage, drought and excessive rains; a land with many languages, kept apart by lack of good communications and by the division of the people into Hindus and Moslems in the ratio of five to two, a gigantic land equal to half of Europe in size, 2500 miles wide, stretching from the salt steppe of the west to the teak forests of Burma to the east and bounded in the north by the eternal snows of the Karakorum on the parallel of Tokio and in the south by Cape Comorin on the parallel of Northern Sumatra. A rich land? If we think in terms of the peasants and the workers, no. But in terms of the harvest, yes. It produces jute, tea, sugar, cotton and – soldiers.

It was the Moslems especially who did not go gladly to the Western front in Europe. Was not the war against Germany also a war against Turkey, the citadel of Islam? Of the Hindus, many seemed to respond to Gandhi who had returned from South Africa and was exercising all his influence on behalf of the British. Mohandas Karamchand Gandhi (1869– January 30, 1948) had gone to Britain in 1888 to study law. He was first a lawyer in Bombay and then went to South Africa. There, particularly in Natal and the Transvaal, lived many migrants from Nearer India who, just as in Kenya, Tanganyika and Mauritius, were treated by the whites as rather troublesome ballast. It was here that Gandhi tried out his tactics of passive resistance (*satyagraha*) against the Dutch Boers. He was successful.

Why, then, on his return to Bombay did he seem, contrary to all the expectations of many of his countrymen, to become pro-British? Partly no doubt because of his earlier liking for Britain and Europe, but surely and mainly because he thought, or at least hoped, that if his country loyally and vigorously threw in its strength against Germany and Turkey it could demand much more of Britain. The agreement between the All-India

National Congress (founded 1885) and the All-India Moslem League (founded 1906) made at Lakhnau (Lucknow) in 1916 was mainly Gandhi's work. The two biggest nationalist organizations now demanded of the new viceroy, Lord Chelmsford (1916–1921), an elected legislative assembly. At the same time the radicals intensified the agitation which they had started at the beginning of the war. Tilak and Annie Besant, the Englishwoman who became spiritually a Hindu, went through the country advocating home rule (*swaraj*) to people roused to passion by the fiery Sarojini Naidu. She was arrested; Annie Besant was interned. Britain, however, realized that all this was the first gusts of a tempest which came at a most awkward moment, and so the Secretary for India in London issued on August 20, 1917, a plan for the development of self-government as the first stage on the way to freedom. In 1918 Montagu went to Delhi and with Chelmsford produced in a final report the somewhat obscure plans for a restricted self-government known as the Montagu-Chelmsford reforms.

They were restricted, very restricted, if they are considered in the light of later events. As is always the case with half-way concessions, their sole result was to spur on the national movement. The All-India Congress lost no time in declaring that the reforms were no basis of discussion. The reader knows the Greek proverb: 'Whom the gods wish to destroy they first make blind'; all the European governments yesterday and today were blind where their Asian policies were concerned. The only exception is the broad-minded attitude of Britain towards India and Pakistan in 1947.

In 1918 Britain was no more liberal than any other colonial government. When the situation, already bedevilled by famine and influenza epidemics – in which, as we have already noted, 5 per cent of the native population died[1] – was made worse and when everywhere, partly influenced by what had happened in Russia, the peasants and workers were showing a revolutionary spirit, how did the government of British India react? Instead of granting the modest wishes of the people, it replied with the Rowlatt Acts under which agitators could be imprisoned without trial (March 18, 1919). A silly move? Probably, even certainly. But one should never forget that, in the history of the awakening of Asia, the Europeans often acted out of fear, fear of the great Asian monster which was now stirred to activity, and fear of the other European owners of the monster. In the present case London and Delhi rightly feared the influence of the Russian revolution and still more of the Moslem agitation in Hither Asia on British India, particularly on its Moslem provinces.

The Rowlatt Acts accomplished just the opposite of what was intended. On the one hand, the opposition, so often disunited, of Hindus, Moslems and Sikhs was now a single united opposition, at least temporarily; on the other, Gandhi had just launched his first great campaign of passive resistance and non-co-operation which showed itself to be much more effective a weapon than the Western mind of the British could have thought. Besides the whole of the Punjab, the whole area of Lahore, Amritsar and Delhi was in a state of chaotic rebellion.

[1] *v.* p. 64.

In this heavily charged atmosphere came like a lightning flash the event which is known as 'the bloodbath of Amritsar' (April 13, 1919). Amritsar is the holy city of the Sikhs. Here General Dyer who, it seems, had become slightly unbalanced after an atttempt on his life, ordered troops to fire on an unarmed mob. Official reports say that there were 379 killed and 1208 wounded. Not content with that, Dyer compelled the survivors to go through the streets on hands and knees. The only comparison is with 'Bloody Sunday' in Petersburg on January 22, 1905. Stafford Cripps, the British Labour leader, was surely thinking of Amritsar when he said: 'You have only to look in the pages of British Imperial history to hide your head in shame.' The bitterness in India and Pakistan was greater and more widespread than over any other incident. The military authorities called it 'an error of judgement' and the House of Commons voiced its disapproval.

As if that were not enough, the Montagu-Chelmsford reforms, which had been weighed in the balance and found wanting, were made law by the Government of India Act (December 23, 1919). British officers and officials in the unfortunate colony found them premature, but London and Delhi realized that, even if the war was over, the reforms must be put in force. On the day that they were put in force Britain was celebrating Christmas. With great gusto the British ate their plum pudding, drank their whisky and their tea without realizing what a child could have seen, that in a third of Asia all was up with foreign domination.

In this period Indonesia was the only Asian country which was not disturbed by the war, for the simple reason that Holland remained neutral. Colonies like British India, Malaya, Indochina and the Philippines were all more or less involved in it, simply because they were colonies; Turkey and the Arab countries, the Russian Empire and Mongolia were all directly involved in the fighting and in revolution; even China was, if to a lesser degree. Japan sent its troops to the German islands in the Pacific, to Manchuria and to Siberia. Iran nominally was neutral, but actually Russian, British and Turkish troops ranged all over the country as if its frontiers did not exist. What happened in Afghanistan we shall relate later,[1] but we cannot call its conduct neutral.

The story of Indonesia in these years is the story of a change in atmosphere, in social-political readjustments and of the coming to maturity of nationalist ideas. What visibly took place gives only a blurred and distorted picture of the reality. It was a period in which trade was being directed to Asia and America instead of Europe; it was also the period when a native bourgeoisie arose, opposed to the European traders whom it regarded as much too enterprising. It was also a time of radicalization, partly in echo of the general transformation in the rest of Asia, and especially of the Arab and Russian revolutions, but also simply as the natural result of nationalist feeling. It was a radicalization which in 1914 began with the discussion within the nationalist movement on the future national defence of Indonesia,

[1] v. pp. 139, 201 sq.

and that movement during the war grew to such a degree of self-consciousness that the resistance against tyranny was no longer the only thing that held the movement together, though it was still clearly the main factor. More and more socialists entered the Sarekat Islam. The majority in this bourgeois organization was still in principle against the ideas of the small communist-inclined minority which repudiated every kind of capitalism and not just the European colonial variety. In 1920 there was founded the Partai Kommunis Indonesia (PKI), a variation on the Indian Social Democratic party which was under the influence of the events in Russia; in 1921 the Communists left the Sarekat Islam.

The first genuine trade union in the sugar refineries dates from 1917. A general union was founded on December 25, 1919, by the Sarekat Islam, the Persatuan Pergerakan Kaum Buruh. This new radicalism was not confined to the archipelago; the Indonesian students in Holland were united in the Perhimpunan Indonesia (1922) in which Hatta was very active, and by its official organ *Indonesia Merdeka* revealed itself as a distant outpost, but one visible even from afar, of the independence movement.

Had the issue depended on the governor-general, Holland in 1918 might have made reasonable concessions to the just claims of the Nationalists. Count I. P. van Limburg Stirum (1916–1921) was a mild and progressive ruler. Unlike the government in The Hague, unlike the planters and sugar barons and all those whose insight was hindered by arrogance or selfishness, he realized that what in Holland was called increasing unruliness of the natives was actually the awakening of the native population. Had not Holland wished, or claimed to wish, this awakening when in 1900 the so-called 'ethical policy' was begun?

But governors-general, and especially the progressive ones, had very little say in the matter. The real government of the Dutch East Indies were the ministers in The Hague, and what stood behind them were the colonial capitalists, the planters, the steamship companies, the tin and oil companies, and, above all, the sugar barons, men like the directors of the Niederländischen Handel Mij who were wont to say that they 'could look after the natives', but who, during the serious rice famine in 1918, wrecked the plans for a diminution in the sugar plantations in favour of rice. Naturally, out of sheer goodheartedness, for when the war was over, there would be a great demand for sugar! But 600,000 of the starving Indonesians died during the influenza epidemic.

In the end the Dutch government in Indonesia reacted just as stupidly and unimaginatively as did the government of British India. In the true Dutch manner it tried to check the progress of nationalism and turn it aside, instead of welcoming it as a fructifying agent. The only official change was the creation of a People's Council (May 18, 1918), a sham parliament with no right of decision, not even in internal affairs. In addition to a president nominated by the crown, the assembly had thirty members – fifteen Indonesians (10 elected, 5 nominated) and 23 Europeans and non-Indonesian Asians (9 elected and 14 nominated). In 1920 the figures were changed to lessen the percentage of elected Indonesians.

What Holland did when faced with the awakening of one of the greatest peoples of Asia was extremely little compared to what, in the opinion of ever-growing numbers of Dutchmen, had become a bitter necessity and compared to what moderate nationalists thought could be demanded. When we look back, we can see that the 1914–1918 War was a not unimportant stage in the advance to freedom, a freedom which did not fall like a ripe fruit into the lap of Indonesia.

During the First World War Indochina was modernized in lesser degree than Thailand, India-Pakistan and Indonesia, although here, too, we can see the various phenomena that characterize the great turning-point in Asian history. In the first place, about 150,000 Annamites went as soldiers or labourers to France, from which, like the Siamese and all the other Asians and Africans, they came home full of new revolutionary ideas and experiences. A second shock to the country was the great demand for rubber during the war, which drew Indochina into the whirlpool of the world economy. The entire colony from Saigon to the Chinese frontier, an area six times the size of Java, was occupied by only 2000 French troops; France needed all her forces against Germany. The ideas of the Chinese and Russian revolutions began to penetrate the country, especially in the north which traditionally is a Chinese cultural domain. Because of these, the government in Paris, and the not inaccessible governor-general Sarraut (1911–1914 and 1917–1919), made attractive offers of rather more freedom once the war was over.

But, like London as regards India and Pakistan, Paris in 1919 suddenly seemed to have forgotten all that had been so generously promised, and as Chelmsford disappeared from British India in 1921 and as in Indonesia Limburg Stirum was replaced by a genuine colonialist overseer, Fock, so in 1920 France replaced Sarraut by the somewhat reactionary Maurice Long, who had little sympathy with the national movement, the less so as the French affection for the garden of the Pacific had become greater during the war. When the radical nationalist Nguyen Ai Quoc – of whom more later [1] – tried to represent the wishes of the natives at Versailles he achieved as little as did the Chinese, the Persians or the Egyptians. But the period of hesitant and emotional resistance was over and the period of conscious active resistance to French domination had begun. Neither the further policy of 'Frenchification' nor the weak tactics of doing things by half and making sham concessions in the years between the wars could in 1953 spare France the necessity to send out a great part of the French colonial army – 25 per cent of all French officers and 40 per cent of non-commissioned officers – in order to remain in occupation at least of some big towns and main roads.

Malaya, the rubber and oil paradise of the British Empire, between 1914 and 1919 carried through a genuine revolution, though in the economic sense, more than any other region. But consciousness of a national idea did not

[1] v. p. 240.

A.C.—5*

show itself, partly because the native Malays had not developed a high enough culture, partly because of the bitter hostility between Malays on the one side and Chinese, Indian and Arab immigrants on the other. In this period there was little consolidation or elucidation of the confused ideas of the British about what could really be called national wishes.

To conclude this section we must deal with the countries in the outer zone, Iran (Persia) and Afghanistan, the two mountain and steppe countries which in 1914 bordered in the west on Turkey, in the north on Russia and in the east on British India. During the war Persia proclaimed her neutrality, but it was an empty word. The country was much too weak to be able to maintain even an appearance of impartiality. The only troops available were a brigade of Cossacks under Russian officers – at least up to the Russian revolution – and a small gendarmerie officered by pro-German Swedes. In fact, the country was partitioned between the Russians in the north and the British on the Persian Gulf. Very remarkable was the activity of a series of German agents who arrived in 1915. We know their names – Wachmuss, the former German consul in Bushire, Niedermayer and Zugmayer. Their plan was to draw Persia into the war on the Turkish side and then advance through Afghanistan to what is now West Pakistan. In Berlin apparently it was believed that, if that happened, the native nationalists would at once drive the detested British into the sea, and that one of the richest colonial regions in the world would fall into German hands without a shot being fired. Regarded seriously, the scheme was a mere pipe-dream, a fact which did not prevent Hitler in the Second World War from sending agents to Iran with the particular mission of acting against the Russian oil of Baku. On both occasions it was the Russians who thwarted the German schemes. In November 1915 Russian troops occupied Teheran, and that was the end of German activity. In May 1916, when the British troops in Kut el-Amara had to surrender, the Turks tried to invade Persia, but were met on the frontiers by the Russians. Not until 1917 was the much enduring country given a respite; in March the Turks were beaten by the British at Bagdad and vanished from Persian soil. In November, after the revolution, the Russian troops likewise departed.

All this is of more than historic importance in so far as this encroachment by the foreigner fanned the fire of Persian nationalism. When in 1918 the British occupied the whole country, not now for fear of the Germans but for greater fear of the Bolsheviks, the Persians could do no more than endure it and bide their time.

The historian can see much if he looks to the sources. In 1919 the Persians sent a delegation to Versailles which demanded the renunciation of the Anglo-Russian partition treaty of 1917, the abolition of the capitulations and the military guards in the European consulates and the restoration of the Caucasus with Batum, a considerable part of the present Soviet republics of Turkmenistan, and of Mesopotamia east of the Euphrates, i.e. Mosul and Bagdad. One must admit that such demands do not say much for the Persian sense of reality, but the feelings of the Persians at that time could not have been more plainly revealed. The fact that on the advice of Britain the delegation was simply not recognized naturally aroused anger in Persia, the same sort of anger as the similar treatment of the Wafd aroused in Egypt. How such humiliations can eat into the heart of a nation was to be demonstrated later both in Iran and in Egypt.

In theory an independent state, actually a semi-colony of Britain, Afghanistan also remained neutral. The large subsidies to the amir Habibulla no doubt played a considerable part in the decision. The numerous German and Turkish agents achieved here no more than they did in Persia, although it is possible that the murder of the amir on February 19, 1919, was indirectly the result of their intrigues. It is characteristic of this period that the interim government of the conservative Nasrulla, Habibulla's successor, was in no position to make changes. None the less, even in Afghanistan the mediaeval system began to go to pieces. The amir Amanulla (1919–1929) chose a different path. He was so anti-British that he began his reign with an attack on Nearer India in the naïve expectation that the Indian nationalists would aid him in driving the British out of it. Naturally the attempt failed; it was none the less a sign of the times. How low must have sunk the power of European imperialism as a result of the war when an amir of Afghanistan could actually think of destroying British rule in India-Pakistan!

If we sum up the results for Asia of the period 1914-1919, we can lay it down that the widespread belief in the West, especially among the bourgeoisie, that the awakening of Asia is entirely or virtually entirely a consequence of the war, is a mistake and one as dangerous as it is tragic. Those who believed that Asia, once normal conditions were restored, would again relapse into slumber had to revise their opinion even before 1940. It is unfortunate that too few people in the West knew then what is common knowledge today, and not only among experts on Asia, that both world wars did no more than further and intensify a process which without war would have gone, perhaps less stormily but in any case, to its fulfilment.

It is futile in a historical study to pass adverse judgement on a definite country, a definite class, an entire cultural domain – in our case the West. It is probable, even certain, that nowhere in history will you find a nation, a class or a culture which voluntarily and against its own interests has given up a colony. No more easily will you find an instance of a government not so far as is possible concealing its baser intentions towards other peoples. These are not characteristic failures on the part of the West, nor are they proof of a total lack of a colonial policy. It would be neither scientific nor fair to demand of European civilization in these matters more than we demand from any other civilization, nor expect of it a higher standard of political morality. Yet it is a terrible thing for Europe and for Asia that in the West so few understood what was happening in Asia and the revolution that was going on in the hearts and heads of half the world's population. Covetousness by itself is a very uncertain basis on which to found foreign and colonial policies, but lack of comprehension and refusal to recognize reality are much more dangerous. That was proved in the First World War and will be even more obvious, as we shall see when we come to deal with the years between 1919 and 1955.

Third Period 1919 – 1941

REACTION AND ACTION

I

SOVIET ASIA

To the reader who has a taste for the magnificent and the romantic, for the history of peoples in a realm of endless plains and distances without horizons, the history of Northern Asia between the Black Sea and the Pacific, the region in which of old Gengis Khan created the astonishing empire of the Mongols, will be a fascinating object of study.

Soviet, or Russian, Asia, which has an area of over six million square miles – the area of the United States and Canada together or one and a half times that of China together with India – is equal in size to three-quarters of the entire Soviet Union and two-fifths of Asia. It can be divided from the cultural and geographical points of view into three regions: Siberia (pop. 8,000,000), Central Asia or Turkestan (pop. 16,600,000) and Transcaucasia (pop. 16,000,000).

The vast Siberian region, where at the time of the revolution of 1917 only Russians and Ukrainians lived, except for a very few Asians, was made part of the biggest state of the USSR, the Russian Socialist Federative Soviet Republic, whose core is European Russia.

Soviet Central Asia, known in the nineteenth century as Western Turkestan, is the country of the Turko-Tatar peoples and under Communist rule has been divided into a series of republics.

1. Kasakstan, the genuine steppe region between the lower Volga and Sinkiang and Mongolia; it is not much smaller than India (pop. in 1956 about 8,500,000 of whom 57 per cent are Kasaks and 35 per cent Russians and Ukrainians).

2. Usbekistan, the cotton-growing oasis region of the Amu Daria southeast of the Sea of Aral and as big as Germany or Japan (pop. in 1956 about 7,300,000, of whom 75 per cent are Usbeks and 5 per cent Russians).

3. Tadjikstan, in the highlands along the Chinese and Afghan frontiers (pop. about 1,800,000, of whom 78 per cent are Tadjiks and 18 per cent Usbeks).

4. Kirghizstan, between Kasakstan and Tadjikstan (pop. about 1,900,000 of whom 67 per cent are Kirghiz, 11 per cent Usbeks and 12 per cent Russians).

5. Turkmenistan, a land of sandy deserts and cotton fields on the Persian frontier (pop. about 1,500,000, of whom 72 per cent are Turkmans, 10 per cent Usbeks and 7 per cent Russians).

Transcaucasia, the region between the Caucasus and Turkey and Persia, contains today three Soviet republics: Georgia on the Black Sea (pop. in 1956 about 4,000,000), Azerbaidjan, the hinterland of Baku on the Caspian (pop. about 3,400,000) and Armenia (pop. about 3,400,000) on the frontier of Turkey. Only the inhabitants of Azerbaidjan belong culturally to the

Turko-Tatar region east of the Caspian. Both Georgia and Armenia have a quite different, a non-Moslem past.

Siberia in 1956 had a population of about 25,000,000, about the same as that of Soviet Central Asia together with Transcaucasia.

Although the First World War (1914–1918) and the Russian revolution (November 1917) mark the beginning of an entirely new epoch in modern history and in the relations between Europe and Asia, the relations between Russia and Asia have a very much longer history.

The military achievements of the Mongol mounted hordes are as well known as they are execrated. From the thirteenth to the fifteenth century they added China and almost the whole of the outer zone of Asia, as well as South Russia and Eastern Europe, to their steppe empire. Their shaggy little horses and their daring mounted archers appeared before Pekin and Delhi and before Bokhara, Samarkand, Bagdad, Constantinople, Kiev and Budapest. Only the forest region north of the grassy steppe escaped, relatively at least, the Mongol invasion. It was in its forests that the Grand Duchy of Moscow arose from which the first czar Ivan IV the Terrible, conquered Kazan on the Volga from the Tatars. With the westward expansion of the new state we have already dealt.[1] Here we can give only a sketch of the expansion to the east and south to Asia during four centuries during which the Tatar Cossacks from the Ukraine and the Northern Caucasus, even as Russian soldiers, maintained for long their savage independence (sixteenth and seventeenth centuries).

The Tatars of the Crimea stormed and looted Moscow in 1571, but the Russian capture of Kazan and of Astrakhan (1556) had opened to the Russians the road to Siberia. In 1582 Yarmak Timofevitch and 840 other Cossacks undertook an expedition for the Russian merchant house of the Stroganovs and took possession of the country between the Urals and the Irtish. This was the first of many expeditions into the less remunerative, but probably safer, forests of Northern Asia; the southern tree and grass steppeland, the region of the true Tatars, was not troubled by the Russians in the sixteenth and seventeenth centuries. In the middle of the seventeenth century (1637) Cossacks, fur trappers and peasants crossed Siberia and reached the Pacific (Bering Sea 1648; Okhotsk 1649; the lower Amur 1651). It is interesting to note that the Russians reached the Pacific before they reached the Black Sea or the Baltic, where Crimean Tatars, Turks and Swedes blocked their path. Azov fell in 1696; Petersburg, the Leningrad of today, was founded in 1703.

By the Treaty of Nerchinsk Peter the Great (1682–1725) recognized Chinese sovereignty over the Amur region – the first diplomatic contact between Russia and China – but none the less the Russians continued to press eastward. In 1697 Russian colonists reached Kamschatka, in 1711 the Kuriles, in 1780 the Aleutians and at the end of the eighteenth century had entered Alaska, where a man called Shelikov, 'the Russian Columbus', founded the first regular trading settlement. His plans for a Russian Pacific empire – Russian peasant farmers in California with a Russian naval base in Hawaii – seemed then quite possible of realization. In 1812 Ivan Kuskov built Fort

[1] v. p. 117.

Ross in California; it was also a farming colony. It was about 1820 that the Russian Empire reached its greatest expansion.

An imperial ukase in 1821 declared Oregon to be Russian territory and the Bering Sea an inland Russian sea. Scientific expeditions were sent to the Pacific and discovered some 400 hitherto unknown islands – names like the Lisianski islands, the Borodinos and Suvarov island witness to their achievements – while in 1825 Wrangel's expedition proved the existence of a sea passage between Siberia and North America. The first scientific description of the Papuan peoples of New Guinea is the work of a Russian traveller. But at this same period, the mid-nineteenth century, the British from Canada and the Americans from the east reached the Pacific. California was added to the United States in 1848 and Russian expansionism turned towards eastern and central Asia; in 1844 the Russians voluntarily relinquished California, and in 1867 all 'Russian America' including Alaska. The abandonment is understandable when one remembers that the British were pressing into Asia from the south (First Afghan War 1839–1842; Kashmir 1845; the Opium War and Hongkong 1842; the Anglo-French expedition to Petropavlovsk in Kamschatka 1854), while in the region between the Black Sea and the Caspian the Turkish Empire stood in the way of Russian conquest.

In 1849 the Russian captain Nevelskoi landed on the lower Amur, a region which was Chinese but in which very few Chinese lived. This was the beginning of the real Russian imperialism in the Far East. In 1855 Nevelskoi took the island of Sakhalin on which the Japanese had already settled; it became part of the Russian Empire in 1875. In the summer of 1860 the first modest wooden houses of Vladivostok were built, and on November 2nd the Chinese emperor in Pekin was compelled to recognize the new Sino-Russian frontier; it is virtually the same as today's. Chinese labourers meantime built the port and fortifications of Vladivostok. In 1880 its inhabitants consisted of 600 Russian civilians and 4000 soldiers, with about 4000 Chinese and Koreans.

As early as 1860 the Chinese had conceded certain trading rights in Tannu Tava and Mongolia, though trading in firearms and alcohol was forbidden. Nor was permanent settlement allowed; the Russians lived outside the towns in tents or boats. In 1881 – i.e. at the beginning of what we have called the golden age of modern imperialism, the period of the partition of Africa and Asia (1880–1919) – all these restrictions were removed.

To this period also belongs the conquest of Transcaucasia and Western Turkestan, which we deal with below, and the building of the Trans-Siberian railway (1891–1901), one of whose consequences was the migration of 6,500,000 Russians between 1895 and 1914; the Russo-Japanese War of 1904–1905,[1] as a result of which Port Arthur was lost to Japan – the Russians had taken it from the Chinese in 1898 – and of the southern half of Sakhalin (Treaty of Portsmouth, September 5, 1905); the Russo-Japanese compromise of 1907, by which Tokio recognized Outer Mongolia as an exclusively Russian sphere of influence; the Japanese occupation of Korea in 1910; and finally the annexation of Mongolia and Tannu Tava by Russia in 1912 and 1914.

[1] v. p. 52.

In the south the Russians between 1812 (Baku) and 1878 (Batum) occupied the Caucasian region between the Black Sea and the Caspian. The native population was partly Turkish and was possessed of an old and rich culture. It offered far more serious resistance than the sparse and primitive inhabitants of Siberia; of that resistance Tolstoy has told in his *Cossacks* (1852) and *Hadji Murad*.

In the second half of the nineteenth century Russia attacked Moslem Turkestan. Here again was a land with an old culture of its own. One need only recall the Arab period (seventh to twelfth century) and the Mongol (thirteenth to fifteenth century). At the beginning of the nineteenth century in what is today Kasakstan there dwelt the independent Kasaks of the grass steppes with their famous cavalry, while to the south there lay the then independent states of Bokhara and Khiva which went back to the sixteenth century. Here the Usbeks ruled. Their territory corresponded roughly to that of the four Soviet republics to the south of Kasakstan. Here virtually the only foreign visitors were British and Russian agents and spies.

These states with their Asian culture could no more than any other hold their own against a higher technical and economic culture which appeared in the guise of Russian soldiers. In 1720 the first Russian peasants came from their forests to the grass steppe of North Kasakstan to farm the land. In 1839 the first Russian fortified posts were built east of the Caspian. In 1847 the 'barbarians' reached the Sea of Aral and the rich valley of the Syr Daria, the gate to the heart of Bokhara. In June 1865 the Russian officer Chernichev took Tashkent with 1500 Cossacks, although it was defended house by house by 30,000 soldiers and many civilians. When in 1867 Alma Ata on the Chinese frontier and in 1868 the cities of Bokhara and Samarkand became Russian, that was the end of the old independence.

Via Krasnavodsk on the Caspian (1869), Khiva (1873), Fergana (1879) and Merv on the Persian frontier (1884), the troops of the czar reached between 1885 and 1895 the snowclad peaks of the Pamir highlands; there they were less than ten miles from the British troops in Southern Asia. Although Khiva and Bokhara were allowed to continue to exist as semi-independent states and were not annexed as the Kasak region was, that was so that there would be a diplomatic buffer state between Russian and British imperialism; from the military point of view Bokhara was as much Russian as Afghanistan was British. The Russians went no farther. The Anglo-Russian entente of 1907, by which[1] Persia was divided and Nicolas II recognized Afghanistan and Tibet as non-Russian spheres, confirmed the frontiers of 1900.

Petersburg secured and russified the new possessions by the building of railways, e.g. the line from the Caspian to Samarkand (1890) and the Orenburg-Tashkent line (1906). The obstinate resistance of the native peoples, especially in the great revolts in Ferghana (1886) and in Samarkand (1892), could not alter the situation.

Thus in this remarkable nineteenth century virtually the whole of Asia apart from Japan was brought under Western imperialist rule. But how tremendously Europe itself had changed in these years! Did not the Commu-

---

[1] *v.* p. 85.

nist Manifesto of Marx and Engels (1848) on a long view alter Asia as much
as it did Europe? Further the 'discovery' of rubber, of oil and electricity
(1840–1880), Monet's impressionism (1867), the beginning of modern art, the
work of Pasteur and Koch (c. 1880) – did they not, if we look back, have the
same significance for Asia as for Europe? There came to Asia Western technology and colonial exploitation; there also came the new ideas of freedom
and democracy. Neither customs-barriers nor oceans could keep them out.

In the years before 1917 the Asian inhabitants of the Russian Empire were
much less governed from above than were the native subjects of the West in
Asia and Africa. Transcaucasia and Turkestan were, however, nothing else
but colonies. And as in other eastern lands – particularly in Egypt, Turkey,
India and China – so in Russian Central Asia a freedom movement had
already developed among the bourgeois and the intellectuals (e.g. the half-
secret Shura Islamia in Usbekistan), when in August 1914 the Russian Empire was involved in a European war.

How general was the feeling against Russian domination was seen in June
1916 when the Government proclaimed its intention to apply military con-
scription to the 24,250,000 inhabitants of Central Asia, and that at harvest
time. A fierce guerrilla war was the result; it lasted four months and cost the
Kirghiz and the Kasaks a loss of 150,000 lives.

In March 1917 the Moslem bourgeoisie was solidly behind the new government in Petrograd. From the pan-Islamic congress of Kokand in November
there arose the 'autonomous republic of Turkestan'. When the Bolshevik
November revolution reached the Asian parts of the empire, independent
bourgeois governments were installed in Transcaucasia. In contrast to what
took place in Turkey and China these republics were but houses of cards
which went down in the storm of revolution, civil war and foreign intervention.

In December 1919 Kolchak's white forces in Central Asia surrendered; in
April 1920 the Red Army occupied Baku and in 1920–1 Caucasia and North
Turkestan were divided into a number of semi-independent republics within
the Russian Empire. At the outset the Bolsheviks did not interfere in Khiva
and Bokhara. The arrest of the khan of Khiva and the expulsion of the emir
of Bokhara – he fled with his wives to Afghanistan in 1920 – were entirely
the work of native bourgeois revolutionaries à la Ataturk.

In consequence, however, of Enver Pasha's pan-Turkish intervention and
the activity of the 'Whites,' the Red Army in August 1922 occupied all
southern Turkestan and Khiva and Bokhara were incorporated into Soviet
Turkestan. Thus the whole of the Moslem Turko-Tatar area between the
Caspian and China remained part of Russia. The Communist government
declared, though not entirely voluntarily, various parts of the former imperial
territory to be independent (Finland, Poland and the Baltic States); it also
gave active help to Asian freedom movements outside its borders (in Turkey
and in China) and denounced Western imperialism and the old Russian imperialism as 'the plague of Asia'. That was partly a tactical move, but behind
it there was comprehension of what was happening in the captive countries
of Asia. Lenin, the leader and theoretician of the October revolution, had

studied imperialism in Asia long before 1917 and had characterized it as 'the latest phase of capitalism'.

The pan-Asian congress of Baku in September 1920, where some 2000 representatives of nearly all the countries of Asia discussed the question of liberating Asia from the West, is a milestone in the modern history of Asia even if one does regard the congress as only a Russian move in the international political game. Three periods in the history of the Soviet Union can be distinguished between the October revolution and the German invasion of 1941. The first is the period (1917–1927) of the civil war, of economic and social experiments and of internationalism, the period of the distribution of the landed estates and of the new economic policy (NEP 1923–1927). This was the period of 'the storm over Asia'. In 1925 the various republics and autonomous regions had their frontiers fixed. Stalin was then Commissar for Nationalities. The second period (1928–1934) saw the completion of the revolution, the beginning of the five-year plans, the collectivization of agriculture and the isolation of the Soviet Union behind a Russian version of the Great Wall of China, the decline of the Communist International and a general revision of foreign policy after the failure of the revolution in Europe (Germany, Hungary) and especially after the Chinese Thermidor of 1927. This was the period of 'socialism in one country'. In the third period (1935–1941) Russian policy was determined by the increasing threat from Germany and Japan. So far as foreign countries were concerned, it was seen in the Russian campaign for the principle of collective security in the form in which Litvinov advocated it in Geneva, i.e. the combination of the Soviet Union with the 'bourgeois democracies' in an effort to meet the fascist danger. As far as Asia was concerned, that meant the recognition of Chiang Kai-shek's regime in China.

Internally the economic and cultural level of Siberia and Central Asia was steadily raised as a measure of preservation for Russia, in case the industrial and agricultural regions of the west should be occupied by an enemy. Several frontier areas with Asian populations became 'independent republics of the USSR', i.e. the three Caucasian republics, Kasakstan, and Kirghizstan. Usbekistan and Turkmenistan had been republics since 1924, Tadjikstan since 1929. At the same time for reasons of security many Korean rice-farmers were deported from the far east of Siberia to Usbekistan and settled there; in 1936–9 there were several frontier 'incidents' between the Japanese Kwantung army and the Red Army. In the bloody 'purges' of 1936–8 throughout the entire Soviet Union many people in the Asian parts of Russia were arrested as Japanese spies, Trotskyists, Bukharinists and bourgeois nationalists; it is probable that most of these last were only asking for more freedom for the Asian peoples of the Soviet Union.

By the division of the Asian population into various republics and autonomous regions, the Bolsheviks' aim was to lessen the natural resistance of many of them to any Russian encroachment. In czarist days there had been general russification; under Soviet rule the Asians in Russia retained their own language and culture. But the old historic kingdoms had been divided up and the development of pan-Islamic and pan-Turkish leanings made more difficult. The process occasionally met with considerable resistance, even from those natives who were Communists.

Essentially the revolution in Russia was a *Russian* and not an Asian revolution. The Communist party was essentially one of Russian workers and' intellectuals with a Western outlook; there was no Asian peasant party like the Chinese one between 1927 and 1949. The Asians in the Soviet Union remained a very small minority of from 10 to 15 per cent, of which two-thirds were Turko-Tatars; in Siberia they were not 5 per cent – Yakuts, Buryat Mongols, etc. When the great crisis of the revolution had passed – in 1927 Trotsky was banished and at the same time the country reached the economic level of 1914 – the Communist party under its iron leader Stalin devoted itself to the consolidation and security of the revolution in the shortest possible time. As in a fairy tale, a very bloody one, a semi-mediaeval kingdom was transformed into the modern USSR. The Asian element did not lag behind the European. Agriculture was mechanized; the villages got electricity. Where before the revolution there was only mountains, forest and steppe, there were now factories, blast furnaces, new fields of grain and cotton. All that demanded of the population a tremendous effort, on the part of the Russians as well as the Asians. The freedoms that are part of Western democracy, like freedom of the press, freedom of speech and freedom to strike, were limited to the point of extinction. Numberless people, possibly millions, were sent to labour camps as criminals and saboteurs, many of whom are described in the Russian literature of the Stalin period as 'creatures beneath contempt'.

The spectre of the fascist danger, which many people in Europe and America thought to be a creation of Communist imagination, had by 1933 become only too real. If the Russian Government had not modernized the country with such ferocious energy it would in 1941, if not earlier, have been divided between Germany and Japan.

This threat from abroad throws considerable light on the modest character of Russian expansion in North China. Tannu Tava, the independent Mongol-Buddhist mountain land in northwest Mongolia, was economically and culturally part of Russia by 1929. In 1941 the Russian alphabet was introduced; in 1941–5 500,000 horses and cattle were transported to Siberia and in October 1944 it became (of its own accord?) an autonomous region of the Russian Socialist Federative Soviet Republic. It then had a population of 100,000, mostly cattle-raisers.

Chinese Sinkiang to the north of Tibet (pop. 4,000,000 Usbeks, Kasaks and Chinese) became as a result of the local revolution (1932) of Sheng Chi-sai economically and militarily semi-Russian (1932–1943). As for Outer Mongolia, when the Japanese in 1933 occupied all Mongolia and reached the frontier of Outer Mongolia, the country hesitated between Moscow and the Chinese – really a Japanese – government in Nanking. In 1937 some Mongolian ministers 'disappeared' on a journey to Moscow and the pro-Russian Marshal Choibalsan (1895–1952), the 'Mongolian Stalin', became prime minister and commander-in-chief. He brought in the Red Army, and that alone prevented the occupation of his state by the Japanese. Its territory was violated before 1941 at the time of the secret war of the Kwantung army on the Amur and the Mongolian frontier (May to August 1939), a war which was described in the international press as a series of 'frontier incidents' in which about 100,000 Japanese troops were none the less employed.

How and to what degree did the Russian revolution show its influence on the Asian regions of Russia? The modernization of Siberia and Central Asia meant:

1. A steady stream of Russians and Ukrainians into many technical and scientific posts. Although the revolution and the civil war had deprived Russia of no small number of its intellectuals, the new regime sent many technicians and revolutionaries into the Asian regions while many others, from peasants to skilled engineers, were banished to Siberia. As early as 1914 the population of Siberia was 85 per cent Russian and that of Kasakstan nearly 40 per cent, and between 1927 and 1939 a further 5,000,000 Russians and Ukrainians went to the Asian districts, two-fifths of them to the Moslem republics. Between 1941 and 1945, the period of the German occupation of western Russia and the Ukraine, more than 4,000,000 non-Asians settled east of the Urals-Caspian line. The Asians in Siberia are thus a dwindling minority; in Kasakstan just under 49 per cent and in Kirghizstan 20 per cent of the population is non-Asian. The situation is entirely different from that in India, Indonesia or Indochina where it is the Europeans who are in a great minority.

The high percentage of non-Asians in Russian Asia naturally affects the 'independence' of these areas, the more so as Russians as a rule fill the higher posts, even if that is not always the case. Certainly it is not a matter of principle, for there also live here many Russian peasants and workers. But to take one example: of the technicians employed on agricultural machines in Kasakstan in 1938, only a fourth to a third were Kasaks. Intermarriage – which is common here, since Russia has neither race nor 'colour' problems – lessens the difference between Russians and Asians, while the 'un-colonial' ideas of the revolution as compared with the ideas before it, imply a fundamental change. Notices like 'Asians forbidden', which are not at all unusual in other colonial regions, or the ban of marriage between white and non-white (as in South Africa and parts of the United States), are not known in the Soviet Union.

2. Modernization of agriculture. The new USSR had too few factories and too few workers. Russia and the Asian parts of the empire were almost entirely agricultural in character. The mechanization and collectivization of agriculture, i.e. the concentration of many small peasant holdings into kolkhozes of on an average 1000 acres, was in principle a scientific method of getting more produce from fewer peasants, which in turn meant more factory workers. But it made the peasant less free. The resistance to the 'second agrarian revolution' of 1927–1933, especially on the part of the more prosperous peasants, was mercilessly suppressed alike in the European and Asian parts of the country. In the winter of 1929 roughly 500,000 peasants with their families were banished to Siberia. In Kasakstan, with its wide grass steppes and its wild horses, the romantic symbol of the freedom of the men

of the steppes, it was a time of terror, famine and chaos in which it is reckoned 100,000 to 200,000 Kasaks fled into Chinese Sinkiang.

The Government realized it had gone too far, for in this period the number of cattle and sheep had fallen by half. It therefore permitted the cattle-raisers in the collectives to have as private property from eight to ten cows, a hundred sheep, eight to ten horses and three to four camels. The peasants who farmed the land could have two to three cows, ten to twenty sheep and ten to twenty pigs. The Bolsheviks, however, generally speaking, were able to carry out their agrarian plans, even if the peasants remained a burning problem for the national economy.

Farm land increased in Soviet Asia from 34,000,000 acres in 1914 to 65,500,000 acres in 1938 and to about 75,000,000 in 1954. Many new canals in Kasakstan, Usbekistan, Turkmenistan and other republics brought water to rice, grain and cotton fields. In 1937 about 9,000,000 acres were irrigated and today about double that figure are, the Ferghana canal (185 miles long; built in 1939) is widely known abroad. In Usbekistan alone about 220 miles of canals were dug. Small republics like Turkmenistan and Kirghizstan by 1940 possessed about 4000 tractors, i.e. one to every 500 acres of plough land, which is nearer the European level than in any other Asian country.

3. Extension of the transport system as the basis of modern economic and cultural modernization. The classic example of this is the construction of the railway from Turkestan to Siberia, the so-called Turksib (just over 900 miles long; built in 1927–30); it was the first modern link between Siberia with its wealth of coal and corn and the treeless cotton areas in the south.

Although the Central Asian republics have, as we have said, no important deposits of coal and iron and the industrial regions of the USSR are elsewhere – on the Upper Volga, in the Dnieper and Don regions of the Ukraine, in the Ural and in the Kusnezk districts between the Upper Ob and the Upper Yenisei – Russian Central Asia is not simply a purely agricultural region which produces virtually all the Russian cotton. Remember the oilwells of Baku in Caucasia, in the Emba district and Nebit Dag north and southeast of the Caspian; the coalfields of Karaganda and the copper-smelting works of Lake Balcha in Kasakstan, which are the biggest in both Asia and Europe; the many calico factories in Tashkent, Fergana and Stalinabad; the factories for artificial manure, farm machinery and tractors in Tashkent and Akmolinsk. All that naturally made for closer ties with the Russian economy. But at the present time, when agriculture has become an industry, are not factories, tractors and artificial manures the only basis of which we know for raising the standard of living of a peasant population?

We need not here go into detail on the romantic conquest and modernization of Siberia, the latter of which was in part the achievement of prisoners from the concentration camps. Although in the geographical sense part of Asia, it has very few Asian inhabitants. It is, however, interesting to note how the primitive herdsmen have got books, films and modern health services; how biologists and engineers have pushed forward the northern edge of agriculture farther into the frozen regions of the north as far as the frozen sea; how meteorologists, port workers and seamen have settled here and grown vegetables in hothouses while on their mission to make safe the strategic sea passage – from the economic point of view the project is a sensible one – through the fogs and icy temperatures of the north. This northeast passage between Europe and East Asia was as early as the sixteenth century a European mariner's dream! Dutchmen will recall the terrible winter stay of Heemskerk and Barentz on Novaya Zemlya. The Swede Nordenskjöld in 1878–9 took two summers and a winter to make the dream come true. But freight-carrying on any significant scale only began after the voyages of the former Scottish whaler the *Siberiakov*, which in 1932 was the first ship to sail from Archangelsk to the Bering Sea in a single summer and of the Russian-built icebreaker *J. Stalin* which in the summer of 1939 sailed there and back, a distance of 3750 miles.

Despite the restrictions on freedom to speak and to criticize, despite the merely nominal independence of the Asian Soviet republics, the revolution in Central Asia and Caucasia did raise the cultural and economic level of their peoples higher than it is in any other part of Asia, including Japan. The peasants of Indonesia, Egypt, Arabia, China and India-Pakistan in 1940 did not possess tractors, harvesters, artificial manure factories and medical and health centres in numbers comparable to those in Russian Asia.

4. An end was put to illiteracy. Where else in Asia was that the case? How far more backward were the Moslems in the Arab countries just a short time ago! In 1914 only 1 – 2 per cent of the population of Turkestan could read and write; in 1940 75 per cent could and in 1945 nearly 100 per cent. Even in Outer Mongolia, which lies outside the actual boundaries of the USSR, the Russian cultural revolution had had effect. In 1950, according to British and American reports, 80 per cent of the population could read and write against only about 1 per cent in 1924.

In 1914 there was not a single newspaper in Turkestan in a native language; in 1940 there was in nearly all the villages newspapers in the local languages. In the Soviet Union today newspapers appear in eighty different languages, reviews in fifty. A relatively small republic like Kasakstan has 4000 libraries, many of which are travelling ones. In a district like Yakutia, the autonomous socialist soviet republic in Eastern Siberia, 3000 books in the native language have been published between the October revolution and the present day.

As for medicine and health, Kasakstan has a doctor for every 2500 to 3000 inhabitants and about half of these are Asians. A relatively small mountain republic like Tadjikstan has 900 doctors today as compared with about twenty in 1925, that is, one to every 2000 inhabitants, a proportion roughly equal to that in Western countries.

But the spectre of general russification still haunts the Asian republics. The Asians will continue to be a small minority in the USSR; their language areas are quite small. Russian, 'the speech of Lenin and Stalin', is the medium of communication in the economic life, in technology and in science. In its Asian cultural policy the Kremlin after 1937 tried in some ways to distort the past of the various peoples of the Soviet Union, to put Peter the Great in the place of Gengis Khan and Moscow in the place of Mecca. This 'covert' russification is reflected in the language, script and alphabets of the Asian peoples and thus in their speech. An interesting example, if perhaps an extreme case, is that of the native newspapers in Yakutia in which a third of the words are Russian. This phenomenon, if it happens quite naturally when areas of various cultures tend to assimilate, is much less evident in the states of Southern Turkestan whose Asianism is much purer. As regards writing, the changes in the non-Russian areas are not uniform. At the outset (1924–1935) the Bolshevik government introduced the Latin script in all their Asian districts on the other side of the Caucasus, just as Ataturk did in the new Turkey; that script is international, whereas the Arabic, say in Turkestan, is an over-strong reminiscence of the Islamic past. But since 1939–40 everywhere east of the Caspian, the Russian (cyrillic) script of Moscow has been substituted for the Latin; even Outer Mongolia and Tannu Tava have not escaped.

How far are such proceedings, how far is the constant assimilation of the Asian districts, offensive to the Asians living in them? To what degree does the feeling in Armenia differ from that in Usbekistan? How do the students from Samarkand and Tashkent think differently from the workers in the oil-fields of Baku? We do not know enough, and the reserve of the Russian Government makes for the moment a really scientific and frank answer impossible.

Was the resistance of the herdsmen of Kasakstan in 1930–2 an example of Asian nationalism or did it in no way differ from the resistance of the rich peasants in Russia itself? Did many Tatar intellectuals fight in 1926–7 against the latinizing of their script *as Asians*? During the campaign for the emancipation of women in Usbekistan in 1927–8 hundreds of 'emancipated' women and girls were murdered by 'reactionaries'. Was that a case of Islamic nationalism or was it merely the resistance of mediaeval peasants to change? Did the Usbek minister, who some time ago wanted to further the growing of grain at the expense of cotton, want *as an Asian* the increasing independence of his country of the *Russian* grainfields of Siberia? That at least is the explanation an expert, but perhaps a rather pessimistic, writer W. Kolarz gives in his book (pub. 1952) *Russia and her Colonies*. Again, others say: Have such unimportant things which are made a reproach to the Soviet government much sense when against them is put the gigantic achievement in these lands of the revolution? The interesting notes of the few foreigners who have travelled in modern Soviet Asia usually leave unanswered the question: Are the Asian republics free states or are they Russian colonies? The peasants and workers there are materially much better off than their counterparts in the rest of Asia. But are they independent and how far do they want to be independent? The coming of the socialist revolution, of new and foreign ideas and techniques, naturally are not incompatible with an eventual Russian imperialism. The penetration by Russians, even if they are revolutionary Russians, the entire assimilation of regions like Turkestan to the economy and culture of the USSR, have in a sense to be considered as colonial. But the emancipation of women, tractor factories, hygienic houses for the peasant and other things may not be in the least romantic but they are the coveted signs of modern civilization; even by 1940 Soviet Asia was very different from the other countries of Asia, the free and the non-free alike.

Further, did not the socialist experiment in the Soviet Union, the mechaniz- ing and restoration of a semi-colonial empire beyond the boundaries of Western capitalism, act as a model for all Asia? Of all the Western govern- ments, only the Russian does not treat its Asians as 'natives'. They are just as free and as unfree as the Russians themselves. It is not the aim of this book to give the reader an appreciation of the Russian revolution and its effect on the Asian districts. But the enormous historical significance of what was begun in distant Petersburg is beyond any doubt at all. The revolutions of today in China, Korea and Indochina may differ much from one another but they are all consequences of the Russian revolution; to a considerable degree it has set its seal on the Asia of the future.

II

JAPAN

In this period the Soviet Union was the country in which there was most change, but it was Japan which, through its military and economic expansion, brought the greatest changes in the world. If one wishes to understand the world's history in the years between the wars and in particular the history of Asia – in our days it is not possible to separate them – then one must understand the Japanese aggression, its basis, its sources, its characteristics and, if possible, its peculiar character.

First and foremost, what was this aggression not? There are in circulation a whole series of legends and ideas which were reinforced during the Second World War. Thus Japanese expansion was not the result of inborn character, an unalterable Japanese national trait. The attractive but dangerous theory that certain peoples are by nature aggressive and others are not is seen as absurd if we treat history as a whole, and do not confine ourselves to the study of a restricted period. Every nation whose history we know has had periods of expansion and aggression, the Indonesians as much as the Danes, or the Mongols, or the Americans; the Russians as much as the Dutch, the Arabs, the Egyptians and the British.

Actually Japanese aggression is as hard to explain as is Japanese isolation in the previous centuries. The real causes and also the exact time and the reason for such changes are as a rule a mystery. As an agriculturist, without knowing the character and mystery of the growth of a plant, can still investigate how these plants react to heat, aridity, rain and manure, so the historian can study a country's reactions to different situations and at different times. He can try to comprehend why a country's internal structure alters, and how these changes affect its history. In the case of Japan we must ask what it was that induced Japan to march into foreign countries with her armies and her products.

Of the many and very different factors which influenced Japan in this century, and particularly in 1919–1941, we naturally can deal only with the most important and that rather summarily.

First, we should note the curious combination of feudal social structure with modern technology, an explosive combination as has often been demonstrated. What does the term feudal really mean in this connection or at least approximately? Feudalism and feudal are terms belonging to the Middle Ages of Europe. Broadly speaking, we can explain feudalism thus: In the eighth century, kings, and particularly the French kings, began to hand out to their nobles part of their estates as fiefs. In return the noble had to serve in the royal army and as a mounted man. In the next centuries the system developed far beyond its original conception and in the fourteenth century had gone so far in many regions that the kings were almost over-shadowed by the independent nobles, counts, dukes and barons in their strong castles. The noble had generally absolute power over the formerly free peasants and their possessions. For their own safety the peasants became soldiers of their lord of the castle and were more his subjects economically, legally and in every other sense than those of the king. It was only when the king made an alliance with the rising commercial and capitalist towns which opposed the nobility (mostly in the fourteenth and fifteenth centuries) that the countries of Western Europe became really national states and, as the fruit of the new capitalist mentality of the town bourgeoisie, the ideas began to ripen which we regard as the fundamental ideas of modern democracy.

If that was generally the course of events in most of the Western European countries, the development was not everywhere the same. In Germany, for instance – another puzzle of history – the feudal system remained, on the whole, intact. In the sixteenth and seventeenth centuries the German Empire contained 300 free cities and states which gave only nominal allegiance to the emperor. As late as the American revolution (1774–1783) many German princes could permit themselves to ship off their citizens as soldiers for the British. In agricultural Eastern Germany it was only after the Russian occupation in 1945 that the influence and power of the great feudal land-owners were broken, after they had for many centuries been a state within the state. Just as in Japan, the dangerous mixture of feudalism and modern technology played a part in modern German history – the alliance of the Prussian junker with the industrial barons of the Ruhr.

Outside Europe the feudal concept was applied after the end of the mediaeval period to many similar social systems, especially in Asia. Today it is used generally to describe a social structure in which a predominantly agricultural population is economically and politically ruled by a landed aristocracy whose status and rights are hallowed by tradition and are more or less treated as something quite natural.

In 1854, when isolated Japan first received the benefits of Western com-mercial and industrial capitalism, the land in its structure was still medi-aeval. It was a country without firearms and without factories; it was ruled by three hundred feudal lords held together for nearly three centuries by the shoguns of the Tokugawa family who, as far as the nation and the nobility were concerned, had usurped the functions of the emperor. Shogun origin-ally meant 'leader in battle'. In the Middle Ages, when the whole northern half of Japan was inhabited by the Ainus, the earlier inhabitants of the Japanese islands, the post of commander-in-chief against the Ainus was an important feudal one. But what was originally the purely military post of 'sai-i-tai shogun', i.e. general against the barbarians, grew into a political one; the shogunate, the office of first minister, is comparable to the office of the mayor of the palace in the early mediaeval Frankish Empire in Europe. About the twelfth century, the shoguns had acquired real power as com-pared to that of the emperor.

Now we must explain two terms which we cannot avoid using when we describe the rise of modern Japan, *Daimio* means great nobleman. Like the feudal baron in Europe, the *daimio* ruled his own domain and saw in the emperor his feudal lord. The *samurai* were the lesser nobility, the equivalent of the English gentry. They were often landowners likewise, but for the most part on a small scale, and militarily were under the *daimio*. A *samurai* who possessed no land got it from his *daimio* for his service in the field.

Like shoguns of other families before them, the Tokugawa shoguns had been appointed by the emperor, but their position became virtually permanent because of feudal wars. The rise of the Tokugawa family dates from the great battle of Sekigahara in 1600. The new Tokugawa political structure was solidly based; one might call it centralized feudalism. The fishing village of Yedo, which is now Tokio, was the new capital far away from the imperial capital Kioto. All feudal lords were compelled to swear loyalty to the shogun. Spies watched for plots and many *daimios'* wives and children lived near the shogun as hostages. Besides, the nobility was sharply divided into two classes. There was the old nobility which at Sekigahara had fought for the Tokugawa, and the newer nobility which had been defeated there. By the granting of all sort of privileges the old nobility was induced to watch carefully the former opposition.

About 1640 the isolation of Japan was complete. But that does not mean that there was no tension inside the country. Many members of the Tokugawa family and other adherents of the old nobility left the land for the towns, the *samurai* especially who had not much to do, and became the basis of a new feudal bourgeois merchant class. And what apparently was only an economic development, the germ of an early capitalism, was the cause just as in Europe of an internal social revolution. When metal money took the place of rice as a medium of exchange, that was simply the external sign that the ownership of land was no longer the only social criterion. The possession of money became as important as the possession of land and grain, as noble title and aristocratic birth. Social mixing, and even mixing by marriage, between the classes began to undermine the purely feudal structure of the country. But where the newer nobility was concerned, especially in the southwest of Japan, the old structure remained fairly intact; up to 1870 for instance the *samurai* were paid in rice.

If one sees the situation as one in which the landed nobility, and particularly the lower nobility in the southwest, the whole feudal and mediaeval thought and feeling and the whole feudal economy was being more and more threatened by the rise of capitalism, the events of the period between 1854 and 1868 can be more easily understood. When in 1854 the American squadron appeared, the whole country was already in a ferment. It was the landowners in the southwest, families like the Satsuma and the Choshu, whose attitude can be compared *mutatis mutandis* to that of the American plantation owners at the time of the Civil War, feudal landowners who were well content to use the threat from abroad for a revolution against the domination of the Tokugawa and for the maintenance of their own positions. Their peasants had muskets, while the army of the shogun had only *samurai* swords; the result could not be in doubt. When the emperor in 1868 resumed his throne it was evident that he had become emperor of a considerable part of the landed aristocracy. In 1871 all feudal fiefs reverted to the emperor, but the *daimios* remained masters of the land and fleeced the peasants as before. Thus, as the Tokugawa barons owned the factories and the commercial enterprises in modern Japan, so the great landowners of the south-west and their *samurai* were commanders and ministers of the army and the navy. National military service introduced in 1872 was on the one hand a defence against eventual peasant revolts, and on the other the foundation on which was built a dreaded state within the state.

The second great factor in Japan's modern history is agriculture. In Western Europe and in North America large-scale industry arose after the peasant generally, and in the United States especially, had been freed from mediaeval ties and mediaeval methods. In Japan, capitalism was grafted on a feudal land. Generally, capitalism has the tendency to regard agriculture as a branch of industry in which capital can be invested. Feudalism demands taxes and rent from the peasant but does not invest. In the Western countries agriculture is made to progress socially and economically as industry advances, but in Japan the landed nobility and the industrialists kept down the peasant as much as possible and apart from other classes in the community. 'Dangerous' elements – students, for instance, and city workers – were not permitted contact with the army, and the peasant girls who worked in the factories were in the period between the wars kept in barracks and supervised as if they were harem women. Nor is there much change unless strikes force it.

A country like the United States can at least at the outset base its big machine-production on a growing internal market. Countries like France, Britain and Holland had, in addition, their colonies. When Japan emerged in 1919 as a Great Power after the war, she had neither the one nor the other. Mediaeval small peasants do not constitute a market for large-scale industry and particularly when the ruling classes, because of well-founded fear of a revolution, keep the standard of living of the peasant as low as possible.

We shall encounter the peasant again when we deal with Japan's domestic history between 1919 and 1941. But before that we must mention two other things in our introduction to it.

Several Japanese governments sought to excuse their expansionist aspirations as due to the agonizing increase of population in their island realm. This argument has been vigorously attacked in certain Western circles. The increase in population was undoubtedly a fact. But two other facts are not mentioned. In the first place, there was the connection between increase of population on the one hand, and agrarian feudalism and lack of machines in agriculture on the other. A peasant economy which lacks machines means much toil and that, for the Japanese peasant as for peasant families everywhere, means many children. In the second place, in the Tokugawa period the number of children was kept within limits by abortion and child murder, a process called in the speech of the peasants *mabiki*, i.e. making thin. But when later there was a general desire for modern birth control, these very governments who put forward excess of population as an argument for their military undertakings, forbade any propaganda for limiting the number of children.

For the Japanese expansion these factors are important – the blending of a social structure that in character remained feudal with modern technology, the feudal unmechanized economy of the village, and thirdly the extraordinarily swift increase in population which, in the opinion of the average Japanese, understandably justified the conquest of regions beyond the frontier.

The three cannot be treated separately. They form a whole which is part of a definite historical situation. But there are still three other phenomena which explain expansionism. The feudal commanders of the Japanese army and navy between the wars constituted a state within the state, which was the more dangerous as there was no semblance of a democracy in Japan. But because of this feudal character and because of all their past history the imperial court and the military nobility were in a certain sense anti-capitalist. The importance of this lies in the fact that, because of this anti-capitalist mentality, a great part of the workers and peasants could be won for a policy of aggression. That such anti-capitalism was out of date, reactionary and anti-social, that it was not prepared to make real improvement in the lot of the peasant and that it was completely dominated by the capitalist munitions industry was seen in 1930, when the peasants and workers threatened to awaken. The answer of the military, as well as of the 'liberal' trusts, was the fascist dictatorship, the classic refuge of capitalism threatened by a crisis. The Japanese rulers, who could no longer endure to look at the witches' cauldron in their own country, turned their eyes to the Asian continent and to the rich islands of Indonesia and the Philippines and Hawaii.

Thus we come to the fifth factor. Japan had no colonies of any importance. In 1919 it possessed Sakhalin, Korea, Formosa and a series of Pacific islands but, compared to powers like Britain, France and Holland, that was relatively little. The solution arrived at by the United States, which had few official colonies but with the aid of dollar imperialism had economically and politically bound to itself great parts of Central and South America, was unthinkable for Japan. Like Germany and Italy, Japan began to think in terms of colonies only after most of the world had been divided up. Germany, for lack of valuable colonies, sought to acquire the iron-ore of Lorraine west of the Rhine (1870, 1914, 1940) and dreamed of a 'pan-German empire' in which there would curiously enough be included the Ukraine, not very German indeed, but rich in coal and iron. So, too, Mussolini's Italy dreamed of a restored Roman Mediterranean empire and for a while held North Africa which was there for the taking. Similarly the rulers of Japan looked enviously across to East Asia and the Pacific to the enormous market that China offered, to its cotton, its iron and coal, to the rubber of Malaya and to the tin, rubber and oil of Indonesia.

Besides – and this is the sixth factor – Japanese policy and Japanese mentality were anti-Western, with the result that for a time they found very fruitful soil for their propaganda in colonial and semi-colonial East Asia. At the same time, official Japan was anti-Russian and in general anti-socialist. The result here was that there was, on the one hand, a reluctance on the part of Western Europe and America to oppose Japanese expansion in Manchuria and in China proper and, on the other hand, there was a direct approach of the fascist powers to Japan, that is, those powers which had no colony to lose in Asia.

The definite tendency towards expansion and aggression against other states dates from 1926. From that year the history of the empire seems to take a new direction. During the First World War – we have already described Japan's rise to power at that time [1] – the working class doubled in number. Cities like Osaka (earlier a modest rice port), Nagoya and Kobe had become great manufacturing centres. Japanese engineers and technicians went to all the countries in the West, smiling commercial spies about whom incredible stories were told by the managers of Swiss motor factories and by the officials of the Indonesian agricultural experimental stations. Ever more did Japan make Western science and technology its own. Up to about 1920–1 the labour movement remained revolutionary as a result of the great increase in the price of rice, cotton and other commodities, of reports about the revolution in Russia, of the spirit of the age and the hesitating attitude of the Government to strike action. The Government may have had the situation well in hand in 1921, but the agitation for universal suffrage rose ever higher. In 1919 the number of voters had risen from 1,500,000 to 3,000,000; in March 1925 all Japanese had the vote, but not the women – they had to wait until 1946, and the number of voters rose in 1925 from 3,000,000 to 14,000,000 in a land with a population of 61,000,000. It can be said that as far as domestic policy was concerned, Japan was taking the quickest way to become a modern democracy, like Britain, for instance, but a rather more radical one; indeed, that was what caused the ruling classes such anxiety.

Foreign policy was at first rather uncertain. In 1919 Japan was more or less isolated. As once before, the powers tried to deprive it of the gains made in the war. Besides, the United States feared that for it the steadily rising sun of Japan could become too hot. At the naval conference in Washington (November 12, 1921, to February 6, 1922) America and Britain held back Japan as much as they could. And, just as the Treaty of Versailles dictated by France had sowed the seeds of the Second World War in Europe, so the Washington treaties became the cause of new wars in the Far East.

The Washington conference was concerned with the naval armaments of the Great Powers and with the problems of the Far East. In addition to the United States, Britain, France, Italy, Belgium, Holland, Portugal, China and Japan sent delegates. The Soviet Union, which was not recognized by the United States, was not invited. The results of the conference were: 1. the Pacific Treaty of December 13, 1921, between the United States, Britain, France and Japan, in which each recognized the others' possessions in the Pacific and in which, much to Japan's discontent, the Anglo-Japanese alliance was dissolved; 2. the Shantung Treaty of February 4, 1922, by which, against the will of Japan, the German port of Kiauchow on the Yellow

[1] v. p. 128.

Sea (captured by Japan in 1914) was restored to China; 3. two nine-power treaties of February 6 in which the territory and political independence of China were recognized. That meant that all the powers could be economically active in China but that none should hold a monopoly in certain areas. This was an American idea, since America thought that, with the most modern production mechanism in the world, it could outdo the colonial methods of Europe and Japan; 4. and, the worst of all for Japan, there was the naval treaty of February 6th which established the following ratio for capital ships of the four powers, $5:5:3:1\cdot67:1\cdot67$, which meant that Britain and the United States would have 525,000 tons each, Japan 315,000 tons and France and Italy each 175,000 tons. The aim was again to curb Japan. Japanese pride was further wounded by the new American immigration law of 1924 whereby the migration of Japanese to the United States was in principle forbidden.

The consequences were soon seen. There were great demonstrations against America and for a boycott of American goods; in foreign policy there was a tendency to pursue a milder course towards China and the Soviet Union. A notable example of that is the Russo-Japanese compromise of 1925 in which diplomatic relations were restored. Russia recognized the 1905 Treaty of Portsmouth, Japan withdrew its troops from North Sakhalin, and in compensation received there oil and coal concessions.

These things were no doubt oil on the stormy waves of Japanese imperialism, but their calming effect was very slight. In 1926 there came a sudden and fierce reaction. Japan prepared to drive Western imperialism from Asia and put Japanese imperialism in its place. Siberia and no less Southeast Asia were dangerous objectives, and so divided and nearby China seemed suitable prey, the more so as there was need for haste. On March 24, 1927, the army of the then revolutionary Kuo Min-tang under Chiang Kai-shek entered Nanking and China seemed once again to be a united country. If that happened, Japan's hopes were ruined. The result of this situation was the 'positive', i.e. anti-Chinese, policy of Baron Tanaka, the leader of Japan's extreme conservative party, the Seijukai, who became prime minister on April 17, 1927. In May Japanese officers appeared in Shantung and sought to prevent the Chinese Nationalists from occupying Pekin. In April 1928, before Pekin fell into the hands of the Nationalists, the Japanese navy intervened. There was bloody fighting at Tsinan and most of the railways in Shantung were seized by the Japanese. But the vigorous boycott action by the Chinese was too threatening and in May 1929 the invaders withdrew to await a more favourable opportunity.

Tanaka was already notorious as the alleged author of a secret report to the emperor, the so-called Tanaka memorandum (1927), which became known in 1929 and in which it was laid down that the occupation of China was only possible if Manchuria and Mongolia were conquered, and that the occupation of China was an essential condition for the conquest of Asia. The genuineness of this document is contested, but it is undoubted that from 1927 to 1941 Japan followed broadly the policy laid down in it.

But the greatest economic crisis which history knows, the result of a

A.C.—6

collapse on Wall Street on October 29, 1929, caused a greater sensation. Japan, or at least the Japanese capitalists, in a sense richly profited. When in September 1931 Britain, which had been badly hit, devalued the pound, Japan devalued the yen a little more, and so drove Britain and other Western countries from many markets. Japanese goods flooded the world, and not merely the colonial and backward countries; they got to London, Paris and New York. The other industrial countries took measures to restrict imports and accused Japan of having no social legislation and practising wage slavery so that its goods could be sold at only a fraction of what the Western countries needed to charge. There was truth in the accusation, for the Japanese workers in the blast furnaces, and the ports, and the girls in the cotton mills worked for wages which were unthinkable in the West even in times of extreme crisis. For instance, in the average cotton mill the managers and the workers together earned what in a similar factory in Indonesia the managers only were paid. What happened to the immense sums which came to Japan from the mass of exports? Where else but to the war industry? The number of workers in the metal and machine factories and in the chemical industry, which were increasingly war industries, rose between 1931 and 1937 from 385,000 to 1,235,000.

The misery of the Japanese factory workers, 40–50 per cent of them women and children, was certainly terrible enough, but the misery of the peasantry is indescribable. Roughly 15 per cent of the land in Japan proper was under cultivation and it did not seem possible to put any more. On the roughly 15,000,000 acres of Japanese fields and gardens, 5,500,000 peasant families lived, i.e. 55 per cent of the whole population. In the period with which we are dealing, exactly 50 per cent paid rent and roughly 30–35 per cent owned their farms. Peasant farms were very small, 50 per cent of them under two and a half acres, 0·5 per cent under an acre and scarcely 10 per cent over five acres.

Japanese statistics distorts the difference between peasants and landlords. It was estimated none the less that the number of landlords who did not cultivate their own land was about 1,000,000. The landlords, the manufacturers of artificial manures, the money-lenders and the State squeezed the peasants like a lemon. A rent of 50–60 per cent of the harvest was the normal thing. Besides, the rent was reckoned in kind not as a percentage of the harvest, but as a fixed amount, a system of which Europe had rid itself in the Middle Ages. Only Asian and African peoples could really understand the situation of the average Japanese peasant. Travellers from the West in the forests of Japan noticed that the trees had no bark. Here was a puzzle, but the solution was barbarically simple. The peasants in the district stripped the trees to have something to eat. The stories of the sale of peasant girls are not fairy tales. Examples of such a traffic can be found in the many books dealing with it, and the numbers and prices involved. In the four northern districts in January to October 1934 some 50,000 girls were sold at prices ranging from 2300 yen for a geisha to five yen for a factory worker.

Japanese agriculture, the entirely rotten basis of Japanese industry, had naturally a very small production as compared with the West. The 14,000,000 peasants produced in 1930 less than did 2,000,000 British farmers, and at that time British agriculture was in no good way. Still more striking is the fact that, while in Holland there were 250,000 peasant and market gardeners as compared to Japan's 14,000,000, the Dutch production was equivalent to two-thirds of the Japanese. The Japanese family on rented land had a monthly income of barely thirteen yen, the value of 100 loaves, twelve gallons of milk and possibly seventy-five eggs.

Once all that has been grasped, one will better understand our view that Japanese aggression was in its way a flight from the problem of that starving desperate peasantry and the awakening working class. Seen in this light, no wonder the ruling class in Japan prohibited the study of sociology in the universities.

In 1930 the time seemed ripe for the Japanese offensive. On the one hand China seemed to be more soundly established than before; the whole land, as well as the majority of the powers, recognized the national government in Nanking; on the other hand, the Western Great Powers were involved in the great economic crisis. The Japanese army was ready. 'Incidents' arose of themselves; on June 27, 1931, a Japanese officer called Nakamura, who was really a spy, was killed by Chinese soldiers in western Manchuria, 'executed' it might be said. In mid-August an official report on the incident was published in Japan, the obvious purpose of which was to rouse public opinion against the Chinese. Everything now went according to plan. In the night of September 18th–19th the Kwantung army was holding night manoeuvres near Mukden; somewhere there was an explosion on a railway line. This was the second 'incident'. Before dawn Mukden and other towns had been occupied. With the fall of Harbin in February 1932, Manchuria became a Japanese colony. To meet all contingencies 70,000 Japanese troops landed at Shanghai and the brand-new colony was now called Manchukuo and declared independent (February 18, 1932). In 1934 Pu-i was formally proclaimed emperor of Manchukuo, the Pu-i who had been driven as a lad from the throne of China (1912). His Japanese 'advisers' held the reins of government.

During its campaigns in China the Western countries put no obstacle of any kind in Japan's way. On the one hand, London, Paris and Washington had their hands tied by the crisis and by troubles in Europe; on the other there was a general belief that Japanese aggression in China and eventually in Siberia was less dangerous, even more pleasant, than an attack on one of the European or American colonies in Southeast Asia. The policy was no different from that which Western diplomacy followed towards Nazi Germany. The only result of a paper protest by the League of Nations was that Japan withdrew from it (May 27, 1933). At the same time the Japanese occupied another Chinese province, Jehol, north of the Great Wall some sixty miles from Pekin. In 1935 they occupied Chahar, the province between Jehol and the southeastern frontier of Mongolia.

A considerable part of the Japanese people seemed, at least at this time, to be against the Government's war policy. At the election of 1936 (February 20th) the moderate liberal party, the Minseito, got a majority. The answer of the reactionaries was the notorious military *putsch* of the 26th, when several ministers were murdered. The Government drew the correct conclusions, and shortly after, Japan began more and more to be a totalitarian state. The prospects were darker; to use a Japanese metaphor, Fujiyama began to smoke.

To show its independence of Britain and America, Japan in November 1936 signed the anti-Comintern pact drawn up in Berlin, which was later (1937) signed also by Italy and (1939) by Hungary, Spain and Manchukuo. Ostensibly the pact was directed solely against the Third International; actually it was a weapon against the Soviet Union and also against China and all the Western countries not belonging to the fascist bloc. As one thing followed another in mad succession, the political fronts of the Second World War began to take shape. In Europe the curtain-raiser to another great war began with the reoccupation (March 7, 1936) of the Rhineland which the Treaty of Versailles had demilitarized, Mussolini's unhindered invasion of Ethiopia (October 3, 1935 – May 5, 1939) and, especially, the civil war in Spain (July 18, 1936 – April 1939) in which the Western democracies followed their non-intervention policy and the German and Italian legionaries killed the young Spanish republic.

In East Asia we may say the same new world war began on the night of July 7, 1937, at the Marco Polo Bridge at Pekin.[1] It was the signal for the great Japanese offensive against China proper; apart from the two world wars it is the greatest war in history.

In March 1938 the sham parliament in Japan passed the law for economic mobilization; the entire production, import and export, shipping, everything, was placed under the direct control of the Army and the Navy. In every sphere conditions worsened and Japan became more and more a police state; workers, and even nurses who worked a twelve-hour day, were arrested if they demanded higher pay. The press and the universities were completely under police censorship. Anyone who protested against the policy of the Government disappeared into the prisons of the secret police.

When the fascist abscess burst in Europe in September 1939 and the Second World War broke out with the invasion of Poland by the Germans, Tokio felt the hour had come to realize its dream. On April 13, 1941, when the Germans had occupied three-quarters of Europe, Japan signed the Russo-Japanese Treaty of Neutrality, which was a protection for their rear when they struck southwards. The Soviet Union could not do anything else but sign, for it realized that by this time the Russo-German Treaty of August 23, 1939, was a thing of the past. On June 22, 1941, the German army invaded Russia on a front of over 1600 miles. On September 29th the Japanese premier, Hideki Tojo, who was to be hanged as a war criminal in the winter of 1948, declared that an end must be put to the influence of the British and Americans in East Asia. On December 2nd, Roosevelt learned

[1] *v.* p. 222.

of the Japanese aims in Indochina. While discussions were going on, the Japanese fleet put to sea and early in the morning of December 7th the bombs fell on the American naval base at Pearl Harbour. At the same time Japanese ships and aeroplanes attacked Guam, Midway, Wake, the Philippines, Hongkong and Malaya. Asia was on the march; the West was tottering. The Second World War had reached Asia and the Pacific.

III

TURKEY

We have already seen how in the First World War the great Turkish Empire with its many peoples fell to pieces and how a new smaller but national state was all that remained. In 1919 the only minorities in Turkey of any importance were Greeks, mainly in the west, and Kurds and Armenians in the east, altogether 20 per cent of a population of some 10,000,000. Today Turkey has a population of 22,000,000 and the only minorities worth mentioning are the Kurds (6 per cent) and the Greeks (2 per cent); of the total population, 98 per cent are Moslems. Turkey was the first small Asian state to free itself from the imperialism of Europe and America. Its example acted as a sort of leaven in other regions of Asia, and for that reason we deal with it first and before many other states which in population or political influence are much more important.

We shall deal in some detail with the two periods – the national revolution (1919–1926) and the period of planning and reconstruction (1926–1930). Between the latter period and the Second World War Turkey's role in world history was again less important.

The first sign of a resurgence of national feeling was seen on May 14, 1919, the day when, encouraged by London and Paris, the Greeks occupied Smyrna (today Izmir) on the west coast of Asia Minor. The Great Powers had drawn up once again and this time finally, a scheme for the partition of Turkey. Britain was to occupy Istanbul and the Straits, the key to the gateway through which the Russian revolution could advance beyond the Russian frontiers; Greece was given freedom of action in central Asia Minor, while the south was divided between Italy and France. The French advanced from Syria; the Italians landed at Idalia (today Antalia), northwest of Cyprus on the south coast (April 29, 1919). A centuries-old Western dream seemed about to be fulfilled; Turkey would disappear from the map; the Cross would conquer the Crescent.

It was all a dream and not a very pretty one at that. The Turkish national revolution fought on two fronts – against the sultan (Mohammed VI, July 4, 1919 – November 1, 1922) and his corrupt government in Istanbul which was guarded by New Zealand troops, and against the powers which had invaded the country and their agents. It was this double threat which was one of the reasons for the powerful reaction and the ultimate victory. On the day the Greek troops entered Izmir (May 15, 1919) a patriotic meeting was held in that town which unanimously declined to allow the annexation of Turkish territory. On May 28th and 29th nationalist resistance fighters were trying to halt the Greeks near Ödemis, some forty-five miles south of Izmir.

None the less it is still rather doubtful if the national revolution would have developed as it did if the sultan had not been scared of Mustapha Kemal (1880–1938); we have met him as a Young Turk in 1908, as a Turkish officer in Tobruk in the war against Italy and at Gallipoli against the British. He was banished to Asia Minor, for that is what his appointment as Inspector-General of the Third Army amounted to. It was a very foolish move, for Asia Minor was just the place where a dangerous man could be more dangerous. There only Turks lived; there was the centre of nationalism. On May 19th Kemal landed at Samsun, a little port on the Black Sea coast. This was the birthday of the new state, a result of nationalism and upheaval, and, like everything really new in history, with its bad as well as its good side. Within a few weeks all Anatolia had rallied to him. The sultan acted like a man who has lost his wits; he roused the Kurds against the Nationalists and declared Kemal an outlaw, acts which, far from helping him, merely strengthened the national resistance. In summer Kemal organized a provisional congress in Erzerum in the mountains of the northeast (July 23 to August 6, 1919). In September came the great Nationalist congress in Sivas, 125 miles inland from Samsun. Here the Turks laid down the broad lines of their new policy, defence of their independence and the indivisibility of the country. All past illusions, all thoughts of a great Islamic empire were deliberately and resolutely given up. Here perhaps we see the real greatness of Kemal. What the average Nationalist politician could not do, he risked doing, throwing a great past overboard like burdensome ballast and beginning something new on a smaller scale. His is the same greatness as William of Orange's, who out of the seventeen Spanish-Dutch provinces between Dollard and Dunkirk made the little realm of Holland the core of the free republic born out of resistance to the king of Spain. The Turkish officer in the twentieth century, like the Dutch prince in the sixteenth, had grasped the truth of Hesiod's words written centuries earlier: 'Fools, do you not see how much more the half is than the whole'.

It was now time for new elections in Turkey. The sultan tried in every way to get votes; he made concessions to the revolutionaries, dismissing Damad Ferid, the head of the government of traitors to their country in Istanbul, and, on the other hand, sent a conciliatory letter to the Powers, the last gesture of the Ottoman Empire before which Europe had trembled from 1500 to 1700. The elections were none the less a victory for Kemal. As far as the interior of the country was concerned, the sultan and his ministers were in the future of no consequence whatever.

On the evening of January 28, 1920, after Kemal had spoken for seven hours, the new parliament adopted the policy of the Sivas congress – in a word, the right of self-determination, the idea which at this time fascinated not only Turkey but all the countries of Asia. Further, Istanbul was to be Turkish; the Straits were to be free and all foreign troops were to leave Turkey. These conditions were made known to the Allies as the *conditio sine qua non* for the ending of the war of independence. In these confused times Kemal's political action shows him possessed of one of the essential qualities of a great statesman; he could see both the dream and the business. Without an apparently unrealizable dream, policy sinks into the quicksands of a reality limited by time; without a sense of reality, policy parts from the facts which serve it as basis and is tossed on a sea of illusions.

The British recognized the danger and again occupied Istanbul. Covered by the guns of foreign ships, Damad Ferid again got together a reactionary government. Kemal's answer was immediate. On April 23, 1920, he summoned in Angora (today Ankara) the first great National Assembly, the basis of the revolutionary counter-government by which Turkey from now on would be ruled. The powers tried in every way to hinder the revolution's growth. They not only, as we have already told, sent in Greek, Italian, French and British soldiers; they also created, in the rear of the new Turkey, the republic of Armenia, partly from Turkish, partly from Russian, territory. The alleged desire was to protect the Armenians and there certainly was reason enough for protection. But there are other explanations of this Allied action; the Bolsheviks thought their oilfields at Baku were threatened. As early as the summer of that year, Turkey and Russia, acting together, dissolved the republic of Armenia, and in the winter of 1921 they signed the Treaty of Kars which settled the frontier between Turkey and the Soviet Union as it is today. As they felt themselves threatened by the same Powers, the two countries had at first pleasant and rewarding relations; the idea of a planned economy was taken over by the Turks from the Russian revolutionaries.

In that same summer the invaders had occupied large parts of the country. In June they marched from Smryna into the interior and also occupied a number of places in European Turkey. By July they were master of all the rich, densely populated coastal provinces. The sultan signed the notorious Treaty of Sèvres (August 20th), the lines of which had been laid down at the inter-Allied conference of San Remo (April 18, 1920). Turkey was reduced to a small area of barren hill country. At that time Lawrence of Arabia wrote in *The Times*, 'Sèvres was a senseless consequence of Allied covetousness'. Its consequences did not come up to expectations. All Turks now were convinced of the treachery of Istanbul; the Russians and the Arabs recognized the kinship of the Turkish revolution with their own.

The further the invading armies progressed, the more intense grew the resistance to them. Near Inonu the Greeks were twice (January and March 1921) driven back by Ismet Pasha; in 1934, when all Turks took on family names, he called himself Inonu. In summer the Greeks embarked on another large-scale offensive against Ankara. At first they were successful. They took Kutahia and Eski Shehr, some 120 miles from Ankara. In August they reached the hot valley of the Sakkaria, about fifty miles from Ankara. The prospects seemed fair, but in fierce and bloody fighting (August 24th to September 1921) it was seen that Kemal's fiery spirit was unshakeable and the Greeks began to retreat; Ankara, the capital of the revolution, remained untaken. The Turks now had the initiative and took the offensive. In 1922 the French evacuated the areas they had occupied; the Italians had withdrawn before that in June. In August the Greeks were in full flight to the coast and at the beginning of September the Turks entered burning Smyrna, from which the unlucky campaign had started.

Britain was now the only one of the invading powers who was ready to go on fighting – on account of the Straits. The others, and also the British Dominions, had had enough of the Turkish adventure and Britain was not strong enough to enforce its wishes. His war policy cost Lloyd George the premiership. In October, at the port of Mundania on the Sea of Marmara, a compromise was reached between the Allies and the 'Turkish bandits'; it was followed by the definite Treaty of Lausanne of July 24, 1923. Here, in a Swiss hotel overlooking the Lake of Geneva, it was agreed that the Turks would get Eastern Thrace as far as the Maritza (the classical Hebrus), which we call the European part of Turkey, and also the two small hilly islands at the entrance to the Dardanelles, Imbros and Bozcaada (the classical Tenedos). Italy got the Dodekanese, a chain of islands of purely strategic importance off the southwest coast of Asia Minor; they had been occupied by Italy in 1912. Cyprus remained British (occupied 1878; annexed 1914); the Straits (the Dardanelles, the Sea of Marmara and the Bosphorus) were demilitarized; in peace-time, passage was to be free for ships of all nations; in war-time, only if Turkey remained neutral. If Turkey became involved in war, passage would be refused only to enemy ships. The compulsory removal of some 2,000,000 Greeks living in Turkey to Greece and the removal to Turkey of some 500,000 Moslem Turks living in Greece was to be arranged by a separate Turko-Greek treaty (1923–4).

On August 23, 1923, the British garrison left Istanbul. October 29th was the official birthday of the Turkish Republic with its capital at Angora; the name was changed to Ankara in 1930. Mustapha Kemal was president (1923 to November 10, 1938). Ismet Pasha, also called Inonu (1923–1937; president 1938–1950), was prime minister. Meantime the sultan fled to foreign parts on a British ship (November 1, 1922). A new democratic constitution did internally what the Treaty of Lausanne had done externally; it consolidated the revolution which had begun in May 1919 in the mountains round Samsun.

Now that the West had been rendered incapable of mischief, it was in Kemal's opinion possible to take in hand and in full peace the plans for reform in the Western sense. Only now was Turkey completely liberated from European intervention, political, economic and military, such as had earlier given an unpleasant after-taste to any modernization. Kemal was a radical; in many things he took Russia as model, e.g. a single political party, no foreign investments and, in general, modernization and yet more modernization. From Ankara, which is badly situated from a climatic and economic point of view, but is far distant from Istanbul with its reactionary tradition and lies in the heart of the land of the peasants, a modern state would arise which would symbolize the revolution.

A measure symbolic in its way was the ban on fez and turban. The liberation of Turkey from an Islamic culture that had in part become rigid and its entry into what we call Western civilization, was helped by the abolition of the caliphate (March 3, 1924), the banishment of members of the former sultan's family and the abolition of the article in the constitution in which Islam is declared to be the State religion (1928). Landmarks in the emancipation of women were the abolition of the harem and polygamy (1925), the modernization of the divorce laws (1925), obligatory civil marriage (1926) and the extension of the franchise to women (1934). In all spheres, laws which often had originated in the Middle Ages were brought up to date with modern practice, the penal code on the Italian, the civil law on the Swiss, and commercial law on the German model (1926). The titles of pasha and bey were abolished and a law was passed obliging all Turks to have a family name (1934). It was then that Mustapha Kemal changed his name to Kemal Ataturk.

The Arab script was not suitable for Turkish, which is akin to the Mongol speech – the Arabs brought it in when the Turks were converted to Islam – and the Latin alphabet was substituted for it. Newspapers in Latin script made their appearance in 1928 and the next year it was forbidden to print books in the Arab. As in the case of the laws against polygamy, the fez and the turban, the change in script was accompanied by intensive propaganda for the new idea. Kemal himself went on great propaganda tours of the scattered Anatolian villages in which he tried to force writing in Latin characters on peasants and their wives who could not write at all. Turkish replaced Persian and Arabic as the language of everyday life in which it must be possible, and so was possible, to say all that one wanted to say. Persian, Arab, Greek and other foreign influences were expunged from Turkish. In 1930 geographical names were 'turkicized'. Constantinople became Istanbul, Angora, Ankara, Smyrna, Ismir, Adrianople, Edirne, and so on. Turkish historians began to treat their own history as a unity going back to the Sumerians, the people who lived in the valleys of the Euphrates and the Tigris in about 4000 B.C. A modern university and an agricultural college were set up in Ankara, although at the outset the professors, for lack of Turkish ones, were foreigners, mainly Germans. In former days 90 per cent of the Turks were illiterate, but as early as 1935 20 per cent of them could read and write Latin characters and today at least 50 per cent have learned much.

For the modernization of the economy Russian experts were imported, and generally, though possibly less radically, the Russian model was followed. Foreign capital was refused; great State factories were built in accordance with what was planned in Ankara; other enterprises had rather more freedom. Many new motor roads provided better transport for the produce of the mines.

In order to increase agricultural production, the forestry industry was nationalized, machines and artificial manures brought in, granaries and irrigation works built. But, instead of drastic collectivization on the Russian model, the ideal of voluntary co-operatives was spread among the peasantry. Although the peasants (about two-thirds of the population) cultivate only a fifth of Turkey and their methods are still pretty primitive, the country today produces besides cherries, apricots, currants and grapes, 4 per cent of the world's olive oil, 3 per cent of its tobacco, 3 per cent of its barley and wheat and $1\frac{1}{2}$ per cent of its cotton. Certainly peasants and farm labourers do not live in luxury, but compared with the peasants in the Arab countries and Egypt one can count the Turkish peasants rich.

In 1936, shortly after the outbreak of the civil war in Spain, and above all as a result of the Italian occupation of Abyssinia (1935), Turkey at the Montreux Conference (July 20, 1936) recovered its rights on the Straits; this was a move in France's and Britain's game against Italy and the Soviet Union. Alarmed lest they should be hindered in their reconstruction by foreign political conflicts, the Turks shortly before the Second World War signed a treaty of neutrality and non-aggression with France and Britain (May–June 1939). Similar treaties had already been signed with the Soviet Union 1925; renewed 1929), with Greece, Roumania and Yugoslavia (1934) and with Iran, Irak and Afghanistan (1937).

During the Second World War Turkey remained deaf to the threats and blandishments of either side. It stayed neutral and only declared war on an already defeated Germany in February 1945. Otherwise, all its time was devoted to preserving and augmenting the gains of the revolution.

IV

THE ARAB COUNTRIES (i)

IN wintry weather the Peace Conference opened in Versailles. At it appeared, besides the Europeans and Americans, who naturally were in a big majority, a picturesque group of Arabs in their white woollen mantles. This was the delegation from the Hejaz led by Faisal, the most intelligent of Hussein's three sons. Now the fruit of the bloody war of liberation would be gathered; all the Arab countries between the Red Sea and the muddy Tigris would be united in a free and independent state under Hussein ibn Ali the 'King of the Arabs' as he liked to call himself. But it turned out that the masters in Whitehall and the Quai d'Orsay had no intention of keeping their word. The Western plan was the maintenance of the *status quo* as it existed in the Arab countries. That meant that Arabia proper, i.e. the peninsula, would be independent but the British areas on the southern and eastern coasts would not be included. Irak would be under a British administration; Syria, i.e. the former Turkish province of that name, all the land between Egypt, the Mediterranean, Turkey, Irak and Arabia, would be divided into three parts and would not get independence. Palestine would be a mixed Arab and Jewish area under the British; in the interior where only Arabs lived the so-called Transjordania would also be British; the northern coastal area, Syria in the narrower sense, would be French. That would, it was said, be only a temporary arrangement, but in it we can easily recognize the plan of partition of the Sykes-Picot agreement of May 1916 which certainly was not meant to be temporary.

The French, besides, were ready to recognize Faisal as delegate of Arabia, but not of Syria. At that time, we must remember, France was again, if only temporarily, one of the most important Great Powers on the continent, possibly one of the great world powers beside Britain and the United States, and so could do very much as she pleased. The moderate Faisal asked that a committee of enquiry should be sent to Syria; his wishes were met, but only because President Wilson favoured them. It is worth noting that only Americans went to Syria, the so-called King-Crane Commission; delegates of other countries were suddenly prevented from going. What the Commission discovered in Syria did not make pleasant reading; it recommended that Syria should be for a time mandated territory but not under France. That was forty years ago, when the Americans could not oppose France and Britain, and so a well-intentioned plan passed into the oblivion to which so much has gone in the course of history.

It was soon seen that the Arabs were not prepared to take all this lying down. On July 2, 1919, the All-Syrian Congress in Damascus declared that Syria and Irak should be independent of foreign control; both countries were ready to accept technical, military and political assistance, but there was to be no regimentation; help was to be got if possible from the United States, and, if necessary, from Britain, but in no circumstances from France. Here we must note again two less well-known factors in the rise of the United States to be a Great Power. Compared to France and Britain, the United States had not only greater productive capacity and bigger gold reserves, but a much less obvious colonial tradition and its policy, if it intervened, would be much more strictly an economic one. To the Arabs it appeared less dangerous. As for the attitude of the Arabs to Britain and France, we can only repeat what has been said in connection with other Asian and African countries. The British were not loved, but were much less detested than the French. As individuals the British may be arrogant – in a sense they are genuinely insular – and they have waged colonial wars as barbarously as anyone else, but they do have political understanding of other countries and other cultures. The French, and especially those in the colonies, understand by culture only French culture. A relation such as exists today between India and Britain is not easily imagined between France and an ex-colony.

When against American advice Lloyd George and Clemenceau sought to carry out their plans, Faisal protested but declared that he would not resist a temporary French occupation of the coastal strip of Syria. The Arabs blamed Faisal for this. There were numerous clashes and skirmishes with the troops of occupation in Syria, especially when the British began to withdraw their forces from the 'French' zone. A second Syrian Congress on March 8, 1920, quickly passed a resolution that there should be created two independent constitutional monarchies; Syria, all the land between Egypt and Turkey, where Faisal would reign, and Irak, which would be Abdulla's kingdom. But Paris and London knew their maps of the Near East; they remembered the oilfields of Mosul and Iran, and in the southwest thought of that sensitive spot, the Suez Canal. So the occupying powers said; No. No independent Arab kingdoms.

At a minor Anglo-French conference in San Remo (April 26, 1920) the powers put their desiderata on paper. What is today Syria and the Lebanon was to go to France, Palestine and its hinterland and Irak to go to Britain. Further 'incidents' in the area affected were the inevitable consequence; once a people knows freedom, it defends it. Paris thereupon sent a very plain ultimatum to Faisal (on July 14th, the anniversary of the French revolution in 1789) that, if there was any further resistance, military intervention would follow. Faisal gave way, but not the Arabs. In a heroic *levée en masse* they tried to drive back the invaders, but their army, which was anything but modern, was destroyed in a week, an event which Ibn Saud took into account and never forgot. The French occupied Damascus (July 25th) and banished Faisal and his family (July 28th). That is what happened in Syria; we shall return to it later.

In Irak also the occupying power was not at all inclined to further independence. The resistance of the Arabs, which in Syria had broken out in a guerrilla war, became in Irak a bitter rebellion. From July to December 1920 several British garrisons were beseiged for weeks, and according to British reports at least 10,000 Arab resistance fighters were killed or wounded. Not without reason is 1920 known in the Near East as the year of catastrophes.

The only apparently considerable concession which the British made there at this period was the recognition (April 1, 1921) of Abdulla as emir of Transjordania, though he was considered merely an amiable puppet, and the recognition of the expelled Faisal as king of Irak (August 23, 1921). After the suppression of the Irak rising, the foundations at least were laid for eventual independence during the high commissionership of Sir Percy Cox. But in Syria, the Lebanon, Palestine and Transjordania, independence remained in the balance. Europe considered herself able to rule the world. But that means something different from actually being able to do so, and that again is not the same thing as actually doing the ruling.

So far the history of the Arab countries can be considered as a whole. Now, however, after international frontiers separated them, and the former Turkish provinces had become states and mandated territories, we must treat of them individually: the Peninsula (Arabia proper), Irak, Syria, Palestine and Transjordania. In this section we shall relate the history only of the Peninsula. We must, however, make it clear that the ideal of a united Arabia stretching from the Red Sea to the Turkish and Persian frontiers never ceased to be the Arab aim. It would truly be a historic achievement if the Arab countries, now that they are in possession of Western techniques and Western ways of thought, refused to continue the balkanization which is the reverse of the nationalist aims. It would be a tragic, though perhaps unavoidable, episode in their awakening if these countries, so Arab in language and culture, stayed apart, as the countries of Spanish America have done.

At this period the peninsula was not a political unity. Besides the British zones in the south the Crown colony of Aden and the protectorates like Hadramaut, Oman and Muscat, there were five states: 1. The Hejaz northwest of the Red Sea, the land of Mecca and Medina, the realm of King Hussein; 2. the sultanate of Nejd, the great desert and oasis region in the centre, which was ruled by the Wahhabite Ibn Saud (1880–1953); 3. the emirate of Shammar in the north of the Iraki frontiers, the part of the great Syrian desert ruled by the Rashid dynasty; 4. the small state of Asir on the Red Sea south of the Hejaz. These four now make up Saudi Arabia and have a population of about 6,000,000, of whom 2,000,000 live in the Hejaz. The fifth state is the Imamate of Yemen, now a kingdom, the famous coffee country in the southwest west of Aden. Official figures give its population as 3,500,000; it is believed to be actually much less.

The course of Arabian history from 1921 to 1941 can be summed up in a few words; Ibn Saud conquered all the states in the peninsula except Yemen. The conquest began in 1919, when he cut to pieces a force of Hussein's cavalry among the sandhills of the interior. Hussein turned to Britain for aid and made an alliance with Ibn Rashid of Shammar. In the autumn of 1921 Ibn Saud wiped the state of the Rashids off the map. He had already annexed Asir in the summer of 1920. In August 1924 the Wahhabites invaded the Hejaz; and Hussein's realm fell apart like a pack of cards. Hussein was not more liked by his own Arabs than he was by the invaders; he renounced his throne (October 3rd) and turned the government over to his son Ali, who was just as unable to cope with the crisis. Mecca fell (October 13th) and then Medina (December 5th) and when Jeddah surrendered (December 23rd) Ibn Saud had reached the Red Sea on a broad front. He now took the title of King of the Hejaz and Sultan of Nejd; the latter title was his original one; in February 1927 he altered it to 'King of the Hejaz and Nejd'.

London recognized his complete independence (Treaty of Jeddah, May 20, 1927), and it was no empty formula. On the other hand, Maan in the north-west and the strategically important Akaba were handed over to Trans-jordania, which thus received a port on the Red Sea. Ibn Saud pledged himself to leave the southwestern coastal strip as it was, that is, British.

By a decree of September 18, 1932, the official name of his state was changed to 'Kingdom of Saudi Arabia', although it still retained its dual character. It had two capitals: Riadh in the interior – oil and the American-built railway were not yet known – and Mecca in the Hejaz. The only further attempt at expansion was the campaign against Yemen. The Imam was besieged, but it was apparent that Ibn Saud could not annex so attractive an agricultural land. Some frontier alterations apart, Yemen remained an independent state. Why this sudden withdrawal? Had the sly fox become a peaceful lamb? Was the Imam the greater politician? Not at all. The reason for withdrawal was Italy, then still a Great Power. In the 'eighties of the previous century the Italians had invaded Eritrea on the opposite shore of the Red Sea and in 1890 annexed it. As early as 1926 the Imam of Yemen, fearing Ibn Saud's increased power, had concluded a security treaty with Italy (renewed in 1937). Manoeuvring between Saudi Arabia, Britain and Italy, Yemen was able, to all appearances at least, to retain its independence.

Why was Mussolini's Italy so active in these regions? When Ibn Saud made his attack on Yemen, Italy had its plans all ready for conquering Abyssinia (October 5, 1935–May 5, 1936), in which it was, half secretly, half officially, supported by the Laval government in France. The hills of Yemen, with their coffee plantations, could become an Italian Aden, perhaps a base against Britain's door to the Red Sea, perhaps, too, the core of an Italian colonial empire in the Arab countries and East Africa. Obsessed with the fantastic dream of a Roman Empire and of 'Mare Nostrum' – the Mediter-ranean – as an Italian inland sea, Mussolini drove his armies to battle in Africa, in Spain, in France, in Greece and in the Ukraine. From Kemal Ataturk we have learned that the hallmark of the great statesman is to unite the dream and the reality. Benito Mussolini's Arab-African empire was never more than a dream, and not a beautiful one at that.

Of just as great significance as the achievement of Ibn Saud is the manner of its achieving. Here we may note three factors:

1. The character of the Arab population of Nejd, the contrast between the Arabs of the Hejaz, partly farmers, partly living in towns, and the Wahhabi nomads of the desert interior. Besides, the Wahhabites were, as is

known, a special, particularly orthodox group in Islam.[1] At the beginning of the nineteenth century they were in possession of Mecca and Medina and threatened Damascus, and not until 1820 were they driven back into the interior by the Turkish governor of Egypt. Now, a century later, they were the great opponents of Hussein who had allowed himself to be hailed as the caliph of all the Moslem peoples after the caliph of Constantinople had been expelled. Hussein's arrogant attitude had its consequences abroad as well as in Arabia itself. In London they had had enough of the 'King of all the Arabs' and in India and Pakistan the Moslem party went over to Ibn Saud.

2. Ibn Saud had not – why should it not be admitted? – refused subsidies from London. That implied obligations. His tactics confirm his right to be called the greatest Arab politician of modern times; he always knew how to outwit the politicians in London.

3. There was modernization. Like Ataturk, though not so radical as he, Ibn Saud, to prevent the Europeans having too much to say in Arabia, sought to make his mediaeval land a modern state. The discovery of oil in it made his task easier. First of all he worked at a project which he had begun in Nejd as early as 1910, to settle hundreds of thousands of nomad Arabs, the cattle-breeders, with their cattle and their herds of goats and sheep. Here we have another case, almost contemporary with what was happening in Russia Kasakstan, of what is common in the history of all the peoples. Nomads become settled peasants, the Bedouin sow and reap grain. This is a change which may put an end to romantic beauty, but which increases agricultural production and so reduces the misery and insecurity of the people; today, because the power of the nomad tribes is a thing of the past, the safety of the traveller in the interior is much surer. The footpad and the caravan robber have disappeared like snow before the sun. The telegram, the telephone and air travel are taking the place of the camel, or, more accurately, the dromedary, as the only means of transport. If today Arabia does not yet possess a great modern network of roads – apart from the roads lately built in the oil region, the roads between Jeddah and Mecca and Jeddah and Medina are the only macadamized roads – the various roads that do exist are made usable for motor traffic.

Apart from camels, dates and a little wool, Arabia originally had little to sell abroad except gold from the mines of Mahad Dhabad between Mecca and Medina. The great stream of Moslem pilgrims to Mecca and Medina, besides bringing international prestige, is also economically quite important. But the years of real prosperity began only after the engineers of the Arabian American Oil Company had sunk the oilwells in 1937 in Dharan in the northeastern coastal province of al-Hasa, which today has 2,000,000 inhabitants. Into the iron pipes flowed from Arabia a wealth hitherto unknown. In a short time the fields of Dharan and Abkaik were universally known. Originally all the oil went to the British refineries in nearby Bahrain, but today there is the great refinery of Ras Tanurah in a place where camels used to graze and the pearl fishers caulk their boats; a thousand-mile-long pipe-

[1] v. p. 31.

line connects it with the Mediterranean *via* the Lebanon. Arabia now produces 5 per cent of the world's oil. And if such an American enterprise is politically very dangerous, it must not be underestimated as a medium of modernization. According to present arrangements Arabia gets half of the oil company's takings. The Americans have built railways, roads, modern houses and water supply, and so helped to changed the isolated primitiveness of the country. In his foreign relations Ibn Saud stands for pan-Islamism or at least pan-Arabism. His treaties with Turkey, Iran, Irak, Transjordan, Yemen and Egypt, all signed between 1929 and 1937, were the germ of the Arab League founded in 1945.

V

THE ARAB COUNTRIES (ii)

IN October 1920, while the great guerrilla war against the British forces of occupation was going on, Sir Percy Cox, the high commissioner for the mandated territory of Irak (1920–1923), arrived in Bagdad. In June 1921 Faisal, the ex-king of Syria, appeared in Basra. In a plebiscite 96 per cent of the voters said they wanted Faisal to be king of Irak. Cox recognized him as king (1921–1923) of a land about the size of Italy or the Philippines, three-quarters of which consists of sandy, stony desert and sterile grassland; on the other hand, it is the classical Mesopotamia, the historic mud valleys of the Tigris and Euphrates where, as early as 4000 B.C., a great culture flourished and later luxuriant gardens and meadows and the great buildings of the kingdoms of Babylonia and Assyria, which are now buried under the sand; it is also the land of Arab Bagdad of the caliphs, of sun-soaked barley, maize and ricefields – Southern Irak is one of the hottest places on earth – where date palms grow everywhere and in their shadow orange-trees and vines: Irak exports three-quarters of the world's dates.

Irak is also the land of oil. Here we touch on a tender spot. The oilfields of the Anglo-Dutch and, to a lesser extent, those of the Franco-American Iraq Petroleum Company Ltd., which now produces 1½ per cent of the world's oil, were much more important in the period between the world wars than they are today. Only Iran had a richer output, when in 1927 at Baba Gurgur near Kirkuk, the famous well No. 1 was sunk. Bahrein, Saudi Arabia and Kuwait, which today produce 8–9 per cent of the world's oil did not appear on the world market until 1934 and 1946. The pipe for the carriage of raw oil from Kirkuk and Mosul to the refineries at Haifa and at Lebanese Tripoli were then, i.e between 1934 and 1935, the biggest in these regions. Like so many Arab countries whose oil problems at that time threatened to destroy them, Irak found it difficult to free herself from the British invasion. What was Faisal's role now? In the distracted period between 1919 and 1921, he had had to abandon his greatest ambitions. But now, a little diminished in stature, he took on the difficult task of freeing Irak from British tutelage. He showed himself a tactician of the first water, nearly as clever a one as Ibn Saud himself. He drove back the invader step by step and without much bloodshed, and it is his achievement that his colonial territory became an internationally recognized sovereign state. The various stages towards independence are embodied in a series of agreements between London and Bagdad. By those of 1921 and 1926 Irak received a constitution which gave it a status between that of a colony and that of a dominion.

The oil districts of Mosul and Kirkuk in the north of the country, where are the ruins of Nineveh, originally belonged neither to Turkey nor to Irak. In Lausanne in 1923 no agreement could be reached on this dangerous problem. The result was a bitter conflict between Turkey and Britain. But Mustapha Kemal did not want any more minorities – the inhabitants of the Mosul region are Kurds – and he did not want an oil war, so he gave in. In the summer of 1926 the greatest part of the oilfields there were recognized as belonging to Irak, but Faisal recognized the dangers as well as the possibilities of their possession. He went to London and returned only when he had got an agreement by which Britain recognized the independence of Irak, and gave prospect of international recognition by 1932. On November 16, 1930, the Treaty of Bagdad was ratified. Independence became a reality and in the autumn of 1932 Irak, as a sovereign state, became a member of the League of Nations. As compensation Britain was given a series of air bases, while a considerable number of British officers were attached to the Irak army.

As far as the outside world was concerned the relations between Britain and Irak were those of independent states, internally the British officers and high officials formed a state within the state. The British were still there and, as oil does not smell, the Iraki Government raised little objection. Two military coups brought no significant change. The *coup d'état* of the pan-Arab politician and soldier Bakr Sidki, a divisional commander, had but one result, the banning of all political parties. The revolt of the pro-German Rashid Ali in May 1941, just before the German invasion of Russia, resulted in a new British occupation and a purging of all elements in the army which seemed too independent and were suspected of being too nationalist.

Like other colonial territories, Irak naturally saw more than just the evil side of European penetration. As in other countries, the coming of Western technology and economic modernization was the cause of much conflict, but it was also an inspiration in the process of awakening and a valuable inheritance when the day of real independence came.

Oil, which constitutes half of all Irak's exports – today Irak receives half of the profits – has already been mentioned. Then, too, Irak has now nearly 4,000 miles of roads, although not more than 200 miles of them can take modern traffic. Basra has become an international airport on the line Europe–the Far East and there is a second big airport in Bagdad.

Four-fifths of the inhabitants are illiterate. Half of them are genuine peasant farmers; half are Beduin, shepherd tribes like the Shammar, the Dafir and the Anaizah. By 1920 an irrigation department had been set up. British and native engineers achieved much, though it is now realized how relatively little was achieved. Water, more tractors, more technical progress, more propaganda could turn one-third of Irak, which is steppe country, once again into the luxuriant gardens which flourished in the long distant past. The peasants and cattle men of Irak have remained Asians – that is to say, in their majority primitive in their agricultural methods and so poor. In this Irak is no different from other Arab lands and from the rest of South and East Asia, where the peasant problem is the burning one for all the states, free or unfree. The position is similar to that of many Asian and

European countries where all relatively radical agrarian reforms have been hindered because they are regarded as dangerous – think of China, Korea, Indochina, Malaya and the rest – and the growing revolt of the population against their often desperate poverty becomes a revolutionary movement with a Communist tinge. Not until 1939 did a Communist paper appear in Bagdad, and then it was a clandestine one; only in the period from 1941 to 1945 could the Communists work openly. The paper was called *Al Sharara* (The Spark), like Lenin's *Iskra* of 1900. As a result of the liberal intermezzo of these years, the Communist party rose to be one of the biggest in the Arab countries, which is why we devote some space to it here.

When the British occupied the country in 1941, all the Nazis were arrested, and the Communists, though still officially banned as a party, had, marvellous to say, almost entire freedom of action. The British obviously intended to encourage any anti-German feeling in Irak. A host of left newspapers and reviews appeared. The market was flooded with Russian publications in English, French and Arabic, and the newspapers in Bagdad of every shade of opinion got their leading articles by telegraph from Moscow. In 1946 the Communist party and other left movements were again banned.

Two domestic problems indicated the way in which the country is divided by religion and by race. Of its 5,000,000 inhabitants four-fifths are Arabs, but in the north there are about 600,000 Kurds who, although they too are Moslems, have good reason for not wanting to have much to do with either Turks or Arabs. Between the world wars there were three great risings of the Kurds against Bagdad (1922-1924, 1930-1931 and 1932). The risings were put down with some severity. In 1932 the Kurds in Irak obtained a certain cultural autonomy, but the Kurdish people divided among four countries – altogether there are about 3,000,000 Kurds living in Turkey, Syria, Irak and Iran – desire to have a state of their own. The mass murders and expulsions of Syrian Christians in the summer of 1933 is a shameful episode in the history of Irak. In Irak 95 per cent of the inhabitants are Moslems, but as a further cause of disunity they are divided in the ratio of five to eight into Sunnites and Shiites. That means a breach in the national unity, and the danger of a disintegration of the anti-British front; it also limits and neutralizes the not-always-healthy mixing of religion and politics, internally and externally, such as is seen in other Arab lands.

But internal differences did not prevent the conclusion of the non-aggression treaties of 1937 whereby Turkey, Irak, Saudi Arabia, Iran and Afghanistan as Moslem states united against any foreign imperialism. Imperialism at home – i.e. the British officers, the oil companies, and the omnipresent intelligence agents – remained. If officially relations between Irak and Britain remained good, there were still areas of friction. That was seen at the death of King Ghazi I (1933–1939, succeeded by Faisal II, b. 1935) in an automobile accident in the suburbs of Bagdad. There was a good deal of rioting and the British consul was stoned because it was suspected that he had engineered the fatal accident to the king. There does not appear to have been any foundation for the suspicion.

The reaction to the king's death shows that the Irakis felt that their independence was limited, and that the British had no intention of leaving Irak voluntarily and especially Kirkuk, Mosul and the oilfields. If one disbelieves this, let him remember the *coup d'état* of the Chief of the Iraki General Staff in the winter of 1952, the 'British cat's-paw' as a well-known Iraki journalist described him in a British newspaper.

As a result of Faisal's expulsion, Syria became definitely a French mandated territory, which to the French meant a colony. For information and for avoidance of geographical misunderstandings let us note that French Syria of 1920 had not quite the same frontiers as the Syrian Republic of later days. It comprised first of all the present republic which is inhabited by an overwhelming Arab majority; of its 4,000,000 population, 80 per cent are Moslems, 8 per cent Christians and 3 per cent Druses. Three-quarters of the Syrians are peasants who live in the western parts of the country and on the Upper Euphrates, where they grow corn, barley and cotton and also olives, grapes, peaches, apricots, lemons and similar fruits. As in Irak, because of the lack of irrigation 70 per cent of the country is grass, stony and sandy steppe land where only Beduin live with their sheep and camels.

The second part was what is now the Lebanon, with 1,500,000 inhabitants, half of them Moslems the other half Christians, an agricultural land like Syria from which it is divided by the Lebanon mountains with their wintry covering of snow. From the economic point of view the Lebanon is important because of the great refinery in Tripoli where part of the Iraki oil is dealt with. The third part was composed of the district of Alexandretta and Antakia (the classical Antioch). This was inhabited almost entirely by Turks and was in 1939 handed over to Turkey.

There were constant troubles in Syria during the years between the wars. The French, as we have said, are notorious for being bad colonizers, not indeed as technicians or as media for the transmission of modern improvements, but in everything which at least for a time makes colonial rule bearable. Compared with the relatively good relations between Britain and Irak, the relations between France and Syria were decidedly bad. The first high commissioner, General Gouraud, ruled like a feudal lord in the worst sense of the word. In the summer of 1920 he doubled the territory of the wealthy Lebanon, gave it a special constitution and divided the rest of the country into four parts. Officially Syria was a federation of autononous states; actually it was a camouflaged colony whose provinces were played off one against the other as Paris wished; Syria was a police state in which the French commercial concerns consumed things like locusts, and French culture by means of tendentious books and censored newspapers sought to suppress the native culture. The few Frenchmen in the country who had other and modern ideas were swamped by a flood of officials who, from their experience in Casablanca, the Sahara, Oran and Tunis were adepts in oppressing Arab populations and ignoring their wish for freedom.

The atmosphere throughout the land was stormy, and in the summer of 1925 when Sarrail was high commissioner the storm began to break. On

July 11th a number of Druses were arrested in Damascus during talks between high officials and Arabs. On the morning of July 18th the Druses rose with other Arabs under Sultan Pasha, occupied villages in southern Syria and attacked the towns. The French military authorities displayed in the streets the corpses of resistance fighters as a warning; the result (October 14th) was a general rising of the population. The French fled from Damascus and only after their artillery had bombarded the city for two days, and tanks and bomber planes laid part of the historic inner town in ruins, did they return. A second outbreak (May 8 and 9, 1926) was likewise crushed. Aircraft was a dangerous new weapon of imperialism; the use of aircraft for gas bombing in the Abyssinian War is the most famous and revolting case of its use. The Druses gave up in the summer of 1927. Their leaders fled to Transjordan. The Syrian revolt roused liberal opinion in France and elsewhere, especially because in these days the Berbers of the Riff under Abd el-Krim were successfully defending their freedom in the mountains of Morocco against 250,000 French and Spaniards.

Perhaps from sheer bewilderment and partly because it was seen that temporary conciliation might bring results, Paris was now less obstinate; Syria should get the same constitution and enjoy the same possibilities for progress as Irak. The new high commissioner, Henri Ponsot (1926–1933), cleared the air a little and recognized – in principle, at least – the right to realization of the desire for independence. He asked the Arabs for their views. When he saw that these were much too much Arab and much too little French, he negotiated; the result was the Republic of Syria, a sham republic of typical colonial stamp. Besides, the country had no access to the sea, nor ports, and it had been robbed of its best agricultural land for, in the meantime, the French had transformed the coastal areas of the Lebanon in the south and of Latakia in the north into allegedly free republics (1926 and 1930). The land was thus geopolitically as well as morally divided. As in other colonial territories, the sham concessions created opposition between resistance as a matter of principle and genuine or interested loyalty to the foreign rule. By 1933 the era of conciliation had passed. As high commissioner France sent out Damien de Martel a man of the type of Kitchener or Lyautey but very much less gifted. He brought with him the draft of a treaty rather like that of 1926 between Britain and Irak, except that the French draft for Syria was in many respects a much less generous document. Also it concerned only the inland districts; it did not mention the Lebanon nor Latakia. Martel dissolved (November 1934) the insubordinate parliament, declared that politics no longer interested him and that he would devote himself simply to economic expansion. But in January 1936, on security grounds, he arrested the Arab leaders and sealed up the buildings of the Nationalist party.

For the Syrians that was too much. Their answer was a successful general strike, fights in the streets and everywhere passive resistance in the Gandhi manner. The French administration yielded; the rebel land got a genuine cabinet (February 23rd); the high commissioner produced a new and more comprehensive plan and an official delegation went from Syria to Paris. On

March 1st the strike was called off without trouble. The storm seemed to be allayed, especially after the Popular Front government of Leon Blum took office in Paris (June 5, 1936). This was a government in which Communists, Socialists and left bourgeois groups were linked in order to meet the threat of fascism inside and outside France. Its hands were tied by the opposition of the French capitalists and reactionaries, but it had good intentions where Syria was concerned. On September 9, 1936, a Franco-Syrian compromise was signed. Syria was to be free within three years and be received as a free state into the United Nations. Lebanon got its own treaty in November. The first really free elections to be held in Syria gave a huge majority to the Nationalists and so confirmed the popular desire for independence.

No one troubled about the 100,000 Kurds who had fled from Irak except the military airmen who, in the summer of 1937, were ordered to drop bombs on the tents and herds of the fugitives; they had asked for the same independence as the other inhabitants of Syria. But the picture soon changed. In October 1938 the Popular Front in France collapsed and reaction returned to power. The government in Paris no longer defended itself against the international menace of fascism; indeed, it soon showed fascist traits itself. In January 1939, when Franco's Spanish fascists, their Moorish mercenaries and the Italian and German army of intervention stormed Barcelona, the last bulwark of the Spanish Government, when Hitler's Germany was concentrating its divisions for the annexation of Czechoslovakia, Puaux, the high commissioner, announced France's denunciation of the 1936 treaty. There were troubles and agitations: one can even speak of a Syrian rebellion. Seven months later the war broke out in Europe. France concentrated a large modern army in Syria and resistance ceased. After Pétain's capitulation (June 22, 1940) the Germans divided France into an occupied region and an allegedly free region under Pétain's collaborationist government in Vichy; Puaux was true to his reactionary instincts. He recognized Vichy and so the capitulation. German officers appeared to superintend the demobilization of part of the French army in Syria; it looked as if the Germans were going to make Syria a base. The avowedly fascist General Dentz replaced Puaux as high commissioner.

To Churchill this was much too dangerous a development. In June 1941 Britain intervened in both Irak and Syria. The British and Free French occupied the latter country. Catroux, the commander-in-chief of the Free French in the Middle East, declared Syria and the Lebanon to be independent in principle but would be so in reality only after the war. Both the mandated territories, however, demanded independence at once (February 1943). Catroux arrested the members of the Lebanese Government, which created a deplorable impression throughout the free world. The United States had already recognized Syria and, despite a stout defence, Catroux was forced to yield a little. The French National Committee under General de Gaulle recognized the absolute independence of Syria and the Lebanon as from June 1, 1944. This is the beginning of independence for Syria and the Lebanon, a day or two before the great Allied invasion of Normandy which liberated France herself. In 1946 all the British and French troops were evacuated. The bitter fight for freedom had lasted for a quarter of a century.

The history of Transjordan between the wars is that of a transformation of a territory freed from Turkey into what was at least in name an independent Arab state. In the winter of 1919, when the old Turkish Empire broke up, the British at first evacuated Transjordan and Abdulla took over the government of the country as emir. In March 1921, when Faisal was passing through the country on his way from Mecca to his kingdom of Irak, the Royal Air Force found it advisable to fill the vacuum in Transjordan, the more so as it had been declared a British mandated territory by the powers. At the same time the colonial secretary, Winston Churchill, T. E. Lawrence and others met in Cairo to decide on British policy toward the Arab countries. The result of their discussions was the official recognition of Abdulla as emir of Transjordan (April 1, 1921). By May 1923 the country enjoyed a pretty wide autonomy. The cause of this British generosity was because at that time Transjordan was part of Palestine; indeed it forms Palestine's natural hinterland. In the partition plans of the Allies during the war nothing had been said about the frontier between the two areas. Now, however, the British, who perhaps were already suspecting that the conflict between Jew and Arab could become a danger to the British Empire, were ready to divide the whole into two parts; to keep Abdulla on their side and to confine Jewish immigration to Palestine proper. The Balfour declaration remained intact, but the Jews had to realize that the promised land had shrunk a little.

A secondary consideration was that the recognition of Abdulla was a blow to the expansionist ambitions of Ibn Saud, Abdulla's enemy and the enemy of the Hashemite house. In the summer of 1922 Ibn Saud had reached the present northern frontiers of his realm, where he was watched by three states under British influence, Transjordan, Irak and Kuwait. The desert in the northeast of Transjordan was perhaps of no economic value but as a line of communication for the British to Irak and beyond, to Persia and India-Pakistan, it was of considerable importance. Through this corridor from 1935 went the pipeline from Kirkuk to Haifa.

Although there were changes in Transjordan – the country, for instance, got many modern roads – the presence of British officers and the loyalty of Abdulla to London remained unaltered. On February 20, 1928, as a result of events in Irak and Transjordan, the independence of Transjordan was recognized in principle; the British Major John Bagot Glubb, better known as Glubb Pasha (born 1897), became commander in chief. Like another Lawrence he identified himself with the native soldiery; he created the famous Arab Legion, for long the only efficient Arab military force.[1]

When in the summer of 1940 the storm of war broke over Europe and Africa, Transjordan was the only Arab country to take an active part in the war and on the British side. No doubt it was still a primitive land, still

[1] v. p. 371.

not modernized either socially or agriculturally, nor was it free from European tutelage, but it possessed a measure of self-consciousness. The soldiers of the Arab Legion fought like lions against the Italians and the Germans who were threatening Egypt and Britain's life-line, the Suez Canal.

In the summer of 1917 the hills and valleys of Palestine formed a Turkish province, a rebellious semi-colony partly at least in the front line dreaming of the 'freedom of all the Arabs', the slogan of the British for the anti-Turkish revolt in the Hejaz in June 1916. It was entirely an Arab region.

None the less, on November 2, 1917, a few weeks before British and Arab troops captured Jerusalem and dream began to look like reality, A. J. Balfour, the British foreign secretary, sent a remarkable document to Paris, a type-written letter of fifteen lines addressed to a Jew, Baron de Rothschild, who had financed many of the Jewish settlements in Palestine, the salient sentences in which are: 'H.M. Government view with favour the establishment in Palestine of a National Home for the Jewish people and will use their best endeavours to facilitate the achievement of this object, it being clearly under-stood that nothing will be done which may prejudice the civil and religious rights of the existing non-Jewish communities in Palestine or the rights and political status enjoyed by Jews in any other country.'

The letter became known, and is now notorious in all Arab countries as the 'Balfour Declaration'. The prime minister, Lloyd George, said in 1937 that the publication was made 'for propaganda reasons'; there is no reason to disbelieve him. The letter was printed as a pamphlet and was distributed in thousands in Germany, Austria and Russia; it was in some cases dropped by air. As in these countries lived the largest number of European Jews, it seemed good British propaganda. At the time it was represented to all the democratic countries as a shining instance of British chivalry to a people driven from their country and become a hated and persecuted race in other lands. Espe-cially in the freedom-loving United States, which had taken a long time to join the anti-German powers (April 1917), the declaration would, it was believed, have great effect.

Before the winter of 1918 the Turkish armies had been driven out of all the Arab countries. Palestine and Transjordan, like Arabia, were in violation of all promises made British mandated territories. And now it was seen how the British had fallen into a bed of nettles. Certainly from the political point of view here was no land 'flowing with milk and honey'. Apart from the 50,000 Jews, there were no minorities in Palestine. Had it not been for the accursed declaration, it would very possibly have ripened gradually to independence like Irak and Transjordan. In the circumstances now created both Jews and Arabs felt they had been tricked. Neither were free, neither had a home of their own; the Arabs were hostile to the immigrants from Europe, the Jews were compelled to come in like thieves in the night to a house which they had thought was their own.

Balfour's defence was childish and sociologically confused. In a speech in the summer of 1920 at the Royal Albert Hall in London, he spoke of Palestine as a 'tiny plot of ground which I hope the Arabs will not begrudge to the people who dwelled in it for centuries'. A notable defence. On this dubious 'plot of ground', actually about less than 1 per cent of the total area of the Arab countries, lived 15 per cent of the Arab peoples, the 700,000 Arabs who had been born in it.

But not unexpectedly the history of Palestine between the wars was that of a tragic conflict between Arabs and immigrants which tells how, despite all bloodshed, all disillusionment on both sides, and the plans and declarations of the government in London, despite all opposition, it became the nucleus of the present state of Israel. The key to the whole development is in a sense, the increase of the Jewish population, and so we give some facts and figures.

In 1922 Palestine had about 800,000 inhabitants; in 1942 more than 1,650,000. The percentage of Jews rose from 10 to 31 per cent, mainly as a result of immigration. Between 1922 and 1942 350,000 Jews arrived, mostly from Eastern Europe. At the start there arrived some 7000 to 10,000 annually, a relatively small figure. But between 1925 and 1926 and between 1933 and 1937 came the great flood of immigrants, 65,000 mainly from Russia and Poland and 175,000 from Germany and Poland where vicious anti-semitic terror was raging.

The majority of the Israelis – an interesting phenomenon in an Asian land – came from the West, mainly from Eastern Europe. The countries from which they came, in order of numbers, were: Poland, 30 per cent; Roumania and other countries of Southeastern Europe, 20 per cent; Germany 15 per cent; the Arab countries with Egypt, Turkey and Iran, 12 per cent; Russia, 5 per cent and North Africa, 5 per cent. Not until 1948 did Asian Jews predominate among the immigrants; in the period between the wars only 20,000 Asian and North African Jews emigrated to Palestine.

All those who came from Europe did not come as in other Asian lands to a colony, but as castaways and squatters, as fugitives who sought a home on any foreign coast even if the natives disapproved. For eighteen centuries the Jews had been forbidden to settle in many a land. Now at their return to Palestine they had at first no speech of their own and owned no piece of land. The land belonged to the Arabs, and of the ancient Hebrew tongue they knew barely two thousand words. But if the language were to be adapted to modern conditions and enriched, then it could fulfil the functions of other languages which have grown naturally. It could become a means of expression and mutual comprehension to the peasant and to the poet or engineer, and so act as a cement to national unity. That is what happened in Turkey and is now happening in Indonesia. As a result of this cultural reorientation there was founded on Chaim Weissman's initiative a Hebrew University in Jerusalem; Weissman, who was born in Russia in 1874 and was a well-known professor of chemistry in Manchester and London, was later the leader of the International Zionist Organization (1920–1931 and from 1935 onwards) and finally President of the Republic of Israel (1948–1952).

The majority of the immigrants settled in the towns. By 1930 half of the Jewish population lived in Tel Aviv, Jaffa, Haifa and Jerusalem, and only some 20 per cent in the villages and agricultural settlements. Tel Aviv, which in 1919 was a village with 2000 inhabitants, became the largest city in the country, with 150,000 inhabitants in 1939 and 350,000 in 1950. It is the only purely Jewish city in the world.

But many of the immigrants very early realized that a collection of towns without land and without farmers is not lightly recognized as a state. In 1919 the agricultural settlements possessed about 100,000 acres of cultivated land. Between the wars land belonging to Arab effendis was bought up; the immigrants who had settled down as farmers possessed in 1939 nearly four times that amount, amounting to virtually a quarter of all cultivateable land. The Zionists worked along three lines. In the first place the principle was to cultivate only waste land, that is, land from which there was no necessity to get rid of Arab peasants. To this the British, and naturally still more the Arabs, objected, i.e. Arab tenants, not the landed proprietors, who had grown rich in idleness. In the second and third places, all the land belonging to Jewish farmers was the collective property of the whole people and it was exceptional for Arab workers to be employed. The colonists were entirely free to manage their farms and villages as they pleased. Most of the settlements were organized more or less on socialist-collective lines. The *kibbutsim*, which we have already mentioned,[1] were worked like the Russian kolkhozes, though on rather more democratic lines. The *moshawim* were more independent; their members for the most part worked their own land themselves – the properties of individuals were equal in size – and had more individual freedom.

Not only among the peasants but also among the new immigrants there were many socialist elements. Naturally it was European workers not tied to Europe by economic interest who came to the new country. The Histradut, the all-embracing workers' organization, in a short time included half the Jewish population. Its leaders, including David Ben Gurion, later to be prime minister, Moshe Shertok (Snaret), later foreign minister, and last but not least Chaim Arlosorov, had close relations with the British Labour party.

Contrary to what many people expected, the Jews turned out to be excellent farmers, working like horses. Everywhere on the coast and in the hills, in the middle of primitive Arab peasantry, they built modern agricultural settlements. Palestine, which, like North Africa and the Arab countries, was exhausted and in decline as a result of centuries of Turkish mismanagement, became once again the blooming garden of the past. The landscape of Galilee, Judaea and Samaria became almost unrecognizable. The colonists planted trees, pumped water on to the parched fields, introduced new plants and fruits – grapefruit, for instance, and lemons – and experimented with cereal crops on dry ground. The tractor became a common sight in a land which up to then had used only wooden tools. As model farms among Arabs who were still in the Middle Ages, the *kibbutsim* had tremendous propaganda significance. The native fellaheen, whose cows gave on the average 100 gallons of milk a year, could see the Jewish farmer get six times that, and the European women on the *kibbutsim* get three and four times as many eggs as the Arab women did.

The economic prosperity of the land colonized by Jews affected the whole

[1] *v*. p. 92.

country. Many Arabs from Syria and Transjordan, perhaps as many as 30,000 migrated to Palestine between 1920 and 1940. Ever more Arabs realized what could be produced if farms were modernized. But what does modernization mean to a feudal country? As in many other Asian lands, it means that the bases of feudal society are undermined. To many the awakening of the peasant in Asia seems purely a technical matter; actually it is first a social-political matter, perhaps Asia's greatest problem, out of which rose the greatest revolution in history, the revolution in China. The resistance of the Arabs to the western immigration can rightly be regarded as a natural reaction, but it can also be misinterpreted. The effendis who incited the resistance were driven just as much by their fear of a peasant rising as by anti-European and anti-imperialist feeling.

So far this account of Palestine has passed over the doings of the British and political events in general. Social and political history is a unity and neither half can be passed over without distorting the whole.

When in April 1920 Britain took over Palestine as mandated territory, London began to interpret the Balfour declaration in as narrow a sense as possible. It did not, for instance, apply to Transjordan. This interpretation was made decisive by the recognition of Abdulla as emir of that country (1921). The Jewish immigration at the outset was feeble, as was the Arab resistance. The Arabs refused to share in the administration and the land was ruled by the British high commissioner. Not until 1929 did the Arab reaction become serious. In the extreme east of the inner city of Jerusalem opposite the Mount of Olives is the high-walled Haram-esch-Sherif, the holy place of Islam. Part of its southeastern wall, in which as is believed are many stones from Solomon's temple, was a special place of pilgrimage for Jews, the Wailing Wall.

As a result, the Arabs in August 1929 began a miniature civil war in which 200 people were killed. The British acted just as what they were here, as diplomatists caught in their own nets, and strove to moderate Arab feeling. The result was restriction on Jewish immigration. The British also were disturbed by the sealed caches of weapons in the Jewish settlements to be used only at moments of extreme need, as had happened in many places between 1921 and 1924. Besides, a White paper signed by the colonial secretary, Lord Passfield (Sidney Webb), called attention to the growing Arab land-hunger and recommended that for a time the purchase of Arab land be forbidden.

To this policy the British Government would probably have adhered had it not been for the outburst of anti-Semitic terror in fascist Germany and Poland. The British were morally bound, obviously against their original policy, to admit a fairly large number of fugitives into Palestine. Between 1935 and 1937 175,000 came in. All this coincided with the effect on British economic interests of the pipeline Kirkuk–Haifa and the erection of a great refinery in Haifa (1934, 1935). That was one of the reasons why the Arab resistance became a conflict with international repercussions. The Germans, and still more, the Italians, who were preparing to invade Ethiopia, looked enviously on the Arab countries and the Suez Canal, secretly sent, as did

Syria and Irak, money and weapons and by radio propaganda stirred up the Arabs against the British.

When in April 1936 the Arab resistance was organized under the Arab High Committee, the country was already convulsed by civil war and revolution, from which it was freed only by the outbreak of the Second World War. The Jews defended themselves with the semi-illegal resistance army, the Hagana (founded 1920), and the more extreme and aggressive Irgun Zwai Leumi (founded 1935). In the period immediately following, the colonists in a single day had to fortify their settlements, provide wells, and searchlights and barricades of sandbags and barbed wire, for when night came a general Arab attack could be expected. In 1936 Arab resistance fighters burned down hundreds of Jewish settlements and hundreds of thousands of fruit trees. A general strike (April–October 1936) made the chaos worse.

London sent out more soldiers and published a report (July 7, 1937) of the Royal Commission headed by Lord Peel, a former Secretary of State for India. This is a document of forty pages and is very critical of British policy. It regarded what it called a 'surgical operation' as the only solution, and so proposed partition; there would be a free Jewish state on the coast between Haifa and Jaffa and a small territory under British mandate between Jaffa and Jerusalem; all the rest, as Arab territory, should go to Transjordan.

At the Pan-Arab conference at Bludan in Syria (September 8, 1937), which was attended by 400 representatives of all the Arab countries, the Arabs turned down the plan on principle. The Arab revolt spread. That was too much for the British. On October 1st they arrested the Arab High Committee and deported most of their leaders to the Seychelles in the Indian Ocean. But the real leader of the Arab movement, Mohammed al-Hadj Amin al-Hussaini (b. 1890), the so-called Grand Mufti of Jerusalem, escaped to Syria, from which he continued to lead the revolution.

In 1939 even Syria became too hot for him. He went to Irak and Iran, and in 1941 appeared suddenly in Berlin where all during the war he conducted wireless propaganda against the British. When Germany capitulated, he went to France after an adventurous journey and, escaping from house arrest there, arrived in Egypt. But his day was past. His fascist learnings were hardly a recommendation in these days, and his effort (1948) to create a state of his own in the Gaza strip occupied by Egypt was a failure. The armies of Israel and Transjordan divided the land.

But before that, in 1938, the civil war had turned into a regular campaign. Britain had now an army of 30,000 men on the scene, yet could not really materially alter the situation. Making a last effort to get a settlement, it submitted all the various plans to a conference in London (February–March 1939), to which were summoned not only the two parties immediately concerned, but also representatives of Egypt, Saudi-Arabia, Irak, Transjordan and Yemen. Officially the conference settled nothing. But to London Arab statements seemed threatening enough and there was no more hesitation. On May 17th it published its own plan. In 1949 Palestine would become an independent state like Irak and Transjordan. Between 1939 and 1944 Jewish immigration would not exceed 75,000. Further, the Arab majority would

have a decisive say on immigration – which meant that it would cease. The
sale of Arab land was virtually forbidden in the whole of Palestine.

The British Parliament did not altogether favour what was clearly a pro-
Arab plan; 100 members of the Government party abstained and twenty-two
voted against it, including Winston Churchill who denounced the plan as a
'second Munich'. In the Munich settlement (September 29, 1938), as is known,
the British and French governments had yielded on Germany's territorial
claims in Eastern Europe. But criticism was not confined to Britain. The
guerrilla war in Palestine flamed out again more fiercely. That was the position when the Second World War caused temporary easing of tension.

VI

EGYPT

IN 1882 Egypt, then in theory a border province of the Turkish Empire, had been occupied by the British. In the winter of 1914 it became a British protectorate and during the First World War was a bulwark against the Turks more or less against the will of the Egyptians. The Egyptian Nationalist movement sought to profit by the circumstance that Britain's hands were tied by the war, and in the difficult days between 1918 and 1921 Britain seemed likely to give in to it. On November 11, 1918, Germany capitulated and fighting ceased on the Western Front. On the morning of the 12th, Said Zaglul Pasha and other leaders of the Nationalists appeared at the house of the high commissioner, Sir Reginald Wingate. To their question when would discussions begin on the constitution Wingate refused to give an answer; such a question he held could be addressed to him only by ministers. When that became known, the country was stirred and demanded that Zaglul should enter the Government. On March 8, 1919, when it was threatened that an Egyptian delegation would go secretly to the Versailles Conference, Britain acted; Zaglul and three of his associates were arrested and deported to Malta. The result was revolt, with strikes and street fighting. As everywhere in the East, as earlier in Europe, the students and many of the intellectuals were in the front rank of the revolt; even the lawyers went on strike. The Nationalist party, the 'Wafd' – 'wafd' is the Egyptian word for delegation – had increased its strength during the war mainly as a result of the measures taken by the occupying power which made unjustified demands, for instance, ordering Egyptians to do compulsory labour behind and at the front.

Field-Marshal Allenby, who had commanded the British and Arab forces on the southern Turkish front, was sent out to clear up the situation. He tried to negotiate. Zaglul and his colleagues were brought back to Egypt. Public opinion was favourable and the revolt died down. But that situation did not last and at the end of April Allenby issued a sharp decree in the true colonial vein. Egyptian resistance was broken.

Allenby was now made high commissioner in place of Wingate (October 1919), and at the same time the Milner Commission came to Egypt to investigate the political situation and report to London. At the beginning of March 1920 Milner returned to London and within a week came the Egyptian reaction. At a meeting in Zaglul's house, fifty-two members of the Egyptian parliament declared the independence of Egypt. It was a sharp warning to Britain and it was not given in vain. All through the summer and into the autumn Milner and Zaglul conferred in London, and by August Britain, as well as his own country, recognized Zaglul as the real leader of Egypt rather than the sultan Ahmad Fuad who in 1917 had succeeded his brother Hussein Kiamil. In February the Milner report was published. Egypt was to be independent if Britain's main interests were secured. The Wafd rejected the plan, Zaglul confirmed the rejection on his return to Cairo in April and resumed his agitation against the British and the weak government of the sultan. When Zaglul was again arrested there were violent outbursts of xenophobia, and many British and Greeks were murdered. After Zaglul was released in June, the Egyptians marked time; there was prospect of renewed negotiation in London. Who was to be Egypt's spokesman? The moderate premier Adli Pasha, or Zaglul the revolutionary? The official line was taken and Adli was sent to London. There he found himself faced with a body of genial but hardened imperialists; at the same time he felt behind him the threatening influence of Zaglul and the Wafd. Negotiations broke down in November. The two British demands – continuance of the military occupation and no independent foreign policy for Egypt – seemed excessive even to Adli, for did they not mean a renewal of the protectorate? The sultan and the British tried to muzzle the annoying Wafd movement by censorship and terror, but the idea of freedom had taken too strong a hold. The third arrest of Zaglul and his deportation to the Seychelles (December 22, 1921) raised a storm of protest and the Egyptians started 'passive resistance' on the model of India-Pakistan. Against that the rifles of the British army and the guns of British warships were impotent.

A year after the publication of the Milner report, on February 28, 1922, London declared the protectorate abolished. Egypt became an independent kingdom; the sultan became King Fuad I (1922–1926). The only limitations of sovereignty were that Britain secured the lines of communication, i.e. went on occupying the Suez Canal zone. Britain was responsible for the defence of Egypt and for protecting foreigners and retained the Soudan, the Nile valley south of the 22nd parallel which has gone into history as the Anglo-Egyptian Soudan because of the condominium set up in 1899–1914 and 1929–1955. In other words, Britain held the guns and the waters of the Nile; otherwise Egypt was free.

Under the changed circumstances, Britain could not any longer keep Zaglul interned; in April 1923 he returned to Egypt. At the same time Egypt received a constitution (April 19, 1923), although it was not really a modern democratic one. Two-fifths of the lower house of the parliament were appointed by the king; women and soldiers had no vote and, thanks to a cleverly worked-out system of indirect election weighted against the agricultural districts, neither peasants nor agricultural workers had much say in things. It was a travesty of real democracy, especially in a country where three-quarters of the population work on the land. The big majority which the Wafd won in the elections in September was a majority of the nationalist bourgeoisie over the king, the great landowners and the British.

There were now two oppositions. First that of the Wafd, as a constitutional democratic party, against the king and the reactionaries, and that of the Wafd as a nationalist party against the British. In all the subsequent conflicts these three elements were responsible for every ultimatum and every use of force against the Wafd. Only the politicians in London kept in power Fuad and his very questionable court.

When Zaglul became Premier in January 1924 the troubles decreased. His appointment and its consequences were due in part to terrorist acts on both sides. In London the well-known Wafd leader, Prince Ali Kiamil, was murdered; in Egypt Sir Lee Stack, the 'sirdar' – i.e. the commander-in-chief of the Egyptian army and governor-general of the Soudan – was assassinated. Such acts naturally were all to the advantage of the Europeans, who promptly branded the Asian and African nationalist movements as the terrorist organizations of hotheads instead of seeing in them the expression of the natural development of oppressed classes and peoples.

The revenge Britain took for the murdered sirdar was notable. In a threatening ultimatum at the end of November London demanded a ban on political demonstrations. But it also demanded the acceptance of a great irrigation scheme on the Blue Nile in the Soudan, as a result of which the British cotton plantations would get more water and Egypt less; that, at least, was what was to be expected. In addition, all Egyptian officers and purely Egyptian troops were to be withdrawn from the Soudan. Zaglul refused, and resigned from the Government. The new premier, Ziwar Pasha, gave in and, while Egyptian troops were withdrawing from the Soudan, British engineers were building the great dam at Makwar (Senaar).

In the second election in March 1925 the Wafd again won a big majority. Fuad and the British were apprehensive. The king ordered new elections, a useless manoeuvre for the Wafd came back 154 strong to the forty of all other parties. Fuad could do no more, but Britain sent out as high commissioner a real imperialist of the deepest dye, Sir George (later Lord) Lloyd (1925–1929).

August 23, 1927, was a black day for Egypt, for it was on that day that Zaglul died, certainly the greatest politician of modern Egypt. His successor as leader of the Wafd was Mustapha Nahas Pasha (b. 1876), who became premier in 1928. But the surge of the independence movement now could not be stopped. None the less, with British help the king strove to stop it, and prevent it having a free course. Now he made no effort to maintain the democratic façade. By a *coup d'état* 'made in Britain' he abolished parliament and the freedom of the press and of assembly. In the years 1928–1935 Fuad and London ruled as autocrats.

Not until 1929 did the situation appear to change. For the second time the British Labour party was called upon to form a government (under Macdonald; June 1929 to August 1931). Just as they did towards Soviet Russia and India-Pakistan, the British now slightly altered their policy towards Egypt. The dictatorial high commissioner Lloyd departed and the constitutional rights were restored. At the election the Wafd won a 90 per cent majority, and in January 1930 Nahas once again became premier. Meantime negotiations had been resumed and London showed a spirit of compromise from which results seemed possible. On the question of the Nile waters it was agreed that the Soudan should use only the waters of the Blue Nile, while those of the White Nile were reserved to Egypt. On the military issue it was laid down that, instead of a British occupation, there should be a military alliance as between sovereign states and only on the Suez Canal would British troops be stationed. Further, Egypt would become a member of the League of Nations and the Soudan would again be administered by Britain and Egypt jointly.

The barometer seemed set fair. But in the further negotiations over the Soudan it fell again. By the early summer of 1930 it was clear that Nahas was no longer master of the situation and a pro-British royalist, Sidki Pasha, became premier. Once again Fuad was a dictator, and his position was further strengthened by the great economic crisis which had particularly unfortunate effects on a cotton-growing country. When the Wafd resumed their tactics of passive resistance, the reactionaries sought to break its influence by means of a party created by Sidki, the People's party. Thanks to the muzzling of the Wafd, to the falsifying of documents, to terror and the encouragement of the reactionary currents in Islam it got an apparent but fictitious majority in May 1931.

Not until 1935 did the situation change. The darkness lightened a little, even if the cause of the lightening was due to events abroad. On October 3rd the troops of fascist Italy invaded Ethiopia in the near neighbourhood of the Soudan frontier. Britain felt that her Empire was threatened, wished to get Egyptian support and sang another song. In December the constitution of 1923 was restored. It seemed a veritable judgement of God when Fuad died (April 28, 1936); Farouk the new king (b. 1920; banished 1952) was at the outset much more popular than his predecessor and appeared much less dangerous.

The result of the elections in May brought back Nahas to power, and on August 26, 1936, he signed the famous Anglo-Egyptian treaty which, despite the controversies that arose later, was a genuine landmark on the road to independence. It provided for the withdrawal of British occupation troops, except in the Canal Zone where they retained 10,000 men and a series of air-fields; in wartime and in times of international crisis these provisions lapsed. Britain retained naval bases in Alexandria and Port Said, but only at the most for eight years; Egyptians were free to migrate to the Soudan and Egyptian troops returned to it; the capitulations were annulled, i.e. foreigners, even Britons, had no longer any special rights; Egypt as a sovereign state would enter the League of Nations. The treaty was to be valid for twenty years.

The Wafd had got all that was then possible. Now there happened what usually happens to resistance movements when the dream suddenly becomes for the most part reality and other and novel problems arise; the Wafd found itself working in a vacuum. It was now visible to what extent the party had been the result of exceptional circumstances, an unstable bundle of opposites at war against foreign invasion. The landowners and the reactionary sections of the bourgeoisie left it, turned right and founded parties like the Saadists and the fascist Blueshirts. The Wafd remained without attraction to the workers in the towns and to the great mass of the peasantry, and at the elections of 1938 it was temporarily wiped off the political board.

Egypt, which was now nearly free, was split internally and orienting itself more and more towards the Arab countries on its eastern frontier. In 1939 it was involved in the war; not actively for it remained neutral, although it broke off relations with Germany, Italy and Japan in September 1939, June 1940 and December 1941, the dates on which Britain declared war on these countries, and gave a host's welcome, if not particularly willingly, to the Allied troops under Wavell and Alexander. Happenings during the war will be dealt with later.[1]

[1] *v.* pp. 285 *sq.*

IRAN AND AFGHANISTAN

In 1919 the Western powers had their plans ready. It was London and Paris who were to take the decisions, not the Egyptians, the Arabs, the Turks, the Persians or the Afghans. The two powers might at least have invited the Middle East to Versailles; instead, Britain interned Zaglul, France kept Faisal out of Syria and such Persians as came to Paris were not recognized. It was Britain which dictated what was to happen in Persia. The Persian Government was forced to sign a treaty – drawn up by Sir Percy Cox, whom we have seen at work in Irak – in which naturally the sovereignty and territorial integrity of Persia were affirmed, but in fact Persia was treated as a colony, carefully disguised of course (August 9, 1919). Persia's reaction was typical of the changed days which were now beginning. The Persian Parliament (Madjlis) refused to ratify the treaty, mainly because it had learned how much money the British had sent to the Government as a tiny mark of their esteem. Such dealings are successful only if they stay secret. If Persia apparently followed in Britain's wake and (January 1920) became a member of the League of Nations, internally there was growing anarchy in which a new era was emerging from a vanishing past.

In the summer of 1920 the Bolsheviks, threatened from every quarter, were apprehensive of British action against Baku and its oil. They occupied a strip of Persia's Caspian coast. The Cossack Brigade under Colonel Storroselski and the British forces of occupation again drove inwards. As in Russia in 1917 and in Turkey in 1919, this was the signal for the new course to begin. The radical tendencies in the Persian bourgeoisie, the Liberals, who were hostile to the corrupt and unpatriotic regime of the Shah and the landed nobility, had long been toying with thoughts of a revolution aiming at a final development such as the left elements in the revolutions of 1906 and 1909 had desired. The leader of the movement, the great reformer and writer Said Zia al-Din, appealed for help to a Persian officer in the Cossack Brigade, Riza Khan (1878–1944). An intelligent patriot, born in the province of Masandaran between the snowclad peaks of the Caucasus and the Caspian, he first of all purged the brigade of its czarist officers and then declared himself ready for a *coup d'état*. In the night of February 22nd–23rd he entered Teheran at the head of 300 Cossacks, and by morning Persia had a new and nationalist government. Officers' revolts of this type, moderate in their aims, are a frequent phenomenon in the history of awakening Asia. In Western eyes they are odd and even embarrassing events, for in Europe the professional soldier is more inclined to maintain the old ways than to make a revolution. But history does not lie. In Persia things took the same turn as in the neighbouring countries. As in Russia of the *coup d'état* of a night in Teheran. As little as did the Egyptian revolution did it involve the whole population, in these countries that population is four-fifths peasants and workers on the land.

Guards who were Peter the Great's best collaborators in his attempt to westernize Russia. A century later it was the officers who were the spiritual inspirers of the abortive revolution of 1825, officers who had served with the army of occupation in France in 1814 and had been captivated by Western political ideas.

Naturally enough czars and sultans and shahs had tried to keep the westernization of the armed forces within limits and to prevent the army having 'dangerous ideas'. But intelligent officers, who often, in spite of the obstacles in the way, had come from the bourgeoisie and had studied English, French and German military books, did not neglect other and revolutionary books. They also learned in their own persons the iron law of history which says that no state can have a really modern army if in other respects it remains in the Middle Ages. It is never possible to adopt just one significant part of a foreign culture.

Just as in other revolutions, the Persian officers were quite as useful . . . and as dangerous to the evolution of the national effort. Riza Khan got rid of Zia al-Din as early as 1923 and from then on ruled alone as a frank dictator. Yet he was no traitor to the revolution, even if about 1940 his rule showed markedly right-wing tendencies. On February 20, 1921, he denounced the Anglo-Persian treaty and reached a compromise with the Bolsheviks. The latter were in the critical and heroic phase of their revolution and, partly from principle, partly because they feared further intervention by the West, were generous towards the Persians. They evacuated Persian territory and declared all capitulations, all debts, all mining concessions and all other Russian claims on Persia of whatever date to have lapsed. The true meaning of the compromise is to be found in the clause in which Russian rights, with regard to Persia are dealt with; if any foreign power (Britain, for example) were to occupy part of Persian territory, then the Russians would be free to march into the country.

The northern front was now secured. The British troops had all gone back to Irak or India and no danger threatened from Turkey where the Ankara government was trying to drive out the European invaders. Actually a Turko-Persian agreement (December 1921) transformed the old feud between the two countries into neutrality, even if it was not too friendly a neutrality, and Riza Khan recognized in Kemal a 'fellow fighter for the revolution'—and still more a model, as we shall see later.

The Persian nationalists between the two world wars did not achieve what Kemal had achieved in his very individual campaign for modernization after the Russian model. Riza Khan could not keep out foreign capital, least of all British capital. It had a tight hold on oil production and from oil production came the greatest part of Persia's national revenue. At this period the cotton crops and the Suez Canal and the oilfields of Kirkuk were the cause of British intervention in Egypt and Irak; the oilfields of Kermanshah and Kusistan afforded reasons for similar intervention in Persia. The oil remained British; Mossadeq thirty years later would change that situation and pay for his daring with three years in prison (December 21, 1953).

It is an open question how far Riza Khan really tried to exclude oil capital, though it is evident that he strove to restrict and neutralize British influence by inviting to Persia technicians and economists from Germany, Russia, Scandinavia and the United States. The American economist and emissary of the Californian oil trust, Dr A. C. Millspaugh, became administrator of the naturally chaotic state finances and of the Ministry of War (1922–1927). The reformed army of Persia, now of greater strength, occupied the recovered provinces in the northwest and the southwest. Azerbaijan was occupied in 1922. After that Riza returned to Teheran and, as we have said, got rid of Zia al-Din, whom he regarded as too democratic, and took over the premiership himself (October 28, 1923). That was a signal for the reigning shah to leave the country; he disappeared into Europe and never came back.

His flight was not an official banishment and when, in the summer of 1924, rumours of his return were widespread a wave of republican agitation swept the country. The Shiite mullahs, who were suspicious of everything which looked like revolution on the Turkish or Russian model, urgently begged Riza Khan to moderate his zeal for modernization and to prevent the spread of republican and anti-religious feeling. The Government bowed to the mullahs' argument, for the time at least, the more willingly as the British Government and the Anglo-Persian Oil Company were urging the Bakhtiaris of the southwestern oil region to revolt against Teheran. This is another instance of the anti-patriotic alliance between a threatened feudal system and foreign imperialism; there are others in the civil wars in Russia, China, Korea, Mongolia and Indochina.

In Persia, Riza broke the revolt of the Bakhtiaris in October 1924. His time now seemed to have come. Just as was the case with Kemal in Turkey after the Kurdish rebellion, the parliament in Persia gave legal standing to the dictatorship which the situation seemed to justify (February 1929) and deprived the shah in Europe of all his functions (October 31, 1925). That was the end of the Kadjar dynasty. On April 25, 1926, the Cossack officer ascended the throne as Riza Khan Pahlevi (1925–1941). He tried now to follow the Kemal policy. A Turko-Perso-Afghan Pact of Security and Non-Aggression inspired by Russia (1926) decreased the danger of Western penetration, and when in 1937 Irak became a fourth signatory of the pact – the Saadabad Pact, or the Eastern Entente – it brought together about 50,000,000 Moslem Asians.

The technical basis of the modernization of Persia was the westernization of its transport and road and rail system. A land of camels and caravan tracks may be romantic, but it is in no way equipped to meet modern requirements. The revolutionary shah summoned engineers, German for the most part, and built roads everywhere between the sleepy villages and the towns across stony desert country and the hills – four-fifths of the country is desert land – between the grain fields and the vegetable gardens, vineyards and apricot plantations which blossom like oases in the western valleys, and the roses of Ispahan which, apart from its women and its oil, are perhaps the fairest – and most transient – product of Persia. For the first time in a turbulent history there was now the possibility of real and direct contact between the scattered peasantry and shepherds and the government in Teheran. It must be remembered that Persia is as big as Britain, France, Spain and Germany put together, and that more than three-quarters of the people are peasants and workers on the land, including 3,000,000 nomads who send to the colder countries the famous Persian sheepskins. In 1939 Persia had nearly 20,000 miles of roads, a fifth of which were first class.

As far as transport is concerned Persia has hardly entered the railway age, yet she has some good railway lines in the west, of which the Trans-Persian railway from Bandar Shah on the Caspian to Bandar Shapur on the Persian Gulf was well known during the Second World War, for it was the one sure line of communication between the Russian front and its material needs and the American war industry. It was constructed between 1928 and 1937, and the first train ran in the winter of 1938–9. German, Swedish and Danish engineers had laid down nearly 700 miles of rails and built 224 tunnels and 1933 bridges all with Persian money which came from the tea and sugar State monopolies. The German Junkers works brought international air traffic to Teheran and Isfahan (1927). British companies operating on the Europe-East Asia route followed in the track of the Germans. A Persian State Bank (Bank Melli Iran, 1928) took business away from the British financial houses like the Bank of Persia and the Middle East.

The establishment of the regime and the growth of self-consciousness in the people expressed itself in the change of the national name from Persia to Iran and also in a changed attitude towards London. For instance, in 1927 the Government asked for the return of the Bahrein islands from which Shah Abbas the Great had driven the Portuguese in 1602 and which had belonged to Persia for two centuries. The British had got the islands from a family of sheiks from Kuwait which had annexed them in 1800. Another 'historically founded' attempt at expansion! The British would not yield an inch. As little realistic were the plans for a Persian navy. In 1928 a number of warships arrived in Persian waters from Italian yards to be the nucleus of a Persian fleet. It did not materialise and in 1955 the Persian navy consisted of two frigates, five warships, the royal yacht on the Caspian and a few tugs. Times change. Persia had won back her independence, but the days when the Greek cities trembled to see Persian ships of war approach will not easily return.

More useful was the nationalization of the inland lines of the British 'Indo-European Telegraph Company' (1931), the state control of foreign trade (1931) and the amendment of the agreement with the Anglo-Persian Oil Company which owned rights of exploitation on four-fifths of the country. As production from the Persian fields was steadily rising – 50,000 tons in 1912; 6,000,000 tons in 1930 – the Government in 1932 demanded a revision of the d'Arcy contract of 1901. Hard bargaining between Persia, the Anglo-Persian Company and the British Government, which was financially interested, resulted in a new agreement whereby Persia got 20 per cent of the dividend as against 16, plus an additional five shillings per ton, and the size of the concession was reduced by a fifth to the southwestern frontier districts between Kermanshah and Bandar Abbas. The profits of the company, however, remained bigger than the total revenue of Persia. The concession was to last for the period 1933–1993; none the less, Persia annulled it in 1951 successfully and without a war.

Internally the shah tried to achieve what the Turkish revolution had achieved. The methods he adopted were a cross between the radical fanaticism of a Kemal and the savage energy of a Peter the Great. During the campaign against the veiling of women, for instance, the queen in 1928 visited the holy city of Kum, and a Shiite mullah reproached her with immodesty, because she was insufficiently veiled. Next day the shah himself thundered into the town in an armoured car, stumped in his officer's top boots into the mosque, arrested some thieves and murderers who had sought asylum in Kum and administered a sound drubbing to the mullah who had rebuked his royal consort.

But it was not only external survivals of the past that were wherever possible combated as obstacles to westernization. In the sphere of law the mullahs were driven more and more into the background. Laws and an administration on French and Swiss models were substituted for the burdensome heritage of the mediaeval Moslem law books. The emancipation of women was energetically taken up. A modern divorce code, the forbidding of polygamy, the change in the marriageable age of women from nine years of age, as the Koranic tradition prescribes, to fifteen – all that was undertaken between 1930 and 1935.

The percentage of illiteracy remained high – more than 75 per cent. But women and peasants were no longer kept in ignorance on principle; wherever the power of the mullahs was lessened, state schools appeared in towns and villages. In 1939 one-third of Persian children were being taught to read and write as compared with barely half of 1 per cent in 1921. In 1935 the University of Teheran was founded

Just as in Turkey, the most significant of the changes was the work of an enlightened dictatorship. The Madjlis pondered and debated; the shah guided. Like the Turkish revolution of 1919, the Persian revolution of 1921 was the work of officers and a number of bourgeois politicians who had risen against a corrupt aristocracy which desired alone to rule the country and felt the claim justified since it owned half of all the land; yet it formed only 1 per cent of the population. In this sense the Persian revolution, like other nationalist movements was a class revolt. That is perhaps one of the reasons for its ardour and intensity, but again perhaps a reason for its hesitancy and lack of drive in the modernization of the agricultural districts.

The origin and causes of the revolutions in Turkey and Iran are fundamentally akin, but in Iran there was a much lesser result culturally and where the peasantry, foreign penetration and investment were concerned. What is the explanation? Perhaps it is this, that Kemal's revolution had, in a savage war of independence which lasted through three winters and four summers, awakened the peasantry of Anatolia from its oriental lethargy and mobilized it against the European invader, while the Persian revolution was the result of the *coup d'état* of a night in Teheran. As little as did the Egyptian revolution did it involve the whole population, in these countries that population is four-fifths peasants and workers on the land.

In the second place, except for the Straits, Turkey had nothing so dangerous as oil. Iran, on the other hand, has a veritable excess of oil. In 1913 8,000,000 tons came from it, as much as the entire contemporary production of Indonesia and between 3½ and 5 per cent of the world's production. Production went on steadily increasing; in 1945 it was 14,000,000 tons, in 1950 32,000,000 tons, i.e. 500,000 barrels of over 40 gallons per day; all of it was refined in Abadan, one of the greatest refineries in the world. It is that which explains the tenacity with which Britain defended her claims. As early as 1921 Persia was fourth among oil-producing countries and remains so still. Today the United States supplies 50 per cent of the world's oil, Venezuela 15 per cent, Russia 8 per cent and Iran 6 per cent. As both Russia and the United States use all their own production themselves, Iran in a sense is in second place.

How Iran, the bone of contention between Britain and Russia, the oil reservoir of the British navy and an attraction to American and German imperialism developed during the Second World War and, ever more liberated from the West, managed to follow a policy of its own, we shall investigate later on in this book.

Directly southwest of the snowy wilderness of Russia's Pamir mountains (20,000 feet) lies Afghanistan, a rugged mountain land between 1600 and 8000 feet above the level of the distant sea, for the most part hard and stony, in summer burning hot, in winter cold and covered with snow. There are milder districts where water is more plentiful, especially on the northern and southeastern slopes of the Hindu Kush. These have been transformed into garden valleys by the primitive Afghan peasants, and here there are fields of wheat, the white and red blossoms of almond and apricot trees, forests of date palms and small holdings where barley and maize are grown. About 20 per cent of the land is cultivated. The country resembles a fortress built by nature. Although its frontiers are shared with the three most populous countries of the world – China, India and Russia – and with Pakistan and Iran, Afghanistan, of all the Asian countries, is the least accessible. It can be reached by car from the Turkmenistan and Uzbekistan republics, but on its eastern side only by a few wild mountain passes like the historic Khyber Pass which links Kabul with Peshawar. Inside the country communications are worse than in any other Asian land. There are no railways, except an old and rusty five-mile line built by the Germans. There are a few modern roads – rather less than 2000 miles of them – which connect the bigger towns. Dromedaries, small horses and donkeys are almost the only means of transport for the semi-nomad cattle-raisers who certainly form a third of the population and whose caracul sheep are a feature of the landscape.

That is what Afghanistan looks like today, a land which modern history

A.C.—7*

has hardly changed, at least externally. In 1919 the vast majority of its inhabitants lived just as they did in mediaeval times. We have already told
how in 1919 Amanulla Khan (b. 1892), of the Baraksai dynasty became amir
(1919–1929). When he took the title of king (padishah) in 1926, the experts
were agreed that his beautiful consort Suriya had as much to do with the
change as he had. We mention this simply as one of the many instances where
oriental wives, despite all appearances to the contrary, have often through
their charm and wit influenced their husbands and so affected their countries
and their histories.

However that may be, Amanulla about 1920, the period when Moslem
Southwest Asia was resisting British and Western influence, declared the
independence of Afghanistan. His invasion of British India failed in a few
weeks. The British reaction was on a considerable scale. Determined, as it
was in Persia, to take the wind out of the Bolshevik sails, London agreed
(August 8, 1919, in the treaty of Rawalpindi) for the first time in the history
of Anglo-Afghan relations to recognize the sovereignty of Afghanistan and
its right to conduct its foreign affairs itself.

The British colonies on the southern and eastern frontiers remained naturally a menace, and at first Amanulla strove to try as a makeweight to get
into touch with anti-British countries. The firstfruits of his efforts was the
Russo-Afghan Treaty of Friendship of February 28, 1921, which was extended by the Treaty of Neutrality and Non-Aggression of 1926. Parallel
thereto was the Russo-Persian defensive and offensive alliance of February
26, 1921, and the Russo-Turkish Treaty of 1925 with which we have already
dealt. Turko-Afghan alliances date back to 1921 and 1928, Perso-Afghan
ones to 1921 and 1927.

It was only after he felt himself externally secure that Amanulla tried to
break down the mediaeval isolation of his people, and make available to
them modern discoveries and improvements. The publication of a constitution on the Turkish model (April 1923) marks a turning-point, even if
the constitution itself had next to no connection with democracy. The
brand-new Parliament, half of which consisted of nominated members
while the other half was returned by indirect election, had very little to say.
The real leader was the enlightened amir. He wasted no time; a mass of
reforms like those carried out by Kemal were imposed on the country from
Kabul. German and French engineers came on camels to Herat, Kandahar
and Kabul to build roads, railways and wireless stations. The recruitment
and organization of a modern army, the emancipation of women, the transformation of a feudally organized land into a single national state, the removal of the many obstacles to modernization, the suppression of those
Moslem elements from which reaction was to be feared, e.g. the many anti-
revolutionary mullahs – Amanulla sought to achieve all that at a stroke. But
what Lenin and Stalin in Russia and Ataturk in Turkey had on the whole
succeeded in doing, i.e. the cramming of the whole achievement of the
French revolution and the industrial revolution into a quarter of a century,
could not be done in Afghanistan.

Tales like that of the betrothed peasant girl somewhere in the northeastern slopes of the Hindu Kush who refused to accept the husband chosen by her family and was murdered by her father, were told in the Afghan villages, and serve as examples of the opposition to Amanulla's reforms. Objectively the country seemed ripe for revolutionary westernization, but subjectively the conditions for a westernization of the population, as was soon seen, did not exist. The pre-capitalist mentality of the peasants and shepherds living isolated as they did, the division of the people into clans and tiny, restless feudal estates – all that had a negative effect.

In 1928 the rule of the Afghan 'Czar Peter' burst like a bubble. The indirect cause was the king's journeys abroad; he went to Bombay, Cairo, Rome, Paris, Berlin, London and Moscow, and his travels were a sort of symbol of his desire to bring his isolated and distant land into the stream of world events. When he and his queen returned to Kabul in summer, the backwardness of his country, as he saw it, drove the king to take measures which were much too radical. His plan for direct elections was an open attack on the position of the feudal chiefs. In November the reactionary opposition broke out in a general counter-revolution and Amanulla abdicated (January 14, 1929).

He was succeeded by his much less energetic brother Inayatulla. A mild man and little interested in what was happening, he was just as little able to achieve anything. In January 1929 a certain Baksha-i-Sagao, a peasant leader, occupied Kabul, crowned himself as Habibulla Ghazi and got rid of every possible claimant to the throne save one. In March the former commander of the Afghan army and ambassador in Paris (1924–1926), Mohammed Nadir Khan (1880–1933), came back from Europe. This unusually intelligent diplomatist and officer got together his own efficient little army, captured Kabul (October 8, 1929) and on October 16th became king (1929–1933) as Mohammed Nadir Shah. Thus ended the Baraksai dynasty which had ruled Afghanistan since 1835. Habibulla was captured and hanged. Amanulla fled to Rome where, in the summer of 1944, he was arrested by British Intelligence Service for pro-German activities.

An interesting consequence of the fall of Amanulla was the creation of the Soviet Republic of Tadjikstan on the northern frontier of Afghanistan between Tibet and Samarkand, the seventh republic of the USSR. The Moscow government – and it was not alone in its belief – was sure that the counter-revolution in Kabul was the work of British agents, and as a countermeasure Stalin gave the Tadjik district the constitution of a Soviet republic within the Soviet Union (December 5, 1929); in theory, therefore, its position was no different from that, say, of the Ukraine. The ideas behind Russian propaganda in Asia played their part; 20 per cent of the inhabitants of Afghanistan are Tadjiks.

Mohammed Nadir had possibly no great affection for the Bolsheviks, but he understood his age and his struggling country. He knew Europe well; he also knew Afghanistan and, though less provocatively, continued Amanulla's campaign for modernization. His assassination in Kabul on November 8, 1933, caused no political upheaval. During the reign of his son Mohammed

Zahir Shah (b. 1914) Afghanistan went on maturing, even if outward signs thereof were relatively few.

Events in Afghanistan during the years from 1929 to 1941 can be grouped under three heads: 1. Further democratization and further diminution of the influence of the mullahs and the landed nobility with the help among other things of the new constitution of 1932. Structurally this was very like that of 1923; now the progressively minded bourgeoisie and, indirectly, part of the peasantry began to play a certain part in legislation and government. 2. The strengthening of the country as a sovereign Asian state; westernization of the army, employment of Turkish officers as instructors, creation of a Military Academy in Kabul (1932). 3. Adhesion to the Saadabad Pact of 1937, the defensive alliance which we have already mentioned between Turkey, Irak, Iran and Afghanistan.

The recruiting of foreign technicians is, as in other independent Asian countries, an important aspect of Afghan policy in this period. German, Russian, British and even Japanese engineers had much achievement to their credit. But an event like the oil concession to the 'Inland Exploration Company' of New York indicates that economic independence had not yet been achieved. The problem of the modernization of Asian countries like Afghanistan, especially in the economic sphere, is not so much the obstinacy of threatened ruling classes, or the lack of technicians and intellectuals, as how to obtain the capital so terribly needed without allowing foreign capitalism as of old to interfere too actively. American capitalism differs slightly from the colonial capitalism of Europe, but fundamentally the relation between rich industrial countries and primitive agricultural states remains the same everywhere. The invasion of certain parts of contemporary Asia by Russian capital and Russian technicians is naturally, in principle at least, the cause of a certain political connection. But there is perhaps a notable difference in that in the case of Russia private interests play no part.

The revolt of 1929 against the 'socialist king', and the tactics of Britain which sought to use Afghanistan as a buffer state between the British colonies in South Asia and the Russian revolution, were big obstacles to the development of a modern state. There is in Asia no country of any significance which is more primitive. The number of factories in Afghanistan is still extremely small; the only one to possess modern American machinery is the fairly modern cotton-spinning factory at Pul-i-Kumri northwest of Kabul. Four-fifths of the population are still illiterate. Unlike Turkey, Iran and the Soviet Union, the power of the conservative mullahs and of Koranic law are, generally speaking, still unshaken. Coal, copper, oil and no one knows what else is still underground. Western traffic and road connections are more than just evidence of cultural progress; they constitute a dangerous threat to the native Asian culture of the past – and not only the Asian – but their increase is a useful criterion of the modernization of a country. At present Afghanistan has one telephone to each 4000 of the inhabitants and one wireless set to each 5000. Compare the figures for Egypt (one to 200 and one to 170), Irak (one to 350 and one to 100) and Holland (one to 14 and one to 8).

Although compared to other Moslem states this romantic mountain land lags far behind in development, none the less modern technique, and with it the ideals of the age of the machine, are spreading increasingly between Herat and Kabul among the cotton growers and the factory workers. And still more influential in driving Afghanistan forward on the road which the peoples of Asia are taking, is the great development beyond the frontiers in Pakistan and India, in China, in the Soviet Union and in Iran.

VIII

CHINA (i)

IN the revolution of 1911 the weaker China did not achieve what the French bourgeoisie achieved in the revolutions of 1798 and 1830. The bourgeois of Paris and other French towns broke the absolute monarchy of the eighteenth century and substituted for it its own rule in the machine age of the nineteenth. The French peasants burned down the chateaus of their masters, divided their land, fought in the revolutionary armies for the revolution and spread its ideas in Europe. The Chinese peasants and workers had virtually no part in the events of 1911. The insignificant Manchu emperor Pu-i was driven from his throne, but not much else was changed. After August 13, 1912, Sun's Tung Meng-hui, the advance guard of the revolution, continued to be, under the name of Kuo Min-tang, a semi-legal party of the merchant bourgeoisie in China and abroad, but it included as well officials and other intellectuals. Actually the provincial governors continued to rule, and the detested war lords and other 'unofficial' bandits and desperadoes. The government, transformed only in appearance, had virtually no power beyond the walls of Pekin and in fact was little more than the mouthpiece of the Japanese and Western imperialists. Amid the chaos that reigned internally, and stifled under foreign economic pressure, China wasted away.

Round about 1919 three factors caused a change in the situation – imperialism, the growth of the native workers' and peasants' movements, and the Russian revolution. They forced the Kuo Min-tang to the left, to the workers and the peasants, and between 1924 and 1927 made it the centre of the second great revolution in opposition to Pekin and imperialism.

With regard to the first factor: At Versailles, the Western powers and Japan ignored the just claims of China. As an example Japan received the former German concessions in Shantung and kept its army of intervention in Manchuria, a bitter pill for Sun and the Kuo Min-tang to have to swallow; this incidentally is an interesting case of what some Marxist writers have called 'the objective revolutionary functioning of imperialism'. The Chinese bourgeoisie had expected much of the West; only a handful of left-wing intellectuals had during the war given a warning of what would happen, e.g. the Marxist writer Professor Chen Tu-chou of Pekin University in his *Weekly Review* (1918). For Chinese Marxism Chen was what Plekhanov was to the Russian.

The second factor in the leftward development of the Kuo Min-tang was the growth of the workers' and peasants' movement. Peasant risings are no novelty in China but resistance movements among the workers were something new; they date from 1919. The best known are the bloody railway strike on the Pekin-Hankow line (1920) and the general strike of Chinese seamen and workers in British Hongkong (1922). The growing radicalism among students and other intellectuals had a similar effect. In 1918 a society for the study of Marxism was formed at Pekin University. In 1920 Chen Wang-tao translated the Communist Manifesto of Marx and Engels into Chinese, the first classic work of Marxism to appear in the native language. In the same year the Communist party of China, the Kuan Shan-tang, was organized in Pekin. Its leaders from 1921 to 1927 were Chen Tu-chou (1879–1942) and Dr Li Ta-chao of the Pekin University library. Simultaneously branches were formed in the cities abroad where many Chinese lived, particularly in France and Germany in which Chou En-lai and Chu-teh held office, and in Moscow and Tokio. The bourgeois left-wingers also threw off the chains of tradition. In these years Confucianism was attacked from many sides, and was replaced by pragmatism or materialism.

The third factor was the Russian revolution, from which developed the Soviet Union.

Sun read these writings on the wall and, at least in part, understood them. In contrast to his views in 1911 he now tended more and more to think of the peasants and workers as an important element in, perhaps even the advance guard of, the revolution against mediaeval China, although, as has often been stated, he himself was not a communist.

In April 1920 Sun formed in Canton a Kuo Min-tang government as a rival to the government in Pekin. It was anything but secure. Foreign warships threatened the port and reactionaries intrigued against 'red Canton'. A *coup de main* of the right parties caused Sun and his wife to leave Canton for the moment. For fifteen days he lay concealed on board the only warship of the revolutionary government, the *Jung Feng*, and then escaped to Shanghai. His house was wrecked and many important manuscripts were burned, including his studies of the economic problems of the new China, even then historic documents.

In Shanghai Sun contacted Joffe and Karakhan the Russian representatives to Pekin, and thus was established the entente between the Kuo Min-tang and the Bolsheviks which lasted until 1927. The Soviet Union was the only country prepared to help to preserve the Chinese bourgeois revolution. Sun went back to Canton, and in the summer of 1923 a number of representatives of the Russian Government and of the Communist International arrived there, including M. M. Borodin, a Russian who had formerly been active as adviser to the revolutionary government in Turkey, and Manabendra Nath Roy, a well-known rebel from India. Acting on their advice and despite many international menaces and naval demonstrations, Sun transformed the Kuo Min-tang into a really revolutionary party on the Russian model. At the first purely Chinese Congress (January 20–30, 1924) the communists were admitted to the Kuo Min-tang, the Communist party remaining intact as a party. That meant a further swing to the left. The less revolutionary section of the Kuo Min-tang reacted at once; by September a number of their leaders had gone to Shanghai, the citadel of the bourgeoisie, and had formed a 'white' Kuo Min-tang in opposition to the 'red' party in Canton.

Meantime the Bolsheviks had sent rifles and other war material, and also some senior officers including General Bluecher. The revolutionary army got its own professional establishment in the Whampoa Military Academy in Canton (May 1924). Officially, its director was Chiang Kai-shek (b. 1887), Sun's chief of staff, who had just returned from a period of study at the Red Army Academy in Moscow, but its real director was Bluecher. Chou En-lai (b. 1898) was its secretary. He is now premier of China and for long was foreign minister as well. The political commandant was the left radical Liao Chung-hai, the Marat of the Chinese revolution.

Sun tried to induce Pekin to recognize the Canton government as the official government of the Republic. During one of his diplomatic journeys in the north the catastrophe happened; on a cold winter morning (March 12, 1925) the great revolutionary leader died in hospital from cancer of the liver. March 12th was as critical a date for the Chinese revolution as was January 21, 1924, when Lenin died, for the Russian.

Possibly it was only the imperialist threat and the military expedition to the north – of which more later – which prevented further splits in the Kuo Min-tang between 1925 and 1927. The real heads of the Canton government in 1924 besides Borodin were: from the left wing, Wang Ching-wei (also known as Wang Shao-ming), the real author of Sun's manifestoes, as head of the executive committee of the government, and from the right, Hu Han-min. Both had been prominent in the party for twenty-five years.

Two other factors contributed to the growth of radicalism, urging it on against foreign imperialism and at the same time more and more making the right wing in the coast cities hostile to the 'red stronghold' of Canton. On May 30, 1925, Chinese workers and students demonstrated in front of a British police station in the international quarter of Shanghai where some strike leaders from the Japanese cotton mills were being held prisoner. The British troops received the order to fire. The incident was promptly described as 'the bloodbath of Shanghai'. The result was a general strike in the city and an economic blockade of the international settlements. Not until October were Chinese, British and Japanese soldiers able to break the strike and the boycott. The story of the events in Shanghai spread like wildfire through the country and provoked protests in all the seaports. In Canton, marines from H.M.S. *Tarantula* and French marines fired on a mob of demonstrating port labourers and students (June 23, 1925). The general strike of Chinese workers in the docks and the factories of Hongkong, and the boycott of the colony, lasted for 450 days, a historic record. The British blockade of Canton, 'the breeding-ground of the revolution', lasted just as long. Most of the Hongkong strikers went during the summer to neighbouring Canton and worked like leaven in the working class, in the city generally and in Kwantung province.

The manner in which the right wing led by Hu Han-min in Canton itself and the 'white' Kuo Min-tang in Shanghai sought to defend themselves was shown in the murder (August 19, 1925) of Liao Chung-hai, the radical, but not communist, minister for finance and agriculture, and political commandant of the Whampoa Academy, who was next to Wang Ching-wei among the left leaders. It was also seen in the *coup d'état* in the early hours of March 20, 1926, of Chiang Kai-shek and others against Communist infiltration. The head of the Government, Wang Ching-wei, went under protest to France for a holiday, from which he did not return until April 1927. Hu Han-min, who not without some reason was suspected of disloyalty, was temporarily banished. Chiang Kai-shek remained and said the whole business was a mistake.

Meantime the revolutionary government, thinking the time ripe, officially declared war on Pekin and the northern warlords (February 25, 1926), which meant in fact war on Wu Pei-fu (1878–1939), poet and bandit on a heroic scale and actual leader of the Pekin government, and on Chang Tso-lin, the buccaneer governor of Northeast China, who as early as 1904 had been pro-Japanese.

In May, Chiang Kai-shek was made commander-in-chief of the revolutionary army. Neither Borodin nor the communists raised any objection. On the contrary, Bluecher became military adviser to the expedition. In the summer of 1926 the revolutionary army advanced from Kwangtung northwards *via* Hunan and the Taiping road, seven divisions of it, each 15,000 strong. The revolution, which had seemed to be confined to Canton, raged like a typhoon over the country. The peasants and workers and a considerable part of the bourgeoisie greeted Chiang's troops as liberators; the towns of South China fell like ripe fruit into the hands of the invaders; Wu Pei-fu's mercenaries fled or surrendered. It looked like a repetition of the French revolutionary campaigns in Europe round about 1800. By October some of the 'iron divisions' had reached the Yang-tse and occupied Wuhan (Hankow), where the Canton government – composed of the left wing and the communists – established itself (November 10th). In December the revolutionary army entered the ports in Fukien province and by February 1927 had occupied all the great towns south of the river except Shanghai and Nanking. It was now about 200,000 strong.

What happened now was a tragedy. Nanking fell on March 24th. As had happened in other cities, the approach of the revolutionary army provoked trouble in Shanghai. All the workers went on strike. As advance guard of the army, a revolutionary committee – in which Chou En-lai and the well-known labour leaders Chao Chi-yen, Ku Chun-chiang and Lo Yi-ming were included – organized 5000 resistance fighters into worker and student battalions. The army of the north left the city, and when, on March 27, 1927, Chiang made his entry the revolution was already in power.

But that was too much for the bourgeoisie. Already embittered by the growth of the left element in the government in Wuhan, it saw danger ahead, a double danger of an active intervention by Japan and the Western powers and of a genuine worker and peasant revolution. It sometimes happens that one day an island rises out of the sea and sinks again next day; the Chinese bourgeoisie feared that the moment they rose free from Western imperialism they would be submerged in the swirling flood of a universal social revolution. What the capitalists and landowners wanted was in the technical sense of the word a counter-revolution. Strange as it may seem, the leader of the counter-revolution was Chiang Kai-shek. Between the middle of April and August, he arrested and executed in Shanghai alone 5000 communist workers and radical intellectuals and students. On April 15 he organized a counter-government in Nanking against red Wuhan, a government in which the only effective voice was that of the capitalists and the landowners. The Wuhan government, which Wang Ching-wei, returning *via* Russia, had rejoined, reacted at once, expelled Chiang from the party and declared him deprived of all his offices.

But that was all. Wang and the official Kuo Min-tang government were not communists; they were bourgeois revolutionaries inclined certainly to the left, but by no means prepared to act against Nanking with the aid of a mass rising of workers and peasants. Thus they could not defend themselves against mutinous generals, and more and more got involved in the counter-revolution. Hesitatingly they took the way of a white terror of their own. Neither Borodin nor the Chinese communists realized the danger in time. Russia, where the opposition between Trotsky and Stalin was reaching its climax, seemed uninterested in what was happening in China. It was only when Wang started an anti-communist purge such as had been carried through in Nanking, removed Borodin from his post and broke off relations with the Third International, that the communists began to think of active resistance. But the communist revolts in Nanchang and Canton were only a sort of death agony of a horrible kind.

In July 1927 a number of extreme left-wing officers and their men fled from Wuhan and on August 1st occupied Nanchang in the middle of Kiangsi province. They were the 20th army and a division of the 11th army in which Chu-teh and Chou En-lai, who had escaped from Shanghai, were staff officers. Within a week the revolting troops were driven out of Nanchang and in mid-August turned south and set up a communist government in the port of Swatow. An international fleet blockaded the port and in October the rebels fled inland. Part of them were scattered, another part got back into the hills on the frontier between Hunan and Kiangsi. It was the latter who formed the kernel of the Chinese red army; their commander was Chu-teh. In April 1928 they joined Mao Tse-tung and his adherents in the fortified village of Ching-kanshan and here far away from the broad highway of official history the China of today was to be born.

We shall not describe here how the primitive soviet government in Kiangsi-Hunan grew and defended itself in the many campaigns which the Kuo Min-tang waged against it in the hope of annihilating it. First of all, the consequences of these happenings do not fall within the period with which this section deals, and second that, if we do, we risk misinterpreting history and think in terms only of the Chinese communist revolution. We should not relate past conditions and events to the Chinese People's Republic as it exists today. The reader will find below the later history of the communists.

In the counter-revolution of April 1927 – the Chinese Thermidor – and during the period of the white terror in the summer of that year, the bourgeoisie, even if only temporarily, had completely defeated the communists. The agrarian revolution was halted, and the workers' movement in the towns broken. In the middle of December, 2000 communist workers, peasants and students were executed in the streets of Canton in revenge for their desperate attempt at a *putsch*. After this episode, which is in history called 'the commune of Canton' – after the Paris commune which was put down in blood in 1871 – the Communist party was virtually extinguished in the towns. What was left of them formed a resistance movement. Of the 130,000 party members in 1929, only 5000 lived in the big cities.

In this same period the left government in Wuhan fell to pieces. As is almost always the case, it was not enough for the reaction to destroy the radical left groups; it attacked everything which was to left of itself. In December Chiang was once again made commander-in-chief – in 1928 he was also head of the Government – and diplomatic relations with Russia were broken off. A week later Wang Ching-wei and other high officials of the Kuo Min-tang who were left wing, including Mrs Sun, went to Europe and the USSR. The government in Nanking was the government of Kuo Min-tang China, that is, China south of the Yang-tse. When he changed his policies, Chiang also changed his wife; on December 1st he married as his fourth wife Soong Mei-ling, of the very rich, pro-American merchant family of Charles John Soong; of his two other daughters, Ching-ling and Ai-ling, the former had married Sun Yat-sen and the latter, the banker Dr Kung Hisang-hui. If there was any single family which had particular influence in Kuo Min-tang China, it was the Soong family. To that same family belonged Soong Tsu-ven (Dr T. V. Soong), the director of the Bank of China (1933–1944) and later foreign minister (1941–1945). Kung Hsiang-hui was finance minister in the Nanking government. The marriage of Chiang and Mei-ling revealed the betrayal, possibly not generally known, of the revolutionary past of his party; he hired for the wedding the biggest hotel in Shanghai and invited all prominent foreigners, including the commander-in-chief of the British forces in China.

In April 1928 the campaign against Pekin and the rest of the North was resumed. Two of the provincial governors and warlords seemed willing to recognize Chiang as commander-in-chief, Yen Hsi-chan of Shansi and Feng Yu-hsian, the self-willed 'Christian general', in the northwest in Shensi and Hopei. North China fell like ripe fruit into the hands of the invader. Only in Shantung was resistance offered – by a Japanese force at Tsinan (May 3–11, 1928) which withdrew in May. Tokio, it seemed, was not ready to risk a full-scale intervention and on June 8th the Kuo Min-tang army entered Pekin. The universal bitterness against Japan found expression in a large-scale boycott of Japanese goods (1928–1929).

Meantime the ally of the Japanese, Chang Tso-lin, the governor of Manchuria, had understood that the situation had changed and now announced his readiness to recognize the Nanking government as the national government of China. That did not please his former masters, the Japanese, and he was murdered; on June 4th his own train, on which he was travelling between Pekin and Mukden, was blown up. The new governor, his son Chang Hsu-liang (b. 1898), remained loyal to China, and in November recognized the Nanking government; to all outward appearance, at least, China was now united.

Although the urge to revolution had much lessened during the 2,500-

mile march from Canton to Mukden, Chiang none the less had realized quite a considerable part of the dream of Sun and the modern Chinese. That, if we think in historical terms, was his special service to his country. No impartial historian will fail to see how the Nanking government gradually became reactionary. The suppression of the workers' movement, the campaign against the agrarian revolution, the strengthening of the mediaeval social structure of the country – these admittedly were bloody mistakes on the part of a threatened bourgeoisie. None the less Chiang remains the leader and the symbol of the capitalist modernization of China, and so of the partial deliverance of the country from the deadly swamp into which foreign imperialism had been driving it since the middle of the nineteenth century.

The change in the situation was reflected in the change in the policy of the Western powers. During the summer and winter of 1927 twelve countries recognized the Nanking government, among them the United States, Britain and France. China was now permitted to fix her own tariffs. About 1930, nine countries lost their extra-territorial rights, though the Great Powers maintained theirs until the Second World War. In 1919 the Russians had declared that they renounced all such rights, and this was officially confirmed in 1924. Only Britain, France, Japan and the United States retained their semi-colonial privileges in the so-called international concessions in the great cities on the rivers. On the coast, Weihaiwei, in the northeast of Shantung province, which in 1898 the British had occupied as a naval base, was handed back to China in 1930.

The transformation in China's foreign relations was also made visible through a number of British and American loans granted to the Nanking government which afforded a financial foundation for economic and cultural modernization. In the seaports and the river ports there appeared side by side with British, American and Japanese concerns more and more Chinese factories which belonged to Chinese. Communications improved; by 1937 some 19,000 lines of railways were working, a figure equivalent to that of India today and to that in the Russia of 1880. It is a small one when comparison is made with Western countries – today the United States has some 230,000 miles of railways, Russia about 88,000 and relatively small countries like France and Poland have respectively 25,000 and 18,700 miles – but for China it meant a doubling of the 1914 figure. Again, between 1927 and 1937 there were constructed in China proper 75,000 miles of modern roads, that is, four times as many as in 1927. The tariff boundaries between provinces – there were about 500 – which were a permanent hindrance to trade, disappeared in 1932; freedom of trade between the provinces also meant that the spread of cultural values was made easier. Through many new newspapers and reviews dealing with the arts and sciences there now was made available to all China what, in the chaos of civil war, had been hitherto confined to distant universities and the studies of individuals.

In 1930 China was to all appearances developing into a modern democratic state, at least as compared with other Asian countries between Turkey and Japan, and within the limits imposed by a bourgeois government; it was no longer a happy hunting-ground for colonialism but a united empire from the tea plantations of Hainan to the pine forests on the Russian Amur.

But it was just this increasing unity and modernization of China, at the very beginning of Chiang's career, that aroused the displeasure of Japanese imperialism. Japanese industry could not function, the desires of its capitalists could not be satisfied, without China's cotton, iron and coal, and, above all, without the Chinese market. The extraordinary expansion of the island empire required it to possess foreign sources of economic wealth. Now possession seemed to be threatened. Even those who do not know the course that history took, can imagine what would happen and what did happen in the summer of 1931. History calls it 'the Mukden incident', with which we shall now deal.

IX

CHINA (ii)

THE relative unity and prosperity of Kuo Min-tang China roused the Japanese imperialists, for it was an excellent basis for the creation of a power which so far from being a support to Japanese imperialism would be a competitor to it. The Japanese army was ready for action by 1930, and, as we have already related,[1] 'incidents' followed as a matter of course. On June 27, 1931, Naka-mura, a Japanese officer or, rather, spy, was killed by Chinese soldiers in Western Manchuria. On August 17th Tokio published an official account of of the incident which was plainly and confessedly intended to rouse public opinion against China. Everything then went according to plan. On the night of September 18–19th the Japanese Kwantung army held night manoeuvres near Mukden. This army properly was confined to the Japanese zone of Kwantung (established by treaty in 1905) in the southern part of the Liautung Peninsula, but was constantly, though hardly legally, employed on the various railway lines belonging to Japan in other parts of Manchuria. Early in the morning of September 19th there was an explosion somewhere on a railway bridge. Were Chinese responsible or were Japanese? Who could say? No matter; it was a second 'incident'. Before morning Mukden and some other Chinese towns like Antung and Changchun had been occupied by Japanese troops. The troops went on advancing over the country; the Chinese con-stantly withdrew, and when Harbin was occupied on February 5, 1932, all Manchuria was in Japanese hands.

The Western powers, and the United States in particular, let it be admitted, did announce that they would not recognize any extension of Japanese terri-tory – we may recall the Nine Power Treaty of Washington of 1922 – but did not go beyond diplomatic protest. Only the boycott of November 1931 seemed to have any effect; it cut Japanese foreign trade by a half. The Japanese answer was delivered without delay. Japanese divisions landed near Shanghai and in heavy fighting drove out the Chinese 19th army (March 3, 1932) and departed only when, under Japanese pressure, the Chinese Government ended the boycott.

Meantime the Japanese declared Manchuria 'independent', and renamed it Manchukuo. The proclamation was made on February 18, 1932, in Hsin-king, which means 'new capital', the former Changchun; today it has reassumed its old name. As emperor of Manchukuo they appointed (1934) the venal Pu-i, alias Kung Teh, the last emperor of China. After his flight from Pekin in 1924 he had at once got into touch with the Japanese colony in Tientsin. He remained as puppet emperor of Manchukuo until arrested by the Russians when they invaded Manchuria in the summer of 1945. The only

[1] *v.* p. 163.

reaction of the Western powers, then involved in the great economic crisis, was the Lytton report to the League of Nations (October 1932) in which the Japanese action was branded as illegal, but there was no mention of any counter-measures.

The Mukden incident is the real beginning of Japanese expansion in China and in southeast Asia. From January to March 1933 they occupied the province of Jehol and so reached the Great Wall. In 1935 the Chinese troops withdrew from Chahar (between Jehol and Mongolia) and from Hopei which contains Pekin and Tientsin. All that, and the ostrich-like policy of the Chinese Government, meant a new economic colonization of China. The territory occupied by Japan contained 40 per cent of the Chinese railways and 80 per cent of the coal and iron mines. During the Second World War Japan got two-thirds of her iron and half of her coal from northeast China, i.e. from the territory which she had occupied in 1933. In what was still free China, Japanese capitalists owned three-quarters of the iron mines and blast furnaces and half the cotton spinneries and wool-weaving mills; they also controlled 40 per cent of China's foreign trade.

Japanese imperialism was certainly dangerous, and any hope of Western intervention became still more an illusion when at this same period the fascist governments in Europe began their dreaded action and expansion. The German reoccupation of the demilitarized Rhineland (March 7, 1936), the Italian attack on Abyssinia (October 1935 to May 1936) and the fascist intervention in the Spanish civil war (July 18, 1936, to April 1939) – these were equivalent to a notice to Japan that she was free to go on her expansionist path, just as the success of its imperialists encouraged the fascists in Europe.

In September 1936 Tokio secretly threatened to take all North and South China if Nanking did not accept these demands: 1, joint Japanese and Chinese action against the 'communists and bandits' in free China; 2, Japanese to be attached to all Chinese government departments; 3, self-government for the five northern provinces, Jehol, Chahar, Hopei, Shansi and Shantung, and 4, reduction of the customs dues to the figures of 1928. The Chinese Government refused, but took no other action. There was no declaration of war, no mobilization, at least not against the Japanese invaders. On the contrary, Japanese agents proceeded with their task unhindered and a new law forbade anti-Japanese propaganda throughout China.

In an earlier paragraph we have called Chiang Kai-shek the strategist of the Chinese revolution, the thinking head of the Kuo Min-tang, in a stormy period of modernization. How came it then that this leader, great in all other respects, turned traitor? The reason may be found in the reactionary views of his government, reactionary in the sense of seeking to turn 'the natural course of history'. Chiang in the twentieth century tried to do what Europe and America had done in the nineteenth; he wanted to modernize his country but had at heart only the real and alleged interests of the bourgeoisie. Beginning with the purge of the left groups in 1927, the Kuo Min-tang went over ever more to the right. The progressive wing of the party, the fraction headed by Mrs Sun who returned to China in 1930, was deprived of all influence. Chiang was dictator in a regime of the higher bourgeoisie, the industrialists, the bankers, the rich merchants and the great landowners. The resistance of the party to the workers' and peasants' movement was the natural reaction of an exaggerated class rule. The reports on the white terror are not fairy tales. The great workers' strikes in the Chinese ports between 1928 and 1930 were as cruelly put down as was the peasants' rising in Hunan in 1927. One of the leaders of the resistance movement, Hsu Hai-tun, told the American journalist Edgar Snow in 1937 that in his family alone sixty persons had been executed by the Kuo Min-tang.

This reactionary tactic of the Government had the inevitable consequence that every active resistance to Japanese and Western imperialism between 1931 and 1937 was ineffective. Chiang not only wasted his few modernly equipped armies in campaigns against the resistance groups, as we shall show later, but at the same time recognized that a genuine war of liberation from the foreign invader meant inevitably a left-wing policy. This episode in Chinese history is a notable example of how, in an Asian country, thanks to a very small but modernized ruling class which is in control, foreign imperialism can be kept at bay, and thanks, too, to anti-imperialist and anti-capitalist feelings on the part of peasants and workers. This is important for the history of modern imperialism and so for the latest contemporary history.

Did Chiang betray China? Certainly not consciously in the manner, say, of the more and more pro-Japanese minister Wang Ching-wei who was later to be head of the puppet government in Japanese-occupied China. None the less Chiang, because he was not prepared to liberate the peasants and workers, tried to curb the natural resistance to Japanese aggression and to sabotage it. The Chinese Government refused to declare war on Japan either at the time of the Mukden incident, or on the occupation of Manchuria, or when Jehol and Chahar were invaded, or at the threats from Tokio in 1936. This would emphatically have been a just war. But Chiang hesitated. It was only in the winter of 1936 that an extraordinary incident – perhaps unique in history – brought about a change for the better in his dangerous tactics of submission. But before we come to that we must describe the action and experiences of the Chinese communists, which alone afford an explanation of the historic change in December 1936.

We have already told of the development of the Chinese revolution between 1919 and 1931 and how after the *coup d'état* of 1927 the party was banned as illegal, how some 25,000 communist and radical workers and intellectuals were murdered in the towns, and how a handful of rebels fled to the hills especially to the roadless districts on the frontiers of Hunan and Kiangsi some 250 miles north of Canton. They seemed to have disappeared from history like a ship torpedoed at sea. Actually the first Chinese soviet, i.e. the first native Communist government, was formed in Chalin in southwest Hainan in November 1927. During the severe winter of 1927–28 some 10,000 resistance fighters were encamped near the snow-covered mountain village of Chingkanchan; their military commander and political head was Mao Tse-tung. In May 1928 more fugitives arrived from Wuhan, among them Chu-teh (August 1927). Out of these primitive formations there was formed secretly the First Red Army of China in southern Kiangsi. The agrarian revolution, the third Chinese revolution in the twentieth century, is the result of their propaganda. By 1929 the rebels were in possession of the whole of southern Kiangsi; the first provincial soviet (Kiangsi's) was formed on February 7, 1930. Simultaneously armies of the resistance and local soviet governments were established elsewhere, notably in Anhui and Hunan.

What were the communists doing? What was their secret? In our view the communists did what, for instance, the French bourgeois in revolt did in 1789, and what the Chinese government had failed to do; they destroyed feudalism on the land, i.e. they distributed the estates of the landowners to the poor peasants and freed them from the yoke they had borne for centuries. Small peasants form the great majority of the population of China. The communists carried on propaganda and gave the peasants what they in their hearts wanted. That was the 'Red mystery'. They were aided in their fight against Chiang's German-trained army less by the inaccessibility of the regions they held, their lack of easy communications and the threats of Japan, than by the small peasants and workers on the land, in the same way as, a little later, Ho Chi-minh was supported against the French and their German legionaries by the peasants of Indochina.

The most prominent leaders of the peasant movement were Mao Tse-tung, Chu-teh and Chou En-lai. Mao was born of a relatively wealthy peasant family in Chaochan in Hunan in 1893. He was a student in Changsha from 1912 to 1918, and studied for a time at the University of Pekin, where he was influenced by the Marxist scholars, Chen Tu-chou and Li Ta-chao. In 1920 he became a communist. During the counter-revolution of 1927 he left his post as director of the Kuo Min-tang's propaganda office and secretary of the peasant committee of the party, and fled to the hills in Hunan-Kiangsi. There he became in 1931 the secretary of the Communist party of China.

Chou En-lai (b. 1898), the diplomat *par excellence* of the party and later premier and foreign minister, like Mao and many other Chinese students and intellectuals, early became a communist. From 1920 to 1924 he studied in Berlin and London, and also in Paris where he founded the youth groups of the Communist party. As secretary of the Whampoa Academy (1924–1927) he organized, in the absence of the Kuo Min-tang armies on their expedition to the north, the workers' revolt in Shanghai (March 21, 1927) which was the direct cause of Chiang's *coup* in April. Chou fled to Wuhan, was active among the rebels of Nanchang and then – dropped out of sight. In 1931, when in Kiangsi-Fukien resistance bands and village soviets were formed, he was found to be their leader.

The third great Chinese communist, Chu-teh (b. 1886), had a very different career. He held high commands in the various bandit armies in the provinces in Yunnan, for instance, and took his ease among his nine wives and concubines, a rich overfed slave to opium. But for such a life he had one great defect; he was intelligent. Also he read too much. About 1922 he began to see how he himself in his harem and with his opium was like to be destroyed along with his country, which was falling into mediaeval chaos. He sent all his wives and concubines packing, and cured himself of opium-taking by living for three weeks on board a ship on the Yang-tse where no opium was to be had. Then he went to Germany, where one of the books he read was Lenin's *State and Revolution,* then to Paris and finally to Moscow, from which he returned to Shanghai a convinced revolutionary. In April as commander of a resistance brigade in the Kiangsi hills, he joined Mao. In 1931 he became commander-in-chief of the Red Army, and by 1934 was at the head of 150,000 disciplined men with 100,000 rifles and 500 machine guns and of as large a number of peasant rebels dispersed about the country.

At the outset very little news came from the forgotten soviet districts either to China itself or to the world outside. All that came out was tales of 'Red bandits', of looting of rich farms and murder of landowners and peasants, and, of course, horrid details of sexual outrages and other fantasies of Western journalists. Nanking's blockade of news was most efficient. It was not until 1937 that news of what had happened in China between the 'Thermidor' of April 1927 and the mysterious kidnapping of Chiang Kai-shek in Shensi in December 1936 reached the West. In 1937 there appeared a book of 450 pages which can now be called a classic, Edgar Snow's *Red Star over China.* Snow who, in defiance of the Chinese Government's order and despite all friendly warnings, visited the soviets in the northwest, stayed with Mao for some weeks and devoted his evenings to interviewing communist leaders.

Meantime Nanking was issuing exaggerated communiques on the government expeditions against the Red bandits. The lack of results from these expeditions to annihilate communism may be gauged from their number and from the numbers of men mobilized. For the first expedition (December 1930–January 1931) 100,000 men were mobilized; for the second (May–June 1931) 200,000; for the third and fourth in the summer of 1931 and that of 1933, i.e. during the Japanese invasion of Manchuria, 300,000. But the Red Army was still there; indeed, it was growing stronger. That Chiang could not endure, and in 1934, instead of mobilizing China against Japan, he concentrated all his modern forces for the siege of the soviet districts. Outside these, on the frontiers of Kiangsi, he built four lines of redoubts, small forts and machine-gun posts and hundreds of miles of roads which armies could use. He mobilized an army of 900,000 men with artillery and planes against the 100,000 rifles of the communists. The civilian population was evacuated, the rice crop was burned down or carried off, as a result of which, according to the Kuo Min-tang's official figures, nearly one million peasants and their wives and children died of starvation or disease.

Now, it was believed, not a single communist soldier could escape from the beleaguered fortress. The tactics in this fifth campaign is easily recognizable as German and due to Chiang's military adviser (1932–1935), Hans von Seeckt, the former chief of staff of the Turkish army (1917–1918) and head of the German Reichswehr between 1920 and 1926. The siege and capture of the soviet territory lasted from October 1933 to October 1934. In these months the Reds lost 60,000 men. Mao and his men lacked everything – munitions, rice and medical supplies. Things became too hot for them and a hard decision was taken. They would not capitulate; on the contrary they planned something really desperate, to flee from their present territory and to carry the Red Army and the soviet government to the northwest of China.

There they would be safer and be the more able, thanks to a new geographical situation, to attack the Japanese. The struggle against imperialism was one of the chief planks in the communist programme, and in fact at the beginning of 1932 the soviet government had declared war on Japan.

On October 16, 1934, 90,000 men of the Red Army had concentrated in Yütu in southern Kiangsi. In the evening, Chu-teh and Mao gave the order to break out while a rearguard of resistance fighters tried to cover the withdrawal. Between October 21st and November 30th the Red Army did surprise the enemy, and in a series of costly night attacks broke through Seeckt's four lines of fortification and marched westward into Hunan.

Thus began what is known in Chinese history as 'the Great March' (Chang Cheng) or the 'march of 25,000 li'. It was a unique feat, unexpected and heroic, which is not surpassed by anything in modern military history, not even in the Russian civil war. When, half-naked and starving, the Red Army after hard and unceasing fighting reached Kweichou province, it had lost in dead one-third of its strength. It stayed four months in Kweichou, fighting a war of manoeuvre, making communist propaganda among the peasants, recruiting many volunteers and destroying several enemy divisions. From there it marched on westwards to the wild mountain country of Yunnan and then turned north.

Chiang's troops and planes went on attacking but could not stop it. These sansculottes pursued their way in disciplined order in spite of all their sufferings, their seemingly aimless wanderings, spurred on by hope of liberation for their class and their country. In the summer of 1935 came the especially critical time when they stormed the only bridge across the great river Tatu. In this region of cold and rocky passes and narrow river valleys in western Szechuan, the last Taiping rebels, the 100,000 men of Prince Shi Ta-kai, had been driven to their deaths by the Manchu army under Seng Kao-fan. Chiang Kai-shek hoped for a similar result from his offensive. But the hope was not fulfilled. The Red Army had still nearly 2000 miles to travel and all the time to fight against nature. In the crossing of the high passes in northern Szechuan from which, looking west, could be seen the tableland of Tibet looking like a sea of snowpeaks, thousands of men fell exhausted in the deep snow. Finally, on October 20, 1935, 90,000 men reached northern Shensi just south of the Great Wall where they were to remain for many a day.

In 368 days the Red Army had marched over 6000 miles, often in a column some forty miles long, carrying with them on donkeys and mules only their ammunition and light machine guns, marching, always marching; even senior officers went barefoot. On the average they marched some seventeen miles a day; if you reckon marching time as taking only 250 days, the average is twenty-five miles. They had to halt constantly – halts amounted to 100 days – when there was constant skirmishing. Of these, fifty-six days were spent in western Szechuan; this is equivalent to forty-four rest-days for a march of roughly 4400 miles, i.e. one rest day per hundred miles.

The march was as significant politically as it was militarily. No longer were the communists confined to their beleaguered fortress in the south. On the Yellow River they were in contact with the Japanese positions, and during their march they had traversed twelve provinces with a population of 200,000,000 and spread their propaganda to good purpose.

It was a weird army that was established in the great bend of the Yellow River, an army without artillery, without a single motor vehicle, with a wonderful assortment of weapons and ammunition, three-quarters of which had been captured from the government troops – modern British, Czech, German and American rifles and machine guns – and yet it was the only politically armed army in China, the only army which was not hated by the peasantry. And it was a singular place, the red loess hills of northern Shensi, northeast Kansu and southeast Ningsia, in which the Chinese soviet government found itself. It is symbolical, for it is the historic cradle of the Chinese Empire where twenty-two centuries ago the emperor Sin Shi-huang, the builder of the Great Wall had been born.

When Edgar Snow travelled through these regions – the Red Army territory was as large as Britain or Korea – the new government was already functioning well. In various towns and villages primitive industries were established – salt, oil, cotton, war material; the Red government was in wireless contact with every part of China; the roads were safe and numerous behind the front. Mao, the ruler of this republic, lived in a small peasant hut made of mud, and his only personal possessions were two cotton blankets and two uniforms; he had no horse of his own, not even a donkey, and no bodyguard. Yet do not such details explain much which non-communist commentators usually fail to understand?

Still more worthy of notice – and here we come back to the point at which the account of official China was temporarily interrupted – is the fact that this Red Army was able to compel Chiang to offer genuine resistance to Japanese imperialism. The reader may remember his mysterious arrest in 1936 which gave occasion for so many rumours and conjectures in China and abroad, in Moscow as well as in London and New York.

This is what happened. In the regions south and west of the communists' territory there were stationed at that time many Manchurian troops belonging to the so-called Tungpei (i.e. northeastern) army. Their commander was Marshal Chiang Hsu-liang, a former governor of Manchuria who had been driven out by the Japanese, and who was the second senior commander in the country. After the Japanese invasion of Jehol he was made the scapegoat and was sent off to Europe (1933–1934) to study there. When he returned in 1935 he was promptly made commander of the Tungpei army, with the mission to destroy the Red Army. He did not carry out that mission. He and his men, robbed of their homes, their wives and their children, had only one desire, to get back to Manchuria, which meant fighting the Japanese. The perpetual civil war against the communists was of no interest to them. Chiang found that out all too soon. He had to go to the scene himself and, on December 7, 1936, he landed at the airfield of Sian (Siking) in southwestern Shensi, equidistant by some 125 miles from the Japanese and from the communist front. He intended to tell the Tungpei officers just what was expected of them. On the evening of the 11th the divisional commanders decided on a plan of action; they intended to arrest

Chiang. That meant that 170,000 men would mutiny. Chiang was living in a hotel in Lingtung, a holiday resort with warm springs about ten miles out-side Sian. On the 12th at 5 a.m. Tungpei soldiers under Sun Ming-chiu, the commander of the rebellious marshal's bodyguard, stormed into the hotel. Chiang fled from his bed to the snow-covered hills behind the hotel and at 6 a.m. was captured, still in his pyjamas.

This action, the only aim of which was to rouse official China against Japan, was very probably a communist idea which could be carried out only by Chiang Hsu-liang. In considerable embarrassment he told Chiang: 'If your Excellency will accept our proposals I will execute any orders your Excellency may give.'

On December 14th Nanking was shocked to read an official communique from the rebels and from the Red commanders about mobilization of the so-called anti-Japanese army. It was 250,000 strong, and held the provinces of Shensi and Kansu. Right reactionaries in the Nanking government, like the pro-Japanese minister of war Ho Ying-chin, at once attempted to organ-ize a punitive expedition against the new army, and at the same time to seize power. But the moderate pro-American group, headed by Soong Mei-ling and T. V. Soong, opposed them, reported the intrigues in Nanking to Chiang, and were wise enough to realize that, if the Kuo Min-tang army intervened, it would find itself in an extremely critical position. The communists had no valid reason for being kind to the 'bloodthirsty counter-revolutionaries'. Yet all through his captivity Chiang was well treated. Mao and his associates were well aware that, on the eve of a national war against Japan, they must not kill the man who at home and abroad had become the symbol of Chinese unity.

The communists and the rebels held Chiang captive for a fortnight. Be-tween December 17th and 25th he surrendered completely. He did not sign anything, but gave his word that he was finished with his policy of tem-porizing and would fight the Japanese. Freed, he hastened back to Nanking. To save his face the communists promised to decrease their activities against the landowners and to recognize Chiang as commander-in-chief on con-dition that they retained control of their own army and government; thereby they had a guarantee of their political independence. The rebel marshal went with him to Nanking, apparently a government prisoner; after a week or two he was set at liberty. A third unbidden guest also came to Nanking, Chou En-lai, as representative of the Communist government.

For the first time Japanese spies and agents were executed and treach-erous elements expelled from the Government. The martyred country flew to arms. The Chinese dragon had awakened and was spouting fire.

Naturally reports of the new course in China, and especially in Shensi, reached Tokio. What Tokio answered we know; it was the same answer as they had given in 1931, only worse. For Japan it was now or never. From the international viewpoint the time was ripe. Fascism was steadily spread-ing in Europe. The Soviet Union internally was at a moment as critical as that of 1927 (Trotsky's banishment), the moment of the execution of Mar-shal Tutachevski (June 1937) and the purges of 1936–1937 to which Zinoviev,

Kamenev, Bukharin, Radek and many others fell victim. Apparently Tokio did hesitate, but the state of things in China put the armies in motion. A suitable pretext was soon found. Such can always be found, just as much can happen before it comes to actual war, if neither side is anxious to fight; compare the events some years later when Russians and Japanese were fighting on the Amur.

On the night of July 7th, a Japanese detachment was, as it was legally entitled to be, on an exercise in Chinese territory; it went into Wanping, a place about ten miles west of Pekin. Shots were fired. Tokio claimed that it was the Chinese railway guards who had fired. This 'incident', at the Marco Polo Bridge, was the beginning of what is called the Sino-Japanese 'conflict' and of what was by far the greatest war between 1918 and 1941. In the middle of July the Japanese had stationed fresh divisions between Pekin and Tientsin. On July 28th Pekin fell and next day Tientsin. Like hungry sharks the Japanese divisions fell on northeastern China. The death of two Japanese marines on the Chinese military airfield near Shanghai led in mid-August to a landing from Japanese warships. The Chinese fought like lions; not until the beginning of November, after more Japanese divisions were thrown in, were the invaders able to drive the Chinese troops from the city. Chiang again appeared as the great commander; his tactics was that of the Russians against Napoleon and against the Nazi invaders. He traded space for time, defending every mile of Chinese territory but always withdrawing before he was totally defeated. The Japanese went on invading. On December 13th they took Nanking and committed worse atrocities there than usual. In the dark winter days at the end of December Hangchow and Tsinan were captured. There is little point in recording the fighting in detail; everything that happened was equally bloody and horrifying – not only the fighting but also its consequences. Between 1937 and 1939 50,000,000 Chinese and their families left their homes and fled inland. The doings of Japan in China cannot be told simply; they would need a whole library of books on atrocities.

In less than three years the Japanese occupied as much as they could occupy, i.e. all northeastern China east of the Yellow River, the valley of the Yang-tse as far as Ichang, and the whole of the Chinese coast; in other words, roughly all the country under 1000 feet above sea level, all the cotton plantations, all the ports, nearly all the factories, a territory in which 250,000,000 people lived. Yet free China did not yield, though, as in 1940, it no longer possessed a single gun-factory and had only two regiments equipped with tanks, light ones. By 1937 the whole world was astonished at the moral steadfastness of the badly governed empire. From Chungking on the Yang-tse, where the Government had been established in October 1937, Chiang waged a bitter war of liberation. The Japanese had pushed into a veritable hornet's nest. It was soon apparent that all they could do was to hold permanently the towns and the main roads, that is to say, about one-tenth of China excluding Manchuria. All the ground behind the widely extended lines from Mongolia to Indochina was the zone of action of the Chinese resistance fighters; by day the peasants were in action, by night soldiers, saboteurs and bombing brigades. A considerable part of these fighters had communist officers who had studied their trade during the guerrilla war against Chiang, and had studied to some purpose. In the Japanese-occupied territory, often far behind the front, whole districts were ruled as tiny soviet republics in which the big estates were divided up, except those whose proprietors were taking part in the national struggle. The peasants, often illiterate, the resistance fighters and their wives and children learned to read and write, and to the greatest extent possible modern democratic and communist ideas were spread among them. No sacrifice was too great for these awakening people. It was a regular occurrence for the railways in Japanese-occupied territory to be put out of use, but there was more than that; the priceless rails were taken away to places hundreds of miles behind the front so that new lines could be constructed there.

In August 1937, when the Japanese navy was blockading all the coast of China, a Non-Aggression Pact was signed with the Soviet Union, and as a result quantities of weapons and ammunitions was sent from Russian factories to the front in China. The Western democracies also sent no inconsiderable amount of arms to free China, but in really worthwhile quantities only between 1940 and 1945; it is still a dark page in the book of history that neither Europe nor America, on their own initiative and through comprehension of what was at stake, put the slightest obstacle in the way of the fascist rulers in Tokio, and, what was worse, almost right up to the day of Pearl Harbour the Americans were sending oil and motor fuel to Japan.

When on December 8, 1941, Holland, Britain and the United States declared war on Japan, the Chinese had for ten years been keeping the Japanese terror at bay. That it was possible by 1945 to drive the Japanese back into their islands was not the least result of the patriotic resistance of the Chinese masses.

X

THE PHILIPPINES AND INDONESIA

WHEN the famous British historian Seeley was reproached for not having made his books interesting, he answered: 'I cannot make history any more interesting than it is.' If the historian of modern Asia fails to be interesting, the fault lies with him and not with his material. The whole process by which Asia, which contains half the population of the world, found again the cruel but noble road to freedom, the road which all its countries from Turkey to Japan, from Siberia to Indonesia had to travel – could any romance be more exciting? Revolutions, guerrilla wars, economic crises and world conflicts, banishments, strikes, thousands of death sentences mark that road and are part of the internal development and shaping of Asia.

Never in history had Europe and Asia been so closely in contact, yet never were they farther away from one another as in the age of imperialism during which both Europe and Asia were more radically altered than at any other period. Is any situation more dramatic than that of the expanding highly developed technical civilization on the one hand, and under-developed lands striving to become modern on the other?

As a rule, Europe and America treated their colonies as plantations and the Asians, the 'natives', as plantation labourers. How and when did Asia react? How far was the nationalist movement in the different countries also a social revolution? How anguished are those periods when the stream of freedom seems to have sanded up, those episodes of internal confusion, those times of demoralization and treachery; how tragic is the conviction of many nationalists that the expulsion of their Western masters itself will solve all problems – the illusion under which every revolution labours. The liberation of the former European colonies in Asia have rather brought up new problems, and in this we have a good example of an especially interesting aspect of history; man has to go on treading the road even if he often stumbles, and if the hoped-for Paradise is never attained but recedes as does the horizon to the sailor.

In a sense our account of China has been a digression for, however interesting the nationalist movement in Asia as a whole may be, that section of Asian history which concerns China is the most attractive object of study. In China, events, domestic or foreign, were more stirring and more intense than those in the rest of colonial Asia where they were less sudden, slower and sometimes almost hidden from view. We think here of the opposition between right and left which played a part in all the nationalist movements of the period, to the anti-Asian action of the West, the role of the Soviet Union, the influence of Japan. China had its Pearl Harbour not in 1941 but in 1931. When the Japanese armies in 1941–2 invaded the countries of

Southeast Asia, where they were by many greeted as liberators, China had already been suffering from them. What to Indonesia, the Philippines and Burma seemed to be liberation from Western interference, was to China but another imperialism coming this time from the east. When it is compared to the tremendous social and political revolutions in China, the history of the other countries in east and south Asia seems pretty uninteresting, not excepting India and Pakistan. Yet we shall now see how in all these countries the thought of freedom grew, if to all appearances less violently and certainly less openly.

We turn first to the two island realms of Southeast Asia, the Philippines, the 'Republika ñg Pilipinas' of today, and Indonesia, now the Indonesian Republic; the former is an ex-colony of the United States, the latter an ex-colony of the Netherlands, that is, of one of the oldest of the capitalist countries, as America is one of the richest.

Indonesia and the Philippines, the former with 20,000 greater and smaller islands, the latter with about 7000, have much in common both historically and otherwise. Both have a Malay population; both in the Middle Ages were Hindu-Malay empires, and both became as early as round about 1600 the objective of the Western nations, notably Holland and Spain. No other Asian countries have had for so long a continuous Western domination. Besides, in the modern period Indonesia, the Philippines and Malaya have been the most important plantation colonies of the West (sugar, tobacco) and the ideal ground for coconut-growing. In 1940-5 the two archipelagoes produced four-fifths of the world's palm-oil. In both, more than half the population lives on a single crowded island and the birth rate is higher than anywhere else in Asia. We have more than once drawn attention to this increase in population as a factor of the greatest importance. We would like to repeat that anyone who fails to recognize the cause and consequence of this phenomenon cannot understand our view on much of his own epoch. In 1800 there were 2,000,000 Filipinos and possibly 8,000,000 Indonesians; today there are 20,000,000 and 80,000,000. This is an increase such as only uninhabited countries inviting emigration like the United States or Australia can exceed. In 1800 there were 7,000,000 Americans; in 1950 there were more than 150,000,000. In Australia about 1000 British landed at Botany Bay in 1788; in 1950 there were 10,000,000 white inhabitants. In the same period the population of Britain rose only from 9,000,000 to 50,000,000, that of all Europe from 200,000,000 to 550,000,000, that of Japan from 25,000,000 to 80,000,000.

In contrast to the Dutch who at first wanted nothing from the Indonesians except nutmegs and pepper, and made no attempt to europeanize the native culture, the Spaniards, just as they did in Central and South America, sought to spread Spanish civilization among the Filipinos – the Spanish language, Spanish Catholicism and Spanish feudal agrarian economy. Nine-tenths of the Filipinos are today Roman Catholics; more than 5 per cent are Moslems, mainly in Mindanao and Sulu. Only the remaining 5 per cent are Protestants, converted by American missionaries in our own times. As regards language,

American has for the most part displaced Spanish; roughly 4,000,000 Filipinos speak English, a higher percentage than anywhere else in Asia, and about 400,000 Spanish. Geographical and personal names on the other hand have often remained Spanish and the Republic still keeps the name the islands got from Philip II. Socially the Filipinos have kept Spanish survivals in the landed nobility and their stewards, the *caciques*. The difference in race between the native peasantry, the landowners of Spanish descent, and the many of mixed blood is intensified by a social and economic difference. Here we see a general phenomenon; race difference is of much less significance than many think; a race conflict only becomes dangerous when it is the reflection of an economic and social struggle.

Under American rule the feudal structure of the country remained unaltered. The great estates, the *haciendas,* were not broken up and the few agrarian reforms, those, for instance, introducd at the time of the economic crisis of 1933, were of little effect. In a country like Indonesia the Dutch busied themselves with agrarian reform on a wide scale. That was not the case in the Philippines. The Americans ruled the country not as a colony in the European sense, but rather as a sort of autonomous plantation, i.e. the rule was not that of American officials, but of the native bourgeoisie, the rich peasants and the great estate owners with their own venal police. From such rulers the peasants had virtually nothing to expect. In a purely economic sense the native agriculture was not really modernized. It is true that more and more land was put under cultivation, 7,000,000 acres in 1913 and 17,000,000 in 1939 but, although the population increased, the peasant economy remained primitive and the rice crop per acre was considerably less than in other Asian countries. In 1939 half of the cultivated land was under rice; a quarter grew coconut palms; the modern plantations producing sugar and manila hemp accounted for an eighth of the usable land. Sugar, palm products, hemp and tobacco were exported, particularly to the United States. That strengthened the ties with America and affected the balance of trade, but the majority of the peasants and workers on the land derived no benefit. Two-thirds of the peasants had farms of less than eight acres, and half less than four acres. The percentage of peasants owning their own land fell during the crisis, and in 1938 the big landowners and the capitalists of the towns held a third of the land. Rent swallowed up half the harvest.

Those who became rich were the Americans and the Spaniards of the sugar and hemp plantations, the mines, the palm-oil refineries, the Chinese of the sago and rice mills, and the small traders, two-thirds of them Chinese and Japanese. Foreigners controlled the foreign trade. Colonial countries do not have a modern industry of any significance. Such factories as there were belonged to foreigners, and the wage of native labour was extremely low.

Dutch writers often declared: 'Look now at all we have invested in the Indies, at what we have brought in the way of technology, hygiene and civilization. And what really have we got out of it? Remarkably little.' Their views were buttressed in the true scientific manner by figures and statistical tables. The nationalists were reproached with lack of understanding; to give them time to understand, they were deported to the Digul River and to remote islands.

Rather differently but with the same underlying thought, many Americans came to a similar conclusion: 'We have invested half a milliard dollars in the Philippines, which is 1 per cent of all American investment abroad. The trade between us and these islands is only 3 – 4 per cent of our total foreign trade. It follows then that we get nothing out of the Philippines; really, they are merely a burden to us.'

There would be little use debating how far American economic policy in the Philippines can be called exploitation. We will deal unemotionally and without economic controversy with what actually did happen in the Philippines, particularly in the sphere of economics.

American rule obstructed both the political development and the technical modernization of the country. It assured the position of the economic exploiter and the feudal landowner, and helped to make them rich instead of troubling about the position of the peasants. The irony of history again! The democratic Americans were compelled everywhere in Asia to support feudalism and reaction. Compare China, Korea, Indochina, Iran, Jordan and Arabia.

American economic policy kept the still agrarian economy of the Philippines closely tied to its own. By 1936 more than three-quarters of Filipino overseas trade went to the United States, as compared with barely 25 per cent between 1880 and 1910.

Finally, the groups in Washington economically interested in the Philippines had very considerable influence. After liberation (July 4, 1946) the United States retained its privileged economic position in the islands and, besides, was granted many military bases.

Herein lies the paradox of Filipino freedom. It was the only ex-colonial territory which achieved a fairly genuine autonomy and that at an early date; Washington fixed 1935 as a definite date for independence. Yet at its liberation it was less free than the others. That could be easily explained by pointing out that it is a keypoint in the domination of the Pacific by the United States (Formosa, Japan, Korea). But that does not appear to us to be the sole cause of this semi-freedom of the Philippines. All through their history the Americans have never been convinced colonialists, for one reason because of their own past history; did not a British king in 1783 withdraw his troops from the rebel colony of America? This anti-colonial mentality is especially characteristic of the Democratic party. The other great American party, the Republicans, who derive their strength from industrial and capitalist circles, has more leanings towards expansion. For instance, in 1893, the American planters and merchants in the sugar kingdom of Hawaii staged a native 'revolution' against Queen Liliuokalani, in the course of which they a little disingenuously asked the United States for protection, that is, they asked for annexation. The Democratic government of Cleveland (1893–1897) refused. When in 1898 the Americans occupied the Philippines, in addition to Hawaii and Cuba, many Americans including Mark Twain protested against what they called 'un-American action', an insult to the principles of democracy. Up to the present the United States, some strategically important islands apart, has only two real colonies in the European sense of the word. These are Puerto Rico (1898) and the Panama Canal Zone (1903). The whole of its overseas possessions contain only some 3,000,000 inhabitants, which is a good deal less than the figure (for 1950) for the British colonies (75,000,000), the French (51,000,000), and fewer even than the Belgian (15,000,000) and the Portuguese (12,000,000).

Because of fears of getting involved abroad the United States was isolationist in the nineteenth century. In that century three-quarters of the land was still unexploited (4,000,000 square miles). American expansion overseas begins in the period between 1900 and 1918, and unlike the European was primarily the result of a financial and economic imperialism; it is usually called 'dollar-imperialism'. In principle the United States does not annex; it makes an economic conquest. It endeavours to bring the countries into its financial empire, and that by attaching to it economically the bourgeoisie and the landed gentry. It was the cause of many revolutions in Central and South America, especially in countries where its aim was to supplant British capital.

In the Philippines, with America's support the aristocracy of Spanish blood and the big landowners grew richer, their position was assured and inside the country they had freedom on a relatively grand scale. That was an effective damper on any revolutionary feeling among the native governing classes and the effect was increased by the constant fear of a peasant rising. In this sense the Philippines are comparable to the China of 1945.

We have now to consider the true history of Filipino sovereignty between 1919 and 1941; a limited autonomy dates from 1907. The Jones Act of August 1916 assured the colony of self-government on a broader basis, even if the majority of the illiterate peasants and workers on the land were excluded from its benefits, the more so as the Democratic governor Harrison interpreted the Act in a very liberal sense. Proof of this are the facts that the civil services were recruited more and more from Filipinos, that a Filipino division (1918) was included in the US Army, that it was decided to recognize Spanish as the second official language; there was also the visit to Washington of forty Filipinos (May 1919); it was then that Manuel Luis Quezon (1878–1914), the Filipino head of the government and leader of the Partido Nacionalista, demanded real freedom as the obvious consequence of the American Government's announcement during the war. Quezon and his friends got evasive answers. Meantime the Republicans had returned to power (1921–1933). Once again American marines patrolled the towns in Cuba, Nicaragua, Haiti and other countries of Central America and an old-fashioned colonial wind blew over the Philippines. 'Immediate independence would be nothing less than a betrayal of the Filipinos and it was the duty of the government in Washington to see that under no circumstances was a situation to be allowed to arise in the islands which should throw a responsibility on the United States without its possessing the necessary authority to deal with it.' The quotation is from an official report of 1921. A letter from Coolidge (Republican President of the United States 1923–1929) added: 'The Filipino people do not have sufficient experience nor the standard of living to bear the burden which independence would lay upon them.'

On this the national movement grew even more quickly than the sugar-cane; in Quezon's classic phrase: 'We should prefer to rule ourselves in Hell to being ruled by others in Heaven.' The Americans were, however, not ready to grant what the Partido Nacionalista demanded. Quezon went again to Washington but in vain; equally in vain did the Philippines Government inter-vene; it demanded in 1926 that a plebiscite should be held on independence, but the governor refused to permit one. There was a certain dishonesty im-plicit in the words of Hoover, Coolidge's successor as president (1929–1933): 'The islands can only attain political freedom when they are economically in-dependent.'

But in 1933 matters took a new and remarkable turn. By the Hare-Howes-Cutting Act the United States declared the islands as from 1945 to be inde-pendent and definitely sovereign. What caused the change? Why this switch in American policy? Have we painted imperialism in over dark colours? Have democratic principles and isolationist tendencies put obstacles in the way of capitalist expansion? Has the United States renounced the historic laws of imperialism and voluntarily set one of its colonies free? These, alas, are but rhetorical questions. The answer to them is in the negative. If the freedom spoken of was honestly meant, why did Quezon's government refuse to ratify the law and why did it simply disappear from sight in the archives of the State Department? What was behind all this? In the first place, the law contained some paragraphs dealing with American military and naval bases and other infringements of sovereignty. In the second, the law put the trade relations between the two countries on a new basis; the United States would raise the import duties on sugar, palm-oil and hemp coming from the Philippines; hitherto trade in them had been free. These changes from a technical juridical viewpoint were possible only if the Philippines were politic-ally independent of the United States. They supply three-quarters of the grounds on which America set the Philippines free.

As is known, the United States in 1933 found itself at the worst stage of the great economic crisis. Certain groups in America were badly hit by the free entry of Filipino products – the beet-sugar farmers, the cotton growers and the American sugar barons of Cuba and Hawaii. Many Americans were in favour of Filipino independence so as to control Filipino competition through tariffs. At the same time the islands, and especially the landowners and planters in them, had no desire for a freedom 'made in USA'. This is the second paradox.

On March 4, 1933, Franklin Delano Roosevelt became president (1933–1945), with the mission to deal with the spectre of economic crisis. American foreign policy took a more progressive line. In March 1934 the Tydings-McDuffie Act – generally known as 'the declaration of Filipino independence' – was passed. It was a more liberal reproduction of the Act of 1933. The American military bases were to go when independence was finally reached in 1946; arrangements about naval bases would be made at a given date. Three-quarters of Filipino exports would be allowed into America duty free and in 1940 the present duties would be abolished. The Act seemed to the Filipinos something more than just an expression of Roosevelt's goodwill and democratic sentiment and so Quezon and his government, if without enthusiasm, accepted this semi-independence of the Philippines.

In May 1935 the Philippines got their constitution. As a result of the elections in September Quezon became president (1935–1941), and on November 15th the islands received the official title of 'The Commonwealth Government of the Philippines'. Apart from control of foreign relations that meant independence, but defence, immigration (e.g. of Americans) and finance and the economy remained tied to the United States. In a word, the new status was that of a protectorate. But for the Philippines the temporary domination of the Americans was not the prelude to colonization as had so often been the case elsewhere in Asia and in Africa; on July 4, 1946 – at least according to the text of the Act – the Philippines would automatically become a sovereign state.

Quezon and the Partido Nacionalista ruled very much as Chiang Kai-shek did, i.e. not so very democratically. The bourgeois of Manila and the great landowners were the pillars of the regime. The elections were not really free, and the small peasants, half of the population, were barred from them as illiterate.

Resistance continued. Socialist and communist movements of importance date from the crisis years, which were for all Asia the years in which the peasantry rose. After the suppression of the Tayung rising in northern Luzon (1931) and the strikes in Iloilo and Manila, a number of left-wing leaders, including the Socialist Benigno Ramos, fled to Japan. The bitter and bloody rising of the Sakdalistas in the neighbourhood of Manila (May 1935) was a critical moment, for the whole of Luzon was aflame.

At this period the parties opposed to Quezon formed a united front like that of the Thakin Party in Burma and the radical anti-fascist parties in France and Spain. They included the Aguinaldists, the Socialists called Sakdalistas (with their leaders Ramos and Pedro Abad Santos) and the Communists (under Chrisanto Evangelista, Luis Taruc and others).

The formation of this front was a factor of importance, particularly in Luzon. In Pampanga province, where only a seventh of the peasants had any land of their own, a third of all the mayors were socialists. The Partido Nacionalista remained the largest political party, but the desire for real independence and the resistance of the left to his undemocratic government made Quezon go again to Washington to ask that the date for independence be put forward.

The 'Pekin incident' (summer 1937) brought closer the threat of a Japanese invasion, and both Quezon and Roosevelt changed their views. To many members of the Partido Nacionalista Dominion status appeared the sole reliable defence against Japanese imperialism. While town after town in China was falling into the hands of the Japanese, Douglas MacArthur was made commander-in-chief of the Filipino army. To the Americans the Philippines appeared not only as an American plantation but as a bulwark against the imperialist ambition of Japan. As always, geographical factors do not change; what changes is the significance they have for historical development.

The richness of a tropical country arouses ambitions. Attracted by its natural wealth, European capital streams in and takes advantage of the possibilities offered. Indonesia is the classic example of an Asian colony. The European colonization of Asia did not mean only the invasion of a foreign civilization and individual Europeans, but above all the coming of a foreign economic system, i.e. that of modern capitalism to a purely agrarian country. Profit is the true motive of any colonization.

Before we come to the history of Indonesia between the world wars we must outline briefly the economic conditions. Two-thirds of the population live in Java, which is four times as large as Holland yet is but 7 per cent of the whole area of the country. The population of the archipelago rose from about 8,000,000 in 1810 to the 80,000,000 of today, but the population of Java rose from 29,000,000 in 1900 to 48,000,000 in 1940 an average increase of 600,000 per annum or 1700 a day. There was virtually no emigration from Java. In 1940 200,000 Javanese lived on the neighbouring islands while 800,000 lived off and on outside Java mainly as plantation workers in Sumatra; 35,000 were in Surinam. The increase in the population was, as in other Asian countries, a consequence of modern hygiene and of modern technological progress as well as of permanently high natural birth rate (in 1940, 30 to 40 per 100; Italy, the most fruitful Western European country, can show only 23 per 1000). The death rate remained high (20 to 25 per 1000 as in Holland in 1870); child mortality was very high, 15 to 25 of every 100 children died before they were a year old (the figures for Holland were in 1870 20 per 100; in 1940 3·7 per 100).

The Indonesian peasants were Asian peasants, i.e. they grew rice (50 per cent of sown land) and maize (25 per cent of the cultivateable land). They worked with extreme diligence but technically and economically were primitive. In Java especially the holdings were very small, on the average they were two and a half acres in extent, i.e. ·05 of an acre per head of the agrarian population including women and children. Three-quarters of them had less than an acre and a half; two-thirds did not possess a cow and only 10 per cent an ox or a buffalo. They had no artificial manure, one of the fundamental bases of American and European farming (in 1940 about 1 per cent of the farms). The copra harvest in relation to the total cultivated area within this period fell by about 10 per cent, just as did the farm area belonging to the peasant, and that was with a very small production, 30 cwt per acre; in China it is 50 cwt per acre and in Japan nearly 80 cwt. Besides, large-scale farming, i.e. on the plantations owned by Europeans, occupied a seventh of the cultivateable area. Naturally that seventh was the best land, but of its owners only 1 per cent were Indonesians.

According to the official figures of the Dutch administration the peasant earned on the average 160 Dutch guilders a year, of which he paid twenty guilders in taxation. For an average family that meant eight cents per day.

Many workers and a quarter of the village population did not earn so much, and only rich peasants (roughly 3 per cent of the villagers, those who owned, e.g., roughly twelve to thirteen acres) earned as much as 1100 guilders per annum. One has only to compare consumption figures, the barometer of agricultural prosperity; salt consumption fell from a little over 6 lb. in 1920 to 4 lb. per head, rice consumption between 1914 and 1940 was 15 per cent less.

All this was well known to the administration in Jakarta and to the government at the Hague; economic treatises and government reports revealed the facts. But despite their knowledge of the Indies they were psychologically prevented from spreading knowledge of Indonesia. Who does not remember the way they argued: 'If there were no Dutch officials the land would sink into chaos; if there were no Dutch planters the plantations would be overgrown . . . the lazy natives are not ripe for self-government. The Dutch colonies are a shining example of modern colonial administration.'

Many Dutchmen genuinely believed that, and not only Dutchmen, not only the reactionary sugar and oil barons; this view was widely held by Western Europeans. None the less, by 1919 many Indonesians had not the same respect as formerly for the Dutch, as may be seen from the writings of the Englishman, J. S. Furnivall. But, unlike him, the Indonesians did not draw comparisons between Indonesia and Burma but between Indonesia and Holland, Indonesia and Japan, Indonesia and the Soviet Union. The Dutch administration thought in terms of the economic interests of Europe. Everywhere in the many scientific and ethical theories about Indonesia's lack of ripeness was concealed, as Hatta said in 1928, the desire of the Dutch bourgeois to bind Indonesia to Holland for ever as 'a great coffee and sugar plantation of the Kingdom of Holland'. The desire is comprehensible and had its effect on the richness and variety of Indonesian plantations and their products. From 1934 to 1938 Indonesia exported 90 per cent of the world's quinine, 80 per cent of its pepper, 60 per cent of its kapok, 45 per cent of its palm products, 35 per cent of its rubber, 17 per cent of its tin, 15 per cent of its tea, 5 per cent of its coffee and sugar, 4 per cent of its tobacco and 3 per cent of its oil. In 1929 5,000,000,000 Dutch guilders were invested in it, four-fifths of which was Dutch capital, a land from which 700,000,000 guilders more were annually taken out than were put in, from which roughly 50,000 guilders per hour were pumped into Holland.

We have already seen [1] how the nationalist movement had become more radical, especially the Sarekat Islam (SI) which had become a really big party. In 1920 it had 2,000,000 members. Just as in the Kuo Min-tang, there was tension within it between the radicals and socialists and the bourgeois leaders who were mostly Moslems. The bourgeois-Moslem element in it defended itself against communist infiltration.

As a result of this tension and of the founding of the PKI (Partai Kommunis Indonesia) in 1920, the SI declined in the following decades. Hesitating between a semi-modern Pan-Islam and a Moslem socialism, it estranged the peasants and the workers and the purely nationalist parties like the PNI as well. Its cultural activity increased. The over-revolutionary plans of the crisis

[1] v. p. 136.

period were, as the realist Hatta said, just fantastic dreams in an imperialist colony. None the less, with their 20,000 members in 1930 it was one of the big parties and one of the pillars of Indonesian independence.

The Communist party grew as possibly no other Asian Communist party did. Like so many Russian and Western communists and the Chinese revolutionaries in this period the PKI expected a general socialist revolution in Europe and Asia. In the European version of Marxist theory, the workers in the factories, not the peasants, were the advance guard of the revolution. Hence the attempts of the PKI, like those of the Chinese Communist party, were directed in the first instance to rouse the workers although both called themselves 'workers' and peasants' parties'. During the period of reaction under governor-general D. Fock (1921–1926) there were strikes. The administration intervened and a number of leading communists were arrested or banished; the lucky ones got permission to stay abroad permanently.

Thus deprived of its leaders and internally split because of the obscurity of the directives from Moscow, the left movement went on to the tragedy of 1926–1927. There was trouble everywhere in Java and also in Sumatra. In the night of November 12–13, 1926, rebellion broke out in various parts of Bantam. The rebels cut telephone wires, occupied bridges even in Jakarta. In Surakarta and other places the general bitterness found expression in individual acts of resistance in which tobacco stores and houses of Europeans were burned down.

The whole 'revolution' in Java was crushed within a few days, although trouble continued for a month. The 'red' rising in Sumatra in January 1927, where two railway stations were temporarily occupied by the rebels, was just as quickly dealt with.

During the 'revolution' of 1926–1927 some 30,000 Indonesians were arrested. 4500 of them disappeared into the gaols; others were sent to the internment camp set up on the Upper Digul in marshy West New Guinea. Four prisoners, selected for no apparent reason, went to the gallows. As an illegal party the PKI had now no significance. It left as its legacy a native socialism, a fairly radicalized working class, and here and there some peasants who could be of use. The contact with the Comintern until the dissolution of the latter in 1943 is hardly worth mentioning.

Anything departing at all from the lines laid down by the administration was dubbed 'resistance', all criticism by the native called 'revolutionary and communist' and all too few Dutchmen understood what Sukarno said in Bandung on December 2, 1930: 'Your imperialism spreads misery everywhere; it oppresses this land and it will be your fault if all over it revolution breaks out.'

On June 10, 1927, the Dutch police arrested four Indonesian students in Leyden and The Hague, one of whom was Mohammed Hatta who was later to be vice-president of the Republic of Indonesia, and another was the diplomatist of today, Ali Sastroamidjojo, a member of the Perhimpunan Indonesia (PI), the union of the Indonesian students in Holland.

They were freed in March 1928; the judges at The Hague were less prejudiced than those in the Dutch East Indies. The significance of the PI trial was much greater than is the case with most political trials. It constituted a

A.C.—8*

historic moment in the history of Indonesian independence. During the pre-
liminary investigation which had lasted five months, Hatta had written an
eighty-page defence in prison. It was published in The Hague in 1928 with
the title *Indonesia free*.[1] Modern intellectuals like Hatta and Shahrir demanded a free and modern Indonesia united and democratic; as nationalists
they attacked capitalism as the cause of Indonesia's enslavement.

The experience of the Indonesian intellectuals in Indonesia was no different
from that of those in distant Holland. On the initiative of the engineer
Sukarno (b. 1901), who, though he was not a communist, was well-read in
Marxist literature, there arose about 1925 in Bandung a students' association
which was in close contact with the PI in Holland; from it there came on
July 4, 1928, the PNI (the Peserikatan Nasional Indonesia, a party since 1928),
the party of Sukarno and others. Dr Tjipto Mangunkusomo (c. 1890–1943)
would have been a member had he not been arrested at Bandanaira in 1927
for complicity in the revolutionary agitation in Bantam. The PNI was the party
of the left bourgeois nationalists, a bright light in the colonial twilight. Its
much-read paper, *Persatuan Indonesia*, demanded an 'Indonesian Merdeka'
(a free Indonesia) and the release of the interned on the Digul. As might have
been expected, the reaction of The Hague government was simply: 'The
natives have too much freedom; what we are facing is revolution.' Did they
really think so? The secret police said so.

On December 29, 1929, came the raid on the PNI. House searches were made
throughout the country; 400 premises were ransacked. Waggon-loads of paper
were seized and eight leaders arrested. The whole Indonesian movement protested; in Holland the only protesters were the Social-Democrats and the Communists. In August 1930 the trial began of four of the arrested leaders,
Sukarno among them, on charges of revolutionary activity. The prosecution
of Sukarno and his colleagues was virtually a prosecution of the whole PNI,
which was thus branded as a revolutionary, a criminal and so a forbidden
party. The classic speech made by Sukarno in his own defence on December
2nd – it was published later in Dutch at Amsterdam by Arbeiderspers under
the title *Indonesia Accuses* – did not in any way affect the Government plans.
The verdict was delivered at Christmas; Sukarno was sentenced to four years'
imprisonment; the others got off with shorter periods.

Meantime it became clear that Sukarno and his friends had a greater sense
of reality than the Dutch Government. It became ever more evident that the
nationalist movement in Indonesia was not simply the creation of wild intellectuals and communists, but was the natural and general reaction of a
colonial people which was resolved to be free, that the ferment all over Asia
(and also in Africa and South America) was not a little fire lit by a few
modernists but a conflagration started by the backward, oppressed majority
of the world's peoples. What was now to be seen was the revolution of our
times. As Sukarno put it: 'The sun does not rise because the cock crows; the
cock crows because the sun is rising.'

The wrong interpretation of the situation offered by the reactionary elements in Holland created, alas, more stir than did the attitude of a handful

[1] A new edition will be found in the 1952 edition of Hatta's collected works.

of liberal European intellectuals who found a medium for the expression of their views in the weekly *De Stuw* (Defence: 1930–1933) to which, among others, Dr H. J. van Mook (director of the Ministry of Economics 1937–1942, governor-general in 1942 and again from 1944 to 1948) was a contributor.

What was of greater significance was the combination of ten members to form an Indonesian fraction in the Volksraad (January 1930). Its chief leader was Mohammed Husni Thamrin (1894–1941), a courageous, able, and intelligent critic of the Dutch administration, even if he and his friends did not adopt the methods of the PNI. The PNI was voluntarily dissolved in 1931, but was continued by two new parties. The first was the Partai Indonesia (April 1931), usually known as the 'Partindo'. Thanks to the initiative of Sartono, one of Sukarno's trusted friends, it was a mass party from which the socialist element in the PNI appears to have vanished. Hatta described it as 'watered down' and chose to fight against imperialism and capitalism through the second new party, the Pendidikan Nasional Indonesia (the PNI–baru, founded at Djokjakarta December 1931), whose president was Sutan Shahrir (b. 1909). It was a smaller but more radical party, and for a long time ranked as one of the three great Indonesian parties.

Sukarno, who was released in December 1931 and on his journey home was greeted wherever his train stopped by a crowd of wellwishers, tried for long to unite the two, but in vain. The government, however, tried to suppress both.

It is possible that Dutch rule might have become more democratic, more modern, had not Indonesia been involved in the general economic crisis. The sugar plantations offer a classic example of its consequences. Of the 180 refineries at work in 1928, only fifty were in use in 1934; the area of cultivation sank to a sixth. The same is true of tea, rubber, coffee and tobacco. On the Java market rice prices fell from seventy-five to twenty-five Dutch florins per ton. Indonesia was starving.

How did the Dutch react to this situation? A growing tendency to reaction found expression in a change in the administration. In 1931 Jonkheer B. C. de Jonge (1931–1936), the former head of the Batavian Oil Company, became governor-general. He was a narrow-minded conservative without knowledge of the 'native movement'. He neither knew it nor admitted its existence. 'We have ruled here for three hundred years with the policeman's club,' he said, 'and things will be no different in the next three hundred.' He tried to put obstacles in Van Mook's way. 'Democratic innovations', like the freedom of the press and the secrecy of private correspondence, were severely curtailed. On the economic plane his administration was a modern version of the policy of the seventeenth century.

In 1933 the bomb literally burst. The suppression of the strike and mutiny on board the cruiser *The Seven Provinces* (February 4–10th) cost the lives of 23 Indonesian members of its crew; 500 Indonesian and 80 Dutch seamen were discharged from the navy. The incident may not have great significance for the general development of the Indonesian movement, but it was none the less a warning signal both at home and abroad. It was news all over the world especially among the workers.

In June Government officials were forbidden to join the Partai Indonesia and the PNI–baru. The parties had 20,000 and 1000 members. On August 1, 1933, Sukarno was arrested; in February 1934 Hatta, Shahrir and many others. Sukarno was banished to New Guinea and was freed by the Japanese in 1942. His internment was typical of the measures taken by the administration against the leaders of the nationalist movement.

In March, behind the bars of the Tschipinang prison, Shahrir wrote the first pages of his able study of the development of Indonesia and the relations between East and West. In it he showed that, like Nehru, he understood the colonial contradiction and also the 'opposition' – the word had become a cliche – between an 'intuitive' eastern culture and the 'rationalist' culture of the West. In these pages of his diary (published in Holland in 1946 under the title *Thoughts on Indonesia*) he described how he himself, Hatta and others had ascended the Digul River on a January night to the camp at Tanah Merah where 400 other exiles were living in the damp malarial forests completely isolated from the outer world and bullied by their Dutch guards. In February 1936 Hatta and Shahrir were taken to Bandanaira (1936–1942). This place of banishment was symbolic, for it had long been a Dutch stronghold in this spicy paradise; the first fort was built in 1617. The original inhabitants had been slaughtered or driven out. During Shahrir's stay there migrants from Buton worked on the nutmeg plantations for ten cents a day.

Meantime the Partai Indonesia went to pieces and the PNI–baru stifled. But what had happened in the administration's counter-action in 1926–27 when the PKI disappeared and in 1930–31 when the PNI vanished from the scene, happened again. The self-consciousness of the people grew as silently as does the rice. Parties, method and theory changed, but the drive to freedom was maintained, the drive to the 'Indonesian Merdeka'. Two new nationalist parties appeared. The Partai Indonesia Raja (Parindra) (1935) was the first. It was the party of the modern bourgeoisie of Indonesia, of the native capitalism, which may be compared as a bourgeois nationalist party to the Wafd in Egypt or to Kemal's party in Turkey. Despite its social, economic and cultural activity through its many peasant groups it was by no means a democratic party. The Perhimpunan Indonesia in Holland and the PNI–baru at home criticized it as a 'bourgeois front' and as a result of the criticism there arose the left socialist party (May 1937), the Gerakan Rakjat Indonesia (Gerindo). In the cultural sphere, Muhammadijah (from 1912) and the Taman Siswa movement, founded in 1922 by Ki Hadjar Dewantoro (Suwardi Surjaningrat), did much to modernize the country.

There was, however, no change in the way in which Indonesia was ruled from The Hague. The European press in Indonesia began to lean towards fascism, just at the time when Japan was threatening to carry its expansion southward; it already held the richest parts of China. Japanese 'fishing vessels' were appearing ever more frequently in Filipino and Indonesia waters; Tokio presented at Batavia what was more than just an economic ultimatum. War was in the air and the secret manoeuvres of Dutch and British warships seemed to confirm all the rumours.

In increasing numbers the people of Indonesia expected Tokio to set them free. Asia for the Asians! Only the Gerindo, which was anti-fascist and internationally inclined and some of the exiles (the communists abroad and Shahrir and Tjipto, for instance, in Indonesia itself), saw as did Nehru the really dangerous imperialism of the German and Japanese expansion, the threat not only to Western but to Asian democracy.

In this charged atmosphere Holland failed completely. A great empire and small minds go ill together, wrote Burke in the eighteenth century. That was seen again in Indonesia. The petition of Sutardjo (1936), in which, taking the Philippines as pattern, he asked for Dutch-Indonesian negotiations and more self-government after ten years, was not by any standard a revolutionary demand, but was allowed to lie on the table in The Hague for two years before the Dutch announced its rejection. At that very time, when London and Washington were relaxing the strictness of their rule in India–Pakistan and Burma and the Philippines, the Dutch Government remained blind nor would it yield an inch. That united Indonesia. In 1939 Sukarno was able to do what had been for so long considered impossible; he united the various nationalist groups into a federation. The general Congress Rakjat Indonesia is well known; it was held at Christmas 1939, when was seen the red and white colours of the old kingdom of Modjopahit and where was heard the national hymn *Indonesia Raja* as symbols of national freedom, and the 'Bahasa Indonesia', which had been developed from Malayan as a cultural language, was accepted as the general language of the country.

After Holland and half of Europe had been occupied by the Germans and the Japanese had invaded Indochina, the Dutch Government, then in exile in London, returned a flat 'No' to a request by Thamrin (August 9th) that the terms Netherlands Indies, Netherlands-Indian and natives should be replaced in official documents and in Government announcements by Indonesia, Indonesian and Indonesians. Once again it used every possible pseudo-scientific argument. It would concede only this, that in official documents 'natives' should become 'Indonesians' or 'native inhabitants'. It was a Dutch writer himself half a child of Indonesia, who wrote: 'There is no more misleading or pitiable a term than "native".' (E. du Perron, *Indisches Memorandum*).

That the Government felt obscurely, and much too obscurely, that if there were no reforms Indonesia would be an easier prey for the Japanese, is shown by the fact that the Visman Commission of autumn 1940 was charged with investigating the feeling in Indonesia. It was a diversionary manoeuvre and it came too late. The day before the full report of the last governor-general Tjarda van Starkenborgh was handed over, the Dutch Government in London on December 7, 1941, had declared war on Japan after the attack on Pearl Harbour.

XI

INDOCHINA, MALAYA AND THAILAND

In general, the picture presented by Southeast Asia between the wars does not greatly differ from that presented by the Philippines and Indonesia. Viewed from the outside the development was less turbulent; natives were taken into the administration: hygiene and medical care became general, illiteracy declined and the numbers of intellectuals trained in European universities grew. Above all, Western influence in the economic sphere became greater; ports and modern roads were built; the mining industry (tin and oil) expanded: Western plantations and cultivation (rubber and palm-oil) were extended. Generally speaking we can, except for Thailand, talk of a linking-up with the economy of the West.

Accompanying all this was a more than average increase in the population. In the whole of Southeast Asia, including the archipelagoes, the population in 1939 had risen to 150,000,000, an increase on an average of 35 per cent in fifteen years. The under-nutrition of the mass of that population was still more widespread.

In these countries a small native bourgeoisie sought to counter the invaders from the West and the immigrants from China. In Malaya, where Chinese formed 40 per cent of the population and, in Thailand, where they formed 15 per cent, the national resistance was against them rather than against the white men.

In the period between the wars that situation remained fundamentally unchanged. None of the Southeast Asian colonies was free, although as early as 1935 the status of the Philippines, so far as the form of government was concerned, approached that of a dominion. Yet, however contrary to the intentions of the West, the situation was in fact ripe for a significant change, i.e. for independence from European–American penetration.

A further and very important element in the latest history of Southeast Asia was its economic structure and its position in the world. There were very few small rice-farmers; there were very many big plantations whose owners were white. From it in 1939 was exported about 90 per cent of the world's rubber, 95 per cent of its rice, 65 per cent of its vegetable oil, 20 per cent of its raw sugar. There were also rich mines and oilfields producing about 55 per cent of the world's tin, 8 per cent of its aluminium and 4 per cent of its mineral oil. Such a situation caused the West much anxiety; it also explains the catastrophic and revolutionary effects of the great economic crisis.

In addition, all its countries from 1935, and very definitely from 1937, lived in the shadow – or was it the grey of dawn? – of Japanese expansion. If in some cases this lessened anti-Western feeling especially among the radical elements, it tended much more to increase it and so further decrease Western prestige.

History is a mingling of general and special factors. If one wishes to have a clear picture, both must be investigated. By special factors we mean the character and past of a country and its people and the typical traits which are characteristic of every imperialism so far as Asia is concerned. We have already compared Spanish, French, Dutch and British imperialism in various Asian countries; when we dealt with the Philippines we were concerned with that relative newcomer, American imperialism.

In Indochina we can study French imperialism in Asia. When dealing with the Arab countries we noted how convinced the French are of the special superiority of their culture, how they think that Paris is the heart of European civilization, i.e. the centre of culture, for culture means French culture. It is certainly true that in the history of culture France has played a unique part. But development continues and the Paris of 1940 has much less significance than the Paris of 1900. More than any other West European country, France tried to 'frenchify' its colonies in Asia and North Africa; it was under the illusion that parts of Africa and Asia could be transformed into parts of France. This was called the policy of 'assimilation'. Remember the complete freedom with which the Algerian Arabs and Berbers could migrate to France.

That implies that the French are relatively free from race prejudices. It was hoped that Arabs, Indochinese and other 'natives' could be drawn into the French cultural world; that in turn meant a denigration of the native culture. But as ever the French themselves did not sufficiently understand the real situation. This inclination to assimilate the colonial peoples was deepened by the fact that the native population of France was not increasing as, say, Germany's was. In the nineteenth century the falling birth rate was a real threat. In 1880 there were 45,000,000 Germans, in 1920 60,000,000 and in 1940 about 70,000,000, while in 1880 there were 37,500,000 French, in 1920 39,000,000 and in 1940 41,000,000, and fewer Frenchmen meant fewer French soldiers.

But Indochina did not become what France had hoped. Actually it remained part of Asia, the more so as the First World War, the Russian revolution, modern Japan and the Chinese revolution set their seals on the history of Asia.

These things were happening when France with her declining manhood was more and more attached to the 'blooming garden of the Pacific' which was her only big colony in Asia, whence came numbers of soldiers and workers and which was one of the pillars of her international status. In it lived one-third of the population of her colonial empire. From the mines on the Chinese frontier France exported much tin and coal; from the plantations in Cochinchina and Cambodia 6 per cent of the world's rubber; from the valleys a fifth of the world's rice. From it French trade and French imperialism pressed into South China. Would not Tonkin in 1885 have remained an outlying province of China if shortly before that a French trader had not brought 600 tons of tin down the Red River from the rich mines of Yunnan to Hanoi?

Generally speaking the French no more than the Dutch or the British understood what was brewing in their Asian possessions. Without much knowledge of it and interested almost wholly in what was happening in his own country and in Western Europe, the French bourgeois thought of Indochina as a rich and exotic land where a primitive peasant people lived eternally happily tending their plots, and where an able but mild European administration had delivered to them the culture of France in their idyllic villages with their palms and bamboos.

The less rosy aspects of the reality were not understood – that of the peasants in the Red River valley two-thirds carried on agriculture in plots of little more than an acre, that the peasants of Vietnam had only a tiny portion of rice twice a day, that economically the peasant population faced crisis. Just as little was it known how many of the native bourgeoisie, the intellectuals and the peasants demanded a 'French revolution' of their own, how the ideas of Marx and Lenin were ever more widely spread and how the whole land was weary of foreign penetration. Indochina, and especially Vietnam (Tonkin, Annam and Cochinchina), had many historical and cultural connections with China, of which they had once been outlying provinces. Canton, the heart of the Chinese revolution, had revivified radicalism in Indochina. All the movements and changes in China had impressed far more people here than in other Asian lands. And just as Dr Sun had established his headquarters in Hanoi, so the leader of the Indochinese revolutionaries at the beginning of the period with which we are here concerned, established his bases in Canton and Hongkong. He called himself then Nguyen Ai Quoc; he is the Ho Chi Minh of today. He was born, it seems, about 1892 in one of the northern provinces of Vietnam, Nghe-An, which the French called the 'rebel province', and went to Europe in 1910 as a kitchen boy. In 1913 he became a waiter in a well-known London restaurant. When the Germans invaded France in 1914 he tried to join the British Army. He was rejected and went to Paris, where, as we have already related, he tried to interest the statesmen of Versailles in freedom for Indochina; the only result was that the French secret police became interested in him. He stayed for some time in Germany, Italy and Switzerland and wrote articles for left-wing papers. Returning to Paris he worked part time in a photographer's, and in libraries wrote his book *French Colonization on Trial* which appeared in 1926 and through which he became gradually known in France and in Indochina.

Meantime he became the first native of Vietnam to be a member of a French political party, the Socialists. The French socialists had split at the historic party congress in Tours (1920) into two parties, the adherents of the Second International (of 1889) and the adherents of the Third (founded by Lenin 1919). Ho joined the latter. From Moscow, where he was prominent in Asian revolutionary circles like Tan Malaka from Malaya, M. N. Roy from India, Sen Katayama from Japan and Chiang Kai-shek from China, he accompanied Borodin to Canton as interpreter. Many Indonesians lived there, and here he founded the Than-Nien, an extremely left, revolutionary Annamite party. From the Whampoa Academy of the Kuo Min-tang government he sent adherents and cell-builders, among them many members of the Young Annamite movement, to Vietnam and Thailand. The aims of the Than-Nien were the same as those of the left-wing Chinese, i.e. collaboration between the bourgeoisie, the peasants and the workers to drive out Western imperialism, in the characteristic Leninist manner to split them, and to take the place of the unruly resistance movement; the desperate character of the movement was seen, for instance, in the attempt by a Tonkinese student to murder the French governor-general Merlin while he was on a visit to Canton.

When the counter-revolution in China came in 1927 Ho fled *via* Hankow and Moscow to Thailand, where he remained in hiding until 1928–9. The Than-Nien in Canton remained free of 'white' Chinese influence and, while the Third International, mainly because of the failure of communist revolutions outside Russia, held aloof from the bourgeois parties and the Asian communists kept apart from the nationalist movements in their countries, Ho remained in principle true to his earlier tactics. None the less the Chinese and international changes were reflected in the attitude of the Indonesian nationalists. The Than-Nien changed its name to the Communist party of Indochina. That was in 1929, and in the same year the Young Annamite party fell to pieces because of the same internal divisions that had driven Red and White China into civil war. During the fairly liberal rule of the socialist governor-general Varenne (1925–1928) the Vietnam Quoc Dan Dang (VNQDD) made its appearance in Hanoi. Quoc Dan Dang is a translation of Kuo Min-tang; it was modelled on the Chinese Government party and was the most influential nationalist party of the Indochinese bourgeoisie in the period between the wars. Just as in India and Indonesia, there were strikes in the ports and scattered risings among the peasants which were a sign of the growing protest against French rule; it became so violent that in 1930–1 it reached a critical stage.

There had been in 1929 an attempt to murder the governor-general Pasquier; the attempt on the life of Bazin, the director of an employment office in Hanoi, was successful. The murder was revenge for the brutal treatment of the miners in the Tonkin mines, the 'hell of Hon Gays' (coal), and the 'valley of death' (tin). But what was really cooking in the colonial witches' cauldron was seen first in the mutiny at Yenbay, a fortress on the Red River, 125 miles northwest of Hanoi. The mutiny, in which the Annamite soldiers of the garrison murdered their French officers and occupied various roads, was ascribed to the VNQDD. And, while everywhere in the north anti-French demonstrations were reported and foreign legionaries from Hanoi crushed the mutineers with great cruelty, the peasants rose. The agrarian movement was directed against the landowners who were often pro-French, and in two provinces of Annam communists tried to set up a revolutionary government – an echo of the contemporary events in the Chinese provinces of Hunan and Kiangsi.

The French press has called 1930 the 'year of the Red Terror'. One might just as well call it the 'year of the White Terror' for, when French troops appeared in 1930 and 1931, many natives were arrested and murdered. The situation in Indochina was very like that in Indonesia, where the PKI and the PNI disappeared.

It was in Saigon and Cochinchina that the nationalist parties were built up again, and not in Hanoi, where things had become too hot for the nationalists. The freedom movement in France's overseas domains was encouraged by the existence of the Popular Front 1936–1938 – there was no such encouragement in, say, Indonesia – and the more so, because Popular Front governments were no more able to alter the mentality of officials and officers in Indochina than to prevent the fall of democracy in the Spanish Civil War. While the words of the socialist minister for the colonies offered good hope, actually, apart from the release of many internees, little was done in Indochina which could truly be described as socialist.

All the same, nationalism got some freedom of action. The VNQDD recovered from the arrests of Yenbay. A second movement of some importance arose in Cochinchina, Caodaism, a modernized Buddhism in which elements from other religions, Western and Eastern, were blended. Originally it was a non-political movement of a native government official, Ngo Van Chien, but between 1936 and 1941 it developed into a right-wing nationalist party which was slightly pro-Japanese. At this period its leader was Pham Cong Tac from Cochinchina, who was banished to Madagascar. The left socialists also built up their party again. While Ho Chi Minh remained abroad (in Thailand, Singapore, China, the Soviet Union and elsewhere), Tran Van Giau (b. 1911, alias Ho Nam) reorganized the Communist party. When a student he had been banned from France for agitation at the time of the Yenbay mutiny; he went to Moscow, where from 1931 to 1933 he studied at the Lenin University; in the latter year he returned to Indochina and made the Communist party there one of the largest in Southeast Asia. Originating in Saigon, a Trotskyist tendency of considerable importance began to spread. Its leader was Ta Thu Than (c. 1910–1945) who, as a student, had been expelled from France. Meantime Bao Dai (b. 1913 and from 1926 to 1945 emperor of Annam and the 'night club king' of the later Vietnam) did little, despite his relatively modern leanings, to further the cause of Indochinese independence. Although he introduced a few administrative reforms and banished many old-fashioned mandarins from his court, he was fundamentally in the French camp.

The third period of Indochina's modern history ended with the French debacle in 1940. On May 10th the German armies occupied Holland and Belgium and, a few weeks later, France. On June 22nd France capitulated. In the unoccupied territory, a new fascist government in Vichy under Pétain strove to keep on the right side of the Germans. In June the governor-general of Indochina, Catroux, under Japanese pressure had forbidden traffic with China on the railway from Haiphong to Kunming. But he would go no farther, and so Vichy sent out as his successor an adherent of Pétain, Lecoux, who offered no resistance of any kind to Tokio (August–September 1940). In theory France was still sovereign; French officials remained at their posts; French citizens were not interned. But no limits were put to the authority of Tokio. Japanese warships appeared in the ports, and in the summer of

1941, when Germany was invading Russia, two divisions of Japanese troops were in occupation of the country. That was the beginning of the invasion of Thailand and the conquest of Singapore and Indonesia in 1942.

'History and revolution are the same thing', Sukarno once said. If we mean by the term revolution, not just street fighting and plundering – as a historical conception the word obviously has a much greater significance – we express a certain truth, and then we may consider the history of Asia actually as a single revolution.

A country like Malaya seems interesting particularly, as an exception to the rule. We have discussed this in our treatment of the period 1900–1914. Neither the course nor the fulfilment of the nationalist revolution was the same in Malaya as in the other Asian countries of any importance. How was it possible for the British to remain in Malaya? Why did the British want to remain whatever the cost? Why was the Japanese occupation not the signal for, and the beginning of, independence? Why in the period 1919–1941 was Malaya much less politically ripe for change than any other country in Southeast Asia? The various factors in its situation have already been dealt with – the relative smallness of the country and the sparseness of its population, its special economic and strategic importance, the racial division into Malays, Chinese and Indians. The influence of each of these factors increased in the period between the wars.

If we look at the map of Asia we see that Malaya is a small peninsula no bigger than Java; including Singapore it had in 1930 a population of about 4,200,000, in 1939 about 5,500,000 and today 6,500,000. To control so small a country with so small a population does not need any great army. In the second place – and this partly explains British policy – Singapore, the British naval base in East Asia, the Gibraltar of Asia, the impregnable citadel of imperialism there, was part of the peninsula. What was a Malay village in 1820 became under British rule the third greatest port and one of the biggest trading cities in Asia, and the port of exit for the goods which Malaya could export, tin, for instance, and, above all, rubber, the product of a Brazilian tree, British capital and enterprise, American ingenuity, and the sweat of many Chinese, Indian and Malay labourers.

In 1875 when the British began to penetrate into the interior from a few trading settlements on the coast, there was no such thing in it as a rubber tree. In Java, indeed, from 1864 the wild *Ficus elastic Roxb.* grew in a few plantations; the *Hevea brasiliansis,* to use the technical term, grew only in South America in the valley of the Amazon. As early as the eighteenth century a French traveller had obtained from the Indians some of the milky juice of the tree and brought it to Europe. But it was not until 1839 that the American Charles Goodyear succeeded in primitive chemical experiments in producing modern rubber from the glutinous caoutchouc by mixing it with sulphur. The Brazilian Government grasped the importance of this and forbade the export of rubber plants.

In 1871 an English botanist called Henry E. Wickham published an account of his experiences during travels in the Brazilian forests. The director of the Botanical Gardens in Kew near London read it and sent his remarks on it to the British Government, and in 1876 Wickham smuggled seeds of the coveted plant out of Brazil. Experienced growers and botanists grew trees from the seed in Malaya, Ceylon and Bandung, and in 1905 the first 174 tons of rubber from their own plantations arrived in London. By 1914 as much rubber was got from the plantations as from the wild trees in Brazil. In 1922 British and Dutch were exporting 90 per cent of the world's rubber from Southeast Asia. Between the wars Malaya alone produced 45 per cent. Four-fifths of Malaya is forest, pathless mountains and marshes, but 80 per cent of the usable land is occupied by plantations which produce rubber, coconuts, bananas and other 'Western' products. Malaya is a colonial Utopia for it produces, in addition to these, a third of the world's tin. The very intensive exploitation of Malaya is seen in its very modern – as compared with many other Asian countries – economy, technology and hygiene. From a medical and health point of view Malaya in 1940 had reached the same level as rural Italy, Spain and Eastern Europe. The position in Singapore corresponds to that of Europe so far as standards are concerned; in 1940 40 per cent of the city's inhabitants could read and write. Modern too is the taxation system. Government revenue does not come from taxes on land or from salt and matches monopolies, but from oil, tobacco and income taxes. The average income in 1940 was £40 per annum, as in Japan, a figure at least three times as high as those for India, China and Indonesia.

All that, the rubber and the tin and Singapore, prevented Britain from voluntarily withdrawing. At the same time Malaya was a paradise for Indian and Chinese immigrants very much as North America was for many migrants from South and East Europe. In 1929 the Chinese formed 40 per cent of the population and the Indians fifteen. But, contrary to what happened in America, the migrants to Malaya were not prepared to blend with the native population. The Chinese were tin-miners; they became small farmers; they also became owners of mines and plantations and capitalist merchants. Singapore was almost a Chinese city. The Indians became plantation and railway workers and also road workers. But both remained foreigners, often strongly separated from the Malays and always cherishing the hope of one day returning to China and India. This division among the immigrants, and the gulf between them and the natives, between Buddhists, Moslems and Hindus, made it possible for the British to stay put. If they could not quite suppress thoughts of a united independent Malaya, they certainly very greatly hindered them from developing.

Whatever political radicalism there was before the Second World War was an importation from China and had no influence on the Malays. The Communist party of Malaya (founded about 1925), the kernel of the resistance to the Japanese and later on to the British, was exclusively Chinese, except for a few Malay intellectuals. The ideas of the Kuo Min-tang, brought in by other Chinese left the Malays uninterested, while the relatively small Moslem movement had no interest for the Chinese.

Various parties and individual leaders tried to unite the diverse elements in the population – the Communist party, for instance, the Chinese intellectual and rubber baron, Tan Cheng Lock, and the aristocratic Malay journalist, Dato Onn bin Jafar – but Malayan nationalism remained a mere shadow of what nationalism was in Indonesia, the Philippines or Indochina.

Malaya is an illustration of the fact that a fairly intensive modernization and a raising of the economic level are not by themselves enough to create a nation. Apart from all other things, nationalism is a sense of loyalty to the state in place of earlier loyalties to the village, the family, the religious group, the prince. In Malaya the question is still Buddhist or Moslem, Chinese, Indian or Malay. In the course of things Malaya will of course become a genuinely independent country. But the question what sort of a country will it become is more difficult to answer than in any other Asian country.

Thailand, too, had fewer wars and revolutions than many other Asian lands in this period, although formally, i.e. in the diplomatic sense, it was among the belligerents in both world wars. Also, during the whole imperialist period it remained an independent state among its conquered neighbours.

One reason why it kept its independence was the rivalry between Britain and France while they were expanding their rule in that part of the world. Thailand was a buffer state between the British in Burma and the French in Indochina, in a position very much like that of Afghanistan between British and Russian imperialism. By 1919 the classic period of European imperialism was over. The German colonies in Africa and the Pacific were divided; the freedom just won by the Arabs was limited but there was no new colony in the old sense of the word; the one exception was Abyssinia, which Italy annexed in 1936.

Again, there were no oilfields in Thailand; it did not lie across Russia's road to the sea as did Persia, whose independence was purely formal. It is significant that Thailand was the last country to recognize (in 1936) the Soviet Union.

From the economic point of view European, and especially British, imperialism was of great importance, but politically of very little. In 1920 Thailand, like Persia, was one of the first members of the League of Nations. This was in recognition of the fact that Thailand had declared war on Germany and Austria in 1917. At the same time the extra-territorial rights of Americans, Japanese (1924), French, British, and others (1925–6) were abolished and Thailand recovered full freedom in tariff and customs policy.

Thus it remained relatively free from anti-Western agitation and feeling. It had an American as foreign minister and British officials were in the ministries of finance and justice. Danes held high rank in the navy, and in the police forces Germans, Italians, Belgians and Frenchmen filled senior posts. What nationalism there was was directed against the French who between 1867 and 1907 had tried five times to cross the eastern frontier, and against the Chinese who formed 15 per cent of the population. Three-fourths of all workers engaged otherwise than in agriculture were Chinese, and their richer compatriots controlled internal trade and possessed three-quarters of the rice-mills and other industries; they had more capital invested in Thailand than had the British.

For a long time Thailand was free from Western penetration, even in the form of modern ideas and capitalist economics. While the revolution was general in Asia, the 'land of freedom' seemed in 1920 to be a typical feudal Asian state, i.e. it had not materially altered in character from what it had been in the middle of the fourteenth century. Of course it had been to some extent modernized, especially during the reign of Chulalongkorn.[1] But his reforms, like those in Turkey in the nineteenth century, were for the most part external, technical and very limited. Thailand's kings were interested in Western economics and technology mainly as a means of defence against Western expansion and against change at home. Modern soldiers and sailors must be able to read and write, and a modern army must be as far as possible made immune to plague and malaria. The tanks of the Bangkok garrison and the guns of the Royal Siamese navy assured not only the sovereignty of the country but the absolutism of the monarch and of a mediaeval system of government that is symbolized by the family connections between the king and the ruling nobility; these connections spring mainly from the royal harem of earlier days.

Such a situation did not please the bourgeoisie, especially the officers and the intellectuals who had studied in the West. Some of them wanted little more than a more modern administration, a very modest reproduction of the French revolution. A smaller group of liberal intellectuals wanted in addition a rise in status for the peasant to be achieved by the use of soap, electricity and the alphabet.

In the reign of Rama VII Pradjadhipok (1925–1935), what had happened earlier in Turkey, Persia and China happened in Thailand. On June 24, 1932, radical officers and intellectuals carried out a *coup d'état* in Bangkok. What was remarkable about it was its very modern methods of revolution. There was no bloody conflicts, no harem intrigues, no murders in the royal gardens, only the occupation of all centres of communications, post and telephone and telegraph offices, the central electricity authority and the railway stations, thus cutting off the court and the government behind the high walls of their own castle. Clearly the rebels, although they were not communists, had studied the events in Petrograd in October 1917.

The king, for a time under house arrest, made no resistance. His privileges were curtailed, the government made democratic. Thailand became a kingdom of a Western type in which the king is in principle merely of symbolic importance. On December 10th a final constitution was promulgated. The king appointed half the members of the new parliament; the other half were elected by universal suffrage; the women of Thailand, at least in theory, received a very modern civic right.

In April 1933 the king, thinking he could depend on his people, withdrew the reforms, but a second officers' *coup d'état* assured the success of the

[1] v. p. 77.

bourgeois revolution (June 20, 1933). Its leader, Phya Rahol Sena, became prime minister (1933–1938) and about the same time an artillery officer, Luang Pibul Songgram (b. 1895; alias Plack Srianing), crushed another attempt at counter-revolution led by Prince Bovaradej (October 1933); there was little bloodshed. Bovaradej fled to Indochina and did not return until 1949. A few princes and nobles were kept in prison for a time. The king in January 1934 went to London intending never to return; in 1935 he wrote a deed of abdication.

Meantime the officers, who were at heart not so very democratic, and other right elements took the chance to suppress the liberal intellectuals; compare similar happenings in Turkey, Persia and China. To carry through a revolution the soldier is indispensable, but he is a danger to its survival. The moderate radical leader of the left elements in the 1932 revolution, Luang Predit Manudharm (b. about 1902; alias Nai Pridi Phanomyong), a former professor of jurisprudence in the Chulalongkorn University who today is once again an exile in Pekin, was for a time (1933–1934) banished for his allegedly communist economic plans of which the king said: 'Either he got them from Stalin or Stalin got them from him.'

Ananda Mahidol (b. 1925, mysteriously murdered 1946) became king in 1935, in theory at least, for he lived in Europe and did not visit his country until 1938. The new Thailand was not particularly democratically ruled and, though in this period a fairly important democratic movement did develop and Pridi, a man with socialist views, was minister of foreign affairs, the extreme right-wing minister of defence Pibul Songgram and his associates saw to it that the government leaned towards fascism.

At this time a radical left-wing movement did not exist. The Communist party, founded in 1925, remained a small one. Communist activity in the northeast of the country and in Bangkok was in the main inspired by foreign influence from China and Indochina. Why was it that there was so little social radicalism in Thailand? If we attempt an explanation – and it will be only an attempt – we shall cite some points which possibly are an aid to understanding. Thailand remained relatively apart from international economic developments. The peasants were in better case than in other Southeast Asian lands; there was no high taxation and workers on the land were still a small percentage of the people; the indebtedness of the peasants was not on the same scale as in China, the Philippines, Indonesia or Japan. The fact that Thailand was independent and Western interference was on a small scale lessened the desire for an anti-imperialist and anti-capitalist freedom movement and, finally, much of the radical agitation and ideas came from Chinese sources and, as in Malaya, aroused doubt and suspicion.

The new regime, however, did show itself more nationalist than its predecessor, but as much towards China and the Chinese as to the West. Foreign advisers were removed from Government offices. State enterprises did their best to depress the Chinese economically. There was a sustained and compulsive effort to win the cultural minorities like the Chinese and the 400,000 Malays in the frontier districts for Siamese culture. The army and the fleet were modernized. Factories were built. Sugar, cigarettes, wine, matches, cement and canned fish were produced. Ships were built in Thailand for the coastal trade, and new river boats which took the place of the English ones. As a primitive country Thailand had no capital – the greatest problem for an 'underdeveloped' country – and was not prepared to ask for much capital from the West – Asia's second problem. Thus only light industries existed.

About 1937 Thailand began to go with the Japanese current. The few left elements in the Government, finally even Pridi, were got rid of after the aggressive Field-Marshal Pibul Songgram became prime minister (1938–1944). He changed the name of the country from Siam to 'Muang Thai' (the 'land of freedom') in commemoration of the period of expansion from the fourteenth to the nineteenth century. After Germany had defeated France and the Japanese had gone into Indochina, he annexed territories beyond the existing eastern frontier (Treaty of Tokio May 9, 1941), and when on December 8, 1941, the day when war broke out in East Asia and the Pacific, a Japanese ultimatum was sent to Bangkok, the army was ordered to offer only token resistance. In the far west of the European heartland the Germans were besieging Leningrad and threatening Moscow and the American Pacific fleet was burning at Pearl Harbour; in Siam the Japanese were pursuing their invasion unmolested.

XII

INDIA-PAKISTAN (i)

WHAT had British India to expect of history in the period with which we are now dealing? Its area is so extraordinarily great (1,500,000 square miles) – only the Soviet Union and China are bigger – its population is so enormous – one-third of all Asians – and it is internationally so important that we divide our account of it into two parts as we did with our account of China; actually into three, as for reasons mentioned later we deal with Burma in a special section.

What we are trying to do in this book is to relate the history of the movement towards independence in the various countries and it is therefore necessary to deal with the development chronologically. In the case of British India, that is easy. Like Palme Dutt in his *India Today* we distinguish between the three great waves of national resistance in the twentieth century – 1905–1910, the period of Tilak and the founding of the Moslem League and abroad the period of the first Russian revolution and the Russo-Japanese War; 1919–1922, the period in which, as a consequence of the First World War, the workers and the colonial peoples in Europe and Asia generally rose in rebellion; and, leaving aside the years 1937–1941, the period 1930–1934, which internationally was the period of the great economic crisis in the capitalist world and of the expansion of Germany, Italy and Japan and the beginnings of the Second World War, whose inevitability was in these years foreseen by relatively few men of insight.

In this section we propose to deal with the events of 1919–1922 and their sequel until January 1, 1930. The revolutionary events which accompanied the end of the First World War in British India have already been described, including some tragic ones, the influenza epidemic, the rough-and-ready Rowlatt Act of March 1919, Gandhi's first campaign and the 'blood bath of Amritsar' in April 1919. All these events combined to drive the independence movement into new courses. On September 8, 1920, Gandhi began his first *satyagraha* campaign, i.e. passive resistance. He declared a boycott (*hartal*) of British goods after a day of mourning and a day of fasting and meditation. As part of the campaign the bourgeois boycotted the elections. Two-thirds of the some 6,000,000 Indians who by the Government of India Act of December 23, 1919, had been given the franchise as being of sufficient means and sufficient education, refused to go to the polls. As the chief move in the boycott campaign Gandhi required the peasants and the townsfolk to undertake in their own homes the spinning and weaving of the native cotton into the raw white *khadi* as substitute for the product of British and Japanese factories. Like a forest fire in dry weather the movement swept over the towns and 700,000 villages of India and Pakistan. It was not only the Hindu districts that were affected. The Moslems, who were already enraged by the partition of Turkey, did not hang back, and the strikes of 1920–1921, particularly in the cotton mills of Bombay, in the mines and on the railways, showed plainly that the working class adhered to the independence movement.

In 1921 the agitation reached its height and also its crisis. Contrary to Gandhi's slogan of passive resistance, the national bitterness found expression in numberless terrorist acts, often quite consciously inspired by the deeds of the Russian revolutionaries and the Irish patriots in the nineteenth century; in Ireland, then a British semi-colony, the extreme nationalist Sinn Fein movement had forced the British into a savage civil war (1919–1923). In several provinces the peasants rose against the landowners; in Malabar Moslem peasants rose against their Hindu landowners in the Moplah rising. Antagonism between Hindus and Moslems in the winter of 1921 at once caused and worsened the chaos in the sub-continent. Meantime, the leaders of the All-India Moslem League, Mohammed and Shaukat Ali, were arrested (September 1921) and were kept in prison for two years.

At the same time – a further example of European tactfulness – the Prince of Wales made a general tour of India. This was the prince who after being king and emperor for a few months preferred marriage with an attractive American to the British crown. It was a notorious and widespread belief in Europe that the mystic 'soul of the East' was very susceptible to the charms of royalty; it was part of the conception of 'the naïve native'. Travellers' tales brought to the West from India and Africa, like that of the Siamese princess who was drowned because no one dared to be so intimate with royalty as to pull her out of the water, were very popular. But this European idea was itself naïve, even if there was an element of truth in it. All colonized peoples, all oppressed classes have a respect for emperors, kings and governors-general if they are still not consciously striving to be free and loyal to their own ideals. But the visit of the Prince of Wales was generally boycotted by the native population. Surrounded by his bodyguard, alone in empty streets, he may perhaps have perceived how India had changed. In the rioting on his entry into Bombay fifty people were killed.

The atmosphere awoke memories of 1857; the Government took alarm. There were numberless arrests; 40,000 in December and January. Of the important leaders only Gandhi escaped arrest. In prison they learned of what happened through censored newspapers and prison rumours; on February 4, 1922, a crowd of peasants burned down the police post in Chauri-Chaura, a small village in the United Provinces, and twenty-two policemen, some of them British, were killed. Gandhi was horrified; he feared things would get out of hand and the effect of the boycott be enfeebled, and ordered that active resistance was to cease. The violence abated but he himself was arrested and imprisoned (March 11, 1922, to February 4, 1924). Were his tactics over the Chauri-Chaura incident wrong as Jawaharlal Nehru and others thought? Was it wise to halt the whole movement towards freedom because of a scuffle in a remote village? By itself, no. Intuitively, it seems, he feared on the one hand that the movement would become too radical and proceed to a workers' and peasants' revolution, and on the other the collapse of his anti-British campaign. It is still an open question how far the ending of the boycott should be considered simply as a defeat or whether it was rather a sign of what the West took to be the supernatural influence of Gandhi over his compatriots.

The effect of all that happened was not confined to the Congress party. Many of the Hindu bourgeois, the basis of the party, began to incline to more moderate policies. In the autumn of 1923 the moderates won a majority in the Congress (roughly from 1923–1930). This group, the *Swaraj* party to which C. R. Das and Motilal Nehru belonged, ceased to boycott the elections and sought by such obstructionism as was permitted to extort from the British Dominion status (*swaraj*, i.e. home rule). But this adoption of 'moderation' must not be interpreted as any weakening or less desire for independence on the part of nationalists like these two. Das went on hunger strike in prison in 1925 and Motilal Nehru, Jawaharlal's father, as chairman of the Congress in the years between 1924 and 1929 became steadily more radical and up to the last moment before his death in 1931 had, in prison and out of it, dedicated all his time and energies to the freeing of India.

If we look back we notice changes in the movement. We are now at the third phase of the awakening of India. In the first phase it was only the feudal and aristocratic elements, and then from 1895 to 1906 only the rich merchant middle class and the pro-Western intellectuals who set their stamp on the nationalist movement. Now the workers and the peasants became the important element with those natives who had themselves engaged in manufacture. Hindi took the place of English in the deliberations of Congress.

The participation of the peasants and workers in the national movement transformed it from a light wind to a tempest, but it also split it. It was soon seen that class conflict between *zamindaris* (landowners) and the peasants and workers on the land, and between industrialists and workers, was not a Marxian invention. The capitalists of Bombay, Calcutta and other industrial centres feared an increase in the power of the workers no less than the landowners feared the power of the peasants, and many of them, seeing the red elements in the movement growing steadily more red, shamefully betrayed their country; these harsh words are Jawaharlal Nehru's.

As Gokkale and Tilak were the embodiment of the earlier phase of the nationalist movement, so in the period between the wars it was the bourgeois intellectuals who held the leadership. Of them, Qaid-i-azam Mohammed Ali Jinnah (1878–1948) was an international figure. He began as a student in Britain, practised in London and Bombay and joined the Moslem national movement in 1913; during the war he held high office in it. As leader of the All-India Moslem League he was in 1947 the first governor-general of the Dominion of Pakistan. A convinced and active Moslem – remember his plan in 1940 for the partition of India – he none the less was generally respected in Hindu circles. Of the Hindu leaders of the Congress party the chief were Chita Ranjan Das (1870–1925), Pandit Motilal Nehru (1861–1931), Vallabhai Patel (1875–1950), Chakravarti Rajagopalachari (b. 1884) who was to become an Indian minister of the interior, Rajendra Prasad (1884), today the president of India, and the Socialists, Subhas Chandra Bose (1897–1945) and

Pandit Jawaharlal Nehru (b. 1889), today prime minister and minister of foreign affairs of India, by far the greatest of the nationalists even if he is not gifted with the religious qualities of Gandhi.

Those who know Mohandas Karamchand Gandhi (1869–1948) only from his writings, e.g. his autobiographical *History of my Experiment with Truth* (1927–1929), can get only a distorted view of his political importance. In his books he seems often to be a complex of contradictions as a confused ascetic idealist who was not understood either in India or abroad. But from history, i.e. from the books and reminiscences of others and from official documents, a very different figure appears, that of the diplomatic revolutionary, the great rebel against the British Raj, the man who stirred modern India and Pakistan to life. In spite of his confused philosophy he set his seal on the period. When he embarked on his first activities in 1919 he came as a sort of gentle rain to bring life to a dry garden. He changed the whole atmosphere in the country, which seemed to find itself again. May we not see the problem of awakening Asia as the rediscovery of its own native cultural sources, as the answer to the challenge of Western civilization in the economic as well as in the cultural sphere?

One of the natural consequences of the advance of imperialism into Asia is the conflict between the primitive native methods of production and those of the more highly developed capitalist countries, more highly, that is, in the purely economic, not in the moral sense nor in the cultural and artistic. We call capitalist methods as opposed to primitive native methods more highly developed because with the former more is produced and manufactured per peasant, per worker, per acre. The Western advance means economic penetration, i.e. trade which originally was the only reason why Europe was interested in Asia. Trade between a capitalist power and its colonies means mainly their exploitation. That is what made Manchester great, what the industrial revolution in Britain and other countries of Western Europe made possible. The steam engine, the invention of a Scot, James Watt, was made about 1770. Factories were built and factories are insatiable. British ships brought raw cotton from India; the products of English and Scottish mills were sent back. The results are known, but not well enough known. The primitive native hand-production was soon put out of business (1850–1880), especially the cotton spinning and weaving in the villages, and not only in India but everywhere cheap cotton goods were brought in. The result was that the peasants, three-fourths of the population, had no work for four to five months in the year – and so still less to eat.

In Western Europe and in the United States the disappearance of the old methods of production was as a rule compensated for by the enormous increase in factories; part of the peasantry became factory workers. That was the case in countries where at the same time agriculture became mechanized. The mowing machines of the American McCormick – in 1860 there were 250,000 in use in the United States – date from 1840, the steam tractor and the steam threshing-machine from 1880.

But in British India, just as in Indonesia under Dutch rule, the growth of a native industry was deliberately thwarted since it might be a threat to

European manufactures. The industrialization of India and Pakistan was below the level of China. Between 1850 and the present day in Western Europe and the United States the percentage of agricultural workers grew steadily smaller; it did not so grow in Asia. Look at the figures. In England and Wales in 1871 21 per cent of the population worked on the land, in 1950 7 per cent. In Germany the figures were: in 1875 61 per cent; in 1919 38 per cent and in 1950 about 25 per cent. In the United States, the classical land of technological experiment, 75 per cent of the people were on the land in 1820 and today only 17 per cent. It was only after soviet rule was established in Russia that there was any notable decline in the peasant population; it was 80 per cent of the whole in 1928; today it is 50 per cent. But in India and Pakistan under British rule 65 per cent of their inhabitants were peasants in 1891; in 1931 the figure was 75 per cent. Statistics are certainly dangerous things, but these are official British figures given, for instance, by A. R. Desai in his *The Social Background of Indian Nationalism* published in 1948 by the University of Bombay; it is a hard book to read, but it is the work of an expert. This situation, typical of colonial Asia, is worsened by the fact that over the last two centuries the population formidably increased. In 1800 India and Pakistan had about 70,000,000 inhabitants; in 1900 about 280,000,000 and in 1940 possibly 400,000,000. It is no accident that the government favours birth control.

In theory there are three possible ways of escape from this 'economic dualism', i.e. the collapse of the native economy as a result of the entry of Western manufactured goods: 1. radical capitalism and westernization, Japan's way; 2. socialization – that is, socialism with mechanization, the way of Russia and contemporary China and the way which Nehru, for instance, seeks to take in India, but not in the Bolshevik manner; 3. return to the pre-capitalist days, i.e. rejection of capitalism, machines and everything which for lack of a better term we call Western technology and civilization.

It was this third way that Gandhi sought to take. In his hatred of the 'unnaturalness' of modern technology, of factories, machines, telephones, railway trains and everything else, which in his view ate like a cancer into the primitive society and culture, he advocated the return to the earlier primitive methods of production (*swadeshi*) and particularly the spinning and weaving of raw cotton in the home. It cannot be denied that the results he obtained were extraordinary. *Khadi*, the white cotton wool made by the peasants, became the badge of freedom. And, what was of greater import, Gandhi with his *khadi* and *swadeshi* carried away the peasantry and roused it against British imperialism. Jawaharlal Nehru tells how the Mahatma and he in the burning hot summer of 1929 went on one of their many *khadi* expeditions from village to village in the United Provinces. In all the villages, only some quarter of an hour's motor-car ride apart, they were met by a crowd of some ten thousand peasants and workers on the land with their wives and children. A speech lasting twenty minutes, and then on to the next village. Apart from the many peasants who did so, many intellectuals and bourgeois also undertook the manufacture of their own *khadi*. From an economic and cultural point of view, the action was in itself liberating. It restored the peasant's self-respect and to some extent it lessened the hostility between the bourgeois in the towns and the mass of the peasantry. That is what Gandhi achieved and it is an element of his greatness.

But his economic theories meant a flight back to the past and were hardly of this world. As far back as historical experience goes, the machine has everywhere destroyed the old production methods, and, what is more important, the more productive methods appear at a definite point in the history of all countries. It is, as it were, a law of nature. As compared to Asia there were many people in wealthy Europe – wealthy, that is, as compared to Asia – who were opposed to the general mechanization of the economy and of culture. It is not so much a question of the people who refuse to eat vegetables and bread which have been grown with artificial manures or of farmers who refuse artificial insemination of their cattle; there are such folk, but they are not very numerous. Rather, it is one of a general longing for the natural which expresses itself in hiking holidays, a typical modern phenomenon, and something that is quite different but just as characteristic, the revolution in art and literature which drove for instance Gauguin and D. H. Lawrence towards the primitive, the 'natural'. Such things have, however, no significance from the economic point of view. The machines remain and new machines are constantly being made, for machines mean higher production, more bread, more houses, more leisure. When the times are ripe, the Asian peasant will not oppose the tractor and artificial manure. Thus the socialists in British India like Nehru regarded the *khadi* and *swadeshi* movements as temporary, though effective, methods; the communists have been against them, the more so as Gandhi always refused to rouse the peasants and workers against the often horrible avarice of the native capitalists and landowners of whom H. N. Brailsford wrote in his book *India in Revolt*: 'Indian moneylenders and *zamindari* are the most rapacious parasites to be found in any contemporary society.' The great landlords (*zamindari*), who were often anglophil, and the princes, generally reactionary, of the Indian States, the 'native states' – they held a third of the whole country and were a quarter of its population – were not directly disturbed by Gandhi's campaigns.

It would seem that Gandhi's 'neutrality' in the class struggle was determined by his second great principle, rejection of violence. His view was that violence only breeds violence, an idea he took partly from early Hindu, partly from modern Western sources. Of the latter we may recall in the first place the nineteenth-century writers deriving from Emerson, Thoreau and, above all, Tolstoy. The great Russian writer and the Mahatma wrote much to each other. Tolstoy, like his comrades of his own class, had been a reactionary and daredevil officer, but in the years from 1880 to 1910 he abandoned many of his earlier beliefs and in speech and writing attacked violence in general and the terrorist regime of the czars in particular. His books circulated illegally in Russia. In protest against machine civilization he lived as a peasant on the land and wore a rough linen peasant shirt though it was bleached white and perfumed. Gandhi demanded complete chastity as part of inward purity; he even called 'unnatural' sexual relations between man and wife. These views Tolstoy shared.

From Tolstoy and other western writers Gandhi and India and Asia learned much. In this book we have painted Europe in very dark colours because we were dealing with it from an Asian point of view. But we must not overlook the brighter side, what Europe has meant in the history of democracy and freedom, including the freedom of Asia. Tolstoy was a Russian, the other two were Americans, but all three were the products of European culture, which is not simply a display of deeds of violence.

Just as Marxism not only interprepted, but altered, history, so the great Indian revolutionary with his philosophy of non-violence changed the history of Southeast Asia. His many campaigns of passive resistance, his own example in his fourteen hunger strikes, mobilized, as it were, the spirit of freedom and possibly more seriously weakened the British Raj than ever bloody resistance could have done. Neither in the West nor in Asia and Africa, did any other independence movement win such prestige. The anti-colonial movement in countries like Indonesia, Egypt and French North Africa have worked in the light of the experience of India-Pakistan.

So much for the resistance struggles of 1919–1922 and the Gandhi period in general. Now to continue. When the government of India on February 4, 1924, released Gandhi and other leaders from prison the resistance flood had subsided. London's reaction was fairly diplomatic. The censorship established by the Rowlatt Act was made less strict, even if the entire news from and to other countries was in the hands of the semi-official Reuter's Agency; India was, as heretofore, isolated, but not so completely. Reuter messages about the bloodbath in Amritsar in April 1919 first appeared in October in British and other foreign newspapers. The British have an international reputation as *the* diplomatists of the West, and not undeservedly. But like other peoples the British believe that their country is the only civilized nation on earth. 'For a Britisher the niggers begin at Calais' a witty Frenchmen once wrote, and the British did seriously mistake the mentality and the desires of other peoples, especially and naturally the peoples of Asia and Africa.

In 1926 a number of Englishmen were commissioned by the Government to go on a mission of investigation to India and particularly to study the workings of the Montagu-Chelmsford reforms of 1919. They composed the Simon Commission; not a single 'native' was on it. The result was that the Commission was boycotted by the whole colony and by all parties including the moderate *Swaraj* party. The excitement grew. Even in the small villages black flags were flown as protest when the visitors arrived, and it was remarked that the Indian peasants knew at least three words of English: 'Simon, go home.' When the Commission produced in 1930 its comprehensive report in two volumes (more freedom, no Dominion status. Who had expected anything else?) the economic crisis now had the country in its grip and changed everything.

In the middle of the revolutionary strike waves of 1928–1929 which proved that the working class were taking a decisive part in the nationalist movement, representatives of almost all the nationalist parties met in Lucknow (August 1928) and adopted a plan that had been worked out for a Dominion constitution, called the 'Nehru report' after its spiritual father Motilal Nehru. It was strongly opposed by those who thought it was not radical enough. The opposition was led by Motilal's son Jawaharlal Nehru. The scion of an aristocratic family in Kashmir, the younger Nehru had returned from a period of study in Europe (1927–1928); he had been before that a pupil at Harrow and a student at Cambridge, where he had studied law, chemistry and biology. His experiences in his journey in 1927 worked liked leaven in his radical socialism. The cruel suppression of a not unjustifiable miners' strike in Wales – he was in London at the time – the little interest which official socialists showed in the independence movements in Asia, as compared to the stormy vitality of a somewhat communist anti-Imperialist league at its congress in Brussels – Nehru represented the All-India Congress at it – these and other things drove Nehru to the left. A visit to Moscow just before he returned home had the same effect.

But there should be no mistake. Nehru did not become a Bolshevik. He only saw once again that in Europe only a handful of left socialists and communists had any understanding of the Asian revolution. He recognized the mighty historical significance of the socialist experiment in Russia especially as it affected Asia. But he was not so enthusiastic about the often much too drastic methods which the Bolsheviks used to muzzle the press nor the fact that everything was conducted in secrecy behind closed doors. In the book he wrote in prison (*An Autobiography*, published in London in 1936) Nehru wrote of how much he owed to the study of Marxist theory, how it was from writers like Marx and Lenin that he had first understood the nature of capitalism and imperialism. His aim was to find a synthesis between Western democracy and the Russo-Chinese version of it.

During the latter part of the Lucknow conference he represented in his 'Independence of India League' (founded August 30, 1928) the extreme aims of the 'most extreme' minority.

This new socialist group, originally very active in the United Provinces, was not given the time to spread to the whole country. In the summer of 1929 the Government arrested many radical labour leaders. But the famous trial in Meerut of the socialists, who were, of course, officially described as communists and terrorists, could not prevent the strike of 500,000 workers in the Bombay cotton mills or curb the rising tide of agitation elsewhere. Now came the third wave of the movement for independence.

In October the London government announced that it was ready to discuss a Dominion constitution for India. During the winter, in spite of the loss of the arrested leaders, the 'extremists' obtained a majority in the Congress, whose demand was now not for a Dominion constitution but for *purna swaraj*, i.e. complete independence. This was determined upon at Lahore on January 1, 1930. The barometer was set at stormy. It was on this basis that Nehru now built his further policy. In 1934 he wrote: 'The idea on which the desire for freedom was ultimately based was this; we wanted to make it clear to the people that we were fighting for a completely new political structure and not just for an Indian edition of the present state of things with the British pulling the controlling strings as would be the case if we had a Dominion constitution. Political independence means only political freedom and brings neither social change nor economic freedom for the masses. But it does mean the loosing of the bonds financial and economic which bind us to the City of London and that will make it easier to change the social structure.' Political freedom was the pre-condition of social liberation.

XIII

INDIA-PAKISTAN (ii) AND BURMA

JUST as the first epoch of unrest in colonial India was more complicated than the second, so the third between 1930 and 1934 was again more complicated than the second. In our confined space we cannot describe all that happened. The true historian describes the past and judges it within its historical setting; the scientific in his treatment mingles with the artistic; he writes not just an accurate but a complete story. 'History only becomes interesting when it is full and complete', said Machiavelli over four centuries ago. In the small space available we have to give an analysis in, so to speak, 'telegraphese' instead of a full description and imaginative treatment.

In the period 1930–1934 the peasants, workers and women are of much greater importance than in the earlier phase. The reader, the Asian more than the European or the American, probably knows the conditions under which most of the peasants lived, the same conditions as prevail in most Asian and African countries. They have an extremely primitive house, often just a hut of mud or straw and reeds; a little rice or maize if the harvest is good, otherwise millet to which is added some fruit and vegetables from the garden; a little milk and butter; no meat, no fish and very little sugar, very much less than the European peasant has of everything.[1] Besides the catastrophes which are natural or almost natural like rained-out and burned-out land, locusts and tuberculosis, there are other things like the way the land is divided into much too tiny plots, the fleecing by landlords and *zamindari*, many of whom especially in Northern India had estates of 40,000 acres and over, and still have, although the regime of today is trying to alter that state of affairs. According to British figures in 1930 only a quarter of the small peasants had land of twelve acres and over, including the *zamindari*. Sixty per cent worked tiny farms of less than five acres, and of these 20 per cent had only about an acre or less. The changes between the wars were the reverse of the usual; the great landowners and other owners who cannot be classed as peasants, rose in numbers from 3,700,000 in 1921 to 4,100,000 in 1931. The number of workers on the land also rose from 21,700,000 in 1921 to 35,500,000 in 1931. The number of those who can genuinely be called peasants, small landowners and leaseholders, fell from 75,000,000 in 1921 to 65,000,000 in 1931. The average family on the land had an income of from 150 to 200 Dutch guilders a year.

The history of Asia, including India-Pakistan, is full of peasant risings in the period of European domination as well as before that. As a rule however, the peasant accepted the caprice of his landlord or moneylender as he

[1] Those who want a full description of the Indian peasantry should read Brailsford's *Rebel India*.

did the caprice of nature. It was the economic and social upheaval of the machine age which came to Asia through imperialism, and events like the Russian revolution and the spread of European socialist thought, that first awakened in some of the Asian peasants a conscious and permanent desire for an adequate share of the world's goods.

In the years between 1920 and 1929 the socialists and communists had succeeded in bringing together part of the peasantry in India and Pakistan into peasant associations (*kisan sabhas*) which, on the whole, followed the policy of the Congress. But the real growth of the peasant movement came, as in China, in 1929 when the economic crisis began which raged like a typhoon not only in the highly developed capitalist countries but also in the hungry parts of Asia. When the first all-India peasant congress (the 'All-India Kisan Congress') assembled in Lucknow in 1935 it was a sign that the social isolation of the villages was at an end.

The crisis period was a turning-point also for the workers' movement. Before the winter of 1918–1919 there were only a few strikes of factory workers in British India, but they were political strikes. The only exception worth chronicling was the strike (1907), commemorated by Lenin, in the cotton industry in Bombay after Tilak's arrest. How the workers helped (1920–1921) on the work of the nationalist movement by, for instance, the protest strikes against the Rowlatt Act has already been described. In the same period the India Trade Union Congress was founded (1920) which at the outset was led by liberal politicians (N. M. Joshi, Lala Rajpat Rai and Joseph Baptista). The first socialist weekly, *The Socialist,* was published in 1923 in Bombay by S. A. Dange. Gradually socialist and communist ideas penetrated the young labour movement. When in 1927 the radical wing got a majority (due, among other things, to Nehru's activity), the less revolutionary section under Joshi founded the All-India Trades Union Federation, but when this threatened to dissolve, the two sections came together again in the All-India Trades Union Federation (1938), which had a left socialist programme. In 1942 the Federation had 350,000 members.

Although in 1927 communist and socialist workers' and peasants' parties were active in various provinces, the real Communist party of India dates only from 1933. In 1934 it was forbidden and remained illegal until 1943. Its leaders, M. N. Roy,[1] P. C. Joshi and S. A. Dange, were not of any great importance in the nationalist movement. The degree to which the party had aroused interest was seen in the election of 1951–2 when it got 6,000,000 votes against the 12,000,000 of the Socialists and the 48,000,000 of the Congress.

The third new element in the nationalist movement was, as we have noted, the women, many of whom were arrested as Congress volunteers. Like the peasants who worked on rented land and who rose not only against the British but against the native capitalists, the women fought a double battle against tyranny, that against the colonial domination and that against the anti-feminist tradition of their menfolk. There are two milestones in the progress of the women's movement, the founding of the Indian Women's

[1] *v.* p. 207.

Conference (1926) and the law against child marriage of 1929 which raised the marriageable age for girls to fourteen. The action against child marriage is an example of feminist rather than anti-British action. In many Indian circles, there was strong support for child marriage, for one reason, to prevent prostitution. The British, true to their traditions, had much earlier opposed child marriage. The law of 1860, which forbade marriage until the age of ten, was not the expression of the British attitude on this matter but of the cultural traditions of India. Why? Terrified by the mutiny of 1857, Britain tried to avoid getting involved in purely native affairs so long as their economic aims were not in danger – for instance, there were no more annexations of native kingdoms, a heritage the bitter fruits of which India and Pakistan are still gathering – and took a neutral attitude where the native culture was concerned. Actually that meant obstructing many modernizing desires of the country and so in a sense was a reactionary policy in strong contrast to the objective liberal and progressive policy of the first half of the nineteenth century.

Apart from action against the trade in women – Madras province alone had 300,000 prostitutes – the women's movement sought to extend literacy, to introduce child hygiene and in other directions to modernize the Indian woman. Several women of this 'revolution of the other sex' were internationally famous like Sarojini Naidu, Kamaladevi Chattopadhaya and Vijaya-lakshmi Pandit, Jawaharlal Nehru's sister.

The adherence to the nationalist movement of workers and peasants meant an injection of fresh blood and an increase in its scope and to its strength. At the same time this new element split the party, and that naturally embarrassed the bourgeois nationalists. The policy of the Congress at this period is incomprehensible unless one grasps how much the bourgeoisie and Gandhi feared the radical socialist movement in their own land.

This lack of political confidence is seen, for instance, in the famous march to the salt pans (1930), the beginning of the so-called second boycott. On the morning of March 12th Gandhi and eighty others walked to the shore at Cambay on the Sea of Arabia and began illegally to make salt, illegally because the British Government held a salt monopoly; the salt tax was a specially hated device. Incidentally there is nothing new in such a feeling; in the fourteenth century the French peasants were up in arms against the salt tax. Gandhi's excursion to the sea shore – he was accompanied by journalists and photographers – set the country in a furore with surprising swiftness. It must surely be admitted that his extraordinary intuition had again achieved what others never could have done. Would, however, a refusal to pay the tax not have been as effective as this direct action? No doubt it would, but for the peasants such a refusal would have encouraged refusal to pay the rent to the landlords, and Gandhi was always careful never to attack their rights. He was not an unworldly idealist but a prosaic and a very clever politician. This was the reason for his zigzag policy, as interesting as it was ambiguous. He put an end to the colonial submissiveness of the peasant and gave the Indian masses new self-respect, but as soon as he saw that the movement was beginning to threaten not just British imperialism but even more Indian feudalism and the native bourgeoisie, he tried to hold it back. The British administration perhaps only half consciously grasped this, and it never knew how rightly to handle the Mahatma. Was he nationalist rebel No. 1 who had to be arrested or was he one of the very much desired insurances against an eventual social revolution?

Gandhi was left unmolested for his symbolic but illegal march to the salt pans, but there were arrests all over the country and press censorship was tightened. But when in April–May 1930 the movement seemed to be taking on a revolutionary character – the attack on the State salt manufactories, strikes of peasants against paying rent and of workers in the factories and the murder of British officials – Gandhi on May 5th was arrested along with 60,000 of his adherents, among them both the Nehrus and the majority of the other Congress leaders. Lacking a leadership which knew what it was doing, the boycott fizzled out, but the report of the Simon Commission (published in mid-June), in which naturally Dominion status was again refused, inside the prisons and outside was felt as a wicked insult. Six months later Gandhi received a letter from the governor-general inviting him to resume negotiations. On January 26th he left his prison for Delhi, and on March 4, 1931, the Government published the famous Delhi Agreement (otherwise known as the Irwin-Gandhi Agreement) which, very much against the will of the Congress leaders still in prison, seemed to amount to complete capitulation. The only consolation was that the Government freed all the political prisoners except the terrorists and would not resist another boycott of a variety of foreign manufactured goods – i.e. not only British – like cotton goods. That meant that *khadi* production would be free and the interests of the Indian cotton manufacturers furthered.

In return Congress had to give up all further resistance, especially in connection with the Anglo-Indian negotiations, then proceeding in London, the so-called Round Table Conference. The first Round Table Conference was held in London (November 12, 1930, to January 19, 1931). A number of Indian leaders and *zamindaris* more royalist than the king betrayed their country at the great banquets. Their smooth 'loyalty' gave pain to many progressive Englishmen. Naturally nothing was achieved. Everything, as Nehru noted in his diary, went as the British wished. As a consequence of the Delhi compromise Britain now invited Gandhi to attend the second Round Table Conference in London (September–December 1931). He accepted the invitation but, as he was completely isolated in London, achieved nothing. And how did London react? It pulled other strings. On January 4, 1932, Lord Willingdon, the new governor-general (1931–1936), arrested all the nationalist leaders of any importance, and Gandhi, too, on his return home. He declared the Congress illegal and issued a series of oppressive decrees in the old colonial style which the British writer J. T. Sunderland in his *India in Chains* (1932) rightly called 'frightful'. How did Gandhi react? A third boycott? No, only one of his heroic hunger strikes as protest against the appalling conditions under which the pariahs lived, those 50,000,000 Indians who were not members of the recognized Hindu castes. It was a noble effort but it was not very dangerous for British rule.

Or was it another case of his intuition? Did he wish in this way to draw into his revolution the 'untouchables', the last group to be affected by the national movement.

In any case resistance grew outside the prisons and, after the Congress had proclaimed the third boycott in Poona (mid-July 1933), many arrests were made – 150,000, the biggest figure yet. Jawaharlal Nehru reckoned the average number of arrests in the period from 1933 to 1937 at 300,000.

The apparent ill-success of Gandhi's dubious policy pushed the radicals into the foreground. Gandhi himself admitted that this period was not completely his. As early as December 1932 the left radical Nehru had been brought into Lahore on a white horse and made leader of the Congress Party on the advice of the Mahatma. The drift leftwards was seen in Lahore in the *purna swaraj* resolution, and in a small majority for Nehru's 'resolution on fundamental rights', the keypoints in which were nationalization of the most important industries like steel, coal and transport, recognition of workers' rights and land reform.

All this did not imply that Gandhi's authority had been broken, but it did mean that it was much decreased. Radical nationalists like Nehru and even Chandra Bose had tolerated the Delhi Agreement though they had really disapproved it. Now, when the increasing divisions in the party threatened to hinder the whole movement, Gandhi again became (October 1934) a member of the Congress; he remained fairly active but in the background.

Meantime London had had second thoughts; it was not only Gandhi's policy that was dubious. Out of the not very fruitful Simon Commission and the two Round Table conferences it had worked out a plan that was not unrealistic. On August 2, 1935, the British parliament passed the new Government of India Bill. The new act meant a material easing of the British system of government in Southeast Asia and showed that, despite all the vacillations of the national movement, the British had realized its significance and that its sense of reality was greater than that of the Dutch or the French. Burma and Aden were separated from India and became Crown colonies. In order no doubt to make things safer if there was an explosion in India and Pakistan, British India itself was divided into eleven provinces, each of which would have a governor representing the Crown and an executive council and an elected assembly with legislative power. The new provincial governments would be autonomous in all purely internal matters; only 'in the case of emergency,' a somewhat obscure phrase, did the governor have a right of veto.

The act also provided for the transformation of the eleven provinces into an all-Indian federation which would also include some 550 bigger and smaller native kingdoms. At the outset the Indian parliament would be concerned only with the eleven provinces. Its composition would be: an upper house of 36 elected members, 24 nominated members and a legislative assembly of 40 nominated and 105 members elected by the provincial assemblies. The governor-general would be entrusted with defence and foreign relations. The act was to enter into force on April 1, 1937.

The Government of India Act was a definite step along the stony road to self-government. There could now be no withdrawal. But how far away was the new regime from what had been demanded for ten years, the *purna swaraj*, the 'liberation from sin' as Gandhi had once translated the phrase.

We have now surveyed the three stages of the resistance movement, 1905–1910, 1919–1922, 1930–1934. Thrice now the waves of nationalism had battered at the foundations of the British Empire. Ever nearer came India to the longed-for freedom, but it was not to attain it in the period between the wars. When in September 1939 the Second World War broke out in Europe, Lord Linlithgow, the viceroy, declared India to be at war without even asking the opinion of a single Indian. None the less the period from 1937 to 1941 was one of steady growth for the nationalists, though perhaps more for the Hindus than the Moslems. The re-creation of the Congress party took less time than had been expected. Although as a result of its internal division and the Willingdon policy of arrests it had only 600,000 members, the results of the provincial elections in January and February 1937 proved its vigorous rebirth. In the eleven provincial legislative assemblies it won 715 out of 1585 seats. In six provinces – Madras, Bombay, the United Provinces, Bihar, the Central Provinces and Orissa – it had a majority. In Bengal and Assam it was the strongest party. In the Northwest Frontier Province a Congress ministry took office. Only in the Punjab and in Sind, which are now West Pakistan and are in their great majority Moslem, had the Congress little success; in the Punjab it won only eighteen out of 175 seats; in Sind seven out of 60.

These results are the more interesting when we remember that only 13 per cent of the population had the franchise, i.e. the bourgeoisie and the few others who could read and write. Yet it was a success; the colony had been able with the help of democratic methods to say what it thought of British rule. But now one of the problems confronting a freedom movement became visible. The party had in principle condemned the new constitution as a British invention. Should, then, Congress members accept office in the provincial governments? And, if so, what should be their tactics? The expected happened. When it had been agreed against the extremist opposition of Nehru and his associates (Party Congress, Delhi, March 1937) that they should, and in seven provinces the Congress formed a government, the differences between left and right in the Congress became acute, especially when the new provincial governments took action against the labour movement when strikes broke out. Besides, many right-wing non-socialists and conservatives were embittered because, apart from releasing prisoners and a measure mainly on paper of land reform, they were not able to make much change.

The left was never able to get a permanent majority. At the party congress in Haripuri (1938) the radical socialist Chandra Bose was elected president, but the illusion of a swing to the left was dispelled in 1939 in Tripuri when Rajendra Prasad, the candidate favoured by Gandhi, now once again a party member, defeated Bose.

At the time all this seemed very important; it seems of hardly any importance today. The war altered much and swept away many former things.

It left unsolved the question whether and when the Congress party would be able by its own strength to enter into freedom.

So far we have said much less about the Moslem League (the All-India Moslem League founded 1919) than about the Hindu Congress for the reason that, even although the Moslem part of British India is now a free republic within the Commonwealth, the Moslem League was of much less importance than the Congress. The Moslems constitute not quite a quarter of the population and the League never had the importance of the party of Gandhi and Nehru. Besides for lack of a strong party of their own many Moslems worked in the Congress party.

It was only in the period 1935–1940 that the great Jinnah pumped fresh blood into the Moslem movement and made the dormant league of the Moslem bourgeoisie a genuine independence movement of all conscious Moslems. At its congress in Lahore he formulated the conception of a Pakistan as an autonomous part of an eventual Indian Union. As they were inferior to the Hindus in numbers and in economic strength, the Moslems feared, and seemingly rightly, to be an oppressed minority once the British withdrew. The Moslem leaders also realized how little significance their minority would have in international Islam if it remained scattered among the masses of Hindus. Their sentimental links with the Moslem peoples from Morocco to Indonesia seemed to them more real, more desirable and more intense than their relations with the Hindus in their own land. The religious tie was stronger than the national.

The rift between Hindus and Moslems, which is as tragic as it is historically comprehensible, could not however prevent the march to freedom; that was another British illusion. During the period of colonial domination the two great nationalist parties could not really remain permanently hostile. In the threatening winter of 1939 Hindus and Moslems, extremists and moderates, felt in their hearts that Jawarharlal Nehru wrote on the eve of his ninth imprisonment:

'For months friends and acquaintances have been coming to me and whispering: Do you know that the lists are already prepared on which are the names of Congress members who are to be arrested whenever there is an opportunity. There is the A-list and the B-list and who knows what others? District authorities are being asked who are the most important propagandists for the Congress in their districts. What is their status? What are their incomes? Are they on the police register? Can they perhaps be persuaded to enter into the British service? What are Congress's financial resources? Where do these come from and how are they being spent?

'Our letters are being censored, our telephones tapped, our bank accounts are being secretly examined by government agents. That is all true, but why should we worry? We keep our self-control if the government proceed to suppress our effort towards freedom and to root it out. We go on calmly at our task and they will not find us keeping hidden if the government presses the button and direct the whole machinery of state against us. Why should we blame the government? A foreign imperialist government can act in no other way. It must have recourse to compulsion, terror, bribery and the secret police. If we combat such a government, how can we complain of their methods? If one goes to bed with a tiger one need not feel surprise if he uses his claws and tries to eat one up.

'None the less even if we face with calm what is and what is to come, it is an inspiring feeling that we live in the shadow of tremendous events and ourselves play a part in them. Even those who belong to an older generation and are accustomed by much experience to the sudden changes which life can bring, can today hardly avoid thinking that we are on the eve of extraordinary events. For a time we thought that the British people after the experiences of last year and because of the danger which they face would perhaps choose new paths. That has not been so. They still bow before the old gods and will not let a fragment of their empire go. The men of "appeasement" failed in Germany, but they will try it again at every opportunity. Always at all times a Halifax, a Simon, a Hoare will be there to decide British policy. And the Labour party stands and looks on.

'We do not know what the future will bring to us – to us, to our country, to the world. What happens to us is not important. Sooner or later we shall cease to live. But what happens to India is extremely important. If India lives and is free we all live and are free. If India ceases to be, how can any of us go on living?

'But India must live and live in freedom, for our country has not lasted all the centuries to be beaten down by brute force. There can be no peace in India and no peace between Britain and India until the pride of imperialism is broken and India is free and independent. A little time ago there was a debate in the British parliament in which Mr Amery quoted what Cromwell once said. He quoted it against the British Government. I quote it to a wider audience, to the British government, to the British financiers, to the British ruling classes, to viceroys, governors and all around them. I say to them in the words of Cromwell: "You have sat too long here. Depart. Let us have done with you. In the name of God go".'

Eight years later Nehru's demand was fulfilled.

The reader who is acquainted with the main events of Asian history will remember how Britain in her expansion in Victoria's reign had, after waiting half a century, incorporated into the British Empire what is today the republic of Burma. The Third Burmese War (1885), after which Burma as an independent state disappeared from the map, was a British move to safeguard her possessions in Bengal and Assam, but also a move in the game against the French imperialism in Indochina. The second half of the nineteenth century, particularly the years between 1885 and 1900, was the period of the 'definite' partition of Asia and Africa between the powers of Europe and North America. In 1886, Burma, a land 261,700 square miles in extent with about 7,000,000 inhabitants, became a province of British India. As it does today, it bordered on China, Thailand and Indochina. In spite of that, we did not deal with Burma along with India and Pakistan. Our reasons were not only geographical (the mountain forest barrier between Burma and Assam) but historical because of Burma's very different past – Chinese influences and Buddhism – and its later history, its separation from British India and its status as a British Crown colony (1937), the Japanese occupation (1942–1945) and its restoration as a free republic (October 1947).

We noted earlier how here, just as in many other Asian regions, the Russo-Japanese War (1904–1905) acted like a lightning stroke in the flash of which appeared as in a dream the vision of a free Asia. As early as 1906 the Buddhist monk Vottama published in Rangoon a much-read account of the Land of the Rising Sun and of the astounding victory over the Russian army and fleet in the Far East.

Imitativeness of British culture and native self-consciousness fused during the First World War into an active resistance mentality. When in 1919 it was seen that the British did not intend to extend the Montagu-Chelmsford reforms [1] to Burma, the agitation in Rangoon made them change their tactics. Relatively unimportant reforms as usual only increased everywhere the desire for real freedom. Burma, i.e. its bourgeoisie and its aristocracy, boycotted the elections, and thereby showed from what classes the national movement would take its leaders and derive its strength. Strikes and boycott action by the students at the University of Rangoon, the rise of the cultural Wantanu movement – comparable to Budi Utomo and the Taman Siswa movements in Indonesia – and the General Council of the Buddhist Associations modelled on the Congress party (all in 1920) were signs of a current which could no longer be held in check; its main inspirers were the intellectuals.

Naturally, of course, the nationalist movement was directed against the British, but it was also directed and more intensely against the immigrants from India. That was no doubt tragic and disappointing at a time when Asians needed to stand together, but it is quite comprehensible to anyone who knows the modern history of Burma. What the Chinese were, for instance, in Malaya, i.e. capitalists, technicians, landowners, coolies and seasonal workers, the Indians were in Burma. In 1930 there were already about 1,250,000 of them; they were particularly numerous in Rangoon where they formed 60 per cent of the inhabitants. The Indians were machine workers, tram drivers, workers in the rice mills, miners in the lead mines, and sailors and dock labourers, but Indians were also directors of half the rice traders' associations. The great Indian landowners lived in sumptuous houses in Rangoon. Above all, 30 per cent of foreign investment was Indian, two-thirds of which was in land. The Chettyars, a famous and hated class of moneylenders from Madras, owned in 1937 a quarter of all the ricefields in the valleys of Lower Burma. Only the small peasant rice-cultivators were natives.

This naturally caused bitterness, especially as under the British rule 80 per cent of the peasants were no better off than before. On the contrary, the typically Asian economic structure had been preserved. The population increased rapidly (from 5,000,000 in 1855 to 10,000,000 in 1900 and to 17,000,000 in 1940). The acres under rice cultivation also increased, but the methods of cultivation on the whole remained as primitive as before. The

[1] v. p. 134.

crop increased, but not in relation to the increase in cultivated land. Western Europe had the same experience – that cannot be often enough said – but in Europe technology developed in the well-established national states. While in 1800 Europe had been hardly richer than Asia, new inventions appeared in the nineteenth century constituting a challenge to which Asia then had no answer: machines driven by steam, factories, steamships, in short, all that we understand by the term modern technology; artificial manure, agricultural machinery, modern chemistry and biology, the colonization of Africa and Asia, the opening up of uninhabited regions like North America (uninhabited, that is, if we discount the 800,000 American Indians) and – emigration. Canada became a great granary for Europe. Cotton and jute and much else came from Africa and Asia. In the nineteenth century the population of Europe rose from 200,000,000 to 400,000,000 despite the fact that 50,000,000 Europeans emigrated, mainly to North America. As a specially crude example take the case of Ireland where, as a result of the mismanagement of the great English landowners, not less than half the population emigrated between 1850 and 1914.

The path of the machine age was not strewn with roses either in Europe or North America. Certainly the countries of the West, thanks to technology, were richer than all others – but were also more dangerous. In Asia only Japan had time to prove itself. The other Asian countries were and remained colonies and semi-colonies. The Asians could not emigrate. Where could they go? India and China were countries from which there was a slight migration. But of the 4,000,000 Indians who emigrated, only 1,500,000 went out of Asia; of the 10,000,000 Chinese migrants, over 9,500,000 lived in Asian countries.

So the Burmans stayed in Burma. Here, as everywhere else, European manufactured goods killed the primitive native industry. In the period 1900–1910 the cotton-spinning and weaving industry in the Burmese villages declined by half. In 1930 the peasant families got nine-tenths of their cotton goods from Manchester, Bombay and Japan. In theory that left more time for work on the land. But because of the low production of the Asian peasant, his primitive methods of cultivation and his dependence on the weather, it remained theory. The typical Asian peasant had not too little time but, from the economic point of view, too much. But he had too little land, too little artificial manure, too little technical and scientific training and too little capital. Besides, the ships which brought European goods to Rangoon took on their return journey the only thing that the valley of the Irrawaddy could supply – rice. In 1930 Burma exported two-thirds of its rice harvest.

The invasion of Asia by Western capitalism is often represented as deliberate exploitation and plundering. That is not quite correct. Where Europe failed was in understanding of Asia, and it brought European methods into countries with a very different social and economic structure and living under very different conditions. In the pre-colonial period in countries like Burma, India and Pakistan, the land was generally the common property of the village. A peasant family worked its own share of land, but could not alienate it. Several countries in Europe in earlier times had a similar structure.

But the nineteenth-century Englishman had no remembrance of such medi-aeval conditions. The London bourgeois expected everything from 'free trade' in which every wolf sought to eat up the other. This ideology, this economic system, was often described as free competition (*laisser faire*), which meant no government interference in the economic process. It was a method under which in 1850, at the time when Marx and Engels published the Communist Manifesto, women and children worked from twelve to fourteen hours a day in the English mines. But such horrors did not remain permanent in Western Europe and, in general, the capitalist lands in the nineteenth century were richer than ever before. Did not capitalism in the economic, technological and scientific spheres achieve infinitely more than the other economic systems in earlier centuries? The British arrived with their preconceived notions and decreed that the individual peasant should be proprietor of his own land. From then on the peasant had to buy his land as he bought a cow or a fowl. He could make money by his land. That might appear to mean, and was intended to mean, a liberation of agriculture; it meant, in fact, its enslavement.

This was seen in Burma and in other Asian countries most clearly in 1929, when the instability of capitalism took its revenge in the greatest economic crisis of all time, when the merchants in Rangoon sold rice at £4 per ton. The peasant received about half of that.

The results on agriculture were terrible. If anyone wants to get a clear picture of the situation let him read the book by Maurice Zinkin, *Asia and the West*, published in 1951. Here he will find a very exact analysis of the relations between Southeastern Asia and Europe and America in this period. In the part devoted to Burma he tells how the peasants were overwhelmed with debts, and how the moneylenders in the towns acquired the land. In the rice districts of Lower Burma in 1870 there lived 540,000 peasants with their own land and only 35,000 on rented land, so that the land was virtually in the hands of the peasants and there were virtually no labourers. In 1931 1,500,000 peasants did not own land any more, and in 1937, after the economic crisis had done its worst, 60 per cent of the ricefields were owned by people who were not peasants and who squandered their new-found riches in the towns.

Zinkin relates how fatefully abstract European law worked. In disputes over rent and mortgages the British judges looked only at the wording of the contract. In theory this was a lofty, a noble conception of law, but was barbarous in its effects when the contracts had been made because of dire necessity, and the peasant could not read what his commitments were. Laws to protect the peasantry were made just before the Japanese occupation, the Rent Law of 1939 and the Land Alienation Law of 1941.

The changes in the economic and social structure of the peasant in Southeast Asia between 1919 and 1941 constitute an entirely new historical pheno-menon, as does their effect. The present-day Asian peasant is fundamentally different from what he was in former days. He is revolutionary and his revo-lution will come to an end when, like the peasant of the West, he gets his proper share of what he earns by incessant toil from the land.

Stormy as the economic crisis itself, the peasant rising of Sayasan spread in 1930 and 1931 from the Tharawadi district of Lower Burma. In appearance and from the reports in the European press, it seemed to be nothing more than a hysterical outburst of xenophobia. Sayasan, a Buddhist priest, called himself King of Burma and roused his compatriots to attack the British 'unbelievers'. The stars had announced the fall of the British tyranny, and everywhere the peasants with their primitive weapons attacked British machine-guns. The rising, naturally, was a failure and died out, but the British official reports recognized and acknowledged its economic background, as it did also in the case of the frequent anti-Indian unrest in Rangoon.

The Burman bourgeoisie was not affected by the Sayasan rising. At the Round Table Conference in London in 1931 it did, however, protest against the refusal to give Burma Dominion status, mainly because of the difficult social and economic situation of the country. 'We are, alas, under a regime that cares only for the well-being and the interests of a small group of capitalists. Exploitation through this regime has reduced to nothing our whole economy and the efforts of our people. The indifference of the present government to the growing poverty of the great mass of the people and the encouragement of foreign capitalists at the expense of our own citizens has caused the present unrest and rebellion in our country.'

Because British, Indians and Chinese occupied all the economic positions of any importance, the growth of the bourgeoisie of Burma was hindered. More than in India, for instance, capitalism and imperialism seemed identical, and the result was to make the bourgeoisie as a whole fairly radical. Its leaders once again were intellectuals, the most important being U Ba Maw, U Saw and Paw Tun. U Ba Maw (b. 1893), who was arrested at the time of the reactionary *putsch* in 1947, studied law in Rangoon and in Europe at Cambridge, where the little hope he had of the British turned to hate, and in Bordeaux, where he took a doctor's degree in jurisprudence. U Saw (b. 1901, executed 1948) lived as a law student in Calcutta and London, and in Rangoon where he worked for the Sun Press. He wrote many pro-Japanese articles after a stay in Japan in 1935. Sir Paw Tun (b. 1883), the 'gentleman' of the bourgeois nationalists, was fairly pro-Western and in principle anti-Japanese; he too studied law in Calcutta where he married an American lady. All three became well known in Burma about 1931, Ba Maw as Sayasan's counsel, U Saw as the author of a banned pamphlet on British atrocities during the peasant rising and Paw Tun as mayor of Rangoon.

In 1934 and 1935 the Socialist party Dobama Asiayone ('We Burmans'), usually called the Party of the Thakins, thakin being a title borne by several of its leaders, came to the front as an active element in the nationalist movement. Its members were radical students and other intellectuals from Rangoon University, most of them Marxists and filled with the desire to be free also of capitalism, once imperialism had been driven out. They did not want Burma to be a Dominion, but to be absolutely independent. Their agitation among students, workers and peasants broadened the basis of the independence movement. In many villages the hammer and sickle were displayed.

The party included both socialists and communists. Its anti-British activity and its guerrilla war against the Japanese during the war was the cement which kept the two sections together. The socialist thakins included Aung San (alias Bogyok, Boh Teza, b. 1915, murdered 1947), who, because of the part he played in the guerrilla war (1943–1945), was called the Tito of Burma. Then came thakin Nu (b. 1907), a writer; in his ways of thought and his artistic temperament he reminds one of Shahrir. The third was thakin Mya (b. 1897, murdered 1947), an able socialist propagandist among the peasants. He was leader of the All-Burma Cultivators' Association, the peasant organization which had been founded in the crisis years; it is comparable to the *kisan sabhas* in India and Pakistan. These three were the secretaries of the Thakin party.

Communist thakins of repute were Soe and Than Tun (b. 1911), both typical intelligent party communists, and Thein Pe (b. 1916), a rather more liberal thinker, a writer of novels and a journalist; all of them came from the University of Rangoon. Originally they held less high office in the Thakin party than their socialist colleagues, but in the difficult days from 1940 onward, as fighters with the resistance and as ministers, they had shown that they were true revolutionaries and had proved their aptitude to hold official government posts.

Although the connection between nationalism in Burma and that in British India was not very close, and the Indian immigrants were not loved, both the bourgeois nationalists and the Thakin party fought fiercely against the plan to separate Burma from British India. They feared to be cut off from the freedom movement across the border. None the less, by the Government of Burma Act of 1935 (entered into force 1937), London did separate them and, instead of being a province of British India, Burma became a Crown colony. At the same time the British allowed the country the same degree of freedom which India got and, despite the undeniable restriction as far as independence was concerned, that was greatly in advance of anything countries like Indonesia, Indochina or Malaya were granted.

The new regime meant autonomy in Lower Burma (which has 60 per cent of the territory and population of the country) except for finance and national defence. The governor, in addition, had a right of veto where the interests of the Crown had to be safeguarded. The mountainous northern districts, where dwell the non-Burmese peoples like the Karens (1,500,000), the Shans (1,000,000), the Chins and others were 'excluded areas' with a governor, but really were ruled directly from London.

As a result of this semi-independence at a time when the world looked like a gigantic powder magazine, Burma strove the harder to get complete independence. The native government – Ba Maw was Burma's first prime minister (1937) – urgently demanded its own army, limitation of immigration from India and, above all, the appointment of Burmese as officials and to the leading economic positions.

As early as December 1938, when the Japanese had occupied the one still unoccupied port in China (Canton, October 1938) and were threatening French Indochina, the independence movement in Burma became more aggressive. U Saw ordered an anti-British boycott; the governor declared a state of emergency, hoping to halt the growing agitation. In 1939 came the notorious secret agreement between the Japanese government and the Burmese nationalists, i.e. Ba Maw, and the great majority of the Thakin party, now united in the National Revolutionary party. What this document meant is clear from the paragraph about the 'independence army of Burma'.

In 1940 Japanese troops invaded Indochina and the Germans occupied Western Europe. Ba Maw and the thakins protested against participation in the British defence in Southeast Asia, and naturally were arrested. In prison their hate for the British increased, but in addition they read there English books written by left-wing authors – the practices of British democracy are unique – and had their Marxist ideas confirmed and strengthened. Aung San and thirty others fled through China to Japan, from which they returned in 1942 as officers of the Burmese army of liberation and leaders of the invasion. When U Saw went to London in 1941, where he begged Churchill in vain to make Burma a British Dominion, the generals in Tokio had already put the red arrows on their maps of Burma. On his return journey U Saw was arrested in Palestine on charges of 'treasonable activities', and during the war was kept in internment in Kenya. In 1942 the rising sun from the East rose over the Burmese mountains and in the summer the Allies evacuated the country. The Japanese occupied Burma; in the fourth part of this book we shall relate what happened thereafter.

Fourth Period 1941 – 1945

STORM OVER ASIA

I

THE SECOND WORLD WAR: A GENERAL VIEW

THE Second World War liberated many countries of Asia from Western imperialism. War is undoubtedly a sorry business, but it can give the politician a deeper insight into the workings of history. Is it not interesting to see how the whole past of a country like Germany which was of relatively little importance to Asia, became through war one of the most important factors in the development of the East?

Wars and revolutions are crises in a historical development. Modern wars are not primarily barbaric outbursts of the desire to kill and of unreasoning hate, but rather, as Clausewitz said at the beginning of the nineteenth century, 'Wars are a continuation of political diplomacy by other, by military means'. Thus wars, like policy, contain many rational elements even if both wars and their causes enter into the sphere of unreason. A war, therefore, has a definite structure and the student of it perceives how a red thread links together what look like isolated events, events which can be understood only if the war is treated as a whole.

It is never easy to answer the question who began a war. A war is a crisis in international relations which arises almost always from events in the past and involves various countries. Threats, humiliations, economic changes and imperialism – these do not constitute war, but they can be the origin of war. In the narrow technical sense the question who started this war is, however, often easy to answer: the Second World War was started by Germany and Italy in Europe and by Japan in Asia.

Why? Despite its highly developed industry and in spite of all its efforts Germany had no possessions in Africa and Asia, as other Western countries had. The new German Empire was founded only in 1871 and so came too late in the period of imperialism. The few areas which Germany acquired in Africa and the Pacific round about 1885 became French, British and Japanese possessions in 1919, and the Versailles settlement put an end to the economic and expansionist dreams of the Reich and its own brand of imperialism. This was the objective cause of the embitterment of many Germans, of the desire for revenge and the dream of finding in the rich corn-lands and metal deposits of the Ukraine and in the oil regions of the Caucasus what Germany could not obtain elsewhere. At the same time the German bourgeois feared socialism, which was highly organized in Germany and was to all outward appearances very powerful. From this medley of feelings grew Hitler's National Socialist dictatorship (1933–1945), nourished by bitterness and supported by the capital of the Ruhr industrialists (Thyssen, Krupp, I.G. Farben, etc.) and by the still semi-feudal landed aristocracy. Possessed by the dream of Germany's greatness, blinded by a 'Germanic' race mania, Hitler's Germany embarked on war.

By mere threats it had already won much. Remember the re-occupation of the Rhineland (March 1936) at the time of the annexation of Abyssinia by Italy, the intervention in the Spanish civil war (July 18, 1936–April 1939), the occupation of Austria (March 12, 1938), the liquidation of Czechoslovakia (September 1938 and March 1939). Britain, France, the Soviet Union and the United States, though protesting, accepted the new dispensation.

In the summer of 1939 Hitler demanded part of western Poland, where many Germans lived. Warsaw refused, London and Paris warned, but in vain. On Friday, September 1st, at 4.45 a.m. Hitler invaded Poland. Europe shuddered; the wild beast had broken loose. On September 3rd Britain and France declared war on Germany. They had become tired of German greed and German double-dealing. The Second World War had begun.

Poland fought alone, for in the west the French and British armies stood in safety behind the French fortified line, while Holland and Belgium declared their neutrality. Poland was bled to death by the now historic, but then new, technique of the Germans, that combination of aircraft, tank divisions and mechanized infantry which is called the 'blitzkrieg'. In a few weeks the Germans were in the suburbs of Warsaw which, after a terrible bombardment, capitulated on September 27th.

Then came something worthy of note. Germany and Russia partitioned Poland, an evil repetition of the notorious partitions in the eighteenth century; these had caused the disappearance from the map of the great kingdom of Poland, which was restored but in much smaller form in 1919. The explanation is that on August 23, 1939, Germany and Russia concluded in Moscow a non-aggression treaty, Hitler because of his dread of a war on two fronts as in 1914, Stalin for fear that Anglo-French help would not come if Russia were attacked by Germany. The Russians occupied Eastern Poland for the same reasons for which the Russo-Finnish War (November 30, 1939, to March 12, 1940) was fought, and the former Russian territory on the Baltic between Leningrad and Poland (June 15, 1940) was occupied, the need to secure Russia's western frontier against a German attack which, in spite of the treaty, was expected.

Britain sent an expeditionary force to France. Otherwise Britain and France waited; perhaps Hitler would seek to take Eastern Europe and the Ukraine and the West would be spared.

On April 9, 1940, German troops like a thief in the night, invaded Denmark and Norway. Denmark was occupied in a day or two, Norway in a month, although it was not until June 9th that British troops evacuated the iron-ore port of Narvik.

On May 10th Holland, Belgium, Luxemburg and France were invaded. The Dutch army surrendered on the 14th; on May 21st the German tanks reached the North Sea at Abbeville; on the 28th the Belgian army surrendered. Between May 26th and June 4th, Britain evacuated 350,000 troops from Dunkirk, of whom a third were French. Seven hundred British tanks and 50,000 lorries were left in France. Britain had but a hundred tanks left.

The West seemed totally defeated. Inwardly in high spirits, outwardly grim, the Germans entered Paris on June 14th and on the 22nd France capitulated. Only the southeastern part of the country remained free, but it received a fascist government under Marshal Pétain, the defender of Verdun and Paris in the earlier World War. With the help of this 'independent' French government in Vichy, Hitler sought to protect the French colonies in Africa against a possible British attack.

But what everyone now expected, a German invasion of Britain – the operation 'Sea Lion', as it is called in the German plans – did not take place. Apparently Germany had not ships enough; perhaps Hitler wished to keep Britain neutral in the hope of thus having his hands free against Russia. Meantime, Italy under Mussolini decided to enter the war (June 10th) and occupied a few towns in southern France. On September 27th Germany, Italy and Japan signed the Three-Power Pact, a renewal and extension of the so-called Anti-Comintern Pact of 1936.

Under Churchill's leadership Britain was the only country which continued the battle despite the terror of air attacks (August 8, 1940, to May 1941), in which there were 45,000 civilian casualties and Germany lost 2000 aircraft. Parallel with this 'battle of Britain', Germany sought to blockade the stubborn islands by sea and so to sever them from their overseas territories and from America, from which they were receiving grain, ships and munitions.

In the terrible months March, April and May, 1941, German submarines sank 450 merchant ships. Up to 1942 the inhabitants of American and Brazilian coastal resorts could actually see British and American, Norwegian and Dutch ships being torpedoed. The Germans during the war sank about 5000 ships (21,000,000 tons), but they lost 650 submarines; the Italians lost 85.

In the meantime Hitler had conquered Southeastern Europe. Roumania, Hungary and Bulgaria had, to some extent voluntarily, accepted the German occupation (October–November 1940 and March 1941). On April 6, 1941, came the attack on Yugoslavia and Greece. Athens fell within three weeks and a British expeditionary force of 50,000 men had to be evacuated; in May German paratroops captured the large island of Crete.

Hitler was now master of the European continent except for neutral Portugal and Sweden, Switzerland and Franco's Spain. He was, therefore, sure that he could defeat the Soviet Union in six weeks. The final plans date from December 1940 (code name 'Barbarossa'). Neither the fact that the Soviet Union was protected in Asia by China and by the Russo-Japanese Non-Aggression Treaty of April 13, 1941, nor the existence of America, seemed to interest him.

In the night of June 21–22, 1941, German, Italian, Roumanian and, a few days later, Hungarian and Finnish divisions, in all some 2,500,000 to 3,000,000 men with about 8000 tanks, advanced into Russia on a broad front of over 1700 miles from the forests of North Finland to the quiet waters of the Black Sea. And again it seemed that the Germans were winning, even if not within the six weeks as Hitler had promised. Smolensk fell in mid-July;

Hitler was half-way to Moscow; as in the Napoleonic invasion the Russians retired on their capital. On September 4th the siege of Leningrad began; Kiev was stormed on September 19th; Odessa fell on October 16th and Kharkov (in the northeast of the Ukraine) on October 24th. Breaking every rule of international law as they went, the German troops continued to advance and behind them came the dreaded battalions of the Gestapo.

In November the German army lay in front of Moscow. The Russian government left, but Stalin himself stayed in the Kremlin. It was now winter; it was to be a hard one. In these days, when German newspapers were keeping space for an announcement of the capture of Moscow, the snow began to fall. The German tanks and lorries stuck in the mud and were frozen in, with night temperatures of 40 degrees below zero. The Russians knew the conditions well; the Germans did not, though any schoolbook on geography could have told them. In December snowstorms, the Red Army and the workers' militia freed Moscow from the threat of investment.

None the less, in the offensive in the succeeding summer the Germans took Sebastopol, Russia's naval base on the Black Sea (July 2nd), Voronesh in part (July 7th) and Rostov (July 24th), and in August were threatening the Caucasus and the Caspian, Astrakhan and Stalingrad on the Volga, in other words threatening the oilfields of Baku, the shipping routes and the railway line Iran–Baku–the Volga region, which was one of the few really good lines of communication between the factories of America and the Red Army.

Compared to the total area of the Soviet Union, what the Germans occupied in the summer of 1942 – the area west of the line Leningrad–Voronesh–Stalingrad–the Caucasus – looks small on the map, but it contained 45 per cent of the Union's population, 65 per cent of its coal and its steel and iron and half of its corn land.

If that was the state of things in Europe, there was no less dark an outlook in East Asia, the Pacific and North Africa. At the beginning of the critical winter of 1941 in Russia, Japan shocked America into action by the attack on Pearl Harbour (December 7th). What did Japan in its madness expect from it? The bold can indeed win success, but not just by boldness and nothing else. On December 8th the United States, Britain and Holland declared war on Japan, and on the 11th Germany and Italy declared war on the United States.

As the Germans had done in Europe, the Japanese armies spread over the Pacific and coastal districts of Southeast Asia. Within a few weeks Indochina, Malaya and Thailand were in their possession. Hongkong fell on December 25th, Manila on January 2, 1942, the islands east of New Guinea in January, Singapore on February 15th, Rangoon on March 7th and on the 9th Indonesia, then called the Dutch East Indies. In April a Japanese fleet bombarded Ceylon. In May the British, fearing a Japanese landing, occupied the French island of Madagascar off the east coast of Africa. In June 1942, while the Germans were advancing to the Caucasus and the Volga, Japanese marines landed on the American islands of Attu and

Kiska, south of the Bering Sea and relatively near Alaska. The Japanese advance into Burma threatened all South Asia, and that to New Guinea and Guadalcanal the line of communication between America and Australia, and Australia itself.

In this same summer, it looked as though the Germans and Italians would take Egypt, and so the whole area between the Suez Canal and the Caucasus was threatened. In June 1942 the 600 tanks of the German Afrika Corps reached the coast village of El Alamein in Egyptian territory, barely sixty miles from Alexandria. In the same month in the Atlantic an average of four Allied ships a day was sunk.

Looking back we can see that these months, May to August, mark the turning-point. Both Germany and Japan had reached the limit of their efforts; El Alamein and the Pacific gave proof that the tide had turned. On August 23rd the Russians announced that the Germans were within a mile of Stalingrad. At the beginning of September their tanks and infantry captured the suburbs and cut the city's communications. Only the river remained and it was under the fire of the German guns. Many people both in Russia and abroad expected Stalingrad to fall and the Germans to be in possession of the whole Volga area within a week. On September 28th Hitler declared to the Reichstag: 'Stalingrad will be in German hands within forty-eight hours'. History and Stalin had other views. The Red Army and the citizens desperately defended their burning factories, railway stations and houses, often from basement to ceiling against the stormers in field grey. The dead lay in heaps, but Stalingrad, or rather its ruins, stayed in Russian hands. When the snow began to fall in November the armies of Rokossovski and Yeremenko counter-attacked from north and south and within four weeks the Red Army had twenty-two German divisions in its grip. This was the first great defeat of the Wehrmacht; 150,000 Germans were dead, and on February 1, 1943, Field-Marshal Friedrich Paulus and his 80,000 half-frozen men surrendered.[1]

In the three winter months the invaders lost 500,000 men in dead and prisoners on the Russian front. But the war went on. In January the siege of Leningrad was raised and the city freed from the hunger blockade and when, in the summer of 1943, the many new factories in the Urals and in Soviet Asia began to produce and much war material came in from America through Iran in the south, Murmansk in the north and Vladivostok in the east – between 1943 and 1945 15,000 aircraft, 5000 tanks, 2000 locomotives and 200,000 lorries – the Germans were driven back 200 to 300 miles along the whole front. By December all Russia east of the Dnieper and the line Kiev–Leningrad had been liberated.

Roosevelt and Churchill had agreed in February 1942 to deal with Germany first and then with Japan so as to safeguard Britain, liberate Europe and relieve the Soviet Union of its burdens. Since the 'Battle of Britain' Russia had been exposed alone to the full menace of the German war-machine; the resistance in Europe did not yet amount to much. Ever more pressingly

[1] For an excellent description of the battle v. Theodore Plievier's novel *Stalingrad*.

Stalin asked for a 'second front' in Europe, that is, an Anglo-American invasion of occupied Europe.

But Churchill shrank from opening such a front. A landing from Britain in Western Europe was no 'military promenade'. It meant the certain loss of many British and American soldiers, and that perhaps was the chief cause of his reluctance. But there were also far-reaching and deep-seated political considerations influencing his hesitation. What he wanted most was action in the 'British' Mediterranean area and in Southeast Europe; without it, the Russians would be the liberators and the occupying power. Against the Americans Churchill opposed the idea of invading Western Europe until December 1943, though he knew that ultimately invasion would have to be undertaken.

On November 8, 1942, 850 British and American ships appeared off Morocco and Algeria, which were then under the Vichy government. The commander-in-chief of the army of invasion, Dwight D. Eisenhower, landed his troops at various ports and within three days the French garrisons of Casablanca, Oran and Algiers had surrendered; this was the turning-point so far as French Africa was concerned. In revenge, and for their own security. the Germans entered unoccupied France; the commander of the naval base at Toulon, as anti-German as he was anti-British, sank his ships in time.

On that same November 8th, the British Eighth Army under Montgomery drove the Afrika Corps out of Egypt and, as Germany was then directing all its strength against Stalingrad and Montgomery had received a host of tanks from America, the British in January 1943 took Tripoli in Western Libya; on May 11th, the 250,000 Germans and Italians in Tunisia surrendered. The African dream of Mussolini and Hitler, the nightmare of London, was over. We shall recount more of the subsequent developments in the next section.

As a natural consequence of the victory in North Africa Churchill's plan of 'attacking Europe at the most sensitive point' was put into action. Early on the morning of July 10, 1943, 160,000 Americans, British and Canadians, together with New Zealanders, Australians, Indians and French, were landed from 2000 ships on the south coast of Sicily. Eisenhower once again was in command and in two weeks he had occupied half the island. The gay Italians had apparently lost what liking they had had for 'the German war'; it was too uncomfortable and bitter. On July 25th a minor revolution stripped Mussolini of all his functions and he was arrested. The new commander-in-chief Badoglio, who had been in supreme command in the Italian campaign in Abyssinia, banned the Fascist party and appeared ready to capitulate. On September 2nd British and American troops landed in Southern Italy and on the 3rd the Badoglio government signed the articles of surrender. Meantime the Germans had occupied the country; in mid-September Mussolini was rescued by Skorzeny and his paratroopers from a mountain fastness in the Abruzzi where the new Italian Government had imprisoned him, but from then on he was without influence on events.

Despite a successful landing at Salerno and the occupation of Naples (October 1st), the Allies in 1943 got no farther than the ill-famed mountain village of Cassino, some sixty miles south of Rome. But the Russians had, to some extent at least, got their way; if they had not quite got what Stalin wanted, a 'second front', they had got a 'third front'.

In the winter of 1943 up to the summer of 1944 almost the whole of Russia was liberated, and the Japanese in a series of savage encounters had been driven from nearly all the Pacific islands.[1] Meantime Eisenhower was making plans for an invasion of Western Europe, the real 'second front', and the greatest overseas expedition in history.

In the night of June 5–6 – on the previous day the Allies had entered Rome – transports left all the ports on the south coast of Britain for Normandy. About 7.30 a.m. the first infantry waded through the water to the beaches and the hills of St. Marcouf and the river Orne on a fifty-mile front. Before they landed 800 naval guns and 10,000 aircraft had bombarded most of the concrete bunkers of the Atlantic Wall and some 10,000 paratroops, dropped behind the coast, had cut the German communications. For a considerable time the situation was critical enough for the British and Americans, but within a hundred days Eisenhower had got ashore from 4000 transports and 5000 landing craft 2,000,000 men – mostly Americans, British and Canadians – and 450,000 tanks and lorries and other war material. A pipeline under the waters of the English Channel provided these half-a-million engines with fuel. Paris was liberated (August 23rd), then Brussels and Antwerp (September 3rd and 5th), then all France and Belgium. Only Holland north of the great rivers (Maas, Waal and Rhine) remained in German hands; a British paratroop division was wiped out at the Rhine bridge near Arnhem (September 17th–25th).

During the winter the Germans stood fast on their Rhine line from the North Sea to the Swiss frontier, while the Russians occupied Finland, half of Poland and all southeastern Europe.

In 1945 the German war machine broke in pieces. Very heavy air attacks by British and Americans worked havoc in the German cities, on factories, bridges and railways. Germany had sown the wind; she was now reaping the whirlwind. By February 20th Russian motorized units were less than thirty miles from Berlin. At the same time the Americans got across the Rhine north of Cologne by the bridge at Remagen (March 8th), one of the few which the Germans failed to blow up in time, and on April 7th seven Allied armies streamed into Western Germany – four American, one British, one Canadian and one French. On April 26th Russians and Americans met at Torgau on the Elbe some sixty miles south of Berlin. It was all over. The German troops in Italy surrendered. Mussolini, in a German uniform, tried to get across the frontier into Switzerland, but near Lake Como he was captured by Italian Resistance men and was shot dead with his mistress on April 28th. On May 1st the German radio reported the suicide of Hitler in a bunker in the Chancellery, and the Russians occupied the centre of Berlin. On May 7th the Wehrmacht surrendered.

For Japan the bitter end came in August; on September 2nd on the *U.S.S. Missouri* in Tokio Bay Japan signed the articles of capitulation.

[1] *v.* pp. 336 *sq.*

The terror which began on the morning of September 1, 1939, in the east of Europe had ravaged the earth for 2194 days and nights.

A few figures give some idea of this bloody period in world history, figures of the dead, soldiers, resistance fighters and civilians in some of the countries who took part in the war: Belgium 160,000 (1 per cent of the population in 1940); Britain and British possessions 655,000 (0·5 per cent); China 20,000,000 (4·5 per cent); Germany 3,750,000 (6·5 per cent); Britain 335,000 (0·6 per cent); France 625,000 (1·6 per cent); Greece 550,000 (7·7 per cent); Holland 255,000 (2·9 per cent); Italy 570,000 (1·7 per cent); Japan 2,200,000 (2·8 per cent); Yugoslavia 1,700,000 (11 per cent); Canada 39,000 (0·3 per cent); the Philippines 125,000 (0·8 per cent); Poland 5,500,000 (16·7 per cent); Roumania 700,000 (6 per cent); the Soviet Union 15,000,000 (8 per cent) and the United States 370,000 (0·3 per cent). More than 13,000,000 Europeans, of which a quarter were women and children, were murdered far away from the battlefields in the occupied villages and towns of Eastern Europe and Russia. It was the Jews who suffered most; of the 16,000,000 who were alive in 1939, there were only 10,000,000 left at the end of the war – a loss of 37·5 per cent.

To conclude this section we give the place, date and some results of a series of diplomatic and military conversations between the Allies. These conversations were for the most part, and naturally, secret and, although the countries concerned sent many experts to them – at Yalta there were present 700 British and Americans, including Roosevelt, Churchill, and their doctors and secretaries – it was as a rule only Churchill, Stalin and Roosevelt who took the decisions.

The important conferences were:

1. Between Churchill and Roosevelt on board H.M.S. *Prince of Wales* off Newfoundland on August 9-10, 1941. Here was signed the Anglo-American Atlantic Charter (published August 14th) which outlined the Allied plans: restoration of the sovereignty of all occupied countries; no acquisition of territory by Britain and the United States; all peoples to have the right to decide their form of government (this was interpreted rather differently for Asia as compared to the West); freedom of the seas; and then the so-called four freedoms – freedom of speech and expression of opinion, freedom of religious belief, freedom from want and freedom from fear.

2. In Casablanca in French Morocco from January 14 to 24, 1943 (Churchill, Roosevelt and the Free French Generals de Gaulle and Giraud), where Western strategy in Europe was laid down in broad outline; agreement to demand unconditional surrender from Germany was reached; and plans for the invasion of Italy and the supreme command of the Free French was discussed.

3. In Quebec from August 11 to 24, 1943 (Churchill, Roosevelt, T. V. Soong for China and others), when the subjects discussed were plans of campaign for Asia; the extension of aid to China (the air bridge) and American activity in the Pacific; and also plans for the invasion of Western Europe.

4. In Moscow from October 19 to 31, 1943 (the foreign ministers of the

United States, Britain and Russia: Hull, Eden and Molotov); the ministers dealt among other things with the restoration of Austrian independence, the punishment of war criminals and the recognition of China as one of the 'Big Four'; France was not yet admitted to that status.

5. In Cairo from November 22 to 26, 1943 (Churchill, Roosevelt and Chiang Kai-shek) on the conduct of the war in the Far East; Manchuria and Formosa were recognized as Chinese territory; Korea was to become independent.

6. In Teheran from November 28 to December 2, 1943 (Churchill, Roosevelt and Stalin). This was the first time Roosevelt and Stalin had met, a portent of the greater confidence shown on both sides in 1944-1945. Previously, despite appearances, there had been no real understanding between Russia and her Allies; it was, for instance, only in 1944 that Britain and Russia exchanged weather reports. Among other things the plans for the campaign in Europe were agreed, the invasion of Normandy in May combined with a simultaneous great Russian offensive in the East. Everything was kept in strict secrecy.

7. In Yalta, a holiday resort in the Crimea from February 4 to 11, 1945. Churchill, Roosevelt and Stalin dealt with the formation of zones of occupation in Germany – the Russians in the east, the British in the northwest, the Americans in the southeast and the French in the southwest; the new frontiers of Poland and Germany; the date of an international conference to approve the plan for the 'United Nations' on which Britain, China, the United States and the Soviet Union had been at work, for instance, at the conference at Dumbarton Oaks from August to October 1944. It was also agreed – this naturally was kept very secret – that Russia within three months of the end of the war in Europe was to turn her arms against Japan.

8. In San Francisco from April 23 to June 26, 1945. Fifty countries signed here the charter of the United Nations. Among them were nine Asian countries – China, India, Irak, Iran, the Lebanon, the Philippines, Saudi Arabia, Syria and Turkey.

9. In Potsdam from July 17 to August 2, 1945. Britain (Churchill at the outset, then his successor the socialist Attlee), the United States (Truman, Roosevelt having died on April 12th at Warm Springs), and Russia (Stalin) dealt with affairs of Europe including the demilitarization and denazification of Germany, Germany's external and internal economic obligations and restrictions, and so the restoration of democratic liberties in a country which ideologically had been poisoned during the National Socialist regime.

II

THE SECOND WORLD WAR IN AFRICA

WHY should we include the story of the war in Africa in our account of the history of Asia? It is because it is not possible to separate the war in East Asia from the war in Africa nor the war in Africa either from the European war or from the development of Asia in this period. In Berlin's plans, or at least in the ambitious dreams of the National Socialists, the campaign in North Africa was, for instance, at once the beginning and the basis of a German invasion of Southwest Asia which would extend to the Caucasus, Russian Asia and India-Pakistan.

Thus to explain the historical background to the war we shall have to look back at past history. In 1915 and 1916 Italy declared war on Austria-Hungary and Germany in the expectation of being able to extend her territory northeast and east. As she was not strong enough to do so – her armies occupied only some six square miles of Austrian territory and only the intervention of an Anglo-French army prevented the fall of Venice – Italy got very little at Versailles. France and Britain divided the former German possessions in Africa and diplomatically and economically pressed into the whole of eastern and southern Europe. The Italian intervention in Greece and Turkey (1919–1921) failed. In Italy itself there seemed likely to be a left revolution, and so the Italian bourgeoisie took refuge in a fascist-nationalist regime under the ex-socialist Benito Mussolini (1922). The fascist 'March on Rome' (October 23, 1922), when the King and the Government capitulated, marks the beginning of the fascist period in Italy. Naturally the new regime was anti-socialist, anti-democratic and extremely imperialist in the sense of territorial conquest. It dreamed of restoring the Roman Empire, and the fulfilment of that dream meant the possession of North Africa.

In the great partition of Africa in 1885–1910, Italy had obtained Eritrea on the Red Sea (1892–1896) and Somaliland on the Indian Ocean. On the north coast of Africa she had conquered Libya from Turkey (1911). Taken together, that was a very large area; Eritrea is about the size of Czechoslovakia; Italian Somaliland is as big as France, and Libya is thrice the size of Germany in 1939. But much of it is deserts of sand and stone and economically it is of virtually no importance. That was what enraged the Italian imperialists.

In Africa there was still one independent native kingdom, the empire of Abyssinia, which lies between Eritrea and Italian Somaliland. That weak empire seemed an easy prey. The frontier incident at Wal Wal in southwestern Abyssinia (December 5, 1934) was the pretext for attack; historically it is a companion picture to the 'Mukden incident' in Manchuria in September 1931. Looking back we can belatedly recognize that these two incidents mark the beginning of the Second World War. Western Europe only half-heartedly opposed the expansionist plans of Mussolini. Italian transports carrying troops were allowed to pass unhindered through the Suez Canal and in the Franco-Italian treaty of January 7, 1935, France gave her secret consent to the occupation of Abyssinia.

On October 3, 1935, the Italians began their invasion. In a barbarous colonial war – air bombardment of primitive villages and towns and the use of poison gas – the Italians under Marshal Badoglio wiped the African state off the map. On May 5, 1936, Addis Ababa was taken and the 'King of Kings', Haile Selassie, fled to Britain. On May 9th Rome announced the annexation of the whole country and King Vittorio Emanuele III became Emperor of Ethiopia.

The unhindered Italian action in East Africa and the contemporary recovery of the occupied Rhineland by Germany (March 7, 1936) mark the beginning of the end of the Versailles Treaty and of collective security. That was seen at the time of the fascist revolt in Spain (from July 18, 1936) which began the civil war in which many Italian 'volunteer divisions', German tank detachments and aircraft squadrons took part without troubling about public opinion.

In the light of these events in East Asia, in East Africa, in the Mediterranean area and in Europe, the Anglo-Egyptian treaty [1] of August 1936 took on new significance. For Egypt it had two consequences. It temporarily lessened the influence of the anti-British Wafd party; it intensified the natural differences within the Wafd; such is the almost universal consequence of crisis within a nationalist movement. The moderates dreamed of a progressive disappearance of the British; the radicals, including the fascist greenshirts and blueshirts, wanted to use Italy to fight the British, thus seeking with the aid of Beelzebub to drive out Satan.

But in 1938, when Austria was occupied by Germany and North China by Japan, the international tension spread to Egypt and, when the Italians were seen to be coveting the Suez Canal, drove it closer to Britain. The Wafd, hesitating between anti-British action and democratic anti-fascism, was defeated in the April elections. None the less Egypt remained a threatened position in the British Empire and, when the Second World War broke out in Europe on September 1, 1939, many Egyptians, particularly in the circle round King Farouk, sympathized with the ideas of the greenshirts, i.e. with the Italians. Now that Mussolini's divisions were firmly established in nearby Libya and on the frontiers of the Soudan the prospects for Britain – and for Egypt – seemed none too rosy.

We have already told how Italy during the German 'blitzkrieg' in France had invaded southern France and declared war on France and Britain (June 10, 1940). In August the Italians, advancing from Abyssinia, occupied British Somaliland. On September 13th an Italian army from Libya crossed the frontier into Egypt. This was the actual beginning of the war in Africa, for the British base in Egypt was in danger of being cut off if Italy blocked the Mediterranean; 'neutral' fascist Spain was a second danger (Gibraltar,

[1] v. p. 194.

Spanish Morocco and the Spanish Sahara). Would Turkey remain neutral? What if the Germans succeeded in taking ports in French West Africa, and from them preventing British ships getting to the Red Sea via South Africa? What value would the Red Sea have if the Italians took Aden?

And this was all happening at the time when German and Italian bombers were by day and by night attacking London and the south of England, and Germany, Italy and Japan were signing their military-economic Three-Power Pact in Berlin (September 27th). 'One shudders as one writes about it', wrote Churchill later, and he does not shudder easily.

But the Italians love the sunshine, the wine and the women, and not the game of soldiering, at least not in the grim reality of war. That was seen in September 1940 when British troops drove Graziani's invading army out of Mersa Matruh in Egyptian territory and occupied Bardia close to the frontier, whereupon many Italians surrendered. Graziani retired via Benghazi (February 7th) by the only road of retreat westward, and on February 8th the British reached El Agheila more than 560 miles from the Egyptian frontier. In an offensive which lasted two months Wavell took 120,000 Italians prisoner.

Almost simultaneously British troops from the Soudan and Kenya, with the help of Abyssinian partisans, liberated Ethiopia. On April 5th Addis Ababa, the Abyssinian capital, was occupied, and by November the whole of Italian East Africa. Of the original 420,000 Italian soldiers in Africa, 220,000 were taken prisoner in Ethiopia, Eritrea and Somaliland alone. The Emperor returned to his capital (May 1941) and the British declared Ethiopia to be sovereign and independent (January 1942), a typical example of the way in which European imperialism abdicated.

Under Italian leadership the Italians had not been really a threat to the British occupation of Egypt, but, when the German Afrika Korps in March 1941 arrived, partly by air, in North Africa, and the German tank expert Rommel succeeded Graziani as commander of the fascist divisions at the front, the situation altered. The 'desert fox' had already shown his remarkable skill in tank warfare in France, and the Afrika Korps with Prussian thoroughness had already been prepared for the peculiarities and terrors of desert warfare and technically fully instructed to combat the scorching heat, the absence of any natural protection in flat barren country, the lack of water and the sandstorms which hindered the movement of tanks and guns and could exhaust the resistance power of the soldiers.

On April 3rd the Germans, reinforced by some Italian infantry divisions, attacked and, as the British had sent four divisions to Greece, which the Germans had invaded from the north, Rommel in two weeks took Bardia and Sollum on the Egyptian frontier. The situation in Egypt and southwest Asia became critical. In April Greece surrendered, so that the Germans were masters up to the frontier of Turkey. In May German paratroops captured Crete, less than 200 miles north of Egypt. German 'tourists' in the Arab countries were as numerous as the sands of the sea. In every report coming from Irak and Iran and from Syria, which belonged to Vichy France, German officers and aircraft were said to be everywhere and the dangerous plans of the Nazis for these countries were revealed. That explains the occupation of Irak by the British in May 1941, of Syria and the Lebanon by the British and Free French in June, and of Iran by the British and Russians in August. The further development of the Arab lands during the war we have related elsewhere.[1]

In all these countries the German plans remained unrealized; even the long-awaited invasion of Egypt failed in May. On the one hand, Berlin at the moment was devoting all its attention to the Barbarossa plan, the attack on the Soviet Union (June 22, 1941); on the other, it may be that Berlin feared to drive neutral Egypt into the British camp.

Whatever the reason, both sides stood still behind their milewide minefields on the Egyptian frontier and it was not until December 1941, when the Germans were attacking Moscow, that the British troops were able to drive back the Afrika Korps (December 25th, the day Hongkong fell), to reach first Benghazi and then El Agheila half-way between the Egyptian frontier and Tunis.

None the less the German army remained intact in a strong position and in spring 1942 they counter-attacked. Although numerically inferior Rommel held the initiative. In a few hours on June 21st he took Tobruk, with 30,000 prisoners, and pushing eastward along the coast crossed the frontier into Egypt; on June 30th he reached El Alamein, just over sixty miles from Alexandria. Cairo and other Egyptian towns were bombed. All this was happening while the Nazi armies from the Ukraine had advanced to the Volga and the Caucasus, the Japanese were occupying Burma and so isolating China on the south, and British troops were (May 1942) landing in Madagascar, which belonged to Vichy France, because a Japanese invasion was feared. The Asian dreams of Berlin and Tokio – the conquest of South Asia and the cutting of communications between Russia and China, on the one hand, and Britain and America, on the other – looked like coming true.

Meantime Britain had radically intervened in Egypt. In February 1942, at the time of the fall of Singapore, the British ambassador in Cairo, Sir Miles Lampson (later Lord Killearn), with British tanks in readiness before the palace, had demanded of King Farouk the recall to power of Nahas Pasha, the moderately nationalist and anti-fascist leader of the Wafd. He became premier and military commander-in-chief of Egypt and held free elections in which the Wafd again won a significant majority. Egypt in the later stages of the war, however unwillingly, was a secure base for the British. The strategic importance of this change cannot be denied, even if it took Egypt, like Turkey, until February 1945 to declare war on Germany officially.

The German plan to reach the Nile by the summer of 1942 failed. On the El Alamein position lay English, Scots, New Zealanders, Australians, Indians, Nepalese, Poles, Czechs, French and South Africans, aided by the shipyards and factories of America, to bar the road to the Nile; all the steel, lead and aluminium were American. It is rare that the influence of historic factors can be expressed in figures or even correctly estimated, but it is probable that American war production had as much to do with the security

[1] v. pp. 371 sq., and for Iran v. pp. 290 sq.

of Egypt and Nearer Asia as the desperate resistance of the British and the Russians.

With our restricted space it is not possible to give proof of this, but here is one example of the significance of the term applied to America, 'the arsenal of democracy'. In 1939 the world had 10,000 big merchantmen in service; the United States alone between 1941 and 1945 built 12,000 warships and merchant ships – landing craft are not included – which means that in 1943 the construction rate was from two to three merchant ships per day.

Two other factors helped to thwart the German-Japanese hopes of uniting their forces in India. The first was the Russian offensive on the Volga and the Caucasus in the summer of 1942 and the winter of 1942–3 which resulted in the catastrophe that overtook the German Sixth Army.[1] The second was the Anglo-American landing in French North Africa (Morocco and Algeria) on November 8, 1942. This invasion[2] in the rear of the Afrika Korps and the Egyptian ports was half-British half-American. But Eisenhower, the commander-in-chief, gave the expedition a wholly American character in the expectation that the French would prefer to be liberated by Americans. However that may be, the French territories capitulated within three days. We have already told how, as a result, Germany occupied the still free territory of Vichy France.

Early in November the Germans began to withdraw from Egypt. In the third week of October the British Eighth Army under Montgomery counterattacked. In a furious tank battle at El Alamein the Germans lost 500 tanks, 45,000 Germans and Italians fell and 30,000 were taken prisoner. As Churchill said it was 'the end of the beginning'.

On January 24, 1943, the Germans evacuated Tripoli in western Libya and withdrew to the fortified line with its cover of palm trees at Mareth in southern Tunisia. But Montgomery's eight motorized divisions were given no rest; they attacked the new German line while the Americans from the west and the Free French from the south invaded Tunisia. Meantime Rommel had gone to Berlin and asked for substantial help from the Wehrmacht chiefs. It was a vain request, for as the Eastern Front needed all that was available, a fresh offensive in Africa was not possible. The war in Africa had passed into history. Egypt was no longer menaced; the sea-lane between Gibraltar and Suez was again open and in May 1943 the first ships from Britain sailed unopposed into the port of Alexandria. In mid-July British, Americans and Canadians landed in Sicily, thus completing the destruction of Mussolini's imperial dream.

The war in Africa had exacted heavy toll from the fascist states. It cost them 8000 aircraft, 2500 tanks, 70,000 lorries, 250 to 300 merchant ships and 950,000 dead and prisoners. The loss of the victors was just as heavy. As every war report does, that on Africa ends in blood, tears and charred ruins.

[1] v. p. 279.　　[2] v. p. 280.

III

IRAN AND AFGHANISTAN

WHEN Iran is genuinely modernized and, in addition to its own economists, technicians and agricultural engineers, has its own historians and archaeologists, many of the latter will dedicate themselves to the study of the unusually varied history of Persia. They will, one may believe, show how even in prehistoric times three millennia before our era begins and even earlier, the period for which we have no sources of any kind, Persia served as intermediary between three cultural areas – the cultural area in the valleys of the Euphrates and the Tigris (the modern Irak); the cultural area of the Indus valley discovered only recently (West Pakistan) and which attained the same high level as did Egypt and Mesopotamia (one recalls here the excavations at the sites at Mohendjodaro and Harappa), and the third, the very old cultural area on the southern slopes of the Caucasus and in Armenia between the Black Sea and the Caspian. Of all these, and of the very early culture of Persia itself (Susa, Persepolis), we still have only a very incomplete picture.

We know considerably more about the Persian Empire between 550 B.C. and 350 B.C., which in these days stretched from Egypt and Istanbul to the Indus and the Sea of Aral. Apart from the Chinese Empire it was the greatest power in the world. Persia's geographical situation, which makes it a landbridge between southwest Asia, the Arab countries, South Russian and India, between Europe and the centres of Asian culture, not only made rich the native culture but gave peculiar character to its history. The country had to endure invasions from every direction. We must not think of 'imperialism' simply as a European and a contemporary phenomenon; it was known also in Asia and at a very early date.

Persia itself is an example. Its kings Darius (521–485) and Xerxes (485–465), not only conquered Asian and African countries but tried to conquer South Russia and Greece. Herodotus (c. 480–436), the first important European historian, described the 'Persian Wars' as a conflict between East and West, and one of the conditions for the greatness and development of Europe was the Greek defence of the West against contemporary Persian imperialism. That is the reason why nearly all European history books begin with the defeat of the Persian invaders (490 B.C.) at Marathon, twenty-five miles from Athens, and the destruction of the Persian fleet at Salamis (480).

If, as Schiller said, world history is a world court, then the Persians were harshly punished; think of the invasion of Alexander the Great (331 B.C.), the conquests by the Arabs (A.D. 636) and by the Mongols (c. A.D. 250). Such dire happenings, however, did not mean only loss and suffering. Looked at from a distance, all historic events have their light and shade. As a result of

Alexander's invasion Persia was brought into contact with the Hellenistic culture of the Mediterranean area; the Arab invasion brought Islam with it.

In modern times the political-strategic importance of Iran was seen in the Napoleonic era. When, in the summer of 1798, a French invasion of Britain was seen to be impossible, Napoleon took an expeditionary force to Egypt, then a Turkish province, with the idea of attacking the British possessions in India by way of Arabia and Persia; he had already sent a letter to the shah demanding right of passage.

The French adventure in Egypt in 1799 failed as disastrously as did the Italo-German venture in 1942–3. None the less the emperor of the French in 1807 sent some flattering inflammatory letters to the shah, and on October 23 of that year the London *Times* wrote these warning words: 'the passage of French troops through Persia to India is part of the gigantic propects of French ambition.' Historic parallels are a prickly business, but a comparison between 1807 and 1941 is very tempting. In 1807 the French were in possession virtually of all Europe save Russia and Britain; the Franco-Russian peace of Tilsit (July 1807) made Russia neutral. Napoleon's power was shattered on the snow-deep plains of Russia and in the flames of Moscow, at Leipzig (1813) and at Waterloo (1815). Hitler's was shattered at Stalingrad (1943), in Normandy (1944) and in Berlin (1945).

In a previous section [1] we have described how Britain and Russia intrigued in Persia in the nineteen and twentieth centuries, the length to which British action went and how in that period the modernization of Persia and its desire for freedom progressed and became stronger. Because of the dazzling many-sidedness of Persian history we have taken the reader back to events which lie outside our period; we now return to that period and to Iran in 1940.

Since the famous February night in 1921,[2] the ex-Cossack officer, the great Riza Khan (crowned shah in 1926), had been all powerful. Like Kemal Ataturk he used a mild dictatorship to modernize his country, but it was a modernization which was confined to technique and as far as the peasant was concerned the feudal basis remained unchanged just as in China, Japan, Arabia and many other countries, including Eastern Europe west of the Soviet Union.

¯One of his innovations was the great Trans-Persian railway (875 miles long, with 224 tunnels and 1933 bridges) from Bandar Shapur on the Persian Gulf to Bandar Shah south of the Caspian. It was Persia's only railway line of any consequence, and was built by Persian capital without any help from either Britain or Russia. Only German, Scandinavian and American technicians were employed on it alongside Persians. Including the new ports, Persia spent on it £40,000,000. This mountain railway acquired in the Second World War an importance which far exceeded any of the expectations of the shah and his German engineers, for it was the line of communication between the Soviet Union and the open sea.

When the war broke out in Europe in September 1939 Persia declared herself neutral, but it was not a neutrality which is to be understood in the Swiss sense of the word. The Persian Government certainly did not so interpret it

[1] *v.* pp. 82 *sq.*   [2] *v.* p. 197.

and covertly, and on occasions not so covertly, turned to Berlin. Like Napoleon, Hitler recognized the strategic importance of Iran and had earlier sent to it engineers, technicians and even professional spies; to Teheran, caught between Baku and Abadan, that seemed almost providential. The Foreign Office in London knew all about this Perso-German friendship and in 1939–40 sought to wreck it and separate Teheran and Berlin.

In May–June 1941 the war came nearer Southwest Asia. In May the German tank divisions were threatening Egypt and on June 22nd came the attack on the Soviet Union. Syria and Irak, where there were too many German agents, were occupied soon after by the British. The case of Persia became immediate.

Iran, with its German sympathies, remained a dangerous vacuum with its wealth in oil; it was, too, a barrier between Russia and the sea, and the readiness of the Americans to deliver war material to Russia could not be utilized without secure communications. Theoretically Russia had then two open seaports, Murmansk in the extreme northwest and Vladivostok in the far east. Leningrad, on the Baltic, and the ports of the Black Sea were blockaded by the Germans; the ports of Northern Siberia are icebound for too long or have poor connections with the interior. But the way to Murmansk was no safe one. The ports of Norway were crowded with German submarines and aircraft, and Vladivostok was far too far away from the fighting front in Russia – it is 6000 miles distant and being near Japan was certainly not safe; in the period December 1941–August 1945 Japan prevented in its area the movements of British and American shipping.

The safest and useable line of communication between America and Russia was through Iran (Turkey's frontiers were now on the borders of what Hitler called the European fortress; there was no inclination in Ankara to make any rash experiments). Between August 25th and 29th British and Russian troops occupied the country, Russia taking the north, the British the south. On September 16th the shah surrendered and was sent to the British island of Mauritius; in 1944 he died in South Africa, an embittered man.

His son, Riza Pahlevi (b. 1919; his first queen was Princess Fawzia of Egypt), became monarch of a more democratic country though temporarily under foreign occupation. In a particular sense it was not free. Foreign officers, among them many Americans on the railway and other ways of communication, really ruled the land. Was that against the will of the Persian people? By no means, for Iran knew great social inequalities, for instance those between the small peasants and the great landowners; in the years just past, these inequalities had become greater and more visible. The autocratic rule of the shah had radically prevented any tendencies in a leftward direction; in 1937 fifty liberal and socialist intellectuals and students were arrested simply because of their political ideas, which were regarded as dangerous to the state. Under the new regime they were released, and almost at once (1941) the 'Fifty', of whom Sulaiman Mirza Eskandari was the best known, founded the Tudeh party (Workers' party), a radical, rather left-wing party of reform; in 1945 the extreme left, the communist element, won a majority in it.

The change, of course, in Persia had as a result some clearing out of Germans from Afghanistan – the technicians and 'tourists' whom we have already mentioned. Some members of the Government too friendly to Germany were removed from office. Apart from that, the kingdom of Afghanistan remained completely neutral, a mountain land standing apart from the wild course of Asian development.

On January 29, 1942, Britain, Russia and Persia concluded a treaty in Teheran which guaranteed the territorial integrity and sovereignty of Iran. American technicians built up the country's transport system, modernized the Trans-Persian railway and many motor roads, constructed ports and brought in locomotives, railway waggons (partly from India-Pakistan) and motor lorries. In the northwest Russians and Persians built a railway line linking Teheran with Russian Azerbaijan, and in the east the British constructed a new road from what is now West Pakistan to Russian Asia.

American and some British war material streamed over the Trans-Persian railway and some motor roads to Russia, to a total of about 5,000,000 tons, brought on some 700 ships, three-quarters of all the material sent to the Soviet Union by America – 2000 locomotives, 5000 tanks, 1100 guns, 150,000 lorries, a great part of the 15,000 aircraft already mentioned, and many other goods which are needed in war – machinery, field telephones, medicines. That was a very large amount, but for a modern war it was relatively little. Various authors have given differing estimates of the importance of Anglo-American help to the Soviet Union. Of all that the United States invested in the war, barely 3 per cent when to Russia while 15 per cent went to Britain; the figures are Roosevelt's. None the less the transports via Iran and Murmansk probably increased Russia's fighting power by 20 per cent. The Persians made a great contribution, even if not a very willing one, and although the Persian declaration of war on Germany (September 9, 1943) – this was the day on which Italy surrendered – and on Japan (1945) had little more than diplomatic significance. Besides the railway there were the oilfields, the ports and the workers, and the agricultural areas in the north from which grain, vegetables and fruit went to Russia.

Iran being the only country in which Russian, British and American soldiers could move freely, it was at Teheran that the historic conference was held (November 28 to December 2, 1943) at which Churchill, Roosevelt and Stalin (who had not wished to go very far from his headquarters), cheered by much vodka and Russian tea, discussed plans for the campaign in Europe.[1] In a document dated December 1st, which is usually called the 'Declaration of Teheran', the three powers in honeyed words again affirmed the 'territorial integrity, independence and sovereignty of Iran', fixed a date by which their troops would be withdrawn – the British and Americans withdrew in December 1945, the Russians in May 1946 – and promised the exhausted land economic aid, for the occupation and the military transports through Iran had wrecked the native economy and the civil transport system. There was in 1942 a regular famine in Teheran. Time was given the shah to read through the declaration and he signed it, if rather unwillingly. Perhaps he already saw clearly how unimportant in international relations are am-

[1] v. p. 283.

biguous terms and obscure designs; he was certainly justified in not basing any great hopes on it. But the very genuine function which Iran discharged in the anti-fascist war, as well as the general feeling of bitterness when concrete evidence of gratitude and economic aid failed to materialize, plus the liberation of many Asian lands from European colonial domination – all that drove Persian nationalism beyond the narrow limits within which it had hitherto been confined. Of this Dr Mossadeq, who became an international figure, was the symbol. Then came the Azerbaijan dispute with Russia (1945–1946) and the dispute with Britain over oil (1950–1954). Thus here, too, the war furthered liberation.

IV

INDIA-PAKISTAN

VERY high mountains separate India-Pakistan from China and Central Asia. The reason why Persia was of strategic importance even in the distant past was primarily because, looking west and north, behind her lay the rich lands of Nearer India with their dense population and their wealth in grain and gold.

Did not the Indus valley and other areas in what is now India and Pakistan possess in 4000 B.C., and perhaps earlier, an agricultural society which in culture did not fall behind the cultures of Egypt and Mesopotamia? Was not cotton grown and cropped here centuries before there was any such cultivation in these two lands? In its long history India-Pakistan has always been more densely populated than, for instance, Europe. The situation was modified only in the eighteenth century when European civilization technically and economically began to surpass the Asian.

Many European and Asian empires coveted the riches of India. There were many invasions and still more plans for invasion. Recall the invasion of the mysterious Indo-Germans (Aryans) *via* Persia and Afghanistan from 2400 to 1500 B.C.; the Greek invasion of the Indus valley under Alexander the Great (c. 325 B.C.); the incursions of the White Huns from Central Asia (sixth century A.D.), which also came through Persia; the raids of the Mongol horsemen under Timur (Tamerlane) of Samarkand (fourteenth century); the occupation (sixteenth century) by the Mongols under Babur (Babar) of Ferghana, a king of Timur's race and on the distaff side a descendant of Gengis Khan. Besides these, there were the Moslem invasions (twelfth to fourteenth centuries) of Arabs, Turks, and Afghans, the arrival and wars of the Portuguese (sixteenth century) of the Dutch, French and British (seventeenth century), the invasion plans of Napoleon (c. 1800), and the Asian dreams in our own era of Hitler and Hirohito.

All through that long history Nearer Asia was strategically always an object; it had, so to say, a feminine function. Only its culture spread beyond its frontiers. The various native kingdoms and cultures naturally stoutly defended themselves against the foreign intruders, but there were virtually no cases of attempts to expand beyond the frontiers of today.

The role of 'object' is very characteristic of India in the nineteenth century, in the colonial period when the Hindu bourgeois class adopted British culture either in Oxford or Cambridge or in their own country. During the First World War the relatively young Indian nationalist movement had no leaders abroad, no international vision. Gandhi and most other nationalists, at least at first, supported Britain in the sincere, if somewhat naïve, belief that, once Germany and Austria were defeated, democratic Britain would help them to freedom from imperialist domination. By 1918 more than 1,200,000 soldiers and workers from India had aided the British Empire in the campaigns in Europe, Mesopotamia, Arabia and East Africa. But freedom did not come; rather, things grew worse.

Meantime the situation had developed internally. By 1927 the Congress party was saying that their country, even if not free, should refuse to be involved in the imperialist wars which were coming. Their rejection of fascist plans for expansion in Europe and Africa (1935-1939) and especially their condemnation of Japanese imperialism in China when the party sent Chiang much medical aid (1938-1939), did not imply any alteration in that resolve.

In 1939 the Congress party avoided committing again the bitter mistakes of 1914 and this time refused to build castles in the air. When in the summer of 1939 the British sent native troops to Aden, Egypt and Singapore, there was general resistance. In a frank communiqué the party made its position clear: 'We are against fascist aggression in Europe, Africa and the Far East; we are equally against British imperialism's betrayal of Czechoslovakia and Spain.'

When war broke out in Europe the viceroy, Lord Linlithgow, announced on his own authority that his portion of the Empire was in a state of war with Germany and stopped the preparations for an All-Indian Union. The Congress leaders took the view of the Communist International and the American isolationists: 'This is a war between two imperialist powers in Europe; we shall keep out of it.' Later (September 14th) they said: 'If Britain will tell us its war plans and its plans in Asia we may be able to see farther. . . . We shudder at the German aggression in Poland, but India cannot take part in a war which is proclaimed one for democratic liberty, so long as democratic freedom is denied to India and the limited freedom which she does have is taken away. . . . If this war is waged to protect the imperialists' possessions, colonies, invested capital and privileges, then India can have nothing to do with it. If, however, the aim is democracy . . . then India is intensely interested.'

On October 15th London sent an answer to the viceroy. Britain, it said, is defending besides its own islands democracy in Europe and the freedom of the world, and as for India Britain will declare it to be a Dominion. 'These are hackneyed phrases', said the Congress, 'which are too obscure to fire our hearts. We want independence; we do not want to be a Dominion. We are as anti-fascist as you are, but we do not intend to shed our blood for the freedom of others while we ourselves are not free. There are limits to everything.'

In protest the ministers installed by the party in the eight Hindu provinces resigned and so, just as in the nineteenth century, the British governors had to rule alone. A second sign of the general desire not to be involved in European affairs was given by the strike of 100,000 factory workers in Bombay.

Only the rajahs of the native kingdoms and a great part of the landowners and industrialists supported Britain. In the three Moslem provinces, the native governments remained in office – in Bengal and Sind only temporarily – although Jinnah made it clear that in his view the times were ripe for the establishment of a free India and Pakistan. During the war 15,000 volunteers joined the army every week; in 1945 the British Empire's forces included 2,500,000 Indians and Pakistanis of all races and from all parts of the country. These Asians on the fronts in Asia, Africa and Europe were not inferior as officers and men to the Europeans and Americans, and that was for India of profound psychological significance. These native divisions trained for modern war were to become the bases of the armies of free India and free Pakistan.

When in May 1940 the war spread, the anti-fascist Congress leaders, including Nehru and Rajagopalachari, declared their readiness to defend an India which was free and independent. Although that meant a revolutionary change of direction and a temporary abandonment of Gandhi's ideals, London remained as blind as ever, as blind as Holland in Indonesia and France in Indochina. A letter of the viceroy in August merely repeated what he had said earlier.

The party turned again to Gandhi. At this time Nehru wrote the articles from which we have already quoted.[1] The *satyagraha* movement was revived and many volunteers arrested; in October 1940 there were 30,000 Indians in prison, most of them from the United Provinces, including all the party leaders. Away in the West German officers were drawing up the plans for 'Barbarossa', and early on June 22, 1941, the German motorized divisions flooded into the Russian plains. Here was a new element – on the international plane – for London and its Asian territories. On December 4th, a few days before war broke out in the Pacific and when it seemed that Hitler's armies would reach Moscow and the Caucasus, the British set Nehru and many others at liberty.

But Churchill would go no farther, and his obstinacy estranged many countries and created new bitterness in Nearer India. Had not Roosevelt and Churchill in the Atlantic Charter of August 1941 plainly stated that 'they, i.e. Britain and the United States, would respect the right of every people to choose its own form of government, and that they desired to see the right of sovereignty and self-government restored to the peoples who had been deprived of it'. At the beginning of September Churchill said in London that he meant only the occupied countries of Europe, and had no intention of diminishing the Empire while he was head of the Government. 'One does not put good whisky into badly washed and cracked bottles', was the opinion of the high officials in Delhi. Admittedly that was plain speaking and without ambiguity, but in Asia it was interpreted as: 'if the British talk today of freedom what they mean is the continued existence of British rule. Churchill and his followers are imperialists from the nineteenth century'.

Aggression spread. On December 7, 1941, the temperature in the Pacific reached boiling-point. It was not only the British who heard with dismay the reports from East Asia; Hawaii, Wake Island, the sinking of H.M.S. *Prince of Wales* and H.M.S. *Repulse,* Malaya, Thailand, Hongkong, the Philippines, Indonesia. On January 1, 1942, between the fall of Hongkong and the fall of Manila, twenty-six states signed the declaration of the United Nations: there was question also of extending the Anglo-Russian

[1] *v.* p. 264.

mutual aid treaty of July 13, 1941. Among the signatories were Australia, Canada, China, Britain, India, the Philippines, the Soviet Union and the United States.

Nehru and his followers declared: 'We too belong to this front.' But many of his party colleagues thought differently. Gandhi was at first opposed to any participation in the war, while Subhas Chandra Bose and quite a few others hoped to get from the Japanese the freedom Britain had refused them. Officially the tactics of the Congress party was that they would enter Churchill's front if they were really free but on no other terms.

While the white men in Singapore and Manila, in Bandung and Batavia, disappeared into Japanese prison camps, various foreign governments strove to persuade London to grant a measure of freedom to British India. At the beginning of 1942, Chiang- Kai-shek, while on a visit with his wife to Delhi said to Lord Linlithgow: 'Give independence to India now; otherwise the Japanese will occupy Burma and cut communications with Chungking.' The Australian foreign minister said something similar, but on the ground of the direct threat to the freedom of Australia by the Japanese establishment of bases in New Guinea and Guadalcanal. And Roosevelt in more than one letter to Churchill said: 'Only a free India will defend itself as we are doing; think of China – and of Indonesia and Malaya.'

It was only when the Japanese took Rangoon (March 7, 1942) and Bandung in the same week surrendered to them, and when some towns in the eastern hills of India were bombed that the British showed readiness to make some concessions. Hundreds of thousands of Indian refugees arrived in India, having crossed the pathless forests of the Arakan hills and told of the horrors of their flight – chaos in the British administration, malaria, banditry, and the forbidding of non-Europeans to cross the frontier and of the retreat of the British army. It was then that Sir Stafford Cripps (from 1940 to 1942 British ambassador in Moscow) was sent to Delhi; he belonged to the circle which Nehru trusted. Cripps brought new plans, but not for freedom. Again it was plain that the right wing of the British government, and Churchill in particular, wished to postpone the hour of freedom for India, so terribly can a great man and a man of intelligence be the slave of his own obstinacy and misread alike the present and the future. Cripps's plan was for an Indian Union as a modern Dominion with the right to secede from the Commonwealth; a new, purely Indian, national constitution for the provinces and the native kingdoms. But this was not to come into force until the war ended. And then the British Government would only consent to a constitution if each province and native kingdom had the right to stay out of the new State of India and minorities were protected.

Closely examined, the plan does not appear to be very different from that of August 1940. The Congress and all other parties rejected it (April 11, 1942). Nehru and his followers shrank from the possibility of a division of the country into various Hindu and Moslem districts and the creation of many anti-democratic and possibly pro-British smaller or bigger kingdoms. The Moslems, like Jinnah, wanted assurance that there would be a free Pakistan and not just hope of one. They were all displeased with the lack of clarity in the text – 'British words seem to change their meaning from the time they cross the Suez Canal' Nehru had written in 1934 – and particularly by the postponement once again of the date of freedom. When we look at it objectively and from a distance in time, Cripps's plan appears a mixture of Dutch conceptions as laid down in the Queen's speech of December 7, 1942, and the partition tactics of Van Mook in Indonesia in 1945–8.

While the Congress was groping its way back to its old policy, Gandhi for the last time assumed the leadership. It was anti-fascist and anti-Japanese, ordered simultaneously a boycott of the British administration and, if the Japanese invaded India, reunuciation of armed resistance and guerrilla war such as Nehru and others advocated. It was characteristic of the way things go in politics that observers in the summer of 1942 said not: 'how stupid and arro-gant are the British imperialists', but: 'Look, a party like the Congress is not mature enough for freedom; they are only bewildered and embittered obstruc-tionists'.

Meantime the Japanese in Burma had occupied various frontier districts from which they were not to be expelled until the middle of 1944. The whole eastern region of British India was now in danger. The British were in no doubt of that and in East Bengal they burned all the river vessels, which were the only means of transport. In Madras a part of the port installations was dismantled on a report that the Japanese intended a landing.

On the evening of August 8, 1942, the All-India Congress published its historic answer to Cripps and Churchill which is known as the 'Quit India' resolution. 'Depart: we have had enough of your evasions and ambiguities', said the resolution in effect. 'Make the country free now and we will defend it as the Chinese and the Russians and the British have defended their countries. The freedom of India will be at once the symbol and the beginning of the liberation of all other Asian peoples.'

'What happened in India in 1942', wrote Nehru in his *Discovery of India* (written in 1944 but not published until 1946), 'was no sudden explosion but the culmination of all that had preceded it. Much has been written about it, but most of the writers miss the real significance of it, for in all their writings they talk in terms of political motives, whereas there was something here much deeper than politics. At bottom it was the passionate feeling that it was no longer possible to endure life under foreign autocratic domination.'

Many party members were arrested on August 9th, 130 in Bombay alone, including Gandhi, Nehru and Abu I-Kalam Azad, the Moslem president of the Congress; they were all detained in Fort Ahmadnagar. Meantime the whole country was in uproar. In many places the people, uninstigated, attacked the symbols of British tyranny – police stations, railways, stations, telegraph and telephone lines, military transports. Everywhere British – and Indian – troops and police fired on unarmed crowds (British reports an-nounced 539 incidents of the kind): the RAF bombed many villages; in various smaller localities people were beaten up in the streets. Strikes almost everywhere caused extreme tension; in the steel town of Jamshedpur all the workers were out for a fortnight; in Ahmadabad the strike lasted three months. The British casualties amounted to 100 dead; those of the native 'terrorists', according at least to British reports, amounted to 1028, but according to Nehru the true figure was in the neighbourhood of 10,000. It must be admitted that the situation in India was very similar to that in the countries occupied by the Nazis. Abroad in America and in Britain itself, little was known of what was happening. The British remained masters and in December made 60,000 arrests, most of the arrested, including the party leaders, were not released until 1945.

But before the chief figures of the Congress party had disappeared from view, a happening which worked to the advantage of Jinnah and his adherents, the communists had changed their tactics. Between 1939 and 1941 many of them had been sent to prison camps for their activities against the imperialist war. But when the Germans invaded the Soviet Union, a high British official brought to the imprisoned communists, among them Joshi the leader of the party, a letter from the secretary of the British Communist party to the effect that, if they helped the government in the 'anti-fascist war' they would be freed. Joshi and his friends yielded. The Nazi armies were driving to the Volga and the Caucasus; the country and party of Lenin and Stalin was in the gravest danger. In July 1942 Joshi demanded the withdrawal of the ban on the Communist party. That was in the middle of the Cripps period and many Indians regarded the change in communist policy as treachery to the nationalist movement; the exchange of correspondence between Joshi and Gandhi (published in Bombay in 1945) makes interesting reading. It was not easy for the communists to interest an Asian population in a matter which many regarded as a purely European concern, in anti-fascism and the liberation of Europe and the Soviet Union from Nazi domination, at a time when their own land was suffering under the British terror. When in the summer and autumn of 1942 the party tried to prevent strikes, they brought on themselves the hate of all right-thinking nationalists. Compared with left-wing parties in other countries (compare Iran and Irak), the communists in India had considerable freedom of action and many intellectuals had an international outlook, so the party maintained itself, and instead of being, as many thought it would be, overwhelmed by the nationalist flood, increased its strength.

Another extreme policy was represented by Subhas Chandra Bose.[1] In 1941 he fled the country and at his instigation there was created in Southeast Asia, in the sphere of 'Asia for the Asians', the Asat Hind party, i.e. the Indian Independence League, and a free Indian government was set up in Singapore (1943). At the same time he formed an anti-British volunteer corps from the Indians in Malaya and Burma; in Germany and in Western Europe the Germans collected 4000 Indians, including prisoners from North Africa, as recruits. In India-Pakistan the Bose movement was of virtually no importance, although many secretly favoured it. Bose was killed in a flight from Japan to Burma in 1945. He and his supporters became in India symbols of a united Asia fighting for freedom.

Meantime the war was having other effects. India-Pakistan was the seat of the great British war industry in Asia even if – in contrast to Canada and Australia – increase in industrial capacity was sabotaged by Britain quite

[1] v. pp. 262 sq.

openly. The same held good for the shipbuilding and for machinery and car production, although the Americans had ready plans to build factories in India. None the less this was a golden age for the landowners and the great industrialists like Tata, Birla and Damia, and for the jute and cotton spinners and weavers. The upsurge in the native economy freed the country from many foreign burdens, notably from its financial debts to London.

What remained unaltered was the poverty and the tiny rations of the workers and peasants; if they did alter, it was for the worse. The most notorious proof of this is the famine of 1943–4 in the northeast and south of the country, in the course of which 3,400,000 people – the figures are those of the University of Calcutta – died of starvation in Bengal; the British Government reported that 1,500,000 to 2,500,000 had died. The disaster was the terrible consequence of the cold indifference of the administration; besides, there were transport difficulties and chaos in the economic machine; money had become devalued by inflation; rice and grain merchants hoarded supplies and no more rice came in from Southeast Asia.

All this, however, was an apocalyptic prelude to independence. In May 1945 Germany surrendered. Negotiations in Simla between the viceroy, Lord Wavell (1943–1947), and Jinnah, Liaqat Ali Khan and the freed prisoners, Nehru, Desai, Azad and others, broke down within a few days (June 25th–29th) and the country in August 1945 seemed no freer than it was in 1939; freedom none the less was on the way. How India achieved it will be told in the following section.

V

BURMA, THAILAND, INDOCHINA AND MALAYA

WARS have played a great part in arousing the self-consciousness of Asia – the Sino-Japanese War of 1894–1895, the Spanish-American War of 1898, the Western expeditions to China round about 1900, the Russo-Japanese War of 1904–1905, the First World War 1914–1918, the Turkish War of Independence 1919–1923, the intervention and civil war in the Soviet Union 1917–1924, the Japanese invasion of Manchuria in 1931 and of China proper in 1937 and, of course, and particularly, the Second World War.

In 1945 foreign observers noted how strong the freedom movement, earlier relatively feeble on the continent, had grown in Southeast Asia during the Japanese occupation. One of the reasons for this relative – we stress the word relative – unimportance of the nationalist movement in countries like Burma, Indochina and especially Malaya was, as we have said already, the divisions among the populations. We must mention it again, for such divisions are still effective at the present time. Should not the study of history ultimately help us to reach a deeper insight into contemporary and future history? Is it not true what an English writer has said: 'History is the politics of the past; politics is the history of the present'? That was not a Western discovery; the Chinese chroniclers knew it long ago, but Europe had developed the necessary method and techniques – first in the eighteenth century – with the help of which historians can delve into the past more deeply, more purposefully and more objectively than before.

How is the strong difference between the freedom movement in the southeast of the continent and that in, say, British India, the Dutch East Indies and the Philippines to be explained? First and foremost, it is because, by and large, and also culturally, that part of Asia long before the coming of the whites was not independent but merely an outlet for Chinese culture, a frontier zone between China and India and China and Indonesia. The name Indochina generally used in Europe is eloquent of this. In modern times the fresh stream of migration from China and India placed nationalism on a double defensive. In all these countries the nationalists were divided in sympathy with regard to white men and Asians. In Burma there were the Indians and the British, in Malaya the Chinese and the British, in Indochina the Chinese and the French, in Thailand the Chinese and the French and British. The fruits of this internal division in these lands and in their nationalisms, which differed in their aims, were reaped by London and Paris and even by Tokio each in its day; Tokio's day was from 1940 to 1945.

In Burma the war began really in the winter of 1940. In April the Germans had conquered Denmark and Norway, in May and June Holland, Belgium and France. Britain was besieged. The Japanese realized what that meant for Asia and sought to isolate China completely from the West. By June 1940 pressure was put upon the French administration in Indochina and obstacles placed in the way of traffice to China by the Haiphong–Kunming railway. In mid-July pressure was applied to Britain, which closed transport by the Burma road, the mountain road completed in May 1939 from North Burma to Chungking and the only relatively secure way of communication between China and other countries save for the difficult northwest route to Soviet Asia. When the invasion of Britain was delayed, the Japanese began to bomb the roads leading out of Indochina inside and outside the frontiers of China. Meantime London tried to win over the Burmese people and draw them into the Western camp. Many persons were released from prison and immigration of the unwelcome Chinese and Indians was restricted. It was in vain. Britain's hour was already over and too many Burmans now hoped for liberation from the East.

The secret agreement between Tokio and the Burman nationalists united in the National Revolutionary party, to which Ba Maw and the majority of the thakins belonged, dates from the beginning of 1940. It included plans for the creation of a Burmese Liberation army and for independence after an eventual Japanese occupation. During the period of British rule many Burmans joined this secret army, sometimes openly, while the Japanese sent *via* Thailand flowery instructions and ambiguous orders but very few rifles.[1] In December 1941, when U Saw was in London where he demanded independence from Churchill,[2] the Japanese army pushed into Southeast Asia and at the beginning of 1942 into Burma; to Rangoon the rice port and seat of government on March 7th; to Lashio at the head of the Burma road on April 30th; to Mandalay on May 2nd. The British fled westwards and Sir Paw Tun became head of a government in exile in Simla.

The masters of the country reached safety by motor-car, but not the 400,000 Indians; their weeks' long painful trek through the forests to the frontier on which famine, bandits, guerrillas and mosquitoes were allied against them is a sad story.

By the middle of 1942 the Japanese were in full occupation of Burma and only the Arakan hills separated the British Empire in Asia from the Empire of Japan; in the north the Chinese were still defending their frontier.

But there was still no move towards the independence of Burma, although the interim government of Ba Maw (August 1942 to August 1943) did by comparison relieve the situation. In Ba Maw's government were included thakin Than Tun (communist) and thakin Mya and thakin Nu (socialists). Aung San was at the head of the war ministry, i.e. the Burma Liberation army, whose commander-in-chief continued to be the Japanese colonel Minami.

But in 1943, when the picture was beginning to change in Africa and

[1] An interesting account of this period is in *What Happened in Burma,* by Thein Pe, published in Allahabad in 1943. [2] *v.* p. 271.

Europe as well as in the Pacific, the Japanese altered their tactics in the occupied territories and on August 1st the Japanese commander-in-chief in Rangoon, Lieutenant-General Kawabe, declared Burma to be completely independent. Tokio saw clearly now that the day for expansion had passed. The bad news from Stalingrad, of the Italo-German surrender in Africa, of the invasion of Italy, of the renewed activity of the Americans in New Guinea and, above all, of the Anglo-Chinese plans for the reconquest of Burma and the opening of the land route to southwest China had their influence on Tokio. Did not the Japanese army plan for the defence of fronts in Arakan and Yunnan, a modern line of communication between Thailand and southern Burma? This was the sadly notorious Burma railway – not to be confused with the Burma road – from Ratburi near Bangkok right through forest and marsh to Moulmein, whose construction cost the lives of so many Asians as well as Europeans.

Despite all the limitations imposed on it, the independence granted was a liberation, even if naturally the country remained occupied until the war ended, and the activities of the Japanese secret police were bad enough. As a result only a minority was really pro-Japanese, including the Freedom Bloc of Ba Maw (founded February 1940) and the right-wing Myochit party of U Saw, who had been a detainee in Kenya since January 1942. Others, including several thakins and Aung San, had accepted posts in the government merely for tactical reasons. Others again, mostly communists and left socialists, held aloof from a regime which was all too fascist in appearance and in 1943-4 started a secret anti-Japanese movement, the Anti-Fascist Freedom League, whose leaders in 1944-5 were thakin Than Tun and Aung San. Besides these two 'double-faced' parties, the illegal movement had many other contacts with the Ba Maw government.

As in other occupied regions in Asia and various parts of Europe, for instance in France, Italy and Yugoslavia, the core of the resistance movement was composed of left-wing people. Thakin Thein Pe was liaison officer between Than Tun, Aung San, and Mountbatten, British commander-in-chief in Southeast Asia, in Ceylon and Sir Paw Tun in Simla. Semi-secretly thakin Soe travelled through the villages where he conducted guerrilla activity and sought to guide the growing agrarian revolution on the right lines. In 1944-5 in many parts of the country, because of the activities of the resistance, the bad communication and the fact that many landowners like, for instance, the Indian Chettyars, had fled the country, rents were no longer collected and, when liberation came, it was apparent that the peasants were not inclined to recognize the old rights of their former masters, native or foreign.

Meantime the Japanese Empire was contracting. The sinking of many Japanese ships made communications between the different parts of the empire ever more difficult. Americans and Australians landed in the east of Indonesia and in the Philippines, and the more the proud edifice erected by the Japanese tottered the greater became the resistance in the occupied countries.

In the winter of 1944-5 the growing Resistance Army managed to smuggle many British weapons into Burma, partly by air, partly across the Japanese lines, and that was the beginning of liberation in the north and west. The British had their Southeast Asian army ready in the east Indian hills. In March Aung San went secretly to Kandy in Ceylon, where he and Mountbatten discussed plans of campaign. A fortnight later the Burma Liberation army mutinied against its Japanese officers and, while guerrillas everywhere were cutting the Japanese lines of communication, the British Fourteenth Army, reinforced by Americans and Chinese, took the offensive. On March 22nd Mandalay was re-occupied and on May 3rd Rangoon.

By June almost the whole country had been liberated, but only from the Japanese, not from the British. From the White Paper of 1945 it is clear that the Churchill government had no intention of giving Burma back its freedom.

But in Burma, no more than in India-Pakistan, Indonesia, Indochina, Korea, Egypt or anywhere else in the world, the course of history could not be altered. On October 17, 1947, it had gone so far as to let thakin Nu and Attlee, the Socialist prime minister of Britain, sign a treaty in London whereby the Union of Burma (Pyee-Daugn-Su Myanma-Naing-gan) became a fully independent country outside the British Commonwealth.

Field-Marshal Pibul Songgram, the head of the Thailand Government in the critical period 1938–1944, saw by 1944 just what the German attack on Western Europe, the Japanese infiltration into Indochina and the bombing of the Burma road really meant. He fitted his foreign policy accordingly. In the spring of 1941 the Japanese forced the signature of an agreement between France and Thailand, by which Thailand, besides some parts of Laos west of the Mekong, recovered three provinces of Cambodia with their wealth in rice and rubber which France had taken in 1907 – Battambang, Siemreap and Sisophon. That in every sense brought Thailand closer to Japan and farther from Western Europe. At the same time Thailand sought to get into touch with Moscow in order to get its tin, rubber and cotton to Germany *via* Vladivostok and the Trans-Siberian railway. But the plans collapsed after the events in East Europe in June and in the Pacific in December 1941.

We have already related how Thailand on December 8, 1941, resisted the Japanese invasion for only five hours, and then not very energetically, and so came into the Japanese sphere militarily and economically. Diplomatically it remained independent, as the cultural treaty of December 24, 1941, concluded in Bangkok declared, and Thailand suffered little from foreign domination as compared with the other occupied territories in Asia and Europe.

On the contrary it drew profit from it. When, in 1943, the Japanese position in the South Seas was shaken, Tokio permitted Thailand to recover areas which it had formerly possessed – the four Malay kingdoms Kelantan, Trengganu, Kedah and Perlis which in 1909 Britain had annexed to Malaya, and the tiny mountain kingdoms of Kentung and Mong-Pan which in 1886 had been added to Burma, as well as the frontier district between Thailand and Chinese Yunnan in the Salween valley west of the Mekong. This second increase in Thailand territory was the reason for the earlier date for the proclamation of Burmese independence.

Meantime Pibul Songgram on January 25, 1942, declared war on Britain and the United States. Britain replied in kind; the United States remained silent, regarding Thailand as an occupied country whose foreign policy was dictated by Tokio.

It was at the beginning of the Japanese period that the 'Free Thai' movement was started by Pridi and his associates (Chiu Chee, the leader of the leftist Chinese, and the relatively few native communists). This movement sent information abroad, conducting espionage, looked after American pilots whose planes had come down in Thailand and put obstacles in the way of the economic pillage of the country. As did the resistance movement in Burma, Pridi maintained contact with the government and in July 1944 when the Americans had several times bombed Bangkok, the all-too-pro-Japanese field-marshal was replaced as premier by one of his opponents, Khuang Aphaiwong. The secret police knew all about the activity of the Free Thais, but Japan had little inclination to stir up new trouble in Asia and contented itself with a warning not to let things go too far. The Aphai-wong government acted accordingly.

As in Europe, British and American airmen flying at night dropped arms for the guerrillas, and also Thai students as liaison officers and instructors.

The whole country became free again in August 1945 and, in contrast to Burma, Malaya, Indochina and Indonesia, remained free. The Allied leaders had agreed on this at Yalta, partly out of gratitude to Pridi and his friends, but so far as America, China and Russia were concerned, to prevent Britain intervening too seriously for, where Thailand was concerned, Churchill had ambitions as well as a desire for revenge.

It must be admitted that Thailand steered as skilfully as in earlier days between the rocks and sandbanks of imperialist policies. Britain recovered the regions in North Burma and North Malaya lost in 1943, France her possessions in Indochina. Thailand sent shiploads of rice to India-Pakistan and other countries on her own initiative, and in 1946 diplomatic relations were restored with Britain, the United States, China and the Soviet Union; nothing untoward happened except the British proviso that a canal between the South China Sea and the Indian Ocean across Thai territory in the Malay Peninsula should not be constructed without the prior consent of Britain. To crown its recovered status Thailand, in December 1946, was admitted to the United Nations in fourth place after Afghanistan, Iceland and Sweden – excluding, of course, the founding members.

In June 1941 Paris fell, the city of the Revolution and to all the world a symbol of freedom; Hitler had now added all western Europe to his empire. On September 27th, Germany, Italy and Japan agreed on their secret plans of campaign – a co-ordination of the fascist expansion in Europe and Africa which had begun in 1935 and the Japanese campaign in East Asia which had begun with the Chinese 'incident' in 1931.

The plan did not remain simply on paper. In the summer of 1940,[1] the Japanese occupied several ports in Indochina by agreement with the somewhat pro-fascist governor-general Decoux. Tokio in August recognized French sovereignty and the territorial integrity of the country, but at the same time began to take possession of Indochina, of course in France's name.

The French administration had never ceased to refuse to increase the very restricted freedom of the native population, therein differing in no way from the Dutch and the British. A communist rebellion in Cochinchina was nipped in the bud, and similar movements in Tonkin and North Annam (in the region of Langson and in Duo Long). Many Frenchmen were more afraid of Indochinese independence and the leftist Chinese there and elsewhere than of the orders and duplicity of the Japanese officers. Are not fascism and imperialism everywhere akin? A narrow reactionary like Decoux, and other French officials too, treated these foreign officers as themselves, as members of a master race even if they were yellowskinned and intruders; the native nationalists they regarded as 'red incendiaries'.

By the winter of 1940–1 the French had to all intents and purposes capitulated. That was seen at the beginning of 1941 when Thailand[1] took the frontier provinces of Laos and Cambodia. In July and August a Japanese occupation force of two divisions appeared. Simultaneously the Germans were advancing in the Ukraine; Moscow, Leningrad and Cairo were threatened and Persia had been divided between Russia and Britain, because it was the bridge between Russia and the sea. The United States, which was not yet at war, was on guard and forbade the export of iron and steel to Japan; for the Americans, Japanese ambition was going too far. That, of course, did not prevent Japan from attacking the American islands in the Pacific in December 1941 and to occupy all Southeast Asia and the western part of the Pacific in less than twelve weeks.

These events brought little change in Indochina. The French officials, the soldiers and the planters remained in their posts. Frenchmen and their wives and children were not interned. Indochina was the only case in which Europeans were allowed to remain free in a Japanese-occupied Asian country.

It must be carefully noted that a small number of Frenchmen who thought differently from most of their compatriots had left the country and travelling via China had reported for service to their chief, the leader of the Free French, General de Gaulle. Others joined the resistance movement inside the country, passed on secret information and circulated wireless news from the free world. Many of them lost their lives. But the great majority of the French did as they were told by the Japanese and shared, at least at first (1940–1943), the fascist views of Vichy, while France was being drained dry

[1] v. p. 242.   [2] v. p. 248.

of her wine and her corn and her coal, and her workers and soldiers were being sent to Germany.

In Indochina the Japanese in the end left off imitating the renowned French courtliness, for in 1945 they interned the French and gave some freedom of action to the native nationalism. From the economic point of view the country was naturally all through the war the scene of Japanese exploitation; in the five-year plan of 1942, Indochina was exploited as the chief jute district in Asia and in 1943–4 Chinese and Indochinese worked on the never-completed motor road from Korea to Singapore. It was a case of forced labour and many of the workers died at their task.

Meantime the revolutionaries had, in the winter of 1940–1, shifted their base of operations from Vietnam to South China. Here at Liuchow, quite near to the Japanese army headquarters in Canton, communists and sympathizers founded in 1941 the 'Independence League' of Vietnam, better known as Viet Minh; it was, and remains, anti-fascist, anti-Japanese and anti-French. Its leader was the communist Nguyen Ai Quoc, who took the name of Ho Chi Minh.[1] The Chinese government welcomed with delight the Indochinese movement. They hated the French administration, which in 1940 had cut the railway to Kunming and so made easy the advance of the Japanese into South China. Had not Paris tried to colonize Yunnan and had not Indochina once been Chinese territory? None the less the communist leanings of the Viet Minh annoyed Chungking. For that reason Ho Chi Minh was arrested as a French spy and every effort was made to further the building-up of a non-communist resistance party in Indochina known as the Dong Minh Hoi (at Liuchow in October 1942); it was an extension of the VNQDD which had been active in the Yenbay mutiny of 1930.[2] It was hoped that it would absorb the Viet Minh, thus diluting the communist poison.

It was soon seen that this was a miscalculation. The Viet Minh, theoretically a part of Dong Minh Hoi (in Indochina), kept apart from it. The centre of the Indochinese resistance was not Dong Minh Hoi; it remained Viet Minh. Ho, who was released in 1943, had, like Gandhi and Sun Yat-sen, many of the qualities of a great revolutionary and in the hour of danger fought with all his power to preserve freedom. When the Indochinese of both parties started the guerrilla war against Japan in North Tonkin – the Chinese, Free French and Americans gave them weapons – it was almost always the Viet Minh who took the lead. Their commander was the man who later was to command in chief in the war of independence against the French, Vo Nguyen Gap (b. 1912). In 1940–2 in North China he had studied the guerrilla tactics of Mao and his associates.

Meantime, and especially in 1944, the atmosphere in Indochina, in Japan and internationally had changed; the Germans were retiring, almost fleeing, from the Soviet Union; France was liberated by the Normandy landing; the Americans were extending their conquests in the Pacific and in October landed in the Philippines. These reports and orders from de Gaulle reached

[1] *v.* pp. 137, 240.   [2] *v.* p. 241.

the French Government in Indochina and many Indochinese sympathized with the new government in liberated Paris.

In February 1945 the Americans recaptured Manila. Because of its huge shipping losses Japan was isolated from South Asia. In March Tokio asked the French for help in an eventual American invasion, Decoux neither consented or refused, and on March 9th the Japanese authories began to intern all Frenchmen. The French army capitulated within a week; only a few regiments cut their way through from Tonkin to China. A few Frenchmen volunteered for service with the Viet Minh and the Dong Minh Hoi.

To keep matters under control, the Japanese on March 11, 1945, declared the whole country, except for Laos and Cambodia, to be independent. The new state was called Vietnam, a name which was used in the eighteenth century to describe Tonkin, Annam and Cochinchina. The emperor of Annam, Bao Dai, became emperor of Vietnam and Tran Trong Kim became premier. The new government was too friendly to Japan and the population generally kept aloof from the fickle emperor and his adherents. Indochina earnestly desired freedom and a real independence under the Viet Minh and the Dong Minh Hoi, whose guerrillas had already (May 1945) liberated various districts in the north.

Bao Dai and Kim realized the situation and, after the Japanese dream of empire vanished for ever in August among the smoking ruins of Hiroshima, both disappeared from the Government, Kim on August 15th, the emperor on the 26th, the latter saying he wished to be a free citizen of an independent country. On August 16th the Liberation Committee of the Viet Minh had formed a broader-based government in Hanoi. Ho was premier and Bao Dai, as 'Citizen Vinh Thuy', was an influential political adviser. On September 2nd, the Democratic Republic of Vietnam announced to the world its declaration of independence. In it there was much reminiscent of the formulae of the French and the Russian revolutions. It began with a translation of the second paragraph of the American Declaration of Independence: 'All men are created equal . . . they have received from their Creator inalienable rights . . . the right to life, freedom and the pursuit of happiness.'

Ho's government was generally accepted in the country as the legitimate government. The relatively few Japanese offered no resistance. Vietnam was ruled as an independent country and was not in the least a political vacuum when in mid-September the British began to occupy it from the south and the Chinese from the north. This occupation had been agreed to at Potsdam in July 1945, and the boundary between the two zones of occupation fixed at Hué in the centre of Annam on the 16th parallel; there was a similar partition in Korea, where the Russians and Americans disarmed the Japanese.

In the north the Chinese were out for loot and rape, and had no interest in the internal affairs of the country. The British acted very differently in the south; they had no feelings against the French. In addition to British and Indian troops, some Free French divisions were landed at Saigon on September 11, 1945. Meantime Paris complained that the British commander-in-chief was not dealing sternly with the native rebels; the French, therefore, occupied Saigon on September 23rd. By the time the British (in February) and the Chinese (in August 1946) had withdrawn their troops, the liberator of Paris, General Leclerc, had already several divisions in Indochina.

Liberation and freedom are not quite the same thing, as was shown once again in Indochina. During the war General de Gaulle had promised to rule Indochina 'in the spirit of the great French Revolution'. Now the French refused its former colony any real freedom. What happened in Indochina was just what happened in Indonesia or in Britain's Southeast Asia possessions. Even the semi-freedom assured the country by the Dalat agreement of March 6, 1946, annoyed the French overlords and the reactionary French circles to which the high commissioner d'Argenlieu belonged.

Their intrigues against the new leftish government in faraway France were not without results. The French bombardment of Haiphong on November 23, 1946, meant the beginning of what was generally called the 'monstrous war', one of the bitterest and most serious colonial wars in French history – at least so far. In 1954 France had some 450,000 men in the field, half of whom came from Europe and North Africa. It was a war in which Indochina bled and France destroyed all her bridges to Asia.

In the northwest corner of the South China Sea off the Indochinese coast lies the large Chinese island of Hainan, some 120 to 180 miles from the coast of Indochina. Early on February 10, 1939, a big Japanese fleet appeared and in a short time the island was in Japanese hands. In the prophetic words of Chiang Kai-shek, this was 'of historic international significance; it marked the beginning of the Japanese attack on the whole Pacific region, was a direct threat to Indochina and in wartime cut the communications between Singapore and Hongkong and between Singapore and Hawaii'.

The Western governments were, however, neither ready nor able to understand the signs of the times, even if the occupation of Hainan, like earlier 'incidents' in the Far East, came at a time of angry excitement in Europe. In January 1939 the rebel fascists had attacked Barcelona, where in summer Nehru had spent a few days during the nightly bombing and had realized that it was in that city and not in Paris or London, Geneva or Munich that European democracy was being defended. In the first weeks of February, at the time of the Hainan occupation, the resistance of Socialist Spain was crushed by Franco and his German and Italian allies. In March Hitler wiped Czechoslovakia from the map of Europe.

Hainan became what Chiang feared it would become, the outpost of Asian imperialism. On December 4, 1941, while the Germans were pressing into the suburbs of Moscow, a Japanese fleet sailed from Hainan southward and on the same day landed 45,000 troops, not at Singapore – which was bombed on December 17th – but on the east coast of Malaya some 270 miles north of it.

The safety of the island of Singapore, the symbol of the domination by the West of Southeast Asia – Britain had just spent £50,000,000 on defence works – was, or so military experts believed, assured by its 15-inch guns pointing seawards, its 350 aircraft and its warships; among the last were the *Prince of Wales* and the *Repulse*, which had just arrived.

On the news of the landings in Malaya both ships sailed to the north to sink the Japanese transports. The reverse happened; under a hail of air torpedoes both ships sank beneath the waters of the South China Sea. Ships alone, even British ships, were not safe against air attack. The Western democracies began to shiver. The loss of these ships in Eastern waters did not fit into the picture which the West had conceived, and Asia thought back to 1905, to the historic destruction of the Russian Baltic fleet in the Straits of Tsushima.

On December 11th, Germany and Italy declared war on the United States, and in that week the invading army of Yamashita began to move southward in three columns down the Malay Peninsula. On February 8, 1942, they were crossing the narrow strip of water that separates the mainland from Singapore, where the oil stores were already ablaze. On the 15th, while the Japanese were invading Sumatra, the proud fortress was in Japanese hands. In seventy days Yamashita had taken 70,000 prisoners; the rubber of Asia had been placed out of reach of Britain and America and the fable of 'invulnerable Singapore' had been exploded. It was, as Churchill said, 'the greatest catastrophe in the history of the British Empire'.

Malaya was the only country in Southeast Asia which the Japanese virtually ruled as a colony, and where there was no mention made of independence, even although the Malayan nationalists had certainly more freedom than under British rule. The division conditioned by history between the native Malays and the Chinese was fully exploited. Many Chinese workers within and outside Malaya were compelled to build roads, ships, ports and bunkers. Many Indians, volunteers and others, were pressed into the labour battalions of the Japanese Second Army and Bose's Indian Army. As in other lands, Tokio pillaged the country economically.

In the resistance movement Chinese were most prominent. Of these some hundreds of thousands were peasants and often dwelt in the pathless savage districts beyond the reach of the secret police; for the most part they had left sympathies.

In the period 1937 to June 1941, when Germany attacked Russia, the British had arrested many communist leaders, mostly Chinese, during the series of strikes in the port of Singapore and in the tin mines and rubber plantations. As in the second half of 1941 these seemed ready to abandon their anti-British activities, they had full liberty of movement while the Japanese invasion was in progress. When British resistance ended they vanished into the hills of Perak and Johore and formed the core of an anti-Japanese guerrilla army consisting of Chinese, Indians and relatively few Malays. When in 1944–5 London began to send weapons and instructors, the resistance movement was already in possession of some 10,000 rifles.

As in Europe, the Resistance Army was not of much value from a military point of view, but it was of very great importance as a fermenting factor in the nationalist and social revolution in Malaya and Southeast Asia. It gathered together the communists and other left-wingers in Malaya, which became British again in 1945. At the signing in Singapore on September 12th of the Japanese surrender in Southeast Asia and Indonesia, the guerrillas, by agreement with Mountbatten the British commander-in-chief, kept their arms, and on their demobilization in December many of them stayed in their hills where from 1948 they waged a bitter desperate communist revolutionary war; they were and are communists, but like Mao in China and Ho Chi Minh in Indochina they were also anti-imperialists.

Even if in 1945–6 there was the passing vision of an independent Malaya, it was plain in 1948 that, quite apart from the rubber and the tin and the fear of international communism (China and the 'cold war'), the permanent division in the population encouraged the British, in contrast to what was done elsewhere, to keep Malaya in the Empire. The parties were small islands in a sea of dissension, parties which sought to unite what nature and history had put asunder: the natives and the Chinese and Indian immigrants. We may mention the Malay Nationalist party (Ipoh, October 1945, the result of Malay-Japanese efforts in 1944–5) which, so far as its ideas went, was comparable to the PNI in Indonesia, especially in its left period; it was pan-Malay in its aims and was generally led by Indonesian immigrants like Mokh Tarrudin and Dr Burhanuddin. We may also mention the equally leftist Malay Democratic Union (December 1945), which aimed at linking up the Chinese and Indian movements with the Malay nationalists.

Not until the parties get clarity in their ideas and these have spread to the population generally will the country be completely free.

VI

INDONESIA AND THE PHILIPPINES

THERE never was any mystery about Japanese aims in the Pacific – the creation of a Japanese East Asia from Korea to Australia and then to take in Eastern Siberia and all the islands of the Pacific.

In September 1939, when France and Britain were involved in the war in Europe, the Japanese imperial armies had already occupied many districts in China, including all the ports and islands amounting in area to a quarter of China and including half of the population. In the early summer of 1940 came the first signs of the final catastrophe. America made it known that she would resist any attempt by Tokio by any means other than diplomatic to alter the political situation of Indonesia, then the Dutch East Indies (April 17th).

When the Germans conquered Holland and France and added them to their European empire, I. Kobayashi, the Japanese minister of economics, went as an observer to Batavia. It was soon perceived that he was there to demand what the French in Indochina had granted, that is, ports, air bases and economic concessions. Unlike the Vichy regime, the Netherlands Government in London and their officials in Batavia refused; they would concede only a little salt and oil. If Kobayashi expected that Britain would give up the struggle while he was negotiating, he waited in vain and went home again. The inclusion of Indonesia in the Japanese Empire did not proceed as the inclusion of Indochina had done; on the contrary, it would need war.

The commercial negotiations were resumed in 1941 by K. Yoshizawa, apparently only to secure what had been obtained by the restrictions on foreigners in Japan itself, secrecy for all that was being prepared in the Japanese shipyards and factories and in the camps in Hainan, Formosa and Indochina.

On December 7th the black day of Pearl Harbour came. Four hours later the government in Batavia declared war on Japan, although it had no one behind it save the Dutch living in Indonesia. Had not Dutch obstinacy and lack of understanding prevented the growth of a free democratic and anti-Japanese Indonesia? The Dutch navy had three cruisers and about twenty smaller ships of little value in Indonesian waters. A very tiny army of some 40,000 men with fairly modern equipment kept in subjection an island realm over 3000 miles in length.

Three weeks later the storm reached the frontiers of Indonesia. Dark clouds lay over the northern horizon. Hongkong fell (December 25th), then Manila (January 2nd) and then Malaya. On December 22nd, Japanese marines landed in British North Borneo and on January 10, 1942, on the Indonesian oil island of Tarakan, and in the second half of January they landed on North Celebes, on the islands north and east of New Guinea and on Ambon (January 31st). A sea battle (January 24th–27th) in the Straits of Macassar could not prevent the Japanese transports moving south.

The invasion of the tin islands of Banka and Bulliton between Sumatra and Borneo and the air landings on the oilfields of Palembang (February 12th–14th), the capture of Singapore (February 15th) and of parts of Bali (February 18th) isolated Java.

Next day Port Darwin, the only port on the north coast of Australia, was bombed. The desperate attempt – known as the battle of the Java Sea (February 27th–28th) – of British, Dutch and American ships to prevent the Japanese transports reaching Java was, considered from the purely military angle, a senseless affair even if it is, and rightly, written in letters of gold in the history of the Dutch navy. Only four small American ships succeeded in escaping; all the others were sunk.

The actual occupation of Java took only a week. On March 9th the capitulation was signed in Bandung. That meant the final defeat of Dutch rule in Indonesia, though at the time no one knew or wished to know it. Long before their invasion, the Japanese had prepared plans for the government of the occupied territories, Over Indonesia there was a difference of opinion. The Japanese occupation authorities aimed first and foremost at 'japanizing' Indonesia and estranging it from the West. With the help of the 'AAA-Action' (Pergerakan Tiga A, April 1942: Nippon the light of Asia, the protector of Asia, the leader of Asia) they tried to convince Indonesia of the high importance of the culture, the language and the history of the liberators. Naturally history, and especially that of modern Japan, had much to teach Asia – and also the West – but the invasion of a foreign, even if it was an Asian, culture no more meant freedom than did economic penetration, introduction of Japanese time, lack of rice, restrictions on transport and movement, and the terror of the secret police.

Those who longed for a free democratic Indonesia were not unaware of the imperialist and fascist tendencies of the new masters. Many Indonesians, e.g. Shahrir and Sharifudin, were opposed to them and formed an illegal movement. Many others, like Sukarno and Hatta, hoped to bring independence nearer by being pro-Japanese and getting the support of the occupation authorities. There was a difference of mentality as well as of tactics. The aim of both was the same, the freedom of Indonesia. They understood each other, and all through the war remained in contact; Hatta and Shahrir, for instance, through Djohan Sharuzah and Dr Abdul Halim. Things were different here from the situation in Europe where collaboration with the Germans was treachery to the freedom of the nation. The Japanese occupation, considered objectively, had functions other than those of the German occupation of Europe.

In the early summer of 1943 it was evident that the Germans would not reach either the Volga and the Caucasus (Stalingrad) or Egypt (El Alamein), and at the same time the Japanese advance was stopped at Guadalcanal. Tokio began to change its tactics. While its plans matured for the independence of Burma and the Philippines (August and October 1943), a union was brought about of all the not-forbidden parties and tendencies in Java and Madura (March 1943) by the founding of the 'Pusat Tenaga Rakjat' (Putera), whose Indonesian leaders were Sukarno, Hatta and Ki Hadjar Dewantoro (Suwardi Sufjaningrat). In a roundabout way through the Putera the occupation authorities tried to increase the production of rice, quinine, tin and oil at the expense of coffee, tea and sugar, to introduce improved methods of cultivation in the villages, to mobilize workers and soldiers, and generally to represent their imperialism as the liberation of Great East Asia.

In this period there was created the Hei Ho, a semi-voluntary labour service, and, above all, the Sukerela Tentara Pembela Tanah Air (Peta), the volunteer legion of Java for the defence of the land against an eventual invasion. The *Sukarelas* (volunteers) were officered by Indonesians only, and the legion, which in August 1945 was 120,000 strong, was the core of the republican army. Actually the Putera and kindred organizations strengthened Indonesian self-consciousness which, in contrast to what obtained under Dutch rule, increased formidably. In the smallest villages the speeches of Hatta, Sukarno and their fellows were heard on the radio. Because of their prominent position and their freedom of movement, which was so much greater than it used to be, they awakened in many hearts the picture of an 'Indonesia Merdeka', which had, to all appearances, only been asleep, in which no foreign imperialists would hinder the rise of their own country. In veiled speech they rejected equally the Asian imperialism from the north. In various ways Sukarno and Hatta influenced the Indonesian officers and soldiers, the intellectuals and peasants, not only against the Dutch but also against the Japanese. This on the whole purely Indonesian agitation, one not blindly directed against the West alone, was not to the taste of the army of occupation. By the side of the all-too-independent Putera there was established at the time of the American attack on the Marshall Islands (Kwajelein, Eniwetok) and the capture of Hollandia in February–March 1944 (i.e. at the time when the Germans were being driven out of South Russia), the Djawa Hokokai (Perhimpunan Kebaktian Rakjat) in which Sukarno, though nominally its leader, had at the outset much less influence in it than the delegates of the Japanese commander-in-chief. There was also the Moslem Madjelis Shura Muslinin Indonesia (Mashumi), through which the occupation authorities sought to win the actively Moslem section of the people. But neither the Mashumi nor the Hokokai came up to Japanese expectations.

Because of these and other events in 1944, something must be said of the real resistance movement. The first and biggest anti-Japanese movement was the anti-fascist group of Amir Sharifudin and others, including many communists from the illegal PKI. The occupation authorities hated and feared Sharifudin's group, and the main effort of the secret police was directed to eliminating it. It is probable that, from 1944–5 at least, the group round Sutan Shahrir was of the greater importance, particularly among the modern intellectual circles in the towns. A third group was the Persatuan Mahasis

(Union of Students) of the students of the University of Jakarta, especially the medical students; it was very close to the Shahrir group. Its criticism of principles was almost open and had much to do with the spread of anti-Japanese feeling.

The chief aim of the resistance movement was to infiltrate into Peta and kindred organizations, get in their own officers, and prepare them and others for anti-Japanese action when the Anglo-American invasion eventually took place.

As in other occupied countries the resistance in Indonesia came in the main, but not exclusively, from the left. It had, however, no contact with the outside world. Dr van Mook and the other Dutchmen in Camp Hollandia and those in London, because of their lack of information but also because of their total lack of understanding of the actual development, had even in 1944-5 a completely wrong view of the situation. As 'children of another age' none of them expected a general revolution in Indonesia; at most Japanese time-bombs, perhaps, and calls to action by 'extremists'.

In Tokio the conflict of opinion had unwittingly served the Indonesian national movement. The foreign ministry wanted the creation at an early date of a confederation free in name at least; only the primitive regions like Borneo and New Guinea would continue to be governed by Japan. But the military authorities in Tokio and Singapore were generally against any independence until the war was over. Indonesia was invited to the famous East Asian Conference in Tokio of November 1943; at it were representatives of Japan, China (the part of it ruled by Japan, with Nanking as capital), Manchukuo, Burma, Thailand and the Philippines; and a representative of Bose's Indian government also turned up.

Early in 1944 Japan's communications were in danger; in summer 800 merchant ships were lost. In July, after the loss of Saipan, the Japanese naval base in the Marianas, the former governor-general of Korea, Koiso, became premier and found the army not inclined to oppose the declaration of Indonesian independence.

On September 7, 1944, while the Americans were getting ready to attack the Philippines (October) and the Germans were fleeing from France, Belgium, Eastern and Southern Europe, the Koiso government promised to declare Indonesia independent very soon; no date was mentioned. Fulfilment of the promise took time, but it was not an empty one. By October the Hokokai had much more freedom, the red and white flag was no longer forbidden and could be seen in most places, the word 'Indonesiazin' replaced the former rather colonial name. Several Indonesians received high posts in the provincial administrations in Java. Sukarno and his associates could speak openly of independence.

One of the most interesting innovations was Asrama Indonesia Merdeka (Institute of Free Indonesia), which was more or less connected with the University in Jakarta and Surabaya. Lectures were held for students on nationalism, economics, political science, sociology, Marxism and so forth. Hatta and Shahrir were among the lecturers, as well as officials of the news services. They had complete freedom of speech, although what they said was often far from the views of AIM. Meantime the Americans, and so independence, were coming nearer. To study the principles of independence and the ways of attaining it, a great commission was set up on March 1, 1945, of which Sukarno, Hatta and sixty others were members.

To it on June 1, 1945, Sukarno delivered his famous speech on the five principles (*pantja sila*). His words, which were taken to indicate the leading ideas and the philosophical basis of an independent democratic Indonesia, had almost revolutionary effect and caused much resentment among the occupation authorities. The five principles are an interesting blend of Western democracy, modern Islam, Marxism and the native agrarian democracy – 1. nationalism in the widest sense of the term; 2. humanism or internationalism: 'internationalism can develop only on the soil of nationalism; nationalism can only be developed within an international framework'; 3. people's sovereignty or political democracy; 4. social justice or social economic democracy, in support of which he quoted Jean Jaurès, the French socialist leader murdered in 1914, and 5. religious freedom.

In February the Americans occupied Manila, and on April 1st they landed on Okinawa only some 340 miles from Japan. A new government, under Suzuki (April 8, 1945), took command of a sinking ship. From April to July, with the British and Chinese occupying Burma, with the Americans and Australians in Borneo and other islands in eastern Indonesia, the Japanese calmly went on with their preparations for Indonesian independence. On August 14th Sukarno and Hatta returned from talks with the Japanese authorities in Indochina with the mission of 'determining when Indonesia shall become independent'. On his return Sukarno spoke to a huge crowd at the Kemajoran airfield: 'If I told you before that Indonesia would be free before the corn is ripe, I can now tell you that Indonesia will be free before the corn is in ear.' That day was the real date of the capitulation of Japan, although the imperial order to cease fire was not issued until the afternoon of the 16th; officially it reached the Japanese in Jakarta only on the 18th.

Slight differences of opinion between Sukarno and Hatta on the one side and Shahrir and others of the illegal movement on the other held things up, but on the night of August 16th–17th the declaration of independence was published in Jakarta. Dated Jakarta, August 17, 1945, and signed 'in the name of the Indonesian people' by Sukarno and Hatta; it said: 'We, the people of Indonesia, hereby declare the independence of Indonesia. All the measures for the transfer of functions will be carried out in a suitable manner and in the shortest possible time.' The text was published that same day about 10 a.m. Indonesian time). 'Pemudas', students and Indonesian officials saw that it was distributed throughout the country. Indonesian journalists of the Domei agency telegraphed it abroad. The revolution had begun and neither British nor Dutch soldiers could check it.

Early on December 27, 1949, the Netherlands recognized the independence of the country off whose coast (at Bantam on June 22, 1596) the first four Dutch ships had cast anchor, over three and a half centuries before.

In the grey of the morning of December 7, 1941, six Japanese carriers were 170 miles off Hawaii. At six o'clock, to the accompaniment of thundering *banzais,* the first wave of bombers flew off towards the American naval base. This was the bloody Sunday of Pearl Harbour. Only bad weather prevented a simultaneous attack on the Philippines. On the afternoon of the 8th the Japanese destroyed the airport of Manila and on the 10th the naval base at Cavite. Meantime the transports of Yamamoto were sailing unhindered eastwards to Guam and Hongkong, to Wake Island and Malaya. On December 17th Japanese marines landed in the north of Luzon, and in a single surge General Masaharu's troops with their small tanks had penetrated to the heart of the archipelago.

Surrounded by masses of Japanese warships and isolated between Formosa, Hainan, Indochina and the Japanese islands in the southwest Pacific the American commander-in-chief MacArthur had little freedom of movement. That was still more evident in these critical weeks when the maintenance of what were essentially colonial conditions took its revenge. The small native army had not a free country behind it; the population's reaction was that which was general in Southeast Asia; it stayed neutral and often secretly friendly to the Japanese. Many greeted the invaders as liberators; even Quezon in the besieged camp of Bataan was not really pro-American at heart. Through MacArthur he wired to Roosevelt his plan to neutralize the Philippines and make them a sort of Switzerland of the Pacific in which neither Washington nor Tokio would have any say.

In general, the Asian leaders, much earlier and much more clearly than the Western governments, grasped – because they wanted to grasp – what was coming in Japan and the rest of Asia. Nehru had good reason to complain as he did in 1939 of 'the total incapacity of the West to read the signs of the times and comprehend what is happening'.

The small American squadron in Philippine waters could not prevent a Japanese landing, and fled southward to be involved and destroyed in the battle of the Java Sea (February 26–27, 1942). Before that, on December 26, 1941, MacArthur and his 20,000 American and 70,000 Filipino troops had retreated to the Bataan peninsula and the rocky island fortress of Corregidor, which like a cork in a bottle lies at the entrance to Manila harbour. On January 2, 1942, Homma occupied Manila, and Cavite and all the islands in a few weeks. In Bataan and on Corregidor, where MacArthur was putting up a fierce defence, troops fresh from the victory at Singapore brought a decision. Bataan fell on April 9th, Corregidor in the bloody night of May 5th–6th.

Meantime, as we have already related, MacArthur, Quezon and Osmena had received orders from Washington to leave Bataan (March 7th). MacArthur landed in Australia where, as commander-in-chief in the Pacific, he established permanent headquarters; the two Filipinos went on to Washington and, while the war lasted, were the leaders of the Filipino Government in the United States.

The Philippines were now Japanese. And not only the Philippines for, as we know, Malaya, Singapore, Burma and Indonesia had already all been conquered. The dark days of the Japanese occupation and the birthpangs of the liberation of Southeast Asia had begun.

As might be expected Japanese rule in the Philippines had the same characteristics as in the other occupied areas of Asia – the imposition of Japanese culture and ideology, economic exploitation and the terror of the secret police directed against everything which opposed the invader. At the same time the islands were, at least to a considerable extent, freed from Western imperialism, a development which Europe and America did not realize in time and the more so as quite early in the occupation Tokio granted the Filipinos a degree of freedom in local administration. This was the period of the Vargas government 1942–3, which can be compared with the contemporary Ba Maw government in Burma. Besides, on October 14, 1943, Lieutenant-General Kurodo declared that military rule was at an end and that the Philippines were independent. Jose Laurel, an important legal figure in the earlier government of the Partido Nacionalista, was made head of a new government, in which the well-known Manuel A. Roxas held several posts; from April 1946 to April 1948 he was president. Despite its anti-American and anti-European leanings, the Laurel government contrived not to antagonize the Americans too much; the Philippines did not declare war on the United States and Britain until October 1944; Burma had done so in August 1943. By and large, it was the rich and the reactionary who were ready definitely to take Japan's side. This is one of the reasons why three-quarters of the Filipino resistance turned left. The guerrillas of the Hukbalahap (Hukbong Bayan Laban sa Hapon, i.e. the anti-Japanese People's army) became active as early as March 1942. Their soldiers were small peasants, workers on the land, and workers from Manila and the towns; their chief officers and leaders were socialists and communists from Manila like Pedro Abad Santos, Luis Taruc, Dr Vincente Lava and Casto Alejandrino. Their movement was particularly strong in Luzon, where they not only carried on their anti-Japanese activity but spread the gospel of the agrarian revolution. In several districts the big estates of the *caciques* were divided up.

At the beginning of 1944 the Hukbalahap got into radio contact with the American command in the Pacific; the Americans sent weapons and munitions, and 10,000 resistance men were ready when, in the autumn of 1944, the oft-quoted promise of MacArthur, 'I will come back', was fulfilled.

On October 20th the American Sixth Army landed on the wooded west coast of Leyte southwest of Luzon, and a few days later MacArthur himself went ashore. Marshal Terauchi knew very well what would happen if he could not hold up the invasion; the Japanese Empire would be cut in two and Japan cut off from Southeast Asia. He removed Kurodo from the command-in-chief of the Japanese land forces, replaced him by Yamashita, the man who had taken Singapore and Bataan-Corregidor, and summoned virtually the whole fleet to Philippine waters. On October 23rd a hundred ships had assembled and three fleets coming from the west sought to reach Leyte through the numerous straits between the islands, while a fourth came down from the north. Only Takeo Kurita's squadron caught sight of the American transports off Samar on October 25th. Between the islands the Japanese were defeated in the thrilling three days' battle of the Philippines (October 23rd to 25th). This was the sixth decisive naval battle in the war in the Pacific – the others were Pearl Harbour, the Java Sea, Midway, Guadalcanal (one of the British Solomon Islands) and Saipan (one of the Marianas) – and it was also the greatest naval battle in history. On the night of December 25th Nimitz, the American naval commander-in-chief in the Far East, announced the sinking of a third of the Japanese ships, including four carriers, three battle-ships (including the *Musashi,* one of the two biggest battleships in the world), ten cruisers and many smaller craft. Yamashita could expect no more naval aid.

The situation in the air was just as bad, even if Japanese airmen began their terrible suicide *kamikadze* tactics, i.e. the crashing of their aircraft on American ships on whose decks they were smashed to pieces. The Japanese say that the first suicide pilot was Vice-Admiral Masabumi Arima (October 15, 1944).

In December the Americans occupied Samar and Mindoro. On January 8, 1945, came the landings on western Luzon, particularly in Lingayen Bay; the troops were brought in 800 ships. The Huks and other guerrillas hindered Japanese operations by blocking roads and destroying bridges. Manila, where every house was defended by veteran marines, was completely invested by the 24th. Mindanao, in the Celebes Sea, was conquered in May. On May 1st the Australians invaded the oil island of Tarakan and on July 1st Balikpapan, showing that Japan was now completely impotent at sea. All this happened when Japanese cities were burning, when their armies were withdrawing from Burma and China, and the Russians were occupying what was left of Berlin. On July 5th MacArthur announced that the Philippines campaign had ended. The island Empire was rent in twain; Indonesia and Southeast Asia were isolated and the islands of Japan itself were defenceless. The obstinate defence put up on Luzon by Yamashita cost the lives of 400,000 soldiers and sailors as well as 9000 aircraft.

On February 27, 1945, MacArthur welcomed Sergio Osmena, returned from his American exile, as head of the civil government; after Quezon's death on August 1, 1944, Osmena had succeeded him as head of the Filipino Government in exile in Washington.

The Americans kept the promise on independence which they had given in 1943. On July 4, 1946, the islands were free, although in the economic and military spheres the freedom was somewhat restricted, just as it was in India in 1947 and in Indonesia in 1949.

That liberation from imperialism does not turn a country overnight into a paradise was painfully felt in the Philippines because of the continued resistance of the small peasants. Neither the Americans nor the national governments were able to root out the Huks. Communist guerrilla activity was the expression of the Asian agrarian revolution at that time. Military action can restrict that activity but it cannot be completely crushed. Only a modern democratic administration, artificial manures, electricity and agricultural machinery can in this age of immense possibilities peacefully transform a mediaeval village population into a modern nation.

VII

CHINA

MORE than once we have indicated how, while the Second World War furthered the awakening of Asia, the undercurrents of social revolution on the land was gaining ground. This is particularly true of China. In 1931 (the 'Mukden incident') and then in 1937 (the 'Pekin incident') the Japanese Government was already endeavouring to prevent the growth of a united Chinese republic, and the development of the double revolution because its ambition was to take the place of China as the dominant land in East Asia. As a minor example of what is known as the irony of history we may note that by its aggression Tokio only achieved, or helped to achieve, what it did not at all desire – a partial reunion of the Kuo Min-tang and the communists, an increase in self-consciousness in those parts of China that remained unconquered, and the spreading of the communist revolution once it became clear that the communists were the real and democratic defenders of Chinese independence.

There is only one word, and that is 'sad', to describe the spectacle which China presented at the beginning of 1942 when the Japanese attacked Southeast Asia, when China signed the charter of the United Nations[1] and Chiang became commander-in-chief of the theatre of war, China–Indochina–Thailand–Burma.

In the period between the commencement of the Japanese occupation of Manchuria in the summer of 1931 and the historic kidnapping of Chiang at the end of 1936, the Kuo Min-tang used up their few modernly equipped troops in not very serious fighting against the communist resistance and the agrarian revolution. Meantime Japanese imperial troops coming from Kwantung had occupied almost the whole of northeastern China which can be called China's Ruhr, and China became an Asian Spain where Tokio experimented with its weapons of war just as Germany did at Madrid, Guernica, Teruel and Barcelona.

In 1937, shortly before the 'Pekin incident', free China, with the civil war hardly over, could not offer serious resistance to the invader. That year saw the fall of Pekin, Tientsin, Nanking and Shanghai, and the Government fled to the inland city of Chungking, over 900 miles away among the mountains. It is the economic capital of Szechuan and the Red Basin where there are very few modern roads and no railways. It was here that Chiang and his associates spent difficult days.

At the beginning of 1939 the Japanese were in occupation of the whole northeast of China proper east of the Yellow River, and also of nearly the whole of the Yangtse valley and the coast of southern China, that is, of all

[1] *v.* p. 283.

the railways, nine-tenths of the factories, all the ports and about half the population.

At the same time the dubious invulnerability of Chungking was exposed by the terrible air raid of May 3, 1939 – it was not the only raid; there were hundreds of them. Wang Ching-wei,[1] one of the Kuo Min-tang leaders, fled *via* Hanoi to the occupied territory where, on a rainy Sunday morning (March 30, 1940), he was made head of a pro-Japanese counter-government in Nanking; the train carrying foreign journalists to the ceremony was wrecked outside the city by guerrillas. The Nanking government did not signify much and, on the whole, was not a genuinely Quisling government. But these things further poisoned the atmosphere.

Meantime collective security broke down in the West – Ethiopia, Spain, Austria, Czechoslovakia. On September 30, 1938, the agreement was signed in Munich by which London and Paris betrayed Czechoslovakia, the only democratic country in the Western sense in Eastern Europe. Now there was no holding Japan back. In three weeks Canton was occupied and British Hongkong isolated. Thus Chamberlain and his friends opened the way for the Japanese attack on Hongkong and Singapore because they 'were totally unable to read the signs of the times'.

The West continued to send the Japanese conquerors coal, oil and iron. The Australian Government put down the strikes of dock workers, who, imitating their comrades in London, Southampton and Marseilles, refused to load ships sailing to Japan. In 1940, according to the calculations of the London *Times,* nine-tenths of Japan's war material came from the United States, Britain, France, Holland and their colonies.

Only the Soviet Union sent any significant aid to China in the years 1937 to 1946 as Soong Mei-ling, Chiang's wife, regretfully admitted in a somewhat bitter article in December 1940; regretfully, for the Kuo Min-tang had no love for the Soviet Union; the presence of Russian soldiers and technicians in Sinkiang and the Russian occupation of Outer Mongolia was in their opinion less a source of security and relief than a threat to China. Cloud-covered Chungking was in verity no summer resort for the Chinese Government. In the summer of 1940 when the Germans were occupying Western Europe, Britain forbade any imports to China through Hongkong, and from July to October forbade traffic on the Burma road, the road from Burma via Kunming to Chungking. In 1938–9 the Chinese had built this 15,000-mile-long highway almost without proper tools and machines, and expected much of it as their only secure and not too roundabout link with the sea and the outside world. Up to then, the only road not passing through Russian territory was the railway from Kunming to Haiphong in French Indochina, and how little secure that was, was seen in June 1940 when the semi-fascist French authorities, because of Japanese demands and threats, hermetically sealed the Chinese frontiers. As for the northwestern route from Chungking *via* Kansu (Lanchow) and the desert of Sinkiang (Tihwa) to Russian Kasakstan, this was a bad road nearly 3000 miles long – that was why Russian transport came over the Burma road from 1937 to 1941 – and it led only to the

[1] *v.* p. 208.

Soviet Union. Neither technically nor politically was it a good road, the more so because neither Britain nor the United States had seaports in Kasakstan! Goods had to come from western ports to Karachi, then by rail from Karachi *via* Quetta to Zahedan, then by motor lorry from Zahedan *via* troubled Persia to Askabad (in Turkmenistan), and from there by the 930-mile long Turk-Sib railway to Alma Ata in Kasakstan. Besides, pleading the Russo-Japanese neutrality treaty, Russia from April 1941 forbade all 'military' transport to free China. Even if Moscow had shut both eyes to such traffic, this route had little importance.

Even so, free China kept its head above water – Chungking and the isolated area of the communists in Kansu-Shensi and the many small guerrilla bands in their own areas – and continued to do so after the Russo-Japanese neutrality treaty was published. Nor did the situation change after the German attack on Russia when the sources of Russian aid began to dry up, nor when, after the attack of December 7, 1941, the white men were swept out of Southeast Asia like straws before a hurricane, when the Burma road was closed and the very existence of Yunnan, all southeast and southwest China, and even India itself seemed in danger.

Although as early as February 1942 Churchill and Roosevelt had agreed to deal with Germany first and then turn against Japan – a bitter blow for free China – many people in the West, especially in the United States, began to realize the importance of China in the war, an importance it had had even while British and Americans were behaving like men in a dream. The danger to Egypt and Australia made immediate aid impossible, but Churchill did at least make a friendly gesture when in February 1942, he presented to Chungking three gunboats; to free China British gunboats had been the symbol of Chinese humiliation since the Opium Wars! This happened when Chiang and his beautiful wife pleaded during a visit to Delhi for the independence of India-Pakistan and declared that China's dearest wish was to see all Asia gain political freedom. The journey they made in the northwestern districts of China in the summer of 1942 was a new sign of the recovery of the Chungking regime, for the world war had freed it from its isolation and made new blood course through its veins.

In April 1942 the first air convoy from northeast India reached free China; it consisted of ten American transport planes flown from Egypt, which brought in oil. Chungking was terribly short of everything except soldiers. Free China manufactured virtually no weapons; it had no oil and far too few lorries. In 1944 China's steel production was less than $\frac{1}{4}$ per cent of America's.

General J. W. Stilwell, the military representative in China of the United States and also Chiang's Chief of Staff (1942–1944), was constantly asking for oil, machine-guns, bombs, medical stores, typewriters and the like. The Americans maintained the air service week after week from the sandy banks of the Brahmaputra over the 20,000-feet-high snow-clad mountains to Kunming and Chungking; another route was opened in 1944–5 from Calcutta to Chengtu. Thus there arrived in January 1943 1200 tons; in December 12,000 tons; in August 1944 24,000 tons, in January 1945 44,000 tons and in July roughly 70,000 tons, an average of 2000 a day, i.e. as much as 400 military lorries could carry.

During the war Chiang wrote a book called *China's Destiny,* in which he described the Opium War of 1840–1842 and the later greedy interventionism of the West based on the eighty treaty ports as the source of China's oppression and the general decline of the country. As he was writing his book Washington and London (October 1942) declared themselves ready to abandon all their privileged positions in China, an announcement of historical importance even if at the time it had no practical significance, since all the rich areas were in Japanese hands; including Hongkong, which Churchill had no intention of giving back. The relevant treaties were signed on January 11, 1943, and that meant that when China was liberated, there would be no longer British and American enclaves in her territory, that no foreign soldiers would control her seaports, that no British or American warships would be in Chinese waters and that the laws of China and her customs regulations would be drawn up by China and not by Britain, and, above all, that there would be no boards with this notice on them: 'Chinese forbidden'.

Nor were the Japanese lagging behind the West. As early as March 1942, the commander-in-chief of the Japanese army, Okamura, handed over to the Nanking government what was once the British quarter of Tientsin. On January 10, 1943, Tokio declared invalid all special territorial rights, including the international settlements in Pekin and Shanghai; Italy followed suit in January and the representative in Pekin of Vichy France in May; Germany had no settlements in China. Wang Chung-wei's declaration of war on Britain and the United States on the same day received no answer. The total prohibition of Chinese immigration to the United States disappeared on December 17, 1943, although the law kept migrants down to a very low figure, not more than 105 a year!

None the less in 1943 China was internally and militarily nearer catastrophe than at any time between 1937 and 1945, even if the optimistic reports of the Kuo Min-tang's news agency and the charm of 'the First Lady of China' which was displayed on her American visit (at the beginning of 1943) glossed it over, and although the Chinese barometer remained firm so far as the outside world could see. The governments of countries like Britain, France and Holland still at bottom feared a united and strengthened China. Churchill, for instance, did not conceal his dislike of any intensive support for what he called 'rotten' Chungking. But many Americans, and Roosevelt especially, had high hopes of China. Did not most American generals think that the Japanese Empire could be reduced only *via* Southeast Asia and China? Was not free China the only place from which American air squadrons could bombard Japan itself? Everywhere in the south of free China the Americans (1943–4) built airfields. Not until the end of 1944 did America develop a Pacific strategy (Philippines, Iwo, Okinawa),[1] as a result of which China and Southeast Asia lost significance. Not until the occupation of the Marianas (Saipan) did the United States (summer 1944) possess an airbase for the bombing of Tokio.

[1] *v.* p. 316.

An Anglo-American-Chinese plan of campaign for Southeast Asia (in particular for North Burma to secure the land link between China and India) was drawn up in May 1943 and was developed in the talks in Quebec (August 11th to 24th) by Churchill, Roosevelt and the Chinese foreign minister T. V. Soong. In Moscow (October 19th to 31st) the Soviet Union, the United States and Britain recognized China as one of the four Great Powers and in the very important talks in Cairo (November 22nd to 26th: the prelude to Teheran) Chiang himself appeared as one of the 'three kings'. He, Roosevelt and Churchill discussed, besides the plan of campaign for the Far East, the frontiers of a completely liberated China; China was to recover all the territory lost since 1894, including Formosa and Manchuria. Korea would 'at a given date' become free and independent; the words 'at a given date' are evidence of Roosevelt's doubts on the fitness of Korea for self-government; the notorious 38th parallel first appears in the talks at Yalta and was further discussed at Potsdam. The Soviet Union, not being one of the warring states in East Asia, held aloof for a time from these decisions, but in Yalta (February 1945) Stalin recognized the plans made in Cairo for China and Korea.

The Japanese army in China between 1941 and 1945 had not advanced on land beyond the line reached in 1931–41, i.e. it did not generally go beyond the 110th degree of longitude. South of the Yangtse valley, where the Japanese did not go farther west than Ichang, only the coastal districts and the ports were under Japanese control. Thus, the railway from Canton to Changsha, the only railway link between south and central China, was held, in part at least, by the Chinese.

The whole of the north of free China was held by the red armies of Mao Tse-tung and Chu-teh based on their 'democratic liberated territories' in Eastern Kansu and Northern Shensi with a government in Yenan (Fushih). The Yellow river here was the boundary between free and occupied China. Every Japanese attempt to cross the sandy plains of Sui-juan north of the river and reach the road from Chungking to Kasakstan failed against the resistance of the red armies and of the Mongolian cavalry. Besides, the communists in northwest China had small guerrilla brigades in the field, especially in the area Hopei-Shansi-Chahar, whence resistance groups from the Wutai hills (miners and railway workers) could penetrate to the centre of Pekin, to Shantung and north Kiangsu and the frontier districts of Shansi, Honan and Hopei; here their base was the Tai Hang hills. Resistance men fought on the sea – was it only in China that this was the case? – and attacked lighthouses, lightships and small coastal vessels. Beyond the great highroads and the railways the Japanese could not do much; for instance, in 1942, the Japanese army (i.e. forced Chinese peasants) built for the defence of the railway line Mukden-Pekin-Nanking seven-foot-high embankments along the whole line; trees and brushwood near the line were cleared away and road crossings were blocked at night. Every railway station in the villages was a small stone and concrete fortress guarded by soldiers day and night.

Possibly the reader will say that all this is just romantic military history, but let him consider how the tactics of the occupying power with its motto of kill, pillage and burn roused hate – in one action, one of many against the guerrillas in Chekiang in 1942, 600,000 Chinese were killed – and how far the 'new democracies' in Kansu-Shensi and other liberated districts inside the Japanese lines had freed the peasants and workers from their former slavery. He should likewise remember what a history the communists had behind them. Very few people in China or anywhere else had so rich an experience of guerrilla fighting as Mao; as early as 1936 he had written his book *Strategy of the Revolutionary War in China* (published in 1941 and translated into several Western languages). What in the turmoil of an Asian country at that time a relatively small guerrilla brigade could achieve against a modernly equipped army of occupation was seen again in Indochina where in the last stage of the eight years' war with the French, the latter were able to use the Hanoi-Haiphong railway for only a few hours of the day.

In 1937 the Chinese Red Army numbered about 100,000; in 1943 it was some 600,000 strong. With the guerrillas it tied down during the occupation about 45 per cent of the Japanese troops in China, that is, twenty divisions. These figures come from Chungking, Washington and Yenan.

At this period relations between Chungking and Yenan were anything but good. The Chinese Government held back behind the lines a third of their modernly equipped troops to blockade 'the red area', and even serious frontier incidents were not avoided. All through history and in any guerrilla war there are dark passages of human error and human failure; in the 'cold civil war' (1938–1945) these are found in Chungking. Far too many Chinese in the free areas controlled by the Kuo Min-tang were neither mature enough nor willing enough to understand Mao's language and to make their area a democracy. As early as the winter of 1935–6 groups of students, intellectuals and journalists, and even many bourgeois merchants and the like, demanded: 'Stop the war against the communists, set the peasants free, drive out the Japanese.' After the temporary kidnapping of Chiang, the civil war came to an end for the moment; Mao's government seemed ready to check temporarily the agrarian revolution. During the latter part of the war rich peasants and landlords were not as a rule deprived of their lands, and Chiang was again recognized as commander-in-chief. The Kuo Min-tang, too, modified their attitude and became a little democratic; freedom of speech and of the press was extended, and in January 1938, for instance, the first communist paper appeared unmolested in 'white' China. But outside the big towns conditions altered very little, and the strong rightish and reactionary elements in the Kuo Min-tang made impossible any accommodation between Chungking and Yenan. Very moderate radical bourgeois groups like the Federation of Chinese Democratic Parties (1941, known between 1943 and 1945 as the Democratic League) had singularly little influence.

The transfer of the government to the interior of the country strengthened anti-democratic leanings. Szechuan, Kweichow and Yunnan were not the most progressive provinces of China. The establishment of the government at Chungking meant separation from the very different outlook of the great seaports with their bourgeois democrats and their farseeing merchant class.

In the primitive interior of the country the great landowners would not hear of reforms or of the modernization of the economy. Everything remained as it was. The peasants had neither land nor freedom. Kweichow, and especially Yunnan, remained centres of the trade in opium and women (peasant girls cost about from 50 to 100 Swiss francs – as both American and Chinese sources report). The American journalist Edgar Snow (author of *Red Star over China*), who travelled a good deal in Chiang's China at the beginning of the war, relates that the *Mintuan* – the police of the big landowners and rich peasants – and the military formations under 'bandit officers' had as many men as the whole official army. The country went from one economic crisis to another. This, despite their evident strength, was the time of reckoning for the Kuo Min-tang.

That explains the repeated failure of Chinese efforts at defence; it is part of the ups and downs of Chinese history. Once again it was the fate of a government, originally revolutionary and recognized throughout the country, to abandon its old ideals and fall into decay. Irresponsible governors, landowners, officers and bandits had too great freedom; the peasantry was oppressed. Lack of land, neglect of flood regulation and irrigation works, civil wars and, in general, anarchy are signs of a coming turning-point in time when the tortured peasants will revolt.

Only a new and better government of a peasant leader emerging from the revolt and a fresh partition and extension of usable land can in such circumstances reunite a people and a country. Did not the first Tang Emperor (about A.D. 600) divide the land in the first years of his reign? Was not the first Ming Emperor (about 1350) the leader of a peasant revolution? Would the Manchus have come to power in 1644 had a garrison commander not summoned these barbarians from the north to put down a peasant leader who had seized Pekin? Admittedly the Western intervention from 1840 hindered this cycle of neglect, anarchy and revolution; it was only with the aid of foreign ships and guns that the Taiping rebellion had been suppressed (1850–1865). Many members of the Kuo Min-tang really wanted to liberate and modernize China, but as a whole the party was unable to solve the triple problem of the agrarian revolution, Western intervention and Japanese imperialism.

In his day Dr Sun had laid down the three principles of the Chinese revolution (San Min Chui) – independence, economic security (land, rice, machinery) and democracy. The second and third principles the Kuo Min-tang – and Chungking – failed to realize. Chiang's China oppressed the peasants still more and squeezed them like a lemon instead of giving them some land and granting them a place in the sun. By so doing Chungking estranged not only the peasants but the intellectuals and the liberal bourgeois.

Marxism is a product of Europe – just like Sun's whole concept of democracy – but in the growth of communism in China within the framework of the agrarian revolution we recognize not just a modern European phenomenon but also a recurrent phenomenon in Chinese history, the history of a peasant people. In that sense Mao and his associates are as purely Chinese as were the peasant leaders of the past.

Because of its fears of the communists, Chungking all through the war

refused to let part of the aid sent by America go to Mao and Chu-teh, neither
lorries nor rifles nor even medical stores. The varied opinions, expressed in
the literature on the new China, on the extent of Russian aid to the Red
Army do not relate to this period.

But it was not only the communists and the democrats who saw the dangers
of a split in 'white' China. An eventual renewal of the civil war – which was
what various influential people in Chungking really wanted – was not just
a Chinese concern; it could change the course of the war in Asia and Africa.
A war between Chungking and Yenan made possible a rift between Chungking and Moscow which, in turn, meant a cooling of the relations between
Moscow and Washington. As early as 1943 the effects of such a split were
realized in Britain and America. Especially in America, government and
press began to ask: What does Chungking, what does Yenan really want?
What is the significance of Yenan for the Soviet Union? What is the significance of China in the war against Japan? Further, did the war demand
democratic reforms in 'white' China? Were American lorries and machine
guns to be devoted to defending Chungking against communism in a China
liberated from the Japanese? In other words: What was the meaning of the
Chinese revolution? Many Americans living then in China, and especially
Stilwell, Chiang's chief of staff, and in charge of the air lift, were not a little
annoyed with the outdated and undemocratic policy of Chungking and with
the waste of military strength – and of American war material – in the
blockade of the Red areas. Frankly, even bluntly, the American general
criticized the regime and tried (1943–4), with the help of Washington, to bring
the two sides together again.

At the beginning of 1944 a Chinese-American army invaded Northern
Burma in order to secure the land link between China and India. In the period
of the air-lift, Chinese soldiers and workers with the help of American
engineers modernized and widened the Chinese part of the Burma road and
worked out plans for traffic from northeast China (Ledo) *via* Myitkyina and
Bhamo to the road. In December 1944 this route was completely liberated
and the first lorries went into free China. The new link – it is sometimes
called the Stilwell road – was extended in 1945 far into Kiangsi, nearly, in
fact, to Canton; it had 600 wooden bridges and ran straight through some
900 miles of malarial swamp and forest. It was, however, a poor road, especially in the rainy season, and the air-lift retained its great importance; in July
1945 land traffic was still only a third of air traffic.

At the same time as the Chinese-American advance from Yunnan, the
Japanese field-marshal Hatta, to relieve the pressure on his troops in Burma,
attacked the Chinese positions in Kwangsi, Hunan and Kweichow. Early in
the summer of 1944 he occupied Changsha, the only big city in free China
apart from Chungking and Chengtu. Advancing from Canton he drove the
Americans from their many air-bases near Kweilin from which they bombed
Japanese shipping in the South China Sea and in the Chinese ports. In that
summer the Chinese army threatened to break up altogether; it looked as if
the 'cold civil war' was taking its revenge.

In July Washington sent to China the well-known Democrat Henry

Wallace who had leftist leanings, to prevent a further cooling of the relations between Chungking and Yenan. He was on the point of getting them together again – it was high time for Terauchi's troops were already threatening Kweiyang and many Americans were beginning to think Kunming too hot a spot – when the Japanese retreat began. Did the Japanese peasant also want to go home? Wallace went away; the split remained unhealed. It was too much for Stilwell. He hated the methods of Chungking and all that it stood for, and he made his feelings very plain to Chiang who, much displeased, sent a furious letter to Washington which revealed very clearly the full extent of the crisis in Chinese-American relations. Washington gave way and replaced the angry Stilwell by Wedemeyer, the former American chief of staff to Mountbatten, the British commander-in-chief in Southeast Asia.

Wedemeyer sided with the anti-democratic views of Chiang's China. Here was the first sign of a new American intervention against the communists, an intervention whose results are still visible in the rift between America and Communist China.

But how could that be foreseen in August 1945? In my opinion by neither a Chinese nor an American. The business of the historian is only with the present and the past. Anything beyond these is but conjecture. The historian who deals with the last few years is dealing with a period which is not yet ended. Twenty-five years earlier many Chinese and foreigners were treating the Chinese revolution as a passing phase which would find its final accomplishment only in general agrarian revolution, but the how and the when remained unrevealed.

In February 1945 at the Yalta conference Roosevelt and Churchill tried to get Stalin to recognize Chungking as the sole government in China. They succeeded, although they had to make concessions which to some extent restored the position before 1904: Russo-Chinese control of various railways; Port Arthur to be a Russian naval base; Dairen a free port; and the preservation of the *status quo* in Outer Mongolia. Chungking, informed by Roosevelt of this agreement, declared its acceptance. Did even one of the leaders in the Kremlin then expect what became reality in 1949, the recognition by Russia of a Communist government which, except for Formosa and a small island or two, ruled all China? The question is asked simply to show how few even of the politicians who make history can foresee it, or to express it rather differently, realize that it is not they who make it.

In August 1945 the Japanese army surrendered, and on the morning of September 2nd the signature of China on the instrument of capitulation beside those of Japan, the United States, Britain, Russia, Holland, Australia, New Zealand, Canada and France marked the end of one of the most terrible periods in Chinese history. But 'red' China was excluded. To Asia and America in liberated Europe, Chiang Kai-shek and Chungking represented the Chinese Empire, one of the 'Big Five' in the United Nations.

That empire was now ripe for the last phase of the revolution. Mao Tsetung and his associates recognized this; so did many democrats outside Kansu and Shensi. Even Chungking seemed to realize it, for it sought to modernize the country and so free it from civil war. In 1945–6 Mao and Chou En-lai

A.C.—11*

had a series of conversations with the Chungking government, at which General Marshall, us Chief of Staff during the war, and Vice-President Wallace, who was in China from November 1945 to January 1947, were present. But the compromise between the Kuo Min-tang and the communists (January–February 1947) was only a flash at the beginning of a storm in which the Kuo Min-tang government crashed down like a rotten tree.

Between 1927 and 1936 Chiang had believed he could destroy Mao's peasant bands. He erred. He erred again in 1947, for now these peasant bands were China. A single historic chain bound 'red' Pekin of the winter of 1949 with the Hankow of autumn 1911 and the Canton of the summer of 1926, from which the tiny revolutionary army of the Kuo Min-tang, then entirely alone, began the anti-imperialist war of liberation and so the decisive phase of the Chinese revolution.

VIII

JAPAN AND THE SECOND WORLD WAR

IT is many years since Japan grasped the significance of Western, i.e. modern technology and particularly its significance for the conduct of modern war. In 1842, at the time of the Opium War, Japanese officers were studying the British conduct of it; in 1855 they were studying the Crimean War; in 1871 the Franco-Prussian War. By 1870 students were going to the West to the shipyards of Britain and America, to the engineering sheds of France and Germany. In 1885 Japan was building torpedo-boats, in 1895 light cruisers and by 1905 was less dependent on the armaments factories of the West than was Russia.

Unlike many Indian and Chinese students, the Japanese did not study at Cambridge, Harvard or Paris. They did not try to acquire Western culture as a whole; they concentrated on learning modern technology and its wide, though intellectually somewhat restricted, scientific background. The Japanese revolution was 75 per cent a technological one. Technical reform apart, the Japanese took for model not the mature democracies of France, Britain and latterly America, but the Germany of Bismarck. What the Japanese attained between 1870 and 1945 – and it was much – was not a modern democracy either Asian or European; they never acquired libertarian ideas such as went with capitalism in Europe and America and which came from them to Asia. The Island empire was ruled by two forces. One was the *Zaibatsu*, the new capitalists; the other was the army which was anti-capitalist and pseudo-socialist like the fascists in Europe, and very undemocratic. Imperialism in its domestic or external forms united these forces at every critical moment in modern Japanese history, while their domination and the secret police kept down the growth of any really socialist or democratic movement.

From 1870 to 1920 Japan sailed in the wake of European imperialism. A few facts show how its empire grew. In 1875 it acquired the Kurile islands; in 1876 the Bonins (Ogasawara); in 1879 the Ryu-kyu islands and in 1891 the Vulcan islands (Kazan). In 1895, as one of the gains from the war with China (1894–1895), it acquired Formosa, the beginning of Japanese encroachment in China. In 1899 was added Marcus Island, some 1400 miles southeast of Tokio; in 1905, as a result of the Russo-Japanese War, the Kwantung peninsula, Port Arthur and the southern half of Sakhalin (Karafuto), and in 1910 Korea. In 1915 Japan occupied all the German islands north of the Equator. Although in general the Asian countries came off badly at Versailles, Japan obtained the Marianas, the Carolines and the Marshall islands due northeast of Indonesia.

The revolutions in Russia and China and the fact that the Western States were occupied fully in Europe and in Asia (intervention against the Bolsheviks, the revolution in Turkey, the Arab countries and Persia) gave the Japanese imperialists the chance to push farther into Asia; hence the temporary occupation of all Sakhalin (1918–1925), of Vladivostok (1918–1922) and Shantung (1918–1922). When the Russian revolution spread and barred the way to Siberia, and the West stood in the path of further expansion in the Pacific, Japan seemed to come to her senses and seek to take the road of democracy.

But the imperialism of Tokio was merely sleeping – and dreaming of China, of coal and iron and cotton, of the way to Siberia and Southeast Asia. On the night of September 18–19, 1931, at the height of the great economic crisis in the West, the Kwantung army provoked the 'Mukden incident'.[1] This was the beginning of the occupation of Manchuria and of the great Asian war. The West was disunited and from the date of the 'Pekin' incident' (summer 1937), which marked the occupation of all eastern China, to the occupation of Hainan (February 1939) did nothing to check the Japanese. Europe had her own troubles; the widespread growth of fascism, particularly in Germany; the Abyssinian War (1935–6); Hitler's remilitarization of the Rhineland (1936); the Spanish Civil War (1936–1939); the crises in Austria and Czechoslovakia (1938); the Polish crisis and the outbreak of war in Europe in September 1939.

When, after the occupation of Hainan, its navy took possession of the first 'Western' possession, the uninhabited Spratly Islands (in the South China Sea half-way on the road to Indonesia and Borneo) which were internationally recognized as French territory, Japan had already had a long experience of military conquest. It had forty divisions in China and 3000 war correspondents whose reports day in day out adorned the front pages of Japanese newspapers. When the Japanese army occupied part of Indochina in the summer of 1940, the Germans were already masters of Paris, Brussels, Warsaw, Amsterdam, Copenhagen and Oslo.

While the city of London was burning, the Japanese foreign minister Matsuoka was in Berlin and signed there on September 27, 1940, the notorious German-Italian-Japanese military treaty which was an extension of the earlier Anti-Comintern Pact of November 1936. Before Matsuoka went home *via* Siberia, Hitler told him of his plans for the invasion of Russia – these date from the end of 1940 – and as a result Matsuoka broke his journey in Moscow where, on April 13, 1941, he signed a Russo-Japanese treaty of neutrality. Berlin knew of it only half an hour before Stalin and Matsuoka signed it. Asia for the Asians!

It was plain that the Japanese wished an accommodation with Germany no more than with any 'white' nation. Tokio was as scared of German duplicity as it was of American intervention.[2]

Tokio waited. The Japanese plans were revealed to no one, not even to

---

[1] *v.* p. 214.

[2] The reader who wishes to study the policy of the United States between the fall of France and Pearl Harbour should read *The Undeclared War*, by W. L. Lánger and S. E. Gleason (London, 1953).

the Germans. Britain was relieved of German pressure, but Hitler kept his word as regards Russia; on June 22, 1941, he began the invasion. Tokio went on waiting. In September the Japanese newspapers were saying that the Germans were fighting at Leningrad like the Japanese. In October Hitler had captured Vyasma, some 130 miles from Moscow, and nearly the whole of the Ukraine. Now, thought the fire-eaters of Tokio, the time really has come. In that critical October Hideki Tojo became prime minister (October 18, 1940, to July 18, 1944. He was also minister of war from July 1940 to July 1944). As became a former chief of staff of the Kwantung army, the core and symbol of Japanese aggression in Asia, he was an imperialist of the deepest dye. His appointment meant war; all that had to be settled was the place and method. The fleet Japan had built was no toy; it was equal to America's – 12 battleships, 20 carriers, 35 cruisers, 125 destroyers and 125 submarines. Japan also had the third largest merchant navy in the world, and its soldiers had learned their business on the snowclad hills of the Amur and in the cornfields of China. In December 1941 the Germans were attacking Leningrad, Moscow and Sebastopol. On the 7th of that month the planes from Nagumo's carriers attacked the American naval base at Pearl Harbour, just over six miles from Honolulu. In half an hour 2000 Americans had been killed and of the eight battleships in harbour, the *Arizona,* the *California* and the *Utah* were sunk; the *Oklahoma* had heeled over; the *Nevada* was burning, and the other three were badly damaged. Three days later the two British battleships, the *Prince of Wales* and the *Repulse,* were sunk by Japanese planes off the Malayan coast, and the southern part of the Pacific was in Japanese hands. The Japanese transports turned south to the Philippines, Malaya and Indonesia. Holland, Britain and the United States declared war on Japan, and so in 1941 the European War became the Second World War. However one regards Japan's action in 1941–2 – it can be regarded as the liberation of Southeast Asia from the West, or as pure imperialism, or as both; the historian must not let his personal feelings influence him – it remains one of the most interesting actions in the history of war. Never in that history had such immense territories been conquered in so short a time, territories, too, which could be reached only by sea and against the will of the two great naval powers. More, the total of Japanese killed from December 1941 to March 1942 was only 15,000.

At the beginning of March the Japanese Empire included, besides the parts of China already occupied, virtually the whole of Southeast Asia with all the islands within the line Guadalcanal–Funafuti (Ellice Islands)–Wake, an area with 500,000,000 inhabitants and of almost unimaginable extent; from Tokio to Funafuti (4700 miles) is as far as from Moscow to New York; from Tokio to Jakarta (3750 miles), as far as from Amsterdam to New York. From April to June Tokio sought to extend that area in four directions – Ceylon-India, the Coral Sea-Australia, Hawaii and Alaska, a theatre of war measuring 8100 miles by 6250; the distance from Jakarta to Amsterdam is 7000 miles.

The war at sea, while Cripps was negotiating in India, was uneventful, although the British lost two cruisers and a carrier (April 6th–7th). In the western area little happened, on sea at least. The British, however, between May and August occupied Madagascar, which belonged to Vichy France, in order, as they said, to secure the sea route to Egypt and Iran against any Japanese action in these waters.

At the beginning of May a fleet under Takagi left the new naval base of Tulagi (on Florida Island north of Guadalcanal), making for the New Hebrides and apparently Samoa in order to occupy these islands and cut the communications between America and Australia. Between May 4th and 8th it was driven out of the Coral Sea by the Americans with a loss of a light carrier, four cruisers and many small craft (100,000 tons in all). It was the first important Japanese reverse.

In the next operations, the attack was directed against Dutch Harbour (on the American island of Unalaska off Alaska) and against the Hawaiian Islands. The relatively few ships at Dutch Harbour were driven off at the beginning of June, and on their way home the Japanese captured the three rocky islands of Attu, Agattu and Kiska south of the Bering Sea, though, apart from a meteorological station, there was nothing there but grass, rocks and snow.

But west of Hawaii, at Midway Island, the situation was much more dangerous. The naval commander-in-chief Yamamoto had concentrated a great invasion fleet of 5 carriers to the American 3; 7 battleships, including the 64,000 ton *Yamato,* Yamamoto's flagship, the Americans had no battleships here; 13 cruisers to 8 American; 45 destroyers to America's 20, and 12 transports with troops for the occupation of Midway. But the Americans divined Yamamoto's plan and besides had available several modern airfields. The attack on Midway (June 3rd–5th) was a bloody repetition of what had happened in the Coral Sea; at midday on the 5th the Japanese fleet withdrew westward, having lost four carriers, two cruisers and many smaller ships. After the battle of the Coral Sea, this was the second naval battle in history in which the big ships far distant from each other did not fire a shot; it was an air battle by sea. It was also the first time that a Japanese fleet had taken to flight since 1592 in Korea. It may not have been so appreciated at the time, but Midway was the Stalingrad of the Pacific; it marked the end of Tokio's possession of the initiative and of the expansion of the empire.

On December 11, 1941, Berlin and Rome had declared war on the United States. On January 1, 1942, twenty-six democratic countries – in some cases the adjective may be taken with a grain of salt – signed the declaration of the United Nations and announced themselves in agreement with the Anglo-American Atlantic Charter. They were: the United States, Britain, Russia, China, Holland, Australia, Belgium, Costa Rica, Cuba, the Dominican Republic, Greece, Guatemala, Haiti, Honduras, India, Yugoslavia, Canada, Luxemburg, New Zealand, Nicaragua, Norway, Panama, Poland, Salvador, Czechoslovakia and South Africa. Of these, only the Soviet Union was not at war in Asia. Eight of them were occupied; China was half-occupied;

Stalingrad, the Volga, the Caucasus, Soviet Asia, Egypt, Australia, India and Hawaii were, it seemed, all in danger in the summer of 1942.

In February 1942, as we have already related, Roosevelt and Churchill agreed that the freeing of Europe should have first priority and that the war with Japan should come second. None the less, that year, 1942, in both theatres marks the turning-point; in Africa (El Alamein), in Russia (Stalingrad) and in the Pacific (Midway and Guadalcanal).

Here we shall deal only with the war for the Pacific islands. It was only American industry, American technology and American forces which drove the Japanese out of their conquests; the Chinese, the Indians, and the Russians in East Asia on the whole merely kept the Japanese attack at bay. The war on land and the occupation period in Southeast Asia has already been dealt with.[1]

No matter how greatly we abhor wars – and, in the eyes of those who think of humanity as a whole, all wars are civil wars – we should not let ourselves underestimate their significance. Wars and revolutions are just as important a part of history as are economics and culture in the narrower sense. The wars of Alexander and the Romans, of the Arabs and the Mongols, the American War of Independence, the campaigns of Napoleon, the French revolution and the Russian, have all put their mark on their times. The expansion and fall of cultures and empires are summed up for most of us in the names of places – Cannae, Constantinople, Trafalgar, Waterloo, Tsushima, Singapore, Stalingrad.

From 1942 to 1945 the Americans attacked the Japanese from two directions: in a northwesterly direction from Australia via New Guinea and the neighbouring island (c.-in-c. MacArthur) and westward from Hawaii *via* the many small islands west of it (c.-in-c. Nimitz). The two forces united in the invasion of the Philippines.

In 1942 in the Australian sector the Japanese had reached the north coast of New Guinea and all the neighbouring islands from the Admiralty Group up to and including the Ellice Islands. Although the battle of the Coral Sea had prevented the occupation of the New Hebrides and Samoa, the Japanese expeditionary force in New Guinea again resumed its southeasterly advance with Port Moresby, the only harbour of any importance still unoccupied, as main objective. The advance was brought to a standstill in the Ioriwaiba Hills (September 1942). On November 2nd the Australians were back, this time for good, at Kokoda in the high mountains between Port Moresby and the east coast of New Guinea. Here, too, as on the Volga and the Nile, the picture had changed.

Meantime the Americans coming from New Zealand had landed on Guadalcanal, where the Japanese army had built an air-base to protect any further operations in the Coral Sea. The terrible campaign in the damp, wooded island, with the accompanying actions at sea in which the Americans as a rule were successful, ended on the night of February 7th–8th with the evacuation of 12,000 Japanese troops; the Japanese newspapers called this a 'regrouping of forces'. The Japanese losses amounted to 24,000 killed on

[1] *v.* p. 278.

Guadalcanal, more than the entire invasion of southeast Asia had cost; the Americans lost 1800 killed out of 60,000. In December 1943 – the Russians had freed virtually the whole of the Ukraine and Italy (September) had surrendered – the Americans occupied all the islands between Guadalcanal and New Britain (Bismarck Archipelago), and New Guinea from Milne Bay in the extreme southeast to Finschhafen which lies opposite New Britain. The recapture of the Admiralty group and the St. Matthias Islands (February–March 1944) completely isolated Rabaul the Japanese naval base in the southeast. MacArthur, therefore, advanced over 1500 miles westward to Aitape, Hollandia and the bay of Tanahmeran (April) to the islands of Wakde and Biak (May) and in July to Noemfour and Geelwink Bay. By September he had reached Morotai in the north of the Indonesian Halmahera Archipelago, some 280 miles distant from the Philippines. In the meantime the Australians had cleaned up the tropical forests and marshes on the New Guinea coast and cut off about 150,000 Japanese troops.

The tactics of 'island-hopping', by which large Japanese garrisons were cut off, is seen again in the American campaign in the east from Hawaii as base. It began in November 1943. Hawaii is more than 2000 miles from the nearest island of Japan and the Americans were still rather unskilled in invasion operations. The carnage on Gallipoli in 1915 had made the West doubt the feasibility of an invasion by sea. In 1940 neither Britain nor the United States – nor Japan – had proper landing craft. Nor had Germany; in 1940 all the shipping on the Rhine was reconstructed for the invasion of Britain. The United States sent what could be spared, first of all, to Britain, Egypt and other Allied bases. Of about 25,000 landing craft built in American yards in 1943, half were sent to British ports for the landings in North Africa, Sicily, Italy and Normandy.

On November 20, 1943, Nimitz's ships appeared at the Gilbert islands. The storming of Tarawa, with its carnage, was typical of what the Japanese tactics were to be in this island warfare. The Japanese had no longer communication by sea; they had nothing but their courage, their patriotism and their bunkers of concrete, sand, white coral and palm wood. The whole garrison of 3500 men was killed, not a single one allowing himself to be made prisoner; the Americans lost 1000 dead. There are many tales told of Japan and the Japanese heroism, and perhaps it is worth noting here that as a whole the Japanese people do not appear to have been very enthusiastic about suicide tactics.

In May 1943 the Americans and Canadians recaptured the bleak island of Attu in the Bering Sea; all the defenders were killed or committed suicide. In August a reconnaissance in force revealed that the Japanese garrison had been evacuated to safer places; Japan heaved a sigh of relief. But courage never failed the Japanese. In the war in the Pacific the number of prisoners was less than 2 to 3 per cent of the dead – which was what the official code of the *samurai* demanded.

Meantime the Americans realized what was happening and used every technical means of preserving their own men's lives. That was seen at the invasion of the Marshalls (some 625 miles northwest of Tarawa and the first outpost of Japan within the frontiers of 1939), and particularly at the attack on Kwajelein (February 2–5, 1944) and Eniwetok; the latter name means the 'land between east and west' (February 17–22, 1944). Both islands were under day and night bombardment by sixty ships, including twelve carriers, before the landing. On Kwajelein 8,500 Japanese were killed (against some 270 prisoners) and 356 Americans; on Eniwetok 3000 Japanese (64 prisoners) and 200 Americans.

Such figures are significant, not so much of the alleged vast difference between eastern and western mentality, as for this particular war in which what was by far the richest land in the world assailed with all its technical resources an island empire whose sea and land communications were destroyed in 1944 and which lacked everything except intelligence and devotion unto death.

At the same time as they took Eniwetok, the Americans by air action mopped up Truk in the Carolines, which was called the Gibraltar of the South Seas and was the most important Japanese naval base in these waters. It was not occupied and here, as on other isolated islands, 80,000 Japanese remained until August 1945, incapable of achieving anything. Neither warships nor transports came to their relief. Up to the summer of 1944 Tokio was receiving nothing from their relatively far-flung outposts but alarming news.

The situation changed when in June 1944 Nimitz appeared off the hilly islands of the Marianas which lay *within* the frontiers of the empire and were only a little over 1200 miles from Tokio. Saipan, Tinian and Guam looked like three hills of stone and concrete raised above the sea. Early on June 15th the first 8000 out of 50,000 Americans were landed in twenty minutes; the intervention of the Japanese fleet in order to prevent an invasion of the Guadalcanal type brought on the naval battle west of the islands (June 18th–20th): it is known as the first battle of the Philippines in which Tokio admitted the loss of three of its 30,000-ton carriers. In three weeks of bloody fighting nearly all the 30,000 defenders of Saipan were killed. The *banzais* of 2000 Japanese who died in a suicidal counter-attack on the night of July 7th–8th marked the bitter end of the battle. The Americans lost 4500 killed. In the battles for Guam (July 21st–August 10th) and Tinian (July 24th–August 2nd), 25,000 Japanese and 2000 Americans were killed. It was indeed changed days since December 10, 1941, when 5000 Japanese captured Guam in a few hours.

The climax of Nimitz's forty-week campaign was the invasion of Peleliu, one of the Palau islands some 900 miles southwest of the Marianas, on September 15, 1944 – the day on which MacArthur landed at Morotai near Halmahera. The retreat of 5000 miles from Hawaii to Peleliu meant the loss of all the outer defences of Japan, the destruction of all Tokio's illusions on the security of the lines of communication between Japanese industry and the troops in 'the garden of southeast Asia'.

How Tokio judged the significance of these and similar events in Europe is seen in the change of government in July 1944. At the beginning of that year differences of opinion on strategy between the army and navy high commands began to be visible. The navy and the minister of marine Shige-taro Shimada (October 1941 to July 1944) wanted to shorten the lines of communication temporarily and withdraw the troops in stations much too far away. Tojo and his associates refused to abandon an inch of ground belonging to the empire; the economists of the *Zaibatsu* on the whole shared the more liberal views of the naval chiefs.

On June 6, 1944, the greatest army of invasion ever known landed on the Normandy coast some 300 miles from the Ruhr, the iron heart of 'Fortress Europe'. The Russians had now liberated their own land and were advancing into Eastern Europe proper. On June 15th the Americans landed on Saipan and on the same day their aircraft, coming from China, bombed the steel town of Yawata on Kyushu, i.e. the heart of Japan itself.

On July 18th the Japanese newspapers announced the fall of Saipan. Next day Tojo's government resigned and the new government of Kuniaki Koiso (July 22, 1944, to April 5, 1945) reverted to the views of the *Zaibatsu* capitalists, as was seen by the appointment of Fidjihara to the ministry of war production. The new head of the ministry of information, Taketoro Ogata, a former journalist, sought at least to some extent to get rid of the old extreme secrecy, the ambiguous communiques and the practice of gloss-ing over unpleasantnesses. The Koiso government, too, by its proclamation on the freedom of Indonesia, indicated that a turning-point had been reached in Tokio and in the Pacific. Now, when Indonesia was directly threatened, Koiso sought to meet the wishes of the occupied territories.

Saipan and Yawata – and the echo of events in Normandy and Eastern Europe – may have been the occasion of the July crisis, but the real cause of the almost revolutionary upset in Tokio was the realization of the true situation, the superiority of the Americans on sea and in the air, in industry and technology, a double superiority which Japan could not challenge.

If ever there was a war in which one economy fought another, one industry fought another, it was the war of 1940–1945 in Europe and in Asia. Germany and Japan had armies that were models and their people were as inventive as those of the Allies. But, apart from the resistance of Britain, Russia and China, it was in the first instance the industry of America, its shipyards and mines – lying in full security between two oceans – which shattered the ambitions of Berlin and Tokio. Today the word 'war' is synonymous with coal, iron, steel, oil, rubber and aluminium. In December 1941 the Japanese Empire had roughly the same productive capacity as France; in production of electricity it was on the same level as Britain. But compared to America, on which Japan declared war in December 1941, that was of little significance. Take these figures:

Percentage of World Production

	Coal		Oil		Iron Ore		Steel	
	1942	1944	1942	1944	1942	1944	1942	1944
U.S.A.	35	35	60	72	30	50	40	55
Japan	6	5	6	2	6	5	5·5	4

What about rubber? Had not Japan in 1942 captured nine-tenths of the rubber plantations (Malaya, Indonesia, Indochina, British Borneo)? The German discovery – it dates from the First World War – of making synthetic rubber from coal and chalk, and the economically more profitable production from potato alcohol, were the basis of American production of synthetic rubber. By 1943 the many new factories in the United States were producing as much rubber from crude oil and alcohol as all the world's plantations produced in 1939. Japan had no surplus of crude oil or coal or potatoes, and the production of her plantations in Southeast Asia fell. In 1944 Japan's rubber production was but an eighth of that of the United States.

Japanese technicians and Japanese industry achieved much in these years – figures like 65,500 aircraft and 4,000,000 tons of new shipping speak volumes – but none the less Japanese production lagged far behind the American. Although in 1940 America possessed only one modern division and in the summer of 1942 had only one carrier, the *Enterprise,* in the Pacific, she was able by 1943 to close all the breaches in the Pacific defences and to restore the technological balance. American material came regularly to the front; remember the length of the line New York–San Francisco–Hawaii–Saipan is 8750 miles. By September MacArthur and Nimitz deployed 100 carriers on the line Halmahera–the Marianas, and so broke the Japanese defensive line while their submarines all over the Pacific and even in coastal waters inflicted heavy loss on Japanese merchant shipping. In 1941 Japan had the third largest merchant navy in the world, roughly 6,000,000 tons gross. During the war it built or captured 4,000,000 tons of iron ships and some 100,000 tons of wooden ships. Shipping for an island empire constituted the only link between industry and the services; in contrast to Germany, land links had very little significance. During 1943 some 300 Japanese ships were sunk; in January–February 1944 200 and in the summer of 1944 about 800. In November 1944 Japan possessed only some 2,000,000 tons, and that in waters which were the reverse of safe.

That alone meant the end, for there was not only the declining capabilities of the shipyards but the isolation of the troops in Southeast Asia from industry and the shipyards at home. In 1943–4, not only were the outer lines separated from the inner fortress but communications between Tokio and Berlin via Southeast Asia, and eventually Siberia, totally broke down. The Germans remained separated from the cotton, rubber, tin and aluminium of Asia and the Japanese from German technicians and factories. It is clear from the book written by Captain Motshisura Hashimoto of the Japanese navy how much less capable of resistance were the Japanese submarines than the Americans, even if in 1943 two small German submarines to serve as models for the shipbuilders reached a Japanese port. How badly Japan missed this communication with Germany is seen by the fact that seven times Japanese submarines tried to reach the German naval base at Brest in order to exchange technical information and bring German technicians to Japan; of the seven, only one got back undamaged to Southeast Asian waters.

It is easy to give examples of the technical superiority of the Americans, to which they owe victory in this war. They knew – and this is more important than would appear at first sight – how to fight malaria; in 1944 only 3 per cent of MacArthur's soldiers suffered from it. When Eniewetok was captured, the first task was to build an airfield. That meant the uprooting of nearly 250 acres of palm-trees, the even levelling of the ground and stiffening it with crushed coral – and all that in three days. It was in this sort of work that the 'Seabees' excelled. These were completely mechanized labour battalions who were next to land after the first wave. The result of this technical superiority was that the Americans were never driven out of a single place on which they had landed, and that, as has already been indicated, they suffered relatively little loss; it was only in very severe fighting as on Tarawa that their losses were a quarter of those of the Japanese; usually they were much less. In addition, the Americans latterly never attempted a landing until the whole area of the objective had been under continuous day and night air and sea bombardment, often for some weeks, so that the defenders were relatively safe only in their yard-thick casemates and dugouts.

From this technical digression, which is indispensable for a correct understanding of events, let us return to the history of the war. We had reached the point at which Peleliu which belongs to the Palau Group was taken by Nimitz, and Morotai near the island of Halmahera, one of the Moluccas, was captured by MacArthur. In October 1944 the two lines of attack converged on the Philippines. We have already described [1] the landing on Leyte of the American Sixth Army, already famous from its campaigns in New Guinea where it had landed in June 1942 in Nassau Bay. That was the beginning of the recapture of the Philippines. Then came the landings on Samar, Mindoro (December 1944) and Luzon (January 9, 1945). MacArthur's troops went on to occupy the ruins of Manila on February 24th; Palawan and Mindanao north of Indonesia in March and May, and then in Indonesia itself, Tarakan (May 1st) and Balikpapan (July 1st). The loss of 12,000 Americans killed in the whole campaign was relatively slight when one considers the enormous significance of the fall of the Philippines bulwark for the course of the war.

Neither Yamashita's 400,000 men nor Tojoda's fleet could prevent it. Soemu Tojoda was the third commander-in-chief of the Japanese navy; the two former commanders were both shot down in the air, Yamamoto in April 1943 off Bougainville and Koga in March 1944 in the Philippines. We have already told of the second battle of the Philippines on October 23rd to 25th in which the American admirals Kincaid and Halsey had covered the landings at Leyte against the squadrons of Kurita, Nishimura, Shima and Osawa.[2]

That same winter the Japanese troops were driven out of northern Burma; the Chinese were threatening the land communications between northeastern China and Southeast Asia, and far to the west the Russians were already on Germany's eastern frontiers while Americans, British, Canadians and French were driving from the west into the Reich itself.

All these events, particularly the invasion of the Philippines and northern

[1] v. p. 318.   [2] v. p. 319.

Indonesia, found their echo in the occupied parts of Southeast Asia. Did not Sukarno's speech on the five principles of a free Indonesia coincide in time with the landings at Tarakan and Balikpapan? Now, too, the Americans could simplify their plan of campaign. Instead of concentrating their whole armament against Formosa and occupied China *via* the Philippines and the Marianas, MacArthur and Nimitz turned to the direct invasion of Japan itself. They captured (February 10th to March 16th) the island of Iwo (Iwojima), one of the rugged volcanic islands of the Ogasawara Archipelago, 560 miles distant from Tokio; once again virtually all the 23,000 defenders were killed against 10 per cent of the invading Americans. At the same time (March 9, 1945) came the terrible night-bombing of Tokio (twelve square miles of the city destroyed, and 80,000 dead), the beginning of a period of intensive air attack (March–August 1945) in which 2,500,000 houses were burned out and 300,000 people killed.

Things did not stay there. In March 450 American transports sailed from eleven ports from Leyte to Seattle to the Ryukyu islands northeast of Formosa. On Easter Sunday (April 1, 1945), the first wave of an army of 180,000 men waded ashore on Okinawa, 300 miles southwest of Kyushu. Behind it were 1500 ships, in front were the 120,000 defenders of the most important fortified island in the Pacific. The desperate resistance of the Japanese passed all known limits. For seven weeks blood flowed and it was not until June 21st that MacArthur could announce the complete occupation of the island; there were 7871 Japanese prisoners and 12,500 American dead.

Besides the numbers of imperial troops who perished on Okinawa, 4000 Japanese aircraft – the weekly production was then 400 – were lost, half of them in suicide crashes on American ships. The suicide attack was known as *kamikadze* ('heavenly wind'), in memory of the great storm which in the thirteenth century shattered the Mongol invasion. The design of heaven in 1945 was very different.

That the Koiso government appreciated. Like the invasion of the Marianas (Saipan) in the summer of 1944, the loss of Okinawa caused an internal crisis, the more so as the Soviet Union on April 5th had made it known that it did not intend to renew the five-year neutrality treaty which expired in April 1946. The Russian plans for intervention in east Asia, which originated in the period of the Teheran conference (1943) and were elaborated at Yalta (February 1945), do not appear to have become known to the Japanese.

On April 7th, the day on which the great battleship *Yamato* (64,000 tons), the biggest warship in naval history, was sunk southwest of Kyushu in the South China Sea, the Koiso cabinet resigned and Admiral Baron Kantaro Suzuki, a figure from the earlier 'liberal' period, became prime minister (April 7 to August 15, 1945).

Tokio had taken pains all through the war not to provoke Russia, although it kept ready for any emergency a strong modern army in Manchukuo. Japanese reporting of the Russo-German War was objective, and in March 1944 Japan had handed back to Russia its rights on the coal and oil production of North Sakhalin in return for a slight extension of fishing rights in Russian waters. When Shigenori Togo became foreign minister, the entire press noted as worthy of comment his experience of Russia and his knowledge of Russian mentality. As early as January Tokio had asked for Russian mediation. In May, when Germany surrendered, Suzuki instructed Sato, the Japanese ambassador in Moscow, to sound the Kremlin again on mediation. On June 20th, when the commander-in-chief on Okinawa committed harakiri, the emperor himself offered to send a prominent statesman to Moscow as a liaison officer. On July 13th Prince Fumimaro Konoye, who had been prime minister from 1937 to 1939, went off with instructions to telegraph to the emperor the little that he hoped to obtain. On that same day there arrived in Tokio Sato's news from Moscow that Stalin and Molotov had gone to Berlin for a conference of the 'Big Four' (United States, Britain, the Soviet Union and China). The conference was held in Potsdam from July 17th to August 2nd. The conferring statesman found no time to discuss conversations with Japan. Except in Japan itself, Tokio's manoeuvres were anything but secret; all the American and European newspapers wrote about them.

Of the Imperial fleet of originally 2,300,000 tons, rather less than a tenth (200,000) was now in service and many of the ships lacked fuel. The few merchant ships left had no freedom of movement. The troops isolated in the distant parts of the empire (250,000 in various places in the Pacific, about 600,000 in Southeast Asia and Indonesia, and more than a million in China) were virtually cut off by sea. Suzuki commanded a sinking ship, a wreck indeed, long before what happened at Hiroshima, in Manchuria and Nagasaki.

What happened was the atom bomb, and to assess its significance we must go back a little. In 1933 a German physicist, a Jew, fled from Hitler's Germany to America. He was Albert Einstein. On August 2, 1939, he wrote to Franklin Roosevelt a letter in which he stated that, on the basis of new work by Joliot Curie in France and E. Fermi and L. Szilard in America, which he had seen in manuscript, it was clear to him that in a short time a completely new and dangerous invention was to be expected as a result of the splitting of the atom of the element uranium. He begged Roosevelt to watch it with the utmost care.

Roosevelt did so. In November 1941 the theory had already been expressed in formulae both in Britain and America. It was high time, for the news agencies were already reporting German progress in the same sphere. In autumn 1942 the well-known American physicist, J. R. Oppenheimer, became the director of very serious experiments and three great workshops were built at Oak Ridge in Tennessee, at Hanford in Washington and at Los Alamos in New Mexico. At the isolated plant in New Mexico, besides the workers, 4000 specially chosen technicians were employed. The 'Manhattan Plan' as a whole cost 2,000,000,000 dollars.

On July 16, 1945, the day before the Potsdam conference opened, the explosion of the first atom bomb at 5.30 a.m. caused the characteristic mushroom smoke formation to rise over the New Mexican desert. In the night of August 5th–6th a mysterious American bomber of the B-29 type left Tinian in the Marianas and early in the morning appeared over Hiroshima in Western Honshu. The explosion (uranium 235), equivalent in its results to the use of 20,000 tons of T.N.T., flattened four square miles of the city and of its 350,000 inhabitants killed between 60,000 and 80,000.

On August 9th, the day of Sukarno's and Hatta's journey to Indochina, a second atom bomb (plutonium, the only one the Americans had available) was dropped on Nagasaki. That same day the Russian troops entered Manchuria; Russia had declared war the day before.

The use of the atom bomb has been defended on the ground that it ended the war. There is a good deal to be said against that view. In a sense Hiroshima and Nagasaki mark the beginning of the cold war between Russia and the United States. The date of the Russian intervention was the fulfilment of a promise given to the United States and Britain by the Soviet Union. The resolve to use the atom bomb was kept secret from Russia and, although nothing was said, it gave Russia grounds for suspecting that its use was also a warning to her to realize that the most powerful weapon ever devised was in the hands of the West. It is true, however, that, if the two bombings did not cause the capitulation of Japan, they certainly hastened it. On condition that the emperor would not be touched and the sovereignty of the Crown remained unimpaired, Japan on August 10th was ready to surrender. This news went *via* Berne to the United States and China, *via* Stockholm to Russia and Britain. The four countries sent their answers on the 11th, and on the 14th Tokio telegraphed that Japan was ready to accept all that had been laid down at the Potsdam conference.

On August 16th, about 4 p.m., the emperor ordered a cease fire throughout the empire and Prince Kanin went to Southeast Asia, Prince Asaka to China and Prince Takeda to Manchukuo to convey the emperor's commands. On the 21st the Kwantung army surrendered to the Russians, and on the 28th the first American troops landed in Japan between Tokio and Yokosuka.

The formal instrument of surrender was signed on September 2, 1945, at 9 a.m. Tokio time, in the captain's cabin of the U.S.S. *Missouri* in Tokio Bay. The first to sign was Mamoru Shigemitsu, the foreign minister, the second was Yoshidyoro Umezu, the chief of staff of the Imperial Army and former commander-in-chief of the Kwantung army. Then MacArthur signed in his capacity of Allied commander-in-chief in east Asia and after him Nimitz as American naval commander-in-chief. General Hsu Yung-chang signed for China, and after him came the representatives of Britain, Russia, Australia, Canada, France, Holland and New Zealand. One of the two identical copies went to Japan; the other to America.

On that grey morning there disappeared the vision that had in those delirious weeks between December 1941 and March 1942 seemed to becoming reality. The proud structure built by the imperialists of Asia turned out to be a house of cards.

Germany, as a result of the war, was driven out of districts which, like East Prussia and Silesia had been German for two or three or more centuries. Italy lost Libya and Eritrea. Similarly, Japan had to give up, in addition to what she won in the war in China and Southeast Asia, many other districts which before the war had been recognized by all the nations as Japanese territory: Korea, Formosa, Kwantung, Karafuto (South Sakhalin) the Kuriles and the islands in the southern part of the Pacific Ocean.

None the less, no other nation in this war did more than Japan to change Asia and the whole course of contemporary history. At the right time it had cleared away that Western Imperialism which stood in the path of the liberation of south and east Asia and sought to prevent any real change in that continent though, for such is the irony of history, it had itself made fundamental change necessary. Satan was driven out by Satan. East Asia was wasted by fire and sword. But India and Pakistan, Ceylon and Burma, Thailand and Indonesia are today virtually free from colonial and semi-colonial domination. Did the militarists of the Kwantung army have any glimpse of the future on that cloudy morning of September 17, 1931, when they sent their troops into Manchuria?

Fifth Period 1945 – 1955

FULFILMENT AND DISILLUSION

I

ASIA AFTER THE SECOND WORLD WAR

In this last part the reader will find a report on the most important events in Asian history in the years after 1945. I use the term 'report' advisedly. That is all that can be given of the immediate past; only later shall we be able to place events in their proper place in a history. Would it then, have been preferable to omit this part altogether? I do not think so, if for no other reason than this, that few have the time and the energy to keep up with the daily stream of news from the agencies, in the papers and in books.

The division according to countries has been maintained to conform to the general plan of the book. Some countries in which there has been relatively little change, or where change has taken place in the direction indicated earlier in these pages, are not dealt with – Mongolia for instance, and the Soviet Republics in Asia, which may be freer in a degree but are not yet independent; Hongkong and Malaya, of which the former remains a British colony while the latter has become independent (1957); Afghanistan, which has managed to maintain its precarious independence although Russian influence, visible in the construction of granaries, oil tanks and roads, has become greater than the old British influence; Irak, of which within our limited space no more need be reported than the treaty with Turkey (February 1955), the basis for the later treaty of Bagdad; and some districts of less importance like Nepal and Kuwait.

We begin with China and then pass to Korea and Indochina, whose destiny lies in the last resort with China. Then we deal with India and Pakistan, Burma and Ceylon; then with Indonesia, which we link to Thailand since both are seeking to build a bridge to the future, the former through its new independence, the latter through an independence long established. Then we come to Japan and the Philippines, both still very much under the influence of the United States, the former probably not for long now, the latter for a period whose duration cannot be estimated. The next sections concern the western half of the continent. If one wished to see how transient worldly power is, one can hardly find a better illustration of it than the most recent history of this old Moslem culture area. It is not yet fifty years since the sultan and caliph was an absolute ruler in Istanbul, and scarcely half that time since Britain had the last word in the area. The three sections deal with Israel, its development and its struggle against the Arab League and against Syria-Lebanon and Jordan; with the old heartland, Turkey and Iran; and finally with Egypt, the Soudan and Saudi-Arabia – it was in the Soudan and Egypt that the old imperialism fought its last battle, and lost.

II

CHINA, KOREA AND INDOCHINA

WE have already told of [1] the renewal of the civil war in China in the winter of 1946-7. Although the 'white' armies in March 1947 succeeded in occupying Yenan the communist capital, the communist armies from Kansu-Shensi, starting from Sian on the Yellow River, spread all over North China and Manchuria where many districts had their own local revolutionary governments. In October 1947 they recaptured Yenan. It was at this time that Chiang's government banned the 'Democratic Association', the only left group [2] in its shrinking empire. The United States was still sending help to Chiang – amounting to $4,000,000,000 between 1945 and 1949 – while Mao and his associates got no aid at all from abroad. That, at least, is the conclusion one comes to after reading the various written statements by American officials, including Marshall.

As compared with the communists Chiang's troops lacked nothing from the point of view of modern military equipment; Amerca thus helped to prolong the civil war. Apart from Washington, Chiang had no one behind him except bandits and crooks. Economically, China, especially in 1948-9, lapsed into endless crisis. Not merely peasants and workers but intellectuals and a substantial section of the bourgeois greeted the new government from the north as liberators. It was not only Chinese and Russian newspapers which said so, but also foreigners who were then in China and were interested in what was happening.

In the winter of 1948-9 the ever-growing armies of liberation under Mao and Chu-teh were in possession of all China north of the Yangtse including Manchuria; they took Mukden in November, and Pekin and Tientsin in January. The Americans, realizing the significance of that advance, now sent virtually all their material to Formosa. The Nationalist government retired from Nanking to Canton (January–October 1949). That was the beginning of the end. In March 1949 the attack on South China began; Nanking fell in April, Hankow, Sian and Shanghai in May, and in summer the provinces of Chekiang, Kiangsi and Hunan, from which Mao's army had started in 1928. In October Canton was taken and Chiang's government withdrew to Chungking, their headquarters during the Second World War. In a few weeks they were chased out of it and fled to Formosa (December 1949), where Chiang and his associates have been ever since. Formosa was their last refuge on Chinese soil apart from the Pescadores and a few off-shore islands like Quemoy and Matsu; the only other Chinese island of any importance, Hainan, became part of 'red' China in April 1950.

The new government of China dates from September 21, 1949. Since then

[1] *v.* p. 330.   [2] *v.* p. 326.

China has been called Chung-hua Jen-min Kung Ho-kuo, i.e. the Chinese People's Republic. Mao Tse-tung became its president; Chou En-lai was premier and foreign minister and Chu-teh commander-in-chief. Mrs Soong Ching-ling, the widow of Sun Yat-sen, received a high post.

Just as thirty years earlier the Russian revolution had been established, so the Chinese revolution was now. It had arrived; it was there, and that fact made it impossible for recognition to be refused it. By the end of 1950 twenty-five countries had recognized communist China; the Soviet Union and other countries of Eastern Europe had done so in October 1949 and were followed by India, Pakistan, Britain, the Scandinavian countries, Ceylon and Holland, and with Holland Indonesia, which became independent in December 1949.

The 'new democracy' in Pekin, as compared with the Russian experiment was an example of moderate revolutionary Asian socialism. The agrarian reform of 1950–1955 was a bourgeois revolution like the French revolution of 1789; only the property of 'the feudal lords 'was distributed, not that of the rich peasants. In industry and trade only 'bourgeois capital' – that is, the former government properties and the property of higher officials – was socialized, roughly two-thirds of non-agrarian capital. Pekin built up a new economy. In January 1950 trains ran again between Pekin and Canton, and for the first time since 1937 all the Chinese lines were operating. In March–April 1950 inflation, which had lasted for twelve years, was ended and there was a general recovery which, if modest by Western standards, had never been known before in China.

In 1842 the emperor Tao Kuang had erected massive iron unicorns along the Yangtse to keep back the floods. During the revolution and the war these had fallen into decay. Now the peasants, with the aid of Chinese and Russian engineers, built modern dams and other protective works.

Even Tibet, in earlier days virtually an independent state and in the nineteenth century virtually a British protectorate, was recovered in 1950–1. The new motor roads and telephone connections were the visible signs of its return. In 1956 Tibet's first newspaper appeared.

At the same time the railway lines built to Mongolia and to Alma Ata in Soviet Turkestan indicated the closeness of the relations between China and USSR. China none the less was the only communist country which was independent of the Soviet Union; Russian penetration had its limits. That is indicated by the history of Port Arthur, the port of Dairen and the Chiang-chung railway to Siberia which had been made temporarily Russian possessions by the Russo-Chinese Treaty of August 15, 1945. In negotiations in Moscow in February 1950, and in Pekin in September 1954, its provisions were revised. From 1950 onwards Moscow and Pekin jointly managed the ports; the railway became Chinese in 1952, and in May 1955 Dairen and Port Arthur became Chinese possessions, although a few Russian naval officers did remain in this communist Gibraltar; it was from here that in January 1904 Japanese expansion had begun.

As far as China's foreign relations were concerned, the American anti-

Pekin policy and American intervention in Formosa, Korea and Indochina helped to determine them. That will be dealt with later; here it must suffice to say that, before the Korean War, Washington had put obstacles in the way of Chinese foreign trade; today four-fifths of that trade is with the Soviet Union, Eastern Europe and East Germany. The United States was mainly responsible for preventing the Pekin government replacing the Formosa government in the United Nations.

When the Korean War broke out in 1950, Washington 'neutralized' Formosa and the Pescadores (June 27th), that is, the American Seventh Fleet had orders to protect them against a possible invasion from the mainland. Formosa became a frontier fortress of the American empire and has remained so. The United States undertook the obligation of protecting Chiang against the results of his own 'impotence', despite the facts that his government ruled Formosa as if it was occupied territory and that the inhabitants as early as 1947 had risen in revolt demanding their independence as they had done in 1895 and 1929. That insurrection was bloodily suppressed; according to reports from the Democratic Independence Party's headquarters in Tokio – this party under Dr Liao dates from 1949 – nearly 20,000 islanders were killed. The United States made it clear to Chiang that an invasion of the mainland would not be allowed. That did not end the danger for, at the beginning of 1955, Eisenhower, if a little obscurely, said that he would regard a communist attack on Quemoy and Matsu as a *casus belli.* These lie in China's territorial waters and would be Chiang's jumping-off ground for an invasion. Chou En-lai, rightly from his point of view, branded this as aggression and intervention in the internal affairs of China. All Asia, but in particular India, and half of Britain – a Liberal newspaper like *The Manchester Guardian* and Attlee's Labour party – agreed with his view.

It is not surprising then that, with Pekin determined to make good its right to Formosa and with Washington determined to keep it in the American power system, the most important areas of conflict were first Korea, then Indochina and Formosa itself.

That does not alter the fact – indeed it proves it – that China today is again recognized as a military and political factor of particular importance. That was clear from the end of the Korean War in July 1953, and doubly clear after Chou En-lai took part in the Geneva negotiations on Korea and Indochina (April to July 1954).

These negotiations marked the end of the 'Western Period' in Asia, for at the same time as Chinese 'volunteers' were at the storming of the French fort in Indochina, Dien Bien Phu, Chou and Nehru in New Delhi (June 1954) and Pekin (November 1954) declared the relations between their two countries to be closer than ever. Nehru is not a communist and, like most other Asian leaders, he regards China primarily not as a communist, but as an Asian, country; indeed, the most important country in the new Asia, in which a revolutionary government has sought to find an answer to those questions which all 'backward' lands must answer if they are not to founder.

When in the summer of 1945 Korea was liberated from the Japanese by the Russian army (beginning of August) and the American army (beginning of September), the latter suggested that the straight line of the 38th parallel should be temporarily the boundary between the Russian and American occupation zones.

The resolution passed in Moscow (December 1945) by the foreign ministers of the United States, the Soviet Union, Britain and China providing for a five-year occupation by the four countries in order to lead to an 'independent democratic Korea',[1] remained a dead letter. Neither Moscow nor Washington wanted the co-operation of other nations and, after the Russian-American negotiations on Korea in May 1946 were ended, the land remained divided into two zones.

Meantime, in the North, a provisional native government had been formed in August 1945 which naturally was left in character as in so many countries liberated after the war. Communists held office in it and from it emerged the government in Pyongyang. On September 12th that government declared Korea independent. The Soviet Union and the East European states recognized the Pyongyang government as the sole legitimate government in Korea; so did Pekin in July 1949. But in December 1948 the United Nations gave similar recognition to the government in Seoul in South Korea which had become independent in August 15, 1948.

The independence of South Korea was more real possibly, but, while in North Korea all objectively necessary reforms – distribution of landed property and the socialization of factories and mines – were carried through, all parties in any way democratic were forbidden in the South and modernization of any sort hindered. The North followed the example of 'red', the South that of 'white', China.

The history of the leaders in both parts of the country is characteristic of the difference between them. The head of the Northern government, Kim Il-sung (b. 1912), studied at the Military Academy in Canton, in the Soviet Union and also, it seems, in Japan. Because of his participation in the anti-Japanese revolution in Seoul (March 1, 1919) he fled to China. From 1934 he was well-known throughout Korea and was revered as commander of the first Korean Resistance Brigade in Japanese Manchuria. In the summer of 1946 he became leader of the Communist party in North Korea.

The Southern leader, Syngman Rhee (b. 1875), was imprisoned (1897–1904) because of his leadership of the students. He studied in the United States from 1904 to 1910, his studies including a theological course in Princeton. In the 1919 revolution he became the first president of the 'Independent Republic of Korea'. When the revolution was suppressed by the Japanese he fled to Washington *via* Shanghai and was very active there; his name became a symbol of national liberty in Korea. When in 1945 he appeared again in his country after the liberation, he showed himself indeed to be a great nationalist, but also a bitter hater of democracy in the Chiang Kai-shek manner.

In 1949 the occupation forces withdrew, the Russians in February, the

[1] *v.* p. 283.

Americans in June and, as the representatives of the United Nations in September 1949 had feared, there now loomed up the spectre of a 'very barbarous civil war'. The American Government expert, Owen Lattimore, in his book *The Situation in Asia,* in vain warned his government against giving aid to what he called 'the reactionary regime in South Korea'. Early in the morning of June 25, 1950, the civil war began, which from December developed into a very grave international crisis. The northern troops, well equipped with Russian tanks and lorries, pressed into South Korea. Although Washington intervened within two days and foreign countries were mostly with it – on July 8th MacArthur became commander-in-chief of the United Nations forces – the Red Army by the middle of August was in possession of the whole country except for a tiny area of some 2000 square miles round the port of Pusan on the southeast coast.

But the picture changed when the first transports from the United States arrived in Pusan, and on September 15th MacArthur landed 40,000 men from 260 ships at Inchon, west of Seoul, and so threatened the northerners' communications. On October 25th South Korean troops reached Chosan on the Yalu, which is the boundary between Korea and China. At the beginning of November American detachments were within twelve miles of Manchuria and some sixty miles from Siberia. 'By Christmas', said MacArthur, 'we shall be home again.'

The stakes were very high. Had not the well-known American journalist, Walter Lippmann (*New York Herald-Tribune* of August 29, 1950), written: 'Because of its geographical position Korea is for China what Florida is to the United States'? In September Nehru and Chou En-lai had warned the United Nations against occupying North Korea, for that, they said, would almost certainly provoke Chinese intervention. Actually Chinese troops were reported south of the Yalu on October 25th. These belonged to a whole corps of 'Chinese volunteers' which included the famous Fourth Chinese Division and were estimated to be about 200,000 strong. In fierce night attacks by infantry, the American line was breached and, on December 4th, Chinese and North Korean troops forced their way into burning Pyongyang and on January 4, 1951, into Seoul. Before that (December 14th–25th) some 100,000 American, British and South Korean troops had been evacuated from the Lake Chosin area in bitter cold and snowstorms through the port of Hungnam on the east coast of North Korea.

This strategic disaster was balanced by a diplomatic success. On February 1st the United Nations condemned the 'Chinese aggression'. Forty-four countries supported the Americans; seven voted against – Russia, the Ukraine, White Russia, Poland and Czechoslovakia and also India and Burma; while the following abstained – Afghanistan, Egypt, Indonesia, Yemen, Pakistan, Saudi-Arabia, Syria, Sweden and Yugoslavia. If one considers the numbers of the inhabitants of the abstaining countries, the diplomatic victory does not look so good. In the countries which voted against or abstained live 42 per cent of the population represented in the United Nations and, if communist China had been able to take part in the vote, the figure would have been 65 per cent. The vote was of no great advantage to Washington. The aloofness of Asia, quite apart from the hostile vote of India, Burma and Russia, made the Western states, and Britain in particular, think again. When the United Nations troops again reached the North Korean frontier, Washington was forced at the twelfth hour to reject MacArthur's too independent plan for war with China. On the night of April 10th–11th President Truman removed him from all his commands in the Far East.

On June 29th the new American commander-in-chief Ridgeway made it known to the North Koreans that he was willing to enter into negotiations on board a Danish ship. Kim Il-sung and Peng Teh-huai, the commanders of the North Koreans and the Chinese, answered that they would meet him at Kaesong on the 38th parallel. Fighting died down, and in October the negotiations were removed to Panmunjon a village near Kaesong, and here, but not until July 27, 1953, the documents in English, Korean and Chinese were signed, which ended the war and slightly enlarged the territory of South Korea.

The consequences of the war were frightful. The deaths in the opposing armies – the civilian toll was far higher – amounted to 350,000: 150,000 Chinese, 100,000 North Koreans, 75,000 South Koreans, and 2000 British, Turks, Canadians, Australians, French, Greeks, Dutch, Belgians, Luxemburgers, Filipinos, Thailanders, Colombians, Ethiopians, New Zealanders and South Africans; the Americans lost 25,000 men.

There is still no union between North and South Korea. Seoul, on August 8, 1953, concluded a security treaty with the United States just as Tokio, Taipeh, Manila, Bangkok, and Karachi have done. A change in the situation is improbable and the problem is still unsolved.

Earlier we related the history of the Viet Minh and the war in Indochina. In the agreement between the Viet Minh and France of March 6, 1944, signed by Ho Chi Minh and the French representative Sainteny, the democratic republic of Vietnam was recognized as free – the word 'independent' was avoided – and there was provision for the retention of only a small French force. But it was soon evident what the French real intentions were; they were determined to stay in their 'fair garden in the Pacific'. In the conversations between Ho and the French Government in Fontainebleau in July–August 1946 no agreement could be reached. In November 1946 French warships bombarded Haiphong and killed 6000 civilians; the Viet Minh forces went into action and began the war which ended in 1954.

Meantime d'Argenlieu, while the Fontainbleau conversations were going on, had sought to keep the Viet Minh Republic within bounds by restoring French control over Cambodia and Laos through agreements with King Norodom Sihanouk (June 1946) and King Sisavang Vong (August 1946), while Cochinchina, the base of French rule, was recognized (June 1946) as an 'autonomous republic'.

The Viet Minh stoutly defended their territory, and by 1948 the 150,000 men of the French garrison were in control only of the towns and the main lines of communication. The French, therefore, tried to undermine the red republic by political means. Paris declared that it would recognize the independence of the non-communist native counter-government of Hue (summer 1948). Finally the magic word was spoken. On March 8, 1949, when the Chinese communist army was beginning the liberation of South China, Vietnam became 'independent within the French Union'; only foreign relations and defence remained in French hands. Once again Bao Dai, who since 1946 had been living safely in Hongkong and in the south of France, was emperor of the new Vietnam to which Cochinchina now belonged (June 1949); he went back again and again to the sunny Riviera, far from the strife in his kingdom, in order to spend there the 50,000,000 francs which for some years France had been giving him. Simultaneously Laos and Cambodia became independent (July and November 1949) within the French Union.

At the end of 1949 three-fourths of the village communities were in the hands of the Viet Minh, with their own newspapers, universities and a growing guerrilla army. Like China and Korea the Indochinese revolution (summer 1950) became an international problem. Washington, which in the Indonesian question had shown itself anti-colonial, now took the French side; the Michelin rubber plantations had come into American hands. From 1949 on, the French Communist party passed from words to deeds; it began a campaign of strikes and sabotage; this was an 'evil war'. In January 1950 Pekin, Moscow and the East European states recognized the Ho Chi Minh government; in February Britain, the United States and some other Western states recognized the Bao Dai government. But the new French commander-in-chief, Lattre de Tassigny (December 1950 to January 1952), and his army of 400,000 men were making very little headway though the war was costing 1,400,000,000 francs a day. The Viet Minh now began to invest towns; from September to December 1950 it was the fortified towns on the Chinese frontier – Lao-Kai, Kao-bang, Lang-son; in February 1952 it was the strategically important road junction of Hoa-binh, forty-three miles west of Hanoi. From October to December 1952 – summer is the rainy season – the whole of the region between the Red River and the Black River fell into the hands of the guerrillas and in it the French could move relatively freely in daylight only between Hanoi and the coast and in Cochinchina.

Although both at home and abroad warning voices were raised, including those of Cambodia's king and Bao Dai's premier Nguyen Van Tam, that the only solution was the genuine independence of Vietnam, the new French commander-in-chief, Navarre (1953-4), took the opposite view. The keynote of his plan of campaign was to prevent the Viet Minh invading Laos and at the same time delude them into attacking a modern fortress outside the usual area of fighting. In November 20, 1953, the first troops of Colonel Castries arrived by air – the only route open – at the mountain village of Dien Bien Phu in the west of North Vietnam. Robert Guillain, the correspondent of *Le Monde* who spent Christmas Day there, described the place as a virtually impregnable fortress in a clearing of some sixty-eight square miles in the middle of thickly wooded hill-country where the Viet

Minh troops lay concealed. He continued: 'When we talk of the Indochinese War we think of a war between Whites and Asians and that was in a sense true in 1947. Today in Dien Bien Phu are virtually only North Africans, African negroes, Vietnamese, Thailanders and – Germans.' All winter the Viet Minh kept away from Dien Bien Phu as a cat does from hot bricks. Meantime Britain, France, Russia and the United States (Eden, Bidault, Molotov and Dulles) resolved (April 26th) to hold an international conference in Geneva on Korea and Indochina. Pekin (Chou En-lai) was also invited. It was high time. In the rice delta technically belonging to France, the relatively small area between Sonay, Phat-Diem and Haiphong, French communications were no longer safe. Of the 6400 villages between the Red River and the motor road from Hanoi to Haiphong 4000 had a Viet Minh administration. The communists did not need to infiltrate here. Guerrilla regiments like the 42nd and the 50th, in the province of Hung Yen and Thai-Binh came to a man from the Red River region. Navarre had sent a force of 100,000 men to break their resistance in offensives which, though they had the code names 'Lemon' and 'Mandarin', were as barbaric as Chiang's offensives in 1930–1935. But the Viet Minh held out and grew in strength.

When the Geneva conference assembled, Dien Bien Phu had become a symbol of final decision. While the French tried to get other Western states to intervene, the Viet Minh commander-in-chief, Vo Nguyen Gap, with his 40,000 men, pressed the siege and on March 12th to 14th launched the first bloody assault against the stubborn defence of Castries and his 15,000 men.

In April Paris reported that many Chinese lorries with Chinese drivers were with the Viet Minh forces. Washington declared this to be foreign intervention, although it was itself carrying virtually the whole financial burden of the Indochinese War. American warships sailed to Indochinese waters, and on April 4th Paris asked the American Government to relieve Dien Bien Phu. It was a critical moment. London, which generally had a better understanding of Asia, declared on April 18th that it would not think of intervention unless the Geneva conference broke down. Behind Britain stood India and other South Asian democracies. And as Dulles, despite his belief in a 'policy of force', did not dare create a second China-Korea situation, deeds did not follow words.

From April 26 to July 21, 1954, representatives were present at Geneva from Britain, France, the United States, Russia, China (Chou En-lai), Viet Minh (Pham Van Dong), Vietnam (Nguyen Quoc Dinh), Cambodia and Laos. At the beginning of May Dulles went home in anger. The presence of Chou En-lai and Krishna Menon marked the end of an epoch.

The discussions on Indochina began on May 8th, the day on which the morning papers announced that on the previous day Dien Bien Phu had fallen after an attack that had lasted for twenty hours. On June 17th the new French Premier, Mendès-France, declared that he wished to bring the war to an end in four weeks; otherwise he would resign. Chou En-lai had talks with him in Berne, with Nehru in Delhi, with U Nu in Rangoon and with Ho in the south of China while, in the gardens of the White House in

Washington, Dulles, Eisenhower, Churchill and Eden held talks of their own.

At the end of June the French evacuated the whole of the Red River area except Hanoi and Haiphong, and on the night of July 20th–21st the Indochinese war was brought to an end in Geneva. Cambodia and Laos remained independent kingdoms. Vietnam was divided along the 17th parallel into Viet Minh in the north and Vietnam under Bao Dai in the south. Free elections were to take place in Vietnam before July 20th. All objective observers anticipated a victory for the Viet Minh if the South Vietnam Government in the interim did not make far-reaching reforms in their territory in a very democratic sense and without foreign intervention. The proclamation by the premier and first president, Ngo Dinh Diem, of a republic and the deposition of Bao Dai at the end of October looked like a step in this direction.

III

INDIA-PAKISTAN, BURMA AND CEYLON

TOWARDS the end of 1946, while France and Holland were trying to keep the new republics of Indochina and Indonesia under their control, the British Government under Clement Attlee (June 1945) began to declare their 'possessions' in Nearer India independent. On September 1st Jawaharlal Nehru became prime minister of an all-Indian Government. In relation to foreign countries it had far-reaching independence; in October Krishna Menon went to Moscow as his country's first 'free' diplomatic representative abroad, but the bloody strife between Hindus and Moslems still prevented the complete independence of a united India and Pakistan.

As a result of the crisis which developed in the winter of 1946–7 Attlee in February 1947 announced a plan involving the withdrawal of the British by June 1948 at the latest. Simultaneously Lord Louis Mounbatten, who had remarkably liberal ideas on independence, replaced Wavell as viceroy of India (February 1947–June 1948).

From this time on Britain continued its policy of not trying to reach a compromise. What Churchill and his party refused to understand, the Attlee government understood very well; Asia had changed; it had awakened. There was no sense in further estranging Asia. On June 3, 1947, the final partition plan was published in Delhi and in London; British India was to become two independent states, India and Pakistan. On July 18th the king signed the India Independence Act of July 4th, and on the night of August 14th–15th at midnight India and Pakistan became two independent dominions. Here was a development and a decision which showed the political maturity and the intelligence of both London and Delhi. Britain remains in South Asia only because she has voluntarily withdrawn from it. Politically London and Delhi, with their rich store of political ideas, are important factors in every international decision concerning Asia in this period – Indonesia, China, Korea or Indochina.

The division of British India into India and Pakistan and the division of the latter into East and West Pakistan meant at the outset much bloodshed and transplanting of populations, particularly in the Punjab and Bengal with their mixed populations. In 1947–8 some 6,000,000 Hindus and Sikhs moved from Pakistan to India, and a similar number of Moslems moved in the contrary direction. In the winter of 1949–50 there was a slightly smaller exchange of populations in Bengal. These migrations, which were at once an exodus and a civil war, cost 500,000 lives. In the overheated political atmosphere Gandhi, the architect of freedom, and Liaqat Ali Khan, the premier of Pakistan, were murdered by extremists because of their moderate views –

the former in Delhi on January 30th, 1948, the latter on October 16, 1951, in Rawalpindi because of the Kashmir dispute.

Kashmir, a strategically important region, in view of its nearness to China and Russia, has an area of about 80,000 sq. miles, partly wild mountains, partly cultivateable land; it is the water reservoir of West Pakistan; it is the land from which the Nehru family comes and it remains today a cause of quarrel between India and Pakistan. The peasants of Kashmir are mostly Moslems – Kashmir has a population of 4,500,000 – but in spite of that the Hindu land-owners and the maharaja declared their adhesion to India rather than to Moslem Pakistan, a preference natural enough. As a result there was a minor war, which raged from October 1947 to January 1949, in which Indian troops occupied the southern part, some three-quarters of the whole country. Attempts at mediation by the United Nations achieved nothing except to show that Kashmir wanted to remain independent, and its Moslem premier, Mohammed Abdulla, earlier one of Nehru's trusted collaborators, who had carried out many agrarian reforms in Kashmir, was arrested in August 1953 by the maharaja because he sought to establish that independence with foreign (American) help.

In June 1948 C. Rajagopalachari (later minister of the interior) was appointed viceroy in place of the deservedly popular Mountbatten. On January 26th, 1950, India took a further step away from the past and be-came a fully independent republic, but also a voluntary member of the British Commonwealth.

In 1947 the great kingdom of Hyderabad was the only one of the greater or lesser kingdoms of British India to refuse to join either of the new repub-lics. Here, however, contrary to what happened in Kashmir, it was a Hindu population (of 17,000,000) which was opposed to a Moslem ruler and desired to be part of India. In September 1948 Hyderabad was occupied by Indian troops and made part of India. From the international point of view it was just a storm in a teacup, even if the Nizam did, though in vain, seek the intervention of the United Nations.

Meantime India did not become the socialist land of Nehru's dream though, as in Burma and Indonesia, there were movements in this direction. The most important industries and the railways became state-owned but all other enterprises were, temporarily at least – the law was passed at the beginning of 1948 – left to free capitalism simply because the State itself lacked capital. Nor was the peasant population with its own cultivation methods and its typical Asian social structure much affected, although Nehru's government did try to modernize the life in the villages by making the villagers literate, teaching them hygiene, introducing them to artificial manures and modern farming methods, and giving them sex instruction. But things have changed too little, and few know that better than Nehru himself. Only here and there have the big landowners voluntarily partitioned their estates. Vinoba Bhave, an adherent of Gandhi, conducts propaganda for such voluntary division of land; this is known as the Bhudan movement – it does not confine its attentions merely to division of land. It has had some success. At the end of 1955 some three and a half million acres had been divided among hitherto landless peasants. Just how far these relatively minor reforms constitute the beginning of the agrarian revolution remains an open question, but it is *the* question for contemporary Asia.

The Indian bourgeois and landowners follow Nehru not so much as the socialist premier of India, but as the foreign minister for Asia. Internally India was governed in the main by S. V. Patel, in no way a socialist, but internationally India is Nehru. That was made clear at the two inter-Asian conferences in Delhi. The first, held in March–April 1947, was the first all-Asian conference at which half the world's population was represented, including that of Soviet Republics of Asia, and the second in the critical weeks of January 1949 when the independence of Indonesia was on the agenda.[1] There were represented: Abyssinia, Afghanistan, Australia, Burma, Ceylon, Egypt, India, Irak, Iran, Yemen, the Lebanon, Pakistan, the Philippines, Saudi-Arabia and Syria. Today London does not decide anything regarding Asia without taking counsel of Nehru, the leader of the 'third force'; that was shown in the cases of Korea, Indochina, China and Formosa.

A minor but very significant episode ended the period 1945–1955 in India. In October 1954 the five French possessions in Nearer India, relics of the French ascendancy in the seventeenth and eighteenth centuries were returned to India. Their total area is just over 300 square miles, with an Indian population of about 400,000 spread over Pondicherry, Karikal, Chandernagore (surrendered to India in 1950), Mahé and Yanaon. Portuguese India – Goa, Damao, Diu and three tiny islands off the Malabar coast with an area of 1600 square miles and a population of 700,000 – is the only land possessed by Europeans within India's natural frontiers. They have been Portuguese possessions since 1510.[2]

'There are', said Nehru in 1953, 'four great Powers today of which two, the United States and Russia, are highly developed industrially and technically, and two, China and India, which are relatively backward.' Yet when he spoke India was building the new city of Chandigarh in the Punjab to Le Corbusier's design; it is, so far as its architecture is concerned, the most modern city in the world.

Pakistan – it became free on the night of August 14–15, 1947 – at first an 'independent Dominion', since 1956 a free republic within the British Commonwealth, has not in either the international or the purely Asian sense the importance of India. One probable reason for this is the death of its founder Mohammed Ali Jinnah (1876–1948) on September 11, 1948, the first representative of the British Crown in his liberated country, and the subsequent murder on October 16, 1951, of Pakistan's second great leader, the premier Liaqat Ali Khan (1895–1951). Pakistan understandably is much more concerned about itself than India is. Pakistan did not take over a great functioning administrative apparatus such as India found in New Delhi. The government in Karachi had to be built up out of nothing, in a land which is

---

[1] *v.* p. 365.
[2] Indian troops occupied Goa late in 1961 and all Portugal's possessions are now part of India.

divided into two widely separated parts. The majority of Pakistanis live in the relatively small area of East Pakistan, some 1100 miles away from West Pakistan; there is only one secure line of communication, the sea-route of 2500 miles. It is a land of peasants and landlords with a small middle class and, in comparison with India, with a very small-scale industry. Economically, and in other respects, Pakistan reaped a poor harvest from the partition of British India; the Kashmir question is an example of that. In East Pakistan particularly, which has always been an area of revolutionary activity and which shared its economic development with the east of India, there has been a good deal of resistance to the not very enlightened, and certainly not at all socialist, government in Karachi. In the year 1954 when the Pakistan Government began its flirtation with Washington, the Moslem League, the party favouring Karachi, was completely routed in the March elections in East Pakistan. Although Karachi managed to avoid a first-class crisis – the East Pakistan government was dissolved and the communist party was banned throughout the whole of Pakistan – it remains doubtful how far Islam, as the only cementing influence in the divided country, can keep it together and whether the Karachi government, if it remains as it is, will not be overthrown by a revolution made by the left.

India's independence and the anti-British movement in Burma were signs that in Burma too a new political situation would have to be created. In December 1946 Attlee invited to London some members of the Anti-Fascist Freedom League [1] to discuss self-government either inside or outside the Commonwealth. In January 1947 there arrived from Rangoon Aung San, U Saw (whom in 1946 the British had sent back to Burma from Kenya where he had been interned all through the war) and Ba Sein (like Aung San, a minister of the Burmese Government during the Japanese occupation), who had been deported by the Japanese to Singapore and Java, where he was living in Bandung when the British occupied that island. On January 27, 1947, Aung San and Attlee signed an agreement leading to a 'free and independent Burma inside or outside the Commonwealth'. U Saw and Ba Sein, who feared the left wing of the Freedom League refused to sign. When the League, apart from the communists, decided to support Aung San, U Saw, supported by Ba Sein and Ba Maw who had returned home from a Japanese prison, tried like lesser Chiangs to clear out the left socialists root and branch. On July 19, 1947, Aung San and six of his ministers, including the much-loved thakin Mya, were murdered in Rangoon. The massacre delayed independence only for a fortnight. While U Saw, Ba Sein and Ba Maw were in prison – the first-named was hanged in May 1948 – U Nu (who had been out of the country in June) and Attlee signed (October 17th) a treaty giving Burma full independence, and on January 4th the land became free except for some minor limitations of sovereignty in the event of a war in Southeast Asia and some provisions for the security of British investments and foreign possessions.

[1] v. p. 303.

Sao Shwe Thaik was the first president of the Republic of Burma. Thakin Nu was premier in succession to the murdered Aung San during the period of negotiation. Thakin Nu, alias U Nu, is a fairly left independent socialist.

U Nu created the system of government according to his own ideas. It is Asian in the modern sense and decidedly socialist but not communist, even if, for instance, in October 1948 no one was allowed to own more than 50 acres of land, and in the same winter the teak forests were nationalized. U Nu took Nehru as his model and, like him, from 1949 on assured foreign capitalists greater freedom of action. As for foreign policy, Rangoon sailed the same course as New Delhi and Jakarta.

Meantime his government, after the somewhat unnatural Freedom League, broke up having secured independence, had to defend itself against three different resistance movements, those of the communists (especially in 1948–1950), the Karens (1949–50) and of the invading bands of Chinese ex-soldiers of Chiang's defeated armies (1950–1954). The first two were very dangerous, and in 1949 nearly brought down the Nu government.

Their history can be told briefly. In October 1944 the Communist party had broken with the Freedom League, which united all the anti-fascists, and so with the interim government of Aung San. The three best known communist leaders [1] were thakin Soe, thakin Than Tun and thakin Thein Pe. The very radical Soe had meantime built up a party of his own known as the Communist Party of Burma (the Red Flag Communists) in opposition to the Burmese Communist Party (the White Flag Communists) which was led by Than Tun and Thein Pe. As in other Asian lands – Malaya, Indonesia, India – and also as in Europe, the Communist party hesitated whether to take part in a leftish 'bourgeois' government or to go on to carry through the socialist revolution.

But in March 1948 Than Tun and his associates went into open opposition at the same time as the Indian communists turned against Nehru and the communists in Malaya declared war on the British. A section of the communists, including Thein Pe, refused to join in the rebellion. Than Tun's forces threatened Rangoon in the summer of 1948.

In 1949 the Karens began their rebellion. These highlanders, who today are scattered all over the country, differ ethnologically and historically from the inhabitants of the river valleys of Lower Burma. Many of them dreaded the departure of the British, who had used them as soldiers in Lower Burma. Although they received a far-reaching autonomy in 1948, many of them thought in terms of an independence such as Pakistan possessed.

In January 1949 they rose, and in March were in possession of Insein just over six miles from Rangoon, and in the summer of 1940 U Nu and his government were virtually besieged by them. Except for Rangoon, the whole country was in the hands of either the communists or the Karens.

Gradually the prospect improved. Thanks to the liberal government of U Nu, both revolutions ebbed away and withdrew to the northern mountains. They had been a terrible danger; they were now only a warning.

Chiang's fugitive soldiers, of whom some 20,000 were living on the

[1] v. p. 270.

peasants in Northeast Burma, also ceased to be dangerous; they were only a nuisance both to Burma and internationally. Half of them, as a result of United Nations mediation, were evacuated to Formosa in December 1953.

Ceylon, because of its small population – about 7,000,000 inhabitants, of which 500,000 are Indians – can only receive summary treatment here, although the history of the island affords an interesting example of Asian-European relations. The Portuguese had built forts and trading posts in it as early as 1505 and, after a period of Dutch colonization (c. 1650–1795), Ceylon became a British Crown colony in 1802.

The limited self-government granted in 1931 was extended in 1945 and, although there was little signs here of a revolution as in India and in Burma, the island by the Ceylon Independence Act of 1947 became on February 4, 1948, the first British Crown colony to attain Dominion status. That meant full political independence for a land in which Britain, from a military point of view, had still much, indeed everything, to say.

D. S. Senanayake (1884–1952), the former minister of agriculture, was premier, minister for foreign affairs and minister of war from 1948 to 1952. The second premier was Sir John Kotelawala, known far beyond his own country as host to the Colombo conference (April 7 to May 2, 1954), where the premiers of India, Pakistan, Burma, Indonesia and Ceylon, on the occasion of the Indochina negotiations at Geneva, gave their views on questions, important today as then, concerning Asia and Africa, e.g. the independence of Indochina and North Africa, China and the United Nations, and the return of the Arab refugees to Israel.

It was these 'Colombo states', the non-communist democracies of Asia, who in December 1954 at Bogor (Buitenzorg) worked out the plans for the first Asian-African conference in Bandung in April 1955.

IV

INDONESIA AND THAILAND

ALTHOUGH it was not until the end of 1949 that Holland recognized the Republic of Indonesia, it had been in existence since the day of its proclamation, August 17, 1945. And it was still in existence when, as a result of the Potsdam decisions, British and not American troops landed at various points to form a temporary army of occupation. The British commander-in-chief, Sir Philip Christison, refused to intervene in the dispute between the republican government and the Dutch administration. Whether or not it was a consequence of his refusal, a war of guerrillas became general.

At first The Hague government forbade all conversations between Holland's chief representative, the governor-general H. J. van Mook (1942 to November 1948), and the republican government (Sukarno and Hatta). It was foreign intervention, the strikes in Australian ports where the workers refused to load ships for 'the Dutch imperialists' and the mediation of Britain (Sir Archibald Clark Kerr, later Lord Inverchapel, and Lord Killearn) which induced the Dutch Government to get in touch with the Republicans on the basis of the much-quoted speech of Queen Wilhelmina of December 7, 1942. But the negotiations (April 23 and 24, 1946) broke down, and in summer the Dutch had again occupied virtually all the Indonesian islands except Sumatra and Java. On November 15, 1946, Shahrir for the Indonesians and Schermerhorn for the Dutch, with Lord Killearn as intermediary, concluded in a village near Cheribon, the internationally famous compromise of Linggadjati, modelled on the Franco-Indochinese agreement of Dalat in March 1946. The agreement meant the *de facto* recognition of the Republic in Java, Madura and Sumatra, and a plan for an interim semi-independent government of the future United States of Indonesia, semi-independent in the sense that the Republic was not allowed to pursue an independent foreign policy. The British forces of occupation were withdrawn. It was, however, soon clear that the Dutch interpretation of the agreement robbed it of all meaning even before it was finally signed at Rijswijk near Batavia. The compromise of Linggadjati was only a paper one. None the less the Arab states in March 1947 recognized the Republic as *de jure* independent, while Britain and the United States confined themselves to *de facto* recognition.

Meantime Van Mook tried to stem the tide of revolution by declaring a variety of Indonesian districts 'free'. Holland still wanted more, and the Indonesian attitude also stiffened when in July 1947 the radical Sharifudin replaced the moderate Shahrir. Concerned lest the radicals should make them lose everything, the Dutch Government for good or ill determined to retain everything. On the night of July 20th–21st the Dutch expeditionary force began the war against 'the house of cards of Djoka' but called it police action. Protests were made almost universally, especially by Asian countries. India and Australia brought the matter to the United Nations. On August 1st the Security Council demanded that the Dutch Government order a 'cease fire'. It agreed and the campaign ended on August 5th. Holland retained the occupied areas, i.e. the most important parts of Java and Sumatra, the ports, the oil and the plantations. Although the Dutch troops, like the French in Indochina, were relatively impotent save in the cities and on the main lines of communication, it was a black day for Indonesia when on January 17, 1948 as a result of United Nations mediation, a second Dutch-Indonesian agreement was signed on board the American transport *Renville*. In it the principles laid down at Linggadjati were re-affirmed, but the free republican area was dangerously limited.

As Linggadjati had caused the fall of the Shahrir government, so the *Renville* agreement caused the replacement of Sharifudin by Hatta. London recognized Dutch sovereignty over all Indonesia and refused to accept Indonesian Republic passports. Thus reduced in size, robbed and occupied, the Republic faced the crisis of 1948. The regime in Jakarta was shaken to its foundations and for the first time the young Republic threatened to fall to pieces. Would the Indonesian revolution remain purely nationalist as India's had done, or would Dutch imperialism push it to the left as had happened in China and Indochina? In August the left socialist groups united with the communist party. What was happening? Was there a general communist plan of campaign for all Southeast Asia? Had not the Malayan and Burman communists begun guerrilla war? Early on September 18 communist forces occupied Madiun and some smaller towns in the Republic. The leaders of this 'Commune of Madiun' were Muso who had just returned from Russia, Sharifudin and Sedjadjit. Their attempt was premature. The Hatta government, which refused Dutch intervention, recaptured Madiun at the end of September, and in October all the revolutionary leaders were killed in a savage guerrilla war in the mountains.

Externally the Republic was also gravely threatened. The Dutch committed all the mistakes and cruelties which the Spaniards had committed in the Dutch War of Independence in the seventeenth century. One of these mistakes, committed through sheer lack of comprehension of modern Asian nationalism, was the second action by the Dutch army which began on the night of December 18th–19th. On the morning of the 19th Jakarta, the heart of the Republic, was occupied by air action and various high members of the Republican government (including Sukarno, Hatta and Sastromidjojo) were arrested and interned on Bangka island (December 31st). In two weeks all the towns and mainroads in Java and Sumatra were in Dutch hands. The more success the action achieved, the more it was shown to have failed. Inside the countery, as was the case after the first 'police action', only the communists and the left socialists protested, but all Indonesia inside or outside the Republic was extremely embittered. While a republican government continued to function from Sumatra and India, the Security Council intervened, and on December 24, 1948, the governments represented on it demanded the abandonment of the police action and the release of the interned leaders. A plan sponsored by various countries, including Russia and China, for the withdrawal of Dutch troops was not carried but the Dutch Government gave in; it finally ended the war on January 5, 1949, having ended it in Java on December 31st. The world outside remained watchful. On January 28th the Security Council ordered the release of the Indonesian leaders; that independence for Indonesia be granted by July 1, 1960, at the latest and the formation of a UN Mediation Commission. This order, and the demands of fifteen Asian countries whose representatives met in Delhi from January 20th to 24th (release of the leaders, and other political prisoners, withdrawal of the Dutch troops, free trade and relations with other countries, independence by January 1, 1950, at the latest), made the Dutch reasonable. On May 7th the third Dutch-Indonesian agreement was signed in Jakarta; the Republican government would be 'free' and would return to Djogjakarta; the Republic would include the former Djogjakarta district (a little over a square mile on the south coast of Java with 2,500,000 inhabitants); Holland would not declare 'free' any other parts of Indonesia; in an all-Indonesian interim government the Republic would have a third of the offices; Holland and Indonesia were to begin negotiations on independence. At the end of June the Dutch left Djogjakarta and in July the Republican government with Sukarno and Hatta in it began to function.

Thus restored, the Republic appointed its representatives to the Round Table conference at The Hague (August 23 to November 2, 1949). On December 27th Queen Juliana for Holland and Hatta as leader of the Indonesian delegation signed the declaration of the independence of the United States of Indonesia, the Republik Indonesia Serikat.

Independence did not mean complete freedom. There remained 'on a basis of free consent and independence' certain ties between Holland and Indonesia where foreign policy was concerned, and in the spheres of finance, economic affairs and education. Both lands were under one and the same crown. This was the constitutional solution, the Dutch Indonesian Union which was Holland's aim. The 'union' lasted only seven years.

Holland retained West New Guinea and, as various discussions between 1950 and 1956 showed, had no intention of altering her position there. This was one of the reasons why the relations between Holland and the Republic of Indonesia – the United States of Indonesia became on August 15, 1950, a single republic in which the federal form disappeared altogether – did not improve. Although every special tie between the two countries were removed at The Hague on August 10, 1954 – Indonesia then finally became completely independent – West New Guinea (Irian) remained a stumbling-block in their relations, for it was considered more and more to be proof of the survival of a Western colonial policy which outraged Asia.

We have related earlier that Thailand, which from 1945 to 1949 was again called Siam, voluntarily returned on July 1945 and November 1946 those regions of Burma, Malaya and Indochina which had been acquired during the war and the Japanese occupation.[1]

The Pridi government, which resulted from the resistance movement (Nai Pridi Phanomyoung, premier from March to August 1946), had not the time to introduce reform and so secure the position against the anti-democratic tendencies from the immediate past. The military *coup* of Field-Marshal Pibul Songgram on November 8, 1947, meant the end of a free Thailand, especially when Pibul himself became premier in place of Khuan Aphaiwong (April 1948). The 'new' policy, whereby the people were denied any share in the government, was laid down in the third Thailand constitution of March 23, 1949; the first constitution was that of December 10, 1932, the second that of May 10, 1946. In the same summer Prince Bovaradej returned from Indochina whence he had fled after his attempt at a royalist revolution in 1933. In March 1950, the Crown Prince Bhumidol (Phumiphon) Adulyadet (b. 1927) returned from Switzerland; he was the brother of King Ananda Mahidol, mysteriously murdered on June 19, 1946. On May 5, 1950, he was crowned in Bangkok.

From the historical point of view this meant a retreat from the new democratic Asia as we have seen it develop in India, Ceylon, Burma, Indochina and Indonesia. Like South Korea, Chiang's China and the Philippines, Thailand under Pibul was in the American sphere. All its rubber and tin went to the United States; Washington had military installations in it. Relations with India and communist China were very restricted for, on the one hand, Thailand refused to take part in the Asian conferences in Delhi in January 1949 where the very critical Indonesian question was discussed, and, on the other hand, the second SEATO conference was held in Bangkok on February 23, 1955.

Pridi and others who had remained in hiding since November 1947 tried several times to give their country a democratic regime by revolutionary action (in September 1948 and February 1949) but without success. In 1949, it seems, he and his associates fled abroad, while four former ministers, all coming from the revolutionary northeast of the country, were executed. In 1954 Pridi appeared in Pekin where he represented 'the other Thailand' at the microphone.

[1] *v.* p. 305.

V

JAPAN AND THE PHILIPPINES

FROM the purely military point of view the credit for the victory in the Pacific and the Far East goes almost entirely to the United States, and it was American forces under MacArthur which in September 1945 occupied the islands that form Japan; during the occupation (1945–1952) other states had virtually no say in anything. The international Far Eastern Commission (from December 1945), in which, besides the United States, Russia, Britain, China, France, Holland, Canada, Australia, New Zealand, India (then including Pakistan) the Philippines and Burma were represented, had practically no significance.

One of the rare examples of joint action was the investigation into the activities of Japanese officers, officials and ministers in East Asia between 1928 and 1945 by an international tribunal (June 1946 to November 1948). As a result of its not very fruitful labours, the occupying powers condemned some 700 Japanese, mostly soldiers, as war criminals, among them (December 1948) the former premier Hideki Tojo. The Soviet Union wanted to bring to trial the 'rapacious emperor'. That was rejected, but MacArthur stripped him of his divine splendour and his manifold functions.

Meantime the Americans had made a beginning of what is called – and in many respects justifiably – the democratization of Japan. In September 1945 many Japanese had expected a regime of terror. But it was soon seen that the occupation brought a new freedom, and caused many Japanese to turn to America, a feeling which lasted until 1950 and then began to disappear. There was at the beginning no opposition of any kind. The communists greeted MacArthur almost as a liberator, and naturally for, for the first time in Japanese history, communists and socialists were able to build up their parties and their press. On May 3, 1945, the empire got a new constitution on the model of the British and American constitutions in place of their undemocratic 'German' constitution of 1889.

Although Japanese officials and politicians continued in office – if for no other reason than that too few Americans spoke Japanese – they were as a rule not democratically inclined. The only 'enlightened' premier was the socialist, Tetsu Katayama (May 1947–February 1948). The better-known Shigeru Yoshida (May 1946–May 1947; October 1948 to February 1949 and February 1949–February 1955) could not be called a democrat or even a liberal in the usual sense of that term.

Nearly all the reforms in these days came from the Americans – the rights of women, the democratization and extension of the labour movement, and agrarian reforms. By the Agricultural Law of October 1946 owners of land who were not peasant farmers were not allowed to possess more than two and a half acres of arable land, and such farmers were allowed only seven and a half acres (in Hokkaido, thirty acres). In 1949 the distribution of land came to an end when the Government had resold to some 4,000,000 small farmers, 5,000,000 acres which had previously belonged to the big landowners. Today almost 90 per cent of the cultivateable land is owned by the farmers as opposed to the 50 per cent they owned formerly.

But when in 1949 and 1950 the friction between Washington and Moscow-Pekin increased, democratization, and, later, the occupation, came to an end. On the basis of the resolutions of Potsdam and Moscow (1945) the MacArthur administration had tried, if no more fundamentally than in the similar operation in Germany, to destroy the Japanese trusts (*Zaibatsu*), and to split them into smaller, less dangerous concerns. From 1949 – the date of the collapse of Chiang's China – the effort ceased on the ground that action against the capitalists 'hindered economic recovery' and also because of the re-militarization of Japan as an island barrier against Red Asia, a barrier less than 125 miles from the seat of war in Korea.

About the same time, when 'Emperor' MacArthur went home on April 11, 1951, John Foster Dulles began secret negotiations in Paris and London on a peace treaty with Japan. Because of a difference of opinion about which China should sign the treaty, neither Taipeh nor Pekin were admitted to the negotiations. On July 12th the text of the Anglo-American draft treaty was published; it was, as the London *Times* said, 'a diplomatic defeat for the position of America in Japan and the Pacific and for the Japanese desire for independence, and is no solution to the problems of the Pacific'.

With only minor alterations the treaty was signed (September 8th) in San Francisco by forty-nine countries; those from Asia were – Cambodia, Ceylon, Egypt, Indonesia, Irak, Iran, Laos, the Lebanon, Pakistan, the Philippines, Saudi-Arabia, Syria, Turkey, Vietnam (the Bao Dai government) and Japan. The Soviet Union, Czechoslovakia, Poland, India and Burma refused to sign, while neither China was given the chance to do so.

The treaty contained, among others, the following provisions: Art. 1. Japan was to be completely independent and sovereign; Art. 2. Japan recognized the independence of Korea and renounced all rights to Formosa, the Pescadores, the Kuriles and Sakhalin and all former Japanese possessions in the Pacific, including the Marianas, the Caroline and the Marshall islands (in 1947 the United States had been given a mandate for these by the United Nations), the Paracel and Spratly Islands in the South China Sea; Art. 3. Japan recognized the full administrative rights of the United States over the Ryukyu Islands, i.e. Nanseishoto, south of the 29th parallel, the Bonins, Rosario and Nanposhoto or Volcano Island, south of the 30th parallel, and also over Parce Vela and Marcus Island; Art. 6. Japan was permitted to retain or station foreign armed forces in her territory. On September 8th Yoshida and Acheson signed a military treaty, extended in March 1954, granting the United States the right to maintain military bases in Japan.

On April 28, 1952, Washington brought the occupation to an end. Japan was once again an independent though a much smaller country.

Criticism by the Soviet Union and India was directed not against the recovery of independence but against Arts. 2 and 6 of the treaty. Both governments regretted the absence of a written recognition of Manchuria, Formosa and other Chinese islands as *Chinese* territory or of South Sakhalin and the Kuriles as *Russian* territory. Both governments desired to forbid the stationing of foreign (i.e. American) troops in Japan. In addition the Soviet Union wanted a more active democratization of Japan; this was virtually a demand for a smaller Japanese army and a ban on the use of the Sea of Japan by warships of any nation other than Russian, Japanese or Korean.

Since the summer of 1954 Japan has begun the creation of a Japanese army, if under another name, for the constitution forbids rearmament. Behind this is a revived *Zaibatsu* which gives the orders. Although the cabinet of Itshiro Hatoyama (February 1955), in which Shegimitsu, released in 1950, was once again foreign minister, was critical of the United States and sought to renew relations, particularly trade relations with Pekin and Moscow, and although in the elections at the end of February 1955 the left parties – the two Socialist parties, the Communist and the very radical Peasant parties – received 35 per cent of the votes, the dream of a really democratically governed Japan remains for the moment a dream. How Japan will develop will be seen in the future. Only one thing can in my view be said with certainty; the course it will follow will be an Asian one.

The Americans kept their promises about the independence of the Philippines. By the law signed by Roosevelt on March 34, 1934, they became on July 4, 1946, a politically independent republic, but only after a little shady bargaining.

Washington wanted to guarantee independence and financial aid on a large scale only on condition that the existing freedom of action for Americans was maintained. So in no very democratic way the Philippines on April 30, 1946, accepted the 'Philippines Trade Act' by which citizens of the United States were the only foreigners who had the same economic rights as the native population and American property and investments were safeguarded.

From the military point of view the Philippines remained an outpost of the American empire. In the treaty of March 14, 1947, the Americans were granted many bases, ports and military installations, while the Security Pact of August 30, 1951, went still farther along those lines and strategically made the islands practically part of the United States.

How all this affected the Philippines is seen in the regime of the Liberal party, a new party made up of the right-wing groups of the former Partido Nacionalista and undemocratic, to put it mildly, under president Manuel Roxas (April 1946 to April 1948) and Elpino Quirino (April 1948 to November 1953). The two milliard dollars which came from the United States between 1945 and 1949 went to the hotels and night clubs of Manila and the country houses of the rich merchants and landowners instead of going, as it should have gone, to the cottages of the peasants in the countryside, where only democracy, modern technique and the distribution of land will complete the agrarian revolution.

Although the government of the rather more liberal Ramon Magsaysay (from November 1953) was able to drive the 'Army of Liberation' of Casto Alejandrino and his associates, the former Hukbalahap (1942–1950), into the mountains and one of the notable partisan leaders Luis Taruc of his own will joined Magsaysay in 1954, the population of the land remained in a state which reminds one strongly of earlier conditions in China, Korea and Indochina.

The foreign policy of the Philippines was very little Asian in character and was dependent on the United States. Manila was represented in January 1949 at the conference in New Delhi, and in December 1954, when the New Guinea question came up in the United Nations was, like nearly all Asia, on the side of the Indonesians. But the government shrank from anything which looked like supporting Mao or even Nehru. It is therefore the more significant of the desire of all Asian countries for independence that the Philippines, too, if a little hesitatingly, decided to go to Bandung in April 1955, although the Philippines belong to SEATO, an American-inspired organization, of which more will be said later on.

VI

ISRAEL AND THE ARAB LEAGUE
SYRIA, THE LEBANON, JORDAN

As we have seen, the civil war in Palestine was virtually over by 1939–1940. When the Germans were driven out of North Africa and Caucasia, a bitter terrorist resistance movement spread among the Jewish population, with the result that the British, despite all their sympathy for the Arabs, could see only one solution – a British evacuation – the more so as many Americans in New York and Washington had come out for the Jewish independence plans as early as 1942.

In August 1945 and several times in 1946, Truman asked Attlee to agree to the settlement in Palestine of 100,000 Jewish refugees from Europe. At the beginning of 1947 the British forces in Palestine were already feeling their position insecure, and British wives and children began to be evacuated; it was then the British Government asked the United Nations to intervene. The result was a plan to divide the contested territory into two independent areas, but the frontiers suggested turned it into much too complicated a mosaic. The Arabs were to have the hill country in the northeast between Beersheba and the Lebanese frontier, including the whole of the Jordan valley north of the Dead Sea except for a strip of land on the Lake of Tiberias. The Jewish area was to consist of virtually the whole of the coast land and the sandy, stony Negeb. Jerusalem was to be an international enclave.

The United Nations, on November 29, 1947, accepted this plan by a two-thirds majority. All the Western countries voted for it, including the United States; so did the Soviet Union, as well as many Latin-American Republics, Liberia and the Philippines, i.e. 33 per cent of the populations represented in the United Nations. While Britain and China (Formosa) abstained, virtually all Asia voted against the plan – Afghanistan, Egypt, India, Irak, Iran, Yemen, the Lebanon, Pakistan, Saudia-Arabia and Turkey (and also Greece and Cuba), i.e. 29 per cent of all the people represented in the U.N. Asia, particularly the Arabs, regarded the plan as a sign of Western intervention in Asia. The Arabs attempted to settle the issue by war. It broke out when at midnight on May 14, 1918, Britain brought her rule in Palestine to an end, and on the same day a Jewish government in Tel Aviv declared the area allotted in the plan to the Jews the independent republic of Israel.

As compared with the situation at the time of the Macmahon correspondence and the Balfour declaration (1915 and 1917), the Arab countries – Egypt, Irak, Yemen, Jordan, the Lebanon, Saudi-Arabia and Syria – were now all independent and united in the Arab League (Dschami'at al-Duwal al-Arabija) which had been founded in Cairo on March 22, 1945, based on the 'Declaration of Principles' (Alexandria, October 7, 1944), the result of the initiative of Irak (Nuri al Said's Blue Book of 1942), Abdulla of Jordan and Nahas of Egypt. Libya, which had become independent, in December 1951, became a League member in March, 1953, the Soudan at the beginning of 1956.

In January 1948 the Palestine Arabs and the international Arab Liberation Army of Fawzi al Kawakji (leader of the Arab rebellion of 1936–1939) began a guerrilla war, and in May the forces of the Arab countries, mainly Jordan, Egypt and Irak, invaded Palestine from all directions with the purpose of driving the Israelis into the sea.

But that same summer the Arab invasion was shattered against the desperate resistance of 75,000 Israeli volunteers. While Israel under the temporary government of Ben Gurion had nearly all the West on its side – modern aircraft were smuggled in from the United States and also from Czechoslovakia – the Arabs were revealed as disunited and their forces, apart from Abdulla's 'British' troops, of little value.

The murder by an Israeli of the Swedish commissioner of the United Nations, Count Bernadotte – he had on the previous day (September 16, 1948) published a new partition scheme in which the Arabs got the Negeb – indeed provoked an international crisis, but the headlong flight of the Egyptian forces from the Negeb meant the end of the war.

As a result of Israeli-Arab negotiations in Rhodes (January to July 1949), Jordan got a fifth of the former territory of Palestine and Egypt a strip of sandy coastline in the southwest round Gaza. Israel received all the rest of the country. This settlement was regarded generally as definitive except in the Arab countries; frontier incidents have ever since been the order of the day. There remains as a dark page in this history the tragedy of 900,000 Arab refugees, of whom four-fifths are in Jordan and Egypt where, driven from hearth and home, they live for the most part in wretched conditions. In their place nearly as many Jewish immigrants have come to Israel, mainly from Europe, a part of those who were not done to death in German concentration camps, from North Africa and the Middle East.

The defeat in Palestine has been the main cause of all the crises in the Arab countries – the anti-British movement in Irak in 1948, the repeated changes in the military command in Syria in 1949, the troubles in the Arab League in 1950 and 1955, the murder of Abdulla in 1951 and the officers' rebellions in Egypt and Irak in 1952.

But is not Israel – a modern, Western, half-socialist 'island in the Arabian Sea' – also an agent towards preserving the unity of these turbulent, often most undemocratically ruled countries whose differences have until today hindered their union in a single Arab Empire? Perhaps eventually three states – Egypt, Saudi Arabia and the Fertile Crescent – will be established.

As we have already related, the British and the Free French in the early summer of 1941 occupied the French mandated territories of Syria and the

Lebanon. On June 8th Catroux, the Free French commander-in-chief as spokesman of the Allies, declared both countries independent and the French Government in London confirmed this in writing for Syria on September 27th and for the Lebanon on November 26th. But the French did not abide by the declaration. That did not meet with the approval of either Churchill or Roosevelt, nor naturally with that of the native governments and populations. This was most notable in Syria which in a sense can be called the cradle of Arab nationalism, where the resistance was led by Shukri al-Kuwatli and Faris al-Churi. The situation was dangerous, and, after repeated international intervention, mainly by Britain, the French Government in exile signed a second declaration of independence for both countries. Although this, in General de Gaulle's words, was only 'in principle total independence', Russia, China, the United States and others did what Britain had done in 1942, recognized both states *de jure*. As independent countries they became members of the Arab League in March 1945.

In the meantime France, herself hardly released from the German occupation, sought to assert her old privileges. On May, 19, 1945, negotiations were to begin between France and Syria. Four days earlier the French landed an expeditionary force at Beirut and bombarded Damascus. Was there to be a repetition of the events in 1920? What happened then could not, however, happen now. At the end of May Churchill intervened, threatened to send a British force to Syria and to take the French troops prisoner; to Britain the support of the Arabs had become more important than the support of France. On June 21, 1945, all Frenchmen in Syria and the Lebanon were removed from their posts in the army and the administration, and at the beginning of July France accepted the end of its rule in the Middle East. In April 1946 all foreign troops left Syria and in December the Lebanon.

Although Syria today has socialist and other left groups the democratic idea has not had time to take root. The military *coups* of December 1948 and March, August and December 1949, all of them the result of the war in Palestine and Abdulla's plans of expansion – it was the last which brought to power the staff colonel Adib al-Shishakli – are characteristic of a country in which freedom may have a future but has no past.

Between 1920 and 1945 Transjordania, as it was at first called, was simply a sandy desert governed from London, which served as a link between Egypt and Irak and where Britain's mercenary Arab army was stationed under Glubb Pasha.

In 1943 and 1944 Churchill seemed ready as a result of events in Syria to declare Transjordania independent in principle. In 1945 it became a member of the Arab League, and on March 22, 1946, the treaty was signed in London by which in terms similar to that of the agreement with Irak in 1930, Transjordania was recognized as independent and sovereign. The British, however, retained many privileges, virtually those they had held before, which was the reason why for a period Transjordania did not attain membership of the United Nations, Russia and other countries asserting that it was not independent.

There were in Transjordania itself protests against 'semi-independence' and, at the time when Egypt and Irak demanded a revision of their relations with Britain, a second treaty was signed in Amman on March 15, 1948, in which these privileges were very much curtailed, at least in peace-time. But British aid was still available for defence and for the construction of airfields, roads and ports; further, Britain retained two air-bases at Amman and Mafrak and the right to pass British troops through Transjordanian territory.

Meantime the emir Abdulla had taken the title of king and his kingdom received the name of the Hashemite Kingdom of Jordan (al-Mamlaka al-Hashimija al-Urdunija). It is usually called Jordan, a name which came into general use in 1949. In December 1948 Abdulla incorporated into Jordan[1] the regions west of the river Jordan which his forces had occupied in the Palestine war, a step which much discontented the other Arab countries. But, as Abdulla thought, was it not his army which alone of the Arab armies had won any successes against the Israelis?

Abdulla's sun had now really risen. He was an international figure. He travelled abroad, visited Bagdad, Riadh and Ankara, and even, as guest in a British warship, Spain. He followed the *fata morgana* of a united Arab empire which would include Egypt, Turkey, Saudi Arabia and Persia. But neither Egypt nor Ibn Saud nor the Syrian republicans took kindly to this 'Great Syrian' plan. Because of that plan he was murdered in Jerusalem on July 20, 1951. Despite his close relation with Britain and his anti-democratic ideas, he was one of the liberators of Arabia.

Little can be said here of his successors, Talal (September 1951 to August 1952), who had to stay long in Europe for medical treatment, and Hussein (from May 2, 1953; he was born in 1935), except the journey of the latter to London in December 1954 where he and the two ministers who had accompanied him asked for a revision of the treaty of 1948; they did not ask for the withdrawal of British officers, but for greater authority over 'their own finances', three-quarters of which came from London (£7,500,000 for the Arab Legion and £2,500,000 for economic development). Even in this feudal state very many of its citizens were beginning to look askance at 'the dependency of their independence' on Britain. Plain indication of this was given by the dismissal of Glubb Pasha at the beginning of March 1956 and the refusal of Jordan to enter the Bagdad Pact.

[1] *v.* p. 373.

VII

TURKEY AND IRAN

TURKEY has a common frontier with the Soviet Union and is the historic line of communication by land between Europe and the Arab countries. Its territory lies between the Black Sea and the Mediterranean. These geographical facts played a part in the determination of Turkish foreign policy from 1940 to 1955. In the Second World War Turkey stayed neutral as long as it could. The increasing threat from the Axis Powers, the Italian invasion of Greece (October 1940) and the German occupation (spring 1941) of that country and of Crete, caused the Turks to sign (June 18, 1941) a non-aggression pact with Germany. The German ambassador in Ankara, Franz von Papen, had no success, however, in his efforts in 1941 and 1942 to obtain a free passage to the Middle East for German troops. Nor had Ribbentrop, the German foreign minister, any more success when he strove to entice the Turks with the prospect of gains of territory in Russian Asia and in Caucasia; at the beginning of 1944 the Turkish Government banned propaganda 'for the liberation of the Turkish peoples in the Soviet Union'. The stay in Turkey of an official of Rosenberg's 'Ostministerium', who called himself 'Gauleiter of Tiflis', had shed a curious light on the German plans.

None the less, this semi-neutrality of Turkey was of considerable advantage to Germany. German ships, including small warships, could steal through the Straits laden with oil from the Caucasus for Rommel's tanks in North Africa. After Stalingrad and El Alamein there was a change and in June 1944 the passage of German warships was forbidden after the ban on the export of chrome in April. In August diplomatic relations were broken off with Germany. From January 1945 Allied shipping had again free passage to the Black Sea, and on February 23, 1945, Turkey declared war on Germany; this step was of no military significance and taken solely to assure Turkey of membership of the United Nations. Meantime Turkey had been since 1941 getting economic help from America (Roosevelt's Lend Lease Act), and for their part London and Washington long strove to get Turkey into the war on their side (Churchill-Ismet Inonu conversations in Adana in February 1943 and the Churchill-Roosevelt-Inonu meeting in the following December).

From 1945 to 1950 the old problem of the Straits arose again. In March 1945 the Soviet Union denounced the Russo-Turkish treaty of 1923 because of 'the help given Germany in the Second World War'. In answer to the Russian attack in Potsdam in November 1945, the United States proposed a 'modernization' of the Montreux treaty by which only warships of the Black Sea states should have free passage, but the Soviet Union in August 1946 demanded a much more serious revision, namely, an independent administration of the Straits by Turkey and the other countries on the Black Sea, including the people's democracies of Roumania and Bulgaria, and the participation of Russia in their defence. Supported by America, Turkey was able in April 1950 to reject these proposals. The Montreux regime of the Straits still remains. Foreign help, however, is rarely without its consequences. In March 1947 the governments of Athens and Ankara had involved their countries in the strategic plans of the United States. In 1950 Turkey was one of the few Asian lands which sent a considerable contingent to Korea, and in October 1951 it was the only Asian land to be a member of the North Atlantic Treaty Organization (NATO) founded in April 1949, which included as original members Belgium, Denmark, Britain, Holland, France, Iceland, Italy, Canada, Luxemburg, Portugal and the United States. From 1942 Turkey possessed the biggest and most modern air-bases in the Middle East, and Alexandretta (Iskanderun) was America's naval base in the Mediterranean; these bases are connected with the Caucasian frontier by secretly built new roads.

Internally, the end of the World War brought with it the end of the revolutionary and authoritarian periods. In November 1945 Inonu in principle proclaimed the end of the exclusive rule of the Republican party (founded 1923), and as a result of the free elections of 1950 Turkey got a government of the Democratic party (founded 1946). Celal Bayar, its leader, became president in succession to Inonu, and Adnan Menderes became premier. This change was not a revolution; it marks rather the disappearance of the revolutionary element. As compared with the past, the atmosphere in Turkey is slightly freer and it can be called capitalist and a little democratic in the Western sense.

The history of Iran from 1945 to the present day has, from the international point of view, been the history of its oil, of the oilfields in the southwest which belonged to Britain since 1901 and of the later designs of Russia in the north of the country.

During the Second World War, as we noted earlier, the independent kingdom of Iran was from August 1941 a line of communication between the American transports and the Russian armies. North of Teheran the country was under Russian influence; all of the south under British. After the war ended the United States and Britain in December 1945 withdrew their troops. But the Russians stayed even after the agreement of March 2, 1946, which arranged for their departure; they wanted to erect an oil refinery in Persian territory south of the Caspian as they had vainly sought to do in the autumn of 1944.

Meantime rebels, adherents of the virtually communist Tudeh party, had declared the northwestern highlands of Iran to be semi-independent as the 'autonomous republic of Azerbaijan' (December 12, 1945) and the Russian troops supported the Red government of Tabriz against the government in Teheran. Iran in vain brought the Russian intervention to the attention of the United Nations. At the beginning of April 1946, the Persian premier,

Kavam al-Saltana, signed in Moscow an agreement on a Russo-Persian oil company. At the beginning of May Russian troops left the country; this was something quite unexpected. This, and the temporary extension of the government in Teheran by the inclusion of some Tudeh ministers, was the signal for an anti-Russian and generally anti-communist propaganda in Iran which came mainly from the British oil districts in the south. It was successful, and one of its results was the recovery of Azerbaijan (December 1946).

When in 1947 the United States got the Middle East (Turkey, Greece) into its scheme for Atlantic defence, and sent weapons and military instructors to Iran, Teheran felt strong enough to cancel the whole Russian oil scheme (October 22, 1947). This step was the result of the immense energy of the premier, Dr Mohamed Mossadeq, inside and outside Parliament. Mossadeq (b. 1880 or 1881), who at that time was to the foreigner still a virtually unknown Persian nationalist, came from a rich landowning family. He had studied law at Neufchâtel and in 1941 had been freed by the Allied troops from the prison to which he had been sent as a result of his over-modern and over-liberal ideas.

Meantime the left and extreme left parties had grown in strength. The government, composed almost entirely of representatives of the landowners and the upper middle class, had banned the Tudeh party and arrested many people (February 1949), but the shah as a sign of his reform plans had distributed a part of his personal estates (February 1950). Teheran in many ways had turned to the United States, yet help did not come from overseas. Perhaps Washington had not recovered from the shock of its Chinese adventure or did not realize what was brewing in Iran.

In any case, in the winter of 1950–1 Mossadeq and his associates started a violent propaganda in favour of nationalization of the oilfields and plants of the Anglo-Iranian Oil Company which belonged to Britain. The premier Razmara was one of the few who were against nationalization; on March 7, 1951, he was assassinated, and on May 2nd, after much hesitation, the shah signed the law of March 20th by which Persian oil was declared to be a Persian possession. 'Eight grammes of powder', wrote a Teheran newspaper bluntly, 'has achieved this.' The London newspapers took a different view. Britain sent warships to the Persian Gulf and held a small expeditionary force in readiness. But no action was taken, for the Foreign Office remembered the Russo-Persian treaty of 1921 by which Russia was at liberty to march into Iran should a third power (Britain, for instance) occupy part of Persian territory. Also, it would seem that Washington did not wish to have another Korean War started; it had had quite enough of the first one.

London prevented the export of oil; at the beginning of August the Abadan refinery (which used to produce daily 700,000 barrels of oil) stopped work; in September Persian troops occupied the oilfields and at the beginning of October all British technicians went home. This end to the 'goose that laid golden eggs' was quite unexpected in Persia, and created the first crisis of the Mossadeq government (July 17, 1952). It brought in a four-day government under Kavam al-Saltana. But on July 21st the populace of

Teheran brought their hero Mossadeq back into power – forty-eight hours before the Neguib revolution in Egypt.

In October Teheran broke off diplomatic relations with London. It is of interest to anyone studying the Persian oil question to note that neither the British nor the native workers and peasants felt any need to hurry a solution. In the meantime British and other Western technicians had been able to increase the oil production in Irak, Saudi Arabia and Kuwait from a total of 49,000,000 tons in 1950 to one of 97,000,000 tons in 1952, so Europe felt no ill effects. Nor did the people of Iran trouble much about the failure of their oil production, because their economy was still agrarian. A restoration of diplomatic relations interested only a part of the ruling class, since the oil revolution threatened the throne and so the whole internal *status quo*. In this sense only was the nationalization of oil a social problem.

Like Sun Yat-sen earlier, and in a rather different way Ataturk, Mossadeq tried to achieve with the help of the left what his own class alone could not achieve. This case, too, shows how a nationalist revolution which meets opposition from outside becomes radical. From July 1952 Western Europe and the United States were entirely on Britain's side.

In May 1953 Teheran lifted the ban on the Tudeh party and at the same time the shah was removed from the post of Army commander-in-chief. Was that too revolutionary? Or was it not radical enough? The first sign of Mossadeq's ultimate fall came on the night of August 15th–16th when the shah ordered his arrest and that of his foreign minister, Hussein Fatemi. The move was premature; the workers and students of Teheran rose. The shah fled abroad and in the streets of the capital the crowd attacked the pictures of the royal family. But on the 18th royal troops were ordered by Zahedi, the minister of the interior, to occupy the excited capital. Mossadeq and Fatemi fled from their homes and after a few days Mossadeq was arrested after he had telephoned where he was hiding. Meantime the shah and Queen Soraya his second wife heard in Rome the news of the changes in Iran and returned to Teheran on the 22nd.

On November 12th Mossadeq was condemned to death, but in December the sentence was altered to one of three years' imprisonment. Hussein Fatemi and hundreds of others were arrested in 1954 and shot.

In December 1953 diplomatic relations with Britain were restored and British and American technicians investigated (January 1954) the oilfields and Abadan, and learned how 'really expertly' the derided Mossadeq government had kept the whole oil industry intact.

Mossadeq's revolution was not completely in vain. In August 1954 a treaty was made between the Zahedi government and the representatives of foreign oil companies, whereby the oilfields and the Abadan refinery remained Persian property and a payment of £25,000,000 was made to the Anglo-Iranian Company. Further, Persian oil was to be produced and shipped by an international company in which there were represented the Anglo-Iranian (40 per cent), five American companies (40 per cent), Royal Dutch Shell (14 per cent) and the Companie française de Petroles (6 per cent). The fields of Naft-i-Shah and the refinery at Kermanshah, belonging to the Persian National Oil Company, were to remain Persian to provide for internal needs.

Thus, as many Western newspapers said, the 'honest Zahedi government' ended the oil dispute although the chief cause of it – we quote *The Manchester Guardian* of August 6, 1954 – 'was almost wholly the arrogant, shortsighted . . . and greedy attitude of the Anglo-Iranian, i.e. of the British Government'.

VIII

EGYPT AND THE SOUDAN

As in the First World War, so in the second, Britain had to intervene in the affairs of Egypt, as, indeed, on the strict letter of the law she was entitled to do, in consonance with the high degree of independence which Egypt had received in 1936. In 1940 Egypt was Britain's most important military base in the Middle East. Its neutrality throughout the war and at the time of the German-Italian invasions was certainly compromised by the permanent British occupation. Only direct intervention brought again to power at the beginning of 1942 the bourgeois nationalist Wafd party, very much against the wishes of King Farouk, who consented only after Sir Miles Lampson (later Lord Killearn) had threatened him with a 'holiday' on an island in the Indian Ocean.

Mustapha Nahas, the Wafd leader since 1927, was premier again from February 1942 to October 1944; he had already occupied that office in 1928, 1930 and 1937. In the winter of 1944 the Germans were driven out of Africa and were soon to leave France and the Soviet Union. Britain gave Farouk back his 'freedom of action' – that is to say, in his case, freedom for reaction. In the years 1944 to 1949 Egypt had only anti-Wafd right-wing governments, one of which was formed by the Saadist party.

The national feelings in regard to Britain changed but little. Foreign soldiers and military installations in the Canal zone – the bridge between Egypt and the other Arab lands in Western Asia – and the British share in the government of the Soudan (1898), Egypt's water reservoir, remained a general cause of discontent. The founding of the Arab League in Cairo in 1945 had increased the country's prestige internationally, especially in the Moslem parts of Africa and Asia, and Egypt therefore renewed her demands for a revision of the 1936 treaty. In 1946 Britain appeared ready to withdraw entirely from Egypt (the London conversations between Sidki the premier and Bevin, the British foreign minister, in October 1946) on condition that the Soudan remained Anglo-Egyptian 'as a transition period before independence'. Cairo rejected this. At the beginning of 1947 the British troops were withdrawn from Egypt except from the Canal zone, and Egypt brought the matter before the United Nations. Negotiations were held up at the time of the war in Palestine; it was only diplomatic intervention by Britain that prevented the Israelis from carrying the war into Egyptian territory. It was this war, with the panic flight of the Egyptian troops and the incompetence of the Cairo government now so plainly revealed, that brought a change and with it the revolution of 1950–1954.

In the elections of January 1950, which were virtually free, the Wafd again obtained a two-thirds majority. Nahas was again premier (from

January 1950 to January 1952) and during this period the anti-British feeling decided the issue. On October 15, 1951, in the midst of the excitement caused by the Persian oil dispute, Cairo denounced the 1936 treaty and demanded the withdrawal of all foreign troops and the surrender of the whole Nile Valley to Egypt. Farouk called himself King of Egypt and the Soudan.

All Egypt was united on these claims. The Egyptian workers at the British bases struck and went off to their homes. But London would not yield. When the British troops in the Canal zone (under General Erskine) were involved in fighting with the native police and fifty Egyptians were killed, the anti-British feelings broke loose in what it known as 'black Saturday'. The Cairo mob, mainly workers and students, attacked the foreign quarter and evidence of what it did was given by the thick clouds of smoke that hung over the city by midday. But the 'red cock' was red in two senses. The possessions of the rich in Egypt were no longer safe and on the 27th Farouk by decree ended the rule of the Wafd.

That was the beginning of the 'revolution of the free officers', though Farouk and many others were too slow to recognize the fact. The movement, which won the upper hand on July 23, 1952, can be called the revolution of the petty bourgeois. Its leaders were Mohammed Neguib, the 'hero' of the Palestine war (premier from September 1952 to August 1954), and Gamal Abd el-Nasser, the present dictator of Egypt. In a few days the revolutionary government got rid of Egypt's biggest landowner, its king. Farouk fled to Italy and on June 18th Egypt became a republic.

Negotiations with Britain brought further liberation. The talks on the Soudan were reopened on February 12, 1953, and ended with the signature in Cairo of an Anglo-Egyptian compromise. This provided for self-government for the Soudan, which would become independent within three years with the right to choose freely whether it would be a kingdom or a republic, and whether it would belong to Egypt or be a member of the British Commonwealth. In the interim, native Soudanese were to fill the administrative posts while a British governor, controlled by an international commission (Britain, Egypt, the Soudan and Pakistan), would see to foreign affairs and defence. All that is now but past history. On January 1, 1956, the Soudan declared itself independent.

The rule of the revolutionary council in Egypt was not without its crises until, in the first half of 1954, a balance was found between its two leaders: Nequib remained head of the state, Nasser became premier. Now Britain declared herself ready to grant all that was demanded and to leave the Canal zone. The resultant treaty, the general lines of which agreed at the end of July, was signed on October 19th. It provided that the British garrison of about 80,000 men would be withdrawn before June 20, 1956. Britain was granted the right to return to her bases in the zone – these were in the interim to be kept in repair – should a foreign power attack Egypt, Turkey or one of the Arab countries between Egypt and Iran; aircraft of the RAF would be allowed to land in Egypt, and the principle of free passage through the Suez Canal, as laid down in 1888, would be maintained. Finally it was agreed that the treaty would expire in October 1961 but could be renewed if both signatories so desired. Thus ended the occupation of the Canal zone, which had lasted for seventy-five years and in its time had been one of the first signs of Western modern imperialism. It is not surprising that Cairo celebrated this notable October 19, 1954, with enthusiasm.

Saudi Arabia, independent since 1927, was not involved militarily in the Second World War and followed in theory a policy of neutrality. Unlike Irak, Afghanistan and the Syria of Vichy France, Saudi Arabia in 1940-1 had no German 'travellers and technicians' in the country That far-seeing tactician Ibn Saud, who had very little liking for democracy, kept his country during the war in 'the democratic camp', although there was little to show that, save for a few trivialities like the visit to Egypt in 1942 of the emir Mansur who delivered an address to British Indian troops before the battle of El Alamein.

At the beginning of 1941, after the Italians had bombed Bahrein (October 1940) and before either the Soviet Union or the United States had entered the war and Berlin was working out its plans for the Middle East, Ibn Saud demanded and received financial help from London, and still more from Washington (after April 1943 through the Lend-Lease Act). Before this time the United States Government had not been particularly interested in Saudi Arabia and did not even have a diplomatic representative there. But things changed now, when America was the only country with the technical equipment for strategic investment in the country. In 1944-6 American technicians built secretly – it was kept secret even from Americans while the war lasted – a great modern air-base at Dharan to secure communication between Africa and India, and also a great oil refinery at Ras Tanurah which was ready by December 1945. This meant a revolutionary invasion of the Middle East by American capital and the expulsion of British capital from Saudi Arabia. On March 1, 1945, the Arab kingdom declared war on Germany, but before that the first Saudi-American talks were held in February between Ibn Saud and Roosevelt at the Bitter Lakes, when Roosevelt was on his way home from Yalta; Churchill was not present. That was the first and only time that Ibn Saud went out of his own country.

In May 1939 Saudi Arabia shipped its first oil. But it was only in 1944 that the expansion of the Arabian American Oil Company (Aramco) began; in 1945 it produced 2,800,000 tons, in 1950 25,000,000 tons and in 1953, 41,000,000 tons, that is 600,000 barrels per day from 140 wells at Abkaik Ain Dar, Dammam and Katif. Nearly one-third of the oil used by Europe comes today from Saudi Arabia. Things have indeed changed since 1933 when a little group of geologists from a Californian oil company landed, hired camels in the coastal village of Ammam and from there journeyed into the burning deserts.

Since 1950 the Saudi Arabian Government is receiving besides the former 34 cents per barrel, 50 per cent of what the oil of Aramco earns. That meant in 1952, the year in which the headquarters of 'Arabian American' was transferred from New York to Dharan, an increase in Ibn Saud's revenues of $200,000,000 per annum. At the beginning of 1954 new oilfields, very rich even by American standards, were discovered. Basing themselves on this profitable arrangement, the first of its kind in the Middle East, others, including Irak and Kuwait, demanded a similar percentage and in 1951 got it. It brings to these countries between $150,000,000 and $200,000,000 a year. It is hardly necessary to say that this is of political significance.

Meantime, in December 1950, the first Arabian oil was delivered to a tanker in the Mediterranean by the 1060-mile-long pipeline which the 'Trans-Arabian Pipeline Company' (Tapline) built from Ras Tanurah to Saida (Sidon) in the Lebanon; it was begun in 1947. There are still camels and rough stony roads to be seen in the oil areas, but between Mecca, Medina and Jeddah there are long motor roads, aqueducts, ports (Jeddah and Dammam 1950), houses for the native workers in the oilfields and . . . 'the king's railway', the only one in Arabia which runs right through the deserts of Riadh and connects the capital with Dammam on the coast; it is 300 miles long and was built in 1947-1951, uses modern diesel engines and employs Arab engineers in most un-Arab dungarees. As in other Asian and European lands, this technical revolution has begun to awaken the people from their slumbers – in 1953 there was a strike in the oilfields – but the government of Ibn Saud holds at a distance both democracy and education. Less than 5 per cent of the people can read or write. Among its representatives abroad are many intellectuals from other Arab countries because there is lack of them at home. In this country, as in all other Arab countries except Syria, women have no political rights, but the men have none either; here is a situation at variance with the spirit of the age, a situation which elsewhere is seen only in Abyssinia.

How far the death of Ibn Saud (November 9, 1953) and the policy of the new king Saud (Abd al-Aziz ibn Abd al-Rahman al-Faisal al-Saud, b. 1902) will bring changes cannot yet be said, but it is certain that change will come just as it has done in other countries.

Saudi Arabia has been a member of the Arab League from its foundation. The American air-base at Dharan is still there, and the Arab-American Defence Treaty of June 1951 strategically attaches Saudi Arabia to the United States even if in international questions which concern Asia and Africa it follows the same policy as the other independent Arab countries.

By 1955 virtually the whole of Asia belonged again to the Asians. Up to that date the most important events were the spread of communism in China and the establishment in India of what in the Western sense is a more democratic regime. These two states are the Great Powers of Asia. Their cultures are Asian cultures; their economic systems serve as examples of what an Asian economic system is and will be in the future.

The progress of Asia towards industrialization is understandable. Factories are the beginning and the basis of the modernization and the mechanization of agriculture, although some western economists and sociologists think that factories mean not more rice and corn but more children. None the less in every country where, as in the West, an industry of importance has been developed, there has in the end been more and not less bread, even in Japan where economic democracy is still almost non-existent. Economic advance for the Asians is not primarily a matter of population, but one of deep social change. It is only the industrialized country with citizens who can at least read and write which has high agricultural production.

It seems likely that Asia will not have time to build up a free capitalist class such as exists in Western Europe and America. But if the future will come swiftly, the disappearance of the past will be slow. European colonialism is dead, but penetration by America, the least colonial of western countries, has created a new kind of imperialism. The United States today has a thousand military bases outside the American continent. Many of them are in Asia. The anti-communist South East Asia Treaty Organization (SEATO), which was founded in Manila on September 8, 1954, is composed of the United States, Britain, Australia, New Zealand, France and, from the countries of Asia, Pakistan, the Philippines and Thailand. A similar sort of organization is the Bagdad Pact. Originally this was a defensive alliance between Turkey and Irak signed on February 24, 1955, on, it would appear, Western initiative. In April Britain adhered to it, then Pakistan in September and in October Iran. The United States has not adhered to it, but let the November conference of the signatories know that it would enter into 'a military and political association' with them. In the other Arab countries the Bagdad Pact was regarded as a move against the Arab League and it should be noted that the attempt to get Jordan to join failed. The failure is one of the many proofs that the issue 'Russia or the United States' or, as the West would call it, 'communism or western democracy' interests the average Asian very much less than the issue 'colonialism or independence'. India, for instance, which is the most democratic country in Asia in the Western sense, has since its liberation very different views on this point from those held by most Europeans and Americans. If the West considers that it is its task to prevent the spread of communism in Asia, then it should realize that the only way to do so is to help socialists like Nehru and thakin Nu in their social policies. But is American capitalism now at its zenith prepared to help on the social revolution in Asia?

In the years between 1945 and 1955 Asia became free to be itself. The West began to understand that more than half the earth's inhabitants are Asians and that Europe and America, for all their present greatness and their long past, are not the only examples and standards of 'culture'. Admittedly Asia is still technologically and politically behind Europe, America and the Soviet Union.

Things of historic growth do not easily change. Relatively few Europeans understand that being ready for self-government is not a necessary pre-condition of independence; the desire for freedom is enough. That, at least, is what contemporary Asians and Africans believe. But they do not stand alone in this belief; behind them is all history, Western European history no less than American.

In February 1927 there was organized in Brussels in the Egmont Palace –

the name commemorates one of the Dutch heroes of the 'colonial' war with Spain – the Congress against Colonial Oppression and Imperialism. Nehru and Hatta both spoke at it. Those who read the report of its proceedings will realize that freedom costs much sacrifice; of the other twenty-five people who spoke then, all are either dead or otherwise eliminated.

But there has been a change, a revolution perhaps wider and deeper than any other in history if we consider it by comparing the conference in Brussels with the conference in Bandung in 1955. In the former a few people assembled more or less in secrecy, obscure people, many of them exiles; in the latter, statesmen met to speak freely to the world.

At the conference in Colombo at the end of April 1954 the premiers of India, Pakistan, Burma, Ceylon and Indonesia agreed that an Afro-Asian conference should be held; preparations were made for it in the Bogor conference in December, and in April 1955 it became a reality in Bandung. Of thirty states invited twenty-nine accepted. Only the young Central African Federation, of which an Englishman was prime minister, was conspicuous by its absence. Except for the Soviet Union, Japan, Mongolia, the two Koreas, Formosa, Israel and the Union of South Africa all the peoples actually or still only formally free from the west coast of Africa to the east coast of Asia were represented. They differed in race, in religion, in culture, in the political system under which they lived, from communism through democracy to the most outmoded despotism; some were industrialized; some were purely agrarian; there were great nations and small alike tending to be 'eastern', or 'western' or 'neutral'. But they were all filled with the same desire, to be themselves the agents of their advance. As Sukarno said in his opening speech: 'We seek the means not just not to die but the means to live.'

At Bandung, which is a little town in the hills and reminds one a little in its upper parts of a Dutch town, the language used was for the most part English. Memories of that other conference in Brussels, where twelve out of the twenty-five speakers were European, were not quite effaced. The liberation of Asia has been an Asian achievement; but recognition of this gives the historian the right, indeed the duty, to state that Europe, even if in most cases unwillingly, played its part. World history, if we study it more closely, often seems to be less a unity than it really is yet from such study comes our hope, our confidence that humanity can in practice achieve that 'unity in diversity' which in principle it has already achieved. The historic significance of that week in April 1955 when Asia and Africa met together in Bandung is the proof it affords that a step forward towards that has been made, that both were ready to play their part wherever world policy is being made.

At Bandung neither the tone nor the content of the speeches was either exultant or embittered, proudly self-conscious as they were. It seemed as if not only the leaders, but the peoples themselves, had grasped the fact that the obtaining of freedom does not make the difficulties disappear. Of the permanent seats in the United Nations Security Council Asia has only one. Yet half and more of the world's inhabitants live there, and that one representative, China's, does not represent the nation of 600,000,000 but the American satellite, Chiang's Formosa.

A.C.—13

From fulfilment comes indeed disillusion, and fresh fulfilment will bring fresh disillusion. Science in its painful development has taught us that behind a solved problem a new problem at once arises. That is an inevitable law, valid not only for science but for all history. That does not mean that in history there is no sense. If we set before ourselves as ideal the happiness of humanity, that is one which with all our efforts we cannot expect to attain. But we can always be getting nearer to realization – if we wish to.

Last Period 1955 – 1960

THE MOST RECENT PAST: CONCLUSION

I

AFTER BANDUNG

THE Bandung conference marked the end of an era, the era of European ascendancy, in Asia. This end was the logical outcome of a development which started at the turn of the century with the growth of national movements aiming at modernization, and resulted in the liberation of the colonial and semi-colonial countries of Asia, with or without social revolutions. Bandung formally rang out the old Asia and ushered in the new; formally, for in reality, the old Asia, though still clinging to a few scattered positions, had already disappeared, while the new Asia had already been born. Bandung must have sounded like a death-knell to those Europeans who found it difficult or impossible to envisage the world without European, or at any rate Western, hegemony. Europe could not easily reconcile itself to what had happened, and even a politically mature country like Britain as late as November 1956 was still trying to put the clock back. Equally the United States, though traditionally more strongly inclined to favour liberated Asia, is essentially little in sympathy with an independence which includes freedom to choose sides in the post-war conflict between the Western and the Communist world. Not infrequently this lack of sympathy shows itself in an underrating of the importance of Bandung.

The desire to belittle Bandung expresses itself in more or less derogatory remarks, implying that, in practice, little of 'the spirit of Bandung' remains, that, in spite of all the talk about Asian solidarity at that conference, the nations represented there seriously disagree and are even hostile one to the other. Apart from the traditional enmity between the inhabitants of India and Pakistan, or between Israel and its Arab neighbours, there is also enmity between Egypt and Jordan, Egypt and Irak, Syria and Turkey, Irak and Iran, Afghanistan and Pakistan, India and China, Indonesia and China, Indonesia and the Philippines. Actually such enmities do not detract from the achievement of Bandung. Asia did not assemble in Bandung to build a model continent – in as many months as Europe has taken centuries and has not yet succeeded – but to demonstrate its independence of the rest of the world and its common solidarity *vis à vis* Europe or, in a wider sense, 'the West'. That the spirit of Bandung in this sense is still alive was clearly shown during the Suez crisis (1956).

In its political-national aspect, the Asian revolution has been accomplished. This does not mean that the newly-gained independence is no longer menaced – the Suez adventure proved the contrary – but a western political domination is no longer feasible. Yet Western influence has not completely disappeared. Asia is glad to receive technical advice and economic assistance, provided that the Westerner – American and Russian alike – plays the part of an equal, not of a superior. After centuries of impotence Asia is at last governing itself.

I have already said that, in its political-national aspect, the Asian revolution has been accomplished; but it has to be recognized that, so far as the solution of social problems is concerned, the 'Asian century' has not yet come to an end. That may serve as a partial explanation at least of the conflicts between the Asian states, and of the extent to which the political influence of the West still makes itself felt. When one examines the systems of government in each of the Asian countries, the political leanings of their governments, the social classes on whose support they depend, and the political and social ideologies – if any – which inspire their actions, one is confronted by a tremendous diversity. There are the communist countries where the social revolution is farthest advanced, and, in direct contrast to these, the mediaeval autocracies which have so far hardly been touched by it. Between these extremes are to be found states with authoritarian governments, where the drive towards social reform is suppressed by a regime of feudal, industrial and commercial interest; 'guided democracies' and military dictatorships where this drive is held back or guided into certain channels; and finally real democracies where champions of social reform are free to have their say, according to whether the government is based on a true social 'centre', or on its right or left. Under these circumstances it is no wonder that conflicts arise; conflicts between states tend to be sharper the more their governments represent different social classes. Nor is it surprising that those groups who are least inclined to social reform seek support from the West, while the West looks on these groups as a useful, if not entirely satisfactory, counter-balance against pressure from below, a pressure which is often deliberately, sometimes unthinkingly, branded as 'communist', i.e. as part of Russia's 'cold-war' tactics.

Despite differences in attitude to social questions, *all* Asian governments are concerned with the supreme problem facing them, i.e. how to overcome the traditional poverty of their peoples. The social background of each government determines how it tackles this problem, either in the direction of completely changing the social structure, or, while leaving the social structure intact, of introducing reforms whereby poverty and misery will be gradually overcome. The only large-scale revolutionary experiment is that being carried out by China; the most important example of evolutionary development is that taking place in India.

II

CHINA

MANY American observers in China during the civil war were afterwards taken to task in their own country for having at the time regarded the communists as little more than 'agrarian reformers' in a society badly in need of reform. Yet in that particular phase of the revolution they were correct. The communist programme of September 1947 was moderate: there was to be no feverish expropriation. Only 'excess property in land, cattle, houses and agricultural implements' was to be confiscated; for the rest, the small proprietors and middle peasants would not be expropriated. Nor would the activities of private enterprise be interfered with. One consequence of this programme was that social measures, such as distribution of the land and rent reduction, won over the mass of the peasants to the communist cause, while, on the other hand, its moderate character did not frighten off the traders and the more prosperous peasants. This moderation was based not only on political, but also on economic considerations; a land distribution carried to extremes would have resulted only in decreased production.

After victory had been won, this policy was at first continued. All over China the big landowners were expropriated and their lands distributed among the small peasants, tenant farmers and agricultural labourers. In many parts of the country this expropriation, which was in effect a revolution affecting, directly or indirectly, 400,000,000 people, was accompanied by extremely harsh measures but these were the result less of the new order of things than of a popular hatred fed by past exploitation, a hatred which needed no encouragement from the communists. In 1950 and 1951 particularly, the Chinese revolution showed its grim aspect. Yet there was no question of total expropriation; small holdings remained in private hands. In the urban centres the banks, heavy industry and foreign trade were taken over by the State; the small factories, businesses and shops remained in the possession of their former owners. The regime was harsher, but at the same time more efficient, and above all more honest, than that of the Kuo Min-tang; corruption was rooted out. This development did not take place entirely without opposition; but when, as in 1952, there was opposition, the cause of it could usually be traced to the conduct of local functionaries whose enthusiasm made them exceed their instructions.

As the Communist government continued in power, the picture began to change: a more rigid policy began to take shape. Thus, in 1955 private trade was abolished as far as possible. Businessmen and works managers were allowed to carry on, but henceforth they were subject to restricting regulations and strict supervision by the State. In the countryside a more radical policy was adopted, involving the small peasants too. After the completion of the agrarian reforms (1953) it became obvious that the splitting up of the large estates into 110,000,000 small farms, sometimes of little more than an acre, had an unfavourable effect on agricultural production.

This became a crucial question for the govenment in Peking. Their aim was to make China more self-sufficient so far as food was concerned, and in order to increase production they proceeded to amalgamate the small hold-ings into larger undertakings: in other words, to collectivize agriculture. At first they went about this cautiously, in order that the support of the peasant masses, won by the earlier land distribution, should not be lost as a result of wholesale collectivization. Under the Five-Year Plan (1953–1958) a pro-gramme was drawn up for collectivization in three stages to be accomplished by 1960. The average size of the big farms was to be gradually increased. Despite all the Government's care to avoid the mistakes which had character-ized the agrarian revolution in the Soviet Union in the 'thirties, they were faced with what was in effect traditional opposition. Collective farming meant a break with the policy which had been pursued hitherto. According to this the peasant was allowed to own a piece of land; naturally he looked upon collectivization as just another attempt to rob him of his right to do what he wanted with his own land, a deep-rooted and traditional feeling that was difficult to combat.

The discontent which in 1956 found expression in Tibet could indeed still be attributed to the land-owning monasteries, but it was eased by the promise that the tempo of modernization there would be slowed up. In China itself more was at stake. Although Mao Tse-tung announced (on February 27, 1957) that in future any further expansion of the socialist sector of the economy was to be brought about by persuasion rather than by force, in actual fact hardly anything changed. Mao's recommendation was followed by the observation that the 'principle of inevitability of gradualness' must guide future activities. Inevitability indeed! The only thing that could be done was to continue on the road that had been chosen, if the basic problem of the hunger and poverty of China's millions was to be solved, yes, even if the present low level of existence was to be maintained. China's population was increasing by 15,000,000 a year, and in spite of the ambitiously high-speed industrialization plan, it was not to be expected that industrialization would be able to cope with such an increase. Very radical measures were necessary, primarily aimed at increasing agrarian production. In this way the systematic reform, which had started with the distribution of land, logically led to the setting up of people's communes.

A short period of freedom of discussion within the country, most likely inspired by a similar episode during the Sung era and heralded by Mao's exhortation to 'let flowers of all seasons blossom and a hundred schools con-tend' (February 1957), preceded the setting up of these communes. Because of the gap which had gradually begun to appear between government and party functionaries on the one hand and the working classes on the other, Mao put forward the thesis of the existence of conflicts within a communist society and encouraged criticism, in the hope that 'out of the conflict of ideas truth would emerge'. He distinguished two sorts of criticism: namely, criticism of the communist system as such, and criticism arising within that system from the clash of major interests of equal importance. The latter criticism was naturally the 'correct' kind. There followed much lively criticism – including that of the system. When, however, in the course of 1958 the most radical phase of China's revolution started – the so-called 'great leap forward' – the old discipline appears to have been re-imposed.

Yet those hundred flowers were more than just a poetic formula for a temporary letting-off of steam with official approval in a situation of threatening conflict. They led to a closer rapprochement between the ideas of the masses and those of the communist leadership. It was not easy for the mass of the people to grasp the overall picture of communist construction that the leadership had in view with all its inherent potentialities and difficulties; on its side the leadership, though clear about the general outline and the common interest, could easily lose sight of the actual situation and the immediate needs of the masses. Free discussion had made possible the exchange of ideas and the recognition of each other's desires and wants; on this kind of understanding depended the team-work between the mass of the people and the leaders, and without it the agrarian revolution could not be carried out.

Team-work is the right word, for the setting up of people's communes was a mass movement of enormous size and strength, and for that very reason could not be imposed from above on an apathetic, let alone unwilling, peasant population. It was not simply an experiment thought up by the leadership. It was a revolution urged on from below at an increasing rate towards a prospect of a more prosperous future, and directed by the Government towards the modern, strong and industrialized welfare state they desired. The expectations of the people and of the rulers thus ran parallel, though they could only be realized by a complete mobilization of all available manpower. In many cases, the initiative in establishing communes was taken by the peasants themselves; afterwards the programme was officially inaugurated (August 1958) and incorporated in Chinese communist ideology – thirty years after the Russians had rejected the idea of communes as unrealistic. At the same time the communes were presented as the first stage on the road from socialism to outright communism.

The communes came into existence by transforming the co-operative farms with their relatively small production into communes of 1,000 to 10,000 families, sometimes occupying a whole district. They also formed an administrative unit, thus relieving the central government of numerous tasks and making for a more efficient system of supervision. In this way local government and commune administration more or less merged together. The commune is primarily responsible for agricultural production and cattle-breeding, but it also concerns itself with the development of industry, with finance and commerce, with education and with the people's militia. The means of production, land, tools, cattle, factories and capital, are collectively owned, but day-to-day expenditure, and also credits and deposits in banks, are allowed to remain in private hands. Life is strongly regimented. There is a strict labour discipline on military lines; the daily programme is laid down; whenever possible common refectories replace private housekeeping; children are

A.C.—13*

educated in crèches, and the intellectuals and women are obliged to do 'productive work', i.e. manual labour.

The ideal of the people's commune is to provide the individual with the main necessities of life free of charge, and at the same time to supply the whole community's consumer-goods requirements, thus eliminating the retail trade and one of the main functions of money. The most important aim of the commune, however, is to make an intensive and rational use of China's labour resources at a time when there are not yet enough machines. In the most literal sense all available hands are being mobilized for agriculture, for the struggle against soil erosion, for industry. The first results of this gigantic effort were overwhelming as regards the production of steel, coal and food-stuffs, even though in 1959 the targets which had been enthusiastically set proved to be unattainable, and the yield of the tens of thousands of primitive little smelting-ovens in the 'iron and steel campaign' did not come up to expectation.

Naturally this revolution was not accomplished without opposition. The sudden break with all forms of individualism, the tremendous speed – by October 1958 740,000 co-operative and collective farms had been transformed into some 26,000 communes – and the chaotic conditions resulting from such rapid changes, all this gave rise to friction. In December 1958 the Communist party warned against excessive haste, and a little later began to use more lenient methods. In 1959, not surprisingly, difficulties of a technical and organizational nature and 'statistical miscalculations' became evident. But all the same China is in the throes of a tremendous revolution, the biggest mass movement in history; if it succeeds, it can have political consequences for the whole world. Most communes have only just started out on a road which, it is estimated, will take ten or twenty years to travel.

The changes that have taken place during the ten years' existence of the Chinese People's Republic have made China almost unrecognizable. The patriarchal character of society has been brought to an end, and the old traditions have gone by the board. The unity of the country has been restored, and at present the government in Pekin makes its authority felt as far afield as Sinkiang and Tibet—in the latter country in spite of the rebellion of the spring of 1959. Both these regions are 'autonomous areas', as is also Inner Mongolia. Their geographical isolation is being overcome by railways and efficient roads which allow the exploration of their mineral wealth and other resources. China has made a start in harnessing her great rivers, on the one hand, in order to counter the chronic, catastrophic floods, and, on the other, with the aim to turning large uncultivated areas into arable land by means of irrigation.

China no longer faces the outside world as the passive sufferer she has been for the last hundred years; she has arisen as a major power even though her seat on the U.N. Security Council is still occupied by a representative of the defeated old regime. Moreover, she is conscious of her strength and conducts her policy accordingly, an 'aggressive policy' as it is called in the West, even when it is a case of taking the offensive in the civil war against Chiang Kai-shek, e.g. the bombardment of Quemoy in 1958. What happens at her frontiers, however, is not of primary importance; internal development is the first concern. She is involved in a tremendous revolution which is carried through, now by persuasion, now by force and sometimes by the use of violence. The outcome of this revolution is being anxiously watched by the whole world, in particular by those parts of Asia which are faced with a similar situation; whether they decide to adopt the Chinese system, or to follow the Indian example, may well depend on the success or failure of this experiment.

III

INDIA

WHEN India's present rulers took over from the British, they were confronted from the outset by bigger problems than the Chinese communists had to face after the downfall of the Chiang Kai-shek regime. In China there was already a sizeable industrial apparatus to build on, utterly inadequate though it was for meeting the country's needs. India, on the other hand, which for many decades had been merely a market for British goods, had to start practically from scratch. China – China proper at any rate – formed ethnologically and linguistically a whole; India was composed of numerous races, peoples, religions, social and political groups including well over 500 native kingdoms. The young state was threatened with 'Balkanization', so that one of the first tasks of Nehru's government was to liquidate the kingdoms. The political map was simplified by the formation of twenty-nine federal states, and in order to nip particularist trends in the bud, provision was made for a strong central authority. All the same, regionalism remained a powerful force, and once the formation of a separate state had been conceded to the Telegu-speaking population of Madras (Andhra, 1952), India's political map had to be revised again. The new administrative partition into fourteen states on a language basis was in effect a retreat from the goal of one Indian nation. Indeed, such a nation has not yet come into existence, and there is still a danger that it could fall apart into a number of states.

Regionalism, however, is not the biggest problem that confronts the Indian government. The most important is the food supply. In 1949 foodstuffs had to be imported; and in 1951 and 1952 certain areas were suffering from famine. Hence measures to increase food production by improving agriculture were urgently needed, and it was mainly with such measures that the first Five Year Plan (1951–1956) was concerned. A 'Grow More Food' campaign was started; irrigation works were carried out which enlarged the arable acreage; courses of instruction were organized and experimental centres established. All this produced good results, which in 1953 and 1954 were reflected in bigger harvests. But, in spite of the progress that has been made, the food situation remains extremely precarious and the poverty is as appalling as before. Moreover, there is a kind of race going on between the rapidly growing population and the increasing food production needed to safeguard a minimum standard of living. In the background looms the grim threat of famine. Hence the tremendous efforts on the part of the Government to popularize birth control, and to raise agricultural production; the beginning of 1960 saw the introduction of another big scheme to that end.

The Government realizes that, if things go wrong, it would be on a scale that would make even a famine like that of 1943 – when according to the official estimate a million and a half people perished – seem small. Unless they succeed in improving the living conditions of the masses and putting an end to a situation in which land shortage, lack of housing and permanent undernourishment are normal, India's continued existence in its present form, i.e. as a parliamentary democracy according to the Western and, particularly, British, pattern will be seriously threatened. The fact that a huge state of roughly 400,000,000 inhabitants should try to cope with over-whelming problems such as these while observing the rules of the Western democratic game is in itself a remarkable experiment. India's achievement to date is of the first order. China, faced with the same problems, solves them by ensuring the participation of the mass of the people, by totally trans-forming the social structure, by persuasion if possible and, where necessary, by compulsion, finally by imposing a very high tempo in order to keep up with the growth of population. India's way of tackling these problems is different: she takes measures which have been expertly prepared, are democratically enacted, and put into practice persuasively and energetically. There is no compulsion, i.e. no personal compulsion; the threat of food shortages and famine is as compelling as in China. Another difference from China is that, in a typically Indian fashion, no attempt is made at involving the mass of the population in any intensive effort to achieve the aims of the five-year plans. There is no organized mass movement, no revolutionary transformation of society, no radical change in the traditional pattern of life of India's peasant millions. One might ask with Walter Lippmann whether in the interests of a speedy solution of the problem of India's poverty and undernourishment, more radical measures should not take precedence over the almost mid-Victorian evolutionary path that the Government is following at present.

The fact that a more radical change in social structure is not being attempted is consistent with the social background of the leaders of India's Congress party. Despite the boldness of its economic and social schemes, the Congress is too closely linked with the interests of the urban and rural propertied classes to risk employing truly revolutionary methods. It is true that certain measures were taken against abuses arising from the great power of the big landlords and usurers, but it never came to large-scale land reform. Vinoba Bhave's campaign for voluntary donations of estates to landless peasants was naïve rather than practical. It scored some local successes, but did nothing to appease the land-hunger of India's peasant mass as a whole. The Congress faces a difficult dilemma: either it must pursue a truly revolutionary policy and, with the support of the popular masses, instigate a social transformation, which because of its social back-ground it is not prepared to do, or else it must take measures which, not-withstanding an appearance of boldness, are no more than temporary ex-pedients. It is hoped that, by means of an essentially conservative pro-gramme, impending disaster may be staved off. But failure to avert it will result in far more radical upheavals than would have to be faced if more progressive methods were adopted. Nor is it entirely unimaginable that the Indian State could fall apart if social discontent, taking the shape either of communist movement or of an extremely reactionary, orthodox Hinduism, were to coincide with regional agitation.

The phenomenon of more or less large-scale social discontent is not new: it occurred in 1948, in the then backward principality of Hyderabad, and was one of the reasons why India intervened to compel this state to join the Union. This peasant revolt was suppressed, but already the first signs of fresh discontent can be discerned. The heavy losses suffered by the Congress in the 1957 elections were due not only to dislike on the part of the electorate for a party which, having held power for a prolonged period, had begun to show signs of complacency; they were no less the result of feelings of social malaise. Closely connected with this was the growth of the Communist party. In one of the constituent states, Kerala, this party even grew so powerful that it was able to form a government. It is true that two years later the anti-communist parties succeeded, by a campaign against it, in creating such chaotic conditions that the president had to intervene in order to make government possible. But the conditions which made the communists powerful, as was obvious from the number of votes cast, though not from the allocation of seats in the February 1960 election in Kerala, were still there.

The Indian communists, however, were in an awkward position. China, so much admired for its 'great leap forward', harshly suppressed the revolt in Tibet (1959) and seemed to be threatening the Indian border. The claims of the Chinese to territories along the northeastern frontier and in Kashmir were rejected by Nehru. But, despite pressure from nationalist groups within the country itself, there was no change in India's policy of non-alignment. India's foreign politics are closely connected with her supreme problem – poverty. If India were to associate herself with one of the two *blocs* in the cold war, military expenditure would rise and schemes to improve her economy would be jeopardized by lack of the necessary finance. Even now, military expenditure is placing a heavy enough burden on the country's financial resources, because of the conflict with Pakistan about Kashmir. The partition of the latter now seems to be definite; on January 26, 1957, the Indian Constitution was declared applicable also to Kashmir, though the UN Security Council – influenced by India's attitude at the time of the Suez crisis – supported Pakistan's demand that no such constitutional change should be made. There was, of course, no question of annexation for ever since Kashmir joined the Indian Union in 1948, it has officially formed part of India. All the new step in 1957 amounted to was the institution at last of normal political relations.

Since 1948 India has become one of the Great Powers, great, not indeed in military might, but in moral prestige. Economically she has made progress, helped by a bold scheme of industrialization. However, the second Five Year Plan (1956–1961) which gave particular priority to industry, subsequently turned out to have been too ambitious; it upset the balance of payments as a result of the enormous imports of capital goods and raw materials.

In 1957, therefore, the programme had to be drastically cut. But, despite great difficulties, India's economy is getting on its feet and has the support of the World Bank and the United States, which, since Secretary Dulles' death, no longer regards India's foreign policy as something utterly immoral! One problem remains – the food situation. If India succeeds in solving this, it will have far-reaching significance for Asia and the whole world.

IV

SOUTHEAST ASIA AND JAPAN

IN the communist parts of the two divided Asian nations, Korea and Viet-nam, the Chinese example is being followed. About North Korea little is known, but it may be assumed that, with the support of China and Russia (in that order), industrial expansion is being energetically pursued. In North Vietnam, too, a programme of industrialization has been introduced, but its execution appears to have met with opposition. The development has therefore been somewhat slowed down, though the ultimate aim has not been lost sight of.

Four countries in south and east Asia on the other hand took the Indian road, but with one exception they have not managed to stay the course. In Indonesia, as well as in Pakistan and Burma, the democratic system was not strong enough to maintain itself, but had to yield to more or less dictatorial regimes. The fourth, Ceylon, is still a democratically ruled state, though its continued existence as a democracy is seriously threatened by the language dispute. In the April 1956 elections the United National party was swept out of office; the United People's Front, a mixed bag of democratic socialists, Trotskyists and orthodox Buddhists gained a majority. The con-servative government of Sir John Kotelawala was replaced by a more or less left one under Solomon Bandaranaike. The dispute about the official status of the two main languages now flared up into a conflagration, fanned equally by extremist supporters of Tamil and by fanatical champions of Sinhalese, and exploited by the conservative groups who made use of the disturbances to embarrass the Government. This conflict resulted in a dan-gerous political crisis, and when in September 1959 Bandaranaike was assassinated by a Buddhist monk, the government coalition was rent apart. In Ceylon, too, democracy is a frail blossom.

One Asian country – properly speaking, the fifth – to follow the Indian example of parliamentary democracy has not been included with those above because its independence is of too recent a date to allow us to judge of its success or failure. This is Malaya. After the communist (mostly Chinese) rebels who carried on a guerrilla war in the jungles had to all intents and purposes been suppressed, the British left behind there the most curious political edifice in the whole of independent Asia. In a century when monarchies have so rapidly disappeared, Malaya saw the birth of a new one, a symbol of the conservative character of the young state. It is an elective monarchy; out of the hereditary rulers of the nine Malay states one is chosen as sovereign, and the only difference from seventeenth- and eighteenth-century Poland is that the term of office of Malaya's head of state is limited; Tungku Abdul Rahman, sultan of Negri Sembilan was the

first. The economic outlook is favourable, but neither the social problem
nor the Chinese problem has yet been solved, and, equipped though it is
with parliamentary machinery, it seems doubtful whether what is an archaic
regime will be successful in dealing with either. Nor is Malaya as yet completely independent. Britain has retained important military facilities. She
has also kept Singapore for the present, one reason being that Malaya's
conservative rulers are not eager to incorporate this town with its unruly,
largely Chinese and left-wing population. In 1958 Singapore acquired internal autonomy, with a government of a very leftist character.

Indonesia is another of those countries which tried to follow the Indian
example, but strayed off the democratic course into a more or less open
dictatorship. After eight years of war and revolution the country gained
its independence in an atmosphere of enthusiasm and constructive energy.
At the same time, however, certain disruptive forces were set free which
sought an outlet now that the unity imposed by the struggle for independence seemed no longer necessary. One of the chief of these was regionalism,
a force more difficult to check in an island empire than in a state whose
territory is continuous. Next there was the political issue which has been
one of the things hitherto preventing the working-out of a constitution,
i.e. the issue whether Indonesia was to be an Islamic republic or a secular
state. Finally, owing to a shortage of experts and specialists, coupled with
a superabundance of factional and private interests, the parliamentary
system functioned defectively and the army failed to adapt itself to the new
post-revolutionary situation.

But the biggest problem any Indonesian government is faced with is once
again that of poverty and social misery. Unlike India, the parliamentary
regime in Indonesia showed itself incapable of coping with this over-
riding problem, the more so as the interests of the over-populated island of
Java, where poverty is most serious, were diametrically opposed to those
of the other, thinly-populated, regions. Thus the opposition against the
central government outside Java was largely an opposition of producer
regions, bringing in foreign currency, against an economic policy which in
their view favoured the consumer island of Java. But if the government was
to remedy conditions there, it had no other choice. Political factors, too,
entered into the situation. The biggest Moslem party, the Masjumi, finds
most support in the non-Javanese regions, while Java is a bulwark of the
nationalist PNI, the main champion of the secular state in Indonesia. Long
before the open rebellion in the spring of 1958, the existence of armed
bands in the Sunda regions, in Atjeh and in southern Celebes was sympto-
matic of this religious-political quarrel; as soon as the Masjumi, during a
short period from 1955 to 1956, entered the government once more, the
activity of these bands diminished.

Under these circumstances it was difficult to start up the Indonesian
economy, nor could the problem of alleviating social distress be tackled
with any chance of success. The consequences made themselves felt in the
elections of September 1955, in which the communists won 6,000,000 votes.
Subsequent local elections in Java further strengthened the position of the

PKI. This growth alarmed not only the Moslem parties, but also the PNI which in the preceding years had been the leading government party. The PNI is a bourgeois party which was from time to time not above making opportunist overtures to the communists, or phrasing its programme in leftist terminology, but in reality it was hostile to the radical social reforms needed to solve the social question.

In an attempt to guide the prevailing discontent into other than social revolutionary channels, nationalist propaganda was revived. Just as in 1916 the bourgeois nationalists had laid down that there was a difference between 'sinful' (i.e. foreign) capitalism and 'un-sinful' (i.e. indigenous) capitalism, so towards the end of 1957 the social unrest was diverted to an attack on Dutch economic interests. Relations with the Netherlands had already been steadily deteriorating in the preceding years, and when the campaign to obtain Western New Guinea did not produce results, Dutch commerce and industry were completely squeezed out. This was not only harmful to Dutch interests, but also added to Indonesia's own difficulties, especially as transport between the islands was virtually a monopoly of the Dutch KPM. The campaign was carried to such lengths that in 1959 the market for Indonesian tobacco and tea was transferred from Amsterdam to Bremen and Antwerp.

In the same years the parliamentary form of government began gradually to be replaced by a 'guided democracy', i.e. by a more or less dictatorial presidential regime. Apart from Sukarno, the chief of staff of the army, General Nasution, is one of the key figures in this regime, while the policy of the PNI, which is regarded as identical with the national interest, sets the tone. This change in constitutional practice, moreover, serves the same purpose as that behind the diversionary manoeuvre against foreign economic influences. Because of its anti-Dutch campaign, the Government gained the support of the PKI, the party that acted as the mouthpiece of social discontent. By the introduction of a strong presidential regime, the danger from communist gains in future elections can, it is hoped, be averted. However, such exploitation of social discontent on the one hand, and severe curtailing of its legal expression on the other, does nothing to eliminate the causes of social misery.

Whether the rebels would have achieved a better solution if they had been victorious is uncertain. The counter-government which was set up in Padang on February 15, 1958, was an expression both of regionalist discontent outside Java with the policies of the centralist administration of Jakarta, and of Moslem opposition against Sukarno's concept of a secular state; it was spurred on by rebellious military elements. From a social point of view the leaders of the rebellion were as far to the right as the Government, and in some respects more conservative; hence the undisguised sympathy with the rebels displayed by conservative and reactionary Asian governments. But with an energy and efficiency which astounded all outside observers, the Government forces put down the rebellion, first in Sumatra (in May), and then in Celebes (in July 1958). About the only results of the rebellion were the establishment of new guerrilla centres and a further curtailment of the power of the Masjumi which had secretly sympathized with it.

Nor did the rebellion interrupt Indonesia's path towards 'guided democracy'. On August 16, 1958, Sukarno announced his programme for a new political structure and a simplified party system. The elections which were to take place in September 1959 were declared postponed, a relief to all those in the West who tended to regard the president as a cryto-communist. At the same time the Constituent Assembly, which since the end of 1955 had been working out a new constitution, was advised to accept the old constitution of 1945. This suggestion was turned down by the Assembly, though on religious grounds rather than out of concern for the survival of democratic institutions. On July 5, 1959, the Constituent Assembly was therefore dissolved by the president, and the constitution of the old Djokja republic reinstated by decree. Sukarno formed a new presidential government and at the same time began to set up advisory bodies in order to isolate parliament.

Meanwhile the fight against foreign economic influences, which indeed are very considerable, is continuing; at the end of 1959, for instance, the Chinese were prohibited from carrying on trade in the countryside. But in spite of all such measures a solution of Indonesia's social and economic problems is not yet in sight. The impression remains that Sukarno belongs to the type of statesman who is indispensable both before and during a revolution, but who is afterwards found to be lacking in vision.

Pakistan, too, seems to be no nearer solutions. It had to deal with a very thorny problem, that of East Bengal. Here, also, social factors played an important part, for that over-populated area with its social-revolutionary aspirations was a heavy drag on the government in Karachi. The same antagonism between advocates of a secular state and supporters of an orthodox Islamic republic existed in Pakistan also. In 1956 an Islamic republic was set up – a compromise, for it is neither a secular, nor an othodox Moslem, state. This was not surprising, for Islam is, or is supposed to be, the only bond between the two parts of the nation. The regional antagonisms were expressed in the frequent *coups d'état* in East Bengal, carried out by the central government. That government was socially a right-wing one; the pressure for the partition of British India was party due to the desire of the big Moslem landlords to retain their feudal privileges, since it looked as if they would stand a better chance of this in a separate Moslem state than in an Indian Union under Nehru, whose views were then leftish. Thus the social problem was hardly tackled at all, and the sharp contrast between property owners and destitute peasants was still painfully visible. An easy diversionary manoeuvre was of course handy, propaganda against India. But the corruption of the successive governments was so blatant that eventually the army, under general Ayub Khan, stepped in. On October 7, 1958, the federal and provincial governments were deposed; three weeks later the president suffered the same fate. The constitution of 1956 did not survive this *coup* for as much as a single day. Since then Pakistan has been ruled by a moderate dictatorship. Whether Ayub Khan, who has certainly taken some important measures towards economic stabilization, will be able to deal with the problem of destitution, it is too soon to say.

There was a similar development in Burma, where in October 1959 the army seized power. U Nu, the leader of the Government and a man of the left, came into conflict in the middle of 1958 with the right wing of AFPFL, with the result that he was expelled from the presidency of that party's executive committee. At the request of U Nu the Government was taken over by General Ne Win, who was given dictatorial powers. Whether here, as in the case of Indonesia and Pakistan, it is a case of dictatorship as a barrier against the rising tide of social discontent, remains to be seen. According to the latest information the contrary is true: the general elections of February 1960 resulted in a majority for U Nu. However, Burma is as yet economically very weak; the opposition of communists and Karens is by no means defeated, and the problem of destitution, above all in the Lower Burma delta, hangs like a sword over the head of each successive government.

The remaining countries of South and East Asia can be dealt with more briefly, as they have remained essentially unchanged. Syngman Rhee's regime in South Korea continued to be as despotic as ever: in 1959 the president caused the opposition candidate in the previous election to be executed. But one feels that the end of the regime is at hand; the students' demonstrations of April 1960, though suppressed in blood and terror, caused the retirement of Syngman Rhee himself and mark the beginning of the end.

The example of the moderately successful revolution in North Vietnam constituted a communist threat which determined the overtly authoritarian character of Ngo Dinh Diem's government in South Vietnam. This country became a republic in 1955, when the emperor, who, in any case, spent most of his time on the Riviera, was deposed.

Equally authoritarian is the government of Thailand. It seems that the downfall of the dictator Pibul Songgram (in September 1957) was the result more of personalities than of principles. A year later this *coup d'état* was followed by the removal of the remaining vestiges of democracy (October 1958): Marshal Sarit Thanarat dissolved the political parties and dismissed parliament.

In the Philippines the regimes of presidents Magsaysay (1953–1957) and Garcia (from 1957) were conservative rather than authoritarian, and, though the world press rarely now makes mention of the Huks, it is unlikely that the problem of poverty on the land has been solved. The preferential rights, moreover, enjoyed by the Americans act as a strong brake on the development of the economy of the Philippines.

A special position in Southeast Asia is occupied by Cambodia and Laos, because the Geneva treaty of 1954 made their independence subject to the condition of 'neutrality'. Cambodia, though exposed to a certain amount of pressure on the part of the pro-Western regimes of its neighbours Thailand

and South Vietnam, has hitherto observed this agreement under the leadership of the fairly progressive ex-king Norodom Sihanouk. In Laos on the contrary, the 1957 agreement between the Government and the Pathet Lao which had taken considerable effort to bring about, was undone in August 1958 when a *coup d'état* put a pro-Western regime in power. Probably the circumstance that the Pathet Lao, organized as a political party, had been victorious in a local election was not unconnected with this. As a result, the Pathet Lao has once more gone over to resistance and civil war continues; the problem is now an international one and the fate of the country in the hands, temporarily at least, of the Great Powers.

Finally Japan saw the return of many of the old politicians, as well as of earlier conditions; Kishi, premier since February 1957, was, for instance, a member of Tojo's war cabinet. After the revocation of the act against trust-formation, the old family concerns regained their economic and financial power. The local autonomous police were abolished and replaced by a national force, though a proposal to give the police increased power was withdrawn as it met with strong opposition (late 1958). With the support of extensive American aid Japan's industry has been built up and its competitive capacity increased. Shipping and shipbuilding were also restored. Yet the country's economic difficulties persisted. Many former Asian markets were now building up their own industries, while the sterling countries blocked Japanese imports. Economic contact with China was tentatively established but, in order not to arouse American displeasure, Japan was not prepared to open diplomatic relations, with the result that in 1958 Pekin broke off all commercial relations. From a military aspect Japan is still closely tied to the United States, despite socialist resistance and growing opposition also in non-socialist circles. Her economic existence remains precarious now that her territory is reduced to the four islands of the Japanese archipelago, for the produce of these islands is not sufficient to feed her growing population; in 1958 it was already 91,000,000.

V

THE ARAB WORLD

BETWEEN Bandung and the present time, nothing that has happened in Asia has been more sensational than the events in the Arab world, culminating in the Suez crisis of 1956 and, two years later, the *coup d'état* in Irak. This is not surprising, for here the nationalist element is more capable of influencing development than in the rest of Asia; theoretically the Arab countries were independent (except for some British strips alongside the Persian Gulf and the Gulf of Aden), but in actual fact most of the states were tied to Britain either economically, politically, or militarily, or even in all three respects. The Middle East, as we still call this area, is a very important part of the world, from the point of view of communications strategy on account of the Suez canal, of military strategy as a base along Soviet Russia's southern border, and of economic strategy because of oil. European influence, therefore, remained strong, even after the nationalist demands for autonomy had been to some extent appeased. In the Arab revolution, the same two currents are discerned that are characteristic of the Asian revolution in general – namely, one directed towards political independence, and the other towards social transformation. Advocates of both were to be found among the intellectuals in the towns and among progressive elements in the army. They could count on the backing of the bulk of the destitute population, who were becoming increasingly conscious of the misery to which they were condemned, and who were no longer prepared to submit meekly to it as if it were 'the will of Allah'. Nationally this hankering after a social revolution conflicted with the aspirations of the ruling classes of feudal landlords and urban property owners. Their desires were purely nationalist: all they wanted was for the mandatory powers to hand over authority to them. Once their political demands had been satisfied they continued to look for support to those same European powers, because of their fear of pressure from below, while these powers in turn continued to rely on them to safeguard their economic privileges.

This situation changed, as it was bound to change, when the idea of a social transformation took stronger hold of the masses, who had grown restive after centuries of exploitation. At first their aspirations were vague and undirected; the ruling classes could still attempt to deflect the mounting tide of revolution into channels that ran counter to European interests, both political and economic. Although it is not an Arab country, I am dealing with Iran here because it provides the clearest example of social unrest deflected by the ruling feudal classes into a nationalist movement with oil as basis. When this movement threatened to get out of hand, it was suppressed; that in 1953 was still possible since the revolutionary element, though vociferous, lacked efficient organization and had, moreover, spent itself in nationalist agitation. Iran has been quiet since, providing front-page news only in connection with a divorce or marriage of its head of state. But under that quiet surface lies the continuing social misery of a primitive peasant mass living in feudal conditions. One can easily foresee that, before long, less idyllic news items than the shah's latest love affair will cover the front pages of the world's newspapers.

The Arab social revolution began in Egypt. Here, too, it was met by a diversionary move culminating in the notorious 'black Saturday' in Cairo (January 26, 1952). But in this case the forces that had been aroused could not be held in check, and, in the resulting crisis of 1952, the army took over from a corrupt government and a debauched king. Soon it was not Neguib but Nasser who came to the fore as the strong man, in 1954 taking power into his own hands. Ruling the country as an enlightened despot, he freed it from the domination of the indigenous feudal classes and such British influences as remained. A certain amount of opposition was unavoidable: it was put up by supporters of the old conditions and the traditional Islamic groups on the one hand, while, on the other, Nasser's social reforms were not sufficiently radical to satisfy the extreme left, in particular the communists. But he persevered. As a social renovator and champion of Arab unity he managed to gain great popularity with the masses, and reinforced by this he got rid of the conservative opposition, and at the same time left the communists no choice except flight or prison.

The Egyptian example greatly influenced opinion in other Arab countries; to the Arabs generally Nasser became the hero of the day, with the result that, among progressive groups in all those states, certain sections who saw their own ideals reflected in Nasser's policy, above all in his concept of Arab unity, began to gather strength either secretly or openly. Nasser did not invent the nationalist movement for a united Arabia; it was older than he was, but he was the first to give it leadership and direction. He was encouraged by and himself encouraged the hope of the popular masses of a better future and of solidarity which would surmount the artificial barriers of frontiers. The force of this movement proved so strong that its repercussions were felt by the governments of all Arab countries. In Jordan young King Hussein, faced with threat of revolution if he persisted in a suspected intention to join the Bagdad Pact, dismissed the real power behind the scenes, namely the British general Glubb Pasha (December 1955).

A year later, the Arab world experienced its most serious crisis since the war in Palestine. As an Arab nationalist, Nasser was no friend of a Europe whose domination in previous decades had sown as much hatred as its duplicity had aroused distrust. The Bagdad Pact (Britain, Turkey, Irak, Iran, Pakistan) was generally regarded as an attempt by the West to maintain its political influence. To counter-balance this, Nasser sought support from the Soviet *bloc*, and got arms from it. This did not turn him into a supporter of communism, though the West promptly branded him as one. Actually he considered communism as serious a danger to the Arab right of self-determination as the Western imperialism he was trying to oust. His approaches to the Soviet Union were nothing but a normal political move in the normal political intercourse between independent states. The West, however, instantly sounded the alarm. It made a show of moral indignation behind which, however, lay nothing but fear for its own position of power in the cold war, fear that the Soviet Union would gain economic and political influence in an area which was of vital importance to it. This was the hidden cause of the Suez crisis.

Other factors, too, played a part in it, especially Nasser's desire to improve the standard of life in his over-populated country by means of large-scale irrigation works. The necessary funds for the construction of a Nile dam near Aswan were lacking, though they had been promised by the United States. Suddenly this promise was withdrawn; Dulles was incapable of regarding Nasser's relations with the Soviet Union as anything but immoral, and pressure on the part of American cotton planters did the rest. Nasser reacted sharply on July 26, 1956, by nationalizing the Suez Canal Company. This touched Britain and France on the raw, but neither their attempt to obstruct shipping in the Canal by recalling the pilots, nor diplomatic pressure, could make Egypt go back on her decision; with the profits drawn from the Canal, Nasser intended to finance the Nile dam. Force of arms was the only way left for the British and French to impose their will. This was strongly objected to by the United States, which had other and more important interests at stake; above all, America feared reactions in Asia. Britain – i.e. Eden – hesitated, but when France, the prime mover in the expedition, went ahead, Britain joined in. In the eyes of the French, Nasser bore the main responsibility, on top of everything else, for the Algerian rebellion which, in spite of all efforts, they had been unable to suppress. They sought contact with Israel and supported the latter when, alarmed at the prospect that Jordan might come under Egyptian influence, it opened a campaign in the Sinai desert to put an end to the Arab raids (October 29, 1956). When it became clear that Nasser was not yielding to threats and aerial bombardments, and that the popular revolt which had been expected in Egypt did not materialize, the British and French made a landing in Port Said to reconquer the Suez Canal (November 5th) – a repetition of 1882, one might say, a typical example of nineteenth century conduct against a non-Western people, but one that was not appropriate to the twentieth century. The Arab countries promptly closed the oil taps. Asia protested vehemently and the United States, which up to the last day had been misled about Anglo-French intentions, also sharply condemned the attack; the Soviet premier Bulganin adopted a threatening attitude. After a day and a half, Britain and France called off the expedition, which had taken several months to prepare. Victory was completely on the side of Nasser: the aggressors, Israel included, had to withdraw.

By now Britain's role in the Middle East was practically played out. The United States, whose attitude during the Suez crisis had earned a certain amount of goodwill, had the tactlessness to speak of a 'vacuum' which it was to fill. This cold-war terminology promptly aroused suspicion. The Eisenhower doctrine (January 5, 1957) – economic aid and military assistance while respecting independence – was seen as a new attempt to keep the Arabs within the Western camp, or force them back into it. This distrust was increased afresh when in April 1957 the king of Jordan, with scarcely-veiled American support, sent his pro-Nasser government packing. Anti-American feeling grew more violent, especially in Syria, where in the summer of 1957 changes occurred both in the Government and in the army which strengthened communist influence. But this did not suit Nasser's book, and the way in which he managed, aided by his supporters in Syria itself (President Shukri el-Kuwatli among them), to solve the crisis was one of his masterstrokes. On February 1, 1958, Syria and Egypt merged to form jointly the United Arab Republic.

Two things were achieved by this. On the one hand the growing communist influence in Syria was eliminated, while on the other a beginning was made to give practical effect to the unification of the Arab world. It was the latter aspect of the fusion between Egypt and Syria which provided the strongest attraction for the popular masses in the other Arab countries. The rulers of Irak and Jordan promptly recognized this, for by way of a counter-move they organized a federal alliance between the two kingdoms. What the average Arab thought of this is best illustrated by the one and only telegram of congratulation from Kuwait that the Irak-Jordan federation inspired; its sender was the king. Thousands of such telegrams had been sent to Nasser from this little state when the United Arab Republic was formed.

The strength of the Arab revolution was most clearly demonstrated in the summer of 1958. In Lebanon a civil war broke out between the predominantly Moslem supporters of Nasser and the mostly Christian adherents of the pro-Western government of President Shamoun. Much more sensational was the revolution in Bagdad (July 14). A single hour was enough to put an end to the authoritarian and feudal-conservative regime in Irak, the strongest pro-Western bulwark that still existed in the Arab world. King Faisal II, Premier Nuri al-Said and Crown-Prince Adb al-Ilah were assassinated; General Kassem took over power.

To these events the West reacted in a mood of panic. American troops landed in Lebanon and British air-borne troops descended on Jordan, to prevent the revolution from spreading. By then the expression 'indirect aggression' had been coined to characterize revolutionary movements in the Arab world. The revolution in Irak, however, did not spread across its borders. Intervention achieved only half its aim; in Lebanon a 'neutralist' was chosen as president, whereupon the Americans departed. That they had come for the sole reason of guaranteeing free elections no Arab believed. In Jordan Hussein managed to hold his own, at first with, later without, the support of British bayonets. His downfall was prevented not so much because his position was strong, and his country's nationalist aspirations weak, but because the Arabs were convinced that a revolution in Jordan would automatically be followed by an aggressive move on the part of Israel.

Since then, developments in the Arab world have proceeded fairly quietly. In spite of great pressure to join the United Arab Republic, Kassem showed himself determined to let economically strong Irak steer a course of its own, a 'neutralist' course, which in this context means Arab nationalist, but independent of Egypt. His position was rather precarious: in order to suppress a pro-Nasser revolt in Mosul (March 1959) he had to seek the support of the communists, and as a result they were able to strengthen their position in Irak. Kassem is very popular with the Irak masses, however, on account of his social reforms, which make him the rival of Nasser. The West derived a certain amount of pleasure from this rivalry, and when it supplied Kassem with the arms it had refused to Nasser earlier on under the pretext that the balance of power between Arabs and Israelis should not be upset, fresh distrust was aroused. This took the form of an accusation that the West collaborated with the communists (of Irak) in order to fight Arab nationalism, for Nasser is threatened with the danger that Syria, with its revolutionary inclinations, will detach itself from the United Arab Republic to join the more radical Kassem, a danger which materialised some months later (1961).

What is happening in the Arab world today is just what is happening on a larger scale in Asia as a whole. Nasser and Kassem are contending for the allegiance of the Arabs in the same way as India and China are competing for the allegiance of the Asians. In the Arab world, too, the central problem is how to alleviate the poverty of the millions; all internal and foreign policies in Asian countries are in a sense conditioned by it.

CHRONOLOGICAL SURVEY

(COMPILED BY DR J. M. PLUVIER)

1830–1847 Algeria conquered by France.

1842 China: the Opium War; British take Hongkong.

1851–1865 China: Taiping rebellion.

1853 Japan: American squadron under Perry compels Japan to open her territory to the rest of the world.

1857 India: the Great Mutiny.

1858 India: dissolution of the East India Company.

1865 Russia: Russians take Tashkent.

1867–8 Japan: revolution; fall of the shogunate.

1869 Egypt: opening of the Suez Canal.

1873 Indonesia: Atjeh War begins.
Russia: the emir of Bokhara and the khan of Khiva recognize Russian sovereignty.

1876 Turkey: Abdul Hamid becomes sultan.

1877 India: Queen Victoria becomes empress of India.

1881 Tunisia becomes a French protectorate.

1882 Egypt occupied by British troops. Cromer becomes resident-general.

1885 India: Founding of the All-India National Congress.

1887 Indochina: Formation of the Indochinese Union under a French governor-general.

1889 Japan receives a constitution on the Prussian model.

1894–5 Sino-Japanese War; Japan gets Formosa. China: attempted rising of Sun Yat-sen.

1896 Philippines: rising against Spanish rule.

1898 China: liberal period of the 'Hundred Days'; Russians lease Port Arthur and get concession to build a new railway through South Manchuria. Turkey: Wilhelm II's visit to Constantinople. Philippines: Spanish-American War, guerrilla war first against the Spaniards, then against the Americans. Soudan: Battle of Omdurman.

1898–1902 Egypt: Aswan dam built.

1899 Anglo-Egyptian agreement on Soudan condominium.

FIRST PERIOD

1900 China: Boxer rising; siege of the Pekin Legations; international campaign against the Boxers; Russians occupy Manchuria. Russia: Trans-Siberian railway prolonged to Vladivostok.

1901 Philippines: Aguinaldo surrenders to the Americans. China: the powers compel China to sign the so-called Boxer-protocol. Indonesia: Queen Wilhelmina's speech from the Throne; 'ethical colonial policy' sanctioned.

1902 Anglo-Japanese alliance signed. India: catastrophic famine in Bombay, Rajputana, Central India and the Punjab.

1903 Turkey: a German company receives a concession for the building of the Bagdad railway.

1904 Japanese attack the Russian fleet at Port Arthur; Russo-Japanese War begins; battle of the Yalu. Egypt and Morocco: Anglo-French entente; Spain receives a sphere of influence in Morocco. Tibet: British expedition under Younghusband to Lhasa. Arab countries; founding of the 'Ligue de la patrie arabe' in Paris.

1905 Japan: battles of Mukden and Tsushima. Morocco: first Franco-German crisis. Russia: revolutionary movement in the towns and the countryside. China: Sun Yat-sen founds the revolutionary organization Tung Meng-hui. India: nationalist agitation over the partition of Bengal. Japan: Peace of Portsmouth; Japan receives South Sakhalin and Port Arthur but no war reparations; Korea becomes a Japanese protectorate. Russia: creation of the Imperial Duma; workers' rising in Moscow suppressed.

1906 Russia: reaction; punitive expeditions; Stolypin's agrarian reforms. Morocco: Conference of Algeciras; end of the first Morocco crisis. Turkey: removal of the 'Fatherland and Freedom' to Salonica. India: founding of the Moslem League; Congress of Surat. Egypt: Denshawi incident. China: peasant rising in Hunan; an Imperial decree foreshadows a constitution. Iran: revolutionary movement; creation of a national assembly; Shah Musaffer-ed-din dies after signing the constitution.

1907 Morocco: rising against the sultan Abd el-Asiz. India: split between extremists and moderates. Tilak arrested. Indochina: Emperor Thanh Thai of Annam compelled to abdicate. Korea: rising against the Japanese suppressed. Iran: Anglo-Russian agreement divides the country into spheres of influence. Thailand compelled to surrender border districts to French Indochina. Philippines; creation of a legislative Assembly; founding of the Partido Nacionalista under Osmena and Quezon. Japan signs with Russia a treaty on fishing rights in east Siberian waters and on the division of North China and Korea into spheres of influence. Egypt: Cromer retires. Mustapha Kiamil summons the National Congress. Iran: failure of the reactionary *putsch* of Shah Mohammed Ali.

1908 Morocco: Sultan Abd el-Asiz deposed. Egypt: Mustapha Kiamil dies. Burma: founding of the Buddhist Young Men's Association. Turkey: Young Turk revolution under Enver and Talaat; founding of the Ottoman-Arab Brotherhood (al-Icha al-Arabi al-Othmani). Iran: reactionary *coup d'état* by Mohammed Ali; revolutionary rising in Tabriz. China: death of the dowager empress. Indochina: risings suppressed; the rebel leader De Tham surrenders. Palestine: first Jewish agricultural colony founded on Lake Tiberias.

1909 India: Morley-Minto reforms (Indian Councils Act). Turkey: failure of Abdul Hamid's reactionary *coup d'état;* Mohammed V becomes sultan; oppression of the national minorities; dissolution of Ottoman-Arab Brotherhood. Arab countries: founding of the literary club al-Muntada al Adabi in Constantinople. Iran: Shah Mohammed Ali deposed by the revolutionaries; founding of the Anglo-Persian Oil Company. Philippines: the Payne-Aldrich tariff eases the import of Filipino products into the United States. Thailand is compelled to surrender Perlis, Kedah,

Kelantan and Trengganu to Malaya. Japan: founding of the Colonial Bank of Korea.

1910 Egypt: murder of Butros Ghali. Thailand: death of King Chulalongkorn. China: the pre-Parliament meets. Japan annexes Korea.

1911 Morocco: French occupy Fez; the *Panther* sent to Agadir; second Morocco crisis; Spain subdues the Riff Kabyles. Iran: Shuster the American finance minister forced to leave by the Russians. Arab countries: founding of the Young Arab movement (al-Fatat) in Paris. India: King George V and Queen Mary crowned emperor and empress of India. Indochina: Sarraut becomes governor-general. Russia: Lena gold mines strike; Stolypin murdered. Turkey: Italian invasion of Libya. China: the revolution breaks out in Wuhan (Hankow); Sun Yat-sen provisional president; Outer Mongolia becomes independent.

1912 China becomes a republic; Yuan Shi-kai president. Morocco becomes a French protectorate; Lyautey resident-general; campaign to reduce Morocco begins; Spain receives the coastal strip. Arab countries: founding of the Decentralization party. Iran: Russian armed intervention; National Assembly closed. India: the Moslem League presents demand for the independence of India. Indonesia: anti-Chinese agitation; founding of the 'Sarekat Islam'. China: Sun's party takes the name of Kuo Min-tang in opposition to Yuan Shi-kai. Turkey makes peace with Italy which gets Tripolitana; attack of the Balkan states on Turkey; the First Balkan War. Japan: Bundshi Suzuki founds the Labour Federation.

1913 Arab countries: Arab congress in Paris. China: Kuo Min-tang rising suppressed by Yuan Shi-kai. Libya: Italians occupy Fezzan. Turkey in the First Balkan War loses its territory in Europe; recovers Adrianople in the Second. India: Gandhi in South Africa.

SECOND PERIOD

1914 Morocco: the French occupy the Atlas region. Libya: Senussi rising; Italians lose Fezzan. China: Yuan Shi-kai dissolves the National Assembly. The First World War breaks out. Japan declares war on Germany; Germans lose Shantung. Turkey at war with the Entente. Egypt: Britain declares Turkish sovereignty over Egypt abolished; the Khedive Abbas II is deposed; Egypt becomes a British protectorate.

1915 Japan presents the 'twenty-one requests' to China. Turkey: Anglo-French expedition to the Dardanelles; Armenian atrocities. China: opposition to Yuan Shi-kai's plan to declare himself emperor. Arab countries: the Macmahon conversations; Britain guarantees the independence of the Arab countries.

1916 China: death of Yuan Shi-kai; dissolution of the Central government; rule of the provincial governors; civil wars. Philippines: the Jones Act envisages more self-government. India: Tilak and Annie Besant found the Home Rule League; reconciliation of the moderates with the extremists; declaration of Lucknow; the Moslem League and the Congress demand self-government. Indonesia: the Sarekat Islam becomes a radical mass movement. Arab countries: secret Sykes-Picot treaty dividing the Arab countries between Britain and France; Arab rising against Turkey. Hussein, sherif of Mecca, becomes king of the Hejaz. Indochina: rising suppressed. Russia: the Amur railway completed.

1917 Morocco: the French occupy Tiznit. Russia: the bourgeois February revolution; fall of czarism. Arab countries; British troops occupy Palestine and Mesopotamia. Egypt: Ahmed Fuad becomes sultan. China: declaration of war on Germany; monarchist rising fails in Pekin. Japan: the United States recognizes Japan's special interests in Manchuria. India: Montagu's statement on constitutional reform. Russia: the left radical October revolution; the Bolsheviks in power. Palestine: the Balfour declaration on a Jewish national home.

1918 Wilson's Fourteen Points. Libya: the Italians subdue Cyrenaica. Tunisia: creation of the Destour party. Arab countries: British troops occupy Syria. India: the Rowlatt report. Russia: civil war in Siberia; intervention of Czechs and Japanese; Japanese troops occupy Vladivostok. Japan: rice unrest; Hara becomes the first premier of non-noble birth. Turkey: armistice of Mudros. Germany capitulates. End of the First World War. Egypt: Zaglul asks for conversations on the political status of Egypt. Indochina: Sarraut opens conversations on the possibilities of independence; Nguyen Ai Quoc's memorandum.

THIRD PERIOD

1919 Egypt: nationalist unrest; the Milner Commission. Korea: nationalist rising suppressed; provisional government of Korea established in Shanghai. India: unrest in the Punjab; the 'blood bath of Amritsar'. Afghanistan: attack of Afghan troops on India is defeated. Iran: Anglo-Persian treaty, acceptance of which is refused by the National Assembly. Russia: founding of the Comintern. Syria: Pan-Syrian Congress in Damascus. Treaty of Versailles. Turkey: beginning of the national revolution; Kemal summons the Sivas congress. China: anti-Japanese students' demonstrations in Shanghai. Japan: extension of the franchise. India: Government of India Act.

1920 Turkey: the National Assembly endorses the National Pact; British troops occupy Constantinople. Syria: Faisal becomes king; conference of San Remo; Syria becomes a French, Irak a British, mandated territory; French troops expel Faisal and establish a military government. Turkey: Mustapha Kemal establishes the National Assembly in Ankara, and begins the war against the Greeks. Palestine: great increase in Jewish immigration. India: death of Tilak; Gandhi becomes leader of the nationalists; Moslem agitation against the treatment of Turkey by the Great Powers; passive resistance; first non-co-operation campaign; Hindus and Moslems work together. Indonesia: founding of the Communist party. Burma: university boycott. Japan: economic crisis. Irak: after months of fighting the rising against the British suppressed. Turkey: the Turkish delegates sign the treaty of Sèvres. Russia: Congress of Eastern Peoples at Baku; expulsion of the emir of Bokhara and the khan of Khiva; defeat of Kolchak.

1921 Iran: march on Teheran; *coup d'état* of Riza Khan and Zia al-Din. Arabia: Ibn Saud annexes Shammar. Afghanistan: treaty with Russia signed. China: Sun forms Kuo Min-tang counter-government in Canton; first congress of Chinese Communist party. Japan: prime minister Hara murdered; founding of Japanese Communist party. Russia: Turkestan becomes an autonomous soviet republic within the RSSR. China: separate peace treaty signed with Germany. Morocco: rebellion of Abd el-Krim in Spanish Morocco; battle of Anual. Indonesia: split between left and right wings in Sarekat Islam. Irak becomes a kingdom with Faisal as king. Turkey: Kemal defeats the Greeks on the Sakharia. Egypt: negotions with Britain on the future political status of Egypt break down; Zaglul is deported.

1922 Egypt: British protectorate ends; Egypt an independent kingdom under Fuad I; British occupation continues. Morocco: Abd el-Krim declared emir of the Riff Kabyles. India: incident at Chauri-Chaura; Gandhi discontinues the non-co-operation movement. China: nine-power treaty on China's territorial integrity; treaty of Shantung; Shantung evacuated by the Japanese. Japan: naval ratios established by the naval treaty of Washington. Turkey: battle of the Sakkaria; Greeks driven out of Anatolia; fall of Smyrna; sultanate abolished. Russia: Japanese troops leave Vladivostock.

1923 Afghanistan: constitution proclaimed. Palestine: British mandate over Palestine and Transjordan enters into force. Burma becomes a province of India. Indonesia: railway strike. Iran: Riza Khan prime minister. India: Gandhi sentenced; Swaraj party gains majority in the Congress. Egypt receives a constitution. Turkey: treaty of Lausanne signed; republic proclaimed; Kemal president. Japan: earthquake disaster. Russia: autonomous Buriat-Mongolian Republic founded; church and monastic property taken over; restoration of property of Islamic organization; Russia becomes the Union of Soviet Socialist Republics.

1924 Soviet Union: death of Lenin. Turkey: caliphate abolished; Turkey gets a constitution. China: Kuo Min-tang congress agrees to co-operate with the communists. Irak ratifies assistance treaty with Britain. Arabia: Ibn Saud captures Mecca and drives Hussein out of the Hejaz. Burma: anti-Indian unrest. Philippines: anti-Chinese agitation in Manila. Mongolia becomes an autonomous people's republic on the Russian model. China: Pekin captured by Feng Yu-hsian. Egypt: Zaglul prime minister; he is compelled to resign after the murder of the British governor of the Soudan. Japan: Kato becomes prime minister.

1925 China: death of Sun Yat-sen. Iran: Riza Khan becomes shah. China. blood bath of Shanghai; anti-British boycott; strikes in Hongkong. Japan: manhood suffrage for the lower house of Parliament. Syria: Druse rebellion; bombardment of Damascus. Palestine: opening of the Hebrew university in Jerusalem. Turkey: Kurdish rising suppressed; dervish order banned; abolition of the fez. Egypt: Fuad dissolves parliament after Wafd's electoral victory. Indonesia: law on the political status of the Dutch East Indies: Indochina: Varenne governor-general; founding of the revolutionary Young Annamite party. Soviet Union: Turkestan and Usbekistan become socialist soviet republics. Morocco: joint action by France and Spain against Abd el-Krim.

1926 Irak gets Mosul from Turkey. Afghanistan becomes a kingdom. Syria: establishment of civil administration; the Lebanon becomes a republic. Philippines: founding of a Consejo Supremo Nacional. Indochina: Annamite appeal to the League of Nations. Morocco: Abd el-Krim surrenders. China: Kuo Min-tang expedition under Chiang against the northern war lords; fall of Hankow. Arabia: Ibn Saud becomes king of the Hejaz. Japan: Hirohito becomes emperor. Soviet Union: expulsion of the counter-revolutionary Basmadjis from Central Asia. Kirghizistan becomes an autonomous soviet republic. Indonesia; communist-inspired rising in Java.

1927 Indonesia: communist-inspired rising on west coast of Sumatra. Indochina: founding of the revolutionary Tan Viet Cach Menh Dang and the nationalist Viet Nam Quoc Dan Dang. China: Kuo Min-tang forces take Nanking and Shanghai; Chiang breaks with the communists and forms a bourgeois nationalist government in Nanking; workers' movement in Shanghai suppressed. Japan: end of the liberal period; Tanaka in power; Tanaka memorandum; bank crisis. Soviet Union; construction of Turksib begins. Syria: Druse revolt suppressed. Egypt: death of Zaglul; Nahas becomes leader of the Wafd. Indonesia: Sukarno founds the Partai Nacional Indonesia. China: peasant risings in Hunan; the Canton commune; white terror throughout Kuo Min-tang China. Iran: construction of the Trans-Iranian railway begins.

1928 Iran: abolition of the capitulations. China: Japan temporarily occupies Shantung; Chiang's troops take Pekin; Chang Tso-lin murdered. Indochina: Pasquier becomes governor-general. Egypt: Parliament rejects the treaty with Britain: Fuad dissolves Parliament. Turkey: introduction of Latin script. Transjordan: agreement with Britain on sovereignty. Syria: Nationalists' electoral victory. China: Manchuria adheres to the Kuo Min-tang. Soviet Union: first five-year-plan; industrialization.

1929 Afghanistan: reactionary rebellion; Amanulla deposed; civil war. Syria: French dissolve the legislative assembly. Indochina: murder attempts by the VNQDD; split between communists and nationalists in the TVCMD; Nguyen Ai Quoc founds the Indochinese Communist party. Korea: risings suppressed. Soviet Union: founding of the Socialist Soviet Republic of Tadjikstan. Afghanistan: Nadir becomes king. Palestine: Jewish Arab unrest. World economic crisis. India; the Congress of Lahore passes independence resolution. Indonesia: PNI action suppressed. Libya: Italians take Fezzan.

1930 Libya: Italians take Kufra and crush Senussi rebellion. Turkey: Kurdish rising. Arabia: Ibn Saud captures Asir; Syria: creation of the Republic of Syria. Indochina: nationalist rising in Tonkin; Yen Bay mutiny; peasant rising in Annam crushed by French. India: Gandhi's march to the salt pans begins the second non-co-operation campaign; the Simon report; campaign against the Afridis in the North-West Province. Burma: peasant rising in Tharrawaddy; Sayasan's rising. Morocco: Allal al-Fasi founds the Nationalist party of Morocco. Philippines: swift rise of the revolutionary Sakdai party. China: war in the north; failure of rising against Chiang; soviet government formed in Kiangsi. Indonesia: Sukarno prosecuted. Egypt: Wafd electoral victory; negotiations with Britain for a treaty break down; Fuad abolishes the 1923 constitution and substitutes a dictatorial one. Soviet Union: agrarian revolution from above; collectivization of farms. Irak concludes an independence treaty with Britain.

1931 India: Gandhi concludes an agreement with Irwin for the ending of the non-co-operation movement. China: temporary provisional constitution; Mao Tse-tung becomes president of the Chinese Communist party; Kuo Min-tang expedition against the soviet districts. Indonesia: dissolution of the PNI; founding of the Partai Indonesia (Partindo) and

Pendikan Nasional Indonesia (PNI-baru). Philippines: anti-Chinese agitation in San Paolo. China: Japanese attack on Mukden; Manchuria occupied. India: Round Table conferences in London.

1932 India: Gandhi resumes the non-co-operation campaign; arrest of the Congress leaders. China: Manchuria independent under Japanese protection; Japanese bombard Chapei; fighting in Shanghai. Morocco: rebellion in the Atlas; French take Tafilet. Japan: premier Inukai murdered by a member of a secret patriotic league. Burma: Sayasan rebellion crushed. Thailand: revolution against royal absolutism; constitution granted. China: revolutionary movement of Cheng Chi-tsai brings Sinkiang into the Russian sphere of influence; Lytton report on Manchuria. Arabia: Ibn Saud gives his kingdom the name of Saudi Arabia. Irak becomes a member of the League of Nations.

1933 Indonesia: Mutiny on *The Seven Provinces*. China: Japanese troops occupy Yehol; Japan leaves the League of Nations; China signs the truce of Tangku with Japan. Irak: Death of Faisal; extermination of the Assyrians. Thailand: Communists banned; king's *coup d'état* fails. Iran signs new agreement with the Anglo-Persian Oil Co. Afghanistan: Zahir succeeds Nadir as king. Indonesia: Government begins to suppress the non-co-operative nationalist groups. Soviet Union: second five-year plan.

1934 Morocco: Spaniards occupy Ifni. Libya divided into four provinces for administrative purposes. China: Manchukuo becomes a kingdom under Japanese protection. Arabia: war – a short one – between Saudi Arabia and Yemen. Japan: Monroe doctrine for the Far East. Philippines: Tydings-McDuffie Act fixes 1946 as date of independence. China: expropriation of Anglo-American oil interests in Manchukuo. Soviet Union becomes member of the League of Nations. China: the Red Army begins the great march from Kiangsi to the north. Turkey: introduction of family names. Egypt: revolutionary agitation; Fuad abolishes the 1930 constitution.

1935 Soviet Union sells the Chinese Eastern Railway to Manchukuo. Indochina: Franco-Chinese treaty on the position of Chinese. Burma: founding of the thakins' party, Dobama Asiayone. Persia becomes Iran; Teheran University founded. Philippines: Commonwealth established; Quezon president. Egypt: Fuad restores the 1930 constitution. Indonesia: founding of the bourgeois-nationalist Partai Indonesia Raja (Pardindra).

1936 Japan leaves the Naval Conference in London and denounces the 1922 Washington Treaty; military *putsch* fails in Tokio. India: Jinnah reorganizes the Moslem League. Irak: short-lived fascist dictatorship of Bakr Sidki. Palestine: Arab resistance to Jewish immigration; strikes; Arab terrorism against Jewish settlements. Soviet Union: Stalin's constitution; Kasakstan and Kirghizstan become socialist soviet republics. China: Japanese occupy Suiyan. Turkey: Montreux convention; Turkey remilitarizes the Dardanelles. Morocco: Moroccan troops in the Spanish civil war. Indonesia: Sutardjo petition for greater independence. Egypt: Farouk becomes king. Treaty with Britain; British troops evacuate Egypt save for the Canal zone; *status quo* remains in the Soudan. Syria: France concludes treaties with Syria and the Lebanon on independence. China: mutiny in Sian.

1937 India: elections for provincial governments; Congress majority in most provinces. Burma: separation from India; Ba Maw premier. Egypt: Montreux convention; abolition of capitulations. Libya: Mussolini's visit. Morocco: nationalist agitation. Irak: opening of the Bagdad railway. Thailand: treaty with Britain; abolition of extra-territorial rights. Indonesia: founding of the left socialist Gerakan Rajkat Indonesia (Gerindo). Japan: Konoye premier. China: incident at the Marco Polo Bridge; fall of Pekin and Tientsin; united front of Kuo Min-tang and communists against Japan. Turkey, Irak, Iran and Afghanistan conclude the Pact of Saadabad. China: Japanese take Shanghai and Nanking.

1938 Tunisia: nationalist agitation. Arabia: discovery of oil in Saudi Arabia. Burma: anti-Indian agitation; civil disobedience movement; Ba Maw resigns. Indochina: French temporarily close the Yunnan railway. Thailand: Pibul Songgram dictator (premier). Soviet Union: completion of the Ferghana irrigation canal. China: fall of Hankow; Chinese Government withdraws to Chungking; Japanese troops land in South China and take Canton. Turkey: death of Kemal Ataturk; Ismet Inonu becomes president. Soviet Union: third five-year plan.

1939 Palestine: London conference; Britain restricts Jewish immigration. China: Japanese occupy Hainan. Iran: Trans-Iranian railway opened. Syria: France delays carrying out the 1936 treaty. Thailand: name (Siam) changed to Thailand. Indonesia: founding of the political nationalist federation Gabungan Politik Indonesia (Gapi); demand for an Indonesian parliament. Soviet Union: 'secret war' between Russian and Japanese troops on the Manchukuo frontiers. Second World War breaks out in Europe. India is declared 'belligerent' by the viceroy on his own authority. Burma: arrest of nationalist leaders. China: Japanese attack on Changsha repelled.

1940 China: Wang Ching-wei forms a pro-Japanese government in Nanking. Burma: Ba Maw forms the Freedom Bloc. Morocco, Algeria, Tunisia: after the fall of France they support the Vichy government as does Syria. Indochina comes under the Vichy government; the French give the Japanese permission to station troops in Tonkin. Burma: under Japanese pressure Britain closes the Burma road. India: Gandhi protests, proclaims 'personal' non-co-operation; Moslem League passes the Pakistan resolution. Egypt: British troops occupy country and defeat the Italian attempt at invasion at Sidi Barrani. Japan, Germany and Italy conclude treaty of Berlin. Indonesia: the Dutch administration rejects the proposals of Wiwoho and Thamrin; the Visman Commission set up.

1941 China: clash with the Fourth Army; blockade of the communist-held areas. Libya: British troops capture Cyrenaica and are driven out by the Afrika Corps. Indochina: the French hand over certain areas to Thailand. Soviet Union: Stalin becomes prime minister. Irak: Rashid Ali's pro-German *coup d'état*; British troops occupy the country. Syria: British and Free French troops occupy the country and expel Vichy representatives; Syria and the Lebanon declared independent republics. Burma: U Saw, the premier, arrested. India: agitation against the Indian Restriction Act in Burma. Indochina occupied by Japanese troops. Iran: British and Russian troops occupy the country and compel the shah to abdicate: Mohammed Riza Pahlevi becomes shah;

founding of the left Tudeh party. Roosevelt and Churchill sign the Atlantic Charter. Japan: militarist government under Tojo. Soviet Union: German attack on Moscow fails; Leningrad besieged. Japan: attack on Pearl Harbour and Singapore; war declared by Britain, Holland and the United States. Thailand occupied by Japanese; Pridi becomes leader of the resistance movement against Japan. China: Japanese take Hongkong.

FOURTH PERIOD

1942 Thailand at war with the Allies. Malaya conquered by the Japanese; fall of Singapore. Indonesia: Japanese take Celebes, Borneo and Sumatra; rising against the Dutch in Atjeh thwarted by the Japanese invasion; battle of the Java Sea. Philippines: Japanese take Mindanao and Luzon; battle of Bataan; fall of Corregidor. Burma: fall of Rangoon and Mandalay; British withdraw to India; anti-Indian agitation leads to a mass exodus of Indians to Bengal; by the conquest of Burma the Burma road to China is closed; thereby China is cut off from the rest of the world. Egypt: German troops threaten Alexandria; Britain compels Farouk to appoint Nahas premier. Japan: battle of the Coral Sea; battle of Midway; end of the great Japanese expansion. India; the Cripps mission; Congress passes the 'Quit India' resolution; the August rebellion; Congress leaders arrested; Bose forms his Free Indian Army. Malaya: anti-Japanese guerrilla forces unite. Indochina: Ho Chi Minh forms the anti-Japanese freedom organization, the Viet Minh. Japan: battle for Guadalcanal; American troops land on the Solomons. Morocco and Algeria: Anglo-American troops land in North Africa; Tunisia occupied by the Germans. Egypt: battle of El Alamein; Germans driven out of Egypt. Soviet Union: Germans advance to the Volga and the Caucasus; battle of Stalingrad.

1943 Libya occupied by the British; British military administration. China: Britain and the United States renounce extra-territorial rights. Morocco: nationalist organizations unite in the Istiklal. Philippines: formation of the anti-Japanese (and anti-feudal) liberation army of Hukbalahap. Indonesia: founding of the Moslem federation Mashumi. Tunisia: Anglo-American armies drive the Germans and Italians from North Africa; French depose Munsaf Bey. Soviet Union: Stalin dissolves the Comintern. Burma: independence under Japanese control; Ba Maw premier. India: famine in Bengal. Cairo Allies' conference; independence of Korea recognized and the reversion of Formosa to China. Syria: the French dismiss the Lebanon government; nationalist agitation.

1944 India: Japanese invasion of Assam repulsed. Palestine: Jewish terrorism begins; Irgun Zwai Leumi and Stern gang. Burma: founding of the anti-Fascist Freedom League under Aung San. Egypt: Farouk dismisses Nahas. Syria and the Lebanon: France transfers the mandatory power to the governments. Turkey: relations broken off with Germany. Philippines: Japan recognizes the independence of the islands. Indonesia: Japanese declaration on Indonesian independence. Japan: Tojo dismissed; beginning of the great Allied air attacks. China: Japanese victories in South and Central China; fall of Changsha and Kweilin. Burma: British troops begin the reconquest of Burma. Soviet Union:

Tannu Tava becomes an autonomous district within the USSR. Philippines: battles of Leyte and Surigao; defeat of the Japanese fleet; American troops begin the reconquest of the Philippines.

1945 'Big Three' conference in Yalta. Indochina: the Japanese remove the French administration. Arab countries: founding of the Arab League. Burma reconquered by the British. Germany capitulates. India: conference in Simla; the Wavell plan to reconcile Hindus and Moslems fails. Syria: unrest; French troops leave. Japan: destruction of Hiroshima and Nagasaki by atom bombs; Soviet Union declares war; Japan ready to capitulate. Soviet Union: Red Army occupies Manchuria; treaty between China and the Soviet Union. Indonesia: Sukarno and Hatta proclaim the independent Republic of Indonesia. Japan: capitulation; American troops occupy the country. Korea: Americans occupy Korea up to the 38th parallel; the Russians occupy the north. Soviet Union; occupation of South Sakhalin and the Kuriles. China: Chiang dissolves the democratic parties of the centre; resumption of the civil war between the Kuo Min-tang and the communists. Indochina: proclamation of the independent Republic of Vietnam; fighting with French troops in Saigon. Indonesia: after severe fighting with the nationalists British troops occupy Surabaya; Shahrir becomes premier.

FIFTH PERIOD

1946 Thailand makes peace with the Allies; Pridi premier. China: Russian troops evacuate Manchuria. Iran: Security Council takes up the question of Russian troops in North Iran. Egypt: British troops leave. Transjordan: end of the British mandate; becomes a kingdom under Abdulla. Indochina: treaty of Dalat; France recognizes the independence of Vietnam, Laos and Cambodia within the French Union. Philippines become politically independent. India: British Cabinet mission arrives. Indochina: the free state of Cochinchina created under French auspices. China: civil war spreads all over China north of the Yangtse. India: Nehru forms a provisional government; violent religious-political strife in Calcutta; thousands dead. Japan receives a new constitution. Soviet Union: fourth five-year plan; Mongolia concludes a treaty of mutual assistance with Russia. Indonesia: treaty of Linggadjati; Holland recognizes the Republic of Indonesia in Java and Sumatra. Iran: separatist movement in Azerbaijan suppressed. Indonesia: under Dutch auspices the free state of East Indonesia is created. Indochina: the French bombardment of Haiphong begins the Franco-Indochinese war.

1947 China: rising in Formosa suppressed; Marshall's mediation effort fails. Truman's 'fair deal'. India: Nehru convokes the first pan-Asian conference in Delhi. Thailand: *coup d'état* of the right. Philippines: military treaty with the United States. The Marshall Plan. Burma: Aung San, the premier, and several of his ministers murdered in Rangoon. Indonesia: first Dutch military action against the Republic; Security Council intervenes. India: British India becomes independent; two dominions created, India and Pakistan; Nehru premier of India; Liaqat Ali Khan premier of Pakistan; partition of the Punjab and Bengal; the Punjab horror; the Hindu-Moslem quarrel costs half a million lives. Soviet Union: creation of the Cominform. India: conflict between

India and Pakistan over Kashmir. Palestine: the United Nations accepts the partition plan.

1948 India: Gandhi murdered. Ceylon becomes a Dominion. Burma becomes independent and leaves the British Commonwealth. China: communist advance into Manchuria and North China begins; fall of Mukden and Kirin. Thailand: military dictatorship of Pibul Songgram. Philippines: guerrilla war of the left Hukbalahap against the Quirinos government. Malaya: founding of the Federation of Malaya. Burma: rebellion of the Karens. Palestine: Britain declares the mandate ended; proclamation of the state of Israel; the Arab attack; beginning of the Palestinian war. Malaya: Chinese communists' guerrilla war against the British administration. Korea: the Korean People's Republic (under Kim Irsen) is proclaimed in Pyongyang; the Korean Republic (under Syngman Rhee) is proclaimed in Seoul. Pakistan: death of Jinnah. Indonesia: commune of Madiun. India: kingdom of Hyderabad annexed. Palestine: Egyptian defeat in the Negeb. Japan: end of the war criminals' trials in Tokio. Indonesia: second Dutch military action against the Republic; occupation of Djokjakarta; internment of Sukarno and other republican leaders.

1949 China: communists take Pekin and Tientsin. North Atlantic Pact (NATO) concluded. Palestine: armistice between Israel and the Arab countries. China: fall of Shanghai and Hankow. Indochina: France recognizes the independence of Vietnam within the French Union; the country gets a pro-French government; the Viet Minh continues the war. India-Pakistan: jute conflict in connection with the devaluation of the Indian rupee and the non-devaluation of the Pakistan rupee. China: Mao Tsetung proclaims the Chinese People's Republic in Pekin; fall of Canton. Indonesia: Round Table conference in The Hague; transfer of sovereignty; Indonesia an independent federal state; Sukarno president.

1950 India becomes a republic; Prasad president. Indochina: Ho Chi Minh proclaims the People's Republic of Vietnam. China: communists occupy Hainan; Chiang flees to Formosa; the United States takes Formosa under its protection; the USSR signs a treaty of friendship with Communist China. The Colombo plan for the economic development of under-developed regions. Egypt: Wafd's electoral victory; Nahas premier. Turkey: electoral victory of the Democratic opposition party; Celal Bayer president. Transjordan annexes part of Palestine and becomes the kingdom of Jordan. India-Pakistan: agreement on trade and the minorities. Indonesia: rebellion in Ambon. Korea: North Koreans invade South Korea; intervention of the Americans in the name of the United Nations; after initial successes the North Koreans are driven back to the Chinese frontier. Indonesia becomes a unified state. China: communist troops occupy Tibet. Indochina: French defeat in Tonkin. Korea: Chinese intervene on behalf of the North; the Americans are driven back to the 38th parallel; battle near Hamhung.

1951 Morocco: Sidi Mohammed ibn Yussuf compelled under French pressure to disassociate himself from the Istiklal. Syria: Shishakli military dictator. Iran: the oil problem; the oil treaty of 1933 annulled by Iran; nationalization of the Anglo-Persian Oil Company; Mossadeq premier. Burma: invasion of northern districts by Kuo Min-tang troops driven out of China. Korea: Macarthur dismissed; armistice negotiations in

Panmunjon. Jordan: Abdulla murdered. Turkey enters NATO. Japan concludes with the Allies the peace treaty of San Francisco; Russia refuses to sign; India concludes a separate peace. Pakistan: Liaqat Ali Khan murdered. Egypt: Anglo-Egyptian treaty of 1936 denounced; conflict over the Suez Canal and the Soudan. Libya becomes an independent state.

1952 Tunisia: nationalist agitation; conflict between the French and Sidi el-Amin Bey; Tunisian Government dissolved by the French; the nationalist leader Bourguiba banished. Egypt: 'Black Saturday' in Cairo; Farouk dismisses Nahas. Korea: the Americans bomb power stations on the Yalu. India, Burma, Ceylon: general elections. Iran: Mossadeq receives dictatorial powers. Egypt: military *coup d'état* of General Neguib; Farouk deposed; dissolution of the political parties. Indonesia: unrest in Jakarta; conflict between Parliament and the Army. Morocco: the sultan demands revision of the protectorate treaty; rioting in Casablanca.

1953 India-Pakistan: conflict over the Sutlej waters. Indochina: Viet Minh offensive in Tonkin and Laos. Soviet Union: death of Stalin. China: new electoral law. Korea: armistice signed in Panmunjon. Egypt becomes a republic; Neguib signs an agreement with Britain on the Soudan. Morocco: Sidi Mohammed ibn Yussuf deposed. Iran: flight of the shah; he returns after a military *coup d'état;* Mossadeq dismissed. Indonesia: rebellion in Atjeh. Philippines: electoral victory of the opposition; Magsaysay becomes president. Palestine: Israeli-Arab clash at Kibia.

1954 H-bomb exploded in the Pacific. Syria: Shishakli driven out. Pakistan: defeat of the Moslem League at the elections in East Bengal; the central government dismisses the East Bengal government; treaty concluded with Turkey. Indochina: fall of Dien Bien Phu; conference in Geneva; armistice in Vietnam. China: air incident in Hainan; general election. Tunisia: agreement between Mendès-France and the Bey; rebellion of the Fellaghas. Southeast Asia Pact (SEATO) signed. Egypt: treaty with Britain on the Suez Canal: Neguib replaced by Nasser. Algeria: rebellion.

1955 Conference of Bandung (April 18th to 24th). Bagdad Pact concluded. Ceylon, Cambodia, Laos, Nepal, Jordan and Libya become members of the United Nations. Turkey: strained relations with Greece over Cyprus. Egypt: deliveries of arms from Czechoslovakia and Russia. Israel: the United Nations condemns an attack on Syrian positions on Lake Tiberias. India: conflict with Portugal over Goa. South Vietnam becomes a republic. Indonesia: general election. China: Sinkiang becomes autonomous. Soviet Union: Bulganin and Kruschev visit India, Burma and Afghanistan. Morocco: general rising leads to the return of Sidi Mohammed. Algeria: war of independence begins.

1956 Twentieth Congress of the Soviet Union Communist party. The Eisenhower doctrine promising help to peoples threatened by communism. China: first rail connection Pekin–Moscow *via* Ulan Bator; all private businesses nationalized or semi-nationalized. Japan: ending of state of war between Japan and the Soviet Union; peace treaty with the Philippines. India: plan of central government to alter the state frontier in Bengal leads to riots in Calcutta; demonstrations in Bombay against the central government's plan to make Bombay a bilingual state; agreement with Pakistan on the frontier between India and West Pakistan. Pakistan: Iskander Mirza elected first president of Pakistan. Indonesia: Round Table conference agreement with Holland denounced; refusal to pay to Holland sums specified in the agreement; military *putsch* begins in Sumatra; creation of the province of West New Guinea (West Irian). Cambodia: Norodom Suramaret again crowned king. Nepal: treaty with China by which Nepal loses extra-territorial rights in Tibet. Burma: U Nu resigns as premier in favour of U Ba Swe; later U Nu becomes premier again. Egypt: nationalization of the Suez Canal; Anglo-French military action leads to the occupation of Port Said by Anglo-French forces and of Sinai by Israelis; British and French forced to withdraw (December 23rd); formation of first United Nations police force. Libya: elections. Tunisia: first National Assembly elected. Jordan: Glubb Pasha ceases to be commander-in-chief of the Arab Legion. Afghanistan: agreement with the Soviet Union by which Afghanistan receives long-term credits.

1957 China: speech of Mao on the tensions within a communist system. Japan: fishing agreement with the Soviet Union; Japanese oil companies active in Saudi Arabia. India: elections; communists form a government in the State of Kerala; Nehru sets to work the first atomic reactor in Asia near Bombay. Indonesia: Sukarno's speech on guided democracy; formation of a national council; Sukarno forms a cabinet under Djuanda; Subandrio addresses the United Nations assembly and announces 'a new course' on differences with Holland on West New Guinea; Dutch concerns taken over; attempt on Sukarno's life fails. Thailand: after proclamation of a state of siege the election results are falsified by the Pibul government; the *coup d'état* by Sarit Thanarat leads to the disappearance of Pibul Songgram and his stooge, the chief of police Phao Saryaanond. Malaya: declaration of independence; defensive treaty with Britain. Burma: U Win Maung elected president. Philippines: Magsaysay killed in air crash. Egypt: Israeli troops withdraw from Sinai. Jordan: end of defensive treaty with Britain; Hussein, while the United States Sixth fleet is in Near Eastern waters, gets rid of Soliman Nabulsi his 'neutralist' premier. Oman: the revolt of the Imam leads to air action by Britain. Laos: representatives of the pro-Viet Minh Pathet Lao (Free Laos) movement enter the government. Ghana: independence declared. Tunisia: republic proclaimed; Bourguiba president. Turkey: financial crisis. Ceylon: Bandaranaike, the premier, wants the British to give up their air base.

1958 Afro-Asian writers' and journalists' conference in Tashkent. China: new crisis in the Formosa Straits; bombardment of Quemoy and Matsu. Japan: peace treaty with Indonesia and agreement on reparations. Pakistan: Iskander Mirza dismisses the central and provincial governments and entrusts power to the Army commander-in-chief, Mohammed Ayub Khan. Indonesia: formation of the 'revolutionary government' in Sumatra and Celebes. Thailand: military *putsch* by Sarit Thanarat. Burma: split in the Anti-Fascist People's Freedom league causes resignation of U Nu in favour of General U Ne Win. Egypt and Syria: creation of the United Arab Republic. Irak and Jordan: creation of a union under Faisal of Irak. Irak: murder of King Faisal, Crown Prince

Abd al-Ilah and premier Nuri al-Said; republic proclaimed. Lebanon: internal unrest; because of the Irak crisis American troops land; General Shebab elected president; Karami government (two Arabs, two Christians). Jordan: landing of British paratroopers because of the Irak crisis. Philippines: tension with Indonesia because of Filipino attitude to the Indonesian rebellion. Tunisia: French aircraft bomb the village of Sakit Sidi Yussef. North Africa: General de Gaulle's constitution accepted except by Guinea. China: the 'great leap forward'; institution of the people's communes.

1959 China: treaty with Soviet Union on economic co-operation; suppression of the revolt in Tibet; Dalai Lama escapes to India. Indonesia: nationalization of all big Dutch plantations and estates. United Arab Republic; financial agreement with Britain on the Suez Canal Company. Irak: military revolt in Mosul suppressed; treaty with the Soviet Union on economic co-operation; withdrawal from Bagdad Pact. Singapore: complete internal autonomy achieved; electoral victory of the People's Action party. Indonesia: Sukarno dissolves Constituent Assembly; return to constitution of 1945; formation of Presidential Advisory Council. India: Communist government of Kerala overthrown; conflict with China over Chinese activities in northern border regions. Laos: campaign of Pathet Lao against pro-Western government (in office since 1958); United Nations Commission investigates charges of North Vietnamese aid to rebels. Algeria: General de Gaulle proposes three alternative solutions (starting from four years after peace is restored) – separation, complete union with France or autonomy (September 16th). Ceylon: Bandaranaike murdered; Dehanaiake premier. Soudan: agreement with the United Arab Republic on Nile waters. China: land reforms in Tibet. Tunis: nationalization of public utilities. United Arab Republic: resumption of diplomatic relations with Britain. Eisenhower's journey through Europe, Asia and Africa.

BIBLIOGRAPHY

I HAVE made no attempt to give a complete bibliography of all the sources used, which would have occupied an excessive space. What are listed here are the more important books likely to be useful and reasonably accessible to English-speaking readers. No references to articles in periodicals, reviews and newspapers are given.

ABDULLA. *Memoirs of King Abdulla of Transjordania*, 1950.
ADAMS, C. C. *Islam and Modernism in Egypt*, 1933.
ADAMS, J. T. *Building the British Empire*, 1938.
AHMAD, M. *Economics of Islam*, 1947.
AKHTAR, S. M. *Economics of Pakistan*, 1951 (2nd ed.).
ALBIRUNI, A. H. *Makers of Pakistan and Modern Muslim India*, 1950.
ALLEN, G. C. *A Short Economic History of Japan*, 1946.
— and DONNITHORNE, A. G. *Western Enterprise in Far Eastern Economic Development. China and Japan*, 1954.
ALLEN, H. E. *The Turkish Transformation*, 1935.
ANDREWS, C., and MOOKERJEE, V. G. K. *The Rise and Growth of the Congress in India*, 1939.
ANSTEY, V. P. *The Economic Development of India*, 1952 (4th ed.).
ANTONIUS, G. *The Arab Awakening*, 1955 (3rd ed.).
ARMSTRONG, H. C. *Lord of Arabia. Ibn Saud*, 1934.

BAILEY, S. D. *Ceylon*, 1952.
BALL, W. M. *Nationalism and Communism in East Asia*, 1953 (2nd ed.)
BELDEN, J. *China Shakes the World*, 1950.
BENDA, H. J. (ed.) *The Communist Uprisings in Indonesia*, 1950.
BERKENKOPF, P. *Siberien als Zukunftsland der Industrie*, 1935.
BEVAN, E. *Thoughts on Indian Discontents*, 1929.
BEY, M. R. *The Awakening of Modern Egypt*, 1947.
BILBY, K. W. *New Star in the Near East*, 1950.
BISBEE, E. *The New Turks. Pioneers of the Republic (1920–1950)*, 1951.
BODDE, D. *Peking Diary*, 1951.
BONNE, A. *State and Economics in the Middle East*, 1948.
BOSSHARD, W. *Gefahrenherd der Welt*, 1954.
BOURKE-WHITE, M. *Halfway to Freedom*, 1949.
BOWLES, C. *Ambassador's Report*, 1954.
BRANDT, C., SCHWARTZ, B., and FAIRBANK, J. K. *A Documentary History of Chinese Communism*, 1951.
BROCKELMANN, C. *History of the Islamic Peoples*, 1952 (repr.).
BROMBERGER, M. and S. *Scenes of Suez*, 1957.
BROWN, D. M. *Nationalism in Japan*, 1954.
BROWN, W. N. (ed.) *India, Pakistan, Ceylon*, 1951.
— *The United States and India and Pakistan*, 1953.

BULLARD, R. *Britain and the Middle East from the Earliest Times to 1952*, 1952 (2nd ed.).

CADY, J. F. *A History of Modern Burma*, 1958.
CAMPBELL, W. K. H. *Practical Co-operation in Asia and Africa*, 1951.
CAVE, S. *An Introduction to the Study of some Living Religions of the East*, 1947 (4th ed.).
CHAMBERLIN, W. H. *Japan over Asia*, 1938.
CHASSIN, L. M. *L'ascension de Mao Tse-tung (1921–1945)*, 1953.
— *La conquête de la Chine par Mao Tse-tung*, 1952.
CHEN, S., and PAYNE, R. *Sun Yat-sen*, 1946.
CHIANG KAI-SHEK. *China's Destiny*, 1947.
CH'IEN TUAN-SHENG. *The Government and Politics of China*, 1950.
CHRISTOPHER, J. W. *Conflict in the Far East. American Diplomacy in China (1928–1933)*, 1950.
CLEGG, A. *New China, New World*, 1949.
CLYDE, P. H. *The Far East*, 1952 (2nd ed.).
COAST, J. *Recruit to Revolution, Adventure and Politics in Indonesia*, 1952.
COATES, A. *Invitation to an Eastern Feast*, 1953.
COATES, W. P. and Z. K. *Soviets in Central Asia*, 1951.
COLBERT, E. S. *The Left Wing in Japanese Politics*, 1952.
COLOMBE, M. *L'évolution de l'Egypt (1924–1950)*, 1951.
COOKE, H. V. *Challenge and Response in the Middle East. The Quest for Prosperity (1919–1951)*, 1952.
CORDAN, W. *Israel und die Araber*, 1954.
CRESSEY, G. B. *Asia's Lands and Peoples*, 1952 (rev. ed.).

DALLIN, D. J. *The Rise of Russia in Asia*, 1949.
— *Soviet Russia and the Far East*, 1948.
DATTA, D. M. *The Philosophy of Mahatma Gandhi*, 1953.
DAVIDSON, M. *Malayan Conflict*, 1953.
DAVIES, R. A., and STEIGER, A. J. *Soviet Asia*, 1943.
DAVIS, K. *The Population of India and Pakistan*, 1951.
DEAN, V. M. *The Nature of the Non-Western World*, 1957.
— , BENDA, H. J., and others. *New Era in the Non-Western World*, 1957.
DESAI, A. R. *The Social Background of Indian Nationalism*, 1948.
DESAI, R. C. *Standard of Living in India and Pakistan*, 1953.
DESCHAMPS, H. J. *La Fin des Empires Coloniaux*, 1950.
DEUTSCHER, I. *Stalin*, 1949.
DEVILLERS, P. *Histoire de Viet-Nam (1940–1952)*, 1952.
DIEZ, E. *Glaube und Welt des Islam*, 1941.
DREXLER, P. J. *Die Front der Farbigen*, 1957.
DUDA, H. W. *Vom Kalifat zur Republik. Die Turkei im 19 und 20 Jahrhundert*, 1948.
DUNBAR, G. *India and the Passing of Empire*, 1951.
DUTT, R. P. *India To-day*, 1949.

EAST, W. G., and SPATE, O. H. K. (ed.). *The Changing Map of Asia*, 1953 (2nd ed.).
EDIB, H. *Conflict of East and West in Turkey*, 1935 (2nd ed.).
EMBREE, J. F. *The Japanese Nation*, 1945.

EMERSON, R., MILLS, L. A., and THOMPSON, V. *Government and Nationalism in Southeast Asia*, 1942.

FAHRENFORT, J. J. *India*, 1950.
FARIS, N. A., and HUSAYN, M. T. *The Crescent in Crisis*, 1955.
FAROUGHY, A. *The Bahrein Islands (750–1951)*, 1951.
FEIS, H. *The China Tangle*, 1953.
FIELD, F. V. *Economic Handbook of the Pacific Area*, 1934.
FINEGAN, J. *The Archaeology of World Religion*, 1952.
FISCHER, L. *The Life of Mahatma Gandhi*, 1951 (2nd ed.).
— *Indonesia*, 1959.
FISHEL, W. R. *The End of Extraterritoriality in China*, 1952.
FITZGERALD, C. P. *Revolution in China*, 1952.
FORBES, W. C. *The Philippine Islands*, 1945 (rev. ed.).
FOSTER, H. A. *The Making of Modern Iraq*, 1936.
FRASER-TYTLER, SIR K. *Afghanistan*, 1953 (rev. ed.).
FREETH, Z. *Kuwait was my Home*, 1956.
FRYE, R. N. *Iran, Key to the Middle East*, 1953.
— *The Near East and the Great Powers*, 1951.
FURNIVALL, J. S. *Colonial Policy and Practice. A Comparative Study of Burma and Netherlands India*, 1948.
— *Studies in the Economic and Social Development of the Netherlands East Indies*, 5 vols., 1934.

GABRIELLI, L. *Abd-el-Krim et les événements du Rif (1924–1926)*, 1953.
GANDHI, M. K. *Autobiography*, 1948.
— *To a Gandhian Capitalist*, 1951.
— *Selected Writings*, 1952.
GHANI, A. R. *Pakistan. A Select Bibliography*, 1951.
GIBB, H. A. R. *Islamic Society and the West*, 1951 (2nd ed.).
— *Modern Trends in Islam*, 1954 (3rd ed.).
GLASENAPP, H. VON. *Die funf grossen Religionen*, 2 vols., 1951–2.
GLUBB, J. B. *The Story of the Arab Legion*, 1952 (3rd ed.).
GOUILLY, A. *L'Islam dans l'Afrique Occidentale Française*, 1952.
GROUSSET, R. *La Face de l'Asie*, 1955.
GUNTHER, J. *Inside Asia*, 1939.
GUPTA, I. B. *Indo-Pakistan Relations (1947–1955)*, 1958.
GRAJDANZEV, J. *Modern Korea*, 1944.
GRUNDER, G., and LIVEZEY, W. E. *The Philippines and the United States*, 1952.

HAAS, W. S. *Iran*, 1946 (2nd ed.).
HADDAD, G. *Fifty Years of Modern Syria and Lebanon*, 1950.
HALL, D. G. E. *A History of South-East Asia*, 1955.
HAMMER, E. *The Struggle for Indochina*, 1954.
HANS, J. *Homo Economicus Islamicus. Wirtschaftswandel und sozialer Aufbruch in Islam*, 1952.
HARDY, O., and DUMKE, G. S. *A History of the Pacific Area in Modern Times*, 1949.
HARRISON, B. *South-East Asia*, 1954.
HARVEY, G. E. *British Rule in Burma (1824–1942)*, 1946.
HATTA, M. *Verspreide Geschriften*, 1952.
HAYDEN, J. R. *The Philippines*, 1942.

HAZARD, H. W. *Atlas of Islamic History*, 1952 (rev. ed.).

HELL, J. *The Arab Civilisation*, 1951 (5th ed.).

HELLER, O. *Sibirien ein anderes Amerika*, 1930.

HITTI, P. K. *History of the Arabs*, 1950 (5th ed.).

— *The Arabs. A Short History*, 1950 (2nd ed.).

— *History of Syria including Lebanon and Palestine*, 1951.

HOLITSCHER, A. *Das Unruhige Asien*, 1926.

HOLLAND, W. L. (ed.). *Asian Nationalism and the West*, 1953.

HOLLINGWORTH, C. *The Arabs and the West*, 1952.

HOLTOM, D. C. *Modern Japan and Shinto Nationalism*, 1947.

HOPKINS, H. *New World Arising. A Journey of Discovery through the New Nations of South-East Asia*, 1952.

HORNER, F. J. *A Case History of Japan*, 1948.

HOUGH, E. M. *The Co-operative Movement in India*, 1950 (2nd ed.).

HOURANI, A. H. *Syria and Lebanon*, 1954 (3rd ed.).

HOYLAND, J. S. *The Case for India*, 1929.

HUREWITZ, J. C. *Middle East Dilemmas. A Review of United States Interests and Politics*, 1953.

HUSSAIN, M. M. *Islam and Socialism*, 1947.

HYAMSON, A. M. *Palestine Under the Mandate (1920–1948)*, 1950.

ISSAWI, C. *Egypt at Mid-Century*, 1954.

IZZEDDIN, N. *The Arab World*, 1953.

JAMES, D. H. *The Rise and Fall of the Japanese Empire*, 1951.

JINNAH, M. A. *Speeches and Writings*, 2 vols., 1947.

JONES, F. C. *Japan's New Order in East Asia; its Rise and Fall (1937–1945)*, 1954.

— *Manchuria since 1931*, 1949.

JOSHI, G. N. *Constitution of India*, 1950.

KAHIN, G. M. *The Asian-African Conference*, 1956.

— *Nationalism and Revolution in Indonesia*, 1952.

KARUNAKARAN, K. P. *India in World Affairs (August 1947–January 1950)*, 1953.

KATRAK, S. K. H. *Through Amanullah's Afghanistan*, 1929.

KERR, G. H. *The Development of Modern Formosa*, 1950.

KHADDURI, M. *Independent Iraq. A Study in Iraqi Politics since 1932*, 1951

KHAN, LIAQAT ALI. *Pakistan, the Heart of Asia*, 1951.

KIMCHE, J. *Seven Fallen Pillars. The Middle East (1915–1950)*, 1953 (rev. ed.).

KIRBY, S. E. *Introduction to the Economic History of China*, 1954.

KIRK, G. E. *A Short History of the Middle East*, 1952 (2nd ed.).

— *The Middle East in the War*, 1952.

KLOETZEL, C. R. *Indien im Schmelztiegel*, 1930.

KOESTLER, A. *Promise and Fulfilment, Palestine (1917–1949)*, 1949.

KOHN, H. *A History of Nationalism in the East*, 1929.

— *Western Civilisation in the Near East*, 1936.

KOLARZ, W. *The People of the Soviet Far East*, 1954.

— *Russia and her Colonies*, 1952.

KROEFF, J. M. v.d. *Indonesia in the Modern World*, 1954.

KRUEGER, K. *Die Türkei*, 1951.

LASKER, B. *Human Bondage in Southeast Asia*, 1951.
LATOURETTE, K. S. *The Chinese; their History and Culture*, 2 vols. 1947 (3rd ed.).
— *The American Record in the Far East (1945–1951)*, 1952.
— *History of Christianity*, 1953.
LATTIMORE, O. *Manchuria, Cradle of Conflict*, 1935 (rev. ed.).
— *Pivot of Asia*, 1950.
— *The Situation in Asia*, 1949.
— *The Making of Modern China*, 1947.
LAWRENCE, T. E. *The Seven Pillars of Wisdom*, 1935.
LE THANK KHOI. *L'Economie de l'Asia du sud-est*, 1958.
LEGER, F. *Les influences Occidentales dans la Revolution de l'Orient (1850–1950)*, 1955.
LENCZOWSKI, G. *The Middle East in World Affairs*, 1952.
— *Russia and the West in Iran (1918–1948)*, 1951.
LEVI, W. *Free India in Asia*, 1952.
LEWE VAN ADVARD, E. J. *Japan from Surrender to Peace*, 1953.
LILIENTHAL, A. M. *What Price Israel?*, 1953.
LONGRIGG, S. H. *Iraq (1900–1950)*, 1953.
LORIMER, F. *The Population of the Soviet Union*, 1946.
LUMBY, E. W. R. *The Transfer of Power in India*, 1954.

MACLAER BATES, H. *Report from Formosa*, 1952.
MCCUNE, G. M. *Korea To-day*, 1950.
MCLAREN, W. W. *A Political History of Japan during the Meiji Era (1867–1912)*, 1916.
MAO TSE-TUNG. *Selected Works*, 4 vols., 1954–6.
MAUNG MAUNG. *Burma in the Family of Nations*, 1956.
MARLOWE, J. *Anglo-Egyptian Relations (1880–1953)*, 1954.
MENDE, T. *South-East Asia between Two Worlds*, 1955.
MICHENER, J. A. *The Voice of Asia*, 1951.
MIKESELL, R. F., and CHENERY, H. B. *Arabian Oil. America's Stake in the Middle East*, 1950.
MIKUSCH, D. VON. *Gasi Mustapha Kemal*, 1929.
MIRSKY, D. S. *Lenin*, 1931.
MITCHELL, K. L. *Industrialisation of the Western Pacific*, 1942.
MOOK, H. J. VAN. *The Stakes of Democracy in South-East Asia*, 1950.
MORSE, H. B., and MACNAIR, H. F. *Far Eastern International Relations*, 1931.
MUKERJI, D. P. *Modern Indian Culture*, 1948 (rev. ed.).

NAOROJI, D. *Poverty and Un-British Rule in India*, 1901.
NEHRU, J. *An Autobiography*, 1953 (20th ed.).
— *The Discovery of India*, 1951 (3rd ed.).
— *Independence and After*, 1950.
— *Before and After Independence*, 1950.
— *Talks with Nehru*, 1951.
NGUYEN AI QUOC. *Procès de la Colonisation Française*, 1926.
NORMAN, E. H. *Japan's Emergence as a Modern State. Political and Economic Problems of the Meiji Period*, 1940.
NORTHROP, F. S. C. *The Meeting of East and West*, 1947.
— *The Taming of the Nations*, 1952.

PANDIT, V. L. *This is India,* 1951.
PANIKKAR, K. M. *Asia and Western Dominance (1498–1945),* 1953.
— *In Two Chinas. Memoirs of a Diplomat,* 1955.
PAYNE, R. *Mao Tse-tung,* 1950.
— *Red Storm over Asia,* 1951.
PHILBY, H. ST. J. *Arabian Jubilee,* 1952.
PIPES, R. *The Formation of the Soviet Union (1917–1923),* 1954.
PRIVES, L. F. L. *Punjab Prelude,* 1952.
PURCELL, V. *The Chinese in Southeast Asia,* 1952 (2nd ed.).
— *Malaya, Communist or Free,* 1954.

REISCHAUER, E. O. *Japan Past and Present* 1952 (new ed.).
— *Wanted: An Asian Policy,* 1955.
RENOUVIN, P. *Les Politiques d'Expansion Impérialiste, Colonies et Empires,* 1949.
RIGGS, F. W. *Formosa under Chinese Nationalist Rule,* 1952.
ROOSEVELT, E. *India and the Awakening East,* 1953.
ROSINGER, L. K., and others. *The State of Asia,* 1951.
ROY, M. N. *Revolution und Konterrevolution in China,* 1930.

SAAB, H. *The Arab Federalists of the Ottoman Empire,* 1958.
SACHER, H. *Israel. Establishment of a State,* 1952.
SAMSOM, G. B. *The Western World and Japan,* 1950.
SCHECHTMAN, J. H. *The Arab Refugee Problem,* 1952.
— *Population Transfers in Asia,* 1949.
SCHWARTZ, B. *Chinese Communism and the Rise of Mao,* 1952.
SEEGER, E. *China,* 1950.
SHEEAN, V. *The New Persia,* 1927.
SMITH, W. C. *Modern Islam in India,* 1946.
— *Pakistan as an Islamic State,* 1951.
SNOW, E. *Battle for Asia,* 1941.
— *Red Star over China,* 1938.
SOKOL, E. D. *The Revolt of 1916 in Russian Central Asia,* 1954.
SOVANI, N. V. *Economic Relations of India with South-East Asia and the Far East,* 1951.
STONE, I. F. *The Hidden History of the Korean War,* 1952.
STRONG, A. L. *The Rise of the Chinese People's Commune,* 1959.
SUKARNO, A. *The Birth of Pantjasila,* 1950.
SUNDERLAND, J. T. *India in Bondage,* 1932.
SYKES, P. *A History of Afghanistan,* 2 vols., 1940.
SYMONDS, R. *The Making of Pakistan,* 1951 (3rd ed.).

TALBOT, P. (ed.). *South Asia in the World Today,* 1951 (2nd ed.).
T'ANG LEANG-LI. *The Inner History of the Chinese Revolution,* 1930.
— (ed.). *Reconstruction in China,* 1935.
TENDULKAR, D. G. M. *Life of Mohandas Karamchand Gandhi,* 8 vols. 1951–3.
TENG, S., and FAIRBANK, J. F. *Chinese Response to the West. Documentary Survey (1838–1923),* 1953.
THAYER, P. W. (ed.). *Southeast Asia in the Coming World,* 1953.
THOMAS, L. V., and FRYE, R. N. *The United States and Turkey and Iran,* 1951.
THOMPSON, V. *French Indo-China,* 1942.
— *Thailand, the New Siam,* 1941.
— and ADLOFF, R. *The Left Wing in Southeast Asia,* 1950.

TOWNSEND, M. E. *European Colonial Expansion since 1871*, 1941.
TWITCHEL, K. S. *Saudi Arabia*, 1953 (rev. ed.).

VINACKE, H. M. *A History of the Far East in Modern Times*, 1946 (4th ed.).

WALDSCHMIDT, E., and others. *Geschichte Asians*, 1950.
WARRINER, D. *Land and Poverty in the Middle East*, 1948.
WEIZMANN, C. *Trial and Error: the Autobiography of Chaim Weizmann*, 1949.
WENZ, H. *Weltmacht Indien*, 1952.
WERTHEIM, W. F. *Indonesian Society in Transition*, 1956.
WHYTE, A. F. *Asia in the Twentieth Century*, 1926.
WILBER, D. N. *Iran, Past and Present*, 1951.
WINSTEDT, R. O. *Malaya and its History*, 1948.
WINT, G. *Spotlight on Asia*, 1955.
WOOD, W. A. R. *A History of Siam*, 1933.
WOYTINSKY, W. S. and E. S. *World Commerce and Governments*, 1955.
WU, A. K. *China and the Soviet Union*, 1950.
WYATT, W. *Southwards from China: A Survey of South-East Asia since 1945*, 1952.

YAKHANTOV, V. A. *Russia and the Soviet Union in the Far East*, 1931.
YANAGA, C. *Japan since Perry*, 1949.
YOUNG, T. C. (ed.). *Near Eastern Culture and Society*, 1951.

ZINKIN, M. *Asia and the West*, (2nd ed.).
— *Development for Free Asia*, 1956.
ZISCHKA, A. *Le Japon dans le Monde (1854–1934)*, 1934.

INDEX OF PERSONS

INDEX OF PLACES

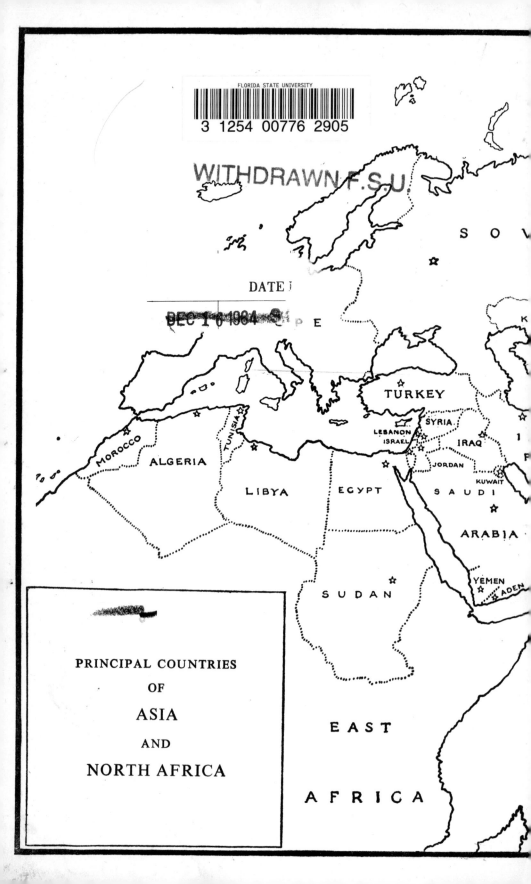

S O

TURKEY

SYRIA

LEBANON
ISRAEL

IRAQ

MOROCCO

ALGERIA

TUNISIA

LIBYA

EGYPT

JORDAN

KUWAIT

S A U D I

ARABIA

SUDAN

YEMEN

ADEN

PRINCIPAL COUNTRIES

OF

ASIA

AND

NORTH AFRICA

E A S T

A F R I C A